Date Due

MANKIND.

THE RACES OF MAN,

AND

THEIR GEOGRAPHICAL DISTRIBUTION.

FROM THE GERMAN OF

OSCAR PESCHEL.

NEW YORK:

D. APPLETON AND COMPANY,

549 & 551 BROADWAY.

1876.

D. H. F.

PREFACE TO THE FIRST EDITION.

——◆◇◆——

INCLINATION without some form of external pressure is insufficient to induce an author to publish a handbook, for though completeness is essential, the work is little attractive. Moreover, in such a subject as ethnology the author finds himself obliged to enter into matters requiring special study. He can no longer bring forward his own thoughts, but has only to repeat the dicta of the recognized authorities, and he never loses the oppressive sensation of gathering roses in the garden of another. It would never have occurred to the present author to reconstruct a doctrinal system of ethnology, had he not in the beginning of 1869 been requested by the then War Minister, General A. von Roon, to edit a fourth and revised edition of his "Ethnology as an Introduction to Political Geography" (Völkerkunde als Propädeutik der politischen Geographie). The wish of a man whose name is closely connected with the creation of our military system, became a duty to a German on whom the newly acquired strength of his nation has imposed obligations of gratitude towards its great originator and promoter. After a short correspondence it was agreed that the new work was to be described on the title-page as the joint production of Herr von Roon and the present author, and that it should be previously submitted to the former for approbation.

Last autumn, however, when after nearly five years a portion of the proof was ready, it appeared that, owing to the shattered state of his health, His Excellency Field-marshal Count Roon was for the time unable to examine the contents of the "Ethnology," and that although he intended to do so when convalescent, yet if such delay should be prejudicial to the author and the publisher, he urged an immediate publication of the work, but that in this case any mention of his name on the title-page must be omitted. Any longer delay was indeed undesirable, for the rapidity with which writings grow old, owing to the present activity of science, more especially in the province of ethnology, was painfully impressed upon the author while his work was in the press, by the appearance of several new investigations, of which he was unable to make use.   Thus in the early chapters the Mohammedan monarchy at Talifu was described as extant and prosperous, whereas, according to the latest intelligence, the Chinese destroyed it in 1872.

The original object of the undertaking, namely, to urge anew the scientific claims of A. von Roon's "Völkerkunde als Propädeutik der politischen Geographie," thus came to naught, much to the regret of the author.

OSCAR PESCHEL.

Leipsic, Jan. 10, 1874.

PREFACE TO THE SECOND EDITION.

THE issue of a Second Edition has been delayed for some time by
the author that he might avail himself of the opportunity completely
to rearrange his work.   But owing to considerations of health
this intention must be postponed to a future time.   Such additional material as has been gathered, as well as all elucidations
derived from critical discussions on ethnology in the press of
Germany and of other countries, and in private correspondence,
have been placed in the list of "Addenda and Corrections"
before the list of "Contents."* Although at present no alteration of
the systematic groups has been adopted, it must be remembered
that new arguments have lately been urged against the combination of the Indo-European, Semitic, and Hamite nations into
a Mediterranean race.   When, for instance, Professor R. Hartmann recognized a remarkable correspondence between the skulls
of the Shillook negroes and the heads of the old Egyptians and
of their descendants, the Fellaheen (Schweinfurth, The Heart of
Africa, vol. i. p. 96), such a fact could not fail to produce a
deep impression.   On the other hand, in the absence of measure-

---

* These have been inserted in the text of the English edition.

ments and distinct physical descriptions of many members of
these groups, a separation could not as yet be carried into effect :
nor is it indeed impossible that proof may yet be obtained of the
common origin.   In the three great groups of languages it is
perhaps unadvisable hastily to replace an old and questionable
arrangement by one which, though new, is also questionable.

OSCAR PESCHEL.

Leipzic, October, 1874.

CONTENTS.

INTRODUCTION.

PHYSICAL CHARACTERS.

LINGUISTIC CHARACTERS.

INDUSTRIAL, SOCIAL, AND RELIGIOUS PHASES OF DEVELOPMENT.

THE RACES OF MANKIND.

III.—*European Races of Doubtful Position.* (*a*) Basque. (*b*) Caucasian Peoples (Daghestân, Tshetsh, Abkhas, Tsherkess, Lazi, Suan, Mingrelian, Georgian).

IV.—*The Indo-European Race.* (*a*) Asiatic, Sanscrit Nations (Neo-Indian Languages, Siah Pôsh, Gipsy). Erânian (Persian, Kurd, Armenian, Osset, Tadshik). Afghan. (*b*) European. α Northern European. Letto-Slavonian (Lett, Slavonian.) Germanic Nations (Scandinavian, Goth, Teuton). β Southern European, Greek, Albanian, Latin (Portuguese, Spanish, Catalonian, Provençal, Northern French, Alpine Dialects, Furlanian, Roumanian). Celtic. Original Abode of Indo-Europeans. Europe as a Place of Abode.

INTRODUCTION.

MANKIND.

INTRODUCTION.

I.—MAN'S PLACE IN CREATION.

In the earliest attempt to classify animated nature Linnæus excited no indignation, though he united Man and Apes in one order of the class of Mammalia, which he designated the Primates. In our days, however, a scientific dispute has arisen whether the human race is to be separated from the apes by the rank of an order or a sub-order, but as this is a question of the value to be attributed to the idea of orders and sub-orders in a systematic edifice, Ethnology is not called upon to join in the discussion. Richard Owen thought that he had ascertained that in man alone the cerebellum is completely eclipsed by the cerebrum, and that a decidedly superior rank was thus secured to us. But even naturalists who, with Gratiolet, oppose the doctrine of historically successive transmutations of species, have acknowledged that this assertion was founded only on erroneous observations.

The distinction between man and apes, as bimanous and quadrumanous, has also been set aside by recent investigations. The tarsal bones of the gorilla resemble those of man in all important respects—in number, arrangement, and shape ; only the metatarsal bones and phalanges of this animal are relatively longer and slimmer, while the hallux is not merely comparatively shorter and weaker, but, in conjunction with its metatarsal bone, is attached to the tarsus by a more flexible joint.[1] But though the attachment of the flexors of the toes may be somewhat different in man, the prehensile foot of the ape possesses three muscles (*M. peroneus longus, flexor brevis, extensor brevis*) which are wanting in the hand.[2] Although the hinder limbs of the gorilla must therefore be recognized as genuine feet, their arrangement differs from that of our foot, and by this alone the morphological rank of man is raised far above that of the highest apes ; for we reckon as higher the bodily construction which restricts special functions to special organs. Conversely, we regard as lower, those creatures which accomplish a variety of actions with the same members, as for instance, birds which are obliged to use their mandibles (which serve us only for the mastication of food) for prehension, and occasionally for climbing ; in other words, for locomotion. The fore and the hind limbs of apes perform the same service, *i.e.*, they grasp and climb, from which it may be conjectured that the locomotion of these creatures is mainly conducted by means of climbing. The anthropomorphous apes, it is true, endeavour to walk erect, but they accomplish only short distances, and this not without effort. In the Malay Archipelago the Hylobates, which otherwise stand far nearer to man than the other three highest apes, always walk erect, although with bent knees, but, to keep their balance, they touch the earth alternately to the right and left with the tips of their long fingers which reach down to the ground.[3] On the other hand it must be admitted that in some races of mankind the foot is used for grasping, especially in the case of certain Nubian tribes[4] who hold fast to the ship's tackle with the hallux, and the natives of the Philippines, who pick up small coins from the ground with their toes ; even in the midst of European civilization, caligraphers and painters have, in consequence of bodily defects, guided pen and pencil with their toes.[5] Still these slight approximations scarcely narrow the wide

---

[1] Huxley, Man's Place in Nature, p. 23.

[2] Claus, Grundzüge der Zoologie, p. 1125.

[3] Dr. Mohnike, Die Affen der indischen Welt. Ausland, vol. xlv. 1872. No. 3, § 714.

[4] G. Pouchet, Plurality of the Human Race, p. 39. London, 1864.

[5] Mohnike, No. 36, p. 847. Waitz, Anthropologie, i. 117.

chasm between us and the apes, which is mainly founded on the division of labour between the fore and hinder limbs. As soon as the child ceases to use its hands for locomotion, it has acquired a high rank in creation. If the foot of the gorilla only preserves the distinction that the hallux can be opposed to the other toes, it becomes by this an organ of prehension and unfit for walking. Apes always tread either on the outer edges of their soles or, like the orang or chimpanzee, on the backs of their bent finger-joints.[6] Man in contrast with the ape, stands, walks, runs, jumps, dances, climbs, swims, rides, sits, and can remain for a long time in a recumbent position. The erect gait has caused the shortening of the anterior limbs, and has also, as Carl Vogt observes, given rise to the dish-like form of the pelvis as a support to the intestines.[7] Our comparatively spacious skull is poised on the support afforded by the vertebral column, and if the jaws greatly protrude, as in the negroes, the balance is restored by the elongation of the occiput. The anterior limbs, released from their functions of locomotion, now serve for prehension only, and as yet they have always been found adapted to carry out every purpose of the human mind.[8]

Naturalists such as Pruner Bey have given currency to the assertion that the vocal organs of the apes are not adapted to the ejaculation of articulate sounds, but this statement has been refuted by Darwin, who cited as an example a monkey of Paraguay,[9] which, when excited, emits six distinct sounds which excite similar emotions in its comrades. And although the dentition of man and apes in the Old World is alike, the permanent canine tooth is developed in us before the last molar teeth, and of the molar teeth, the front before the back ; in the

---

[6] Darwin, Descent of Man, vol. i. p. 139.

[7] Vorlesungen über den Menschen, vol. i. p. 172.

[8] Steinthal (Psychologie und Sprachwissenschaft, vol. i. p. 342, § 453. Berlin, 1871) maintains that our eye is assisted by the arms in the recognition of the relations of space, and that hence the knowledge of space is more developed in man than in animals. But the same service is rendered to the apes by their arms, and to the elephant by its trunk, and the antennæ of the insects perform perhaps better services.

[9] Cebus Azarae. Darwin, Descent of Man, vol. i. p. 53.

apes, on the contrary, the development of the canine teeth forms the conclusion of dentition, and the second back molar tooth appears before the front ones. Finally, the early disappearance of the intermaxillary bone in the human infant may be cited as a distinction from the apes.

These last facts oblige us to glance at the evolutionary history of man, which has gained great importance since Johann Friedrich Meckel, of Halle, asserted in 1812, that every animal in its immature condition (and this lasts from the fecundation of the egg to the first sexual functions) passes through all the forms which occur during the entire life of the animals of every grade beneath it. At the time of birth the gap between the child and the young of the ape is as yet very narrow. Novices might be puzzled to distinguish between the skulls of children and young chimpanzees. The brains of children and young apes approach very closely in size, but of all parts of the body, the brain of the ape grows the least. Thus, although the brain of the anthropomorphous ape contains all the main parts of the human skull, its development nevertheless assumes quite another direction. In the course of growth, the young of the orang or chimpanzee, which closely resemble our children in their ways, gradually lose their resemblance to the human structure. Before the change of teeth has begun, the brain of the ape has usually attained its completion, whereas in the child its proper development is just then actively beginning. In the apes, on the contrary, the facial bones grow in an animal direction, so that finally the largest ape has the brain of a child and the jaws of an ox. Thence it follows, that a man would never originate from the progressive evolution of the apes, for their development is directed to different ends, and the longer they advance towards these ends, the greater are the contrasts. It is in quite the lowest species of apes, the Uistiti of Eastern Brazil, which are, as it were, behindhand in their evolution, that the bony portion of the head presents a greater resemblance to that of man than in the anthropomorphous species.[10] It is only a popular misapprehension that, by the theory of the transmutation of species, man is supposed to be descended from one of the four highest

---

[10] Virchow, Menschen und Affenschädel, pp. 25, 26. Berlin, 1870.

species of apes. Neither Darwin nor any of his adherents ever asserted anything of the sort, but on the contrary they maintain that the ancestors of mankind branched off, in the first or earliest part of the tertiary period, from species of the Catarrhine group long since extinct. If this conjecture is to be recognized by science, the intermediate and transitional forms from these apes of the eocene period to the man of the present time, must be somewhere discovered. From the moment that the separate links in the chain of transmutations of form become known to us, no thoughtful man will longer doubt as to the process. But till then every other hypothesis is equally justified, and so far geological discoveries afford no promise that this gap will necessarily be filled up either sooner or later.

We cannot conclude these observations without answering the accusation which may perhaps be silently made, that we leave out of sight the intellectual functions of mankind. We at once repeat what Darwin[11] has already said, that the motions of conscience as connected with repentance, and the feelings of duty, are the most important differences which separate us from the animal; that in the latter there is no capability of solving a mathematical problem, or of admiring a landscape painting, or a manifestation of power; neither can any reflection take place respecting the correlation of phenomena, and still less as to the hypothesis of a First Cause or a Divine Will.[12]

The greatest differences between man and animals will first claim attention during the investigation of the evolutionary history of speech ; and the history of national customs likewise tacitly contains the best argument for the superior dignity of mankind. Yet all these facts in no way concern us in assigning to man his position in the animal kingdom, any more than the position of the elephant in a zoological system can be affected by its sagacity. Man is only entitled to that rank in a morphological system which, in future ages, when nothing is left of our race but a sufficient number of fossil bones, a thinking being

---

[11] Darwin, Descent of Man, vol. i. chap. ii. Haeckel, History of Creation, vol. ii. p. 344. London, 1876.

[12] Darwin, Descent of Man, vol. i. chap. ii.

would assign to him in a scientific arrangement of the animal kingdom. According to the principles of comparative anatomy and by systematic requirements, he would then be separated from the apes of the present geological era only as an order or a sub-order.

II.—THE UNITY OR PLURALITY OF SPECIES OF THE HUMAN RACE.

THE attempt to classify all the most similar creatures under one name, dates from the time when in the growth of language the invention of the name perfected the class. In nations which have remained at a low stage of civilization, we find names for different species of oaks, but none for the genus oak, nay, not even one for tree. The distinctive marks are therefore apprehended before the analogous qualities. Names for dog, wolf, and fox arose from a need of intelligible communication respecting the outer world, and with the names, a classification was already accomplished. Linnæus was the first who scientifically justified such use of language. Scarcely a century and a half therefore has elapsed since the idea of species was first instituted ; and Linnæus himself did not imagine species to have been created for ever invariable in number, but believed that new ones might be produced from the mongrels of dissimilar representatives of the genera. Goethe, on the other hand, still maintained that Nature knows only individuals, and that species exist only in school books. As soon as terms were to be invented for the typical varieties of the human race, a dispute arose as to whether the nations of the earth are divisible into different species or only into different varieties. Often, as in this instance, it is the highest and most obscure problems which most strongly attract the inexperienced, hurrying them on to premature and utterly worthless conclusions. Nor was it even with unprejudiced minds that anthropologists approached this difficult question, for some endeavoured to harmonize their conclusions with the Hebrew legend of the creation of a first human pair, while others strove to establish the plurality of species in order to withdraw the sympathy of humanity from the negro, and to hush the appeals of conscience against the degradation of man into a beast of burden in tropical husbandry. It is a remarkable fact, that this dispute as to the unity or plurality of species should have occupied the attention of men before a single definition of species had found universal or even general acceptance. " We reckon in one and the same species," says Blumenbach, " those animated beings which are so analogous in structure and form that their differences can have originated only from variation. But we regard as separate species, those of which the differences are so essential that they cannot be explained by the recognized influences of variation, if this expression is allowable." [1]

It is strange that Blumenbach, otherwise so acute, should not have perceived that in this play of words everything remains vague, since he assumes the idea of variation to be known, and therefore leaves it undefined. Moreover, if we can imagine that a being exactly similar to ourselves both in bodily structure and in mental functions, had miraculously descended from the planet Mars, Blumenbach must have agreed with us in reckoning it a member of the same species. This would have been the case in Cuvier's opinion also, for " the species," he says, " is the sum of all living beings descended from one another and from common ancestors, and those which resemble them as much as they resemble one another." [2] Thus Cuvier and Blumenbach did not as yet insist that all the members of the same species should possess common ancestors.

A common descent was however postulated by the elder De Candolle. " The species," so ran his definition, " is the association of all individuals which reciprocally resemble each other more than others, and from whose union proceed fertile offspring, which again, in their turn, reproduce themselves in successive generations, so that their descent from a single being can be inferred." [3]

Here at last species seemed to be sharply and well defined. All animated beings, however striking the differences perceptible in their structure and form, would be included in one species

---

[1] De generis humani varietate nativa, p. 66. Ed. 3.   Göttingen, 1795.

[2] Quatrefages, Rapport sur les progrès de l'Anthropologie, p. 56. Paris, 1867.

[3] Ibid. p. 104.

whenever they generate fertile offspring which, as well as their descendants, effect fertile crosses in their turn. Sterility in the offspring, or even in the second generation, was decisive of the contrary.   Flourens also adhered to this mark of recognition. "Fertility," he says, "is the foundation of the persistency of specific character. Different species generate hybrids of limited fertility."[4] Drawing the definition still closer, De Quatrefages says, "The species includes all more or less similar individuals which descend, or can be supposed to descend, from a single ancestral pair in unbroken succession."[5]

Before we decide as to the value of this definition of species, we will first inquire whether the hybrids of different races of mankind possess the characteristic of fertility.   That Aryan Hindoos and Dravidas, Chinese and Europeans, Arabs and Negresses can generate hybrids, and that these hybrids in their turn produce offspring, has probably never been disputed, but on the other hand, it is frequently maintained that Mulattoes die out in subsequent generations, and in Central America, women of mixed blood are commonly considered barren. The cause of this phenomen, which is certainly frequent, is not however physiological, but an immoral course of life.[6] The fact that in the islands of Cuba and St. Domingo, the half-caste population has increased to hundreds of thousands, attest at least that the offspring of South European Creoles and Negroes are fruitful.   Only one observer has affirmed the entire sterility of Mulattoes in Jamaica, and the statement was not left without contradiction.[7]   In America a hybrid race, the Zambos, has arisen, descendants of Negroes and the women of the so-called red aborigines.[8] They

---

[4] Flourens, Examen du livre de Mr. Darwin sur l'origine des espèces, p. 21. Paris, 1864.

[5] Unité de l'espèce humaine, p. 54. Paris, 1861.

[6] On this point of dispute, which it is impossible to settle in the absence of strict observations, the author has questioned German merchants long resident in Cuba, and invariably received the answer that mulatto women of every conceivable degree of fertility are not uncommon, and that the frequent unproductiveness of such women must be ascribed to early excesses.

[7] P. Broca, Hybridity in the Genus Homo, p. 36. London, 1864.

[8] Cases in which negresses form unions with the indigenous men of America are, as might be expected, very rare.

are frequently found [9] among the Creek Indians of the United States, as well as in Central America ; and on the coasts of Ystmo and New Granada the population already bears distinct marks of semi-African blood. In the former dependencies of Spain, the hybrids of Europeans and American women may be reckoned by millions ; Ladinos, as they are termed in Mexico ; Cholos, in Ecuador, Peru, and Chili, and collectively known as Mestizios. If hybrids are rarities in Australia, this, as judicial investigations have attested, is because the natives themselves habitually destroy the half-castes. [10] Tasmanian women have likewise given birth to numerous hybrids, for James Bonwick knew and names the mother of thirteen half-caste children. [11] Paul Broca was therefore falsely informed when he denied the existence of half-caste Australians and Tasmanians, [12] and thus fall to the ground the conclusions which he pronounced with unwarranted assurance. But it is still more significant that half-castes are born of unions between Europeans and Hottentots, for if any race of men have a claim to be regarded as a separate species, it is undoubtedly these aboriginal inhabitants of the Cape. [13] Finally in remote islands, such as Tristan d'Acunha, various crosses between English, Dutch, Mulattoes, and Negresses have taken place. [14] To judge by experience in the vegetable kingdom, as Darwin observes, threefold crosses betwixt Negroes, Indians, and Europeans, as they occur in America, afford the most certain proof of the reciprocal fertility of the parental forms. [15]

Even were it no longer disputed that all the families of mankind, however different, were capable of generating hybrids, we should still be no nearer a decision as to the unity or plurality of the human

[9] According to the Second Annual Report of the Board of Indian Commissioners, vol. iii. p. 412. Washington, 1871.

[10] Charles Darwin, Descent of Man, vol. i. p. 194. Also Edward John Eyre, Central Australia, vol. ii. p. 324 London, 1845.

[11] The Last of the Tasmanians, p. 316. London, 1870. [12] Broca, p. 47.

[13] In their own country, these mongrels are sometimes called hybrids, sometimes Griquas, but this latter designation has been so misapplied that it no longer conveys any strict anthropological idea. Fritsch, Die Eingebornen Südafrika's, p. 376.

[14] Quatrefages, Rapport, p. 477. [15] Descent of Man, vol. i. p. 198.

2

species. For modern science acknowledges that animals which when in a state of freedom avoided one another sexually, can be induced to form an entire mixture of blood and specific characters. We do not say so much of the commonly cited hybrid productions of the dog, the wolf, and the fox, of the goat and the sheep, of the rabbit and the hare, for in some cases the mongrel forms were not successfully established, while in others the fertility of the hybrids was not continued beyond a few generations. But we will cite the experiment for which we are indebted to Mr. Buxton, who has naturalized two species of cockatoos, in his park in Norfolk, which not only breed every year, but have crossed in the open air and produced a hybrid race which, unlike both its parents, is decorated with a scarlet hood, so that creation here seems to be enriched by a new species. Moreover our canine races are certainly the result of a mixture of species. In shape and make the Eskimo dog approximates to the Arctic wolf; the Indian dog to the prairie wolf; the Nubian domestic dog and its mummied examples clearly testify to their descent from the jackal.[16] Again, the peculiar smell of the last-named animal was acquired by dogs which Geoffroi St. Hilaire had for some time fed on raw meat. Our present breeds of cattle have moreover been evolved from two distinct European species : *Bos primigenius*, which was still wild in Cæsar's time, and *Bos longifrons* or *brachyceros* of the Swiss lake dwellings.[17] As long as they lived side by side in freedom they preserved their specific characters in full purity, whereas their structure and form are now completely blended by intercrossing. European cattle are capable of generating hybrids even with the zebu (*Bos indicus*), the

---

[16] Herr Jeitteles, who has been long studying this question, and has diligently collected the skulls of animals, maintains the complete accordance of the dog of the lake dwellings and the Algerian jackal (*Canis Sacalius*). Alterthümer der Stadt Olmütz, p. 79. Vienna, 1872.

[17] Rütimeyer arrived at the conclusion that the cattle of Chillingham Park are the descendants of the tamed ure-ox (*Bos primigenius*), also that the Trochoceros and Frontosus forms are likewise derived from the ure-ox, whereas the Bos brachyceros represents a distinct so-called species. Art und Race des europäischen Rindes im Archiv für Anthropologie, vol. i. pp. 240–247. Brunswick, 1866.

Indian buffalo. Again, our domestic swine are mongrels of the wild-boar, or *Sus scrofa*, and the *Sus indica*, which no longer exists in a wild condition. We owe this statement to the craniological investigations of Herr von Nathusius, who in other points ranks among the enlightened opponents of the Darwinian school. That the same can be said of Agassiz gives double weight to the fact, that he declared the endeavour to employ fertility of union as a limitation of species to be a complete fallacy.[18] If this be the case, no obstacle remains to the opinion that the several races of man are distinct species, provided they fulfil the condition which Grisebach holds to be essential for the formation of a species, namely, the absence of transitions not arising from crosses.[19] Occasionally a distinct line may really be drawn, as for instance between Hottentots and the Kaffir tribes ; the Papuans of New Guinea and the true Polynesians. Facts such as these have encouraged the pluralistic school of anthropologists to assert a multiplicity of human species. To the United States of America, where this school formerly found its most energetic champion, we may trace the doctrine which teaches that the various inhabitants of the earth were created in those regions which they now inhabit, and that they are not descended from single ancestral pairs, but, like seed sown broadcast by the Creator, at once peopled the earth in hordes, being already in partial possession of their present vocabulary ; for in its zeal, this school assumed a plurality of species even within a family connected by ties of language as in the Aryan. These strange opinions were primarily based on the assertion that the characters of specific variety have been maintained in historic ages, especially by the Jews and Brahminical Indians.[20] These examples are incapable of converting sincere

---

[18] Essay on Classification, p. 250. London, 1849.

[19] Die Vegetation der Erde, vol. i. p. 8. "The sytematiser's method of distinguishing between varieties and species consists in this," that in the first case he can point to intermediate forms, but none in the latter.

[20] Tyros in ethnology must be warned against mistakes with regard to the "Black Jews" of Cochin, which were formerly erroneously cited as an example that the sun is capable of altering the colour of the skin. The black Jews are natives of India, purchased as slaves by true white Jews, and received into the community after the fulfilment of the Mosaic rites.

sceptics, for we know that during thousands of years, Jews as well as Brahminical Indians have intermarried only among themselves, while the experience of breeders of animals proves that racial characters must thus necessarily become established.   Even in modern societies, in which the precepts of caste enjoin marriages in the same rank, it is acknowledged that an aristocratic type occasionally appears; in the Hapsburgs and in the Bourbon families peculiarities of physiognomy have become hereditary in a comparatively short period.

It is furthermore supposed that this high antiquity and persistency of type is shown in the representations of various races in the monuments on the Nile.   Egyptologists are certainly unanimous that the people of the Pharaohs are distinctly recognizable in the Fellaheen of the Nile, and that, although much defaced, the negroes of the Soudan are beyond all doubt so distinctly portrayed beside them on the wall-paintings that there can be no confusion.   It is, however, a suspicious circumstance that the old Egyptian artists unnaturally distorted their figures according to fixed prototypes; they draw the face always in profile, the eye always full face, and the hands invariably as two right hands. Hence we are surprised at the temerity of the pluralists who would infer from these portraits of kings and queens an admixture of Semitic or European blood in the Pharaohs.   Of the wife of the founder of the 17th dynasty, Amunoph I., ascribed to the year 1671 B.C., it is said that she most strongly and evidently bears the characteristics of Hebrew blood, and this is at once adduced as proof that the Chaldean type has been traced in Egypt, prior to the arrival of Abraham.[21]   The head of Rameses the Great is spoken of as highly European and Napoleonic in type.   In Rosellini's representation the portrait of Rameses does certainly vividly recall the first Emperor of the French, but that this copy was either unsuccessful, or was purposely endowed with Buonapartist features, is shown by a more accurate drawing published by Robert Hartmann.[22]   Darwin relates that, in a visit to the British Museum, he and two officials of that institution, whom he speaks of as competent

---

[21] Morton, Types of Mankind, p. 163, fig. 33.

[22] Zeitschrift für Ethnologie, p. 153. Berlin, 1869.

judges, were struck by the strongly marked negro character of the statue of Amunoph III.[23]   Yet this is described by Nott and Gliddon as a "hybrid without admixture of negro blood." Robert Hartmann was unable to satisfy himself that the Egyptian type had undergone alteration by mixture with Asiatic races, but on the contrary he perceived modifications such as might be accounted for by Nubian conquests and invasions.[24]   If the monuments of Egypt prove on the one hand that, after the lapse of 4000 years, the inhabitants of the Nile valley still resemble their ancestors, they teach us on the other that, even at that time, the so-called types were merged into one another by intermixtures.   No one can feel more forcibly the weakness of the opinion which holds to the immutability of racial characters, than one who has endeavoured to describe various nations, for no single characteristic is strictly the exclusive possession of any race of men, but each loses itself by imperceptible gradations.   If it were easy to draw the line between the various races, anthropologists would not so far differ from one another, that one feels himself obliged to separate mankind into two, another into a hundred and fifty species, races, or families.[25]   The method followed in these divisions is usually founded on error, for it is not the frequent occurrence of definite characters which is established, but among the numerous representatives of a type, that one is selected which differs most strongly from the members of other races of mankind.   Thus the German traveller before he crosses the Alps, possesses a definite conception of the Italian countenance and figure.   At Naples he expects everywhere to meet men on whose heads he has only to put a Phrygian cap, in order to recognize in them the well-known operatic figures, and he imagines that he has but to place a trunkless head on a silver plate in the hands of any girl to transform her

---

[23] Darwin, Descent of Man, i. 217.

[24] Zeitschrift für Ethnologie, p. 147.   Berlin, 1869.

[25] Quatrefages, Unité, p. 366. According to Darwin (Descent of Man, i. 226), Virey assumed 2, Jacquinot 3, Kant 4, Blumenbach 5, Buffon 6, Hunter 7, Agassiz 8, Pickering 11, Bory St. Vincent 15, Desmoulins 16, Morton 22, Crawford 60, and Burke 63 species or races.   Haeckel (Natürliche Schöpfungsgeschichte, 2 Aufl., p. 604) and Friedrich Müller (Anthropol. Thl. iii. der Novara-Reise) are satisfied with 12 species, and we ourselves have been led to accept 7 divisions.

into a Judith.[26] The delusion does not last long, and the traveller soon confesses that what he had pictured to himself as the Italian type is only to be found at Rome assembled on the steps of the Trinità di Monte, where models selected from among thousands offer themselves to the artist. The same thing occurs in Germany. If we see a child with delicate skin, rosy colour, flaxen hair, and modest blue eyes, we congratulate ourselves that we have found such a genuinely German type of girl, without considering that we are thus declaring thousands of others to be not genuine, that is, belonging to no race.

In our days, belief in the persistency of specific characters hitherto current has been profoundly shaken by Charles Darwin. Even before his time the fanciful idea of the older geologists had been refuted, that each of the sectional periods, which teachers are obliged to assume for the sake of clearness of expression, had closed with a total annihilation of organic nature, and that then, by a creative fiat a new organic world had followed in its place. As long as our planet has harboured organic life, single new forms of living creatures have silently mingled with the old ones, others have silently disappeared, until, after the lapse of certain periods, new species, all differing from the older ones, are found associated. The succession of time in which the different forms replaced one another was not arbitrary, but presents a morphological chain, each link holding the other, each innovation (in obedience to the law of all genesis) is connected with that which previously existed.

Perhaps there is not a single expert in Europe who would not acknowledge that the organic world of the present age presupposes with imperative necessity that a tertiary creation preceded it, for in Australia and South America, as well as in other portions of the earth well-secured against an interchange of species, the animal world is most closely allied to the local fauna now extinct.

Hence if Darwin's doctrine consisted merely of the proposition that the succession of species is connected with the past by some cause or other, all geologists, botanists, and zoologists would belong to the school of the great Englishman. But, not satisfied

---

[26] Peschel is thinking of Bernard Luini's picture of the daughter of Herodias, not of Judith, at Vienna.

with this claim, he believes himself able to disclose the process itself and its necessity. According to his theory, parents or sexual couples will transmit all their characters, including even the smallest varieties, so that the offspring resemble their parents and yet differ from them in a useful, indifferent, or detrimental direction in some exceedingly minute peculiarity. The detrimental deviations would lead to the speedy destruction of their possessors, nor would the indifferent have any prospect of permanent preservation; the useful alone would effect the transformation of the creatures. But by continual accumulation, imperceptibly minute variations may in the course of considerable periods gradually grow up into specific differences. In this development of new forms, creation at the same time, as it were, criticizes its own works, for as each individual or parental pair usually generates far more descendants than can prosper on the earth, there arises between the offspring of the same, as well as between the representatives of the different species, a struggle for existence in which the more vigorous competitors overpower those less favourably equipped. By continued elimination of the feeble members of the species, and by constant transmission of the favourable newly acquired variations, a change of form gradually occurs. The gist and novelty of Darwin's doctrine consists in the selection just described and which is supposed to be carried on by Nature. This process of transmutation of species has therefore been justly spoken of by Nageli as a utilitarian system. When enthusiasm for this novel and bold idea had given way to cooler reflection, it became more and more evident that selection on utilitarian principles could not always have taken place. The evolution of new organs, or the transformation of old, would certainly have required long periods, during which the incomplete novelty, if not directly detrimental, must at least have remained neutral in the struggle for existence. Moreover, it became evident that organs may exist before advantage can be taken of them. Even among the most different races of mankind, a majority of their number possess vocal apparatus admirably adapted to song, although not employed for musical purposes.[27] Nor does natural selection explain how the shape and

---

[27] This is admitted by Darwin himself.

appearance of the organic world can arouse æsthetic dispositions in sensitive persons.   We find not only the beautiful, the graceful, the agreeable, but also the repulsive, the terrible, the ridiculous, and the demoniac, represented in animals or plants.   Darwin, in his book on the descent of man, has attempted to overcome this difficulty by a new article of belief, namely, in sexual selection ; the female animals being supposed to prefer the male which most actively excites their senses.   But in butterflies, particularly in the Sphingidæ, the lower wings are coloured with peculiar brightness and are adorned with gaudy eyes; yet this creature conceals its own decorations when at rest, while all perception of penciling and colour is precluded by its rapid movements when in flight.[28] Many finely formed men and women in America and Africa habitually disfigure themselves by placing discs and plugs in their lips and cheeks, and thereby prove that their taste is still undeveloped, so that their other physical beauties are certainly not due to a fortunate selection.   Again we find beauties in such members of the animal kingdom as fecundate themselves, and even in the motionless vegetable kingdom.   The aspect of an oak during a storm, the mournful appearance of a Deodara, the hues of many a corolla, the graceful lines of trailing vines, the fabric of a rosebud, are all capable of affording us æsthetic satisfaction, and yet any idea of the exercise of sexual selection by these objects is absolutely impossible.

Still less can the transmission of prejudicial characters be reconciled with intentional selection.   Darwin indeed appeals to the correlation of the constituent parts of an animal body, in consequence of which changes in one part are accompanied by changes in remote portions of the body ; but as we cannot demonstrate, or even imagine, the necessity of this correlation, this argument has no foundation.

According to the Darwinian theory, the ancestor of modern man must have been a hairy creature, protected from changes of temperature by a furry coat.   Yet the loss of this fur could only

---

[28] Darwin, who never conceals anything that disturbs him, gives in his Descent of Man, vol. i. p. 354, a number of cases in which the lower surface of the wings of nocturnal butterflies are brilliantly coloured or adorned with splendid eyes.   When at rest these beauties are invariably concealed.

act prejudicially in the struggle for existence.[29] In the case of birds the same observation applies to gaudy plumage, which favours the schemes of their enemies, to the boat-like excrescences of their beaks, as well as to the trailing tails which hinder flight and incubation. Thus it is just the new pith of the Darwinian doctrine, namely, natural selection, which still remains unaccredited ; nay, Darwin himself, truth-loving as he always is, has openly confessed with regard to the objections made by Nageli and Broca, that in the earlier editions of " The Origin of Species " he has probably ascribed too much to the effects of natural selection and the survival of the fittest.[30] We may add that the older history of the organic world exhibits cases in which the extinction of families of animals has been originated by profound alterations of structure which, as far as such inferences are justifiable with regard to phenomena exhibited by fossils, must have been prejudicial to them. The Ammonites, which died out during the cretaceous period, previously began to pass into so-called cripple forms. Their shells, originally curled into a planiform spiral, subsequently become perpendicularly spiral, extend themselves lineally, or bend like a bow, a hook, or a shepherd's crook, or at least distend themselves so much, that the individual convolutions are no longer in contact with one another.[31] But this abandonment of the old type was followed by the complete extinction of the family.

We, nevertheless, hold the Darwinian doctrine, not indeed as a successful, but yet as the best attempt to explain the connection of the older with the newer creation, and it will only be supplanted by a more satisfactory solution. It is scarcely comprehensible that pious minds can be disquieted by this doctrine, for creation

---

[29] Inveterate disciples of Darwin remind us that if graminivorous animals, such as horses, take to animal food, their bellies lose their hair. Seligmann, Fortschritte der Racenlehre, Geogr. Jahrbuch, vol. iv. p. 288. Gotha, 1872. The ghost Lemur (Tarsius) is, however, a beast of prey. Carl Semper himself witnessed how one of these creatures killed a mouse with a bite, and devoured it (Allgem. Ztg., p. 239. 1873.) Yet we do not find that baldness has been caused by these articles of food.

[30] Descent of Man, vol. i. p. 152.

[31] Credner, Elemente der Geologie, 1 edit. p. 435.

gains in dignity and importance if it possesses the power of renovation, and of evolving higher perfection. We may remind the religous world of the danger to which they expose themselves by contemning an investigator so highly esteemed as Darwin. When Copernicus came forward with his, as yet, feebly substantiated doctrine of the planetary character of the earth ; nay, even later, when the telescope had discovered in the crescent shape of Venus, as well as in Jupiter and its satellites, a testimony confirming that of the senses ; and Kepler by his laws had furnished strict proofs of the truth of the Copernican theory, the new revelation was condemned not by the Roman Curia alone, but also by Protestant zealots. The true Creator, because he had acted on the plan pointed out by Copernicus rather than that of Ptolemy, was placed on the Index in the person of those who had made known his system of worlds ; they were persecuted as heretics, for whom, as Kepler writes of himself, God waited six thousand years, in order that they might recognize his works.[32] Once more, two creators are represented to us ; the Creator as Cuvier pictured him, who destroys his works because he has devised better ones, and the Creator as Darwin pictures him, who created life variable, but foresaw the tendency of this variation of form, and now allows the clock to go undisturbed. A single fossil discovery, which, however, we will not either desire or predict, might any day testify that the true Creator more nearly resembles the Darwinian conception than that of Cuvier ; the rash zealots would then have to lament, as did Galileo's tormentors, that they had persecuted the true God for the sake of a scientific phantom. The history of the transmutation theory can already claim a brilliant case of refutation. Cuvier silenced Lamarck, Darwin's precursor, by requiring him to discover the intermediate form between the Palæotherium and the horse of the present day, if a transformation from the older into the newer animal was supposed to have taken place. Were he still alive, Cuvier, seeing in any of our museums the graceful Hipparion of prehistoric times, with its two aborted hoofs, would have been forced to acknowledge with shame that his demand had been strictly fulfilled.[33]

---

[32] C. G. Reuschle, Kepler und die Astronomie, p. 127. Frankf. 1870.
[33] Richard Owen, Anatomy of Vertebrates, vol. iii. p. 791. London, 1868.

Although Darwin has not been able to give strict proof of his theory of the transmutation of species, he has, nevertheless, thoroughly shaken the credit of the opposite theory of the immutability of specific characters, and, in the sphere of ethnology, has corroborated the conjecture that all races have sprung from a single primordial form, and by the accumulation of small differences, rendered persistent by undisturbed transmission, have developed into varieties. This opinion is favoured by a number of facts, which lead us to infer the high antiquity of our race as well as the capacity of man to adapt himself to the greatest contrasts of temperature found on the face of the earth.

As far as man has hitherto advanced in the direction of the poles, traces of inhabitants have been discovered ; for not long before the sailor Morton and the Eskimo Hans reached Cape Constitution on the west coast of Greenland (81° 22′ north lat.), on June 24th, 1854, they noticed the fragments of a sledge.[34] Traces of inhabitants, such as walrus ribs which had been used as sledge-runners, an old knife handle, and some circular stones for fastening tents, were found by the crew of the *Polaris* at the extremity of West Greenland.[35] These testified to the previous presence of Eskimo, whom in Homeric language we must regard as the " uttermost men " (ἔσχατοι ʼανδρῶν). With the men we also discover the tracks of at least one domestic animal, for the dog has always been his companion. That portion of the earth has yet to be found which could not be inhabited, or at least visited by some race or other. It is true, the transitions from different climates must not be too sudden. Even Icelanders who immigrate to Copenhagen, are apt to perish from consumption,[36] although they are of common origin with the Danes, and only eight hundred years ago spoke the same language. While in the New World, and in the Philippine Islands, the Spaniards have adapted themselves to a tropical life,[37] the English have been unable to populate India, and the Dutch to people Su-

---

[34] Kane, Arctic Explorations, i. 297. Philadelphia, 1856.

[35] Proceedings of the Royal Geogr. Society, vol. xviii.

[36] Waitz, Anthropologie, vol. i. p. 145.

[37] Jäger, Reisen in den Philippinen, p. 29. Berlin, 1873.

matra and Java with the descendants of Europeans. Children born of English parents in India, sicken and die when they pass the age of about six years. Hence the English send their children to Europe on the approach of the dangerous moment, and the same occurs among the Dutch. In the Dutch possessions in India a European woman reflects maturely before she consents to a marriage, for the first child-bed usually costs the life of the mother. Even the Portuguese women at Tete, on the Zambesi, succumb to this fatality, as is stated by Rowley, the English missionary. But if the transitions to other climates follow gradually and at great intervals of time, there is no doubt that men of the same breed can people every zone of the earth, for no one disputes that the Hindoo of high caste, whether in Bengal, in Madras, or in Scinde, or any other tropical portion of his own country, is of the same Aryan origin as the old northern inhabitants of Iceland, and that the unknown primordial ancestors of both must have dwelt in a common home. Nor will any one maintain that the Gothic conquerors on the other side of the Pyrenees did not long preserve the purity of their " blue blood," and give birth to children of their own stock, Spaniards in Spain. From the Spanish peninsula again were derived the settlers in Madeira and the Canary Islands who, some twenty years ago, after the outbreak of the vine disease, emigrated in multitudes to Trinidad and British Guiana. All ethnologists agree that the aborigines of America, with the exception perhaps of the Eskimo, constitute a single race, and that this race has succeeded in adapting itself to every climatic condition in both hemispheres from the Arctic circle to the equator, and beyond it as far as the 50th latitude. We meet the Chinese at Maimaitchin (Kiakhta) on the Siberian boundary, where the mean temperature is below freezing point, and the thermometer falls in winter to 40° Reaumur ; and we find them also on the island of Singapore, which almost touches the equator.[38] Turkish races, such as the Yakuts, are settled on the Lena, where Kennan found them [39] gossiping in the open air at a temperature of 32° Reaumur, clad only in a shirt and

---

[38] Pumpelly, Across America and Asia, p. 256. London, 1870.
[39] Tent Life in Siberia, p. 218.

a fur coat. The Kirghiz pasture their flocks on the Pamir plateau, perhaps the highest steppe in the world, and they dwell as the dominant race in the tropical part of South Egypt,[40] as well as at the ill-famed Massowah on the Red Sea.

In the examination of racial characters, we shall show how little these great fluctuations permit fixed limits to be drawn ; but meanwhile we may prove by a number of facts, that nations and races of men the most remote from, and least resembling each other, are so analogous in their mental habits, that at least it is impossible to question the unity and identity of the intellectual faculties of the human species. We shall refer later on to the fact that the language of signs and gestures used by the deaf and dumb of Europe coincides with the method of communication employed under similar circumstances by the North American Redskins. With but few exceptions, all nations have arrived at a single or double decimal system, because they have used their fingers in counting. Skin-painting and tattooing reappear in every part of the world. Knocking out the front teeth is not only a negro custom, but occurs also in Australia. Again, the teeth are filed to a point in Brazil,[41] as well as by the Otando, Apono, Tshogo, and Ashango tribes in Western Africa.[42] Hippocrates even, or whoever else may have been the author of the book on "Air, Water, and Situation," mentions that by the people of the steppes of Southern Russia, the skulls of free-born children were pressed between boards to give them a more upright form ; [43] and we meet the same fashion among the Conivos on the Ucayali, in South America ; [44] it was observed by Ch. Bell and Berthold Siemann in the Mosquitia among the Smu ; [45] it is practised also on the northern continent, especially by the Tshinuks of British Columbia, and generally by all the so-called Flatheads, who further only permit the pressure of the skulls of the children of the

---

[40] Latham, Varieties of Man, p. 77.

[41] Von Martius, Ethnographie, i. 536.

[42] Du Chaillu, Equatorial Africa, p. 74, and Ashango Land, p. 431.

[43] Cap. 80.   [44] Grandidier, Perou et Bolivie, p. 129.

[45] Journal Royal Geogr. Society, vol. xxxii. p. 256, and Siemann, Nicaragua, Panama, and Mosquitea, p. 308.

free-born.[46]   Sanitary considerations have induced many nations to introduce circumcision.   Herodotus [47] considered that the Egyptians and Ethiopians were the inventors of this preventive measure, which was only borrowed from them by the Phœnicians and Syrians.   At the time of the conquest, the Spaniards found circumcised nations in Central America,[48] and on the Amazon, the Tecuna and Manaos tribes still observe this practice.[49]

In the South Seas it has been met with among three different races, but it is performed in a somewhat different manner.   On the Australian continent, not all, but the majority of tribes practise circumcision.   Among the Papuans, the inhabitants of New Caledonia [50] and the New Hebrides adhere to this custom.   In his third voyage, Captain Cook found it among the inhabitants of the Friendly Islands, in particular at Tongataboo,[51] and the younger Pritchard bears witness to its practice in the Samoa or Fiji groups.[52]   Another Mosaic statute requires that the Jew should endeavour to raise posterity to his brother's widow.[53] This view of fraternal duty was met with by Plan Carpin, the ambassador of St. Louis to the Mongols,[54] and by Martius among the Brazilian tribes of Tupinamba,[55] and it prevails also among the Kolush, in the north-west of America,[56] and the Ostiaks in Northern Russia.[57]   We even find an instance in which we come upon two Mosaic statutes, namely, circumcision and the above-mentioned duty of brothers-in-law, which is quite beyond suspicion of any connection with Judaism, that is to say, among the Papuans of New Caledonia.[58]   The strange custom of greeting by rubbing noses, is not only peculiar to all Eskimo even as far as Greenland,[59] but is also ascribed to the Australians.[60]

---

[46] Paul Kane, Indians of North America, p. 181.   [47] Book ii. 104.

[48] Herrera, Historia general, Dec. IV. lib. ix. cap. 181.

[49] Von Martius, Ethnographie, i. 582.

[50] Cook, Voyages in the Australian Hemisphere, vol. iii. p. 156.

[51] Cook and King, vol. i. p. 384.

[52] Polynesian Reminiscences, p. 393.

[53] Deut. xxv. 5-10.   [54] Receuil de Voyages, iv. 613.

[55] Ethnographie, i. 153.   [56] Waitz, Anthropologie, iii. 328.

[57] Castrèn, Ethnolog. Vorlesungen, p. 119.

[58] Rochas, Nouv. Caledonie, p. 232.   [59] Barrow, Arctic Voyages, p. 30.

[60] Waitz (Gerland), Anthropologie, vol. vi. p. 749.

Darwin observed it among the Maori of New Zealand,[61] Lamont noticed it among the Polynesians of the Penrhyn and Marquesas islands.[62] Wallace, who was startled to see it in practice among his crew on taking leave of Mancassar, calls it the Malay kiss,[63] and Linnæus observed it in Lapland.[64]

The descriptions of Cook's first and second voyages by Hawkesworth and the two Forsters, made us acquainted with the Polynesian custom of ratifying a bond of friendship by an exchange of names. The same practice prevailed among the Mohawks in North America,[65] and in South Africa, a bond of fraternity was concluded in the same manner by a Makololo and a Zulu Kaffir in Livingstone's presence.[66] Every possibility that such community of custom is the result of intercourse is removed, when we find that both among the Fuegians of South America, and the inhabitants of the Andaman Islands in the Gulf of Bengal, widows are obliged to wear the skulls of their dead husbands suspended round the neck [67] by a cord.

From the lofty plains of Peru and Bolivia may be seen cairns or so-called Apachetas on the mountain tops, which no mule driver will pass without adding a new stone to the memorial.[68] This custom extends all over the world. Captain Speke observed it in the region of Usui to the south of Karagve and south-west of the Ukerewe Lake.[69] Colonel Meadows Taylor in a romance [70] esteemed for its ethnographic delineations, describes the same custom in the Mahratta districts of India. Adolphe Bastian saw similar pyramids of stones in the mountain passes in Burmah, and among the Kayans in Borneo,[71] the brothers Schlagenweit

[61] Voyage in the Beagle, vol. ii. p. 198.
[62] Wild Life among the Pacific Islanders, pp. 18, 269.
[63] Malay Archipelago, ii. 165.
[64] Tylor, Early History of Mankind, p. 66.
[65] Ibid. p. 161.   [66] Zambesi, p. 149.
[67] Frederick Mouat, Andaman Islanders, p. 327.
[68] Grandidier, Perou et Bolivie. In more detail in J. J. von Tschudi, Reisen durch Südamerika, vol. v. p. 52. Leipzig, 1869.
[69] Source of the Nile, p. 193.
[70] Tara, a Mahratta tale, i. 144.
[71] Völker des östlichen Asiens, vol. ii. p. 483; vol. v. p. 47.

in Thibet,[72] Michie during his journey from Pekin across the Mongolian steppes,[73] Ebers on the Sinaitic peninsula.[74] In Switzerland stones are piled upon the graves of the victims of fatal accidents,[75] and in Venezuela these monuments have precisely the same signification at the present day.[76] Spenser St. John relates that similar cairns are erected by the Dyaks of Borneo to the eternal disgrace of any man guilty of a shameless falsehood or a breach of promise.[77]

Lastly, it is to all appearance a perfectly meaningless custom that a man, when a child is born to him, should stretch himself on a couch, and behave like a lying-in woman. Diodorus was acquainted with this custom in Corsica, Strabo notices it among the Spanish Basques,[78] among whom it is still maintained under the name of "couvade;"[79] Marco Polo ascribes this habit to the population of Zardandan or the "people with golden teeth," whom, according to Pauthier's explanations, we must look for westwards of the Chinese Yunnan on the upper Mekong;[80] and not very far from it, namely, in Borneo among the Dyaks, the father of the new-born child is for eight days allowed to eat nothing but rice, must take care not to expose himself to the sun, and must give up bathing during four days.[81] In South America, east of the Cordilleras, the custom of the paternal lying-in has been observed by Martius among the Mundrucus and Manaos on the Amazon, and it extends to the Caribs[82] and to the Macushi of Guayana, among whom it was met with by the younger Schomburgk;[83] according to James Orton[84] it

---

[72] Indien und Hochasien, vol. ii. p. 330.

[73] Siberian Overland Route, p. 136.

[74] George Ebers, Durch Gosen zum Sinai, p. 188.

[75] Carl Vogt, Vorlesungen über den Menschen, vol. ii. p. 119.

[76] Dr. Ernst im Globus, vol. xxi. p. 124.

[77] Life in the Far East, vol. i. p. 76. London, 1862.

[78] Geogr., lib. iii. cap. 4. Tauchn. ed. i. 265.

[79] Lubbock, Prehistoric Times, p. 580.

[80] Marco Polo, lib. ii. cap. 41. (Vol. ii. p. 52, in Yule's edition.)

[81] Spenser St. John, i. p. 160.

[82] Spix and Martius, Reise in Brasilien, vol. iii. p. 1339, and Martius, Ethnographie, pp. 392 and 538.

[83] Reisen, vol. ii. p. 314.

[84] The Andes and the Amazon Land, p. 172. 1870.

is also customary among the Jivaros on the Napo. Even yet we have not exhausted the list of nations which adopt this custom,[85] but we will merely add that in the beginning of the last century it was also met with by the missionary Zucchelli among the negroes of Cassango.[86] Heedless travellers have not failed to revile or ridicule this practice as a senseless absurdity ; profound judges on the other hand inform us that it is founded upon a misguided solicitude. Dobrizhoffer, who describes it among the Abipones, informs us that the fathers avoid draughts and fast strictly only because they consider that a material connection still exists between themselves and the new-born infant, so that their excesses or abstinence might affect the child. If the infant dies during the first few days, the women accuse the father of heartless frivolity.[87] In the Antilles, the father who is expecting offspring might not eat the flesh of the turtle or the manati, for in the first case deafness and deficiency of brain, in the second disfigurement by small round eyes, might be apprehended for the child.[88] Similarly, among the Indians of British Guayana, on the occasion of a bite of a serpent, the parents and brothers of the wounded person inflict fasts and privations upon themselves for several days.[89] Thus the inhabitants of the four quarters of the world have hit on the same ideas and superstitions, a coincidence which can be explained only in two ways ; either these errors originated when all the varieties of our race still dwelt together in one narrow home, or they have been independently developed after the dispersion over the entire globe. If the latter be probable, then the mental faculties of all families of mankind are alike, even in their strangest twists and aberrations.

---

[85] Since the above was printed (Ausland, 1867, p. 1108), Dr. Ploss has published a treatise on the paternal child-bed with a greater profusion of testimony, in the 10th Jahresbericht des Leipzigers Vereins für Erdkunde, pp. 33–48. Leipzig, 1871.

[86] Antonio Zucchelli, Missione di Congo, vii. 15, p. 118: Venice, 1712.

[87] Geschichte der Abiponer, vol. ii. p. 273.

[88] E. B. Tylor, Early History of Mankind, p. 372.

[89] C. F. Appun im Ausland, No. 31, p. 440.

III.—THE FIRST HOME OF THE HUMAN RACE.

WITH few exceptions all oceanic islands, that is, such as lie at a considerable distance from the nearest continent, have been found uninhabited when first visited by European navigators. That Barent should have discovered no inhabitants on Bears' Island and Spitzbergen in 1596, does not surprise us when we remember their inhospitable position, but it is strange that the same should have been the case in Iceland, for the opposite coast of East Greenland is inhabited by Eskimo as far as $75°$ north latitude. The earliest colonists of Iceland seem to have been Celtic Christians in the year 795 ; for there are legends which say that when the Normans first set foot on the " Ice Land," they found croziers, bells, and Irish books on an islet on the south coast, still called Priest's Island.   In the Atlantic Ocean the coral-built group of the Bermudas, the volcanic Azores, the volcanic group of Madeira, the volcanic group of the Cape Verd Islands, the volcanic islands in the Gulf of Guinea,[1] the lonely volcanic islands of Fernando Noronha, Trinidad with the Martin Vaz-Klippen Islands, St. Helena, Ascension, Tristan d'Acunha, and even the numerous Falkland Islands, not to mention those in the Antarctic Ocean, were all uninhabited.   The volcanic islands of the Marion, Croset, and Kerguelen groups, with those which lie southwards, and the two island volcanoes of St. Paul and Amsterdam, and even Mauritius and Bourbon, and the granitic island of Rodrigue, which is reckoned with them, were all void of human beings.   Even New Zealand, extensive as it is, has been inhabited only in modern times, for according to the statements of the Maori, though these are unreliable, their forefathers landed on the northern island about 1400 A.D., while the volcanic group of the Chatham Islands, lying eastwards, was colonized by New Zealanders only during the last century, and the volcanic Auckland Islands to the south are still uncolonized.

In the whole ocean hitherto examined, the Canary Islands

---

[1] They were discovered by the Portuguese, 1470-1486, and were untenanted. Ghillany Martin Behaim.

alone were inhabited; here were found the Guanches, now extinct, who at the time of their discovery were no longer aware that a continent existed in their neighbourhood, for on being asked by the Spanish missionary how they had come to their archipelago, they gave the ingenuous answer, "God placed us on these islands, and then forsook and forgot us." Fragments of their language have, however, since indicated that they were scattered members of the Berber family. We know moreover that they were in the habit of making their dead into mummies, and also that they brought goats with them when they first settled in the islands.

Again, the islands in the Pacific Ocean to the west of South America were found uninhabited; among them Juan Fernandez, the scene of Alexander Selkirk's adventures, and Massafuera, S. Felix, and Ambrosia, likewise Sala y Gomez, the volcanic Galapagos Islands, chosen by the buccaneers for their hiding-places, Cocos Island, and the Revillagigedo group. In some cases even islands which were extensive, and situated near the mainland, remained uninhabited, such as Behring's Island, notorious for the shipwreck of its discoverer, whose name it bears.

Arguing from these historical facts, we may venture to state that the first human beings were inhabitants of a continent. The diffusion of the Malay tribes to which, besides the actual Malays of Sumatra and Malacca and the Javans, belong also the brown tribes with straight hair which, under the name of Polynesians, are distributed over all the tropical or subtropical islands of the South Sea, might be quoted as a single but only apparent exception. Since Wilhelm von Humboldt's researches on the Kawi language, we know that the dominant race in Madagascar also belongs to the Malay family, a fact which was previously disputed. This race of mankind has spread from the Comoro Islands, where the language is Malayan, to Easter Island, from 43° 30″ east long. to 109° 17″ west long., that is to say, over five-ninths of the circumference of the world. Nevertheless, it is not *primâ facie* very credible that the original stock of the Malay family should have arisen on islands. The resemblance of their languages proves that before their dispersion the widely remote members of this family must have inhabited a common home. But this home must be sought only where the Malay nations are still most densely populous. The point from which these hordes spread, lay therefore somewhere between Sumatra, Java, and the peninsula of Malacca. We may even go somewhat further and look for it on the South Asiatic continent, for in their physical characters the Malays are allied to the great Mongolian race. The extension of the Malay family more than half-way round the world, suffices as an example of how far the migratory instinct may scatter a human family which has once procured means for crossing the sea. But on continents also, the migrations of the earliest human families extended to the remotest districts. A single great language with various shades of dialect fills the whole of South Africa as far as the equator, so that Suaheli of the east coast is not entirely unintelligible even to the Africans on the Gaboon in equatorial West Africa. In language, we ourselves belong to the great circle of Aryan nations, which includes the Celts of Gaul and Britain, all Germans, the Italians, Greeks, and Albanians, all the Sclavonians, the Armenians, the Ossets of the Caucasus, the Kurds, the people of ancient Persia, and the Brahminical Hindoos.

In America, though the case is not quite the same, a similar fact is observable. Setting aside the Eskimo and certain tribes of what was once Russian America, all the inhabitants of the New World, according to the unanimous testimony of all anthropologists, belong to a single stock, so that we might believe them to have sprung from a single parental pair. Although a confusion, such as exists in the districts of the Caucasus, prevails in the vocabulary of their languages, yet the construction of the sentences, or rather the formation of the words, is so peculiar and homogeneous that Spanish missionaries in South America have preferred to preach the Gospel sometimes in the Peruvian Quichua language, sometimes in the Brazilian Tupi or Guarani languages, because the Indians of those parts easily enter into the spirit of those languages, while Spanish and Portuguese are unintelligible to them.

It is true that a family likeness in language, or even a close analogy, is no infallible proof of a common bodily pedigree, for otherwise the nations to the east of the Elbe which formerly spoke Sclavonian and now speak German, must always have been Germans; the English-speaking negroes of the United States must have been Anglo-Saxons, and the Spanish-speaking Indians of Central or South America, blood relations of Calderon. Yet identity or family likeness in language unquestionably proves that all nations included in it must once have been united by a social tie. We may, therefore, conclude that before the separation of their language the whole of the Australians, the South Africans, the Aryan nations, and the Americans possessed a common home, from whence they spread by migration. But if the New World could be gradually peopled from any one starting-point, we can easily imagine that time alone was required for all continents to become peopled from a single point.

We have as yet merely shown that our race, starting from a common habitat, may gradually have ranged over all continents and peopled them. But what is possible may not be probable, and still less inevitable. Fortunately, geology and our knowledge of the distribution of animals enable us to set narrow limits to the district within which we may expect to find the original home of the human race. Geology teaches us that the layers of the earth's crust are ranged in chronological sequence, so that where abnormal disturbances have not occurred, the most recent lies at the top, the most ancient at the bottom. If we now descend from the highest layer, the forms of creation change; with imperceptible transitions they become more and more alien to those of the present time. That which is modern we find above, that which is primitive below, for the history of creations resembles the history of fashions. For we at once observe that, as a rule, the more highly integrated creatures are the newer, the less perfectly integrated, the older. But the zoological forms have not changed everywhere with equal celerity. They have been transformed most rapidly in the Old World, less quickly in North America; they have remained somewhat behindhand in South America, and are most primitive in Australia. Small and remote localities laid aside their organic forms more slowly, or in some cases preserved them altogether.

The fauna of Australia preserves the characters of the age in which forms such as the kangaroo were still usual, while at home we now find marsupials only as fossils of the tertiary period; with the exception of some few smaller species, they have entirely vanished from the face of the earth in the New World. Australia is destitute of all kinds of monkeys, beasts of prey, ungulates and edentata. Of its 132 mammalian species, 102 are marsupials, and the remainder consists of rodents, bats, and strange monotremes. It is true man has made his way into this fauna, and with him— for like associates with like—a carnivorous animal, the dingo or wild dog of Australia. But that they set foot in this zoological province as strangers [2] is held by all who have profited by the historical lessons afforded by a study of the distribution of animals.

The same applies to South America, which contains a peculiar and completely distinct mammalian kingdom of which the edentata are considered the representatives. All the species, the majority of the genera, and even of the families, are different from those of the Old World. Our argument gains much weight from the observations made by Andreas Wagner, that the existing mammals of Australia and South America approximate much more nearly than do ours to the fossil forms of the tertiary period; [3] so that in both these districts the characters have changed much more slowly. South America was however an island within a recent zoological period, before the isthmus of Panama united the two continents. This district therefore, which has remained so primitive, is not a province of which the mammalia are of such a character as to point to its being a possible birthplace of the most modern of all creatures.

It is more reasonable to suppose that the cradle of the human race was in North America. The animal and vegetable world in North America is to some extent similar and is closely analogous to that of Asia and Europe. The physiognomy of nature changes completely only in Central America, nearly, if not exactly, at the southern limit of the true pines, of which, as is well known, South America is destitute.

It is however precisely in the second highest order of mammalia that America has remained more primitive. The falsely so-called Quadrumana of America are so different from ours, that they constitute a separate family, and might in a zoological system be termed the apes of the New World, if they were geographically

---

[2] This is admitted even by Agassiz in the Essay on Classification, p. 60. London, 1849.

[3] Abhandlungen der mathem. physik. Classe der K. bayr. Akademie der Wissenschaften, vol. iv. pp. 1, 18. Munich, 1846.

classified. The American family differs in dentition, in the lateral position of the nostrils, in the absence of ischial callosities and cheek-pouches; nor is any tailless monkey to be found in the whole of America. It is where the highest animals appear—the chimpanzee, the gorilla, and the orang—that we must also look for man.

All these inferences are independent of the fate of the Darwinian dogma; they stand or fall with the doctrine of a single centre of creation for the species of the animal and vegetable kingdom. Even this doctrine by itself meets with stubborn opposition because it is not yet capable of explaining all the facts. Nevertheless, the greatest difficulty, namely, the occurrence of fifty northern species of plants in Terra del Fuego, has been overcome by the acuteness and learning of a German botanist.[4] In the chapter which treats of the primitive inhabitants of America, we shall endeavour to prove their derivation from Northern Asia. We will only observe in anticipation, that the more rude, and hence the more frugal and hardy, a people is, the more readily does it change its abode, so that, in their lowest stages of development, all families of people were capable of accomplishing the migrations which we have ascribed to them. The difficulties generally exist only in the imagination of the spoilt children of civilization.

In Central Australia, where European explorers were exhausted by starvation, hordes of black men roam about, free of care; and if we are startled by the idea that, thousands of years ago, Asiatic tribes are supposed to have crossed Behring's Straits to people America, we quite forget that even at the present day, a naked nation of fishermen still exists in Terra del Fuego, where the glaciers stretch down to the sea, and even into it.

We have already demonstrated that the first appearance of man must have been on a continent; we proved from migrations which have actually taken place, that the dispersion of our race from a single starting-point over the whole world might be only a question of time; we have ascertained from the geographical distribution of animals, that neither Australia nor South America, nor even North America, was a fitting position for the cradle of humanity; con-

---

[4] Grisebach, Vegetation der Erde, vol. i. p. 96.

sequently, it is in the Old World that we must look for it. Then, again, we may confidently set aside the lowlands of Siberia, for at a time geologically recent it was still covered by the sea. This objection would not exist with regard to Europe ; but if Europe had been the starting-point, we should assuredly have found so-called fossil men among us, just as two very highly organized tertiary apes have been discovered, one in Greece, the other in Switzerland.

If we give up Europe also, it is only in Southern Asia or in Africa that we have any prospect of finding the oldest vestiges of our race. Of these regions, British India has already undergone the most thorough geological research, and as many precursory types of the present mammals have already been found, the prospects of localizing our primordial parents in that district are diminished.

It is possible, however, that the first appearance of man may have taken place neither in Southern Asia nor in Africa, but in the Indian Ocean itself. There at one time existed a great continent to which belonged Madagascar and perhaps portions of Eastern Africa, the Maledives and Lacadives, and also the island of Ceylon, which was never attached to India, perhaps even the island of Celebes in the far East, which possesses a perplexing fauna with semi-African features. This continent, which would correspond with the Indian Ethiopia of Claudius Ptolemæus, has been named Lemuria by the English zoologist, Sclater, because it would include the entire range of the lemurs. Such a continent is required by anthropology, for we can then conceive that the inferior populations of Australia and India, the Papuans of the East Indian islands, and lastly, the negroes, would thus be enabled to reach their present abode by dry land. Such a region would be also climatically suitable, for it lies in the zone in which we now find the anthropomorphous apes.

The selection of this locality is, moreover, far more orthodox than it might at the first glance appear, for we here find ourselves in the neighbourhood of the four enigmatic rivers of the scriptural Eden—in the vicinity of the Nile, the Euphrates, the Tigris, and the Indus. By the gradual submergence of Lemuria, the expulsion from Paradise would also be inexorably accomplished

To this may be added that ecclesiastical writers, such as Lactantius,[5] the Venerable Bede,[6] Hrabanus Maurus,[7] Kosmos Indicopleustes,[8] and also the anonymous geographer of Ravenna,[9] placed the scriptural Paradise in South-eastern Asia, and some explicitly on a detached continent, and that the ingenious maps of the Middle Ages exhibit the first parental pair on a land surrounded by sea, lying beyond India. This explains how Columbus after the discovery of South America, taking it for an insular continent lying south-east of the mouth of the Ganges, wrote home to Spain, "There are here great indications suggesting the proximity of the earthly Paradise, for not only does it correspond in mathematical position with the opinions of the holy and learned theologians, but all other signs concur to make it probable." [10]

This suggestion is, however, a mere hypothesis which need not disquiet those who like to imagine Paradise in the land of the lotus blossom, or who turn to the papyrus-fringed shores of the newly discovered lakes of the Upper Nile, or perchance prefer to believe it still nearer to the eastern lands of the scriptures. The value of the hypothesis is, that it challenges a geological investigation of Madagascar, Ceylon, and the island of Rodrigue, as well as deep-sea soundings in the Indian Ocean, to ascertain whether vestiges exist of the higher points of the vanished Lemuria. All that we require is the vindication of a single starting-point for all human *races*, in opposition to the anthropological school of the Americans which has recently constituted above a hundred human *species*, not *races*, of men; as many species, that is, as it is possible to find natural types, and these it is imagined were at once sown broadcast by the Creator, in numbers as vast as swarms of bees, in the localities which they now inhabit. An hypothesis such as this does not explain why the islands were left fallow at this general seed-time, nor why the several quarters of the world admit of being characterized as provinces by means of their fauna and flora. Any explanation of the present by the past

---

[5] Div. Instit. ii. **13.**   [6] De Mundi constit. p. 326.
[7] De Universo, xii. **3.**   [8] Ed. Montfaucon, tom. ii. p. 188.
[9] Geogr. lib. i. cap. 6.
[10] Navarrete, Coleccion de los viages y descubrimientos, vol. i. p. 259. Madrid, 1825.

3

is thus abandoned, although it lies deeply rooted in human nature not to rest satisfied with observed facts until they have been reconciled with some law of necessity.

IV.—THE ANTIQUITY OF THE HUMAN RACE.

THOSE who pronounce in favour of the development of the different races from a single human species which, making its first appearance within a limited region, gradually spread over the whole earth, must admit that events such as these demand periods of vast duration, and on them falls the burden of proof that vestiges of our species may actually be traced up to remote pre-historic times.   These objections would be removed by the dis-covery made by the Abbé Bourgeois, who extracted stone knives and axes from strata of unquestionably miocene date, in the neighbourhood of Tenay (Loir et Cher), which would testify that France was inhabited as early as the middle of the tertiary period.   But at the Archæological Congress at Brussels, in 1872, the best judges of such articles decided against the artificial origin of these so-called human relics of the miocene period.   On the other hand, the highest probability of a human origin must be attributed to the flint implements which were first discovered by Boucher de la Perthes, in 1847, at Menchecourt, in the valley of the Somme, between Abbeville and Amiens, intermingled in the chalky clay with remains of the mammoth, the woolly rhinoceros, an extinct species of horse, the European hippopotamus, and other animals of the diluvial period ; a discovery which has attracted to the site the best geologists of the present time. Human remains have as yet been sought in vain, for the jaw-bone discovered near Moulin Quignon, is supposed to have been inserted for purposes of fraud.   The absence of remains of human bones must not however excite too much distrust, for after the draining of the lake of Haarlem, which was once a gulf, scanty fragments of ships but no human bones were found, although vessels had been wrecked and naval engagements fought on it. According to Prestwich's ingenious conjecture, it is conceivable that in the glacial period, at the end of the tertiary age, the inhabitants of Picardy, like the Eskimo of the present day, broke open the ice of the Somme and harpooned the fish with their missiles through these openings, which they kept free from ice. The stone flakes which in an unsuccessful cast fell into the bed of the river, and were then enveloped in the diluvial deposit, are those which now decorate museums and rejoice the hearts of archæologists. Among these treasures there really are some so regular in outline and so accurately pointed that there can be no question of their artificial origin. But it would be important to ascertain whether they have been selected from among hundreds or thousands of similar but ruder stones in the same neighbourhood. In countries where masses of flint are found on the surface, and where they are readily broken by a sharp blow, they frequently splinter into chips and flakes, from which a very fair collection of stone implements might be put together, for the trouble of picking them up. Among the stone implements which Boucher de la Perthes had placed in the museum of St Germain, Virchow remarked many objects quite familiar to him in his home in Pomerania as sports of nature.[11]

Fortunately, there is a profusion of unimpeachable evidence which confirms the testimony of these flint implements of the Somme valley. As early as 1833–1840 deposits of human remains were discovered by Dr. Schmerling, in Belgian caves, mingled with bones of diluvial mammals, but they were for a long time disregarded in deference to Cuvier, who had denied that man had appeared on the scene before the animals of the present age. These discoveries were much misinterpreted, and it was assumed that the human bones had been transported by beasts of prey, or washed down into the caves by streams, and deposited among the diluvial remains. But since archæologists have been willing to recognize new truths, discoveries of similar bone-caves in other countries rapidly succeeded one another. Occasionally the remains of the diluvial denizens of the earth were extracted

---

[11] Comp. Virchow in the Zeitschr. für Ethnologie, p. 51 (1871), in reference to Pomerania. His statements could be supplemented by Wetzstein in regard to the southern parts of Syria where in the tract of 'Ardh e'-Samân, three days' journey in length, the ground is covered with splinters of flint stone.

from beneath a flooring of calcareous stalactite, and flint implements of certainly artificial origin from beneath a stratum containing bones of prehistoric animals. The examination of one of these caves at Brixham, by a geologist as trustworthy as Dr. Falconer, convinced the specialists of Great Britain as early as 1858, that man was a contemporary of the mammoth, the woolly rhinoceros, the cave-bear, the cave-hyæna, the cave-lion, and therefore of the mammalia of the geological period antecedent to our own.

With the animals just mentioned was associated the reindeer, which, as is well known, belongs not to the extinct, but only to the expelled species. Formerly it roamed over Western France, where its vestiges are now abundant in the valley of the Vezère. In the district of Périgord, in the department of Dordogne, through which the railway between Orleans and Agen passes, six caves have been found. They contain among their detritus remains of reindeer's antlers artistically worked, as well as stone implements. In one of these old hiding-places near Cro-Magnon, the skulls and skeletons of two men and two women were found beside the remains of the cave-tiger (*Felis spelea*), of a colossal bear, of the ure-ox, and also of animals belonging to the far north, such as the jisel (*Spermophilus erythrogenus*) and the ibex. These cave-men of France maintained themselves on the produce of the chase, the horse especially being pursued as game. As the bones of the animals exhibit no traces of fire, the meat must have been either eaten raw, or seethed in water-tight plaited baskets, as is still the custom of certain North Americans, who, having no earthen vessels, heat their water in wooden vessels by dropping in heated stones. Indeed, pebbles which suggest a custom of this sort are found among the ash heaps in the cave of Cro-Magnon.

The ancient inhabitants of the Dordogne already attempted to portray objects of the outer world, such as fish, reindeer, or men, in carvings on horn and the ivory of mammoth's teeth, with a distinctness and animation which compels recognition.[12]   Among

---

[12] Sir John Lubbock, in his Prehistoric Times, ed. 2, 1869, has published the portrait of a mammoth scratched on bone, found in the cave of la Madeleine in Périgord. Critical observers, however, are of opinion that archæological imagination has filled in the outlines of this piece of animal portraiture. Our

the horn implements, mostly awls and arrow-heads with or without barbs, our attention is attracted by the occurrence of needles,
with which, doubtless, the inhabitants of the caves sewed together
the hides of animals.

A soft red ochre which occurs amongst the remains, enables us
to infer that they painted their skin. Their love of finery is also
betrayed by the discovery of necklaces of animals' teeth and shells.
The latter, moreover, were derived from the far-distant shores of the
Atlantic, and could, therefore, have come into their possession
only by means of barter; the same must have been the case with
the rock crystals, which are found, but which do not occur naturally,
within a large radius of the deposits in which they have been found.
Even the horns of the Saiga antelope, of which the nearest range
must have been in Poland, were among the possessions of these
old hunters, and serve as records that even at that time valued
merchandize was distributed over great distances by means of
commerce. Judging from the remains of bones, the hunters of the
Dordogne were not, like the Belgian cave-dwellers, a small race of
men, but of large size and powerful structure. The skulls were of
a long or dolichocephalic form, and the bones of the face, notwithstanding a slight tendency to prognathism, surprise us by the
beauty of their oval outlines. The capacity of the brain-case of a
man (1590 cubic centimetres), and a woman (1450 cubic centimetres),[13] would also indicate high mental endowments, if any such
inference were reliable.

We may here notice the fragment of a skull found in August,
1856, in a cave in the Neanderthal, not far from Düsseldorf, and
which was at first regarded, on account of its huge brow ridges
and its flat brain-case, as a testimony to the rise of our race from
the animal kingdom. It soon appeared, however, that its proportions were tolerably near those of average Europeans of these

---

text refers to a work which we believe to be still unfinished, of Edward Lartet
and Henry Christy, Reliquiae Aquitaniae. London, 1865–69. An extract from
this work, with some of the original woodcuts, was published by Alex. Ecker,
in the Archiv für Anthropologie, vol. iv. p. 109. Brunswick, 1870.

[13] A. Ecker in the Archiv für Anthropologie, vol. i. p. 116. The skull of the
man could actually be measured, the capacity of the woman's could only be
estimated, on account of injuries received.

days. In its present condition, this brain-case encloses a space
of 63 cubic inches (zollen), which, according to an estimate
made by Schaafhausen, would rise to 75 cubic inches if it had
remained uninjured.[14]   Charles Darwin was thus able to describe
the Neanderthal skull as " very well developed and capacious." [15]
European skulls, however, vary from 55 to 112 cubic inches.
Virchow ultimately stated before the Anthropological Society of
Berlin, April 27th, 1872, that this skull belonged to an old man
afflicted with the rickets, that it was to be rejected as a racial type,
and that its dimensions also were very moderate, and that in
regard to the masticatory muscles it does not show signs of brute-
like coarseness, as in Eskimo and Australians.[16]   The value of
this discovery is thus reduced to very common-place dimensions.

Germany also possesses remains of cave-dwellers, such as those
examined since the year 1871, in Hohlefels near Schelklingen,
not far from Blaubeuren.   The fauna of the valley of the Blau
included not only mammoths and elephants, but also a majestic
tiger (Felis spelæa) three extinct species of bears (Ursus spelæus,
U. priscus, and U. tarandi), and the reindeer, the antlers of which
were made into instruments.   Fragments of earthenware vessels,
which from their shallow form must have served for roasting and
broiling,[17] also occur among these relics of a past civilization.

All the discoveries hitherto made merely enable us to put back
the antiquity of our race as far as the times of the extinct cave
fauna.   On the other hand, the existence of the reindeer in central
France does not justify us in presupposing any important alterations of climate, for even those who hesitate to recognize the
Cervus tarandus in Cæsar's description[18] of the Rhine, must yet
admit that the reindeer is not strictly confined to polar regions,
for the caribu, its representative in America, was found in lat. 43°,
that is, on the parallel of Toulon, at the time of the first colonization of the eastern coasts of the United States, but it was speedily

---

[14] Fuhlrott, Der fossile Mensch aus dem Neanderthale, p. 69. Duisburg, 1865.

[15] Descent of Man, vol. i. p. 146.

[16] Verhandlungen der Gesellschaft für Anthropologie, pp. 157-161.   1872.

[17] See Oscar Fraas, Uber die ausgrabungen im Hohlefels in the Würtemberg. naturw. Jahresheften, § i. p. 25.   1872.

[18] De Bello Gall. VI. 21 and 26.

scared away to the far north by the presence of Europeans. Bones of the sheep and goat have, moreover, been found with those of the reindeer, in a Belgian cave, so that the cave-men who dwelt there must have been peaceable shepherds.[19] The disappearance from Europe of the cave fauna, consisting in part of noxious beasts of prey, in part of huge pachyderms, which latter are always represented locally by a scanty number of individuals only, might have been accomplished in a comparatively short time, as soon as our part of the world became more densely colonized, and the inhabitants combined more efficacious weapons with greater skill in hunting. The rapid disappearance of many species of animals within the last few centuries, such as the wingless auk in northern Europe, the sea-cow (manatee) in Behring's Straits, the dodo in the Mauritius, the Moa species in New Zealand, greatly modifies our notions of the time necessary for the disappearance of the diluvial species.

Fortunately, however, we possess tokens that the Suabian district was inhabited at a time when mighty glaciers filled up the valley of the Rhine and the Lake of Constance. Near the old Abbey of Schussenried, in some earthworks at the source of the Schuss—a small stream which falls into the Lake of Constance, in the neighbourhood of Langenargen—a lower stratum was uncovered in the summer of 1866, in which carved antlers of reindeer, bodkins with eyes, a smooth-scraped needle, fish-hooks, flints in the shape of lancets and saw-blades, lumps of red material for skin-painting, ashes, and remains of charcoal were found intermingled.[20] Even if we attach less weight to the fact that these relics of civilization were enclosed between two layers of glacier mud, their antiquity is marked by the fact that with the human implements were found bones of a species of polar fox, agreeing in structure with one which now inhabits the neighbourhood of Nain in Labrador as well as of a species of glutton (*Gulo borealis*), and of two species of moss, of which one (*Hypnum sarmentosum*) now exists only in Lapland, in Norway on the limits of perpetual snow, and on the highest Sudetic mountains and the Tyrol, and

---

[19] O. Fraas im Archiv für Anthropologie, vol. v. p. 480. Brunswick, 1872.
[20] Ibid, vol. iii. pp. 38, 39, 42, 44.

the other (*Hypnum fluitans*, var. *tenuissima*) in marshy Alpine meadows and in Arctic America.[21] These are facts which firmly convince every one versed in geology that man inhabited Suabia as early as the glacial period. The prevalence of glaciers in this district at an earlier period must not, however, be explained by the solar system having passed through colder regions of the heavens, less warmed by stellar light, nor yet by the precession of the equinoxes during a period of increased eccentricity of the earth's orbit, for in both cases the glacial period would have extended equally over every portion of the northern hemisphere, whereas its traces are very faint in the Caucasus, and totally wanting in the Altai.[22] But the prevalence of glaciers in Switzerland and the neighbouring countries may be easily explained by a different distribution of land and water in Europe. Nevertheless, as changes in the outlines of continents require periods of extremely long duration, the presence of man in the glacial period of Suabia is quite sufficient to bespeak a high antiquity for the first appearance of our race.

Far more recent are the memorials which former inhabitants of the Baltic coast have piled up like embankments on the shores of Jutland and the Danish islands, of the shells of edible mussels; archæologists have bestowed on these the suitable name of kitchen-middens. Among this refuse of food were found stone implements, with roughly chipped or occasionally smooth surfaces, fragments of earthen vessels, the remains of dogs as domestic animals, and even a spindle, but no traces of extinct animals of the diluvial period. Hence, at the time of their accumulations, these eaters of shell-fish either did not yet practise, or were just beginning to exercise, the art of polishing flint. A better idea of the age of these shell heaps is suggested by the circumstance that Jutland and the Danish islands were at that time covered with pine forests. These fir-trees had disappeared by the time that the

---

[21] O. Fraas, Die neuesten Erfunde an der Schussenquelle, Wurtemb. naturwissensch. Jahreshefte, § i. pp. 7–24. 1867. In the Archiv für Anthropologie, vol. ii. p. 33, Fraas cites among the discoveries a third moss (*Hypnum aduncum*, var. *Greenlandica Hedw.*), now found only in the northern regions.

[22] B. v. Cotta, Der Altai, p. 65. Leipzig, 1871.

inhabitants had supplied themselves with bronze implements, and oaks took their place. But, since the bronze period, the oak forests have gradually been supplanted by the beech, which now occupies that district almost exclusively. The kitchen-middens, however, contain the bones of the black cock, which feeds on the sprouts of the fir-tree, and presupposes the presence of conifers. Since the time of the mussel-eating inhabitants of these shores, this region has therefore twice changed its vegetation, a process which assuredly must each time have required thousands of years.[23] This is also confirmed by the occurrence of oyster-shells in the Danish kitchen-middens, for the oyster no longer thrives in the Baltic, on account of the small proportion of salt contained in its waters. Consequently, currents from the North Sea must then have reached the Danish islands by channels much wider than the Sound, as it now exists.

Among the most recent remains of prehistoric ages are the villages on the Alpine lakes, which were built over the water on platforms of piles as was Venice originally, and as is the case even now with the dwellings of the natives of the Gulf of Maracaibo with the town of Brunai in Borneo, and the huts of the Papuans on the northern coast of New Guinea.[24] The custom of building huts on platforms erected in the water, must have continued through long periods; for in the older lake dwellings there are stone blades polished, but not pierced or, in other words, prepared for the reception of a handle ; in the more modern villages, on the contrary, the pointed stones are pierced ; and in the most recent, bronze implements already appear amongst the stone. Although the greater number of lake dwellings were destroyed by fire, it is not necessary to suppose that this was always caused by hostile invasions, for we shall presently find

---

[23] Sir Charles Lyell, Antiquity of Man, pp. 9–17. London, 1863.

[24] The Gulf of Maracaibo was called the Gulf of Venice by its first discoverers, because an Indian lake village at the entrance had previously received the name of Venezuela (See Peschel, Zeitalter der Entdeckungen, p. 313). Even at the present day dwellings are built on piles in the middle of the Gulf of Maracaibo (Ramon Paez, Wild Scenes in South America, p. 392). On the Papuan lake dwellings, see Wallace, Malay Archipelago, vol. ii. p. 282 ; and on Brunai, see Spenser St. John, Life in the Far East, vol. i. p. 39. London, 1862.

races of men who have been induced by Shamanistic superstition,[25] to set fire to their own abodes when they are about to migrate. There is nothing at present to hinder us from considering the lake dwellers of Switzerland to have been an Aryan people. Thus, the skull of a child about thirteen years of age, found near Meilen, and the skull of the bronze period discovered at Auvernier, both belong to the so-called Sion type, of which the Celtic Helvetian is the representative.[26] The Swiss lake dwellers practised husbandry and ate bread, planted fruit-trees, and dried apples. Cattle, sheep, and goats inhabited the lake buildings in company with their owners ; provision must therefore have been made for their forage in the winter-time ; even cats and dogs had already been domesticated as companions. The pig alone remained in a wild condition, at least at the time of the oldest settlements ; the ure-ox, the bison, and the elk were still, though perhaps rarely, among the booty of the chase. Except these animals, which have been extirpated within historic times, the fauna has suffered no losses ; and in the vegetable kingdom the change is limited to the disappearance of one species of conifer and two aquatic plants, which have disappeared from the plains.[27] These lake buildings are in some cases buried beneath layers of peat, in others removed inland from the shore by the silting up of the lakes ; or the stone implements were buried beneath the detritus of torrents, as in the delta of the Tinière, near Villeneuve, on the Lake of Geneva. From the size and extent of these new formations, an attempt has been made to refer these relics to a period some five to seven thousand years ago. But all the ingenuity of investigators was baffled by the unfortunate circumstance that neither the growth of peat nor the deposition of mountain detritus proceeds with the same regularity as the sand in an hour-glass, but in such formations, periods of repose alternate with periods of activity. At present, therefore, no fact necessitates our regarding any of these remains of lake dwellings as older than the pyramids of the Nile, nor would it

---

[25] This is Peschel's term for all priestcraft.

[26] His u. Rütimeyer, Crania Helvetica, pp. 36, 37.

[27] Rütimeyer, Die Fauna der Pfahlbauten in der Schweiz, pp. 8, 228, and 229. Basle, 1861.

even be possible to disprove an assertion that the remnants of the stone age in Switzerland belong to a period between one and two thousand years before Christ.

The attempt to find a reliable date for the very ancient evidence we have of man's presence in Egypt has never met with complete success.

In 1851–54, no less than ninety-six shafts in four rows, at intervals of eight English miles, were sunk at right angles to the Nile, by an excellent engineer, Hekekyan Bey, under the super-intendence of Leonard Horner,[28] an extremely cautious geologist. The greater number of these borings furnished remains of domestic animals, fragments of bricks, and pottery at various depths. These relics did not always afford a satisfactory date of their antiquity, for the strata which were pierced were often broken by layers of sand, due to the action of the desert wind. In the immediate vicinity of the statue of Rameses II. at Memphis, from beneath strata of pure Nilitic mud, over which the desert sand had not been wafted, a red baked potsherd was extracted from a depth of thirty-nine feet. Since the statue of Rameses II. was erected, that is, since about 1361 B.C., a Nilitic stratum of nine feet four inches has accumulated round it, without reckoning a stratum of sand eight inches in depth ; the rate of alluvial formation in this place has therefore been three and a half inches in the century since 1361 B.C. Hence if this potsherd has been covered by Nile mud at the same rate, earthen vessels must have been baked on the Nile 11,646 years before the commencement of our era. Many groundless objections have been raised against this calculation. Some conjectured that in old times the Nile flowed beneath the statue of Rameses, others, forgetting that we were not dealing with a single fragment but merely with the one lying deepest among countless others, that this potsherd was extracted from an ancient well or tank. Again, it is urged that at any given point sediments of great depth may be accumulated in a short time by the influence of water, but it is entirely overlooked that this would have affected the whole district occupied by the four rows of shafts, so that as

---

[28] Leonard Horner in Philosophical Transactions, vol. cxlviii. pp. 74–75. London, 1859.

the base of the statue of Rameses stands 78′ 3″ above the sea level,[29] the potsherds were therefore found at a positive elevation of only 39′ 3″. Even the consideration suggested by Sir Charles Lyell that, according to Herodotus, the old Egyptians protected their temples and monuments from the inundations of the Nile by means of embankments,[30] does not seem unanswerable, for if these bulwarks were once broken down, the deposits on the depressed surface would increase all the more rapidly, and the stream might in a few years make amends for what, during thousands of years, it had been prevented from accomplishing. But it may be justly objected against the above calculation that the thickness of the Nile mud since 1361 B.C. cannot serve as a reliable standard, as the plains through which the river flows have by no means an even surface. Horner himself observes that when the Nile reaches the 24-ell mark at Pegel on the Island of Rhoda, it varies in depth from 20′ to less than an inch, so great are the inequalities of the ground.[31] Hence it follows that the mud strata must increase far more rapidly in the depressions than on the elevated spots, and that if the Egyptians, as may be conjectured, erected their stone Rameses on an eminence in close proximity to a depression, the later increment of Nile mud can have raised the surface but slowly. Few, in defiance of this, will venture to dispute that this potsherd from a depth of thirty-nine feet must be at least 4000 years older than the monument of Rameses the Great.

---

[29] Horner, Phil. Trans., vol. cxliii. p. 56.

[30] Sir Charles Lyell, Antiquity of Man, p. 38.

[31] Horner in Philos. Trans., vol. cxlviii. p. 56.

THE PHYSICAL CHARACTERS OF THE RACES
OF MANKIND.

THE PHYSICAL CHARACTERS OF THE
RACES OF MANKIND.

I.—THE PROPORTIONS OF THE SKULL.

IT is universally admitted that domestic animals by careful select-
tion transmit all parental peculiarities to their offspring.   In the
same manner a human tribe, scanty in number, which in old times
separated itself from the rest of mankind by migration, remaining
for thousands of years in a remote region of the world, was, as
it were, constrained by circumstances to preserve the purity of
its breed, thus necessarily developing the family features of the
first emigrants into racial characteristics.   But the purity of the
acquired type was preserved only as long as the seclusion lasted.
As the single tribes and families before and even after their
adoption of agriculture were constantly in a state of migration,
one variety mingling with the other, some of the distinctive
characters were necessarily obliterated by intercrossing ; for the
infertility of crosses between human varieties cannot be proved.
At most therefore we must hope to meet with even moderately
well-defined races only in those cases in which, either by the
remoteness of their abode, or the precepts of caste, a separation
from other varieties has been maintained during long periods;
everywhere else they will merge into one another.   It may be
shown that no one physical characteristic belongs exclusively to
any single race, but that each may be found in a transitional

state in other races. Hence ethnological description must deal with many distinctive marks, and must not despise any, however much they may vary in degree. In seeking characteristics of the human frame, such as serve to mark difference of race, we instinctively look in the first place to the shape of the head, the seat of our highest functions. The industry and ingenuity of modern anatomists have therefore developed a new branch of science devoted to the bones of the skull. A death's head, as it is vulgarly called, is a skilfully arranged case, narrower and smaller in the head of a child, more capacious in adults. It must therefore expand until a certain age, and cease to grow only in mature years. The separate bones of the brain-case, where their edges come in contact, are usually joined only by sutures with serrated notches, so that no insuperable impediment opposes the continued growth. A premature consolidation of the cranial bones must, on the contrary, prevent the full development of the brain ; hence, if an obliteration of the sutures is observed in youthful crania, these heads are abortive formations. Now, as science is bound to compare only normal phenomena, it follows that we must exclude the measurements of all skulls of which the sutures are prematurely effaced or, what amounts to the same, become anchylosed. One of the plates of the skull, *i.e.*, the frontal bone, consists originally of two halves, a right and a left, which in apes become completely anchylosed after birth, in children in the second year. In many cases, however, they never close, and as in that case the frontal suture, being a prolongation of the sagittal suture, bisects the coronal suture at right angles, the course of the sutures forms a cross, whence skulls in which the frontal suture is open are termed in German, *Kreuz-köpfe.* These also, as the representatives of a peculiar form to be compared only with each other, must be excluded from our list of measurements. The disjunction of the frontal suture in no way injures the normal functions of the brain; rather, as it admits of its growth forwards to a later age, the skulls with open frontal sutures combine greater width of brow with greater capacity, so that it has even been conjectured that the average efficiency of man's intellectual power would be raised if the permanent disjunction of this suture were to become the prevailing character of the normal cranium. In connection with the frequency of cross-heads, Hermann Welcker has furnished us with the following statistics :—

| Nationalities. | Skulls | | Proportion of Cross-heads to ordinary Skulls. |
| | With | Without | |
	an open Frontal Suture.		
Germans of Halle ...	70	497	I : 7·1
Inhabitants ot Petersburg ...	70	1023	I : 14·6
Other Caucasians ...	14	129	I : 9·2
Mongols	7	96	I : 13·7
Malays	5	87	I : 17·4
Negroes	I	52	I : 52
Americans	I	53	I : 53

Other observers are of opinion that skulls belonging to the diluvial period more rarely exhibit this favourable character.[1] But if the forehead remains open, the sagittal suture generally closes later, and we are to a certain extent justified in supposing that an endeavour on the part of the brain to find room may be the cause of this phenomenon,[2] yet we ought not to forget that frontal bones with open sutures also occur occasionally in idiots.[3] But, on the other hand, the full development of the brain may be impeded by the premature anchylosis of the bones if it proceeds in such a manner as to overcome the counter-pressure.[4] In the less gifted races the anterior, in the more highly gifted the posterior sutures are said to be earliest obliterated.[5] In the skulls of negroes, Pruner Bey thought he had perceived a premature closure of the frontal suture, followed by the anchylosis of the sagittal and of the middle portion of the coronal sutures, while the lambdoidal suture at the summit remained open the longest. Occasionally even the basilosphenoidal suture does not completely unite, while even in adults the incisive suture

---

[1] Canestrini. See Darwin's Descent of Man, vol. i. p. 125.

[2] Hermann Welcker, Wachsthum und Bau des menschlichen Schädels, pp. 97–102. Leipsic, 1862.

[3] Virchow, Entwickelung des Schädelgrundes, p. 87. Berlin, 1857.

[4] Virchow, l.c. p. 13.

[5] Gratiolet. See Quatrefages, Rapport, p. 302.

may still be distinguished.[6] But the value of such remarks can be established only by the statistical average of a large number of observations, and these can only be obtained by long-continued accumulation. For the present the only result is that skulls with prematurely or abnormally closed sutures must be excluded from the measurements and not compared with the others.

The sexual distinctions of crania are yet more perplexing. Welcker believed that in German skulls of which the sex was known, the female cranium was intermediate between the infantine and the male in all points susceptible of measurement. Our anatomists have therefore endeavoured to discover indications by which the sex of the skull may be determined. Craniological statistics have already shown that in highly civilized nations all secondary sexual distinctions are far more strongly developed than in those families of mankind which have remained in a state of barbarism. In the former the male brain-case is perceptibly more capacious than the female. On the other hand, it remains undecided whether the female cranium is narrower than the male. While Welcker found the cranium of women to be in nearly all races more dolichocephalous than those of men, Weisbach on the other hand obtained an average of 82·5 in Austrian women, and perceives a slight tendency to brachycephalism.[7] On the other hand the inferior height of the cranium in the female sex has been pointed out by Alexander Ecker, who also attempts to recognize the female skull by the somewhat sudden transition from the flat crown to the vertical line of the forehead.[8] Greater delicacy in the osseous prominences, diminished length of face combined with the greater size of the orbicular cavities, and inferior width of the lower jaw, are likewise supposed to distinguish the female cranium. Nevertheless, we are far from being able to determine with certainty the sex of an unknown skull. Several years ago, the English craniologist, Barnard Davis, wrote to A. Ecker that he had been compelled by the presence of the received sexual characters to pronounce a certain Bengalese skull to

---

[6] Pruner Bey, Mémoire sur les Négres, pp. 328, 329. 1861

[7] Archiv für Anthropologie, vol. iii. p. 61. Brunswick, 1868.

[8] Ibid, vol. i. p. 85. 1866.

be that of a man, and yet he knew positively that it belonged to a woman.[9] The sex of skulls taken from old tombs cannot therefore be determined with certainty by their structure. Hence Virchow says, in his work on the ancient northern skulls at Copenhagen, "I do not in all cases feel competent to distinguish, definitely, between male and female crania, and I have therefore determined not to enter into an inquiry of this sort, that I may avoid arbitrary and doubtful divisions."[10] His and Rütimeyer in the same spirit observe, "We have not made a division of crania according to sex. Sexual distinctions based on mere appearance are too apt to lead to gratuitous assertions to be in any way trustworthy." Barnard Davis also states with respect to the catalogue of his craniological collection,[11] "The sex was determined by the appearance, and follows no infallible rules; so that mistakes may easily have occurred."[12] Strict science, however, still demands a classification of skulls according to sex, in which the classes shall be no more comparable with one another than are two completely different species. Future collectors should therefore make every exertion to ascertain the sex of each skull at the site of its discovery. If ancient skulls, of which the sex is undecided, are thrown together, it may occur that two types or intermediate forms representing not two nationalities, but merely the sexes of a single nationality, may be based on the measurements. There is, moreover, a danger that if we accept the average of the sum of both sexes as types of the race, the average differences will be much smaller in amount than if men alone were compared with men.

The proportions of the human skull have recently been determined even to the minutest details, so that the number of dimensions measured in a single skull has increased to 139.[13] When we note this diligence and zeal, we may still hope that some acute observer may sooner or later succeed in detecting in some

---

[9] Archiv für Anthropologie, vol. ii. p. 25. 1867.

[10] Ibid. vol. iv. p. 61.

[11] Crania Helvetica, p. 8. Basle, 1864.

[12] Thesaurus Craniorum, p. 15. London, 1867.

[13] See the three tables for twenty skulls of gipsies supplied by Isidor Kopernicki to the Archiv für Anthropologie, vol. v. p. 320.

apparently unimportant proportional relations a key to the solution of this difficulty. Perhaps it may yet be discovered by what increase of the individual bones the form of the head is determined,[14] and for this reason the length of the individual sutures should be most carefully registered in all statistics. But the ethnology of our day must dispense with these preliminary labours to future knowledge, and must be content with the distinctions already established.

Unfortunately, there is no universal system of measurement. In England and in France they set to work differently, while in Germany scarcely two craniologists follow the same method. "The object of the ordinary as well as of the scientific observer," says Virchow,[15] "is to detect a definite connection between the shape of the cranium, the conformation of the face, and the structure of the brain."[16] Each will turn his attention to the measurement of those points in which he hopes to recognize this connection. But until such a connection is actually discovered we must content ourselves solely with measurements of the capacity. Retzius was the first who taught us to distinguish long and broad crania (dolichocephalic and brachycephalic) by comparison of diameters of length and breadth, although he did not distinguish accurately between the two forms. Even in obtaining the diameters of the skull, different methods are adopted, for the thickness of the cranial bones is very variable. If we apply a measure to the surface of a vertical section of a skull wall, we shall generally find the thickness of the bone plates to be from two to five millimetres. These variations do not affect the measurements as they would raise the longitudinal as much as the lateral diameters. But in other parts, and especially when we have to look for the longest axis of the skull, the frontal bone parts into a double (an external and an internal) osseous plate, and encloses cavities of considerable size. In the occiput, again, the internal and external layers are forced asunder by spongy capsules, and in the several cases the skull attains a thickness of 20 and 15 millimetres or more. Now, as these internal inflations of the bones

---

[14] Virchow, Entwickelung des Schädelgrundes, p. 81. Berlin, 1857.
[15] Ibid. p. 9.   [16] Ibid. p. 81.

have assuredly no relation to the functions of the brain, and vary greatly in different members of the same family, and moreover increase with age, in determining the longitudinal diameter it does not seem right to place the points of the compass just over those bony enlargements. Barnard Davis therefore measures from the forehead (glabella) to the most prominent point of the occiput. Welcker, like him, places one point of the compasses on the forehead, but the other about an inch above the point of the occiput.

Both thus avoid the places where the bones of the brain-case are most enlarged. After all, perhaps the most accurate plan, although at first sight it appears the roughest, would be to take the greatest axis in whatever place it may be found, for the development of the frontal sinuses, unimportant as it may otherwise be, certainly conduces to lengthen the cranium, while the amount of this elongation can be found with the aid of compasses. But as every system of measurement is justifiable, and none has hitherto acquired universal acceptance, we must for the present follow those craniologists who have furnished the greatest number of measurements susceptible of mutual comparison ; these are Barnard Davis and Hermann Welcker.[17] If we prefer the results gained by the latter, we do so with a reservation. The breadth of the skull is now measured at no fixed anatomical point, but search is made for the point at which the skull is broadest. Welcker, on the contrary, measures the breadth in a plane which, passing through the occipital foramen, divides the cranium into an anterior and a posterior half. Now, as all crania which are not perfectly oval, or, in other words, the great majority of crania, widen behind this plane of section, Welcker's measurements make all skulls appear on an average two per cent. more elongated than they seem to the eye.

The longitudinal diameter is rated as 100, and the lateral diameter is expressed in a percentage of these units. This percentage itself is termed the index of breadth. Completely circular skulls, of which the index of breadth amounts to 100, and even more than 100, occur both in North America and among the Peruvians and the Chibcha of New Granada ; they

---

[17] Comp. Appendixes A and B.

owe their form, however, to an artificial pressure of the skull, and must, therefore, be excluded from all comparisons. Otherwise complete roundness is most nearly attained by a skull from Tartary, of which 97·7 is the index of breadth; with this Huxley contrasts a head from New Zealand, though it is perhaps of Australian origin, of 62·9 as the narrowest of all known skulls.[18]

EXTREME FORMS OF CRANIA ACCORDING TO HUXLEY.

(*Norma verticularis.*)

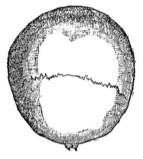

Fig. 1.—Skull of an Inhabitant of Tartary.   Fig 2.—Skull from New Zealand.

Nevertheless, Barnard Davis possesses a so-called Celtic skull which, with a longitudinal axis of 8·2 inches, a width of only 4·9, has an index of only 58.[19] The indexes of breadth, therefore, fluctuate between 58 and 98, if we take the most extreme cases into consideration. But the average is only between 67 and about 85. In this scale of nineteen notes all the average proportional breadths of human skulls are included.

Welcker believes [20] that the index of breadth fluctuates from 74–78 in nations which in point of numbers include one-half of mankind, and these he terms "orthocephali;" they are better named

---

[18] Huxley, On two Extreme Forms of the Human Skull. Archiv für Anthropologie, vol. i. p. 346. 1866.

[19] Thesaurus Craniorum, p. 63.

[20] In his craniological communications to the Archiv für Anthropologie, vol. i. p. 346.

by Broca "mesocephali." If the index sinks below 74, we speak of "dolichocephal," narrow or long skulls, and if it reaches 79 or more, of "brachycephali," broad or short skulls. Statistics have now proved that a medium form of skull prevails in the majority of inhabitants of a given region, so that the further the grades of deviation are removed from the medium form, the more rapidly does the number of skulls diminish by which these grades are represented. This is exactly what every one will expect who considers specific and racial characters as something variable, who recognizes in animated nature only individuals, and who assumes with Goethe that species exist only in the school-books of systematists. Even the average proportions of the skull vary within the limits of individual races. The dimensions which Welcker has found in the Malay nations, are especially surprising. We will first notice only the index of breadth, and setting aside the highly dolichocephalic skulls (68) of the inhabitants of the Carolinas, because as Micronesians they are not free from suspicion of mixed blood, we find the Maori of New Zealand, with an index of 73, still on the verge of dolichocephalism. Next in the scale of mesocephalism are the skulls of the Marquesas islanders (74), the Tahitians (75), the inhabitants of Chatham Island (76), the Kanakas of the Sandwich archipelago (77). On the large islands between Australia and Asia we find the Dyaks of Borneo with 75, the Balinese with 76, the Amboynese with 77, and skulls from Sumatra with 77, and from Mancassar with 78, given as their index. To these mesocephali must be added, as brachycephali, the Javans and Buginese with 79, the Menadorese with 80, and the Madurese with 82.

Of the nineteen gradations of breadth the skulls of the Malay family occupy no less than nine, from 73 to 82. It cannot be said in this case that the Malay skulls present mongrel forms, for surrounded as they are by dolichocephali, they cannot owe their brachycephalism to intercrossing. But if they had originally been brachycephalic this would have been preëminently displayed in the Dyaks, for they must be regarded as the purest representatives of the old Malay type. The results of measurement thus compel us to acknowledge that the relative proportions of the skull vary considerably within the same race. It is now believed that all the Polynesians distributed themselves over the South Seas, from the Samoa or Navigators' group, in three directions. These migrations commenced at least 3000 years ago. The Samoans themselves have remained free from any foreign mixture, and the islands to which the emigrants repaired were totally uninhabited. Here, therefore, we have before us facts which could not have been better arranged for an anthropological experiment. Here we may carefully ascertain by measurement what alterations have taken place in cranial proportions in the course of 3000 years, as the results of emigration and isolation. It is true we have already founded some statements on Welcker's measurements ; but the number of skulls at his disposal is not sufficient to establish reliable averages, and, moreover, he has no indexes from the two most important groups of islands. Samoan and Tongan skulls are the most essential, for they probably represent the original dimensions of the Polynesian type, and next, skulls from the Paumota islands, or Low Archipelago. These latter coral islands were an extremely unfavourable abode, so that on its atolls the Polynesian race must have greatly deteriorated from the social elevation which it occupied at the time of the migration. The interest with which anthropologists look forward to consignments of skulls or cranial measurements from the Paumotas may therefore be conceived. Barnard Davis, who had a larger number of Polynesian skulls at his disposal, arrived at similar results, although he found smaller fluctuations. According to him, the Maori, with an index of 75, are most inclined to dolichocephalism, while the Javans (82) appear still more brachycephalic than the Madurese (81).

Experiences in Germany have been eminently peculiar, but they confirm the statements we have already made in speaking of the condition of the Malay race. Retzius reckoned the Germans among the dolichocephali, although he subsequently ascertained that other proportions preponderated in Southern Germany. He formed his first opinion because it was chiefly the northern representatives of the Teutonic family that he examined. In Swedes the index of breadth averages 75·2, in the Dutch 75·3, and according to another Dutch table, in the English 76, in Danes and Icelanders 76·1. As mesocephalism commences with an index of breadth of 74, and ceases at an index of 79, the Teutons of Northern Europe are rather dolichocephalic than brachycephalic.

German skulls, on the other hand, give the following figures: in Hanover 76·7, in the neighbourhood of Jena 76·9, in Holstein 77·2, at Bonn and Cologne 77·4, in Hesse 79·2, in Suabia 79·3,[21] in Bavaria 79·8, Lower Franconia 80, in Breisgau 80·1. To explain this increasing index of breadth in Southern Germany, our first impulse might lead us to ascribe it to an intermixture with the Celts, but that the Celts have not a very strong tendency to brachycephalism; the French, for example, are represented by no more than 79·5, and the Irish by only 73·4. In Scotland, where we ought to find a mixture of Teutons and Celts, the index stands only at 75·9.

If we must give up the Celts we must think of the Sclavonians. With them we find very considerable indexes, such as 78·8 in the Servians, 79·1 in the people of Little Russia, 79·4 in the Poles, 80 in the Roumanians, 80·1 in Russians, 80·4 in the Ruthenians, 81 in the Slovaks, 82 in the Croats, and 82·1 in the Czechs, these latter being therefore the most brachycephalic of all the Sclavonians. Now an intermixture with the Sclavonians might well explain brachycephalism in Thuringia, but not in South-western Germany, and, above all, not among the Teutonic Swiss, where the index rises to 81·4.[22] Moreover, the German Austrians, who are surrounded on all sides by Sclavonians, ought to be more brachycephalic than the Germans. But the average index of the Germans is 78·7, and that of the German Austrians 78·8,[23] consequently, the difference is much smaller than the liability to error in the measurements. We thus arrive at the conclusion that the Teutonic skull is highly variable, and that in Germany it perceptibly tends towards brachycephalism as it passes from north to south, and especially to the south-west.

---

[21] Schiller's skull had an index of 82.

[22] Weisbach found the index of breadth to be 81·1 in German Austria, 83·6 in the Czechs. As he measures the skull at the widest part, the divergence of his figures from those of Welcker is fully explained. Archiv für Anthropologie, vol. ii. 293.

[23] His attributes to the skulls of the German Swiss (Disentistypus) an index of breadth of 86·5, of height of 81·8. His u. Rütimeyer, Crania Helvetica, p. 11.

4

If we are to make further progress in craniology, the indexes of European populations must first be ascertained in greater numbers. With respect to Italians, we are indebted to Luigi Calori of Bologna for work of this description. He designates skulls with indexes of breadth from 74 to 80 as orthocephali (for which, however, we will substitute mesocephali), those with higher figures as broad, and those below 74 as narrow skulls. He examined no less than 2442 Italian skulls, exclusive of female specimens, and found 1665 brachycephalic, with an average index of 84 among them. The other 777, on the contrary, gave an average of 77. In Italy, as in Germany, broad and narrow skulls are locally intermingled. Of 100 Bolognese skulls of both sexes, 79 were broad, 16 medium, and only 5 narrow. Of 852 heads from Emilia, 733 ranked as broad, 110 as medium, and 9 as narrow skulls. Again, among 254 heads from Venetia, Lombardy, and the Italian Tyrol, 230 exhibited the broad, 23 the medium, and only 1 the narrow form. On the Adriatic shores, south of Bologna, out of 377 skulls, 265 were broad, 105 medium, and 7 narrow. Crossing the Apennines, out of 213 Tuscan skulls, on the contrary, only 134 are brachy-, 59 meso-, and 20 dolichocephalic. In the former Papal States, out of 200 skulls, only 52 belong to the brachy-, 100 on the other hand to the meso-, and 48 to the dolichocephalic type. Finally, out of 356 Neapolitans, 131 were reckoned among the broad, 162 among the medium, and 63 among the narrow skulls. From this it is evident that the northern Italians belong to the highly brachycephalic nations, but that towards the south of the peninsula, the skulls become elongated, and the medium form finally predominates.[24] Here again a variation of the indexes is displayed, corresponding with changes of locality. Nothing else, however, could be expected, since all modern investigations impress upon us that all physical characters are liable to great fluctuations, that living beings in general are not developed in accordance with rigid primæval types, but undergo constant transformation. Above all, we cannot expect persistency of type in the human species, in which the greater number of races are capable of fertile crosses.

It is scarcely necessary to observe that the racial derivation of

[24] Journal of the Anthropological Institute, vol. i. p. 110. London, 1872.

any skull can never be inferred from its index of breadth. The narrowest Sclavonian skull, 72·8, might, from its index, be taken for a negro skull, for individual negro skulls go as far as 77·8, but negro skulls below 72 cannot be confounded with Sclavonian skulls. Among 237 German skulls, only one has an index as low as 69, falling nearly to the average of the negroes, 66, so that negro skulls below 69 can never be mistaken for German.

Statistical averages, when used with caution, have hitherto only confirmed what had already been made known by other means. All Egyptologists are agreed that the old type of the monuments has been preserved in the Fellaheen and Copts. The index of breadth, 71·4, agrees exactly with that of the Egyptian mummies. Even if Fallmerayer's extreme views are not accepted, the modern Greeks must yet be regarded as much mixed with Sclavonian blood, and the index shows us that the modern Hellenes with 77·1, have become considerably more brachy-cephalic than the ancient Greeks with 75. The same result was to be expected in Italy, where we find the ancient Romans recorded at 74.

As a caution that cranial characters alone are not to be relied upon, we will mention that Barnard Davis thought it necessary to divide the Eskimo into three races, according to the degree in which the pyramidal form of the skull was more or less highly developed. He designates the Greenlanders as the purest, the eastern Americans as the medium form, while the western Americans are completely divergent from the normal type. That the Eskimo of the arctic regions are of one and the same race is an inadmissible opinion, however frequently they may have been confounded by travellers, or whatever may be the evidence afforded by their language.[25] Their physical divergencies are self-evident. Now, a great expert in northern archæology has recently proved that the Eskimo did not settle in Greenland till after the middle of the fourteenth century,[26] and Barnard Davis might, moreover, have learnt from Captain Hall's descriptions

---

[25] Thesaurus Craniorum, p. 224.

[26] Konrad Maurer in der zweiten deutschen Nordpolarfahr, i. 234. Leipzic, 1873.

that Eskimo mothers apply lateral pressure to the skulls of their newly born children, and draw over them a tight-fitting leather cap to produce the desired pyramidal form.[27]

Cranial measurements are as yet deficient from the want of a sufficient number of observations, which can be only increased by a continued augmentation of our collection of racial skulls. In this respect the greatest dispatch is urgently recommended, now that so many and various races are intermingling before our eyes.

Of the same importance as the transverse diameter is the height of the skull. For the purpose of determining it, Welcker placed one point of his calipers on the anterior margin of the occipital foramen, the other on the apex of the head, at the intersection of the planes which divide the skull into a right and left, and at the same time into an anterior and posterior half.[28] Here also the result of the measurement is expressed in the hundredth parts of the longitudinal diameter, and it is termed the index of height. By means of an instructive arrangement of Welcker,[29] we perceive that on the average the height increases in inverse ratio to the breadth, so that narrow skulls are, generally speaking, high, and broad skulls flat ; in other words, that in dolichocephali the index of height exceeds the index of breadth, and in brachycephali does not equal it, so that a smaller lateral extension is compensated by an increase in height. This ratio is however neither constant nor equal. The variation in the index of height is far smaller than that of breadth ; it fluctuates between 70·2 and 82·4 for the index of height of 86·8 in the ancient Peruvians is suspected of artificial origin. Moreover, we find nations in which the index of height is far too small for that of breadth, such as the Hottentots, who, although dolichocephalic, only attain to an index of height of 70·2, whereas it ought to be at least three units higher.

---

[27] Life with the Esquimaux, p. 520.   1865.

[28] Alex. Ecker on the contrary measures first from the anterior and then from the posterior margins of the occipital foramen and the highest elevation of the occiput (Crania Germaniae merid. p. 3.) The mean between the two measurements would probably be the " height " most desirable for purposes of classification in the interest of ethnology.

[29] Craniologische Mittheilungen, p. 154.

On the other hand, the inhabitants of the island of Madura combine one of the greatest breadths of skull with the largest index of
height, namely, 82·4, whereas we should expect one of about 75.
Cases such as these furnish ethnology with excellent descriptive
terms, enabling us to designate the Hottentots as flat narrow
skulls (patystenocephali), the Malay inhabitants of Madura as high
broad skulls (hypsibrachycephali). The index of breadth represents
the shape of the skull as it appears when the brain-case is inspected
from above, with the eye perpendicular to the central point of the
longitudinal axis (Norma verticalis). The index of height, on the
other hand, represents the view of the skull as seen from the back
(Norma occipitalis). With similar indexes the outlines may, it is
true, be sometimes angular, sometimes curvilinear ; the greatest
widths may occur sometimes in the middle and sometimes further
back. The comparison of the figures of these measurements is
nevertheless the only process which science has hitherto had at
its disposal, while the selection of types by the eye would lead
to artificial and arbitrary definitions.

II.—THE HUMAN BRAIN.

WHEN we separate the parts of a dissected head we acknowledge that we hold in our hands nothing but the shell of an
exploded cartridge, or the larval husk from which the winged
imago has escaped. We also understand that all cranial forms
possess only an artificial value, and tell us nothing respecting the
several grades of mental power contained within a dolichocephalic
or brachycephalic bony covering. Artificial malformations of
the brain-case by pressure of the infantine head, such as took
place in the nations of olden times, and such as still occur
among countless inhabitants of America, and is even the custom
of foolish mothers in the north of France,[1] although perhaps not
completely harmless, have not perceptibly impeded the healthy
functions of the artificially remoulded apparatus of thought.

The brain, the noblest of our organs, varies in point of weight,

---

[1] Ausland, 1866, p. 1095. Delineations of Artificial Compressions of the Skull.

from two or three to four pounds, while we find the brain of the elephant to be from 8–10 lbs., of the whale from 4–5 lbs., of a narwhal 18 feet in length 2 lbs. 15 oz., of a dolphin 7 feet long $2\frac{1}{2}$ lbs. "Who could venture," observes a celebrated French physiologist, "to infer from the bulk of brain, the nature and power of a human being or even of an animal?" Who, we might add, can judge by the weight whether a church clock or a pocket chronometer will keep the most accurate time? Yet both are merely the work of our own hands. Neither does man take the highest place in the relative weight of brain as compared to the total weight of the body, for although the brain of the whale is only $\frac{1}{3300}$, that of the elephant $\frac{1}{500}$, of the dog $\frac{1}{250}$, while that of man is from $\frac{1}{37}$ to $\frac{1}{35}$ of the weight of the body, yet we are surpassed by the song-birds, among which the weight of the brain reaches $\frac{1}{27}$, by the titmouse and the sparrow, in which it reaches respectively $\frac{1}{12}$ and $\frac{1}{27}$, and by the American apes, in which it amounts to from $\frac{1}{28}$ to $\frac{1}{13}$ of the weight of the body.[2]

Hence if the rank of the brain is to correspond to man's high rank in creation, we must look for differences other than those of weight. The human cerebrum, which can alone be considered the seat and organ of intellectual power, consists of an internal white substance traversed by delicate fibres, which is regarded as the conducting apparatus and focus of nervous action; and secondly, of an external grey covering in which granules, spherical forms, and ganglia may be recognized, and which is held to be, if not the originator, at least the seat of the psychical functions. The more profusely convoluted is the surface, and the more furrowed it appears, the more does the outer covering or grey substance increase in superficies.

We also know that more or less extensive disease of this outer layer is capable of destroying the higher functions of the mind, especially of co-ordinate thought. It was therefore obviously permissible to recognize the abundance of convolutions as a sign of the superior rank of the brain, particularly as the elephant, the most intelligent of all animals, affords a good example of a

[2] Th. Bischoff in the Naturwissenschaftlichen Vorträgen Münchener Gelehrten, p. 139. Munich, 1858.

brain deeply furrowed by multiform convolutions. The primary distribution of the furrows, observes A. Ecker, seems to be generally symmetrical, and asymmetry is prevalent only in the the secondary furrows ; so that greater symmetry in the furrows and convolutions may be regarded as the expression of arrested development, especially as the brain of idiots displays this character.[3] On the other hand, Rudolph Wagner points out that the brain of the dog, when compared with the complex system of convolutions of the unintelligent sheep, exhibits an extraordinary poverty, and that the brains of our great mathematicians, Gauss and Dirichlet, were without any peculiar folds,[4] although among the most richly endowed of any that he has seen in point of depth and multiformity of the furrows, especially in the frontal regions.

Huxley was able to pour 55·3 cubic inches of water into the brain-case of a woman of sound mental powers, and $34\frac{1}{2}$ cubic inches into the most capacious cranium of a gorilla ;[5] but it should first have been ascertained whether the brains of men and apes are so strictly analogous as to justify this comparison in point of size. Unfortunately, investigations respecting the embryonic brain of the ape are still very meagre. Von Bischoff has nevertheless announced his conviction that although the human brain possesses no important furrow and no important convolution which is not represented in the orang, yet the human brain by no means exhibits a mere advance, and the brain of the orang an arrest of growth, but that they each take a different course of evolution, developing in different directions, and at no time coin-

---

[3] Archiv für Anthrop. vol. iii. p. 221.

[4] Wagner, Wendungen der Hemisphären, pp. 6, 7, and 24.

[5] He reckons 252·5 gr. of brain = to 1 cubic inch of water (Man's Place in Nature). Carl Vogt (Archiv für Anthropologie, vol. iii. 186) more precisely estimates the average capacities of the interior of the skulls of the higher apes—

	Males.	Females.
	Cubic centimetres.	
In the Orang and Pongo ...	448	378
,, Chimpanzee and Chego	417	370
,, Gorilla...	500	423

ciding with one another. This is, as yet, merely the conviction of a scholar highly esteemed by his compeers, but at the same time it corresponds with our expectations. It is a common experience that diseases still latent in the parents at the time of procreation, and only breaking out at a much later period, are nevertheless transmitted to their children, to make their appearance in them also only at a mature age. Hence, if even the causes of future disturbances are hereditary, specific, generic and ordinal differences must be still more so. It is therefore impossible to free one's self of the idea that even at the first awakening of life, the morphological end is preordained for the human germ as well as for that of the ape. Their development may be compared with two lines of rails which long run side by side on the same track, and finally separate right and left in different curves. Bischoff moreover admits that by reason of their great morphological proximity, it requires the closest examination to recognize differences between the brains of man and of the orang, the chimpanzee and the gorilla. Relying on Rolleston's measurements, Bischoff considers that the hemispheres of the human cerebrum are specially distinguished from those of the apes by their superior height. To ascribe little importance to differences in quantity, is to overlook the fact that in chemical compounds the quality of the combinations is dependent on the quantity—that by the addition of a single atom of oxygen, sulphurous acid is converted into sulphuric acid, that a numerical increase in frequency transforms dark into luminous vibrations, that is to say, changes the temperature which excites the visual nerves; and that even in numbers slight changes of quantity lead to differences of great importance.[6] In the obscurity which still prevails as to the relations of the several portions

---

[6] The relative difference in quantity between the numbers

$$0,99999999$$
$$1$$
$$1,00000000$$

is very slight; yet the first possesses the property of diminishing to infinity when persistently raised to higher powers, while by the same process the third increases to infinity, and the middle one remains constant at every power.

of the brain to the functions of the intellectual powers, the conjecture is still permissible that the higher psychical functions may be connected with an externally insignificant accretion of the brain.

Again, it is usually held that unimpaired intellectual faculties exist in man only when the weight of brain exceeds a minimum limit which varies according to sex and race. Quatrefages wanted to fix the weight of brain in Europeans at 1113 grams for males, and 977 grams for females.[7] Carl Vogt assumes only 1000 grams in the first case, and 900 grams in the second;[8] while H. von Luschka pronounced 1000 grams to be the minimum weight of a brain of unimpaired efficiency.[9] Weighed in a fresh condition, he found the brain of a microcephalic woman only 30, and of a man even 20 Loth,[10] or about 10 oz. With the exception of the elongated form of the brain-case, and a great projection of the jaws, there is nothing of an animal character in the skull of these unhappy beings, for Virchow has decisively contradicted Carl Vogt's assertion that the position of the occipital foramen is abnormal. The same observation applies to the conditions of the basisphenoid bone, which of course ought to be compared in adult microcephali and adult apes of a high order, not between adult microcephali and young apes.[11] Carl Vogt had ventured to compare the skulls of these abortive human beings with the skulls of apes. According to his tables the capacity of the brain-case amounted to 622 cubic centimetres in one idiot, to 460 in another; while that of a male gorilla reached 500 cubic centimetres.[12] Relying on these researches, he supposed himself to have perceived in these human malformations a reversion or, in the language of the Darwinian theory, an atavism, which, by the reappearance of ancestral characters of remote times, affords testimony of the animal

---

[7] Rapport sur les progrès de l'Anthropologie, p. 324.

[8] Vorlesungen über den Menschen, vol. i. p. 103.

[9] Dritte Versammlung der Deutschen Gesellsch., p. 17.

[10] At the time this was written 32 Loth = 1 German lb. = 1·1023 English lb., but by the new regulations there are but 30 Loth in the German lb.

[11] Menschen und Affenschädel, p. 31.

[12] Mémoires sur les Microcéphales, in the Mém. de l'Institut National Genevois, vol. ix. p. 54.

derivation of our forefathers. But at the third meeting of the German Anthropological Society, all the specialists remonstrated against this interpretation of the facts. With almost an identity of expression the microcephali were recognized as human creatures which, by reason of morbid arrest of development, were rendered incapable of development, and in no way as intermediate links filling the chasm which separates man from the creatures most resembling him in the animal world. That reproductive powers are wanting in idiots, is enough to prove that the ancestors of man never occupied a microcephalous grade—that no part of the world was in past ages peopled with Crétins.[13]

The human brain must therefore be compared only with other human brains. This is approximately accomplished by measuring the capacity of crania of various races of mankind. Water is not generally used, because it necessitates the closing of the numerous apertures in the bones. Lime or plaster of Paris can be used only after transverse sections have been made, that is to say, only in damaged skulls, and afford no really comparable results, as these materials have different specific weights; these substances have therefore been abandoned, even by those who previously recommended them.[14] The brain capsule is now filled either with millet seed or small shot, and the contents are then poured into a metrical gauge. Sand is sometimes used, but with very unreliable results. Wyman, in the fourth volume of the Anthropological Record, states that the capacity of one skull, which was measured with sand eight times, appeared to vary between 1290 and 1350 cubic millimetres; when measured with shot the variation was only between 1200 and 1205. By these means we ascertain the capacity of the brain-capsule in different races. Lucae's measurements tend to show that the broadest negro skull does not reach the average of the Germans, nor the best Australian skull the average of the negro, and also that the individual fluctu-

---

[13] Comp. the speeches of Von Luschka, Virchow, Ecker, Schaaffhausen, and Jäger, in the account of the third meeting of the German Anthropological Society, pp. 16–25; and also H. Schüle, in the Archiv für Anthropologie, vol. v. p. 444–446. 1872.

[14] Lucae, Morphologie der Racenschädel, § ii. p. 45. 1864.

ations increase with the rise of the numbers.[15] Broca's results seem to confirm these. Assuming 100 as the average capacity of the Australian skull, he estimates that of the negro at 111·6, and of the Teuton at 124·8.[16] The suspiciously high averages at which Barnard Davis arrived, based on the richest of all collections, do not seem so unfavourable to those human races which we regard as low.[17] He found the capacity of the cranium to be in—

	Cubic Inches.	Cubic Centimetres.
Europeans	92·1	1835
Americans	89·0	1774
Asiatics	88·7	1768
Africans	86·2	1718
Australians	81·7	1628

In addition to these averages derived from numerous individual estimates, it is advisable to glance at the fluctuations. Thus Morton, among skulls of all races, found one minimum specimen of 63 cubic inches, and one maximum of 114 internal capacity.[18] But Barnard Davis has in his possession an ancient Roman skull of only 62 cubic inches, and an Irish specimen of 121·6. Another Irish skull in the Bateman Museum even reaches 124·2 cubic inches.[19] Even within the same family of nations the greatest differences may occur, for some Tuscan skulls are far behind the

[15] Lucae, Morphologie der Racenschädel, § ii. p. 45. 1854. (These capacities were taken with millet seed).

Number of Skulls.	Minimum.	Maximum.	Average.
		Cubic Centimetres.	
13 German	1300	1725	1531·6
6 Chinese	1400	1575	1482·5
5 Negroes	1190	1505	1344
5 Australians	1115	1300	1186

[16] Broca, cited by Quatrefages, Rapport, p. 306.

[17] Thesaurus Craniorum, p. 360.

[18] Huxley, Man's Place in Nature, p. 77.

[19] Thesaurus Craniorum, pp. 65 and 360.

narrowest Australian specimens in point of internal capacity.   In
a Florentine servant maid, 23 years of age, Paolo Mantegazza
found only 1046 cubic centimetres, but in an adult Florentine
man 1727 cubic centimetres, and in a supposed Etruscan warrior
even 1750 cubic centimetres.[20]

If the smaller average capacity of the cranium is causally
connected with arrested intellectual development, we might expect
that the skulls of ancient Europeans would be of smaller size than
those of their descendants : many facts point this way.   Broca
thinks that he has found an increasing capacity in the crania
of modern Parisians (1482–1484 cubic centimetres) contrasted
with those of the 12th century (1426 cubic centimetres).[21]   Skulls
of ancient Greeks recently exhumed at Athens, especially those of
a wealthy lady of the Macedonian period, Glykera by name, with
only 1150 cubic centimetres, and of a man 1280 cubic centimetres, both favour this opinion.[22]   On the other hand, His and
Rütimeyer have given, as an average for their Disentis type,
to which belong three-fourths of the modern Swiss, 1377 cubic
centimetres; for the Hohberg type, nominally ancient Romans,
1437 cubic centimetres, and for the Sion head, which corresponds
with the skulls of the lake dwellings, 1558 cubic centimetres
$\left(\begin{smallmatrix}\text{min. } 1450\\\text{max. } 1800\end{smallmatrix}\right)$. According to this computation the Swiss population
must have lost considerably in cranial capacity ;[23] but as this is
hardly credible, the fact ought to serve as a warning against
measurements of skulls taken from graves.

The investigation of these dimensions is obviously a means
of inferring, at least approximatively, the size of the brain.   On
the weight of this organ we for a long time possessed only an
introductory work by Rudolf Wagner.   Unfortunately, the majority
of the 964 skulls examined were derived from individuals of
unsound mind, and ought therefore to have been excluded from

[20] Archivio per l'antropologia, vol. i. p. 53 et seq.   Firenze, 1871.

[21] Broca as cited by Carl Vogt, Vorlesungen über den Menschen, vol. i.
pp. 105–108.

[22] See Virchow's account in the Verhandlungen der Berliner anthropol.
Gesellschaft, p. 174 et seq. 1811.

[23] Crania Helvetica, p. 44.   Basle, 1864.

the comparison. Again, the estimates of weight were taken from various anatomists, who do not appear to have adopted the same method of procedure. It was also to be regretted that the bodily dimensions of the corpses examined were only occasionally stated. As a weight of 1861 grams was found in Cuvier, and in Lord Byron (though this is founded on equivocal statements) 1807 grams, a high weight seemed to be accompanied by high intellectual endowments. Yet among eminent scholars of Göttingen, such as Dirichlet (1520 gr.), the great Gauss (1492 gr.), the pathologist Fuchs (1499 gr.), the philologist Hermann (1386 gr.), and the mineralogist Haussmann (1225 gr.), the weights sank to the general average, and even far below it.[24] As the only permanent result of this first attempt, it may be noticed that Wagner found the average weight of the female brain to be lighter than that of the male. This fact was strictly corroborated by Weisbach as regards the German and Sclavonian populations of Austria. Calori, moreover, relying on a large number of estimates of weight, taken from Italian specimens, has found that the female brain is lighter by 150–200 grams. The capacity of the skull is likewise different in the two sexes according to the following statistics arranged by Weisbach.[25]

CAPACITY OF THE FEMALE AS COMPARED WITH THE MALE CRANIUM, THE LATTER = 1000.

		Observer.			Observer.
In Negroes	984	B. Davis.	In Marquesas Islanders	902	B. Davis.
Hindoos	944	,,	Germans	897	Welcker.
Negroes	932	Tiedemann.	Dutch	883	B. Davis.
Malays	923	,,	Germans	878	Weisbach.
Dutch	919	,,	Javans	874	B. Davis.
Irish	912	B. Davis.	Germans	864	Tiedemann.
Kanaks	906	,,	English	860	B. Davis.
Sclavonians	903	Weisbach.	Germans	838	Huschke.

[24] Rudolf Wagner, Die Wendungen der Hemisphären u. das Hirngewicht, Göttingen, pp. 32, 33. 1860. In his published letter to Barnard Davis "on the skull of Dante," Welcker has, however, proved from the estimates given by Wagner and others, that the brains of 26 men of high intellectual rank collectively surpass the average weight of brain by 14 per cent. Dante's brain (1420 gr.) is nevertheless but little above the average of 1360 grams.

[25] Der Deutsche Weiberschädel. Archiv für Anthropologie, vol. iii. p. 63. 1868.

In these estimates it is specially significant that, as in other physical characters, the differences of sex appear more strongly in highly civilized nations.

Other surprising revelations were likewise obtained from the researches made by A. Weisbach, which, although they extended to only 429 brains of inhabitants of Austria, were exclusively restricted to persons of sound mind.[26] The total weight was always first ascertained, and then the several weights of the cerebrum, of the cerebellum, and the pons varolii. But the most instructive fact was that the brain attains its greatest weight between the 20th and 30th year of life, and then till the 80th year undergoes a diminution which increases to 10 per cent. This diminution extends simultaneously to all parts of the brain with the exceptions of the pons varolii, which increases till the 50th year. From this we see that brain weights are comparable only at the same time of life. These researches have also confirmed a previous conjecture, namely, that the specific gravity of brains is variable; for the more capacious crania of the Germans contained a smaller weight of brain than other and smaller skulls, namely—

Men.	Capacity of the Skull.	Weight of Brain.
	Cubic Centimetres.	Grams.
Germans	1501·66	1314·5
Magyars	1421·66	1322·8
Sclavonians	1484·55	1325·2

Thus the capacity of the skull is of more importance in ethnology than the weight of the brain. We will further add that the minimum weight (986·5 gr.) of German male skulls was found in a person of 65 years of age; a minimum of 889·1, female skulls, in one of 83 years of age.

We owe another discovery to Calori of Bologna, who by numerous measurements had already performed valuable services in the cause of science. He gives the weight of the brain in

---

[26] Die Gewichts verhältnisse der Gehirne österreichischer Völker. Archiv für Anthropologie, vol. i. p. 190. 1866.

Italians of both sexes, but separates the cases according to the form of the skull.

No. of Cases.	Weight of Brain in Grams.	
	Total Weight.	Cerebrum.
	In brachycephalic Skulls.	
201 Men	1305	1145
72 Women	1150	1004
	In Skulls with an index of breadth below 80.	
104 Men	1282	1122
44 Women	1136	992

Here we not only again see that the female brain is the lighter, but it also appears to follow that in both sexes the brachycephali have heavier brains than the dolichocephali. The lightest brain in a brachycephalic man of 22 years weighed 1024 grams, in a dolichocephalic of 34 years 1088 grams, while the minimum weights in broad and narrow-skulled women were respectively 909 and 918 grams.[27]

III.—THE OSSEOUS FACIAL APPARATUS.

In the perpendicular section of a skull, even the unpractised eye at once recognizes the region of the brain-capsule and the facial apparatus. In man, the latter occupies a relatively much smaller space, for it is not half so long, nor half so high, and is invariably narrower than the other. In apes, on the contrary, even in the highest, the size of the facial bones preponderates, and the animal expression of the head is chiefly due to the protrusion of the jaws.[1] A slight tendency to this formation of face in human races is termed prognathism. Peter Camper was the first who attempted to measure these structural proportions by means of the so-called facial angle. He drew a line from the external auditory passage to the nasal partition, and intersected it by a line from the front of the closed teeth to the most prominent part of the fore-

[27] Journal of the Anthropological Institute, vol. i. p. 117. London, 1872.
[1] Peter Camper über den natürlichen Unterschied der Gesichtszüge, vol. xv. pp. 17, 21, 22. Berlin, 1792.

head. The magnitude of the angle he took as a standard of a noble expression of countenance. Virchow has justly objected that this angle must decrease in old people by the development of the frontal sinuses, as well as by the retreat of the dental apophysis.[2] But it was yet more unfortunate that Camper should have selected the nasal partition and the auditory passages as points on which to lay a so-called horizontal plane of the skull. A plane of this description has been sought by craniologists almost as eagerly as the philosopher's stone by the alchemists. This plane was supposed to lie horizontally through the head when the latter is poised over its centre of gravity with the least assistance of the muscles. The direction of the zygomatic arch seemed to fall in this plane, and the position of the skull was arranged to correspond with it. But it was soon found that this plane takes quite a different course in skulls of different races; that the zygomatic arch cannot always be followed, and that the skull must be a little raised, sometimes in front, sometimes behind.[3] In this system the investigator relied on his own artistic feeling, which may occasionally vary. As H. von Ihering has shown, it has happened that an anatomist who, venturing on this slippery path, had repeated his measurements on the same skulls, after an interval of three years, found differences which amounted to more than 50 per cent.[4] Moreover, such angles can be determined only on outline drawings of skulls. Consequently, science has at last been enriched by the system of the so-called geometric, or, perhaps more correctly, orthographic projection of the skull. Lucae, its inventor, placed the skull in the requisite position upon a firm support. Upon the skull, and parallel to the support, rested a glass plate, on which a dioptric instrument with a cross thread was moved in such a manner, that its optic axis constantly touched the outlines of the skull. The intersection of the threads was followed on the glass plate by a pen which registered in ink the course pursued.[5] In this way he obtained a picture of the skull

---

[2] Schädelgrund, p. 119.
[3] Lucae, Morphologie der Racenschädel (1861), § I. p. 42, and (1864) § 2, p. 31.
[4] Archiv für Anthropologie, vol. v. p. 396. 1872.
[5] Morphologie der Racenschädel, § I. pp. 10, 11.

as it would be seen from an infinite distance, somewhat as is the case with the moon seen from the earth ; these drawings are not merely free from all the defects of perspective vision, but they admit of measurements by the compasses.

Even less unanimity has been observed in the angular measurements of the facial apparatus than in the estimates of the size of the brain-capsule. Each anatomist went his own new way regardless of his predecessors, and very often applied the same appellations to angles which some other had sought at a different point. The results of the various kinds of measurement do not therefore admit of mutual comparison, and the painful spectacle of this dark mass of contradictions has drawn upon craniology a contumely perhaps not entirely undeserved, for the inducement to make increasingly factitious systems of measurement was often not so much the endeavour to provide ethnology with useful numerical formulæ as to find in the skulls of various races a corroboration of morphological theories.

In this state of things anthropology can but follow Welcker, the anatomist who has measured the greatest number of skulls ; his system, although, as he himself admits, imperfect and susceptible of further improvement, is fortunately the most satisfactory. Welcker searches for no horizontal plane, but merely determines the position of certain points in the facial apparatus, and does this regardless of the frontal bones.

The animal expression of the human countenance is due to the protrusion of the jawbones, and the degree is best determined by angular measurements. Virchow, even before Welcker, pronounced that prognathism, or the snout-like form of the face, is dependent on the shape of the base of the skull, although he did not conceive such a dependence as is shown by Welcker's measurements. The size of the angle at the sella turcica may be determined by a triangle, of which one side (fig. 3) is equal to the distance from the root of the nose to the sella turcica, the second to the distance from the sella to the anterior margin of the occipital foramen ; the third (*b n*) from the latter back to the root of the nose. This angle of the sella turcica exceeds a right angle even in man, but in animals it becomes considerably greater. In the child and the young ape its size, or the degree of flexure of the basisphenoid plate differs but little, that is to say, it amounts to 141° in the first, and 155° in the second case; but with increasing age this flexure becomes more acute in the human being, reaching 134°, while in the ape it becomes more obtuse (174°). In this divergent tendency of growth Welcker recognizes a profound difference between man and beast.[6] Yet, since this angle of the sella is neither visible nor measurable in a complete skull, it possesses a merely theoretical value for our purpose, arising from the fact that another angle of the face is correlatively dependent upon it. This angle is situated at the root of the nose, and is measurable in all skulls by the aid of a triangle, of which the

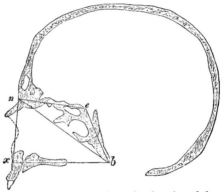

Fig. 3.—Section of the human skull in the direction of the sagittal suture. *n*, root of nose; *e*, sella turcica; *b*, anterior margin of the occipital foramen; *x*, point on the super-maxillary bone above the alveoli.

sides correspond with the distances from the root of the nose to the anterior margin of the occipital foramen (*b*), from this to the insertion of the alveoli (*x*), and finally from this back to the root of the nose. It is obviously the angle at the beginning of the alveoli which controls the expression of the face, and in proportion to its magnitude the countenance appears to us ennobled. Weisbach found this angle to average from 70° to 72° in Amboynese, Javans, Banjarese, Chinese, and Buginese, 73° in 50 German men, 75° in Northern Italians, 76° in 24 German women, 77° in 28

---

[6] Bau und Wachsthums des Schädels, pp. 80, 81.

Czechs.[7] Welcker, however, prefers to determine the position of the jaw indirectly by means of the angle at the root of the nose ($b\ n\ x$), because this latter increases with the angle of the sella, whereas it is the reverse with the angle at the alveoli ($b\ x\ n$), which decreases while the others increase. The angle at the root of the nose varies from 60° to 72° in the skulls of different races. Welcker speaks of a skull in which this angle amounts to 68° or more as prognathous; of one in which it remains below 65° as opistognathous; of skulls of from 65° to not quite 68° as orthognathous, for which latter term we shall substitute mesognathous. An examination of skulls shows that prognathism prevails as a rule in narrow skulls, while medium and broad skulls are mostly mesognathous or occasionally opistognathous. This correlation is not however invariable, for, according to Welcker, Eskimo, Mexicans, Hottentots, and the Highland Scotch belong to the mesognathous dolichocephali, while conversely the Sumatrans and Bashkirs combine an index of breadth of 80° and 82° with prognathism of an angle of 69° 5′ and 67° 6′. It seems strange perhaps that in determining the direction of the jaws, the points of the compasses are placed above the alveoli and not at once upon the lower edge of the sockets, or even on the incisor teeth, as the protrusion of the facial apparatus is greatest at these points. But very many skulls are damaged just at these points, and it would therefore be necessary to reject them as useless. Again, it is still more important that the prognathism produced by the oblique position of the alveoli depends on non-essential directions of growth.

Virchow has shown that the prognathous type of face is inconsistent with the full development of the brain.[8] This fact is most significant when we remember that this unpropitious position of the jaw is confined almost exclusively to nations in which civilization appears somewhat immature. Only here again it must be remembered that various forms occur side by side within the same nations. In England and France cases of prognathism are not unknown, and in Paris they are said to be tolerably common.[9]

---

[7] Weisbach, der deutsche Weiberschädel in the Archiv für Anthropologie, vol. iii. p. 75. 1868. His facial angle is nearly identical with Welcker's angle $b\ x\ n$.

[8] Schädelgrund, p. 121.　　　　　[9] Quatrefages, Rapport, p. 311.

The Chinese are, moreover, reckoned among the prognathous nations by many craniologists ; and in Welcker's statistics we even find the Dutch with an angle of 67° 8' at the root of the nose. With such great variability, the average numbers can only show the frequency of a certain form of facial apparatus, while the individual fluctuations serve as links to a higher or a lower type.

The expression of the human countenance is very greatly affected by the prominence of the zygomatic arch, although this characteristic is not constant, yet where it occurs in a preponderating number of cases, we must be content to use it in the description of nations. If a skull be so placed that the eye of the beholder strikes the centre of the major axis perpendicularly (norma verticalis), it can be determined with certainty whether the zygomatic arches project like two handles beyond the outlines of the skull (phanerozygous), or whether they remain concealed behind them (cryptozygous skulls); in the first case we are able to say that the cheek-bones are prominent. Much attention has recently been given to the form of the orbicular cavities in the osseous face, but these measurements have not hitherto enabled us to recognize any characteristics available for ethnology. The osseous frames appear to have no influence on the oblique position of the opening of the eye,[10] which, although not quite constant as a characteristic of all nations of a Mongolian cast, must yet find place in description. The shape of the nose, again, was taken into account by the older ethnologists. The Papuan is recognizable by the Jewish type of his nose, the Mongols of Northern Asia by the flatness of this feature. In the inhabitants of Thibet the bridge of the nose is said to be so low that, seen in profile, it projects but little beyond the eye-ball, or even disappears behind it in some muscular individuals.[11]

The lower jawbone was formerly neglected by craniologists, and has only recently been noticed. In proportion as it is pointed or flattened, the face acquires oval, angular, or square outlines. But if we look round among our daily companions, we see such a confusion of types, so many transitions from one to the other, that it

---

[10] Von Schlagintweit, Indien und Hochasien, vol. ii. p. 51.

[11] Ibid. vol. ii. p. 48.

would require a vast number of measurements to enable us to say which of the divers forms is most prevalent. The mouth is another subject on which much stress has been laid in the description of races. The thick lips of the Central and Southern Africans are especially opposed to our idea of beauty. The thin lips of Europeans and their American descendants are, however, a character which brings them nearer to the apes. But even among the negroes themselves, this portion of the facial form varies considerably, and although a marked intumescence of the lips may be generally attributed to them, it implies nothing more than that the European form of mouth does not occur among them more frequently than does the negro form among ourselves. Among the Jews, who for thousands of years have intermarried among themselves, we find the two extremes side by side, the delicately chiseled mouth and the intumescent lips.

IV.—THE PROPORTIONS OF THE PELVIS AND THE LIMBS.

If we cast a glance from the head downwards, it is at once evident that there is a harmony of proportion between the skull and the female pelvis. But if the number of skulls of different races was too small to inspire implicit confidence, the stock of pelvises of various races does not equal the hundredth part of the skulls. Nevertheless, M. J. Weber has already ventured to distinguish an European or oval, an American or round, a Mongolian or square, a Negro or wedge-shaped pelvis. Joulin, on the other hand, maintained the identity of form of the Mongolian or, more accurately, the Javan or Papuan pelvis and that of the negro. Lastly, Pruner Bey believes that no race exists of which the woman cannot give birth to children of a European or any other father, that from the same womb proceed children with different forms of skull, although, according to observations on Javans and North Americans, parturition is easier when the child is of pure breed and not a hybrid.[1] Fritsch has recently imported to Europe a comparatively large number of pelvises of South African nations,

---

[1] Pruner Bey, Etudes sur le Bassin, p. 13. Paris, 1855.

but owing to the inconstancy of characters, he has not ventured to distinguish types. In the course of his studies he has, however, made a discovery calculated to cause serious reflection. In European skeletons, male and female are recognizable with tolerable certainty by the capaciousness and form of the pelvis. The pelvis is thus one of the secondary sexual characters. In the case of Bushmen, on the contrary, the female pelvis might be mistaken for the male, and the same holds good of Hottentots and Kaffirs.[2] Should this phenomenon be recognized in other parts of the world, we should be able to declare that the complete evolution of sexual differences is accomplished only under the protection of the higher civilizations.

We owe the most numerous measurements, although exclusively of female pelvises, to Carl Martin, who for a considerable time practised as a physician in Brazil, treating negresses as well as native women and hybrids. He compared the dimensions in the case of eight Papuans, two aboriginal Americans, eighteen Malays, four Bushmen, and fifteen negro women, with the averages of European collections. As far as a result may be deduced from this small stock of anatomical records, the pelvises may be divided into those with a circular inlet, as in the aboriginal Americans, Malays, and Papuans, and those with a transverse-oval inlet, as in African and European women. The inlet is called round when the conjugata is as large, or nearly as large, as the other diameter ; and transverse-oval when it is exceeded more than 10 per cent. by the transverse and oblique diameters. It may also be said with more precision that, in European women, the pelvis combines the greatest capacity and width with an essentially transverse-oval inlet ; and that the pelvis of the negress, although of similar shape, is smaller and narrower in other respects. The pelvises of Bushwomen, corresponding with their small bodily stature, are smaller than those of any other race, and have an inlet which is sometimes of an upright oval form. At page 1008 of the 31st number of the *Literar. Centralblatt*, it is stated that the side bones of the Bushman are relatively longer than the haunch bones, and are higher than in any other race, so that the pelvis

---

[2] Fritsch, Eingeborne Südafrika's, pp. 39, 299, 415.

is of animal form in an extreme degree. The Malay pelvises are narrow, the inlet round, or not unfrequently uprightly oval. In size the pelvis of aboriginal American women closely approach the European form, but differ from it in their circular entrance. Lastly, the Papuan pelvis, although tolerably round, yet approaches the transverse-oval form.[3]

Turning to the dimensions of the body, we must not expect that they will afford us any invariable marks of distinction between the various human families. Most of the observations directed to this end were obtained during the late civil war in the United States. The measurements extended to 1,104,841 men. It first became evident from these large numbers that growth visibly diminished in the 20th year, yet continued slowly till the 24th in all those who were drafted into the military service in the North American States; indeed, growth in native Americans does not completely cease till the 30th year.[4] It was also a curious fact that the inhabitants of the Western States, such as Kentucky and Tennessee, surpassed the natives of the East, and still more the Canadians, Scotch, Irish, English, and Germans in their bodily dimensions.[5]

	Average size.
Kentucky and Tennessee	176·62 Centim.
Ohio and Indiana	175·19
Michigan, Illinois, and Wisconsin	174·91
New England	173·53
New York, Pennsylvania, New Jersey ...	173·00

It is uncertain whether a fuller development of the body by hard work on virgin territories may be cited as the cause, or the fact that it is usually men of high stature and superior physical power who decide on emigration, while the more weakly prefer to stay at home; and that this form of segregation is reflected in this average of many individual cases. But as the native Americans surpass the Scotch, Irish, English, and German immigrants in bodily dimensions, there can be no doubt that the

---

[3] Monatschrift für Geburtskunde, xxviii. i. p. 23–58.

[4] Gould, Investigations in the Military and Anthropological Statistics of American Soldiers, p. 108. New York, 1869.

[5] Gould, p. 125.

descendants of the European emigrants have perceptibly increased in stature in the United States within a short period. It is the more conceivable that this effect is caused by the change of locality, as the aboriginal inhabitants are likewise remarkable for their size, and in them also the arrest of growth takes place only in the thirtieth year; at least five hundred of the Iroquois who were measured, were on an average a trifle taller than the Americans of the United States in the same recruiting districts.[6] That good and abundant food promotes bodily size is shown by the universally more portly figures of the Polynesian chiefs in the South Sea Islands.[7] Similarly among the Kaffirs, six men of a chieftain's family yielded an average of 1830 mm. or 110 mm. more than is otherwise found among the Bantu negroes of Southern Africa. The strikingly low stature of the Bushmen on the southern edge of the Kalahari may likewise be attributed to bad nourishment, for Chapman found their stature greater in the north, where game is more plentiful; the Koi-Koin, or Hottentots, their kindred by consanguinity, perhaps surpass them in height merely because they are shepherds and not hunters like the Bushmen.   Yet food and the nature of the abode can by no means account for all differences, otherwise the Kaffirs could not in their turn outstrip the Hottentots, though both gain their livelihood in like manner and in the same region.   Gustav Fritsch[8] determined the following averages :—

Men.						Bodily Dimensions.
55 Bantu Negroes ...	...	...	...	...	1718 Mm.
10 Koi-Koin ...	...	...	...	...	1604
6 Bushmen	...	...	...	...	...	1444

Difference of stature is therefore to a certain extent attributable to parentage, and so far bodily dimensions may be used as a distinctive mark in the description of nations.   Yet we have no averages derived from a great number of statistics; while measurements even of the same race are extremely various.   With regard

---

[6] Gould, Investigations, pp. 151, 152.

[7] Darwin, Descent of Man, vol. i. p. 115.

[8] Eingeborne Sudafrika's, pp. 17, 277, 397.

to the Maori of New Zealand, for instance, we find the following statements : [9]

Observers.						Height in Mm.
Thomson	...	...	...	...		1695·4
Scherzer and Schwarz		...	...	...		1757·6
Garnot and Lesson		...	...	...	...	1813
Wilkes	...	...	...	...		1904

Of these, Thomson's averages obtained from 147 measurements are probably most trustworthy.[10] The average dimensions may also increase or diminish within the same race, owing to separation during thousands of years, migrations to great distances, and altered habits of life ; for, notwithstanding the fluctuations of the figures, it is impossible to doubt that the Asiatic Malays belong to the small nations, while the Polynesian Malays are preëminent for their stature.[11]

ASIATIC MALAYS.

Observers.						Height in Mm.
Crawford	Javans		...	...		1549·4
Scherzer and Schwarz ...	...	,,	...	...	...	1679
Keppel	Dyaks...		...	...		1574·8
Müller	... Timorese ...		...	...		1586
Scherzer and Schwarz	...	Madurese	...	...		1625
,, ,,	...	... Sundanese		...	...	1646
,, ,, ...	...	Buginese	...	...		1653·9

POLYNESIAN MALAYS.

Wilkes ...	...	...	Sandwich Islanders ...		...	1676·4
Gaimard ...	...		,, ,,		...	1755
Wilkes ...	...	...	Marquesas Islanders ...			1689
Marchand ...	...		,, ,, ...		...	1786
Batare ...	...	...	,, ,,	...	...	1800
Garnot and Lesson			Tahitians ...	...	...	1786
Wilkes ...	...	...	,, ...	...	...	1803·3
La Pérouse...	...		Navigator Islanders	...	...	1895
Wilkes ...	...	...	,, ,,	...	...	1930·4

In every family of mankind popular report speaks of certain persons of unusual size as giants. Statements respecting such

---

[9] Weisbach, Anthropol. Theil der Novara-Reise, p. 217.
[10] Gould, Investigations, p. 146.   [11] Weisbach.

5

extreme cases are however of no ethnological value.[12]   It is more noteworthy that almost every circumnavigator of the world has contradicted the old anthropological fictions spread by Pigafetta the companion of Magalhães, as to the superhuman size of the Patagonians.   It is true these South American families belong to the nations of high stature, as is shown by the following measurements :—

						Height of the Patagonians.
Observers.						
D'Orbigny	...	...	...	...	...	1730 Mm.
,,	...	...	...	...	...	1780
D'Urville	...	...	...	...	...	1732
Wilson	...	...	...	...	...	1803·4

yet the Polynesians are in no way inferior to them in stature.   The lofty volcanic islands of the South Sea and the two continents of America are in truth the regions in which the human race has locally attained the highest stature.[13]

The lowest stature in man may fall to surprisingly low figures in single cases, for dwarfs of 920 mm. (3 ft. 0·2211268 in.) and even 750 mm. (2 ft. 6·5280925 in.) are described as perfectly well formed.[14]

But here again ethnology can make use only of averages derived from large numbers.   The Bushmen of South Africa have hitherto been considered the smallest of men ; their height having been stated by Barrow as 1300 mm., although Knox estimated them at 1372 mm., and the accurate Fritsch at 1444 mm.[15]   Du Chaillu found the same dwarfish proportions in the Obongos in Equatorial Africa, who resemble the Bushmen in other characters.[16]

---

[12] According to Gould (Investigations), in every million of men measured for military service there are :—

47 above 2007 Mm.		7 above 2083 Mm.
22 — 2032		6 — 2108
11 — 2057		2 — 2134

[13] According to Gould (Investigations, p. 152), of 500 Iroquois, 159 men of 31 years and upwards reached a height of 68·6 inches.

[14] Gould, p. 153.

[15] Weisbach, p. 216.   Fritsch, Eingeborne Südafrika's, p. 397.

[16] Ashango Land, p. 319.   The average stature of six women was 4ft. 8¼ in. or 1420 mm.

Again, the Acka, seen by the traveller Schweinfurth in the region of the Gazelle Nile, are somewhat similar, although they attain the height of 1500 mm.[17] It is a significant fact that the polar nations of both the Old and the New World must be added to this list of tropical families. The statements made by Pauw, giving 1300 mm. (4 ft. 3·182027 in.) as the average stature of the Eskimo, are, it is true, totally discredited by other measurements now before us, *i.e.*

HEIGHT OF THE ESKIMO.

Observer.	Locality in which the observation was made.	Mm.	Eng. feet. inches.
Beechey	Melville Island ...	1659	5 ft. 5·23514061
,, ...	Boothia Sound ...	1689	5 ft. 4·41526431
,, ...	Kotzebue Sound ...	1714	5 ft. 7·38479248
Chappel ...	Savage Island ..	1670	5 ft. 5·97644404

1380 mm. (4 ft. 6·18094862 in.) is also certainly less than the average of the Laplanders;[18] still both these nations are universally reckoned by travellers among the diminutive races of mankind. At all events we may confidently assert that human families remarkable for their small size exist in every latitude.

Hitherto we have taken the size of the men only into consideration, but we have now to note that a lower stature is one of the secondary characters of the female sex. Among women the average size fluctuates within much narrower limits, namely, from 1395 mm. (4 ft. 6·77151047 in.) to 1662 mm. (5 ft. 5·32625298 in.)[19] The measurements which have already been made also show that the difference of size in the two sexes almost disappears among the diminutive nations.[20] Thus Fritsch found 1448 mm. (4 ft. 8·57690392 in.) to be the average of five Bushwomen, or 4 mm. more than in the case of men, and this is corroborated by the statements of Weisbach. Accordingly, it is the male sex which is

---

[17] Petermann's Geograph. Mittheilungen, pp. 139–150. 1871.

[18] According to Tenon as cited by Gould (Investigations), p. 144, and Weisbach, p. 216.

[19] Weisbach.

[20] Fritsch, Eingeborne Südafrika's, p. 398.

specially contemplated in speaking of tall or short nations.[21]   The average stature of the male sex we shall take to be from 1600 mm. (5 ft. 2·993264 in.) to 1700 mm. (5 ft. 6·930343 in.), the medium height of the female sex at 1525 mm. (5 ft. 0·04045475 in.) to 1575 mm. (5 ft. 1·96899425 in.), and according to this standard we shall separate mankind into the short, medium, and tall families.

Venturing to express some conjectures concerning the causes of variations in stature, we would point out that this mass of measurements of recruits made during the American war, show that large bodily dimensions are dependent on a prolonged period of growth. This we conceive to be shortened in the case of women by the earlier maturity of their sex.   It is also probable that the full development of the body is impeded by precocious marriages, which, as we shall see, occur among the polar nations and the Bushmen.

Numerous measurements are alone capable of enlightening us as to what proportions the individual parts and members of the human frame attain in different districts.   Quetelet thought that the human type in Belgium harmonized with the estimates derived from the works of Grecian sculptors.[22]   But it appears that the ancient artists did not blindly follow an invariable rule, just as in later times great masters, such as Leonardo da Vinci and Albert Dürer, did not agree in their notions of so-called symmetry.   A Belgian painter, moreover, is wont to study drawing so constantly from the great masterpieces of antiquity that their proportions become at last impressed upon him as strictly imperative.   He will often hire or reject a female model for his studies from nature according as to whether she approaches or departs from the desired ideal.   Hence, if in ten of the female models employed by the sculptors or painters of Brussels, the average proportions of individual parts of the body approximated very closely to the like

---

[21] Beechey as cited by Weisbach gives the following measurements of Eskimo:—

	Men.	Women.
Melville Island	1659 mm. ...	1536.6 mm.
Savage Island	1679	... 1549.3
Boothia Sound	1689	... 1571.3

[22] Anthropométrie, p. 86.   Brussels, 1870.

averages in antique statues, Quetelet ought not to have inferred an identity in the Belgian and ancient Greek types, but rather to have admired the quick eyes of the Belgian artists, which were able with unerring glance to eliminate from among the candidates for this profession such as differed too much from the recognized ideal. The height of the head, which with many artists constitutes the standard of measurement, varies, as we will here note, with the dimensions of the body. Taking the perpendicular height of the skull as the unit, the stature, according to Welcker's estimate, is in new-born infants as 5 : 6, in boys of eight years of age 8 : 4, in short men it is as 11 : 9, in men of average stature 12 : 1, in tall men 13 : 2, so that tall people have, relatively, the smallest heads.[23]

The proportions of the human limbs cannot be expressed unless the height of the body be taken as the standard. During the voyage of the frigate Novara, Von Scherzer and Schwarz extended their measurements of living men to the minutest details. The length of lower and upper limbs must always appear of the greatest importance. The part of the leg below the thigh is usually so related to the thigh that greater shortness of the former is compensated by increased length of the latter. This lower part of the leg is always longer than the thigh. If the latter be estimated at 1000, we find that in a native of Stewart's Island the lower leg reaches 1238, and in New Zealanders may, in exceptional cases, sink below 1000, even to 965. But it appears that the native of Stewart's Island, if we reckon the height of the body at 1000, has a very short thigh of 198 mm. (7·81341642 in.), the New Zealander a very long one of 229 mm.[24] (9·02491101 in.) The length of the leg also varies considerably. In the Chinese it may be only the 0·444th part of the height of the body, and in Bushmen it may be the 0·515th.

But the proportions of the upper limbs are much more important, as their comparative shortness forms a character which separates man from the animals which most resemble him. Carl Vogt has expressed this relation by stating that the orang, in an erect posture, is able to touch its ankles, the gorilla the middle of the

[23] Bau und Wachsthum des Schädels, p. 31.
[24] Weisbach, Reise der Fregatte Novara, part ii. p. 255. Anthropologie.

tibia, the chimpanzee the knee, with the tips of their fingers ; whereas man can scarcely reach as far as the middle of the thigh.[25] In the recruits for the American war, special attention was paid to this particular proportion of the human frame, and measurements were made of the interval between the middle finger in a stiff military attitude, and the upper edge of the knee-cap.   In white men, American and European, the average amounted to $5''036$,[26] in the negroes of the Free States $3''298$, or somewhat more than in the negroes of the Slave States ($2''832$) ; while in the latter, the variations were so great that, in individual cases, the tips of the fingers actually rested on the edge of the knee-cap.

DISTANCE FROM THE FINGER-TIPS TO THE UPPER EDGE OF
THE KNEE-CAP.

No. of Measurements.	Medium.	Minimum.	Maximum.
2020 Pure-bred Negroes	$2''88$	$-0''5$	$7''6$
863 Hybrids	$4''13$	$+0''2$	$7''2$

It is also a curious fact that habits of life are capable of affecting these variations, for in the case of 1146 sailors the average of this distance was somewhat greater than in landsmen.

DISTANCE FROM THE FINGER-TIPS TO THE UPPER EDGE OF
THE KNEE-CAP.

	New England.	New York, New Jersey, Pennsylvania.	England.	Ireland.
Soldiers ...	$4''93$	$4''92$	$4''90$	$5''08$
Sailors ...	$5''57$	$6''06$	$5''55$	$6''07$
Difference ...	$''64$	$1''14$	$''65$	$''99$

Thus the sailors' arms were shorter and their legs longer than those of the recruits who offered themselves for service in the

---

[25] Vorlesungen über den Menschen, vol. i. p. 193.

[26] Gould, Investigations, p. 279.

field. According to the average of the different States, the length of the arm varied in American whites and Europeans from 0·429 of the height of the body (Michigan, Wisconsin, Illinois), to 0·441 (Scandinavia).[27] Pure-bred negroes of the Slave States (0·452) displayed a relatively greater length of arm than the negroes of the Free States (0·447), a proportion occurring also in mulattoes (0·445 and 0·460). The value of averages taken from large numbers is again palpable, for we here perceive far slighter fluctuations than other racial measurements would have led us to expect. According to Weisbach,[28] we find the arms of the Germans reckoned at 0·469 of the length of the body, that of the Sclavonians at 0·467, of the Roumanians at 0·452, in a native of Stewart's Island at 0·511, and in a Sulu Malay, measured by Wilkes, at 0·409. With such an amount of individual fluctuation, no characteristics, reliable in the delineation of races, can be deduced from existing statements, until we multiply our measurements of the different human families at least a hundred-fold.

Finally, the relative length of the fore-arm, as compared with the upper-arm, was statistically ascertained by measurements of the body taken during the voyage of the frigate Novara round the world. In the case of the orang, the result was a proportion of 877 : 1000. Precisely the same ratio was found in the Madurese. In the Roumanians the fore-arm even reaches a relative length of 883, and in the Sclavonians of at least 868. The proportions of Australians, Sundanese, and negroes also are nearly those of the orang ; those of German men differ most from these (835) ; while the proportions sink as low as 822 in German women.[29] Once more we must deplore the scanty supply of measurements ; yet from those which we already have we find that the proportions of the human limbs vary considerably in the nations of the same race, and again individually in the nations themselves ; that even habits of life may influence growth, so that difference of dimensions in the structure of the limbs must be declared inconstant.

---

[27] Gould, Investigations, pp. 298, 299.
[28] Weisbach, p. 251.   [29] Ibid, pp. 242, 243.

V.—THE SKIN AND HAIR OF MANKIND.

THE old geographers believed duskiness of skin to increase in proportion to the nearness of the equator, and that the latitude of a people's abode may be inferred from their colour.[1]　No experience within the territory then known contradicted this dogma. In the North dwelt fair, in Southern Europe and the north of Africa light-brown nations, on the Upper Nile negroes, and in India dusky people.　More correct views were attained only when the Spaniards encountered people of a swarthy tint in every latitude of the New World, some lighter, some darker, according to the locality, but in no way corresponding to their equatorial position. Among the Abipones of Paraguay the hair was so fair, especially among the women, that in European costume they might have been mistaken for European women, while the Puelchas and Aucas, whose territory lay ten degrees of latitude further from the equator, were of a much darker hue.[2]　It was even noticed that exactly in the most northerly parts of the Old World, the brown Laplanders, Voguls, and Ostiaks lived nearer the pole than the fair-haired nations.

Microscopic research as yet only teaches us that the human skin consists of two layers, of which the external one is designated the outer skin (epidermis), the inner one, the true skin (cutis). The outer skin again consists of two parts, namely, the upper transparent cuticle (stratum corneum), and the lower stratum mucosum or Malpighian tissue (rete Malpighi).　The true skin (cutis) and the outer layer of the cuticle are recognized as homogeneous in all families of mankind, and it is only in the Malpighian tissue, enclosed between them, that the cells containing the finely granulated colouring matter are seen.　According as these pigment cells are limited to the lower surface of the Malpighian tissue, or are more and more massed together, in rare cases are extending upwards into the cuticle, so does the darkness

---

[1] Pliny, VI. 22.

[2] Dobrizhoffer, Geschichte der Abiponer, vol. ii. p. 18. Vienna, 1783.

of the complexion proportionately increase. Certain parts of the body are coloured in all human races, such as the nipple, which, moreover, becomes darker during pregnancy.[3] Freckles, moles, and claret-marks are also exactly analogous to the skin of the negro.[4]

The negro child is not born black, but of a colour almost like that of European children. Pruner Bey describes the colour as reddish tinged with nut brown, and adds that the full colouring makes its appearance in the first year in the Soudan, but in Lower Egypt only in the third year.[5] Camper also saw a negro child which was reddish at birth, but became coloured first on the margin of the nails, on the third day in the sexual parts, and during the fifth and sixth days over the whole body.[6] The eyes of negro infants are blue at first, their hair chestnut, and crimped only at the ends.[7] Among the Pimos, or Pimas, in the north-west of Mexico, as well as among the Australians, infants are fair or dirty yellow at birth, but after a few days resemble their parents in the darkness of their skin.[8] The Prince of Neuwied was informed that the Botocudo children are born yellow, but soon turn brown,[9] although he inconsistently extols the fairness of the adults. The children of mulattoes and mulatto women are said to come into the world with black patches, especially in the region of the reproductive organs. On the colour of the skin depends the odour of the effluvia. Especially obnoxious are the strongly ammoniacal, rancid, goat-like exhalations of the negro,[10] which,

[3] Blumenbach mentions a young woman who, during pregnancy, became as black as a negress. A similar case of melanism was observed by Dr. Guyétant. Quatrefages, Unité de l'espèce humaine, p. 65. Paris, 1861.

[4] Flourens as cited by Waitz, Anthropologie, vol. i. p. 113.

[5] Pruner Bey, Mémoire sur les Nègres, p. 327.

[6] Waitz, vol. i. p. 114.   [7] Darwin, Descent of Man, vol. ii. p. 318.

[8] Waitz, Anthropologie. In Latham (Varieties), on the other hand, we find it asserted that at Hawai (Sandwich Islands) the Polynesian children are born completely black. vol. iv. p. 202, vol. vi. p. 713.

[9] Reise nach Brasilien. The Jesuit Lafitau says very decidedly that the children of the North American Redskins "are born white like our own" (Mœurs des Sauvages amériquains, vol. i. p. 104. Paris, 1724).

[10] Bacmeister, Reise nach Brasilien, vol. i. p. 433. Berlin, 1853. It is said that the skins of Arabians returning from Africa emit a noxious smell, which is only lost in course of time; and in corpulent South Europeans, in a feverish condition, an almost negro-like exhalation is said to be developed.

wafted over the ocean by currents of air, used to give notice of the distant approach of a slave-ship. We, too, are recognizable by the gases we emit, or the dog would not be able to follow the track of his master. The nations of the New World are distinguished from the Europeans by their odour, while the Creoles even have expressions for the slight effluvia of the Americans (catinca), and for the exceptionally strong and repulsive smell of the Araucanians (soreno).[11]

It is only in the absence of other and more constant distinctive marks of the various human families that we venture to employ the colour of the skin for such a purpose, for the degree of darkness, and even the tone, varies in every race, and often even in the members of a single horde. Even in Europe, we meet with people of fair or dark complexion. The former is more common in the north, the latter in the south. There are many fair Italians, Spaniards, and Portuguese ; while, on the other hand, dark complexions are not rare in England. The Celts of Gaul are described by the old geographers of the imperial age as a fair race of men ; so that, as the epithet is no longer applicable to the French of the present day, we may conclude that characters of this sort may alter in comparatively short periods. Among the Wakilema of Eastern Africa, German travellers noticed a light negro colour with a tinge of blue in some individuals, but others surpassing mulattoes in fairness, although there were no grounds for suspecting an intermixture.

It is undeniable that latitude does affect the colouring of the skin in some degree, though in a manner as yet unascertained. We find the deepest shade of black only in the neighbourhood of the equator, in Africa, India, and New Guinea. The natives in the vicinity of Moreton Bay, in Australia, were as dark as any negro, while ten degrees southwards copper colour became more common.[12] Among the members of the Mediterranean race, the Abyssinians are very dark ; among the Indo-European, the gipsies and Brahminical Hindoos are the darkest of all. In the latter, an admixture with the aboriginal inhabitants might be conjectured ;

---

[11] Waitz, Anthropologie, vol. i. pp. 114, 118.

[12] Ibid, vol. i. p. 52.

yet Graul was able to distinguish a man of high caste, *i.e.*, an Indian of Aryan origin from the Tamuls, by the almost European fairness of his skin.[13] That it is not the rays of the sun which produce the darkening of the complexion is evident from the fact that, in coloured men, the covered portions of the body are equally dark. But if a higher temperature were the cause, we should find darker skins in all lowland than in elevated regions. This hypothesis is indeed somewhat confirmed by a comparison between the inhabitants of Bengal and the hill people of the Himalayas, who are much fairer, and the same is observable in the inhabitants of the mountain plains of Enarea and Kaffa in Abyssinia. Other observers in the very same regions have, however, found the inhabitants of the valleys the fairest.[14] Munzinger adds that the sultry shore of the Red Sea is occupied by fair people, and the mountain districts by dark people.[15] Still more conclusive is the fact that, of all the aborigines of America, in whom no suspicion of admixture is possible, the Aymara, who occupy plateaux of the same altitude as the summits of the Bernese Oberland, are most remarkable for their black-brown colour, which is deepest precisely in the coldest tracts.[16] Other observers imagined the skin to be darkest in places where a hot temperature is combined with an atmosphere highly saturated with moisture. Livingstone thinks damp heat is the cause of the deep colouring in South Africa.[17] The dark Aymara in the dry, cold land of Peru and Bolivia, bear witness against this conjecture, while the Yuracara, whose very name indicates a pale countenance, occupy the eastern slopes of the South American Cordilleras, which are constantly dripping with moisture.[18]

Still we must always bear in mind that a European who lives long in the East Indies is obliged to adapt himself to an alteration in his customary physiological functions. The difference in colour between arterial and venous blood is strikingly diminished in

---

[13] Reise nach Ostindien, vol. iv. pp. 151, 152. Leipzic, 1855.

[14] Quatrefages, Rapport, p. 155.   [15] Ausland, p. 954. 1869.

[16] Von Tschudi, Reisen durch Südamerika, vol. v. p. 212.

[17] Missionary Journeys in South Africa, vol. i. p. 378.

[18] Darwin, Descent of Man, vol. ii. 347.

Europeans in tropical countries, because, owing to a feebler process of combustion, the absorption of oxygen is smaller.[19] On the other hand, the biliary secretions become more active in hot countries. So that by overwork of an organ destined for comparative repose, namely, of the liver, in a native of high latitudes, of the lungs, in a native of the tropics, the former frequently falls a victim to bilious fevers in the hot climate so uncongenial to him, while the latter when transferred to cold regions frequently perishes of consumption.[20] A European who has survived the change, loses his rosy complexion under the tropics. It is even recorded that an English gentleman, Macnaughton by name, who long lived the life of a native in the jungle of Southern India acquired, even on the clothed portions of his body, a skin as brown as that of a Brahmin.[21] A negro boy, brought from Bagirmi to Germany by Gerhard Rohlfs, changed his colour after a residence of two years, from " deep black to light brown." [22] If an increased secretion of bile influences the accumulation of pigment cells in the mucous layer of the lower skin, the darkness of the Lapps and Finns may be ascribed to their uncleanliness, the impure air of their dwellings, and their unwholesome food, since these also affect the biliary secretions.[23]

It had long been known that negro races enjoy complete health in Equatorial Africa, while Europeans are quickly carried off by coast fevers. In America the yellow fever spares the negroes and even the mulattoes. Now, if there were a causal connection between the darkness of the skin and immunity from local diseases, it would be evident that on the first colonization of fever districts those individuals who were already brown or who became swarthy, would readily overcome the perils of the situation, while those who were paler would be earlier swept away, and in consequence of this elimination a darkening of the skin might gradually become

---

[19] J. R. Mayer, Die Mechanik der Wärme, p. 97. Stuttgart, 1867.

[20] Bastian in Zeitschrift für Ethnologie, part i. 1869.

[12] Pruner Bey, Questions relatives à l'Anthropologie, p. 5. Paris, 1864.

[22] Zeitschrift für Ethnologie, p. 255. 1871. Other instances of negroes becoming lighter are given by Waitz on the authority of Blumenbach. Anthrop. i. 60.

[23] Richard Owen, Anatomy of Vertebrates, vol. iii. p. 615.

hereditary.[24] This is a mere conjecture as yet incapable of proof, but possessing the single advantage of being the only attempt at an explanation. It must be added, however, that Dr. Nachtigal reports that the black natives of the Soudan succumbed to the marsh fever after the inundations in Kuka as rapidly as the foreign immigrants.[25]

Among the preëminently hereditary physical characteristics of man is his covering of hair. It is true the colour of the hair is variable, even in individuals, since it arises from a pigment, the disappearance of which produces the whiteness of old age. Red hair occurs in almost all parts of the world, except America. Dumont d'Urville [26] says he saw it even among Australians. It is not uncommon among Finnish tribes, nor among the Berbers of Northern Africa. In Morocco there are even some of the latter with light eyes and fair hair,[27] while even Scylax knew of the Gyzantis in the Lesser Syrtis as fair Libyans.[28] According to Manetho, the Egyptian queen Nitokris, who belonged to the sixth dynasty, was distinguished for her fair complexion, rosy cheeks, and light hair.[29] Fair hair is also traceable in mummies of the Guanches, the extinct inhabitants of the Canary Islands, who were a branch of the Berbers.[30] Even among the Monbuttoos, on the Uellé, Schweinfurth saw many fair negroes of a grayish tinge.[31] Of the Federal soldiers in the American civil war, 5 per cent. of the Spaniards and Portuguese, and 51 per cent. of the Scandinavians, had red, or some sort of light hair.[32] These shades of hair occasionally appear among Armenians, Semitic Syrians, and Jews, and in hybrids of European and native Peruvians about Moyobamba.[33] Hence, although we must not entirely overlook

---

[24] From an address by Dr. Wells before the Royal Society in 1813. Darwin, Origin of Species, p. 3 ; and Descent of Man, vol. i. p. 214.

[25] Zeitschrift für Erdkunde, vol. vi. p. 335. Berlin, 1871.

[26] Voyage de l'Astrolabe, p. 404.

[27] G. Rohlf's Erster Aufenthalt in Marokko, p. 60. Bremen, 1873.

[28] Scylax Periplus, cap. 110. Geogr. Graeci Minores, ed Müller, i. p. 88.

[29] Lauth, Aegyptische Reisebriefe, p. 1335. Allgem. Zeitung, 1873.

[30] Peschel, Zeitalter der Entdeckungen, p. 54.

[31] Zeitschrift für Ethnologie, vol. v. p. 15. Berlin, 1873.

[32] Gould, Investigations in Military and Anthropological Statistics, p. 193.

[33] Raymondi's Geografia del Peru in the Globus, vol. xxi. p. 300.

the colour of the hair, in describing nations, it is certainly a very inconstant character. The form of the hair is of far greater importance. Neighbouring nations may sometimes be easily separated from one another by this character, although it is impossible to draw an invariable line. The aborigines of America, without exception, have stiff, coarse hair ; the Papuan is distinguished by his crown of hair from the Australian, whose hair, although frizzly, does not unite in tufts. The character of the hair, and especially that of the hair of the head, may be described as smooth or straight, as curly or gracefully waved, as frizzly, or finally as tufted. The causes of the crimping and twisting are manifold ; one is, the size of the diameter, for the finer the hair, the more readily is it affected by the causes of crimping ; since the human hair is never as soft as sheep's wool, no genuine wool like that of animals is found on man. But for our purpose, the form of the transverse section is of greater importance ; this is sometimes circular, sometimes elliptically compressed, so that hair may vary from the form of a cylinder to that of a doubly convex band. Although considerable variations occur in individual representatives of a race, yet Pruner Bey hoped to make use of the averages of size, as a serviceable means for the classification of human races. If the greater diameter of the section is taken at 100, the flatter the hair, the lower will be the number expressing the short diameter. The most perfectly cylindrical form, with a short diameter of 95, occurs in the South Americans, while the mummies of the Aymara in Peru have an average diameter of 89. The Mongols, in whom the compression fluctuates between 81 and 91, approach nearest to the inhabitants of the New World in this point. In the Papuans of New Guinea, the smaller diameter of the hair is shorter than in any other people, varying from 26 to 56 in extreme cases, with a mean of 34. This is another point of difference between the Australians, who have an index of 67 and 75, and the Papuans. It is also significant that the Hottentots nearly agree with the Papuans, for in them the smaller diameter is as low as from 55 to 50.[34] Yet sharp distinctions cannot be drawn by this means, but

---

[34] Pruner Bey, De la Chevelure, p. 15. Paris, 1863. Goette on the other hand found only a small diameter among the Afandy.

we learn that with greater flatness of the hair, especially if combined with greater fineness, the tendency to become curly and frizzly is considerably increased.

It is necessary to distinguish between frizzly hair and the fascicular agglomeration of many hairs into separate ropes, which have not been inaptly compared to the matted locks about the ears of a thorough-bred poodle. Both Dr. Maklucho Maclay and Dr. A. B. Meyer say that the hair of the Papuans is as evenly distributed on the scalp as in the case of Europeans ; the latter adds that it is only when the hair is not combed that it becomes matted into tufts. This tuft-like combination is aided by an external cement, that is to say, by the secretion of grease and tallow.[35] By their tufted locks it is possible actually to distinguish the separate branches of the Papuàn race from Malay and Australian tribes. This character is far less trustworthy in South Africa. There the tufted growth of hair is most distinctly marked in the Hottentots, in the Bushmen who resemble them in bodily structure, and in some scattered tribes in the interior of Africa, extending to the neighbourhood of the equator. The agglomeration of the hair into separate tufts was supposed to be visible in heads recently shorn, which, to quote a prosaic but accurate remark of Barrow's, look and feel like a worn-out blacking-brush. The coarseness of this hair, however, prevents its comparison with sheep's wool. Unfortunately, neither is this character quite peculiar to one family of nations, for according to Gustav Fritsch, the hair of the South African Bantu negroes is matted, though in a slighter degree, into small tufts.[36] This growth of hair occurs not only in the Amaχosa Kaffirs,[37] in whom there is probably some admixture of blood, as they have adopted some of the clicking sounds of the Hottentot language, but is also often plainly perceptible, and is indeed never entirely absent, in the Betschuans who live more in the interior. Hence, owing to its gradual transitions, this character affords no means of sharply separating nations into classes. Frizzly hair, which marks African negroes and Australians, is distinguishable

---

[35] Goette, Das Haar des Buschweibes, p. 34. Tübingen, 1867.

[36] Fritsch, Die Eingebornen Südafrika's, pp. 15, 16, 275, 276.

[37] Fritsch, Atlas, plates xi.-xx.

from the matted form by the absence of tufts, and from the curly hair by its shortness, its strong spiral twist, and a longitudinal division which separates the hair into two flat bands.[38] Without this last character, if the hair be coarser and more cylindrical, we get a slighter curvature of the masses of hair such as we see in the curls of Europeans and Semites. Finally the coarsest and roundest hair is a persistent character of the American Indians and their kindred in Northern and Eastern Asia. Where a mixture has taken place between the frizzly-haired Africans and the coarse and straight-haired American Indians, the hair preserves its crispness but increases in length and rigidity. In these Cafusos, as such hybrids are called in Brazil, a profusion of hair standing up from the head is developed, which gives them a deceptive resemblance to the Papuans.[39] The hair of the latter probably surpasses that of all other nations, in point of thickness of growth. In length of hair on the head, the hunting tribes of North America are unrivalled.[40] That of the men of the Blackfeet, and of the Sioux or Dacotas, reaches nearly to the heels, and in one Crowhead it actually attained a length of 10 ft. 7 in.[41]

The hairy covering of other parts of the body is more or less abundant, but is sometimes wanting in both sexes. The covering most rarely disappears about the parts of generation. Its scantiness or entire absence in North Asiatic Mongols, in American and Malay families, as well as in Hottentots and Bushmen, afford some of the most persistent and best authenticated racial characters, only it must be added that the natural baldness of the body is artificially exaggerated by the careful extraction of single hairs. The beard is either wanting or is extremly limited in all nations with stiff coarse hair, namely, in American Indians, Northern and Eastern Asiatics, as well as in Malays. It is scantily developed in Hottentots; it appears more abundantly and more frequently in negroes of Central and Southern Africa. In all those races,

---

[38] Goette.

[39] On the origin of the name Cafuz, see Martius, Ethnographie, vol. i. p. 150. In Guayana they are called Cabocles, or Capucres. Appun in the Ausland, 1872, p. 967.

[40] Pruner Bey, Chevelure, p. 4.

[41] Catlin, North American Indians, vol. i. p. 49.

whiskers are not to be found, or only as a rarity. The Australians may easily be distinguished from their Malay and Polynesian neighbours by their scanty beards, while a profusion of beard distinguishes the Papuans. A luxuriant growth of hair on the body is one of the distinctive marks of the Semitic as well as of the Indo-European families. In Southern Europeans, especially in Portuguese and Spaniards, this character is most strongly developed. Beyond all the nations in the world the Ainos, the inhabitants of Jezo, Saghalien, and the Kuriles have had the reputation, since the visit of La Pérouse, of possessing an almost animal-like covering of hair on the upper part of the body.[42] Recent observers have considerably modified this exaggeration, and it appears that the Ainos could not even be compared with European sailors. Wilhelm Heine found the beards of the Ainos only five or six inches long, the chest and neck were bald, and only in a single individual were seen a few tufts of hair on the above-named parts.[43] Nevertheless, even this moderate degree of hairiness in the neighbourhood of such beardless people as the Japanese and Chinese, is perplexing when we try to place the Ainos in our division of races, for we are obliged to reckon the appearance of hair on the body among the most persistent distinctive marks of human races. Although among 2129 mulattoes and negroes of the 25th Army Corps who, at the time of the American civil war, were observed by physicians while bathing, only 9 proved to be quite hairless, while 21 on the other hand exhibited the highest degree, and two-thirds were on the average as hairy as white soldiers,[44] we must not infer that the exchange

---

[42] La Pérouse (Voyage autour du Monde, vol. iii. p. 125. Paris, 1798) contents himself with asserting that among the inhabitants of Saghalien in the Bay of Crillon, an amount of beard and hair on the arms and neck, such as is rare in Europeans, is with them the rule.

[43] W. Heine, China, Japan, and Ochotzk. H. O. Brandt, German Consul in Japan, expressed himself in accordance with the statements of W. Heine at the sitting of the Anthropological Society of Berlin, held December 16th, 1871. (Compare their Verhandlungen, p. 27. Berlin, 1872.) In the Narrative of the Expedition under Comm. M. C. Parry (Washington, 1856), vol. i. p. 454, by Francis L. Hawks, mention is made only of the strong growth of beard and great hairiness of the legs in the Ainos in the vicinity of Hakodadi.

[44] Gould, Investigations, pp. 568, 569.

of an African home for the New World has occasioned the growth of the hair of the body. This is perhaps the place in which to refute the mistaken idea that negroes belong to the smooth-skinned nations. Their beard, it is true, is not so fully developed as in the Mediterranean nations, but it is more abundant than in the Koi-Koin (Hottentots), and incomparably more so than in the Mongoloid families of the Old and New World. Even whiskers are not entirely absent, as some people have maintained, and in some tribes the chests of the men are always overgrown with hair, and in others occasionally.[45]

In summing up, we must needs confess that neither the shape of the skull nor any other portion of the skeleton has afforded distinguishing marks of the human races; that the colour of the skin likewise displays only various gradations of darkness, and that the hair alone comes to the aid of our systematic attempts, and even this not always, and never with sufficient decisiveness. Who, then, can presume to talk of the immutability of racial types? To base a classification of the human race on the character of the hair only, as Haeckel has done, was a hazardous venture, and could but end as all other artificial systems have ended. In the separation of the Koi-Koin from the Bantu negroes, this system has led to errors, and the combination of Australians, as a so-called straight-haired people, with the Mongols is due to ignorance of facts.

---

[45] Comp. the Barolong negro in Fritsch's Atlas (Eingeborne Südafrika's), and the description of the Kissama negro given by Hamilton in the Journal of the Anthropol. Institute, vol. i. p. 187. London, 1872.

LINGUISTIC CHARACTERS.

LINGUISTIC CHARACTERS.

IF speech be but the means of communicating emotions or intentions to other beings, even invertebrate animals possess faculties of the same nature. We see insects, such as ants, which live in so-called communities, carrying out elaborately preconcerted warlike undertakings and attacks. A beetle which, in rolling the ball of dung enclosing its egg, has allowed it to slip into a hole, from which it is unable to extricate it, flies away, to return in a short time with a number of assistants sufficient to push the ball up the sides of the declivity by co-operation of labour. These creatures must, therefore, unquestionably possess some means of communicating with each other concerning this combination. It requires no long observation of our song-birds to distinguish the different tones by which they warn their young of danger, or call them to feed, or by which they attract each other to pair. These animals, therefore, have at their control a certain number of signals, which are quite adequate to procure for them some few of the wants of their life, and these signals, as far as we can at present guess, have been acquired and inherited in the same manner as were their instincts. The need of communication is almost more various and urgent in the dog than in any other animal. We fully understand his bark, whether it signifies pleasure, dissatisfaction, a warning of danger, a definite wish, or a declaration of hostility. The dog does not use his voice only, but snarls and gnashes his teeth. With some justice the bark of the dog has been described as an animal's first attempt to speak.[1] But this talent was acquired by intercourse with talkative man, for European dogs, deposited on solitary islands, lost the habit of barking, and produced a dumb posterity, which reacquired the use of the vocal apparatus only after renewed association with mankind.

Human speech, however, is distinguished from the sounds of intelligence used by animals, not only by a greater range of communications, but also by the power of proclaiming not only perceptions, but cognitions which lie beyond the mental faculties of animals. If the bark of the dog be the first attempt at speech, we may add that the attempt is as yet a failure. The animal has not even got so far as to appropriate a call to any particular person. As soon as the child is so far matured as consciously to call its father or mother, its first attempt to speak has been completely successful. An animal can never communicate such simple cognitions as are implied in the words light, warm, sweet, hard, sharp, blue, red.

As history and experience daily teach us that languages alter, and at the same time increase in compass; that their formation, therefore, never stands still, and that these transformations and additions are certainly derived from ourselves, it ought never to have been disputed that man was the creator of his own language. Yet an endeavour has been made to ascribe the first beginning to a supernatural process. But if human speech be regarded as the only difference which, as it were, at once divides us from our fellow-beings in the animal world, our mental faculties are degraded, and this chasm is narrowed by those who maintain that man did not evolve his noblest distinction by his own resources. If this denial is due to morbid bigotry, we need but call to mind that the Scriptures themselves emphatically describe speech as man's own creation (Gen. ii. 19, 20).

Whoever wishes to obtain a clear conception of the first beginnings of human language, must first take warning that all comparisons of existing vocabularies mislead him. If we only trace back for a few centuries the names of towns and countries, we shall see how, in the course of time, they have been

---

[1] C. Geiger, Ursprung der Sprache, p. 190.

deceptively metamorphosed beyond recognition. A. Bacmeister tells us that Wildenschwerdt was originally Wilhelmswerd ; Waldsee (Würtemberg) is corrupted from Walchsee, Oehringen from Oringau, Welzheim from Walinzin, Holzbach from Heroldsbach. Only 300 years ago Martin Luther could still write that "Gott thue nichts als schlechtes, und das Evangelium sei eine kindische Lehre"—*God does nothing but what is bad, and the Gospel is a childish doctrine.*[2] But at that time schlecht (bad) meant something schlichtes (smooth, honest, upright), as in the idiom " recht und schlecht " (upright and downright), and kindisch (childish) something kindliches (child-like). It is with no malicious significance that in the south of Germany every male child is termed a *Bube,* while in the north this expression now signifies only a reprobate ; just as in English the word *knave,* corresponding to *Knabe* (boy), has acquired an unfavourable interpretation. We thus learn the important lesson that the meaning by no means adheres firmly to a phonetic combination, but that even in allied languages it is imperceptibly withdrawn, and even transferred to other phonetic groups.

The fact that the idea is thus independent of its phonetic expression, refutes the assertion so often made, that we think only in inwardly spoken language. On the contrary, thought without the aid of language accompanies nearly all our every-day acts. The musician also constructs his creations with a rhythmical succession of sounds ; the painter selects colour to express his thoughts or his frame of mind, the sculptor selects the human form, the architect lines and surfaces, the geometrician limitations of space, the mathematician expressions of quantity. Were language, on the contrary, the strict and necessary phonetic embodiment of thought, thought would everywhere be expressed in the sounds.

We must, therefore, regard the connection of a certain meaning with certain phonetic combinations as something merely transitory. Philologists who have traced back the development of the Indo-European languages as far as records make it possible, were ultimately able to collect a number of roots which we must con-

---

[2] L. Geiger, pp. 64, 72.

sider as the oldest philological material obtainable.[3]   Yet we
have no positive evidence that these roots were the primordial
elements ; we may rather assume that they also had undergone
phonetic transformation before they reached us.   Some nations,
it is true, have the power of preserving phonetic combinations
longer and more accurately, while others deal less steadily with
the apparatus for the expression of ideas ; still it may be asserted
generally, that the stability of a language increases with the number
of speakers, and at the same time with the more perfect organization of society.   The extraordinary number of languages in
North America is closely connected with the restless habits of the
wandering hunting tribes.   Where, on the contrary, well-organized
societies existed, as in ancient Peru, the predominant Ketshua
language prevailed over more than twenty degrees of latitude.

It has been explained by earlier writers that the belief in an
existence after death accelerated the metamorphosis of language.
The names of the departed were not mentioned for fear of sum-
moning the ghost of the person mentioned.   Many nations do not
even dare to utter the real name of their deity, and something of
the sort is enjoined in the third Sinaitic commandment.   When
the black small-pox broke out among the Dyaks of Borneo, every
one fled in terror to the solitudes of the forest.   No one ventured
to call the disease by its name, but it was spoken of as the "jungle
leaves," or "Datu" (chieftain), or people simply said, "is *he* gone?"[4]
But as, amongst most half-developed nations, proper names are
compounded of words in daily use, new expressions must be invented to replace them.

When King Pomare died at Tahiti, the word *po* (night) vanished
from the language.   The same custom is, or was, observed by the
Papuans of New Guinea, the Australians, and Tasmanians, the
Masai of Eastern Africa, the Samoyeds, and the Fuegians.   The
influence of this habit on the metamorphosis of language must
not, however, to be over-estimated, for when a new generation has

---

[3] Steinthal, Psychologie und Sprachwissenschaft, vol. i. pp. 54, 361. Berlin,
1871. Whitney, Language and the Study of Language, pp. 413-420.
London, 1867.

[4] Spenser St. John, Far East, vol. i. pp. 61, 62. London, 1862.

grown up which does not know or fear the deceased,[5] it may revert to the old word ; or where the prohibition only extends to one horde, and the forbidden word survives in another, it may be reintroduced by intermarriages. Nor must it be supposed that new syllables are invented, but merely that new words are concocted out of the existing ingredients of the language. Among the Abipones on the western shore of the river Paraguay, in South America, the old women are entrusted with the business of creating the new appellations. On account of deaths which had occurred, they changed the name of the tiger (jaguar) three times in seven years, and finally into *laprirctrae*, the " speckled " or " variegated."[6]

Language is exposed to far greater risk of metamorphosis among tribes which roam over thinly populated hunting-grounds in small bands, or sometimes in single families. The requirements of daily life constrain every member of a large society to speak distinctly that he may be understood by all. Ill-trained children often invent syllables which for a time are tolerated in the household, and would become permanently established if they were not rejected in general intercourse as unknown coin. But these bad habits of children find a parallel in the customs of men among the Brazilian hunters, whose single tribes, on account of the rapid development of dialects, not only become incomprehensible to their kindred of the same language, but each obstinately adheres to his peculiar pronunciation. Martius, the traveller, complained that among his escort, although they belonged to the same horde, each clung to small dialectic differences of accent and inflection. His companions understood him as he understood his companions.[7] For this reason the syllables naturally change with great rapidity.

It is easy to conceive the gradual growth of languages, when once the great leap was accomplished, by which the communication of an idea, or even of a want, was expressed by the

---

[5] Pallas (Voyage dans l'Empire de Russie) expressly says that the Samoyeds at first most scrupulously avoid the name of a deceased person, but afterwards give it to a grandson or great grandson, to recall the memory of the departed.

[6] Dobrizhoffer, Geschichte der Abiponer, vol. ii. pp. 235, 361.

[7] Ausland, p. 891. 1869. Verbally communicated by the traveller.
6

speaker by any particular sound and understood by a fellow-creature. This first step, however, is still enveloped in profound obscurity, for the connection of a particular idea with a sound of the human voice depends on a compact between the speaker and the hearer;[8] but it is hard to see how this compact or agreement as to the first word could be concluded when there were as yet no means of communication. According to the oldest conjecture, the process was one of phonetic representation, for by the selection of imitative sounds the attention of the listener was directed to some object of sensory perception. As all languages are rich in sonorous forms which, as it were, give a musical representation of that which they are intended to express, the first commencement was supposed to have been onomatopœic experiment. In consequence of the rapidity of phonetic changes, it was very easy for the opponents of this opinion to refute the hypothesis by observing that the older forms of the present imitative words bear no traces of phonetic representations.

We may easily be deceived by the German word *rollen* (roll), particularly if we think of rolling thunder, into a belief that it is an attempt to represent the noise. Nevertheless L. Geiger easily traced this verb, through the French *rouler*, the Latin *rotulari*, to *rota* (wheel), in which the sonorous imitation is totally absent. Yet this ingenious analyzer of languages overlooked the important circumstance that, in its transfer to the German language, a word must have arisen out of *rouler* sounding something like *ruhlen*. The fact that *rollen* (roll) was formed out of *ruhlen*, betrays an endeavour to give the word onomatopœic force, and at the same time to make it more intelligible by an alteration of sound. But as geologists infer that the changes of form such as are now taking place on and in our planet, took place from the first in like manner, we may presume, from the still undiminished love of phonetic representation, that the same propensity must have operated also in the first beginnings of linguistic evolution. Max Müller has tried to discredit this explanation with the contemptuous epithet of "bow-wow theory," because at the first creation of language the cow would be called moo and the dog bow-wow, in imitation of their

---

[8] Ursprung der Sprache, p. 27.

lowing and barking. But he himself endeavours to explain the
process by the aid of mysticism. Each material body, such as
glass or a bell, he says, has its own peculiar resonance, and thus
thought has, as it were, constrained the vocal apparatus to produce
appropriate vibrations. In allusion to the sound of the bell,
Max Müller's explanation has therefore been ridiculed by others
as the " ding-dong theory."

In recent times the tendency has been in favour of the older
view. A. Pott, the philologist, collected the various local expressions for thunder from every part of the world, and found that
the majority of nations endeavour to render the sensation of this
noisy phenomenon by an echo in the expression.[9] Tylor has
shown that families of mankind in distant regions of the world
employ the same syllables for noisy movements in other instances.
The explosion of gases under high pressure, everything that is
violently blown, is designated by Malays, Australians, Africans,
Asiatics, and Europeans with sounds very nearly approaching *poo*
or *puff*. Again, the name for ox, βοῦς, *bos, bou, bo*, recurs among
Hottentots and Chinese.[10] Neither must it be overlooked that
our children in their first attempts to speak are apt to imitate
with their vocal organs any sound they hear, and designate animals
almost exclusively by the sounds which they emit. The circle of
perceptions that may be expressed by the phonetic representation
is however limited to events connected with the production of
sounds, for no such representation is possible of that which is
perceived by sight or the sense of touch.

The first beginnings of speech were supposed to be enriched by
the spontaneous action of our vocal organs on occasions of strong
internal excitement. The cry of joy and of horror still exists
even in civilized nations. At birth we bring a cry with us into
the world, for the infant's first sign of life consists in an exercise
of its vocal organs. The cry is intelligible to us all without either
instruction or practice ; nay, during the first months of life, crying
fully suffices for the announcement of the various requirements.

---

[9] Zeitschrift fur Völkerpsychologie und Sprachwissenschaft, vol. ii. p. 359.
Berlin, 1865.
[10] Primitive Culture, vol. i. p. 209.

Without the existence of any intention to speak, crying is understood, and for a time, even for a long time, children employ
crying as a means of making themselves intelligible, and very
soon learn to do so consciously and intentionally.   At the time of
the origin of language, the screams of adults may for a long time
have represented speech in like manner, especially as shrill sounds
are still preserved as exclamations.   Only it must be remembered
that our *ah* and *oh* cannot be referred to the age of the first
origin of language, for exclamations such as these, in all appearance
spontaneously wrung from the agonized feelings, have frequently
been unmasked and shown to be abbreviated words or even
idioms.   The English *zounds* originated from *by God's wounds*,
and *alas* from *oh me lasso*.[11]   The negro of Western Africa exclaims in terror or surprise, *Mâmâ, mâmâ*, and the Indian of New
California, *Anâ*.   Both signify mother, so that, like children, they
call the guardian of their youth to their assistance.[12]   The only
important fact is that these phonetic outbursts cannot even yet
be dispensed with in any civilized language.   The language of
animals is entirely composed of similar explosive sounds emitted
by the vocal organs, and to suppose that man in every age expressed his inward emotions—pain, joy, fear, surprise, aversion—
by signals such as these, needs reflection only and not proof.[13]

Accentuation is as an important auxiliary.   Our *yes* and our *no*
admit of a series of pronunciation by which the inquirer or petitioner
may plainly hear whether the acquiescence or assent be willing or
reluctant, the denial vacillating or decided, and generally in what
frame of mind the utterances are made.   The meaning of the
German word *pfui*, when quietly pronounced, might remain completely unknown to any one not acquainted with German, but if
uttered with the full emphasis of abhorrence, even a Fuegian
would be able to guess that this syllable expressed the reverse of
assent.   Accentuation, which is intuitive and not acquired, and on
the other hand not intentional but spontaneous, might materially assist mutual comprehension in the earliest stage of the con-

---

[11] Whitney, Language and the Study of Language, p. 277.

[12] Tylor, Primitive Culture, vol. i. p. 202.

[13] Steinthal (Pyschologie und Sprachwissenschaft, p. 376.   Berlin, 1871),
regards interjections as reflex sounds.

struction of language. It is assuredly not accidental that it is precisely the formless monosyllabic languages which still employ accentuation as an important auxiliary in the discrimination of like-sounding roots.

Pantomimic action and gesticulation did for the eye what accentuation did for the ear. So-called savages, without instruction, unconsciously, or at least only half consciously, exercise the art which, by laborious practice before the looking-glass, our actors are obliged to acquire afresh. The Bushmen, observes Lichtenstein, communicate with each other more by gesticulation than by speech.[14] There are, however, a number of bodily movements of this description of which the sense is by no means identically interpreted by all families of mankind. It is even questioned whether, in every part of the world, clenching the fist is to be recognized as a threat, or stamping the foot as an explosion of anger. Among the Bantu negroes a popular public orator is rewarded with hisses.

Many gestures have acquired their meaning only by mutual agreement. The Turks and others assent by a shake of the head, and reply in the negative with a nod. In ancient Greece a petitioner was repelled by throwing back the head (ἀνανεύειν) ; in Southern Italy the back of the hand is laid upon the chest and the fingers are waved at the person addressed, as a summons to approach.[15] And yet in every human being there is a latent power of making himself intelligible by signs. All navigators who have set foot upon a strange shore have communicated with the inhabitants by this means, and have succeeded in obtaining water or food. All over the world mankind has adopted the same pantomimic representation for the expression of their thoughts. The deaf and dumb were the inventors of their own language, which leads us to the beautiful thesis that even without vocal organs mankind would have attained the means of rendering themselves intelligible. The greater number of their signs, especially such as consist in drawing outlines in the air, are intelligible

---

[14] Reisen im südlichen Afrika, vol. ii. p. 82. Berlin, 1811.

[15] Kleinpaul, Zur Theorie der Gebärdensprache. Zeitschrift für Völker-psychologie, vol. ii. p. 362. Berlin, 1869.

without further explanation, so that we may say that the deaf and dumb make use of the very same gesticulations which were customary in the pantomimic intercourse of the Indians from Hudson's Bay to the Gulf of Mexico. Thus by means of his usual signs a deaf and dumb Englishman was able to make himself understood by some Laplanders at a show. Finally, it is said (though the statement is subject to grave doubts) that the unfortunate Laura Bridgeman, a blind deaf-mute, cut off from all external instruction, used the ordinary pantomimic movements.[16]

Thus at the period of the first development of speech, there were a number of expedients for the communication of thought, while at the same time, as man is of all creatures the most sociably disposed, necessity urged him in some way or other to make himself intelligible to his neighbour. Yet it is still difficult to explain the first attempt at speech. A purpose of communicating an idea to another person by means of the vocal organs must not be assumed, for that would imply a consciousness on the part of the speaker that a sound would serve to communicate an idea. Even if the first speaker had connected a particular sound with a particular idea, yet as any sound may be connected with any idea, he had no prospect of being understood.[17] Any elucidation of this obscure process would be inconceivable, had not each of us been at one time obliged to work himself up from a speechless condition. In speech, each child is obliged to repeat the experiments of mankind, only that in his course of development a great number of intermediate stages are passed over by the aid of instructors. The awakening of the power to comprehend speech, and the creation of speech, may therefore be observed anew in every child. L. Geiger rashly asserts that no new words can be invented. Young America ought to have taught him the contrary. The party name Locofoco, the name of a secret society Kluklux, the sectarian name Mormon, are arbitrary inventions. Schurlemurle, as a beverage of mixed wines is named in Würzburg, and picnic, can scarcely be derived from older expressions. Any one who has watched children must be astonished

[16] Tylor, Early History of Mankind, pp. 21, 44, 69, 86.

[17] Steinthal, Psychologie und Sprachwissenschaft, pp. 84, 370. Berlin, 1871.

at the doubt whether articulate sounds can be combined into new groups.[18] In South Africa the inhabitants of barren districts quit their settlements for a time, leaving the children under the care of a few aged people. The young ones forthwith begin to make a language of their own; the more lively are followed by the less developed, so that in the course of a single generation the nature of a language may be altered in this manner. Two words which are echoed in every language were created by children, and are created anew by every child, namely, the sounds papa and mamma. The elementary sound *ma* or *pa* is by no means an attempt to speak, but merely an exercise of the vocal organs proceeding from an inward physical impulse without purpose or consciousness, in no way better or higher than the twit-twit of our chaffinches. But as long as man has wandered on this earth, parental love in blissful delusion has misunderstood the child as if a call had been intended, as if the child were yearning for its father or its mother. That these first exercises of the vocal organs determined the sound of the future word, whereas the interpretation of the parents determined the meaning, is shown by the fact that, in a certain number of languages, the sound *ba* stands for father, and *ma* for mother, while in an equal number the converse is the case.[19] Other childish words for mother are *aithei* (Gothic) and *atta* (Sanscrit), the latter applying also to the elder sister. *Atta* exists also in Latin and in Greek, and also in Gothic, as an endearment for father, whence comes also the term *atte* for grandfather in German dialects. The lisping child has to pass[20] through various stages in the comprehension of language; for it must first learn by experience that when it cries *ba* or *ma* the parents approach or that pleasure is given to those present; the sound is then for the first time purposely uttered by the child, and it is not till much later, and not without the aid of the parents, that one sound is used as a call for the father and the other for the mother. Months and even years pass by before it dawns upon the perception that *mama* and *papa* are not proper names, but

---

[18] Max Müller, Science of Language, vol. ii. p. 54.

[19] A list of names for father and mother in every part of the world is to be found in d'Orbigny, l'Homme américain, p. 79.

[20] Bacmeister in the Allgem. Zeitung. 1871.

that with all children they are the designations of their nurses and guardians. Only at a later age does the child further discover that these names are given to its progenitors, and their full and true purport is understood even by adults only when they have experienced the joys and anxieties of parenthood. The course of development in tender years is thus approximately, if not completely, similar to the first attempts to speak made by our race.

The richness of a language is always determined by the need for communication; and we must suppose this to have been very small in the earliest evolutionary stages of our race. The English boast of a vocabulary of 100,000 words, but their field-labourers are said to be satisfied with 400. A clergyman in a Friesland island states that he could reckon no more in the case of a workman of his parish. As Kleinpaul[21] informs us, a man of average education has from 3000 to 4000 different words at his disposal, a great orator 10,000, while in the institutions of the deaf and dumb, at Berlin, no less than 5000 signs are employed. That the number of expressions increases with the need for expression is shown by the numerical terms, which among barbarous nations seldom extend beyond 20. Alexander von Humboldt was the first to trace the origin of numerical groups of 5, 10, and 20 units to the number of the parts on the hands and feet, so that with six-fingered hands we should have arrived at the duodecimal system.[22] Exceptions exist, however, especially in the Australian family, which make use of only two numerical terms; thus for 1 is said netat; for 2 naes; for 3 naes-netat; for 4 naes-naes; for 5 naes-naes-netat; for 6 naes-naes-naes.[23] Other Australian dialects have an independent expression for three, and in one linguistic region of those parts, the numerical terms reach as far as 15 or 20.[24] Orton maintains that the Zaparos on the Napo river in Ecuador can count only up to three, but express higher numbers by raising the fingers;[25] and the Prince of Wied[26]

---

[21] Zeitschrift für Völkerspsychologie und Sprachwissenschaft, vol. vi. p. 354. Berlin, 1869.

[22] Life of A. von Humboldt, edited by Carl Bruhns, vol. iii. p. 9.

[23] Latham, Opuscula, p. 228.   [24] Tylor, Primitive Culture, vol. i. p. 220.

[25] James Orton, The Andes and the Amazon, p. 170. 1870.

[26] Reise nach Brasilien, vol. ii. p. 41. Frankfort, 1825.

declares the same of the Botocudos. Closer research might, however, reveal more favourable facts respecting most of the nations mentioned, for it also has been disputed that numerical terms above three exist among the Abipones. In reality, however, they say, instead of four, "ostriches' toes;" for five they use two expressions, for ten they say "fingers of two hands," for twenty, "fingers and toes on hands and feet." [27] We ourselves have no expression for ten thousand such as exists in Greek, nor for a hundred thousand (lak), or for ten millions (kror), such as exist in Hindostanee, the richest language of the world in expressions for high numbers, reaching as far as 51 figures, owing to the fact that these terms were employed in many ways by the Sankhjâ philosophers and the Buddhists in their numerical juggleries. The word million was unknown to the nations of the classical age, while the term milliard has come into circulation only in this century.

A comparison of languages of scantily developed races shows that the perception of specific differences arose much earlier than the recognition of generic characters. Savage hunting tribes have names for the beaver, wolf, and bear, but none for animal. [28] The Tasmanian languages are wanting in expressions for tree, fish, and bird; but there is no lack of appellations for the individual species. [29] The same may be said of the North American Indians, for in the Chocta language, while there are names for the white, red, and black oak, there is none for the genus oak. When we take nourishment, whether it be soup, bread, meat, vegetables, or porridge, we always use the word eat, but the Hurons vary the expression according to the nature of the food. [30] The Eskimo again, have particular expressions for fishing, depending on the implements employed. [31] The

---

[27] Dobrizhoffer, Geschichte der Abiponer, vol. ii. p. 202.

[28] Greek has also no word for animal in so far as ζῶον includes man, for which reason the song, "Mensch und Thiere schliefen feste" (men and animals were sleeping fast), cannot be translated into Greek. Steinthal, Zeitschrift für Völkerpsychologie, vol. vi. p. 480. 1869.

[29] Lubbock, Prehistoric Times, p. 466.

[30] Charlevoix, Nouvelle France, vol. iii. p. 197. Paris, 1744.

[31] Latham, Varieties of Man, p. 376.

Malays distinguish between red, blue, green, and white, but they have no word for colour. The Tasmanians have no adjectives, so that they say "stone-like" instead of hard; "moon-like" instead of round; "long-legged" instead of high.

Languages are variously provided with sounds. The Arabs are destitute of the clicking sounds of the Hottentots, and we are deficient in many Arabic consonants, but the greatest paucity is found in the South Seas. The Polynesians have only ten consonants at their disposal, f, k, l, m, n, ng, p, s, t, v, and even these exist in full purity and completeness only at Fakaafo and Vaitupu,[32] while the inhabitants of the Tupuai group to the south of Tahiti have preserved only eight, m, n, ng, p, r, t, v, and one with a marked guttural sound.[33] A like paucity of sounds has arisen in the Sandwich Islands by deterioration, and is not primitive and simple, for other Polynesian languages, which have remained richer in consonants, have preserved the more archaic forms. If with this be connected the fact, that the enunciation of the Bushman language, especially owing to its clicking sounds, imposes the greatest exertions on the vocal organs, we might be induced to conclude that in the primordial attempts at speech a greater stock of sounds was brought into use.[34] Still there are scholars who maintain the opposite,[35] so that a universally valid rule must not as yet be laid down.

II.—THE STRUCTURE OF HUMAN LANGUAGE.

THE foreign languages, whether ancient or modern, which we Europeans study during our school years, all possess a greater or less number of grammatical forms, by the help of which a definite function in the sentence is allotted to the radical sounds. This

---

[32] See Gabelentz, Die melanesischen Sprachen in the transactions of the phil. Gesellschaft der Wissenschaft, p. 253. Leipzic, 1861.

[33] Hale, Ethnography, p. 142.

[34] W. H. J. Bleek, Ueber den Ursprung der Sprache, p. 53. Weimar, 1868.

[35] Whitney, Language and the Study of Language, p. 467 : "The tendency of phonetic change is always towards the increase of the alphabet."

gives rise to the delusion that every language must admit of the formation of substantive, pronoun, verb, preposition, and conjunction by means of appended syllables or sounds. The novice meets with his first surprise in the Semitic languages which, although not deficient in forms, employ unwonted means of effecting their definitions of meaning. An examination of the African and Northern Asiatic languages discloses the yet more surprising fact, that in these not only the gender but the verb disappears. But we fall into incredulous perplexity on learning that languages exist which have not risen even to the formation of words, especially when it is added, that a highly civilized people with a language of this description have composed works exhibiting profound knowledge of the world, and stories of artistic polish and great subtlety. Yet there is the best evidence to show that all languages have proceeded from such rude beginnings.

All monosyllabic languages are destitute of those phonetic or syllabic suffixes which elsewhere mark noun, adjective, or verb, and still more of those which distinguish the subject of a transaction from its object; for as yet there are no words at all, but only roots. We would however at once warn the uninitiated not to mistake the monosyllabic sounds of German and English with the radicals of true monosyllabic languages. We can certainly construct long sentences with monosyllabic words, as for instance, Der Mann ging auf die Jagd, und schoss ein Reh, etc. (The man went out to hunt and shot a deer), but in this example *gin-g* and *Jag-d* are only apparently monosyllables, and *schoss* accidentally so. English, to a far greater extent than German, has declined towards a rigidly monosyllabic condition by dint of phonetic decay and abrasion, though it has preserved the clear distinction of the grammatical categories [1] and only in a few cases, such as *butter, oil, pepper. cudgel,* the hearer or reader has to guess from the context whether the substantive or the verb is intended.[2]

The Chinese language dispenses with all grammatical distinctions of meaning. It is destitute of all inflections, of all distinctions between substantive and verb, and of verbal structure

---

[1] Whitney, Language and the Study of Language, p. 264
[2] Tylor, Early History of Mankind, p. 80.

of any description. The syllable *sin* may signify honour, honourable, to be honourable, to act honourably, and even to trust. What it means in any given case is decided by its position in the sentence and the context.[3] By the contact of root with root the meaning is defined, and thus the sense is conveyed to the hearer as by verbal structure. In English also synonyms are sometimes multiplied for the sake of clearness, as in *pathway*, or classificatory suffixes are appended as in *maple-tree.*[4] In German, too, we say Hai-fish, Tannenbaum, Elenthier, (dog-fish, fir-tree, moose-deer). These examples are, however, only remotely analogous, for, strictly speaking, combinations of words ought not to be compared with the grouping of roots. In Latin no special arrangement of words is prescribed in the structure of a sentence, and the position of the parts of speech is left to the artistic feeling of the speaker; Chinese, on the contrary, follows the strictest precepts in regard to syntax. Roots which are to serve for a closer definition (attributes), whether as adjective or genitives, must precede the subject or verb which they are to define. Supplements (objects) must follow that which is to be supplemented (the verb.) The grouping of two roots is naturally, in countless cases, liable to ambiguity. If *tschung* (faith) and *kyün* (prince) are combined, a European might be in doubt whether the good faith of the prince or the loyalty of the subject be intended. But in all such cases custom has long ago firmly fixed the sense in which alone such a group is valid; as the Chinese recognizes only the duty of subjects, this group signifies loyalty. The Chinese groups of roots often consist of several parts. For difference of opinion the Chinese say, I east, thou west, *ni tung, wo si*; and for conversing, thou asking, I answering, *ni wen, wo ta.* Weight is called light-heavy, *khing tschung*, and distance far-near, *ywan kin.* In German we have a similar form of word in hell-dunkel (light-dark, *i.e.*, twilight); pianoforte; in Spanish, we find calofrio (warm-cold) for fever, and

---

[3] Steinthal, Characteristik der hauptsächlichste Typen des Sprachbaues, p. 117. Berlin, 1860. Where other authorities are not cited, the present chapter has been borrowed from this invaluable book.

[4] Whitney, Study of Language, p. 335.

altibajo (high-low) for depression.[5] As they have no word for
virtue, the Chinese say loyalty, respect for parents, temperance,
justice, *tschun, hyau, tsye, i,* thus enumerating what they regard as
the highest duties of a Chinaman. In all such combinations of
roots the sequence is invariably prescribed. Neither can any one
speaking by means of roots, as do the Chinese, say simply read or
eat, but he must say read book, or eat rice.

Even in Chinese there are feeble beginnings of a formation of
words. All roots indeed preserve their independence, yet there
are some by the addition of which other roots are raised to the
value of substantives. Of this sort is *thau,* head, so that according
to its position *tschi* may signify show or finger, but *tschi-thau*
always means finger. Again, the root *tsz,* signifying son, is
applied as a diminutive, so that from *tau,* sword, *tau-tsz,* sword-
son, is formed, signifying knife. In the enumeration of objects a
descriptive designation is always added, much as we say in
German, ein Laib Brot (a loaf of bread), ein Blatt Papier (a sheet
of paper), ein Bund Heu (a truss of hay), eine Elle Leinwand
(a yard of linen). A Chinaman, enumerating idols, learned men,
or officials, affixes the predicates, honours, dignities, jewels, to the
number mentioned.[6] The sex of animals is indicated by the
addition of two roots, which in this connection confer the sense
of man or of mother. The plural is formed in Chinese by the
addition of roots signifying many or all.

The rules of syntax are thus sufficient to give perfect clearness
to a language consisting entirely of monosyllabic roots. The
Chinese may therefore claim to have supplied every requisite for
the interchange of thought by these simple means. Nevertheless,
of all languages of the world, Chinese is in the lowest stage of
development. It burdens the memory with the recollection of an
immense number of combinations of radicals on which custom

[5] Tober, Psych. Bedeutung der Wortzusammensetzungen, in Zeitschrift für
Völkerpsychologie, vol. v. p. 209. 1868.

[6] The Mexicans and Malays always append to the number the word *stone,*
the Javans *grain,* the Niasmalays *fruit.* In these languages therefore it is not
customary to say three chickens, four children, five swords, but three stones
chickens, four grains children, five fruits swords. Tylor, Early History of
Mankind, p. 208.

alone has bestowed an unalterable signification, and thereby need-
lessly enhances the difficulty of acquiring the language.   We are
therefore at a loss to comprehend how a man of such sagacity
as Steinthal could reckon it among his inflected languages, for
he himself admits that, "If morphological structure be alone considered, the order would necessarily be different.   Chinese in
particular, which now occupies such a high position, would then
be transferred to the lowest." [7]   Steinthal would think little of a
zoologist if he were to rank the highly endowed ant among the
vertebrata because it is psychologically superior to the lancelet.
Yet his classification is of this sort.   Among the Siamese and
Burmese, the southern neighbours of the Chinese, we also find
purely monosyllabic languages.   Yet they already surpass the
Chinese in the number of roots which are applied to the definition of meaning.   Their rules of syntax prescribe that in Siamese
the auxiliary root precedes, while in Burmese it follows the principal root.[8]   By the addition of these roots, substantives and verbs,
active as well as passive, are differentiated.   We may presume
that if these two languages are left to develop undisturbed, the
formation of words will be effected in one preëminently by means
of prefixes, in the other by means of suffixes.

In the Malay languages, geographically connected with the
Burmese and Siamese, the syllables which define the sense are
sometimes placed before, and sometimes, though less frequently,
after the principal root.   A great chasm separates them from the
types hitherto described, for they contain polysyllabic roots.   But
no part of speech is as yet strictly differentiated, so that the same
root or group of roots is capable of executing the functions of
a substantive, an adjective, a word expressive of action, or even of
a preposition.   There are no syllables by the addition of which
gender, case, number, tense, mood, and person can be expressed.
Pronouns only, demonstrative particles, and a few prepositions,
already perform their special grammatical duties.   Personal pronouns alone are susceptible of a sort of plural definition by combination with numerical expressions ; this gives rise to a dual and
a plural, both of which forms may also be used either inclusively

---

[7] Typen des Sprachbaues, p. 328.   [8] Steinthal, p. 145.

or exclusively, as the person or persons addressed are or are not to be involved. Genuine verbs are totally wanting; they are replaced by substantives expressing an action, much as if we were to render the idea, " I walk to the east," by the words, " my walk to the east." Thus in the Dyak language the prefix *ba* means, to be affected by something. From *tiroh*, sleep, arises *batiroh*, to sleep; from *kahovut*, cover, *bakahovut*, covered; hence *iä batiroh bakahavut*, literally, he with sleep with cover, represents the idea, he sleeps covered.

A characteristic of these languages is the frequent use of such repetitions and reduplication as, in older stages of development, occurred also in highly advanced languages. In Latin a vestige of such word formations has been preserved in *quisquis*, and similar traces of past ages in *dedit* and *peperit*. The Malay languages moreover distinguish simple repetitions, in which the accent remains unaltered, from reduplication, in which the anterior word loses the accent. By repetition they express multiplication, augmentation, or duration; by reduplication enfeeblement or instability is implied, so that *téndäténdä* signifies often, *téndä téndä*, on the contrary, to stop from time to time.[9] This poverty in expedients for the definition of meaning does not, however, exclude a wealth of expressions. In Malay there are no less than twenty sounds expressive of the idea of striking, according to whether it be with thin or thick wood, gently, downwards, upwards, horizontally, with the hand, the palm, the fist, a club, a sharp edge, a flat surface, with one thing against another, with a hammer, or driven in like a nail.

Scattered over the north of Asia and Europe in five large groups, the Tungús, Mongolian, Turkish, Samoyed, and Finnish, we find a linguistic structure strictly limited to the addition of suffixes. The grammatical functions of each word in the sentence are pretty sharply defined by means of these appendages. The suffix *sit* signifies a person occupied with the subject of the preceding root. From *ati*, wares, the Yakut constructs *ati-sit*, merchant; from *ayi*, creation, *ayi-sit*, creator. An action is signified by the addition of *ir*, and therefore, from *tial*, wind,

---

[9] Steinthal, Sprachtypen. Whitney, Study of Language, p. 319.

arises *tialir*, to blow. This grouping of roots is unlimited, and, to recall an example often employed, the Osmanli is able to express in a single word the idea of *incapable of being induced to love one another*, by the group *sev-isch-dir-il-eme*. Inflected languages also admit, however, of an extraordinary accumulation of defining particles; for instance, the following series occurs in English, true, tru-th, truth-ful, truthful-ness, un-truthfulness. The simplicity of the system of adding suffixes, the prospect of expressing a complex idea in a single group of syllables, may at first appear seductive, yet such languages have never succeeded in forming a verb, but rest contented with naming the subject of the action (nomina verbi), which almost answers to such expressions of ours as the living (nomen presentis), the deceased (nomen perfecti), the imprisoned, the sender.[10] In Turkish the construction is—

> *dog-mak*, to beat
> *dog-ur*, a beater
> *dog-ur-um*, a beating $I = I$ beat
> *dog-ur-lar*, beating they $=$ they beat.[11]

The languages spoken by the Ural-Altaic nations illustrate the process of verbal construction. The structure of their language is confined to the agglutination of syllables. Something similar still occurs even in languages in which fusions are otherwise habitual. If two syllables are joined without alteration, and without losing their independent meaning, they are but loosely agglutinated. If we divide such words as note-worthy, care-less, trace-able, into their two halves, the substantive and the defining suffix can each exist alone. The Ural-Altaic languages, in common with all merely agglutinative languages, are confined to constructions such as these. But where these roots were long employed chiefly as definitions of meaning, and were no longer used independently, but solely as auxiliaries, their original and independent signification was presently forgotten and a higher degree of integration of linguistic structure was already attained. This case is represented in English by formations such as *virtu-*

---

[10] Steinthal, Sprachtypen, p. 193.
[11] Whitney, Study of Language, p. 319.

ous, bare ly, in-distinct. The suffixes *ous* and *ly*, and the affix *in*, can no longer stand independently in our language, but have forfeited their liberty, since their original form and their old signification have been removed beyond ken. A third case is conceivable; namely, that, in consequence of agglutination, the defining root has effected a phonetic modification in the principal root, and both combinations are fused in such a manner that neither can any longer exist independently, as in such formations as *scholar.*

A germ of phonetic modification is already latent in the Ural-Altaic languages, though it is only due to a desire for euphony (Vocalharmonie). The eight vowels of these languages are divided into heavy and light, hard and soft, and by the custom of the language the same or some other particular vowel must be contained in the succeeding suffix-root. Thus in the Yakut language, the plural suffix-root consists of the syllable *l—r*, but which vowel is to be inserted between *l* and *r* is determined by the vowel of the principal root, so that the formula is *aχa-lar*, the fathers, *oχo-lor*, the children, *äsä-lär*, the bears. This musical attempt may in the course of time effect the complete fusion of the suffix with the principal root. The fact is significant that in another linguistic province, namely, among the Dravida group or non-Aryan inhabitants of Southern India, we likewise find laws of euphony, but acting in the reverse direction. There the vowel of the defining syllable is dominant, and compels the vowel of the principal root into harmony with itself. The words *katti*, knife, and *puli*, tiger, are transformed by the suffix *lu*, indicating the plural, not into *katti-lu* and *puli-lu*, but into *kattulu*, the knives, and *pululu*, the tigers.[12] Whereas the Ural-Altaic languages always place the defining roots after the principal root, and are, therefore, reckoned as suffixing languages, we find in the whole of South Africa, as far as the equator, with the sole exception of the languages of the Hottentots and Bushmen, closely allied languages, which all place the defining syllable before the principal root, but yet do not exclude the use of suffixes. Southwards from Delagoa Bay, on the east coast, we find rivers bearing the names of Um-komanzi,

---

[12] F. Müller, Reise der Fregatte Novara. Language, p. 81.

Um-zuti, Um-kusi, Um-volosi, Um-hlutane, Um-lazi, Um-gababa, Um-kamazi, Um-tenta, and so on.[13]   It might, therefore, be inferred that the prefix *um* signifies water, as does the suffix *ach* in German names, such as Bacharach, Aichach, Stockach, Lörrach, Elzach.   Yet there are South African names for mountains and places, which are preceded by the syllable *um*.   Names of tribes are formed by the prefix *ma*, Ma-tabele, Ma-sai, Ma-kua, Ma-ravi, Ma-kololo, or by the double prefix a-ma, as Ama-χosa, Ama-pondo, Ama-tonga, Ama-zulu, for which we might substitute the people of the chief Xosa, Pondo, Tonga, Zulu.   Perhaps, at a period not very remote, there was a chief of the name of Suto, the eponym of the Ba-suto ; each individual was called a Ma-suto, their territory Le-suto, and their language Se-suto.   This example indicates the definitions implied by the prefixes *Ba*, *Ma*, *Le*, and *Se*.   Where these series of prefixes have been maintained in their full integrity we find sixteen, or perhaps eighteen, of which the greater number indicate either the plural or the singular exclusively.   Only two of these syllables unequivocally distinguish natural differences, namely, *Mu* and *Ba*, of which both represent persons, one in the singular, the other in the plural ; possibly *Mu* formerly signified person, *Ba* people.[14]   Each substantive and each expression of activity (we can hardly say verb), is provided with an antecedent syllable, so that a prefix thus becomes an ingredient of the word, as inseparable as is the suffix in the older branches of the Aryan family of languages.[15]   We may confidently assert that the prefixes were once independent words, but their significations are now unknown to the existing generation, and in this case the linguistic integration has advanced so far that certain phonetic combinations are applied exclusively to grammatical purposes.   The employment of prefixes requires, among other things, that the same syllable should be affixed to the adjective as to the substantive.   Were Latin a

---

[13] Bacmeister in the Ausland, p. 577.   1871.

[14] W. H. Bleek, Comparative Grammar of South African Languages, p. 95. 1869.

[15] Whitney, Study of Language, p. 345.   1867.   In the Suto languages they say *ba-ntu* (men), *ba-otle* (all), *ba-molemo* (good), *ba-lefatse* (the world), *ba-ratoa* (the beloved), which means, in the world, all good men are beloved (Casalis, Les Basoutos, p. 339.   Paris, 1859).

prefixing language, instead of vin-um bon-um, it would run um-vin um-bon. In Zulu *tyi* signifies stone, and *bi* ugly, *i* is the indefinite article, and *li* the indispensable representative prefix. Thus arises *i-li-tyii-li-bi*, an ugly stone. Even the genitive is expressed by the prefix of the nominative, and in Zulu the woman's dish is called *i-si-tya s-o-m-fazi*, and the food of the woman *u-ku-dhla kw-o-m-fazi*. *S-o-m-fazi* and *kw-o-m-fazi* are the genitives of *u-m-fazi*, woman, and harmonize with the prefix of the substantive.[16] South African languages, however, employ suffixes also in the construction of highly compound words.[17]

We find a different linguistic structure among the American nations, with the exception of the Eskimo. Wilhelm von Humboldt has termed their system "incorporative," because the structure of the sentence may be entirely supplanted by the structure of the word. The aborigines of America are able to build up a complex idea into a single word. In the Cherokee language *wi-ni-taw-ti-ge-gi-na-li-skaw-lung-ta-naw-ne-le-ti-se-sti* is equivalent to "they will by this time have come to an end of their declarations (of favour) to you and me."[18] Even in those American languages which allow only a moderate use of "incorporation," the object is always placed between the subject and the verb. Moreover, some syllables of the inserted words are suppressed, and the phonetic combination, thus mutilated, remains intelligible only in its context. In the Delaware language, from *opik*, white, and *assuun*, stone, is formed *opposuun*, or white stone, by which silver is meant.[19] Although it is not an invariable law that among highly civilized nations we find also highly developed languages, for we have just observed the contrary among the Chinese, while conversely from the Hottentot language we shall presently learn that a highly developed language does not always imply a correspondingly high civilization, yet a highly developed

---

[16] Bleek in the Journal of the Anthrop. Institute, vol. i. p. 71. London, 1872.

[17] From *bona*, to see, arises *isi-bono*, the object seen, *isi-boniso*, vision, *bon-akala*, to appear, *isi-bonakala*, appearance, *isi-bonakaliso*, revelation. F. Müller, Reise der Fregatte Novara, vol. iii. p. 112.

[18] Whitney, Study of Language, p. 349.

[19] Schoolcraft, cited by Tylor, Early History of Mankind, p. 273.

language leads us to expect to find a more matured social constitution in its territory. In America, the most highly civilized
people, the ancient Mexicans, spoke the most developed language,
Nahuatl. The name alone, by its termination *tl*, indicates an
advance. The Ural-Altaic languages were still quite incapable
of any true word-construction when substantives were already
recognizable by the termination *tl* in ancient Mexican. In composition, the word *teo-tl*, God, loses the appended consonants,
as in *teo-calli*, God's house or temple, and in *teo-tlaltolli*, God's
word. These examples also show that not all Nahuatl substantives have the suffix *tl*. Ancient Mexican, in common with
all American languages, is incorporative, inserting the object
between the subject and the verb, so that from *schotschi-tl*, flower,
and *ni-temoa*, I seek, is formed *ni-schotschi-temoa*, I seek flowers;
but another arrangement of the sentence is also used, in which
only the pronoun it (*k*), or somebody (*te*), or something (*tla*), is
intercalated between subject and verb, while the object is placed
last. From *ni*, I, *k*, it, *miktia*, to kill, *se*, one, *totolin*, chicken, the
Nahuatl forms *ni-k-miktia se totolin*, I it kill a chicken. The excessive tendency to incorporation is thus again checked. Plurals
which occur only in the case of living things (in which category
the stars are included), are expressed by the addition of the
suffixes *mê* and *tin*, as *itschka-tl*, sheep, *itschka-mê*, sheep (in the
plural), or *ta-tli*, father, *ta-tin*, fathers. Nor is there any lack of
ingenuity in the formation of words; from *ome*, two, and *yolli*,
heart, arises *omeyolloa*, to doubt; from *nakastli*, ear, and *tsatsi*, to
scream, *nakatsatsa-tl*, in whose ear one must scream—a deaf
person.[20]

In the prefix languages of the South African negroes *um-tu*
signifies a man, *um-fazi*, a woman, *um-ti*, a tree. The same prefix,
therefore, serves for objects which ought to be viewed as masculine,
feminine, and neuter. When the substantive is once distinguished
from the verb by perceptible phonetic terminations, the gender
of the substantive can also be distinguished. We have hitherto
been dealing only with languages which do not distinguish grammatical genders, but we shall now turn to those which express

[20] Steinthal, Characteristik, p. 203.

differences of sex.[21]   The important influence which this improvement in language has had on the formation of myths can only be explained further on; at present we will merely remark that the requirements of a grammatical gender induced a keener observation of external objects.   Traces of a distinction of gender, at least in the pronoun for the third person, may be found in Tarawa,[22] the language spoken on the Gilbert or Kingsmill Islands ; others in South America among the Abipones,[23] the Arowaks, and the Maypures,[24] and in Khasi, the language of the Khasians of Assam.[25]   In Africa the languages of the Hottentots, the Hausa negroes, and the ancient Egyptians, are remarkable for their twofold grammatical gender.   The distinction of the sexes is the most important advance in the linguistic structure of the latter highly civilized people.   In other respects the roots in ancient Egyptian are mainly monosyllabic, and many of them may be used as substantive, verb, and adjective, as in Chinese. The same syllable denotes to write, a writing, and a writer, while another may mean to live, alive, or life.   Some roots, however, serve exclusively as substantive or verb.   A prefixed article, which is, however, only loosely attached, marks the substantive, but there is as yet no declension, prefixed prepositions acting as substitutes. In the formation of the verb, pronouns are loosely attached to the radical, but tense and mood are expressed by prefixing auxiliary words.   But as these pronominal suffixes may also be appended to substantives, and in that case indicate possession, the separation of the verb from the substantive is not yet fully effected.   *Ran-i* may be translated, I name, or my name ; while literally it signifies my naming.[26]   In many of its verbal constructions this language is as

---

[21] In the Algonkin language also a distinction is made between animate and inanimate objects, but among the former are reckoned the sun, the moon, the stars, thunder and lightning, sacrificial stones, eagles' feathers, tobacco, pipes, drums, and wampums.   Tylor, Primitive Culture, vol. i. p. 274.

[22] Horatio Hale, United States Exploration Expedition, Ethnography. Philadelphia, p. 441.   1846.

[23] Dobrizhoffer, Geschichte der Abiponer, vol. ii. p. 200–206.

[24] Bleek, Journal of the Anthropological Institute, vol. i. p. 93.

[25] Bleek, p. 67.

[26] Whitney, Study of Language, p. 342.

ill-developed as, and sometimes more ambiguous than Chinese, which ensures perspicuity by its strict rules of syntax. But it stands higher than Chinese, inasmuch as the defining suffixes have entirely lost their independence as well as their original form and import, having for the most part been reduced to a few consonants by dint of contraction and curtailment, so that they now serve only for grammatical purposes.[27]

There is a wide chasm between the best developed of the lower languages and those of the Semitic and Aryan families. In these the defining element is mostly firmly welded together with the principal root. The root is completely lost in the substantive and the verb, and a real inflection and a real transformation have arisen, though they are effected in totally different ways by Aryans and Semites. The Semitic languages of Western Asia are recognizable by the circumstance that their radicals always exhibit three consonants, although the third is often scantily or abortively represented. Vowels affecting the definition are interposed before, between, or after these consonants. As Steinthal happily expresses it, the consonant is the substance of the thought while the vowel invests it with its shape. The former might be compared to the block of marble, the latter to the sculptor. This may be illustrated by an example frequently employed. For everything that refers to the shedding of human blood Arabic applies the triple group of consonants, *q-t-l.* Thence are formed:—

qatala	...	•••	...	...	*he kills*
qutila		•••	...	...	*he was killed*
qutilu	...	...	...	...	*they were killed*
uqtul		...	•••	•••	*to kill*
qatil	...	...	•••	...	*killing*
iqtal		...	...	•••	*to cause killing*
quatl	...	•••	•••	•••	*murder*
qitl		•••	...	•••	*enemy*
qutl	...	...	...	...	*murderous*

In the verb the middle vowel bestows a transitive or intransitive signification; by the vowel of the first syllable of the radical the active (*a*) is distinguished from the passive (*u*), and the vowel of the last consonant denotes the mood, *u* expressing the

---

[27] Whitney, Study of Language, p. 342.

indicative, *a* the subjunctive, while in the imperative, which conveys a demand, the vowel totally disappears. The other transformations of the verb are effected by prefixes and suffixes, which also have a phonetic influence on the vowels of the syllables to which they are prefixed or appended. Terminal syllables distinguish singular and plural as well as the three cases, nominative, genitive, and accusative.

We may well wonder at the manner in which, in the construction of the Semitic languages, the human intellect has been able to bestow a symbolical meaning on the sounds produced by the organs of speech, and, as it were, inspire this apparatus for the interchange of ideas. The evolutionary history of this process is as yet entirely obscure, for there are not even any conjectures as to the earlier stages which have been surmounted in the formation of language.

An equal or, as many think, a higher rank is occupied by the Indo-Germanic or Aryan languages, akin to Sanscrit. Their superiority over the Semitic group may be primarily founded on their recognition of three instead of two genders, or rather of sexual and sexless objects. But this superiority has been again partially lost in the course of time. With few exceptions modern English still distinguishes gender only in men and animals. In the German language also, as Steinthal remarks, the good times are past in which *zweene* was still said for two men, *zwo* for two women, *zwei* for two children, or for a man and woman. Armenian ignores all distinction of gender.[28] It is more significant that Aryan languages alone possess a verb *to be*, which is wanting even in Semitic languages, so that the latter cannot express the idea of the graciousness of God by the words God is gracious, but are obliged to say, God the gracious, or God, he the gracious, so that in such languages it would be impossible to maintain "cogito, ergo sum."

The evolutionary history of this group of languages is much more easily seen than in those of the Semitic family. All inquiries tend to show that in the dark times of past ages our forefathers effected their interchange of ideas by means of a comparatively

---

[28] Mordtmann, Allgem. Zeitung, p. 6374. 1871.

small number of monosyllabic roots, and that their language was then in the same stage as is now Chinese. Yet the separation of the pronominal roots took place so early that many observers regard it as primordial.[29]   Jacob Grimm's idea, that the stock of the root *tu* is reducible to the conception of being great, of growing, so that *du* properly signifies magnitude, and in a manner represents the titles of modern days, such as your grace, is supported by Kleinpaul with the observation that from civility the Chinese abases himself and, instead of *I have*, uses the expressions *servant has, slave has, blockhead has.*[30]   The formation of words originally took place by the agglutination of the defining root at the end, while prefixes were only very sparingly employed, and this chiefly in negatives with *un*, as in *un*grateful, or *a* as in *a*theism ; also by antecedent prepositions, such as *fore*cast, *out*-spread, *over*throw,[31] finally, by the prefixed *a* or *ä* of the so-called augment in the primitive past tense.   German has many prefixes of which the original meaning has become unintelligible, such as *be*schreiben (to *de*scribe), *er*gründen (to fathom), *zer*fleischen (to lacerate), *ver*kaufen (to sell), etc.   The original meaning of these auxiliary words has long been forgotten, and they are therefore serviceable only as defining syllables, or before the principal root. But in modern times a deterioration of morphological structure has taken place, especially in Germanic languages.   When the inflectional terminations had been worn down beyond recognition, linguistic structure, as a compensation for significant affixes and reduplications, seized on a medium for the definition of meaning which had previously been only casual and incidental, namely, the metamorphosis of vowels.   The conversion of *a o u* into *ä ö ü* was employed in the formation of the plural and the subjunctive (vater, väter ; mutter, mütter ; konnte, könnte ; truge, trüge).   By modifications (as in English woman, women), various functions were fulfilled, especially in marking the time, in expressions referring to actions—hebe, hob, Abhub (lift, lifted, leavings) ; gebe, gab, gibst (give, gave, givest) ; graben, Grube (dig, ditch).   The

---

[29] Whitney, Study of Language, p. 261.

[30] Zeitschrift für Völkerpsychologie, p. 363.   1869.

[31] Whitney, Study of Language, pp. 256, 257.

German language thus acquired the use of a metamorphosis of vowels very like that in the Semitic; possibly the Semitic languages owe their symbolical use of vowels to the same cause.

III.—LANGUAGE AS A MEANS OF ETHNOLOGICAL CLASSIFICATION.

IN order to separate the manifold phenomena of the human race and to arrange them in groups, we require persistent and distinctive characters. Hence, if languages are constantly modified, so that not only the meaning of certain phonetic combinations is altered within a suspiciously short period, but even the structure of the languages may be changed, we can scarcely hope to employ language as a means of classification. We know that before the Roman dominion the inhabitants of France spoke a Celtic language, and exchanged it later for a new Latin tongue. The inhabitants of Germany eastwards of the Elbe belonged, some two thousand years ago, to the Sclavonian family. On the other hand, the inhabitants of Iceland and Norway spoke the same language eight hundred years ago. In Iceland it has been preserved almost without alteration, whereas in Norway it has been developed into Danish. Even if, in this case, we supposed that these metamorphoses took place within a group of languages which were primordially related, and that the transition was thus exceptionally easy, we must remember that English is spoken by the descendants of Africans, who were brought as slaves to the United States, and that Spanish is spoken by many of the aborigines of America. Were we therefore to classify nations according to language only, we should be obliged to place negroes in the same division with English, and pure-bred Indians with the descendants of Roumanian Europeans.

Hence, before we infer any sort of relationship from identity or similarity of language, we must ascertain as an historical fact that the identity of language has not been produced by the requirements of social intercourse. Even where we need not suspect this, language must be regarded as a distinctive mark only of the second order. Community of language in tribes and races

7

merely proves that, in some past age, the various members of the same linguistic group inhabited a common home, and maintained a close intercourse with one another. This, however, is all that we require; for as all races of mankind generate fertile hybrids with one another, residence in a common home is sufficient to produce a new mongrel race, even from stray portions of the human family physically unlike. But here again the consideration arises, that a common home may be inhabited by two physically distinct races united by a predominant language, and yet little or no admixture of blood may have taken place. We see these cases realized in the United States and in India, where admixture of blood only rarely occurs between white and coloured people, or between Aryans of high and natives of low caste. This consideration should be kept in view, though these instances are solitary. The aversion of the English and Germans to intermarriage with negroes is not shared to the same extent by Semites and Hamites, nor, among Europeans, by Spaniards, Portuguese, and French. This feeling of caste only restrains nations of very high culture from an admixture of blood with nations of a very low order. In the newer races of mankind nothing of the sort is to be apprehended. Moreover, as structure of language requires long periods for its development, during which the families with a common language maintain the closest intercourse of ideas, common descent or continued affinity may be inferred in the case of nations connected by a community of verbal structure and parts of speech. No one who has studied the subject any longer doubts that the so-called Indo-Europeans, the Semites, the Bantu nations of South Africa, all derive the rudiments of their languages from intercourse in a common home, where they used a common vocabulary. Yet no comparison of the bodily characters of Icelanders, of Hindoos of high caste, of the natives of Madagascar and Easter Island, would have suggested to us that they were all descendants of ancestors inhabiting a common home and intermarrying. But having observed every rule of critical caution, none but those who have formed exaggerated ideas of the persistency of physical characters will neglect language as a means of classification, or make light of the results of the philological researches of the present day. But where a comparison of languages gives results inconsistent with the racial characters, we necessarily suspect an admixture of blood. Hence, we have no hesitation in reckoning the inhabitants of Kashgar among the Turkish hybrid nations, for by their facial type they would otherwise be classed among the Indo-Germans. We must assume that the conquering Turkish-speaking race mingled to such a degree with the subjugated Tadshiks of Iranian stock, that their original bodily characters were entirely obliterated.

Linguistic relations, founded on a community of defining auxiliary syllables, are recognized without dispute by all philologists. Those cases in which the similarity depends only on conformity of structure, are more suspicious and more liable to objection. But even in these relationship is admitted, at least with regard to the aborigines of America. Their common use of the "incorporative" system has induced all philologists to regard them as members of a single family of mankind, and to separate them from the Eskimo, who form their words by means of suffixes, especially as there are no distinct bodily characteristics which would suggest a real separation in the former. The association of the Ural-Altaic nations, in which the community of the various groups depends only on the type of linguistic structure, and its restriction to the suffix as its morphological element, is far more doubtful. Yet even in this instance we may assume a derivation from a common home, because the special character of their rules of euphony at least is peculiar to them ; and we may conjecture that if the records of their language reached back some thousands instead of hundreds of years, as is the case, a closer kinship might probably be discovered, and, lastly, because their bodily structure favours this association. On the other hand, it seems inadmissible to elevate the Ural-Altaic groups into a Turanian family, and to assimilate with them the Dravida languages of the aboriginal Indians because they likewise observe laws of euphony in the formation of words. Since these laws differ from those of the Ural-Altaic languages, and also because their physical characters render it imperative, we shall treat these South Indian people as a separate branch of the human family.

THE INDUSTRIAL, SOCIAL, AND RELIGIOUS STAGES OF DEVELOPMENT.

THE INDUSTRIAL, SOCIAL, AND RELIGIOUS STAGES OF DEVELOPMENT.

———◦◦◦———

At the time when Europeans were astounded at the condition of the so-called savage nations, as shown by the trans-oceanic discoveries of ancient and modern times, many imaginative people supposed the human species, on its first appearance, to have been endowed with the highest perfections, bodily, intellectual, and moral, and ascribed the absence of these advantages in the coloured inhabitants of forests and islands to a culpable degradation from that golden condition. In refutation of these now harmless errors, it is sufficient to refer to the change of opinion undergone by such a student of the subject as Herr von Martius. At the meeting of German naturalists at Freiburg, in 1838, he still asserted that, " Every day that I spent among the Indians of Brazil increased my conviction that at one time they had been quite different, and that in the course of obscure centuries, manifold catastrophes had overtaken them and reduced them to the peculiarly deteriorated and stationary condition in which I found them." Before thirty years had elapsed, we hear from his lips the following words respecting the same people : " As yet no evidence is before us that the barbarous state of these regions at that period was secondary, that it was preceded by one of higher civilization, that this resort of ephemeral, unstable hordes was ever occupied by a civilized people." [1] Nor do those other views

---

[1] Ethnographie.

survive which, at the end of the last century, were entertained by travellers who, like George Forster, filled with dreams worthy of Rousseau, envied the people of the South Seas as a fortunate race in a state of nature, and not yet deprived of the ideal condition of man by the follies of civilized life.   Only the night before the savages killed him, Lamanon, the companion of La Pérouse, maintained, in conversation with his comrades, that savages were far better than civilized people.[2]   The physical beauty so frequently extolled in the unrestrained children of nature is generally wanting in the photographic portraits which now reach us in such abundance.   Even where it actually exists, unmarred by the disfigurements inflicted by misguided taste, cleanliness, the best attention to the human body, is often lacking.   The hair is in disorder and the teeth uncleaned.   We expect to find certain vices only in highly cultured but deteriorated nations, as among the Greeks and in imperial Rome, yet any one who is but slightly versed in the older Spanish records of American tribes, is well aware that the latter knew of refinements of vice which never occurred either to the Romans when Tiberius dwelt at Capri, or to the Byzantines when Theodora, afterwards the consort of the Emperor Justinian, roamed about with strolling players.[3]   We may add, that nearly all these people were acquainted with poisons which destroy the human embryo, and that they were used with wanton recklessness.[4]   This dark side of the life of uncivilized nations has induced barbarous and inhuman settlers in trans-oceanic regions to assume a right to cultivate as their own the inheritance of the aborigines, and to extol the murder of races as a triumph of civilization.

---

[2] Schaafhausen, Archiv für Anthropologie.   In the same spirit Helfer wrote in his journal before he was murdered by the Andamans, "These are the much dreaded savages !   They are timid children of nature, happy as long as no harm is done to them."   Joh. Wilh. Helfer's Reisen in Vorderasien und Indien.   Leipzic, 1873.

[3] Vespucci, Quattuor Navigations, passim.   Of this in the case of the Aleutes see Erman, Zeitsch. für Ethnologie (1871), of the Tshuktshi see Wrangel, Reise in Siberien, of the Itelmes see Steller, Kamschatka.

[4] A list of the nations in which this vice is tolerated was recently given in the Archiv für Anthropologie.   Brunswick, 1872.

Other writers, led away by Darwinian dogmas, fancied they had discovered populations which had, as it were, remained in a former animal condition for the instruction of our times. Thus, in the words of a History of Creation, in the taste now prevalent, "in Southern Asia and the east of Africa, men live in hordes, mostly climbing trees and eating fruit, unacquainted with fire, and using no weapons but stones and clubs after the manner of the higher apes." It can be shown that these statements are derived from the writings of a learned scholar of Bonn, on the condition of savage nations,[5] the facts of which are based either on the depositions of an African slave of the Doko tribe, a dwarfish people in the South of Shoa,[6] or on the assertions of Bengalese planters [7] or perhaps on the observation of a sporting adventurer, that a mother and daughter, and at another time a man and woman, were found in India in a semi-animal condition.[8]   On the other hand, not only have neither nations nor even hordes in an ape-like condition ever been encountered by any trustworthy traveller of modern times, but even those races which in the first superficial descriptions were ranked far below our own grade of civilization, have on nearer acquaintance been placed much nearer the civilized nations.   No portion of the human race has yet been discovered which does not possess a more or less rich vocabulary, rules of language, artificially pointed weapons and various implements, as well as the art of kindling fire.

Sir John Lubbock asserts in his book on Prehistoric Times, that certain inhabitants of the Pacific Islands have no acquaintance with fire.   We are sorry to find this asserted also of the aborigines of Van Diemen's Land, for Sir John need only have opened the record of Abel Tasman [9] to ascertain that even the first discoverer saw columns of smoke rising in the interior of the island.   With as little justice Lubbock asserts that the inhabitants of Fakaafo were unacquainted with fire.   This island belongs to the Union

---

[5] Archiv für Anthropologie.   [6] Krapf, Reisen in Ostafrika.

[7] G. Pouchet, The Plurality of the Human Race.   1864.

[8] Ausland.   1860.

[9] Burney, Discoveries.   The Tasmanians moreover possessed a tradition respecting the derivation of fire.   See Tylor, Early History of Mankind, p. 301.   See also Lubbock, Prehistoric Times, p. 453.

group, and is situated in the north of the Samoan Archipelago, the inhabitants of which have been named navigators on account of their nautical skill and extensive voyages, so that they would long ago have conveyed fire and the art of kindling it to their neighbours at Fakaafo, if these had been without it. For any one else it would have been warning enough, that in the dialect of Fakaafo the word for fire occurs which, according to the various dialects of the Malay language, is pronounced *api, afi, ahi*.[10] Sir John Lubbock, on the contrary, evades this by the supposition that, as in the allied Maori language, the word may stand only for light and heat. As the only foundation for his assertion he appeals to the famous American navigator Wilkes, who noticed the absence of cinders in every part of Fakaafo, and therefore conjectured that the aborigines consumed their food in a raw condition. The great work of his companion, Horatio Hale, on the languages of the South Seas, appeared only a year after the publication of Wilkes's discoveries. This excellent anthropologist testified not only that a word for fire existed on this island, but, in order to refute Wilkes's mistake, he expressly remarks that, on the evening before their embarkation, he and his companions saw a column of smoke rising from Fakaafo.[11] We may therefore confidently maintain the proposition that no human family unacquainted with fire has yet been found.[12]

Fire is an instructive and powerful auxiliary of man. It is a means that has no substitute for producing those modifications of matter, without which our most important articles of food would be unfit for consumption. With the aid of fire, trunks of trees were first, and are still, hollowed out into canoes. Fire alone scares away the fierce beasts of prey of the forest and desert—the African lion, the Asiatic tiger, the American jaguar. By fire

---

[10] According to the vocabulary in Mariner's Tonga Islands, *tolo-afi* signifies to rub fire, and *tolonga* the grooved wood in which it is rubbed.

[11] United States Exploring Expedition; Ethnography. Philadelphia, 1846.

[12] The death of the author prevents an appeal to him to alter this passage, in which he certainly misrepresents Sir John Lubbock, who sums up his remarks on this subject with the words: " The fact, if established, would be most important ; but it cannot be said to be satisfactorily proved that there is at present, or has been within historical times, any race of men entirely ignorant of fire." See Prehistoric Times, pp. 453, 454. London, 1865.

primitive man hardened his rude weapons and the points of his wooden spears. In the absence of trained dogs, prairie fires serve to drive the game into the hands of the hunting tribes of Australia and South Africa. Traces of charred wood and ashes are found in the caves of Périgord,[13] and with yet greater significance in the source of the Schussen, among implements of reindeer's horn, which belong to the glacial period of Northern Europe.[14]

If we now consider from what source man originally obtained fire, the first thought will probably be that he received it as a gift from on high by means of a flash of lightning, which set fire to a tree. But before man could render himself master of fire as a useful auxiliary, he must first have had a knowledge of all the purposes to which man alone is able to adapt it. The conservation of fire must therefore have been preceded by familiar handling of it. If we may draw an inference from the observations of those who have watched nations in a semi-natural condition, we may add that primitive man would have fled in terror from the spectacle of the blazing tree whenever a kindling flash darted from the threatening cloud. The most probable conjecture is, therefore, that it was in the vicinity of volcanic lava streams that man first and permanently became acquainted with the benefits of fire.[15] Alexander von Humboldt reports that twenty years after the eruption of Jorullo, shavings could still be kindled in the fissures of the Hornitos, or dwarf-craters.[16] Thus throughout the life of a whole generation this lava mass offered continual opportunities of obtaining fire. At the bottom of many craters, as in the volcanoes of Hawai, and in the so-called Hell of Masaye, the glowing lava has seethed for ages without intermission. Again, in some few districts there are numbers of so-called mud-volcanoes, or vents, emitting inflammable gas, namely, carburetted hydrogen. We refer to phenomena of this description in the United States, in China and Italy, but especially to the perpetual fires of the peninsula of Absheron near Baku, on the Caspian Sea, which day and night, summer and winter, throw up blasts of flaming gas from fifteen to twenty feet in

---

[13] See above, p. 36.   [14] Ibid. p. 39.
[15] Darwin, Descent of Man, vol. i. p. 53.   [16] Kosmos.

height,[17] to which pious Parsees make pilgrimages from Gujerat and Moultan in order to behold the presence of their fire-god.

A period must, however, have occurred in prehistoric times when the flaming stream of gas was extinguished, the lava stream grew cold, and man must have contemplated the artificial production of fire. The realization of this problem, a great event in the history of our civilization, was subsequently accounted for by the myth of Prometheus, who stole fire from the king of gods. As this legend still endures as a national possession among the Ossets, or Irons, in the Caucasus, and the language of this hill tribe is of the Indo-Germanic family, it must have existed before the later dispersion of the Aryan races; but as in the glacial period fire was artificially produced at the source of the Schussen, far from any volcanic phenomena, we must not look to this myth for the traces of an historical event. On this point we may even appeal to Æschylus who, in the now lost conclusion of his trilogy, makes Prometheus say that he has lain in fetters for thirty thousand years,[18] so that he also refers the theft of fire to a period far beyond the limits of man's memory.

The most primitive method of kindling fire has been retained by the Polynesians. A stick is rubbed obliquely up and down the groove of a stationary piece of wood until it begins to glow. Chamisso found fire-implements of this sort on the Sandwich Islands, and in the Radak group of Micronesia,[19] and they are common to the other Polynesians in Tahiti, New Zealand, the Samoan and Tongan groups,[20] and even in New Caledonia.[21] Less muscular exertion was required by the fire-drills. The earliest contrivance of this kind is described by the Spaniards as in use in the Antilles and the shores of South America. Two pieces of wood were tied together, between which was jammed a pointed stick, which was revolved until fire was kindled.[22] It was soon discovered, however, that a single piece of wood was

[17] Naumann, Geognosie, vol. i.

[18] Westphal, Prolegomenen zu Aeschylus Tragödien. Leipzic, 1869.

[19] O. von Kotzebue's Entdeckungsreisen, vol. iii. Weimar, 1821.

[20] Tylor, Early History of Mankind, p. 303.

[21] Knoblauch in the Ausland. 1866.

[22] Oviedo, Historia general de las Indias, lib. vi.

sufficient for a framework, if a cavity was previously made for the reception of the fire-drill. This apparatus, one of the oldest inventions of our race, reappears in all parts of the world. We recognize it in well-known sculptures of the ancient Mexicans,[23] it is still used by the Indians of Guayana,[24] and by the Botocudos of Brazil,[25] while in South Africa it is used by the Bushmen,[26] Kaffirs, and Hottentots,[27] by the Veddahs in Ceylon,[28] and by the aborigines of Australia.[29] It must not be supposed that success in kindling fire is easy. The labour is so fatiguing that among the Botocudos at Belmont, several individuals were in the habit of relieving each other in the work of turning the drill.[30]

Theophilus Hahn records the same of the Kaffirs,[31] although they live in extremely dry regions. Hermann von Schlagintweit, in his excursions in the Himalayas, first noticed a fire apparatus of this sort among the Leptsha, which was peculiar in that the framework was made of hard, and the drill of soft wood. He also adds that the labour is very fatiguing, and that as the air is highly saturated with moisture, success is very uncertain.[32]

When we realize the fact that the difficulty of kindling fire by friction is so great that even in such a dry region as South Africa, several persons take part in the fatiguing labour, the artificial production of fire presupposes a mutual understanding between the participators, from which fact we may draw the forcible and incontrovertible inference that language must have preceded the artificial preparation of fire; hence that the Suabians of the glacial period already mentioned must have been in possession of such a language, and that the psychical chasm separating man from animals even then existed. Yet the greatest interest attaches itself to the question whether the artificial production of fire was

---

[23] Recently again figured by O. Caspari, Die Urgeschichte der Menschheit. Leipzic, 1873.

[24] C. F. Appun in the Ausland. 1872.

[25] J. J. von Tschudi, Reisen durch Südamerika. Leipzig, 1860.

[26] Fritsch, Eingeborne Südafrika's.

[27] Kolben's Vorgeb. d. G. Hoffnung.

[28] Emerson Tennent, Ceylon, vol. ii.   [29] A. Lortsch in the Ausland, 1866.

[30] The Prince of Wied, Reise nach Brasilien, vol. ii. p. 18.

[31] Globus. Sept. 1871.   [32] Reisen in Indien und Hochasien.

an invention, or only a discovery. Was some powerful thinker of primitive ages led to argue that as heat was generated by friction, fire might be obtained by a very great increase in degree of frictional heat? In that case the truth had dawned upon his mind that luminous heat is distinguished from latent heat only in its amount, and in the effect on the optic nerves, and his attempt to kindle a fire by friction would have received Nature's assent to an inquiry correctly propounded. In acuteness of intellect, such a Prometheus of the glacial period would have been in no way behind a Copernicus or a Kepler, a Champollion or a Grotefend, a Kirchhoff or a Faraday; we could be certain that the highest grade of intellectual power, manifesting itself now and again in individuals, is no greater in our day than it was in classical or biblical antiquity, and in those times no greater than in the glacial period. When we reflect thus we must remember that mediæval scholastics believed a diminution to have taken place of the powers of the human comprehension, so that even in the sphere of the exact sciences the mighty intellects of Greeks and Romans were regarded as unattainable prototypes. At the present time the Chinese, whose mental development has recently been very inactive, are persuaded that the intellectual powers of their thinkers of past ages far exceeded the present standard. The hypothesis of an increase or a diminution of human powers of comprehension varies, therefore, with the self-appreciation, or the absence of self-appreciation, of individual periods, so that at the present time, when, owing to the highly integrated state of society, every intellectual luminary, methodically fostered, is far more readily enabled to diffuse his splendour, we are inclined to assume that human sagacity is now in its meridian.

But mindful of the golden rule, that inferences must be made only from the known to the unknown, we confess that the first stages of civilization of our species are still far too obscure to invalidate the conjecture that a fortunate accident revealed the possibility of generating fire by means of friction. Yet we cannot suppose with Adalbert Kuhn, that a dry tendril, whirled round by a storm in the hollow of a branch, was ignited. We even doubt the physical possibility of the assertion of the Voguls of the Ural mountains, that a broken tree rubbing against a neighbouring stem until it ignites, can cause a conflagration of the forest. As the same mode of producing fire and the same kindling apparatus have been found among all nations of both hemispheres, the accidental discovery must have resulted from an attempt to drill a hole: we meet with pierced implements —though only of horn—even among the relics of the inhabitants of Europe of the glacial period. Yet as one individual must have become exhausted before fire was kindled, and as the heat would be expended during each interruption, the fact that the drilling was continued without a pause still remains without explanation. But the list of possibilities cannot be exhausted, so that we cannot yet hope to understand the sequence of events in ages so remote.

The old frictional apparatus, uncertain in its result, and requiring for its management two workmen at the least, attained its highest development when it was discovered that the drill might be set in motion by a string caused to wind itself on and off. This invention spread over North America to the Sioux, or Dahcotas,[33] as well as to the Iroquois.[34] The Aleutians still more ingeniously sunk the point of the drill into the tinder, and held the upper end fast in their teeth by a mouthpiece made of bone. Chamisso saw tinder set on fire in a few seconds when the string was pulled quickly.[35] All oriental nations made use of the same apparatus in ancient times. Even Pliny speaks of rubbing fire as of a well-known fact.[36] According to Adalbert Kuhn, the Brahminical Hindoos, by means of a string winding itself on and off, used to make a stick, called *Pramantha*, rotate between two pieces of wood, named *Arani*. This philologist leaves us to decide whether the name of Prometheus is to be derived from *Pramâtha*, theft, or from the drill *Pramantha*, and at the same time reminds us that the Thurians formerly worshipped a Zeus Promantheus. However this may be, the ancient Greeks produced fire in the same manner as the Indians of the time of the Vedas.[37] Their *pyreia* or fire implements consisted of two parts, a base, named

---

[33] Tylor, Early History of Mankind, p. 343.
[34] Waitz, Anthropologie, vol. iii.
[35] O. von Kotzebue's Reisen. Weimar, 1841.
[36] Hist. nat. lib. ii. cap. 3, humani ignes . . . attrita inter se ligna.
[37] A. Kuhn, Die Herabkunft des Feuers. Berlin, 1859.

eschara, of soft wood, ivy by preference, and the *trypanon*, answering to the drill, made of laurel wood.[38] This mode of kindling fire was retained till quite recently in Germany, for popular superstition attributed miraculous power to a fire generated by this ancient method. The English word *wildfire* also refers to the kindling of fire by the friction of wood. In Germany a cylinder of oak was revolved by a rope in the space between two oaken beams, in order to generate the so-called Nothfeuer (need-fire), which was supposed to avert epidemics. At Edessa, in Hanover, even in the year 1828, such a need-fire was kindled on the outbreak of the quinsy among the pigs, and the murrain among the cows.[39] In other nations of the Indo-Germanic family, it was necessary that every fire with claims to sanctity should be kindled by . friction. If the fire in the Temple of Vesta at Rome was allowed to die out by the neglect of a priestess, a new flame was kindled, not by flint and steel, though this had long been in use, but by friction on a consecrated board.[40] At the beginning of each of their short centuries, fire was rekindled by friction by the ancient Mexicans ; in the same spirit the Suaheli extinguished their fire on the first day of the year, and kindled a new one with the fire-drill.[41] In Europe the striking of sparks from hard stones, with or without steel, is of post-Homeric antiquity ; Pliny preserves for us the name of a supposed inventor.[42]

As no people has yet been discovered in a fireless condition, the term savage is inapplicable, and has arisen from an erroneous view. Nor should we speak of the children of nature ; we must at least term them half-civilized nations, for the natural condition of mankind is too distant for our observation, or even for our conception. Let us rather picture to ourselves some one who had never seen a rose, coming by chance upon a rose-bush in full bearing ; side by side with the ripening fruit, he would see withered

---

[38] Theophrastus, Hist. plantarum. v. 9.

[39] Kuhn, Herabkunft des Feuers.

[40] Hermann Göll, Die Geheimnisse der Vesta. Ausland, 1870.

[41] Steere in the Journal of the Anthropol. Institute, vol. i.

[42] The greater part of the above was published by the author in the Austrian Zeitschrift für Kunst und Wissenschaft. 1872.

flowers, blossoms in every stage of development, opening and closed buds, shoots with swelling nodes, and, finally, new eyes nestling in the axils of the leaves. If he carefully traces the gradual transitions, the history of the plant's life lies unfolded before him. Past, present, and future do not here follow one another, but exist side by side. Looking only to the sequences of the various stages, it may be asserted, paradoxical as it sounds, that the fruit is younger than the rose, the rose younger than the bud ; for the fruit followed the blossom, and the flowers were preceded by the swelling of the bud, as yet hardly distinguishable from the leaves, just as in a morphological sense it may be said that the boy is an older phenomenon than the aged man. Nor must we expect to find nations still in a budding condition, although it is possible to pronounce in which race of mankind the oldest or, rather, the most primitive condition may still be observed. The lowest grades of civilization have hitherto been usually sought among the Hottentots and Bushmen of Southern Africa, among the Veddahs of Ceylon, the Mincopies of the Andamans, the Australians and the kindred Tasmanians, and, finally, among the Eskimo, the Fuegians, and the Botocudos of Brazil. With the exception of the last, we find all the people enumerated either at the extreme margin of continents, and mainly on their southern extremities, or on remote islands or island continents ; it is doubtful whether, as feeble tribes, they have been driven to the outskirts of continents, or whether, having prematurely separated themselves from other races of mankind, they could no longer be reached by the increasing blessings of civilization, or perhaps, owing to the diminution of their own numbers, were unable even to preserve those advantages of culture which they had formerly acquired. But it is only the misapprehension of the unlearned that could rank nations of such high intellectual powers as the Hottentots and Eskimo with these still primitive people. Whether the Australians and Tasmanians rank among the lowest human beings will be sufficiently shown in a later chapter devoted to these people. But the other nations previously mentioned have risen considerably in our estimation on nearer acquaintance.

The Bushmen, or Sān, have hitherto been regarded as the link connecting monkeys with men. And I willingly admit that, in 1852, I saw Bushmen in London whose animal appearance might well have cured any one of the beautiful delusion that all men were made in the image of God. But Livingstone soon afterwards warned his countrymen not to believe that the piteous objects exhibited were genuine types of an African race, since ugly individuals were alone selected and brought to Europe to gratify curiosity.[42] It is only in the desert of Kalahari that the race of Bushmen has degenerated to a dwarfish size. Livingstone and Chapman [43] describe some of those further north, near Lake Ngami, as well-grown and handsome men. Their demeanour and appearance exhibit the self-respect characteristic of all races living in unrestricted liberty.[44] Although naked, the strictest modesty prevails among them, and the delicacy with which they woo a maiden, as well as the circumstance that their marriages are made only from affection, places them high above many other nations. Chapman relates with emotion his surprise, when out of gratitude for his having given them a share of his game, some Bushmen presented him one morning with a cup of water, the most costly gift in those thirsty regions.[45] It is also noteworthy that these lowly people find pleasure in artistic experiments. With great firmness of hand they have painted the cliffs from the Cape to beyond the Orange River with figures of men and animals in red, brown, white, and black colours, or etched them in light tints on a dark ground ; the copies which we possess justify the assertion that the outlines appear more true to nature than those of many of the Egyptian monuments.[46] Lichtenstein contends that Bushmen have a conception of a supreme Being,[47] but later travellers suppose them to believe in a male and female deity,[48] and they certainly maintain priests or sorcerers.[49] As it

---

[42] Missionary Journeys in Southern Africa, vol. i. p. 64.

[43] Travels into the Interior of South Africa. 1868.

[44] G. Fritsch, Drei Jahre in Südafrika.

[45] Chapman, Travels into the Interior of South Africa.

[46] G. Fritsch, Die Eingebornen Südafrika's.

[47] Reisen im südlichen Afrika.

[48] Waitz, Anthropologie, vol. ii. p. 346.

[49] Fritsch, Eingeborne.

is proverbial among them that death is merely a sleep, it is almost a matter of course that they pray to the deceased as Livingstone ascertained. Intemperance and dirt are the only vices laid to their charge.

Another primitive people is to be found in the gloomy forests of Ceylon. There dwell the Veddahs, now said to be reduced to 8000 heads, a nearly naked hunting tribe, whose language is supposed to be Cingalese uncontaminated by Sanskrit or Pali. Their skulls are narrow (index of breadth 66 to 78) but always of considerable height, tolerably mesognathous, and with the cheek-bones but little prominent.[50] They traffic with their neighbours in dumb show, exchanging ivory and wax for implements and utensils such as were used in the iron age. They do not reject the most disgusting food, such as putrid meat, but on the other hand bind themselves by dietary laws, never touching victuals prepared by a Kandyan from fear of losing caste, for strangely enough they claim a higher rank for their race, and their claim is admitted by their neighbours. When they are described as worshippers of the devil, this implies that they endeavour to appease the powers of evil by their worship. Their hunting grounds are distributed among the families and are regarded strictly as property.[51] In the midst of polygamous nations, the Veddahs are remarkable for marrying only one wife, and among them it is considered that death alone can part man and wife.[52]

As of the Veddahs so of the Mincopies, the inhabitants of the Andaman Islands, we possess but scanty information, although for nearly twenty years past the English have been in the habit of transporting their Indian criminals to this archipelago. As there is no lack of four-footed game on these islands, hunting is a common means of procuring food among the aborigines, who are dreaded by their enemies as good marksmen.[53] They make nets admirably adapted for catching fish,[54] and are yet more famous for the graceful lines of their canoes, which are made

---

[50] Barnard Davis, Thesaurus Craniorum, p. 132.

[51] Sir Emerson Tennent, Ceylon, vol. ii. pp. 439–451.

[52] Tylor, Primitive Culture, vol. i. p. 51. Lubbock, Prehistoric Times, p. 344.

[53] Frederic Mouat, Andaman Islanders, p. 321. 1863.

[54] Ibid. p. 326.

of trunks of trees scooped out until the sides are no thicker than those of a wooden band-box.[55]   They venture far out to sea in these canoes to spear fish by torchlight.   As their language has not yet been thoroughly investigated, it would be quite premature to deny that they have any religious feelings.   Their mutual intercourse is courteous and genial, and the affection between parents and children is peculiarly tender.   They have been classed among the inferior races on account of their nudity, and probably also because they have always offered armed opposition to any attempts to land upon their shores.

The inhabitants of the Straits of Magellan, a region of constant damp and comparative cold, have always been described as the scarecrows of mankind.   The people ethnographically most nearly allied to them are the Araucanians ; we must regard them as a physically feeble tribe which could only find refuge from more powerful oppressors in the inhospitable district of Terra del Fuego.   Two inventions, which are peculiar to these people, prove that, although the lowest of mankind, they are not destitute of all intelligence.   As will be shown when we speak of the nautical skill of shore-dwelling populations, the Fuegians are the only South Americans who undertake voyages in hollow trunks of trees, from Ecuador to Cape Horn, and from Cape Horn to far beyond La Plata.   They constantly keep a fire in these canoes, to which circumstance they and their country owe the name given to them by Europeans.   In air so highly saturated with moisture, it is very difficult to set fire to wood.   The fire-drill would most likely be useless, and therefore the inhabitants of the Islands of Magellan are among the few races of mankind who strike sparks from iron pyrites and catch them on tinder.[56]   In breeding their sporting dogs they pay attention to the rules of cross-breeding.[57] Sad to say, they kill the old women rather than the dogs in periods

---

[55] Frederick Mouat, Andaman Islanders, p. 316.

[56] W. Parker Snow, Off Tierra del Fuego, vol. ii. p. 360. 1857. Perhaps, however, they may have borrowed this invention from the Patagonians, who use flint and steel like Europeans. Musters in the Journal of the Anthropological Institute, vol. i.

[57] Darwin, Variations of Plants and Animals under Domestication, vol. ii. p. 207.

of famine, alleging that the dogs catch sea-otters, and that the old women do not.[58]   Charles Darwin also says, "I was incessantly struck, whilst living with the Fuegians on board the *Beagle*, with the many little traits of character showing how similar their minds are to ours." [59]   Fitzroy ascribes to them a belief in a just deity, who sends adversity as a punishment for delinquencies.[60]

Perhaps the Brazilian Botocudos, of all the inhabitants of the world, are most nearly in the primitive state.   Although they do not live at the southern extremity of a continent, their native country is inhospitable, and was the last of the coast districts of Brazil to be colonized by Europeans.   The Botocudos live in complete nudity and disfigure themselves by inserting wooden plugs in their lips and cheeks, from which habit they have received their name, which is derived from the Portuguese *botoque* (stopper) ; they call themselves Engkeräkmung.   They gain their livelihood by the arrow, and with a forethought rare in other tribes, wrap a cord round their left hands as a protection against the recoil of the string.   They live in the age of the polished but unpierced stone implements, build huts, sleep on matting, cook in earthenware vessels, and are said to worship the moon as the author of creation.[61]   The use of their hunting-grounds is permitted only to the proprietors, and poaching is avenged in single combats not unlike duels.[62]   To provide communication in their territory, suspension bridges are constructed with the stems of climbing plants (çipo).[63]   Let us add that their language possesses an expression for blushing,[64] and that they enliven their feasts with songs, which are however rude and deficient in imagination.   In the second half of the seventeenth century the Engkeräkmung were still so powerful that they were able to destroy three landing-places, totally expelling the Portuguese from the province of Porto Seguro, a deed which they could never have accomplished had there not been some national feeling binding all the various tribes together. But their greatest achievement has yet to be related ; the Nakenuk,

---

[58] Darwin, Journal of Researches.

[59] Descent of Man, vol. i. p. 232.

[60] W. P. Snow.

[61] Prince of Vied, Reise nach Brasilien.

[62] Ibid.   [63] Ibid.   [64] Ibid.

one of their tribes, presented themselves regularly on September 6th, for three successive years, at a Brazilian settlement, to be entertained, according to agreement, at an annual carousal; they must, therefore, have adopted some means of calculating time.[65]

Possibly we are altogether mistaken in considering the races just described to be lower than all others. Their languages are very imperfectly known, and until these have been investigated, it is impossible for anybody to understand their mental conceptions. It has always been passing travellers who have drawn the most doleful pictures of so-called savages, and especially have asserted the poverty of their language. This, for instance, had been the fate of the Carib language until Alexander von Humboldt declared that "it combines wealth, grace, strength, and gentleness. It has expressions for abstract ideas, for Futurity, Eternity, and Existence, and enough numerical terms to express all possible combinations of our numerals." [66]

As the tribes above mentioned live by hunting or fishing, and reside mainly on islands, they will, before long, become extinct. We do not mean to imply that pastoral tribes will not also die out, as is the certain fate of the Hottentots and all the nomads of Northern Siberia. The North American hunting tribes, in the territory of the Hudson's Bay Company, have continued to thrive under the protection of favourable laws, but now that the privileges of the Company have been abolished, these tribes will probably meet with the general fate. The opening of the great western railroads to California will greatly accelerate the extinction of the Bison tribes and the other remnants of the Indian race, and the next century will not find any Redskins in the United States, or at most as domesticated curiosities they may drag on a miserable existence for a few years. This process by which the beings of a past age pass away ought to be no mystery to us.

Above all, the idea of sanguinary suppression must not be entertained. The Spaniards are very frequently reproached for special barbarity. We have no intention of denying that they were deeply

---

[65] J. J. von Tschudi, Reisen durch Südamerika.   1860.

[66] Alex. von Humboldt, Eine wissenschaftliche Biographie.   Herausgegeben von Karl Bruhns.   1872.

stained with Indian blood, but this was caused by greed and not by cruelty; the extermination was always lamented, and an attempt to counteract it was made by lenient though powerless laws. The transatlantic history of Spain has no case comparable in iniquity to the act of the Portuguese in Brazil, who deposited the clothes of scarlet-fever or small-pox patients on the hunting-grounds of the natives, in order to spread the pestilence among them; [67] and of the North Americans who used strychnine to poison the wells which the Redskins were in the habit of visiting in the deserts of Utah; [68] of the wives of Australian settlers, who, in times of famine, mixed arsenic with the meal which they gave to starving natives; [69] or, finally, of the English colonists in Tasmania, who shot the natives when they had no better food for their dogs. [70] Yet neither cruelty nor oppression have anywhere entirely extirpated a human race, nor have even new diseases, including the small-pox, annihilated nations; still less is it due to the brandy epidemic: a far more powerful angel of destruction now acts on races once joyous and happy, and this is, weariness of life. The unfortunate inhabitants of the Antilles killed themselves wholesale by mutual agreement, partly by poison and partly by the halter. [71] A missionary at Oaxaca told the Spanish historian Zurita, that whole tribes of the Chontals and Mijes had agreed to renounce all intercourse with their wives or to destroy the unborn progeny by poison. [72] The true cause of the extinction of so many various races of mankind is that no new generation springs up among them. It is the decrease of births in the Sandwich Islands [73] and Tahiti which is bringing about the disappearance of the tribes. The inhabitants of Taio-Hae, an island of the Mendana group,

---

[67] Prince of Vied, Reise nach Brasilien, vol. ii. p. 64. Tschudi, Reisen durch Südamerika.

[68] R. Burton, The City of the Saints, p. 576. 1862.

[69] Waitz (Gerland), Anthropologie, vol. vi. Eyre, Central Australia, vol. ii. p. 175. 1845.

[70] Bonwick, The Last of the Tasmanians, p. 50. 1870.

[71] Las Casas, Hist. de las Indias.

[72] Zurita, Chefs de la Nouvelle Espagne.

[73] In the first census in the Sandwich Islands in 1832, 130,315 individuals were counted, in 1853 they had diminished to 73,138, and in 1872 to 49,044. Globus, June, 1873.

diminished from 400 to 250 inhabitants in the course of three years, during which period only three or four births took place.[74]

Certain misunderstood instances help to explain this fact. A young Botocudo boy was brought up by a Brazilian family at Bahia, attended the schools and the university, obtained a medical diploma, and for a time practised as a physician at Bahia. Profound melancholy had always been the chief feature of his character. One day he disappeared, and years afterwards his adopted parents received intelligence that he had discarded clothes and education, and was roaming about the forests with his tribe.[75] A similar case was witnessed by Dobrizhoffer among the Abipones; and he also relates the story of a Spanish lady who, with her children, fell into the hands of this warlike tribe, and remained with them till a ransom was obtained. Her son Raymond and her daughter, who had grown up among the Redskins, entirely refused to return.[76] The late Admiral Fitzroy brought a Fuegian to England, where he was christened and brought up under the name of Jemmy Button, and was for a time made much of as a pet in good society. He was taken back to his native country in the expedition in which Charles Darwin went round the world. On his return to his own home, Jemmy Button, who in Europe had always worn gloves and polished boots,[77] at once became a naked, unwashed, unkempt Fuegian, as he had formerly been, and in 1855 no longer differed from his fellows.[78] Another well-known case of this sort is that of an Australian named Bungari, who was educated at Sydney, where he gained prizes at the college, and spoke Latin well, but who afterwards escaped from civilization into the bush, and declared that education had been of no use but to make him conscious of his misery.[79] The hydrographer Neumayer also relates that, having lost his way on the Lower Murray in 1861, he was taken by

---

[74] Quatrefages, Rapport.

[75] J. J. von Tschudi, Reisen in Südamerika.

[76] Geschichte der Abiponer. Wien, 1783.

[77] C. Darwin, Journal of Researches, p. 207.

[78] Philipps, The Missionary of Tierra del Fuego, 1861; and Parker Snow, Off Tierra del Fuego, vol. ii. p. 29.

[79] Bonwick, The Last of the Tasmanians, p. 359.

the natives to a naked black man, who noted in his pocket-book, in faultless English, the names of the most important localities through which he was to pass on his return. This literary Australian, who was at that time twenty-four years of age, had been educated at a missionary school in Adelaide.[80]

Unsympathetic anthropologists have endeavoured to prove by such cases as these that men of a different colour from their own belong to other species. These examples show principally that the measure of mental capacity is not unequally distributed, but we are also surprised to see that the so-called savage prefers a life of freedom to all the advantages and conveniences of civilization. The difficulty of accustoming hunting tribes to a sedentary life, is not that they are incapable of living in our way, but that they choose to live in their own way. They look upon all labour as degrading, and on hunting as the only dignified and manly occupation.[81] " The black man does not work," say the Australians, " for he is of high birth." [82] When the English and Dutch colonists settled on the eastern shores of the United States, a native was here and there observed watching from an elevation how the farmer followed his plough, not in order to learn his secret, but first to gaze in wonder, and then to turn away in pity, as if he silently thought, with the Latin poet, that life could not possibly be worth more than the pleasures which render it desirable (non propter vitam vivendi perdere causas). That this is the final impression of the native we may perceive from another trait. The Red Indians of North America imagine the next world to be a continuation of the present existence. The Great Spirit, as they hope, will transplant them to regions abounding in game.[83] Thus the warlike Maori of New Zealand imagine life after death as a constant series of skirmishes and battles in which the blessed are always victorious. Our Germanic forefathers cherished the same hopes. The life of the

---

[80] Neumayer, at the meeting of the Anthropological Society at Berlin, April 15th, 1871.

[81] According to Charlevoix this is the case with the Algonkins and Iroquois (Nouvelle France. 1744). They show great industry, however, in the preparation of their hunting and fishing tackle.

[82] " White fellows work, not black fellows ; black fellow gentleman." Hale, United States Exploring Expedition ; Ethnography, p. 109.

[83] Charlevoix, Nouvelle France. 1744.

8

uncivilized man appears to him so full of enjoyment that he can think of another life only as an enhancement of the same. Now let us ask ourselves whether we should be satisfied with an enhancement of our present existence; whether an artisan would like to imagine the life after death as a cotton mill a mile in length. Or can we suppose that a Londoner, who goes into the country a very few times during the year, and some years not at all, could imagine the next world to be an exaggerated London? We must therefore conclude that in the lowest social grades the sense of physical ease is far greater, the appreciation of life far smaller; that the so-called savage prefers to renounce existence rather than undergo the burdens of civilization. Had the home of the ancient Teutons, as Tacitus describes them, been in North America, they would in all likelihood have succumbed, after the discovery by Europeans, to the same fatality which has destroyed the Algonkins and the " Five Nations." The transition from hunting to careful husbandry must be slowly effected during several generations, or the extinction of the race is inevitable. We therefore see that those natives of the New World who had already reached a higher grade of civilization, such as the natives of Mexico, Yucatan, Central America, Ecuador, Peru, and Chili, not only do not die out, but that now, after about three hundred years, are again becoming the dominant races in their own country, although in a less advanced state of civilization.

When comparing hunting tribes with literary nations, there is one circumstance which we ought never to forget. We are all slaves of society, laboriously tutored from our youth upwards to perform the work of a wheel, or often enough of a mere peg or a screw, in the machinery of civil life. Freedom is enjoyed only by the Botocudo, the Australian, or the Eskimo. We never feel the loss of natural liberty, for it is impossible to lose what has never been possessed. But, lest these words should be deemed a lamentation over a lost Paradise, we will add that on the other hand civilized man enjoys one liberty which coloured hunting tribes may well envy him, namely, intellectual liberty. It has frequently been asked whether all savages have religious feelings. No ethnologist will put this question. He knows that the nearer the state of nature, the greater is the belief in Nature. The sway of the incredible is nowhere stronger than in the mind of the so-called savage, who trembles all his life before the creations of his own imagination. A choice was offered to our species ; we were free either to become slaves in an organized society, but to be free from the terrors of imagination, or, disencumbered of all social bonds, to range as lords over wide hunting-grounds, but to be scared by every frivolous and ugly dream, and to remain the prey of a childish fear of spectres.

II.—FOOD AND ITS PREPARATION.

WHEN first considering the primitive development of the human race, we regarded it as self-evident that the scene of its first growth must have been in a region where daily food is freely offered for the mere trouble of taking it. This is the case only in the tropics, so that it was impossible to conceive that sacred garden in which our first parents were as yet free from the cares of providing sustenance, except as adorned with the feathered crowns of palm trees. There are even now small communities which are allowed to reap where they have not sown, and to gather where they have not planted. In the region of the sago palm in the Sea of Banda, Malays and Papuans find supplies of food always awaiting them. In many coral groups of the South Seas and the Indian Ocean, the meals throughout the whole course of the year consist only of cocoa-nuts, or, at most, fishing occasionally supplies a change. The whole family of palms in general is the readiest foster-mother of mankind. Among the trees cultivated by the natives in the tropical parts of South America, is the *Guilelma speciosa*, which bears the pupunhas, resembling the apricot or the egg-plum. It must have been cultivated from time immemorial, and propagated by grafts, as the originally hard stone has been reduced to fibres or entirely changed into pulp.[1] The forests on the Amazon are like a neglected orchard, in which the Brazilian chestnut (*Bertholletia excelsa*) ripens its almond-like seeds, and the cocoa, the pine-apple, the Sapodilla plum (*Achras sapota*), the Avocado pear (*Persea,*

---

[1] Martius, Ethnographie.

gratissima) grow wild, as well as many berries, and plum and cherry-like fruits; the Miriti (*Mauritia flexuosa*) also furnishes palm wine and food. Here, then, food is constantly supplied, and in abundant variety.[2]   In Central Africa the doom palm (*Hyphaena thebaica*), differing from all other palm trees in having a branched stem, annually bears above two hundred nutritious nuts as large as oranges.[3]   By the side of this palm, the date, in the oases of the Sahara, affords sustenance not only to the rider but also to his horse.   It is true that it no longer grows wild anywhere, and to secure a harvest the blossoms of the male tree must be artificially placed in connection with those of the female plant.

The bread-fruit tree has been transplanted by the Polynesians from its home in the Moluccas and the Philippines, across the South Seas.   During eight successive months of the year it ripens fruits as large as melons, which, when buried in the earth, may be preserved in an edible condition during the other four months.[4]   This latter custom is however not universal, for the younger Pritchard observes,[5] that the yams ripen in the six months during which the bread-fruit is failing or altogether absent; yams, however, certainly presuppose some degree of cultivation.   According to J. R. Foster's calculation, twenty-seven bread-fruit trees, which would about cover an English acre with their shade, are sufficient for the support, during the eight months of fruit-bearing, of from ten to twelve people.   If we knew with certainty the original habitat of the pisang or plantain, which three times a year bears from seventy to eighty pounds of fruit in clusters, and according to an often-cited calculation of A. von Humboldt,[6] yields on an equal surface of ground fifty times as much nourishment as wheat, we should be inclined to believe that the first appearance of our race was under the picturesque shade of the tattered oar-like leaves of the Musaceæ.   Outside the tropics, however, there are also dense thickets of trees, showering edible and easily preserved fruits on men who shun labour.   The Mezquite forests in North

[2] Martius and P. Gumilla, Orinoco.

[3] Sir Samuel Baker in the Proceedings of the Royal Geogr. Society. 1866.

[4] Charles Martins, From Spitzbergen to the Sahara.

[5] Polynesian Reminiscences. 1866.

[6] Bemerkungen auf einer Reise um das Welt. 1783.

America cover the ground to the depth of an inch with fallen pods, which are not only greedily devoured by horses and mules, but from which an acid beverage is prepared for man's consumption, while in Mexico the beans are said to be ground and baked into bread. It is at any rate certain that these seeds of the *Algarrobia* or *Prosopis glandulosa* are carefully packed in baskets and stored by the Mohave tribes on the Western Colorado, to serve as a resource in case of the failure of other and more favoured fruits.[7] Pods like those of these acacias of the dry western parts of North America, are produced in the Pampas of La Plata by the *Prosopis horrida*. The present inhabitants call the fruit St. John's bread (algarroba), but except in name it has nothing in common with the pods of the *Ceratonia siliqua* of the south of Europe. The fruit is picked up twice a year by the Abipones, and eaten either raw or mixed with water, and converted by fermentation into a vinous beverage.[8]

Although the supplies of food hitherto enumerated belong chiefly to the plains, the mountain sides are not totally destitute. In the Cordilleras of Chili the araucarias, which there take the place of our conifers, produce spherical fruits, which are as large as a man's head, and which contain from two to three hundred nuts, each of which is twice the size of an almond, and when roasted fresh resembles a chestnut in flavour. As two hundred of these nuts are sufficient for a day's food for the greatest eater, eighteen araucarias are sufficient for a year's sustenance.[9] But we need not go to the Andes of Antuco for such instances. The pine forests of Southern Europe might also be cited; nay, even in the stone-pine of our mountains, which rarely grows at an altitude of less than four thousand feet, we ourselves possess a tree yielding food and growing wild. The fact may be mentioned here that the potato was found wild in the highlands of Chili; and that in Peru the quinoa (*Chenopodium quinoa*) grows at an altitude equal to Mont Blanc; without this plant it is hard to believe that a dense population on Lake Titicaca could have built the famous temple dedicated to the worship of the sun.

---

[7] Möllhausen, Tagebuch.   [8] Dobrizhoffer, Geschichte der Abiponer.
                       [9] Pöppig, Reisen.

Although the native habitats of our cereals are still unknown, there yet exist in boggy marshes wild graniferous plants which have hitherto escaped cultivation. In North America the natives collected, and still collect, the ears of the marsh millet (*Zizania aquatica*).[10] The banks of the pools, back-waters, and igarapes (side streams), of the Rio Negro in Brazil are covered with wild rice (*Oryza subulata*), the ripe grains of which the colonist as he passes in his boat has only to strip off.[11] Quite recently Schweinfurth[12] has mentioned another species of rice (*Oryza punctata*), which at the rainy season makes its appearance in all the pools in the Bongo country, in the neighbourhood of the Gazelle river, and which, though not collected by the negroes of that district, is considered a pleasant article of food by the Baggara Arabs and also at Darfur. Even the arid plains of Kalahari produce many edible roots, bulbs, beans, juicy fruits, and the esculent maguli, the milky juice of which allays thirst.[13]

The examples given by no means exhaust the list of the esculent plants of the desert. Those who have studied the subject will be able to add many others, or some will even be surprised that we have overlooked important instances. Yet enough has been said for our purpose. Nor is our enumeration of different sorts of food intended to uphold the idea that man in his earliest stages of development depended solely on the vegetable kingdom for his nutriment, and, like Brahmins and Buddhists, passed over the animal kingdom with holy awe. Vegetable products claim precedence because man is fitted for a vegetable diet, both by his dentition and digestive system, so that hunger must have driven him to change his mode of nourishment. But even animals which are classed among graminivora by comparative anatomists do not adhere rigidly to the diet allotted to them. As the apes of the New World are exactly analogous to man in dental structure, which is the point with which we are here primarily concerned, it is a significant fact that a similar abnormal mode of

---

[10] The Acclimatization Society of Berlin has since 1870 undertaken the cultivation of Indian rice, and, as it appears, successfully. Ausland, 1872.

[11] Von Martius, Ethnographie, vol. i. p. 679.

[12] Im Herzen von Afrika.

[13] Chapman's Travels into the Interior of South Africa, vol. ii. p. 297. 1868.

subsistence has been observed in them also. Thus, according to Otto Kersten's[14] description, baboons gather leaves and leaf buds, blossoms and half-ripe fruit, dig up bulbs and roots, but also pursue such animals as they are able to overpower. They turn over stones in order to find the insects on the lower side. Pupæ of ants and butterflies, larvæ of beetles, smooth-skinned caterpillars, flies, and spiders are welcome prey. They are also most inveterate birds-nesters, devouring the eggs and nestlings of any but the largest birds; nay, they catch the fledglings and seize mice, devouring them with manifest satisfaction. Not unlike the description of these baboons are the remarks of Alfred Lortsch on the Australians, who not only eat marsupials, but all sorts of birds, even carrion kites, eels, fish of every kind, bats, flying foxes, frogs, lizards, snakes, and worms.[15] We have lately seen a similar list given by Schweinfurth, who says of the Bongo or Dor negroes, that they allow no animal food, with the exception of dogs and men, to escape them; they take rats, snakes, carrion kites, hyænas, fat land scorpions, winged ants, and caterpillars.[16]

F. Appun says of the Indians of British Guiana, that "Game and fish constitute their chief food, but they do not despise rats, monkeys, alligators, frogs, worms, caterpillars, ants, larvæ, and beetles."[17] The disgust caused by any article of consumption is merely conventional, or arises from fear of the unknown. Nor are civilized Europeans justified in shuddering at the Chinese for considering swallows' nests and trepang (*Holothuria*) as great delicacies, or because in Arabia a flight of locusts is greeted as a feast given by God, when they themseelvs do not shrink from the trail of snipe, nor from lobsters and crayfish, although the latter, as water scavengers, act both as grave-digger and grave. Hence, in picturing to ourselves the mode of subsistence in use among the original stock of our race before the institution of husbandry, and even before the adoption of hunting, we must not suppose that vegetable fare alone appeased their hunger, but that everything was seized that seemed fit to eat. Turning first to

---

[14] Reisen des Baron von der Decker in Ostafrika.

[15] Ausland. 1866.

[16] Globus, Bd. xxii. No. 5.   [17] Ausland. 1872.

the sea-side at every season of the year, we may gather edible shell-fish from the shoals, and even from the bottom of the sea, as well as snails in considerable quantities. The accumulations of shells of edible molluscs, which extend in heaps along the shores of the Danish islands, and are known to archæologists under the name of kitchen-middens, consist of the shells of four species of molluscs found in the Baltic, which formed the sustenance of the inhabitants of the shores from the palæolithic to the neolithic age.[18] As soon as attention was directed to these remains, similar accumulations were recognized in Scotland, the United States, Brazil, and Australia.

The capture of fish without the use of fishing apparatus, either net or line, is an every-day occupation in Kamtshatka. Fifteen miles in the interior of this peninsula, Kennan [19] found the sluggish streams polluted by the bodies of dead and putrifying salmon. He saw fish of this species from 18 to 20 inches long, laboriously wending their way upwards in brooks scarcely deep enough to cover their backs with water, so that they could be taken out with the hand. In Cambodia, where fishing-tackle is not used, Adolf Bastian [20] observed that the natives let the water of the river Tasavai into a canal, dammed it up, and then drained it off again, in order to catch in their hands the fish which had entered during the interval. A Chinaman at Calumpit, in the island of Luzon, was seen by F. Jager [21] to do exactly the same thing. Poisoning the water, as it is practised in South America, presupposes more reflection and more protracted observation of nature. The process in use in Guiana has been elaborately described by F. Appun,[22] who saw the Cambodian system of damming and draining in use among the Indians of that district.

It would evidently be a hopeless undertaking to point to any one region of the earth as that which, by a constant supply to meet daily needs, was best adapted for the home of our first ancestors before they were strengthened by thought and practice ; on the contrary, innumerable districts of both continents of our

---

[18] See above, p. 40.   [19] Tent Life in Siberia. 1871.

[20] Völker Ostasiens. Jena, 1868.

[21] Reisen in den Philippinen, p. 74. Berlin, 1873.   [22] Ausland. 1870.

planet were fully adapted for the reception of man. The facts which we have put together may, however, free us from the old mistake of supposing that the spread of our race from one centre of creation to remote continents, could only have taken place under more mature conditions. Of food, at least, there can have been no want: the profusion, greater in some localities than in others, and the narrow regions to which palatable articles of food were originally confined, may have contributed much to entice tribes which had roamed abroad and had discovered these new sources of food, to settle in the uttermost corners of the world. Throughout historic and such prehistoric times as are susceptible of investigation, nations have constantly been in a state of migration, adhesion to the soil being peculiar to highly advanced states of society.

We must not here entirely omit to mention a custom unworthy of the human race.[23] While it seldom occurs that animals devour their own species, we meet with cannibalism in nearly every part of the world. In some cases, this horrible custom is less depraved, in that it is founded on the lamentable superstition that the estimable qualities of the person devoured are thus absorbed. At the time of the Taiping insurrection, an English merchant at Shanghai met his servant in the street, carrying home the heart of a rebel, with the avowed intention of eating it to increase his own courage.[24] Sometimes it is not the sensual appetite but the desire for revenge which prompts this most dishonourable mode of interment for the fallen enemy. Occasionally the deity himself is made to take part in the transaction, when human sacrifice is followed by a revolting feast on human flesh, as was the custom in ancient Mexico.[25] On the other hand, it is quite inadmissible to justify cannibalism by a plea of physical compulsion, as if our bodily welfare urgently depended on an alternation of animal

---

[23] Richard Andrée has lately published a work on the spread of cannibalism in the Transactions of the Ethnological Association of Leipsic, from which it appears that this vice is more common among the Australians than was supposed. A distinction should be made between cannibals by taste and those who are so from superstition.

[24] Tylor, Early History of Mankind, p. 167.

[25] Prescott, Conquest of Mexico, vol. i. p. 78.

and vegetable food, for in India more than a hundred million people are satisfied with a vegetable diet. It is usual to quote the case of the Maori who on their arrival in New Zealand found no terrestrial quadruped there, and driven by an uncontrollable natural impulse, were forced to eat human flesh.[25] But cannibalism is common to all other Polynesians. It has been proved to exist on the Marquesas Islands, the Hawaï group, Tahiti, and elsewhere, where pigs and dogs are bred for the sake of their flesh, so that the Maori must assuredly have been polluted by this disgusting vice before they[26] separated from their kindred tribes. Moreover, even nations which were in the habit of breeding cattle, such as the Immithlanga, a Zulu tribe in South Africa, were not free from this abomination,[27] and among their kindred, the Basuto, it was only suppressed by the chief Moshesch.[28] It would be a mistake to regard this as a vice peculiar to the so-called inferior and less responsible nations. The Australians, although they cannot be entirely exculpated, are yet not habitual cannibals. As far as we know, neither Hottentots nor Bushmen have ever been suspected, but there can be no doubt of the cannibalism of the Botocudos. The detestable custom is most frequently encountered exactly among those nations and groups of nations which are distinguished from their neighbours by their abilities and more mature social condition, such as the ancient Mexicans, who have already been mentioned. Papuans in general, including the inhabitants of New Guinea and the Solomon Islands, the New Hebrides, New Caledonia, and the Fiji group, are cannibals by taste, and yet as a race we must rank them as high or even higher

---

[25] The same might be said of the inhabitants of Rapa-nui, near Easter Island. Revue maritime et coloniale, tome xxxv.

[26] While alluding to the fact taht cannibalism was suppressed on the Western Paumotu Islands by the Tahitians, Meinicke conjectures that the latter were free from this vice, but Gerland (Waitz, Anthropologie) has given evidence of the contrary.

[27] Waitz, Anthropologie.

[28] Casalis, Les Bassoutos. 1859. Among the cave-cannibals were two Betschuan tribes, the Ba-fukeng, or Ba-brukeng, and the Ma-katla, as well as two Kaffir tribes, the Ba-makakana and the Ba-matlapatlapa. Their hiding-place was in the vicinity of Thaba-Bosigo, near the source of the Caledon river. Anthropological Review. April, 1869.

than the Polynesians. Among the Asiatic Malays, the Batta of Sumatra are so advanced as to have framed an alphabet of their own, although after the Indian model.[29]   The statement made by a Dutch governor of Padang to Bickmore [30] the traveller, respecting the supposed recent origin of cannibalism, is a legend invented by the Batta themselves, for they were cannibals as early as Nicolo Conti's time,[31] and even in the days of Marco Polo; [32] nay, if the island of Ramni of the old Arabian records has been rightly indentified as Sumatra, the Batta disgraced the dignity of the human race by this vice a thousand years ago.[33]   In Equatorial Africa we find two tribes equally degraded, namely, the Fans of the West Coast, described first by Du Chaillu and afterwards by Burton, as remarkable for their work in iron and generally for their high degree of intelligence,[34] and the Niamniam, or Sandeh, in the region of the Gazelle Nile, who excel their neighbours in civiliza- tion, both of which tribes are cannibals according to Petherick and Piaggia. Finally, Schweinfurth brought to Europe the first account of their southerly neighbours on the Uelle, the light-coloured Mon- buttoos, whose semi-civilization is very wonderful when compared with the primitive condition of the Nile tribes; yet there can be no doubt of their cannibalism. An old experience was confirmed by their case, namely, that the consumption of dogs' flesh generally accompanies, and is the first step to, cannibalism.[35]   Schaaff- hausen [36] maintains that even Europeans within this century have not abstained from human flesh, but we must leave him to answer for the trustworthiness of his authority. In the last siege of Messina, the flesh of the captured soldiers is said to have been

---

[29] Waitz, Anthropologie.

[30] Reisen im ostindischen Archipel. Jena, 1869.

[31] In the only correct version of Poggio, recently published by Fr. Kunstmann (Indien im 15 Jahrhundert. Munich, 1863), his words are : "In ejus insulae (namely, Sumatra), quam dicunt Bathech parte anthropophagi habitant."

[32] Lib. iii. cap. ii.

[33] Peschel, Gesch. d. Erdkunde.

[34] Winwood Reade (Savage Africa, 1863) speaks of the Fans as an extremely civil and amiable race. According to Zucchelli (Missione di Congo. Venezia, 1712), the Congo negroes are also cannibals.

[35] Im Herzen von Afrika, vol. i. p. 442, and vol. ii. p. 98.

[36] Archiv für Anthropologie. 1870.

sold on the Giudecca, and that of the Swiss at a higher price than that of the Neapolitans.

From all these facts, we learn that cannibalism does not pervade entire groups of nations, with the exceptions of the Papuan and the Polynesian, but occurs only in very isolated cases in Africa and America, while it is almost entirely absent in Asia, and in Europe belongs to past ages of uncertain date. The supposition that all human societies in their more barbarous stages have been guilty of this vice, and have overcome it, is incapable of proof, especially as it has lately been acknowledged that legends of cannibalism have easily spread from one nation to another, so that their local occurrence by no means proves anthropophagy in prehistoric times. It was also assumed with unjustifiable haste that where human sacrifices were customary, human flesh had previously been eaten, as if nothing had been laid upon the altars of the gods which was not esteemed as valuable food by those who brought the offering. Cannibalism was never associated with the numerous human sacrifices in Khondistan. As may be ascertained from Campbell's minute descriptions, they were offered to the deified Earth in order to obtain the boon of a productive harvest. Sacrifice of women and of domestic slaves on the tombs of the deceased is certainly quite unconnected with anthropophagous habits. Thus the Ada, or "great custom," of Dahomey is founded solely on a belief in immortality. Hundreds of men perish at the grave of a king, victims to the delusion that their spirits will follow and aid the departed, or convey to him the latest tidings from this world.[37] For thousands of years the Hindoos have abstained from all animal food, and yet at the great festivals of Juggernaut, these people, in a paroxysm of religious frenzy, were wont to cast themselves by dozens under the wheels of the idol's car in voluntary self-sacrifice. Because Abraham bound his son on an altar of wood, it does not follow that before Abraham's time the Hebrews were cannibals, nor that the Romans had once been in the habit of eating their fellow-creatures, because Pliny[38] mentions that an edict against human sacrifices was published at Rome in U.C. 357. We may therefore assume that here and there, not only

---

[37] Ausland, p. 407. 1861.   [38] Hist. nat. xxx. 3, 4.

barbarous, but even superior races of mankind yielded to the horrible temptation, and that cannibalism has assuredly not been a disease inevitable in the evolution of our species.

It is extremely difficult to prove the effect exercised by diet on the civilization of individual nations. All that we can confidently assert is that insufficient or unsuitable fare has always been followed by physical and mental deterioration. In the prolific hunting-grounds of Australia, travellers have found vigorous and well-made people, instead of such shrivelled deformities as are seen on the west coast. It is only in the deserts of Kalahari that the Bushmen are small and emaciated.

As to the choice of diet, we can only repeat a general and well-known rule. Food abounding in carbon is more eagerly seized in cold than in warmer climates. The arctic circle would be uninhabitable to the Hindoo without a change in his dietary rules, as on the other hand it would be difficult for the Eskimo transported to India to devour enormous quantities of raw seal's blubber. If we add Moritz Wagner's accurate observation,[39] that in Southern Asia, and in Central and Southern America, wherever there is a want of animal food, vegetables are largely consumed, and that where rice constitutes the daily food, fishing is zealously pursued, we shall have given all the information which can be looked upon as certain. On the other hand, it is not proved that bodily strength, physical courage, and acuteness of intellect, are not as possible with vegetable as with animal diet. Of all the Polynesians, if we except the inhabitants of solitary islands, the Maori of New Zealand were the only people who did not fatten either pigs or dogs, and unless it be assumed that their occasional repasts on human flesh may have supplied this deficiency, it must be admitted that, on a diet of fish and roots, they have become the most powerful, courageous, and warlike race of their family of nations, and the one which has made most advance in the social arts.

Probably each of us has at some time had personal experience of the effects of alcohols and narcotics, and has perhaps observed that a moderate use of wine is capable of raising us above the

---

[39] Allgemeine Zeitung. 1871.

prosaic state of our every-day life. With many the excitement produced by tea or coffee is still more powerful. When we feel ourselves thus strengthened, it seems as if we were able to see more clearly and to argue more acutely. Ideas previously eagerly but unsuccessfully sought now crowd upon us in rapid succession, and new truths seem to be within our grasp. This would seem to show, perhaps, that the movements evoked by our mental functions have been accelerated by narcotics, or their length of vibration increased. Mental progress must perhaps have become perceptibly more rapid in human society since the discovery of these magic potions.

Let us be warned by the errors of Buckle, who, lured on by deceptive facts of this description, deceived himself and a willingly deluded multitude into a belief that it is possible to explain the course of the history of the most highly civilized nations by the chemical constituents of their food. The rapid rate of intellectual progress in our days is primarily due to the adjustments of modern society, which furnishes science with many more disciples, and these all better prepared than formerly. The greatest inventions of mankind, hieroglyphic and phonetic writing, the division of time, weights and measures, the positional value of figures, are older than the acquaintance with narcotics, and to wine alone could we ascribe any share in this service. The Mosaic conception of God, the Zoroastrian dualism, Christianity and Islam, Indian legends and philosophies, have all arisen without the aid of narcotics. During the age of Chinese invention, that is to say, during the first three dynasties, tea was unknown in China. Copernicus devised his system, Galileo confirmed it, and Kepler proved it by his laws, without coffee and without knowing its very name. Hence it is more prudent not to enter upon the obscure inquiry as to the excitability of our intellectual faculties by means of stimulants.

Of equal importance with food is its preparation. The consumption of raw flesh and fat is habitual only among the Eskimo, although it occurs exceptionally elsewhere. Among other people glowing embers and a wooden spit are generally employed for roasting. The rinds of gourds, or the shells of nuts, mostly serve as drinking vessels, and among Bushmen occasionally the eggs of the ostrich. Their neighbours, the Betchuans and Kaffirs, plait baskets so closely that liquids are retained in them.[40] Unserviceable as wooden vessels may seem for boiling water, human sagacity hit upon the expedient of making stones red hot, and then dropping them into water in such wooden vessel. In this manner cooking was first carried on. A yet simpler method is pursued by a tribe of Red Indians in the north of the prairies. They line a hole made in the ground with the skin of the slaughtered game, pour water upon it, and heat the water with red-hot stones, hence the Ojibwas called these tribes the Assiniboins, or stone-cookers.[41] Since commerce has supplied them with earthenware vessels and cauldrons, this primitive mode of dressing meat has been practised only on festive occasions.[42] Beyond the Rocky Mountains, the Ahts of Vancouver's Island,[43] as well as the Tshinuks of Oregon, use heated stones and wooden vessels for cooking,[44] and the Kolushs further to the north occasionally employ their canoes as kettles for boiling large fish. The Kamtskadals also cook by means of heated stones dropped into wooden troughs.[45] Even in Europe, as Linnæus records, cooking with stones had been retained in Finnish East Bothland as a remnant of remote past ages.[46] Tylor has ascertained that heated stones were used in Ireland for warming milk even in the year 1600, and that in the Hebrides in the sixteenth century meat was still cooked in the skin of the animal.[47] This last method was customary in the woodless southern steppes of Russia at the time of Herodotus. He says that the Scyths used the bones as fuel, and the skin of the animal as a vessel in which the meat and water was placed during the process of cooking.[48] The Polynesians, who had no earthenware utensils, prepared their food in pits lined with leaves, on which the

---

[40] Casalis, Les Bassoutos. Paris, 1859. T. G. Wood, Natural History of Man ; Africa, p. 63.

[41] Catlin, Indianer Nordamerika's. Leipzic, 1851.

[42] The Patagonians do the same when on their hunting expeditions, although at home they use iron kettles. Musters, Journal of Anthrop. Institute. 1872.

[43] Ausland. 1868.

[44] Waitz, Anthropologie, vol. iii. p. 336.

[45] G. W. Steller, Kamtschatka. 1774.

[46] Linnæus, quoted by Tylor, Early History of Mankind, p. 270.

[47] Tylor, Primitive Culture, p. 272. [48] Herod. lib. iv. cap. 61.

animal or vegetable food was placed with some heated stones; the holes were then filled up with leaves and covered over with earth. From all this we get a clear idea of the mode of dressing food implied, when it is said of a people that they cook with stones, or that they possess no earthen vessels.

Mankind may have discovered how to manufacture earthen vessels in various ways. Sir John Lubbock points out that Captain Cook saw stones surrounded with a rim of clay in use among the Aleutians on Unalashka; but this might be an imitation of European vessels with which the islanders had already become acquainted through Russian sailors. The practice of the Australians on the Lower Murray river, of puddling holes in the earth with clay, and cooking food in them, might perhaps have led an inventive mind to the manufacture of earthen vessels. But the process is better explained by the account of the French sailor Gonneville, who, in 1504, landed on a South Atlantic coast, probably in Brazil.[49] He describes certain wooden vessels in use among the natives (in whom D'Avezac fancies that he recognizes Brazilian Carijo), enveloped in a coating of clay as a protection from the fire.[50] If by chance the wooden bowl separated itself from the covering of clay, an earthen vessel would remain. In examining the site of an old pottery manufactory of the Red Indians on the Cahokia, which falls into the Mississippi below St. Louis, Carl Rau discovered half-finished vessels, that is to say, baskets of rushes or willow, lined inside with clay. When the vessel was baked the fire naturally consumed the external covering. Half-finished vessels from the Southern States show that the rinds of gourds instead of baskets were lined with clay.[51] Hence the art of making pottery was independently invented in America and in the Old World, in centres of civilization unknown to us. From this centre it may have spread over the whole of Africa, with the sole exception of the Bushman district, but not to the extreme north-east of Asia, and not across Behring's Straits. That the Europeans of prehistoric times also originally

[49] Pierre Margry, Les Navigations françaises. 1867.
[50] D'Avezac, Voyage du Capitaine de Gonneville. 1869.
[51] Carl Rau in the Archiv für Anthropologie, vol. iii.

lined basket-work with clay, may be inferred from the decorations of vessels of the stone age. These decorations consist merely of rows of marks made with the finger nail, as if to represent the traces left by the basket work.[52] When some bold individual began to shape the clay by hand, his earthen vessels were perhaps regarded as not genuine, or of inferior quality, as they had not originated in the time-honoured fashion ; in order to meet these doubts he may have counterfeited the impressions of the rushes with his nail. In South America even the Botocudos possess earthen vessels, as do all the natives with the exception of a few tribes of the Pampas.[53] Nor are they wanting among the Papuans ; but they do not exist among the Polynesians and Australians.

All races use their cutting implements to divide the meat into large pieces, in which operation barbarous nations generally exhibit great anatomical dexterity. Forks, which, as we shall see, were unknown in Northern Europe only a few centuries ago,[54] are, as a rule, found only in nations of mature civilization, but they are in use among the Papuans of the Fiji Islands.[55] The mussel shell suggested the first idea of the spoon, and still performs its functions on the Atlantic shores of Morocco.[56] On the White Nile the Bari negroes eat their meal porridge with wooden spoons, and the Kitsh negroes with the shells of fresh-water mussels.[57] In Southern Africa the Hottentots use spoons made of mother-of-pearl or of tortoiseshell ;[58] among the Bantu negroes these utensils are artistically carved out of wood and adorned with figures of animals.[59] Chop-sticks, after the Chinese fashion, and cooking spoons are in use among the Papuans of New Guinea.[60]

[52] G. Klemm, Allgemeine Culturgeschichte. 1843.

[53] D'Orbigny, l'Homme américain.

[54] Little is known about the use of forks in Europe. Tylor has ascertained that in Ruysbroek's time (1253) forks were in use among the Mongols as well as in the west. (Early History of Mankind, p. 22).

[55] Williams, Fiji, vol. i. p. 212.

[56] Gerhard Rohlfs, Erster Aufenthalt in Marokko. 1873.

[57] W. von Harnier, Reise am obern Nil.

[58] Kolben's Reise an das Vorgeb. d. G. Hoffnung.

[59] Casalis, Les Bassoutos. Paris, 1859.

[60] Otto Finsch, New Guinea, 1865 ; and Nieuw Guinea, ethnographisch en natuurkundig onderzocht, uitgegeven door hetv. Kon Institut vor taal-land-en volkenkunde. Amsterdam, 1862.

Alexander von Humboldt observes that the uncivilized natives of South America, who, like caterpillars, are restricted to one species of vegetable food, on a change of abode with difficulty accommodate themselves to any other diet, and generally sicken in consequence. The alternation of the seasons in temperate quarters of the world, he continues, enabled man to obtain, and accustomed him to digest, various substances, while at the same time he acquired greater freedom in the choice of his abode.[61] Hence the preparation of food gains great importance in ethnology : it is an interesting fact that at Tongataboo, one of the Friendly Islands, by skilful variation in the dressing, forty different dishes are prepared from the few indigenous edible plants.[62] Future observers ought always to note carefully whether the natives eat salt with their provisions. This is not done, for instance, by either the Papuans[63] or many Malay nations,[64] nor by the Hottentots in South Africa.[65] In the districts of the Soudan negroes there is no rock salt, but it is brought from the Sahara by caravans. The negroes living between the Gambia and the Niger suck pieces of salt as eagerly as our children suck sugar-plums. It is there said of rich people that they eat salt at their meals.[66] Zucchelli, the missionary, describes the process of evaporating sea-water in use among the natives on the coast of Congo ; but it is uncertain whether this mode of obtaining salt was in use before the settlement of the Portuguese.[67] In South America the nations of the coast of Brazil adopted this new article of food in imitation of Europeans, and very quickly recognized its value. The Patagonians consume a large quantity of salt which they procure without trouble from the natural brine-pits of their own country.[68] Even at the time of their discovery the people on the coast of the Caribbean Sea used salt as money in their commercial transactions. This salt was in the brick-like shape in which they

---

[61] Handschriften. Eigene Gedanken.　　[62] Quatrefages, Rapport.

[63] Otto Finsch, New Guinea.

[64] Waitz, Anthropologie, vol. v. p. 129.

[65] Kolbe, Reise an das Vorgeb. d. G. Hoffnung.

[66] Mungo Park, Reise ins Innere Afrika's. Berlin, 1799.

[67] Zucchelli, Relazioni del viaggio e missione di Congo. 1712.

[68] Musters in the Journal of the Anthrop. Institute, vol. i.

obtained it from the natural salt-pans on the peninsula of Araya.[69] Saltpetre procured from vegetable ashes is used as a substitute for salt on the Orinoco.[70] P. Charlevoix[71] expressly remarks that the Algonkin and Iroquois nations were not in the habit of salting their food. On the other hand, during de Soto's hazardous expeditions, the Indians of the present Southern States of North America were supplied with salt from the province of Cayas by native merchants.

III.—CLOTHING AND SHELTER.

WHEREVER European seafarers saw the inhabitants of newly discovered shores in a state of nudity, they at once concluded that these natives were in the lowest grade of human development. Nor is it only among highly civilized nations that a covering for the naked body is looked upon as the first step upwards from a so-called savage state. The missionary Williams relates that a shaman or priest of Somosomo, one of the Fiji Islands, who, like all his countrymen, was satisfied with a masi or scanty hip-cloth, on hearing a description of the naked inhabitants of New Caledonia and of their idols, exclaimed contemptuously, "Not have a masi and yet pretend to have gods!" But the more familiar we have become with foreign customs by means of thorough research, the more frequently have we found that nudity is not incompatible with modesty, and, above all, that in different nations modesty enjoins the veiling now of one, now of another portion of the body. Were a pious Mussulman of Ferghana to be present at our balls, and see the bare shoulders of our wives and daughters, and the semi-embraces of our round dances, he would silently wonder at the long-suffering of Allah, who had not long ago poured fire and brimstone on this sinful and shameless generation. Before the appearance of the Prophet the veiling of women was not customary in the East. Countess Pauline Nostiz abashed the ladies in the royal harem of Mascat by approaching them without

---

[69] Peter Martyr, De orbe novo, Dec. i. cap. 8.
[70] Gumilla, El Orinoco ilustrado. 1741. · [71] Nouvelle France.

a wire mask. There, not even the mother sees her daughter with uncovered face after the twelfth year, but, on the other hand, the transparent garments allow the body and limbs to be clearly seen.[1] Karsten Niebuhr says that women who, while bathing at Basra on the Euphrates and in a bath at Constantinople, were surprised by men covered their faces only.[2] Similarly the Fellaheen women in Egypt uncover themselves unabashed before men, provided that their faces remained veiled.[3] The Arab women, says George Ebers, will, without embarrassment, allow foot, leg, and bosom to be seen, but, on the other hand, it is reckoned even more indecorous to uncover the back of the head than the face, though even that is carefully concealed by every respectable woman.[4] The oldest Christian community were of a like opinion, for the apostle commanded women to veil their hair during their devotions.[5] Strangely enough the Hottentot women also wear a cloth like a cap upon their heads, and many cannot be induced to remove it.[6] In nations of the Malay race, modesty takes another form. The traveller Jagor told the author that while he was drawing a little naked girl at Samar, one of the Philippine Islands, the mother angrily interrupted them, and obliged the child to put on a shirt, of a length which, according to our notions of propriety, might as well have been dispensed with;[7] still it covered the most essential part according to the manners of the country, namely, the navel. Among the inhabitants of Navigators' Island also it is considered the greatest disgrace for this part of the body to be visible.[8] In China a woman is considered immodest if she shows her artificially distorted foot to a man; it is even improper to speak of it, and in decent pictures it is always concealed under the dress.[9] Longobard women also considered themselves mortally disgraced if men saw

---

[1] Joh. Wilh. Helfer's Reisen in Vorderasien und Indien. 1873.

[2] Reisebeschreibung nach Arabien. Kopenhagen, 1774.

[3] Waitz, Anthropologie, vol. i. p. 359.

[4] Durch Gosen zum Sinai. 1873.

[5] 1 Cor. xi. 5–6.   [6] Fritsch, Eingeborne Südafrika's.

[7] Representation of the child in Jagor's Reisen in den Philippinen.

[8] Waitz, Anthropologie, vol. i. p. 359.

[9] Wilh. Stricker im Archiv für Anthropologie. 1870.

their legs from the feet to the knees.[10] With these strange freaks of the sense of modesty we may compare the fact that we, on the contrary, regard uncovering as a token of respect. Thus we take off our hats as a salutation in the street, at church, and generally in every covered place. The English officials in India always require every native, of whatever caste, to lay aside their shoes before entering the audience chamber.

Thus habit and custom decide what is permissible and what is offensive, and not until an opinion has become established does any neglect of it become a reprehensible act. Nudity prevails among both sexes of the Australians, the Andaman islanders, sundry tribes on the White Nile, the red negroes of the Soudan, and the Bushmen, all of which tribes have as yet no sense of shame. The Guanches, or old inhabitants of the Canary Islands, those at least of Gomera and Palma, may be added to this list.[11] The inhabitants of the Bahama Islands, the Lesser Antilles, and a number of coast tribes in the present Venezuela and Guiana, to whom the name of Caribs is often incorrectly given, are described by their first discoverers, the Spaniards, as completely naked. In the time of Eschwege and Martius, the number of naked Brazilians, such as the Puris, Patachos, and Coroados was much greater than at present, when the Botocudos alone have not adopted any clothing.[12]

The supposition that the sense of modesty arises earlier in the female sex than in the male is entirely erroneous, for there are many races of which the men alone wear clothes. The missionaries on the Orinoco assured A. von Humboldt,[13] that the women show far less sense of modesty than the men. Among the Obbo negroes east of the outlet of Baker's great Nile lake, the only covering of the women is a bunch of leaves, whereas the men wear an apron of skins.[14] In the interesting kingdom of the Monbuttoo negroes, on the Uelle, the men wear a garment of bark

[10] Chron. Salernit, cited by Pertz, Monumenta. Hanover.

[11] Kunstmann, Afrika vor den Entdeckungen der Portugesien. 1853.

[12] As to the clothing of the Coroados at the present day, see Burmeister, Reise nach Brasilien. 1853.

[13] Reisen in die Aequinoctialgegenden. Stuttgart, 1860.

[14] Baker, Albert Nyanza, vol. i. p 273.

which reaches from the breast to the knees, while their wives merely fasten pieces of banana leaves no larger than the hand to their girdles.[15] Speke found that extreme strictness in the matter of decency of clothing prevailed at the court of Mtesa, King of Uganda. Although the apprehensions of his friend Rumanika were unfounded, that admission to this country would be denied to him and Grant because they wore trousers only and not flowing garments after the Arab fashion, it afterwards transpired that the king punished with death every man who appeared in his presence with only an inch of his leg uncovered, while at the same time the service of the house was performed by completely naked women.[16] The Arabian traveller, Ibn Batoutah, declares that it is only when unclothed that women, even if they are princesses, may approach the king of the Mandingo state of Melli.[17] Livingstone was received by the Queen of the Balonde negroes, in South Africa, when she was in a state of complete nudity, and the women of the neighbouring Kissama negroes appear in the same condition on festive occasions.[18] In half-clothed races the covering is assumed only on reaching adolescence, and it is an exceptional case, which moreover requires confirmation, if it is true that the Australian women go naked only after their marriage.[19]

Fair-skinned nations feel the need of clothing far more keenly than dark ones. The Africans are fully conscious of the advantages of their dark skin.[20] We remember reading a statement of Adolf Bastian, that when he was bathing near some brown-skinned Asiatics, his own white skin appeared to him abnormal and by no means beautiful. Von Maltzan also says "Nudity was never displeasing to me if the skin was black, but in fair people it is always repulsive."[21] In like manner, F. Jagor describes his coachman at Singapore, a black Kling from the coast of Coromandel, whose

---

[15] G. Schweinfurth, The Heart of Africa, vol. ii. p. 110.

[16] Speke, Sources of the Nile, vol. i. p. 262.

[17] Voyage d'Ibn Batoutah. Paris, 1858.

[18] Livingstone, Missionary Journeys, vol. i. p. 315. Hamilton, in the Journal of the Anthropological Institute, vol. i.

[19] Dumont d'Urville, Voyage de l'Astrolabe. 1830.

[20] Darwin, Descent of Man, vol. ii. pp. 381, 382.

[21] Globus. 1872.

dress consisted simply of a turban and a waistcloth, adding significantly, he did not look indecent, for dark colour almost removes the impression of nudity.[22] By the majority of American Indians clothes are replaced by skin painting. Where this is the case, shame is felt by women and men if they are seen unpainted. A. von Humboldt, to whom we owe this observation, adds that on the Orinoco the extreme of poverty is expressed by saying, " The man is so wretched that he cannot paint his half body." [23] Tattooing, which is another substitute for raiment, consists of drawings on the body, produced either by the injection of coloured pigments under the skin, or by the artificial formation of raised scars. That it actually takes away from the impression of nudity is declared by all who have seen fully tattooed Albanese. Tattooing may still be seen in every quarter of the world with the exception of Europe. In the South Sea Islands it not only serves as ornament where it extends to covered portions of the body, and where the etched drawings represent emblems of the deities, but has a religious signification.

That clothing frequently serves only for personal adornment or is worn as a protection from cold, is proved by the case of the well-clad Maori of New Zealand, who have no notion of decency.[24] This applies to the highly civilized Japanese, among whom the bathing of both sexes in common, in enclosed areas as well as in the open air, has only recently been prohibited by the authorities.[25] The Eskimo, who in the winter are enveloped to the face in furs, nevertheless, according to Kane's strongly expressed description, completely lay aside their garments in their subterranean dwellings, and the demeanour of the wife of Hans the Eskimo, on board Hayes's ship, plainly shows that she had no idea of decency. G. G. Winkler[26] found that even the Christian and thoroughly conventional population of Iceland had not yet arrived at the perception which the scriptural parents of the human species had already acquired in the Garden of Eden.

These facts ought to render us extremely cautious in estimating

[22] Reiseskizzen.   [23] Reisen in den Aequinoctialgegenden.
[24] Waitz, Anthropologie, vol. i. p. 357.
[25] Wilhelm Heine, Japan.   [26] Iceland, p. 107.

the moral worth of a people by its standard of bodily covering. But although, as we have shown, chastity and morality are quite independent of the absence or vividness of sexual modesty, yet in every nation, the awakening of this latter feeling is a mark of progress. Before the idea of covering himself dawned on any human being, he must have discriminated between the beautiful and the ugly. For clothing we are therefore indebted to the earliest æsthetic emotions experienced by the human species, and in so far as reverence for the beautiful has an ennobling effect upon us, these emotions promoted the education of mankind. Correlatively with the decline of rigid morals at ancient Rome, arose a contempt for the maxims of propriety. The desire for clothing is first awakened by the consciousness of a higher dignity, which urges man to endeavour to increase the separation between himself and animals. It is not mere vanity endeavouring, it may be, to hide the loss of youthful charms, for at a much earlier period a wish is felt to throw a veil over, so to speak, unmerited degradations imposed upon us by the constitution of our animal body, and the desire arises to appear before others as if we were as pure and pleasant to the sight as the lilies of the Gospel. Notwithstanding all the strange freaks of the sense of modesty which we have just recounted, the majority of people have known exactly what most required covering. The sensitiveness of the women of ancient Lydia is known from the narrative of the wife of Candaules, as given by Herodotus;[27] and how carefully the modesty of the female sex is guarded by the Mandanas in North America, is told by Catlin.[28] Among the semi-Papuan inhabitants of the Palawan Islands, the women have an unlimited privilege of striking, fining, or, if it be done on the spot, killing every man who makes his way into their bathing-places.[29]

We find traces of clothing as far back as the so-called reindeer period of Europe. Bone needles were discovered in the caves of Périgord; and a similar discovery in the stratum of relics of civilization in the source of the Schussen, shows that the inhabitants of Suabia knew how to sew even in the glacial period. But in both

---

[27] Lib. i. cap. 8–12.   [28] Die Indianer Nordamerika's.
[29] Karl Semper, Die Palauinseln.   1873.

cases, the occurrence of lumps of vermilion pigment points to the co-existence of skin painting.

The material of clothing always depended on the food of each race. Thus among hunters and shepherds the skins of slaughtered animals were used. But it is instructive to notice that human invention has devised the same expedients in widely distant places, as we have already shown. The simplest form of dress consists of leaves or twigs stuck into a girdle. In other places reeds or rushes are strung upon the girdle as is done by the Papuan women of New Guinea and the Pelew Islands. As it was necessary to renew these rushes too frequently, they were replaced by bands of bass or strips of leather ; this was the origin of the fringed girdle worn by the females of the Mohave tribes and their neighbours on the Colorado in North America, by the Fijians in the South Sea, where it is called Liku, by the New Caledonians, and the Kaffirs. The Tapa is exclusively Polynesian; this, as is well known, is the bark of the paper mulberry tree (*Broussonetia papyrifera*) beaten to make it soft. Where refinement had begun and higher pretensions had arisen, the plaiting of baskets and mats led to weaving. When the Polynesian Maori migrated to New Zealand they brought with them the secret of the manufacture of mats. In their new abode they found an excellent fibrous material in the leafy tufts of the *Phormium tenax*, or New Zealand flax, and they invented for themselves the art of preparing and manufacturing a sort of linen. The use of cotton has been discovered in both worlds, for the natives of America independently discovered the process of twisting the threads which they found at home, and of converting these threads into a tissue. Cotton was also indigenous in ancient Egypt and was woven into stuffs.[30] Still the preference for linen. kept it completely in the background. Cotton was naturalized from the earliest ages even in Syria. The English word *cotton* is derived from *keton* which, with small variations in the vowels, signifies cotton in all Semitic languages, and is still *kutn* in modern Arabic.[31] Phœnician

---

[30] G. Ebers, Durch Gosen zum Sinai.

[31] H. Brandes, Antike Namen der Baumwolle. 5th Jahrsbericht der Ver. für Erdkunde. Leipzic, 1866.

9

sailors therefore conveyed not linen but cotton fabrics under the name of *Kitonet*, or *Ketonet*, to the Grecian ports, and from this term arose words such as χιτών and κιθών. The word *linum* (flax) originally vaguely used in Latin and Greek, passed, with little alteration from its Latin form, to the Basque, Celtic, and Germanic languages [32] and thus appears to have spread from South-eastern to Northern and Western Europe. If spindle wheels have been found in the Danish middens, and if the weaver's bench already stood in the lake dwellings of Switzerland,[33] the art of spinning and weaving must have originated at an age so remote that it can no longer be decided which tribe or which race was the first discoverer. Hemp is certainly an acquisition for which civilization is indebted to the so-called barbarous nations. The cultivation of hemp was found by Herodotus even among the Medo-Persic Scyths.[34]

A. Bacmeister confidently maintained that *Hemd*, *Hut*, *Haube*, *Schuhe*, *Rock*, and *Hosen* (shirt, hat, cap, shoes, coat, trousers), are primordial words in the German language.[35] It is noteworthy that the use of trousers first spread from Northern Europe to the classical shores of the Mediterranean and then over the whole world. But even this article of dress has been invented in various places. All Northern Asiatics wear trousers, and have worn them in the most remote ages of which we have any knowledge. Even if we suppose that in their emigration to America the Eskimo brought this novelty with them from their western home, we yet find the same garment in use among the Red Indians in the northern parts of the New World. The American aborigines had one small advantage over the old civilized nations, in that they were already in the habit of manufacturing an excellent covering for the foot; these were not sandals, but half-boots or mocassins. It is remarkable that the Patagonians, in the extreme south of the New World, also use mocassins, whereas they are unknown in Central America and the other parts of South

---

[32] Von Hehn, Kulturpflanzen und Hausthiere.

[33] See above, and Wilhelm Baer, Der vorgeschichtliche Mensch.

[34] Lib. iv. cap. 74.

[35] *Ausland*, 1871. *Hemd* is certainly derived from ἱμάτιον.

America. It was among the barbarians that the Romans first saw shoes; the idols of the old Egyptians are also barefooted. Shoes and sandals were also entirely wanting in Babylon, where, however, to judge from the cylindrical seal of King Uruch (2326 B.C.), great luxury in dress must have been customary.[36] Barefooted nations are still everywhere to be found in low latitudes, whereas in regions of perpetual snow, where it freezes, or where the ground is greatly chilled by radiation, the necessity of protection for the feet must soon suggest itself. In Africa, sandals are used by the Mandingo negroes of Musardo,[37] and, strange to say, by the otherwise naked Bari negroes of the White Nile,[38] the Kissama in Angola,[39] the Kaffirs[40] as well as by other Bantu negroes, and by the Hottentots.[41]

As many animals, and even inferior animals, provide themselves with an artificial protection against the vicissitudes of the weather, and no race of mankind has been found without a shelter of some sort, the instinct of building must be as old as our race itself. It is in caves that we meet with the first traces of our ancestors, but we must not therefore infer that these natural refuges, which exist moreover only in rocky districts and especially in calcareous mountains, were the earliest dwelling-places of man, or first suggested the idea of constructing artificial shelter. When the Bushmen are away from their caves during their excursions, they cover themselves with sand whenever they spend the night in the open air, or weave a shelter of branches and brushwood for themselves in the thicket. In the temperate season the Australians shelter themselves from the wind by screens of foliage, but at other times they stretch pieces of bark, often 12 feet in length, and from 8 to 10 feet wide, over a dome-shaped framework something like a tent.[42] A similar summer tent of birch

---

[36] G. Rawlinson, Great Monarchies, vol. i. p. 107.

[37] Anderson's Journey to Musardo, in the Transactions of the Geographical Society of Vienna. 1871.

[38] W. von Harnier's Reisen am obern Nil.

[39] Hamilton, Journal of the Anthropological Institute, vol. i.

[40] G. Fritsch, Eingeborne Südafrika's.

[41] Kolbe, Kap der Guten Hoffnung.

[42] Dumont d'Urville, Voyage de l'Astrolabe.

bark sewn together, is sufficient for the Ostiaks of Siberia. [43] Charlevoix, the Jesuit, describes the shelter of many hunting tribes in Canada as being but little superior. [44]

In the extreme north of the Old and New World, beyond the limit of trees, or where the stems of the trees are not of the requisite thickness, and also on the treeless steppes, bark walls are replaced by hides of animals. Thus the leathern tent of Lapland [45] is used throughout Siberia and as far as the prairies of the United States to the 35th degree of latitude. [46] It disappears in Equatorial and Southern America only to reappear among the Patagonians, who cover a framework of stakes with the hides of the Guanaco sewn together. [47] The felt tent, an invention of the Ural-Altaic nations, is doubtless of high antiquity. From Central Asia it has spread in the direction of the monsoon, and within the zone of the trade winds, over the Sahara, and to the wooded districts of Central Africa, but it is transformed on the way into an airy tent of a woven fabric, and rendered architectural in the Arabian style with its domes and slender shafts, the latter of which are represented by the tent-poles.

In the lofty forests of tropical America the itinerant hunting tribes are sheltered from the rain by a sloping roof of the oar-shaped leaves of palms and other trees, laid like scales one above the other. When nations finally become stationary they are at first satisfied with a quadrangular or circular framework of poles, bound together with basket-work or strips of bark. A pointed or dome-shaped roof covered with leaves, tufts of grass, or bundles of rushes, completes the simplest form of hut. Whole tribes frequently live in a single cloister-like structure, within which a cell is allotted to each family. Dumont d'Urville describes two such buildings of the Arfaki of New Guinea, which together accommodated 150 people, and on the Utanete river in the same region

---

[43] Pallas, Voyages. Paris, 1793.

[44] Nouvelle France.

[45] See the representation of Lapp summer tents given by J. A. Frijs in the Globus. 1873.

[46] Möllhausen, vom Mississipi nach der Südsee.

[47] Musters, Journal of the Anthropological Institute, vol. i. p. 197.

there are similar structures.[48]   At Borneo, Spenser St. John saw a Dyak building 534 feet in length.[49]   Similar rows of cells are also customary among the Ostiaks,[50] but the most extensive of these wooden structures are inhabited by the Haidahs on Queen Charlotte's Island in North America, and by the Colquiths on Vancouver's Island, for they accommodate from two to three hundred people, and in Nootka Sound even eight hundred.[51]   The bark huts of the Indians in the east of the present United States, as described by Charlevoix, are not so thickly populated, but yet contain several families.[52]   Even in South America such common dwellings occur. Wallace found them on the Uaupés (Rio Negro) among the tribe of the same name, as far as latitude 75° and longitude 115°.[53]

In Australia and the South Seas plastic earth is never used to thicken wicker walls. Building with sun-dried bricks or adobes is peculiar to the dry highlands and lowlands of New Mexico, Mexico, and Central America, while Central Africa again has its earthen huts, the walls of which are formed of stamped clay, on which a straw roof is placed. Stone architecture at first attempted only the humblest undertakings, for the difficulty of erecting perpendicular walls with mere fragments of stone was insuperable. In Central America, as in Mesopotamia, ancient temple structures consisted of pyramids in steps. The earliest attempts at such works of art may have resembled the simple terraces, or Morai, of the Polynesian Islands, but they attained their fullest development in the smooth Pyramids of Egypt. It was in dry, treeless regions that the inhabitants were first compelled to build walls, by the necessity of finding a substitute to replace the beams which could not be procured. Architecture is therefore nearly four thousand years older in Egypt than in India, where the earliest works of the kind were the rock temples, in which, however, the roofs were supported by trunks of iron-wood (Sideroxylon), while according to Fergusson's researches, self-supporting stone structures were

---

[48] Otto Finsch, New Guinea.   [49] Life in the far East.

[50] Pallas, Voyages.   Paris, 1793.

[51] Waitz, Anthropologie, vol. iii. p. 332.

[52] Nouvelle France.

[53] Martius, Ethnographie.

only introduced under King Asoka, in the middle of the third century before Christ. To pierce the walls for light and air, as well as afford access to the inhabitants themselves, was a severe problem to human ingenuity. This was at last done by placing the stones so as to project one beyond the other, like inverted steps, until the highest stones approached each other so nearly that the aperture could be bridged over by a broad stone laid transversely on the top. The temple gates, which are wider at the sill than at the top, show that the art among the Egyptians and Greeks must for a time have remained stationary at this point, for even when, at a later period, the art of stone-masonry had so far advanced that it was possible to construct rectangular entrances, the primitive form was retained either from old affection or artistic taste. In ancient Babylon spurious vaults converging obliquely, and false arches, were made in like manner, namely, by projecting layers of bricks.[54]

These timid attempts serve to make us recognize the full merit of the invention of the stone self-supporting arch. In the Old World the Assyrians were probably the first to adopt this expedient, and the Romans the first to advance from the construction of door and window arches to that of vaults and domes. To justify this digression into the history of art, we need only state that these facts are of importance in estimating the intellectual rank of American peoples. On the Puna, the plateaux of the Cordilleras, we find stone huts and stone tombs[55] in the district of Inca-Peruvian civilization. Humboldt[56] made sketches of arched vaults in the Palace of the Ataohuallpa, at Caxamarca, while further to the south, vaulted buildings and round arches at Tiahuanaco, as well as in the Temple of the Sun at Cuzco, have also been described by Desjardins and J. J. von Tschudi.[57]

No small credit is due to the Eskimo for the tunnel-like stone

---

[54] Rawlinson, Monarchies of the Ancient World, vol. i. p. 86.

[55] Clement Markham, Proceedings of the Royal Geogr. Society, vol. xv. 1871.

[56] Alexander von Humboldt, Eine wissenschaftliche Biographie, ed. Karl Bruhns. 1872.

[57] F. von Hellwald im Ausland, No. 41. 1871.

vaulting of the entrances to their huts, and of the huts themselves.[58]   The idea suggested itself more readily to them than to
the denizens of more temperate zones, for they had long been in
the habit of piling up snow grottoes, and of constructing domed
huts with blocks of snow.[59]

IV.—WEAPONS.

IF we follow the course of any of the old Spanish, Dutch, or
English discoverers who preceded Captain Cook on a voyage across
the South Seas, we are greatly puzzled if we attempt to assign the
names accepted in modern geography to any of the islands which
they saw.   Even if the calculations of latitude are correct within
half a degree, the error of the longitude given may on the other
hand increase twentyfold, so that we must search about among
countless islands which all look alike, for they are either mere coral
reefs, or are recent or ancient volcanoes.   Our task would thus be
hopeless were we not able to ascertain the longitude by two indications.   When the discoverer sailing westwards describes nations
with crowns of hair, this must be close to the 180th meridian of
Greenwich, for the twin islands, Hoorne and Alofa, are the most
easterly points reached by the Papuans, to whom this character
exclusively belongs.   Again, when we read that the traveller was
greeted by the natives on land or water with volleys of arrows, we
may conclude that this was in the neighbourhood of New Guinea.

The Polynesian races of the South Seas have never opposed
Europeans by means of bows and arrows, and, strange as it may
sound, the reason of their not doing so is purely geological.   If
any one attempted to explain this circumstance by stating that the
Polynesians, like other Malay nations, were unacquainted with
these missiles, because the bow was not invented when they
abandoned Southern Asia for their homes in the Pacific, we should
tell him that the bow and arrow is a boy's plaything on
Nukufetaw, in the Ellice group, and even much further east, at

---

[58] Waitz, Anthropologie, vol. iii. p. 306.
[59] Chas. F. Hall, Life with the Esquimaux, p. 461.

Tahiti.[1]   These missiles were known to the Malay Polynesians at the commencement of their migrations, and it was only at a later period that they fell into disuse.   It is just the same with the Papuans, in whose original home, New Guinea, bows and arrows are never laid aside by the men, although these weapons are totally wanting among the kindred inhabitants of New Caledonia. On the other hand, the Fijians, a race with crowns of hair, like those of the Papuans of New Guinea, certainly brought bows and arrows to their island, but they now use them only for throwing burning missiles into fortified places, or they leave them to the women who are thus able to assist in the defence of their stockades.   The favourite weapons of the men are the club and the spear.[2]   The Tongans relearned to use bows and arrows from their neighbours on the Fiji Islands.[3]

It is easy to see why bows and arrows were forgotten on the South Sea Islands.   The management of these weapons requires great skill and constant practice.   Where they are in use among savage nations, travellers inform us that even the boys practise shooting with miniature implements.   In the hands of an expert, the bow is far more effective in the chase than our fire-arms, for it kills in silence.   An arrow which has missed its mark falls unobserved, so that the marksman can aim two or three missiles without alarming the game.   We need not wonder therefore that the traveller Marcou met hunters in New Mexico, with white skin, and of Spanish descent, who had laid aside their guns and taken to the Indian weapons, which they considered better adapted for the chase.[4]   As a further confirmation, Reinhold Hensel records that the Coroados of Brazil refused to exchange their bows and arrows for fire-arms, as, on account of their noisy report, their weight, the loss of time in loading, and the difficulty of procuring ammunition, the latter were ill suited for hunting in tropical forests.[5]

But excellence in the use of this instrument requires incessant practice, a condition which among savage nations will only be ful-

---

[1] Waitz, Anthropologie der Naturvölker.
[2] Thomas Williams, Fiji and the Fijians.
[3] Mariner, Tonga Islands.   Edinburgh, 1827.
[4] Lartet and Christy, Reliquiae Aquitanicae.
[5] Zeitschrift für Ethnologie.   1869.

filled by those who live on the produce of the chase. The first rude implements of man originally served all purposes. The hunter seized his missiles to repel an enemy ; and the stone axe of the savage, which felled the tree, also split the skull of an opponent in the fray. Hence, the oldest, the truest, and the noblest implement of war is the sword, which can never have been used indifferently for war and handicraft.[6] We may here observe that, so far as we yet know, the invention of swords in Europe dates only from the bronze age, whereas we shall presently find a case in another part of the world in which there were swords elsewhere, even in the stone age.

Bows and arrows necessarily disappear entirely wherever the chase is no longer a means of livelihood, or where hunting is impossible. As we pass in an easterly, northerly, or south-easterly direction from New Guinea, hunting ceases, for, with the exception of bats, tame pigs, dogs, and rats, all the islands are destitute of mammals. Hence the interest excited some years ago by the discovery by Haast of a wild mammal, although an aquatic one, namely, an otter, on the southern island of New Zealand. That there should be no mammalia on these islands is simply accounted for by their origin ; for coral islands arise only where polyps build up wall-like reefs of their calcareous branches on the shallow surfaces of submerged continents. The only other islands are volcanic structures, originally formed below the sea, and then gradually upheaved above the surface by eruptions. These islands, New Zealand included, have never, at least since the tertiary period, been connected with any continent, so that no mammals incapable of flying or swimming were able to reach them. Hence it is that the disappearance of bows and arrows is due to their geological origin.

That this is the true and ultimate reason is substantiated in another locality. In the West Indies we have before us, not small and narrow coral structures, but large areas, such as Cuba, Haïti, Jamaica, and Porto Rico. But, with the exception of Cuba, even these spacious islands were destitute of any large mammals ; for, at the time of the Spaniards' arrival, there were, besides bats, only

---

[6] *i.e.,* the sword of the bronze age, which was intended for striking only.

five species of small rodents, of which the largest was but slightly bigger than a rat. These islands, the remains of larger tracts of country, must have lost their connection with the nearest continent, which is South America, in the early part of the tertiary period. North America was at that time far more distant; for the peninsula of Florida is a recent and still incomplete creation of the coral animal. As hunting was impossible on these islands, the inhabitants did not use bows and arrows, though all the tribes of the adjacent continent carry these weapons. For the sake of accuracy it must be added that, on the Antilles, on the eastern shore of Haiti, the eastern half of Porto Rico, and in the Windward Islands, there were people who wielded these weapons with dexterity. But these were new-comers, the Caribs, who, being better sailors than any other American tribes, invaded the peaceful inhabitants of the Antilles in their own abode, slew the men, and carried off the women as captives, from which circumstances there arose among them separate languages for men and women, unless we accept the other explanation, that, as among the Kaffirs, husband and wife speak different languages, because the wife may suffer no word to pass her lips which occurs in the name of any man allied to her by marriage. As these Caribs came from the continent, where they lived on the produce of the chase, we can easily understand that when they spread to the Antilles they had not completely laid aside the bow and arrow.

The blow pipe is another characteristic weapon for shooting, which is used by the Malay tribes in Borneo, and also on the continent of Asia by the Malayo-Chinese Laoti on the Mekong, as well as by the Orang-kubits [7] and the Semangs of the peninsula of Malacca.[8] The Papuans of New Guinea may also have borrowed it from the Malays.[9] But the blow pipe was not invented in South-eastern Asia only, for we find it also in the hands of the Indians on the Amazon, whose aim is certain at a distance of 250 feet.[10] The blow pipe has the same advantage over other weapons as a breechloader has, and a practised hand can despatch

---

[7] Peschel, Zeitalter der Entdeckungen.

[8] Mouat, Travels in Indo-China, Cambodia, and Laos. 1864. F. Jagor, Singapore, Malacca, Java. Berlin, 1866.

[9] Waitz (Gerland) Anthropologie, vol. vi. p. 599.   [10] Martius, Ethnographie.

several projectiles in the space of a minute. The small slender darts escape the notice of the victim still more easily than the arrow, and the marksman may continue to fire his missiles from his concealment until the object is struck. As the projectile force is derived from the muscles of the thorax, the strength of the percussion is very slight. To produce a deadly effect it is therefore requisite for the dart to be poisoned. Hence the poison itself is the weapon and the missile merely the vehicle. On the Malay islands this purpose is served by the Ipo, or the juice of the upas tree (*Antiaris toxicaria*), which produces very malignant but rarely mortal wounds. At least Dr. Mohnike maintains that a considerable number of arrows are required to produce tetanic rigidity in an old orang-outang.[11] On the other hand Spenser St. John asserts that in a conflict in Borneo with the Kanowit Dyaks, in 1859, the English lost thirty of their men by small and scarcely perceptible wounds made by the poisoned darts;[12] and Lieutenant Crespigny saw a native of Borneo die in two hours after being wounded in this way in the calf of the leg and in the shoulder.[13] Similar effects were produced by a poisonous unguent used by the warlike and bloodthirsty inhabitants of the shores of the Caribbean Sea. According to the accounts of the old Spanish navigators, the death of the wounded took place somewhat tardily, amid delirium and agonies of suffering, frequently only after the lapse of twenty-four hours. They state that the poison was made of the juice of the manchineel tree (*Hippomane mancinella*), mixed with snakes' poison;[14] but their assertions are all very obscure and questionable.

We are better informed as to the most terrible of all poisons. namely, the urari, curaré, or woorali, of the Indians of the river Amazon[15] and of Guyana. Neither Lacondamine nor Spix and

---

[11] Ausland, vol. xlv. 1872.   [12] Far East, vol i. p. 46.

[13] Proceedings of the Royal Geographical Society, vol. xvi. 1872.

[14] Oviedo, Historia general y natural de las Indias, lib. xxvii. cap. 3.

[15] This dreaded poison is prepared on the river Amazon by the tribes living near the sources of its northern affluent, between Rio Negro and Japura (Bates, The Naturalist on the Amazon, vol. ii. p. 238. London, 1863). The Indians on the Napo river procure the urari from the Tecunas; and the return voyage of the boats occupies no less than three months. In their own country the poison is weighed against silver (James Orton, The Andes and the Amazon. 1870.)

Martius witnessed the preparation of this arrow poison. Alexander von Humboldt was the first to penetrate into a manufactory of this poison on the Orinoco, and bring samples of curaré back to Europe. But it was the younger Schomburgh at Pirará who first assisted at the preparation of the unguent.[16] The urari, as he calls it, was made of various vegetable substances, but the actual poison is the bark and alburnum of the *Strychnos toxifera.* In small warm-blooded animals the smallest wound is followed by instant death, and even larger animals stagger and collapse. Humboldt even declares that the earth-eating Otomaks kill their antagonists by the pressure of their poisoned thumb nails.[17] Samples of urari, or curaré, were brought to Paris about ten years ago, and were there employed in experiments by the celebrated physiologist, Claude Bernard.[18] It then became apparent that the poison operates only if it is able to mingle with the blood. The cessation of nervous power in muscular movements then commences, but ultimately the action of lungs and heart is stopped, and death results quite painlessly from the greatest conceivable degree of lassitude, like the stopping of a pendulum when the clockwork has run down. When the poison is fresh even animals as large as the tapir collapse after a few steps.

The practice of poisoning missiles is also common in Africa, According to the records of the Portuguese discoverers, the Jolofers in Guinea, as well as the negroes of Rio Grande, formerly poisoned their arrows.[19] The Mandingo negroes did the same in the days of Mungo Park,[20] and, according to Benjamin Anderson, it is even now done by the Mandingoes at Musardo.[21] On the White Nile the Moro negroes, who live near 5° north latitude,[22] as well as the Bari negroes, are said to anoint their arrows with the poison of snakes or plants.[23] Du Chaillu says that the Fan

---

[16] Richard Schomburgh, Reisen in Guayana. 1847.

[17] Ansichten der Natur.

[18] Revue des Deux Mondes. 1864.

[19] Peschel, Zeitalter der Entdeckungen.

[20] Mungo Park, Reisen im innern von Afrika. Berlin, 1799.

[21] Globus, vol. xx. 1871.

[22] Petherick, Central Africa. 1869.

[23] W. von Harnier Reise am obern Nil.

negroes in South Africa do the same.[24] Ladislaus Magyar[25] relates that the southern neighbours of the Kimbunda in Bihé, poison the points of their spears. Livingstone speaks of kombi, a poison made from a species of Strophanthus by the people living on the Shiré, and of another arrow poison used on Lake Nyassa; he also states that the Bushmen of Kalahari procure a poison for their missiles from the entrails of a small caterpillar named Nga.[26] Theophilus Hahn, on the other hand, asserts that the Bushmen obtain the poison for their arrows used for hunting from the bulbs of *Hæmanthus toxicarius;* but for their weapons of war from the poison glands of snakes and the juice of a kind of spurge (*Euphorbia candelabrum*).[27] Kolbe saw Hottentots anoint their arrows with the poison of the hooded snake.[28] Pliny speaks of the Arabian pirates in troglodyte Africa, that is to say, on the southern shores of the Red Sea, as poisoners of arrows. Another Arabic race, the Bhortans of the Himalayas, completes the list.[29]

The nations enumerated are all within the tropical, or at least within the subtropical, zone. The whole of North America is free from this evil practice, which, according to Moritz Wagner, has its most northerly limit in the New World at the Isthmus of Darien, and at Choco on the Atrato.[30] The single exception yet known to us is the case of the Ceres, or Seris, of the Bay of California, who make use of these hateful weapons.[31] The use of the blow pipe in South America has been already noticed; we will now only add, on the authority of Dobrizhoffer, that the Chiquitos in Paraguay anointed their darts with a poison so fatal that, if the least blood was shed, the smallest injury produced death in the course of a few hours.

But it would be a mistake to suppose that this means of inflict-

---

[24] Explorations and Adventures in Equatorial Africa. 1861.

[25] Reisen.

[26] Livingstone, Zambesi, p. 466. A representation of this larva is given in Wood's Natural History of Man.

[27] Th. Hahn in the Globus. 1870. G. Fritsch, Eingeborne Südafrika's.

[28] Vollständ, Beschreibung des Vorgebirges der guten Hoffnung. 1719.

[29] H. von Schlagintweit, Indien und Hochasien.

[30] Naturwissenschaftliche Reisen. 1869.

[31] Waitz, Anthropologie der Naturvölker.

ing death is peculiar to sultry or warm regions. Chinese writers mention the poisoning of weapons as practised by a Tungus tribe in the third century A.D., and by the Mongols in the fifth century.[32] Even now it is practised by the bearded Aino [33] at Saghalia and the Kuriles; in Steller's time the Itelmes of Kamtshatka used monkshood (*Aconitum napellus*)[34] for the same purpose, and even the inhabitants of the Aleutian Islands knew and used a poison for their darts.[35]

We read of these treacherous instruments of death in classical antiquity. Horace mentions them in his odes.[36] Ovid accuses the Pontic nations in the vicinity of his place of exile of the practice of this crime.[37] Pliny gives an antidote for poisoned wounds, and blames the depth to which human nature has descended in adding the effects of a serpent's bite to the sharpness of iron.[38] Even the Celts of Gaul made occasional use of this expedient,[39] as did the Saracens in the war of Granada in 1484.[40]

This custom had therefore spread through every region of the world, with the exceptions of Australia and the Polynesian Islands, where bows and arrows do not exist. We have dwelt longer than usual on this subject, which we were the first to review,[41] because the suppression of this crime affords one of the rare instances in which man's social instinct has not only raised the level of his morality, but has induced him to strive towards still further improvement; for the crude impulse of self-preservation would certainly warrant the use of poisoned weapons. A passage in Homer shows that some nations even then began to be ashamed of such unworthy means of defence. Odysseus wants to purchase a deadly arrow-poison from Ilos at Ephyra, who, however, refuses it to him from fear of the eternal gods.[42]

---

[32] Alex. Castrèn, Ethnol. Vorlesungen, p. 26.

[33] Herr von Brandt, Berlin Anthropological Society's Transactions. 1872.

[34] Kamtschatka. 1774.

[35] Waitz, Anthropologie, vol. iii. p. 316. [36] Lib. i. 22.

[37] Tristium, lib. iii. Eleg. x. v. 62. [38] Hist. nat. lib. xx. 81.

[39] Forbiger, Handbuch der alten Geographie.

[40] Hernando de Pulgar, Cronica. Valencia, 1780.

[41] Ausland. On the Influence of Local Conditions on some Weapons. 1870.

[42] Odyss. I. 260. Ephyra must be either in Epirus, or in some island of the Argolic bay.

The reason of this refusal suggests why poisoned arrows are used only in the tropics and their vicinity, for the barbarous races of those parts are not troubled about the wrath of the eternal gods.

Another projectile apparatus, the sling, can occur only where there are stones, which are not everywhere to be found. The Amazon and its huge tributaries pass at once from the slopes of the Cordilleras through a flat table-like plain, with a scarcely perceptible fall, throughout which no shingle is to be found, for a fathom of loam covers the finely triturated clay or marl.[43] If all parts of the world had resembled these South American plains, mankind could never have advanced to the stone age, but must have remained at a stage of wood and horn. It is obvious that slings could not be used in the forest country of the Amazon. In North America we find slings only among the Eskimo. They are very common, on the contrary, in the South Sea Islands, among the inhabitants of the Marianne Islands,[44] on the Samoa group,[45] in Tahiti and the Sandwich Islands.[46] The Papuans of the Fiji group and New Caledonia use them.[47] On these islands the sling was also habitually used to knock cocoa-nuts down from the trees. It is less evident why the Guanches, the extinct inhabitants of the Canary islands, employed this weapon; it may be that they brought their slings from their earlier home in Northern Africa. The best slingers of classical times were also islanders, from the Balearic group.[48] The sling does not occur in the Soudan, or only rarely, but it is very common among the nations of biblical history. Among the Hebrews the slingers of the tribe of Benjamin were famed for fighting with either hand, and could sling stones at a hair's breadth and not miss.[49] It was by slinging a stone against a gigantic Philistine that the royal dynasty was founded in Judah. Stony pastures,

---

[43] Ed. Pöppig, Chile, Peru und der Amazonenstrom.

[44] Waitz, Anthropologie, vol. v. p. 30.

[45] Fr. Müller, Reise der Fregatte Novara; Anthropologie, vol. iii. p. 39.

[46] Heinr. Zimmermann, Reise um die Welt mit Capt. Cook. 1781.

[47] F. Knoblauch. Ausland, 1866.

[48] Forbiger, Handbuch der alten Geographie.

[49] Judges xx. 15, 16.

such as extend throughout Palestine, provoke practice with the sling, especially as all shepherds are in the habit of throwing, partly for the defence of their animals, and partly to punish either their dogs or stray members of the flock. Adolph von Wrede saw formal practices in shooting at a mark, and throwing stones, among the Bedouins of Hadhramaut in Arabia.[50] The sling has become a national and favourite weapon in South America. While the hunting tribes of the wooded plains to the east of the Andes are armed only with the bow, the sling is used both for the chase and for war in the land of the Incas, by the civilized Quichua and Aymara nations, on the treeless plateau of the Cordilleras called the Puna. All the nations of the South American Andes use the sling as far southwards as Cape Horn, where the Fuegians use it in hunting the llama or, rather, the guanaco. The Patagonians of the steppes in the south and west of the Argentine Republic are allied by race to the nations of the Andes. Here slings, and the art of using them, have reached their highest development. The stones, which are rounded and held by a leather band, are swung above the head. This is the origin of the bolas, a casting-line with balls.[51] In the course of time the casting-line was even used without any stone; the Gauchos, or half-bred shepherds of the Argentines, still fling their lasso with such dexterity that they use it for defence in preference to a gun.[52] The ordinary sling was superseded by the line and balls in ancient Egypt. In the hunting scenes depicted on the monuments, is a huntsman of the age of the Pharaohs whirling a line with balls round the hind legs of a buffalo.[53] It need not be rashly inferred from this that the Patagonians are descended from the ancient Egyptians, or that Egyptians straying from the Phœnician fleet which sailed round Africa under Pharaoh Nika had perhaps reached South America.

[50] Wrede's Reisen im Hadhramaut.

[51] On the use of the bolas among the Quichua nations in Peru, comp. Markham, Proceedings of the Royal Geographical Society vol. xv. Meeting of July 10th, 1871.

[52] Von Tschudi, Reisen in Südamerika. That the lasso was employed by the allies in the war against the Paraguayans, comp. Ausland and Max von Versen, Reisen in America. Breslau, 1872.

[53] Wilkinson, Ancient Egyptians, vol. iii., and in Lepsius' Monuments.

This is rather one of the innumerable instances in which the same implements have been independently invented by nations remote from and perfectly alien to one another.

As yet we have only traced the connection between the nature of certain regions and the weapons used in them; but we will now turn to a more important view of the subject. Just as comparative anatomy has raised the Latin proverb, that from the claw the lion may be known, into a scientific truth, so is ethnology able to infer accurately the grade of a nation's civilization from its arms. Density of population proportionate to space is the first essential of all high social conditions, for this alone admits of a division of labour. From the census and the extent of land occupied by the Redskins of the United States in 1825, it was calculated that hunting tribes require for their maintenance $1\frac{3}{4}$ square miles per head, whereas in a district in some ways not dissimilar, namely, in Belgium, 320 persons live in one square mile.[54]

Prosperous agriculture alone renders density of population possible. But a husbandman cannot wield arms which require constant practice and unusual dexterity. He will rather guard his body from the missiles of hunters by a covering of wadding, as in America, or with leather or metal. Moreover, abandoning that desultory fighting which has much in common with hunting, he and his fellows will combine into bands. In America we may see this innovation adopted by all civilized nations. The Mexicans and Yucatecs not only possessed defensive weapons, but also wielded the sword of the stone period, made of wood, and provided with a groove, into which separate sharp flakes of obsidian were inserted to form a blade. All the Nahuatl nations of Central America would have remained at a very low stage had they not found obsidian or iztli in the lava of their volcanoes. This mineral may be said to require but one dexterous stroke of the hammer to cause it to fly into knife blades, which are so sharp that long after the conquest the Spaniards allowed native barbers to shave them with such flakes. The Inca-Peruvians had wooden helmets, padded doublets, copper swords, battle-axes, spears, and

---

[54] Sir John Lubbock, *Prehistoric Times*, p. 582.

lances,[55] as well as flags, which are the best evidence of the existence of a system of tactics even at that time.

These transitions must have required long periods. Nomadic tribes did not suddenly lay aside their hunting implements. Husbandmen and herdsmen fought in the Trojan war. Hence in the ranks of the Achaians only two or three experts carried bows and arrows; and in the Odyssey, when Penelope cunningly challenges her suitors to a shooting-match, it appears that they are no longer able to manage such an old-fashioned weapon. Similar changes are now observable in Africa. We find clubs, lances, and shields among all the cattle-breeding negroes on the White Nile, as well as among the Shillooks and Nuers,[56] while we find bows and arrows among the Kitsh, Dshur, Moro, and Niamniam negroes, who still hunt. Schweinfurth found an exception among the remarkable Monbuttoos on the Uellé, who used shield and spear as well as bow and arrows, but he expressly adds that such a combination is very rare in negro countries.[57] The true Kaffirs, says Theophilus Hahn,[57] never use the bow and arrow, but fight in companies of 600 to 1000 men. Chaka, the great king of the Zulus, even abolished the five or six casting spears of the old accoutrement, and substituted a short lance for thrusting, and long shields, under the protection of which his warriors charged their enemies, striking them in the body with the short weapon. The Hottentots and Bushmen, who are akin to each other, belong to a perfectly distinct family. The Hottentots are shepherds, the Bushmen hunters; with rare exceptions, the former no longer use the bow and arrow, which is the sole weapon of the Bushmen. The Celts of Gaul, and our own forefathers, had ceased to be archers in the time of Cæsar and Tacitus.[59]

To say nothing of the Chinese, it might be urged as an objection to this view that innumerable archers are depicted on

[55] Prescott, Conquest of Peru, vol. i. p. 67, et seq.

[56] Petherick, Central Africa, vol. i. pp. 98, 120, 319.

[57] Im Herzen von Afrika, vol. ii. p. 115. 1874.

[58] Globus, vol. xx. 1871.

[59] At least bows and arrows were only occasionally used by the Celts of Gaul. Strabo, Geogr. lib. iv. cap. 4.

the Egyptian monuments and on the sculptures of Chorsabad, Nineveh, and Babylon. But the Old Testament explains why these ancient civilized nations adhered to the old weapons of the chase. The victory gained by the Philistines over King Saul was attributed to their body of archers, and David, although the best slingsman of his nation, made the children of Judah practise archery again in order to neutralize their disadvantage, and from this time forward the art was not neglected. Again, the wars which were then waged in Western Asia centred principally round cities ; but as the walls of cities were already flanked by towers, a missile like the arrow, effective from a distance, was indispensable for covering both the siege works and the besiegers themselves. Even in the Roman order of battle we find a body of archers with special duties in the fight, although the real weapons of the legions were only the sword and the javelin.[60] It was mentioned above, that the Fiji islanders still use bows and arrows in the sieges of fortified villages, as well as in the defence of their stockades. But in all these cases it is no longer the same implement as the weapon of the herdsman, indeed we might almost say it has become a scientific instrument. The monuments of the old biblical nations all show the warriors in array. The division of labour has already begun, and war is carried on either by a trained militia or by a caste, not with the implements of daily labour, but with specialized weapons. But when war is systematically practised, the nature of the locality exercises less and less influence over the choice of weapons ; in modern civilized nations it is scarcely traceable. Even now, however, the people of the Cossack steppes or the Hungarian pusztas are incapable of excelling as sharpshooters, nor are mountaineers fit material for light cavalry.

V.—BOATS AND NAVIGATION.

ALTHOUGH the nautical powers of nations are among the last to reach maturity, they yet produce the most important results on the history of human society, for, however highly we estimate the creations of any people in the sphere of arts, however highly we

---

[60] Mommsen, History of Rome.

value its scientific knowledge or its religious institutions, yet when we consider merely the physical history of our world, we see that the work of a single bold and persevering navigator surpasses all others in its effects. When we speak of a strange world of nature and of strange countries on our globe, we do so in allusion to the strange plants and the strange animals peculiar to them. But if there had been no geographical obstacles to the spread of animals and plants, all climatic zones would have exhibited the same forms of animated life. The seas have been the most effectual barriers, yet the seamen who connected the Old and the New World removed them, and thus deprived America of the character of a separate region. Since its discovery, America has been invaded not only by Europeans, but at the same time by all the cultivated plants and domestic animals of Europe—by wheat, rye, oats, and barley, by cattle, horses, and sheep; and these vegetable and animal immigrants have proved so powerful that in a short time they have changed the aspect of whole regions, and even altered the climate by converting the wooded wilderness into sunny, arable land. This adds interest to the inquiry as to whether America might not have been discovered from some other part of our world, or whether the Americans themselves might not have discovered the Old World; and also what conditions in that hemisphere favoured such a chance As these questions can be answered only by the help of historical comparison, we must turn to those regions in which seafaring nations have reached the highest development. The great rivers of the Old World have not encouraged nautical dexterity in the inhabitants of their shores, and the same may be said of America. Looking at the map of the valleys of the Mississippi, the Amazon, or the La Plata, we are impressed with the idea of an incalculable capability for civilization; we seem to see their waters covered with laden vessels and their densely peopled banks studded with towns; yet the history of our own country tells us that it was not until the days of the Romans that rivers became a requisite for the foundation of cities, and that it is only since the employment of steam that they have acquired their present value as a means of communication. It is true that in ancient times great works of civilization were caused by the presence of rivers, as by the Nile and the twin rivers of Mesopotamia, but in both instances they mainly served for the irrigation of plains in dry countries. A favourable rainy season would have compensated for the Euphrates and the Tigris, and formed a substitute even for the waters of the Nile, though not for its mud. But the aborigines of America were by no means in a condition in which their vast network of rivers could have served to spread civilization. Broad and deep rivers are rather barriers and impediments in the first beginnings of society, as, for example, even in Cæsar's day the Rhine quite separated the Celts and the Teutons. The smaller and more tranquil currents are more fitted for the hunter in his bark canoe, and for the fisherman who has only to poison their waters in order to obtain his prey. It is for these reasons that no advance in the civilization of the wild tribes of the Mississippi district warns us of our approach towards its waters, while the neighbourhood of the Amazon is only slightly better.

This is the case also with the great chain of inland seas in North America, for the hunting tribes inhabiting their shores were in no way superior to the rest; nor need we look for nautical skill on other inland waters. In Asia, neither the Lakes Balkash, Baikal, or Aral, nor even the Caspian Sea, influenced the inhabitants of their shores to seamanship. On Alpine lakes, except where better lines have been introduced by English amateurs, we might till lately have found, and indeed we still find, boats of the most inferior and unsuitable build which have resisted all improvement during thousands of years. It is not on rivers or inland seas that we must look for the nations which connect country with country but on coasts. The words of the Eleusinian mysteries, " To the sea, ye Mystæ !" apply with unusual force to the history of civilization.

Among the nations conspicuous in antiquity for their nautical enterprises were the Phœnicians and the inhabitants of the south coast of Arabia. Profitable transmarine products are the strongest inducements to the first attempts to abandon the shore. Cyprus, the " Copper Island," attracted the Phœnicians in this way; the Arabians were tempted by the neighbouring coasts of Africa. The coasts of Syria, and of Yemen, Hadhramaut, and Oman in Arabia, extend in a more or less straight line. Beyond the narrow strip of coast the land rises, and from this elevation stretches the so-called deserts. On coasts such as these not only is the water generally the quickest, and often the sole means of communication between inhabited places, but the land and sea winds are so regular as to ensure an easy passage. As the population of the narrow coast-line becomes more dense, fishing must contribute more and more to subsistence, and if it be not sufficient some portion of the increased population must roam beyond the sea. It was thus that the Phœnicians passed over to Cyprus, from Cyprus to Crete, from Crete to Carthage, to Spain, and even to Senegal. In this way also the inhabitants of Southern Arabia sailed along the east coast of Africa now called Ajan, but known to the Greeks as Azania, and probably in ancient times reached Kilva at the entrance of the Mozambique Channel. From ship-owners from Aden, Claudius Ptolemæus derived his knowledge not of these coasts only, but also of the great Nile lakes which then, as now, were visited by Arabian merchants from what is now Zanzibar.[1] Arabian colonies subsequently spread from Hadhramaut and Oman to the shore of Africa as far as Sofala, a distance to a coasting vessel equal to that from a Phœnician port to the Columns of Hercules.[2]

If in the New World we seek coasts of similar formation, with a narrow strip of shore, backed by rising mountains, and with comparatively dense populations, we can find the Phœnicians of America only on the western coast of South America, from the boundary of Chili northwards, to the shore of Ecuador. It is well known that the greater portion of these shores never receive a drop of rain; but during the wet season mists prevail, producing a transient growth of plants on the sands and shifting dunes. It is only on the banks of the small coast streamlets, which rush down the sides of the Cordilleras, that agriculture is capable of supporting the population. Here we should expect to find that fishery and coast navigation had been developed. Unfortunately, there are no islands near the mainland to entice the natives to sea, for the Galapogos Islands are at a greater distance from the

---

[1] Ptolemæus, Geogr. lib. i. cap. 17.

[2] Peschel, Geschichte der Erdkunde.

nearest point of land than Cape St. Vincent is from Madeira. Nor is there any evidence that these were visited in ancient times, and our nearer acquaintance with them dates only from the fourtcenth century. The shores of the former Inca-Peruvian kingdom are moreover destitute of trunks of trees fit to be hollowed out into canoes.

Yet along this very coast there existed a sea traffic, of a kind occurring only in few other places in the New World prior to its discovery. When Pizarro, sailing in 1526 from Panama, under the guidance of the pilot Bartolomeo Ruiz, reached the Bay of San Mateo on the shore of the present Ecuador, to the north-east of Cape San Francisco, traders of Inca-Peru fell into his hands, who were conveying jewellery and cloth of llama wool from Tumbez. Their vessel was a mere raft, on which a coasting voyage of about four hundred miles had been accomplished. No want of skill or ingenuity, but the absence of timber fit for shipbuilding,[3] compelled the inhabitants of the coast to construct such clumsy vessels, with which, however, they even now undertake voyages of eight hundred miles, from Guayaquil to Lima (Callao). The natives of the desert of Atacama, where trees are yet more scarce, do not use even rafts for fishing, but employ a pole with an inflated skin.[4] The raft from Tumbez, seized by the Spaniards, was moved by a sail and steered by a helm. At the time of the discovery, sails were very rarely employed by the aborigines of America,[5] so that such an advance on the part of the Peruvians ranks among the highest nautical achievements of the New World.

In the Old World it is not only on coasts, such as those of Syria and Southern Arabia, that we find sea-going people. Norway, beyond all other countries, has bred the most daring seamen, who in the ninth, tenth, and eleventh centuries, while yet unacquainted with the mariner's compass, made their way to Iceland,

---

[3] D'Orbigny, L'Homme américain. 1839.

[4] J. J. von Tschudi, Reisen durch Südamerika. Lesson, Voyage autour du Monde. 1839.

[5] Prescott, usually so accurate, terms (Conquest of Peru) the Peruvian sailors' raft, "the only instance of this higher kind of navigation among the American Indians." We shall see with what justice.

Labrador, Greenland, and the present States of New England. In Norway the severity of the climate has broken up the coast into islands and fiords.[6] A rugged and disintegrated coast, with a sea as rough and yet as productive as the Northern Ocean, is the best school for seamen. The passage between Norway and the Shetland Islands[7] was made even in Pliny's time: a longer distance than from any island in the Mediterranean to the nearest point of the mainland. As we must regard coasts with fiords and a fringe of islands as an excellent school of navigation, when we again examine the New World we shall find that a coast formation of this description exists there only on the Pacific Ocean, where it extends along the island-fringed shores of British and of what was formerly Russian America, from Vancouver's Island to Behring's Sea, and in the south, from the boundary of Chili to Terra del Fuego.

In the latter region we again see that the achievements of the inhabitants do not invariably correspond with the advantages of the abode, unless the inhabitants themselves are of a disposition to make the best use of the favourable circumstances surrounding them. The southern extremity of America, which is rent and cleft in every direction into islands and ravine-like sounds, where glaciers stretch down to the edge of the sea, while parrots fly about, and even colibri do not dread the snow storms, the home of evergreen fuchsias, of impenetrable forests, must, one would think, be inhabited only by sea-going tribes. As to the descent of the present inhabitants of Terra del Fuego, ethnographers can only repeat the words of d'Orbigny,[8] namely, that their language approximates in sound to that of the Patagonians and Puelchians, but to the Araucanian in structure. We need not inquire whether the inhabitants of Terra del Fuego and the islands of Magellan are derived from the Patagonian or Araucanian nations, especially as the two are closely allied, and some genuine Patagonians are certainly to be found among the Fuegians. The Patagonians are hunters and do not possess even the simplest raft only fit to cross a river. The Araucanians are also hunters, although

---

6 Peschel, Neue Probleme.　　　　7 Hist. nat. lib, iv. cap. 30.
8 L'Homme américain.

they inhabit mountains instead of grassy plains. We look in vain for bark canoes on all the great rivers of the pampas or steppes. Formerly the hide of an ox was turned up at the edges and bound together at the corners with thongs so as to resemble a flat open box. Goods were conveyed across rivers in such a pelota, as these leathern rafts were termed. The native of the steppes yoked himself by a thong to the front of the ox-hide, and dragged it after him, swimming from shore to shore.[9] At the time of the discovery of America, no nation, from La Plata to Cape Horn, or from Cape Horn along the west coast of South America to Panama, had conceived the idea of constructing any vessel other than a raft; consequently the manufacture of canoes must have been invented independently on the waters of Magellan, by the Pesherah of Bougainville, or Fuegians, as they are now called. Yet the formation of this coast has always given rise to special customs and skill. At the Chonos Islands rude rafts are alone in use.[10] The Fuegians, again, with whom Captain Wilkes had dealings, possessed only canoes of bark stretched upon a frame and sewed together, and which required continued bailing out. Better craft were seen in other parts, and Cordova even praises their mode of caulking, and mentions canoes at Cape Providence which were cut out of the trunks of trees. In looking at these feeble attempts of the Fuegians, we must remember that they were merely beginners in boat-building, for, as Araucanians or Patagonians, they previously lived the life of hunters on the mainland, as we may infer with great certainty from the fact that they possess slings, which are otherwise rarely found among maritime tribes, and can render them but little service. But the Fuegians still hunt a little, as herds of guanacos exist on Navarin and on other islands of the Straits of Magellan. We may therefore safely conclude that the Fuegians are a feeble horde of hunters, who being driven from their hunting-grounds by more powerful neighbours, were finally compelled to hazard a passage to the nearest island on the coast, and to apply themselves to the pursuit of marine animals. Seals

---

[9] Dobrizhoffer, Geschichte der Abiponer, vol. ii. p. 150.
[10] United States Exploring Expedition, vol. i. p. 124.

10

of many species were once unusually numerous in Terra del Fuego, but the destruction caused by ruthless seal hunters has compelled the Fuegians, who, like so many other natives, are dying out, to content themselves with crustacea and fish.

Although but the rudiments of sea-craft have been developed in the Patagonian fiords, in the north, on the contrary, from Vancouver's Island to the Aleutian Islands, there are many small tribes of Redskins, with distinct languages, who represent the northmen of the New World, inasmuch as they inhabit a coast similar in formation to that of Norway, and are not easily surpassed in their own hemisphere as bold seamen. The slender structure and the pointed and really apt lines of the boats in the Nootka Sound have recently been praised by Catlin the artist : there are canoes there of fifty-three feet in length, and large enough for a hundred men. It is noticeable that south of the Juan de Fuca Straits, where the coast loses it fiord-like character, as far as the boundary of ancient Peru, only the rudest boats are used by the aborigines, while conversely from Nootka Sound northwards, the nearer we approach the continent of Asia, the more skilful is the construction of boats, and their management the more admirable. Even among the islands of what was formerly Russian America, inhabited by the Thlinkites, there are hunting boats of the true Eskimo build ; these baidars, as they are there called, are intended only for a single person, and have closed decks, so that but one seat is left, which the boatman covers closely with his apron. These contrivances have been imitated as far as was suitable in Europe. The coast tribes from the Straits of Juan de Fuca to the Aleutian Islands are quite distinct from the so-called red hunting tribes to the east of the Rocky Mountains. It is uncertain whether they emigrated from Northern Asia in ancient times, or, having borrowed their nautical skill from their Asiatic neighbours, they spread a knowledge of it as far as Vancouver's Island. Both views seem to be admissible, and all that is certain is that the advance was confined to the fiords.

It is immaterial to us whether Asiatic people or only Asiatic culture spread along the north-west coast of America as far as the Straits of Juan de Fuca, for both were facilitated by the shape of the northern part of America, which is very significant. In

Australia, the peninsula of Carpentaria (Cape York), stretching towards New Guinea, still made intercourse with the Old World possible. We may perhaps succeed in convincing ethnologists that this tongue of land was, geographically speaking, the means of again raising the social condition of the Australian aborigines. The north-west of America possesses an analogous limb in the peninsula of Alaska, which stretches like an arm towards Northern Asia, while the chain of Aleutian Islands is suspended like a string of beads towards the outstretched arm, forming an interrupted passage to Kamtshatka. If predestination were conceivable, we should say that this was the preordained pathway for a union between the civilizations of the Old and the New World. If America had not been discovered in 1492 under the Spanish flag, and if Europe had reached its degree of maturity of 1492 only half a century later, a civilized Asiatic nation, that is to say, the Japanese, would have anticipated us, by way of the Caspian Sea, in the discovery of America. We do not in the least mean to imply that Japanese navigators would have been wafted across the Pacific as they were in 1832 and 1833 to the Sandwich Islands, and to America itself in the neighbourhood of the Straits of Juan de Fuca, for history knows of no instance in which advantageous relations with unknown regions were due to the discoveries of castaways or shipwrecked sailors.[11] We are rather arguing from the fact that the Japanese visited the Kuriles, occupying the southern islands before any Europeans had done so, and that no less than three times, in 1697, 1710, and 1729, did tidings come to Russia that Japanese trading vessels had penetrated as far as Kamtshatka, so that if the Russians had not anticipated them, they, as the Russians eventually were, would have been led on

---

[11] The voyage of Bjarne Herjulfson might be quoted against us. Sailing in the year A.D. 1000 for Greenland, he missed his course and discovered America, probably Labrador. But this accidental acquaintance of the Northmen with America in no degree affected the history of civilization. The case of the Portuguese, Cabral, might also be quoted, who, on his second voyage to the East Indies, discovered Brazil. But that the successors of Vasco da Gama must sooner or later have come in sight of South America on their voyages to the Cape of Good Hope, depended in no way on accident, but was a physical necessity brought about by the trade winds prevailing on the Atlantic.

by the fur trade from the Kuriles to the Aleutians, and thence to America in the course of a century.

Islands lying near a coast are especially favourable to the development of seamanship. Thus the proximity of Elba, and of Corsica to Elba, attracted the Etruscans on to the Mediterranean before the time of the Romans. Austria still mans her fleet with excellent sailors from the island-bound Dalmatian coast, and Genoa owed her former greatness not merely to the size of her natural harbour, but to the circumstance that, in clear weather, Corsica, which to the Ligurian fishing-boats is the first goal of a longer voyage, is visible from the Riviera. The British Isles in former centuries attracted various nations in succession, each surpassing the other in seamanship. Before the Northmen, Danes and Saxons, even the Celts, ventured out into the Atlantic; for we know that the Northmen who first landed on Iceland found Irish antiquities of Christian times there, indicating a previous settlement of pious Celtic anchorites.

Large portions of continents which have become detached from the mainland by the subsidence of the intervening land, become groups of islands in shallow seas. We meet with this phenomenon, in the Old World, between Southern Asia and Australia, which were formerly bound together until the land connecting them was dissolved into the Sunda,[12] Banda, and Molucca Islands. From these the Malays, a race eminent for seamanship, have ranged over the ocean to a distance exceeding half the circumference of the earth, spreading in the Pacific as far north as the Hawai or Sandwich Islands, to Easter Island on the east, and southwards to New Zealand, while in the Indian Ocean they have spread to Madagascar. Where Asia approaches so near to Europe that the basin of the Mediterranean is narrowed into the Dardanelles, the Grecian archipelago is the remnant of a former connection of the two continents. These islands trained a people surpassed in nautical skill but by the Phœnicians of all the nations of antiquity. Their colonies and markets extended in time over both the basins of the Mediterranean, in the Euxine as far as the mouth of the Don, and through the Red Sea as far as the East

---

[12] Peschel, Neue Probleme der vergleichende Erdkunde.

Indies. A similar dissolution into islands is traceable on a smaller scale between the mainlands of North Germany and Scandinavia, which is the home of the Danes, who contributed to British blood, and hence may claim a share in the nautical fame of the greatest maritime power of Europe. The Dutch also inhabit a region of islands which originated by subsidence, and did not exist at the time when the British Isles still formed part of the continent of Northern Europe.

In those regions of the New World which owe their configuration to a like cause, we may, therefore, expect to find a similar development of the inhabitants. But from physical comparisons elsewhere made, it appeared that the archipelago of the so-called North-west Passage must also be regarded as the remnant of a former connection between the small continent of Greenland and the continent of North America; and further, that where North and South America approach each other, on the Atlantic shores of the shallow Gulf of Mexico and the Caribbean Sea, the Antilles still exist as the residue of a former connection. Hence, if the development of human civilization depends on favourable local configuration, we ought to find the highest degree of nautical skill in the American Polar Sea, and in the two gulfs of Central America, which in the New World supply the place of the Mediterranean, once so highly favoured. Nor do these expectations altogether mislead us.

Archipelagoes have, however, frequently served as asylums for weak or decrepit beings, for whom the struggle for life on the continents has become too fierce, and who could only continue to exist where the sea protected them from their more hardy oppressors. Both the Lesser and the Great Antilles, as well as the Bahamas, were inhabited prior to 1492 by a gentle and extremely unwarlike race of men, whom Von Martius has named Taini. The few remnants of their language that have been preserved, chiefly names of places, do not afford any certain testimony of their origin, yet it has recently been assumed that they were related to the Arowaks of South America, who still inhabit the Guayanas. These people made no long voyages; at the most, those who lived in the south of Hayti ventured occasionally to

Jamaica, or the inhabitants of Jamaica to Hayti.[13] But in 1492 they had already been partially driven from their islands by the Caribs, a race extraordinarily gifted, both physically and intellectually, whom we must not condemn too severely for their complete nudity, their inclination to piracy, their craving after human flesh, and the poisoning of their arrows. The Caribs of these islands, whose language was a dialect of that of the Caribs of the mainland, had even then conquered the so-called Lesser Antilles, occupied the eastern half of Porto Rico, and extended their kidnapping excursions into Hayti, where some of their adventurers had founded monarchies, and the older comers had taken possession of the country on the eastern shore. Their ships of war, or pirogues, were forty feet in length, and broad enough to afford room for a Spanish cask (pipa) lying crossways. They carried fifty seamen, and were moved either by cotton sails or by oars plied to a time set by a singer. They must not be blamed for their piracy, for Thucydides tells us how the Greeks owed their maritime power to the same trade. Piracy is in fact one of the evils inseparable from the development of national intercourse ; hence maritime customs have remained extremely barbarous even up to our own century. Many of the renowned English circumnavigators and discoverers of the 16th and 17th centuries were also pirates nay, the Dutch West Indian Company was able to pay fabulous profits to its shareholders only because their ships pursued the Spanish galleons. The customs of war at that time certainly ennobled piracy.

Just as the Caribs became pirates where the Antilles approach nearest to the South American continent, so we also find a very highly civilized people, namely, the Yucatecs, at the spot were Cuba approaches the shores of Central America. Here there is, indeed, no piracy, but Columbus, when on his fourth voyage, steering from Bay Islands towards the coast of Honduras, met with a trading vessel from Yucatan, which, if it kept along shore, had to traverse at least 400 miles before reaching the nearest native port. It was eight feet wide and as large as "a galley," and was pro-

---

[13] The largest boats of the Antilles were built in Jamaica ; these were 96 feet in length, and eight feet in width. Bernaldez, Reyes Catol.

vided with a roof of palm leaves for the protection of the merchandize, which consisted of woven fabrics and articles of clothing, wooden swords with obsidian blades, brass and earthenware utensils; in other words, manufactures which the merchants had exchanged for a cargo of cocoa. They were seen to stoop and gather up with care every fallen bean, for even then these seeds, or "almonds," as the discoverers called them, served instead of small coins in Mexico and in Yucatan, to which they were laboriously brought from Honduras. The Yucatecs must also have made occasional visits to Cuba, for on the 1st and 29th of November Columbus notes in his log, that he found a piece of silver and a cake of beeswax among the natives of Cuba, both of which articles could have come there only by way of Yucatan. It is unfortunately impossible to state positively whether sails were even then used by the Maya races.[14]

The archipelago between North America and Greenland would be peculiarly fitted for the development of maritime skill did not its sea, fast bound by the arctic winter, leave the passage by water open only during a few weeks in the year. Nevertheless the Eskimo, one of the most sea-going nations of the world, have spread themselves over this very region. In another place we shall give a more detailed account of their achievements.

Our task is accomplished if we have succeeded in showing that both in the Old and the New World the analogous formations of coast have promoted the nautical achievements of their inhabitants in a similar manner; and that in America it is only in very limited and specially favoured tracts that we find rude germs of navigation. All who know the stories of the voyages in the Pacific, from the times of Schouten and Le Maire to that of Wilkes, or even

---

[14] Don Fernando Colombo, describing in the biography of his father (Vita del Almirante) the Yucatan galley on the coast of Honduras, makes no mention of a sail. On the other hand, Bernal Diaz, an eye-witness, relates that when Francisco Fernandez di Cordova, in 1517, first discovered Yucatan, near Cape Catoche, five large boats containing forty or fifty people approached with oars and sails—á ramo y vela (Histor. verladera). In Herrera the words are *cinco canoas con gente, que iban al remo*, that is to to say, with oars. In Oviedo and Peter Martyr also there is no confirmation of Bernal Diaz's statement.

of later discoveries, are accustomed to regard boats, full of inquisitive and importunate native crowds, as always present round the European vessels off those shores ; nay, in certain favourable places in the South Sea, even where land is not in sight, the sails made of matting of Polynesian natives may be seen passing in the distance. In the records of the discoverer of America, on the contrary, instances in which Europeans meet with natives on the sea even near land are extremely rare. We have already cited the most notable cases. The comparatively small advance of the American natives in the arts of sailing and paddling may perhaps be ascribed to the absence of a Mediterranean Sea or of a coast formation such as that of our North Sea. Yet in all respects the human race has developed far more slowly in America than in the Old World. If we sum up the industrial feats of the great civilized nations of America, the Mexicans and the Peruvians of the time of the Incas, as if they had been found side by side instead of apart, the two together would still not present such a picture of a civilization as we see in Egypt under the fourth dynasty, the earliest of which we possess monuments. In other words, the American race, even in the districts of its highest development, had not attained a maturity in the year 1492 equal to that of the highest local civilization of the Old World three thousand years before Christ. But let us imagine that in the year 3000 B.C., discoverers from America had come to Europe in decked sailing vessels and with the compass in their hands, they would scarcely have found the waters on the northern shores of our continent occupied by better seamen than the Eskimo and the Kolushs, or Thlinkites, of North America, and in the Mediterranean they would probably not yet have encountered Phœnician ships of Tarshish, but perhaps trading galleys, such as went from Yucatan to Honduras, or ships such as the Caribbean sailing pirogues, and manned by the pirates of Asia Minor of whom Thucydides speaks in his first book.

VI.—THE INFLUENCE OF COMMERCE ON THE LOCAL DISTRIBUTION OF NATIONS.

IT is not easy to overestimate the advantages arising from the interchange of local products. The merchant spreads abroad not only his goods, but with them, samples of art, inventions, knowledge, morals, customs, and poetry ; and his footsteps are usually followed by the missionary. Of these facts we shall say no more, but we will rather show the extent to which valuable products of different regions have affected the distribution of nations and languages. Let us first note that commerce already existed in those ages in which we find the earliest signs of our race. It must have been by barter that the cave-dwellers of Périgord, of the reindeer period, obtained rock crystals, Atlantic shells, and the horns of the Polish Saiga antelope.[1] The obsidian blades which are occasionally met with in ancient graves to the east of the Mississippi, must have reached the places where they are now discovered by barter either from Mexico or from the Snake River, an affluent of the Columbia to the west of the Rocky Mountains.[2] We must not imagine that the so-called Redskins of the Union had no intercourse but that of murderous feuds. Merchant boats passed along the great rivers, and transit duties were taken by the chiefs.[3] In South America, curaré, the arrow poison, the preparation of which was understood only by a few hordes, formed a valuable article of commerce among the Indians of the Amazon, so that people living near the Napo were obliged to make canoe voyages of three months' duration in order to procure it.[4] Even where bands of hawkers and pedlars did not wander through the country, goods were bartered betwixt horde and horde, and such a system of intercourse might extend throughout an entire quarter of the world. English wares deposited at Mombas, on the eastern side of South Africa, have been recognized at Mogador, on the west coast of Northern Africa.[5] Since from these circumstances

[1] See above, p. 37.
[2] Carl Rau, Archiv für Anthropologie. 1871.
[3] Lafitau, Mœurs des sauvages amériquains. Paris, 1724.
[4] Von Martius, Ethnographie, vol. i. p. 504, and above, p. 187.
[5] Waitz, Anthropologie, vol. ii. p. 101.

we may assume that commerce has existed in all ages, and among all inhabitants of the world, the circumstances of modern times serve to throw light on the dark ages of ethnology.

When, in the year 1492, three Spanish vessels were sailing westwards, striving to reach the distant lands of the Atlantic, a sort of council of war was held on board the Santa Maria, on the 7th of October, between the two chiefs of the enterprise, Christopher Columbus and Martin Alonzo Pinzon. Until then a direct westward course had been held, the squadron lay between latitudes 25° and 26°, so that in four or five days the trade-wind would have carried it either to the most northern of the Bahamas or to Florida. The elder, Pinzon, nevertheless insisted on directing the course to the south-west, assigning no other reason than the inspiration of his heart (el corazon me da). From no conviction, but from conciliatory motives, the discoverer of the New World actually allowed the course to be altered 45° for a few days, so that on Friday, October 11th, the coral island of Guanahani was sighted. The great Alexander von Humboldt has stated that had this change of course not taken place, the ships would have arrived at Florida, and the Spaniards would have peopled the United States instead of Central America, so that but for the inspiration of Martin Pinzon's heart, the New World would now have had quite different ethnographical features.[6]

But in reality it made no difference at what point America was first sighted, for even before the discovery the region to be occupied by the Spanish colonists was tolerably well defined by the distribution of the precious metals. For as soon as Columbus saw the golden ornaments in the ears and noses of the harmless Lucayans, he endeavoured to ascertain by signs whence the precious metal had been procured. He felt his way from island to island as far as Cuba, going first towards the north-west, and when this direction did not satisfy him, turning towards the south-east till he came to Hayti. Here, from whence gold had been spread over the Antilles, he founded his first settlement. Much has been written of the Spanish thirst for gold, but had they not followed the traces of gold, transatlantic colonies

---

[6] Kosmos, vol. ii.   1847.

could not have arisen so early as the end of the fifteenth
century. All agricultural colonies which the French and English
attempted to found on the shores of the United States in the
sixteenth century, literally perished by starvation. Cut off from
their own country, where division of labour was already practised,
the settlers, when they had exhausted the outfit brought with
them from the Old World, necessarily fell back into the same
grade of civilization as the red aborigines, unless constant fresh
supplies were conveyed to them from their old home. Such
supplies required high remuneration, as the voyage to the New
World still involved great perils. The consignments could not be
paid for in cereals, for these were not yet worth the cost of freight.
It was the discovery of tobacco, an article of commerce worth the
cost of carriage to Europe which, in the beginning of the seventeenth century, made Virginia, the first purely agricultural colony
of the New World, flourish. It is therefore primarily owing to
tobacco, and perhaps to the fur trade, that the present society of
North America is of Anglo-Saxon origin. That Canada was once
purely French, and is still half French, is due to another natural
product. Round about Newfoundland lie incredibly rich cod
fisheries, the produce of which, even in the beginning of the sixteenth century, repaid the cost of carriage across the Atlantic ; for
even in the middle ages it was brought from Iceland. Fishermen
from the north of France, who gave their name to Cape Breton,
have visited Newfoundland annually ever since 1503. From these
well-known waters Jacques Cartier then discovered the St. Lawrence, and, following in his track, the French reached Canada.
A valuable article of export is required to enable a first settlement to strike root : but if it has once obtained a footing, it grows
like the mustard seed of the Gospel. The Spaniards in no way
interfered with the French and English colonists in the United
States as long as the two latter did not venture dangerously near
their southern possessions. They had no reason to disturb the
pious Puritans. The present domains of the United States bear
upon the charts of the Spanish discoverers, the legend, *worthless
territories* (tierras de ningun provecho), because they produced
no gold. All must therefore acknowledge that it was quite
indifferent to the history of civilization whether the Spanish ships

did or did not bear off from the west to the south-west on October 7th, 1492. The Spaniards went in pursuit of gold, and when they had stripped a district of its treasure they abandoned it again, as was the case in the Isthmus of Darien ; but colonies of planters first grew up on tropical islands, where the cultivation of sugar by means of negro slaves yielded profits.   It is certain that America became Spanish and has remained Spanish in all such districts as produce gold and silver, and that it is only later settlements that have taken root in regions where tropical agriculture or profitable cattle-breeding might be carried on.

It is strange that the Spaniards knew the richest gold district of the New World for two hundred and fifty years without suspecting its treasures.   California was theirs ; there their missionaries preached, there their soldiers kept watch in castles (presidios) over the rapacious Comantshes and Apatshes, yet not one among them guessed that they were in the midst of the El Dorado which they had so long sought in vain.   Yet they may find some comfort in the fact that the Russians also held California for a time, and vacated it only a few years before the name of this country served as a trumpet-call to draw all the adventurers of both worlds to the Sacramento.   Had the gold of California been discovered at the close of the sixteenth century, then, indeed, the course of the world's history might have taken another direction.   California and Australia are the best witnesses at the present day, that the local distribution of nations depends on the existence in larger or smaller quantities of tempting treasures on or in the soil.   Gold alone prompted the national emigrations to the Pacific Ocean.

Australia was affected as was California.   An old map lately found in the British Museum has unexpectedly shown that the Portuguese visited a northern point of this continent in the year 1601.[7]   After them the Dutch frequently reached the western and northern coasts, and on two occasions, the southern shore ; hence this part of the world is still often called New Holland.   Yet these regions were to them what the United States were to the

---

[7] P. H. Major, Discovery of Australia by the Portuguese in 1601. London, 1861.

Spaniards in the sixteenth century—*worthless territories.* The English regarded their discoveries on the east coast of Australia in the same manner when, at the end of the last century, they degraded them to a place of exile for their convicts. Thus Australia continued to be neglected by Portuguese, Dutch, and English, until the cry of gold was raised, when a new period of immigration instantly dawned.

About five years ago we heard that the Russians had sold Alaska to the United States. But how did the Russians come to Alaska? Did they go by the Baltic or the White Sea, round Cape Horn, or the Cape of Good Hope? Certainly not; they passed over the Ural mountains in the year 1577 to the Ob, not because their own country had become too small for them, but in the hope of great gains in the far East. As the Spaniards stripped the Caziques of the New World of their rings and anklets, so did the Cossacks, as the invaders of Siberia were named, with the valuable furs which they found in the possession of the chiefs of the hunting tribes. The thirst for plunder urged them with incredible rapidity eastward; and even in 1639 they had reached the shores of the Sea of Okhotsk. In Behring's Sea they found the most highly prized of all furs, that of the sea-otters, which in Steller's time were extremely numerous, but are now dying out, if not already extinct. Of course it was constantly necessary to seek for new and virgin hunting-grounds, and thus the Russian fur merchants reached the New World, where they founded New Archangel at Sitka. Up to the recent advance of the Russians across the steppes of Kirghiz, it may be said that the extension of their power in Northern Asia has been coextensive with the distribution of the animals yielding fur.

Although we have hitherto seen the destiny of great regions and great nations determined by the occurrence of valuable commodities of the mineral and animal kingdoms, yet many vegetable products have had a similar effect; this was especially the case in the earlier times when the present skill in packing and naturalizing of plants had not been acquired. Thus it was the desire for the treasures of the East Indies which first led the Portuguese on the African shore of the Atlantic to venture southwards. India (which name at that time included the whole of

Southern Asia as well as China and Japan) was erroneously considered a metalliferous country, although it is really much poorer in gold and silver than Africa itself. But the jewels of Ceylon and of the future Golconda, the pearl banks in the Gulf of Manaar, in the Persian Gulf, and in the Red Sea, were realities; and in addition to these there were various costly spices and valued drugs. The well-known fact that the various spices, medicinal and aromatic plants, were distributed within very narrow regions, produced great effects. Pepper, which at that time ranked from a mercantile point of view as the first of spices, could be procured only from the Malabar coast, India, or from the island of Sumatra. The nutmeg was as yet confined to the islands of the Sea of Banda; cloves were found only on five small volcanic islands near the Island of Gelolo, which are, properly speaking, the Moluccas. True, camphor was and still is to be obtained only in two small districts—one in Sumatra and the other in Borneo. The Portuguese were thus obliged to sail to the limits of the then known world before they reached the original habitats of these vegetable treasures. It may appear strange that such baits were requisite to allure the Dutch after the Portuguese, and after the Dutch the French and the English, to Southern Asia, but the spread of civilization is in a great measure due to the fact that these treasures were so capriciously distributed, and existed in such small quantities, for otherwise Europeans would not even yet have spread over the whole globe. The Portuguese were in all the original habitats of the spices, that is to say, on the west, but not on the east coast of Hindustan, in the great commercial centres of the Malays, and on the spice islands of the extreme east of Asia.

The cause of their settlement in Brazil is told by the very name of this empire. In 1493 the Pope had distributed the globe between the Spaniards and the Portuguese, and on the western boundary of the latter, or under the "first meridian," as it was termed, lay a large portion of the South American territory, which, after the discovery, and for a long time subsequently, was named the "Land of the Holy Cross;" but it was called Brazil, or *The Land of Logwood*, after the first and most important consignment that it was able to send home, for it was only much later that gold and diamonds were obtained behind the mountains on the coast. Africa, hardly less than Australia, has also been looked upon as hardly civilized. Karl Ritter accounted for the inferior grade of its inhabitants by the absence of indentations of its shores in proportion to its circumference. It is indeed very boldly formed ; it is destitute of peninsulas, and its bays, such as the Gulfs of Sidra and Khabs, are but slight indentations, or are merely formed by some angle of the coast, as is the Gulf of Guinea or the shores of the Red Sea and the Somali coast ; but even the Red Sea is so difficult of navigation that, in comparison with other coast indentations, it offers very slight advantages for communication. Had great rivers, like the Mississippi, the Amazon, or the La Plata, in America, rendered Africa accessible, civilization could have made its way more rapidly into the interior, as is shown by the fact that the shores of the Nile were the site of a very mature, and probably the earliest, civilization. But in addition to the impediments to the spread of civilization which we have already mentioned, the land was almost entirely destitute of treasures such as might tempt foreign colonists. Gold is only found near the sources of the Senegal and Niger, and in a few streams on the Guinea coast, formerly also at Sofala in East Africa, and now in some districts of Kaffirland, but everywhere in very small quantities; so that Africa, possessing no golden fleece, has never attracted Argonauts : it contains no districts equal in mineral wealth to Peru, Mexico, California, or even to Minas Geraes. Hence, even at the present day, the African colonies of the Portuguese, French, English, and Dutch have remained poor and insignificant in comparison with the settlements in South America.

The Cape districts alone have developed prosperously since the time of trans-oceanic emigrations, first as a place of call on the road to India, and subsequently as agricultural colonies. Without metals, without spices, and without drugs, or any vegetable treasures, Africa remained free from conquerors, but also untouched by civilization ; sad to relate, for three thousand years she was fain to pay for European baubles and intoxicating liquors with her own children. The slave trade was thus, not justified, but in a measure explained by the want of any important article of export. But though the slave trade connects the interior with the coast, it does not convey a higher civilization from the coast to the interior.   At last, after the lapse of ages, a treasure has been discovered in our own days even in Africa, which within a moderate period will be the means of revealing the long-preserved secrets of this continent.   This is not a product of the mineral nor of the vegetable kingdom, but the tusks of the elephant.   Ivory hunters roam about South Africa in all directions on the track of Livingstone, and they are followed by missionaries, merchants, and the earliest settlers.   The region lying to the east and west of the White Nile has been explored, and is annually traversed by Italian ivory hunters, who are obliged to penetrate further every year, leaving exhausted hunting-grounds behind them.

Although the examples hitherto given have been derived from modern history, we might also quote from ancient times the early appearance of the Phœnicians, or their descendants, the Carthaginians, in Spain, where they were retained by the quarrying of silver ore.   In the early stages of development tin promoted civilization even more than silver, for without tin bronze cannot be produced.   But tin is found in but few places, and many even of these were completely unknown in ancient times.   History proves that tin was not obtained from the Erzgebergs until the middle ages, and it still seems doubtful whether tin from Crete or the trans-Caucasian tin from Georgia reached the Mediterranean.   In Pliny's time, however, Spanish tin from Gallicia was an article of Roman commerce.   In Gaul tin was washed on the Aurence, and ancient tin mines have also been discovered in Limousin, in the department of the Loire Inférieure and in Morbihan.[8]   So skilful were the Celts in metallurgy that the Romans first learnt from them the art of tinning utensils.   Celtic miners worked the most important of the ancient quarries on the Scilly Islands and in Cornwall.   It must not be supposed that Phœnician travellers communicated their skill in mining and smelting to the old inhabitants of Brittany, or that they even discovered the veins of tin ore.   Never before the days of Abel Tasman were voyages to unknown regions made without a special aim. The seafarers invariably had some object in view; they always

---

[8] Rougemont, Die Bronzezeit.   1869.

endeavoured to reach the emporium or the original source of the treasures of commerce. Hence, if Carthaginian or Phœnician vessels ever reached the west coast of France or entered the Channel, they must have been in quest of known sources of tin ; consequently this metal must already have been excavated, and must have reached the Mediterranean by land in the course of traffic. That such land traffic existed is proved by the early foundation and the prosperity of Marseilles ; moreover, the lumps of tin ore which have been found among the Swiss relics of the bronze age, must have reached Helvetia by an inland commerce, and could have reached Marseilles as easily as Switzerland. It was also owing to the presence of tin that the Celts of Gaul and Britain were of far higher social development than the Teutons of the time of Cæsar. The Romans found an excellent system of husbandry in use among the ancient Britons, in which the yield was increased by the use of marl as a mineral manure. The Britons also used artistic war implements of their own invention, namely, the scythe cars. The possession of an article of export so indispensable, and the fact that tin was in such great request in the age of bronze, was in itself the means of promoting civilization, for commerce at a very early period brought the Britons into contact with the Mediterranean nations, and aided in hastening the maturity of their condition.

The inhabitants of the coast of the North Sea, and still more of the Baltic, possessed an analogous property in amber. At a very early period amber must have reached the shores of the Mediterranean, although perhaps it was at first only bartered from tribe to tribe. Even if the conquering Romans had not appeared at the mouths of the Ems and Weser, and if Drusus had not even then pushed on his ships to the northern point of Jutland, amber alone would certainly have been able to attract the civilization of the Mediterranean to the north ; for even in Nero's time (A.D. 56) a Roman knight undertook a journey, for the purpose of exploring the continent, across the Carpathian mountains to the amber districts of East Prussia, and returned with a supply of the precious commodity to the metropolis of the world. It is doubtless to amber that the early civilization of which we find traces on the shores of the Baltic is due, for the numerous " finds " of Greek and

Roman coins as well as of bronze instruments are owing to the presence of this substance; as these metal implements probably served the native artists as models and patterns, it is perhaps to amber that the advanced condition of the bronze age in the north of Europe is due.

We thus see how much we owe to the rare and precious products of the animal, vegetable, and mineral kingdoms, as the means by which human culture was spread, and as the baits which attracted national migrations, and we perceive that the regions which were fortunate enough to possess such treasures were the first to be drawn into the sphere of a higher culture : the direction in which civilization has moved has frequently been prescribed by this influence. We have but a very slight knowledge of the laws which direct the distribution of mineral treasures ; the treasures of the animal and vegetable kingdoms, on the contrary, are, it is true, restricted to limited climatic zones, but their local abundance, rarity, or total absence within the zones in which they might occur, is not so much a question of law as of history, for it appears to depend on the locality in which the species first occurred, and also on the power of migration of the species, and on the geographical impediments which obstructed their extension.

VII.—MARRIAGE AND PATERNAL AUTHORITY.

THE generation of successors, which is the first and highest purpose of marriage, can only be effected after the commencement of sexual maturity, which is reached somewhat earlier in the female sex than in the male : in Northern Europe it is about the fourteenth and seventeenth year, in Southern Europe somewhat sooner. In warm countries the recognized characters appear at an earlier age ; in Egypt in boys of twelve to fifteen, and in girls from eleven to fourteen years of age.[1]   Klunzinger, who recently described the marriage of one of these childish couples in Upper Egypt, states that boys of from fifteen to eighteen years of age marry girls of

---

[1] Hartmann, Nilländer.

twelve to fourteen years, and adds significantly that in these marriages, which we should deem so premature, no evil consequences appear to affect the fecundity.[2] In Northern Persia the tokens of fertility appear in the female sex during the thirteenth year, and in Southern Persia even as early as the ninth and tenth years.[3] In the Philippines twelve years is prescribed as the legal age for the female sex, but Jagor found the marriage of a girl of nine years and ten months entered in the church registrar of Polangui.[4] Among the negroes of South Africa marriage is also entered upon precociously, but it is difficult to determine the exact times, as the inhabitants are too careless to be in the habit of accurately fixing their age by dates. Among the Hottentots Kolbe saw mothers of thirteen years of age.[5] The Australians give their daughters to husbands in their twelfth year and often earlier.[6] But it appears still doubtful whether this apparent marriage is not a preliminary ceremony of betrothal which is followed by the real marriage at a later period.[7]

These facts, but few of which are new, will not surprise any one who has studied the subject; nor is it a new fact that the polar nations also acquire the power of reproduction at an early age. As yet this has been remarked with especial reference to the Eskimo; but Adolf Erman has recently stated that on the Aleutian island of Atcha, marriage is contracted by the boy as soon as he can manage the baidar; by the girl as soon as she can sew quickly; in both cases in the tenth year.[8] No physiological explanation has yet been given of the fact that the period of immaturity is curtailed in inverse proportion to the approximation to the equator or the polar circle. Probably the latitude of the abode has no reference to this phenomenon; it may more probably

---

[2] Ausland, No. xl. 1871.

[3] Polak, Persien.

[4] Reisen in den Philippinen.

[5] Vorgebirge der Guten Hoffnung.

[6] Eyre, Central Australia, vol. ii. p. 319.

[7] On the age of marriage in different races of mankind, compare the exhaustive work of Dr. Ploss, Jahresbericht des Leipz. Vereins für Erdkunde. 1872.

[8] Zeitschrift für Ethnologie. 1871.

[9] Catlin, The North American Indians, p. 89.

have some connection with the darkness of the skin, for in other North American tribes the girls marry in their twelfth or fourteenth year, and occasionally as early as the eleventh.[9] The Patagonians in the south, on the contrary, are immature till the sixteenth year.[10]

Beauty fades earlier when the natural desire is early aroused, so that by the thirtieth and often by the twenty-fifth year all the beauty of the female is gone. Tacitus was right in ascribing the prolonged youth of our forefathers to their late marriages.[11] So that we must recognize the postponement of marriage, either by habit or by law, as a great advance in the self-education of nations. In ancient Peru, the establishment of a household was only permitted to men in the twenty-fourth and to women in the eighteenth year.[12] The austere Abipones, who possessed the southern half of the Gran Chaco on the River Paraguay, also tolerated marriage only at a mature age.

We must not omit to mention that a great many races of mankind are quite indifferent to juvenile unchastity, and only impose strict conduct on their women after marriage. Yet it is unjustifiable to infer indifference to sexual purity from the want of a verbal expression to distinguish the maiden from the wife, as Lichtenstein ventured to do in the case of the Bushmen,[13] whereas Chapman extols their modest behaviour, and adds that marriages are made among them only from inclination. Even the Abipones have no word for maiden,[14] and yet Dobrizhoffer invariably eulogizes their austere morals and chastity. This deficiency of language may, on the other hand, bear an unfavourable interpretation among the Comantshes, who are in the habit of ceding their wives to their guests.[15] We find this objectionable practice again among the Aleutians,[16] who are in other ways also notorious for their unnatural excesses, among the Eskimo,

---

[10] Musters, Among the Patagonians.

[11] Sera juvenum Venus, eoque inexhausta pubertas, nec virgines festinantur. Germ. cap. 20.

[12] Prescott, Conquest of Peru, vol. i. p. 113.

[13] Reisen im südlichen Afrika.

[14] Dobrizhoffer, Geschichte der Abiponer, vol. ii. p. 218.

[15] Waitz, Anthropologie, vol. iv.

[16] Ibid. vol. iii.

and, lastly, Adolf Erman relates that he found the same custom in his travels through Kamtshatka.[17]

The most profound instance of depravity of this sort is the so-called three-quarter marriages which occur in Nubia among the Hassiniyeh Arabs, among whom married women have free disposal of themselves on every fourth day.[18] History teaches us that all highly civilized nations have carefully guarded conjugal purity and chastity in general, and also, on the other hand, that every relaxation of morals has been closely followed by the disintegration of society.

We need hardly recall the fact that marriages are called polygamous when the man shares his household with several wives, and polyandric when the wife belongs simultaneously to several husbands. Polygamy extends throughout Africa; it was also permitted to nearly all Asiatic nations, but in America, on the contrary, it is very rare. The census has hitherto shown that the numbers of the two sexes are equally balanced, and the excess of one over the other is generally very slight. The greatest trustworthy difference of numbers occurs among the European Jews, among whom male births greatly preponderate.[19] Although, according to the statements of travellers, among the Ladinos, or hybrids of Europeans with the aboriginal inhabitants of Central America, the number of girls is half as much again as that of boys, and in Yucatan, according to Stephens, is twice as great, and at Cochabamba is supposed to be fivefold,[20] yet these statements are

---

[17] Marco Polo records the same respecting the oasis of Kamul (Hamil) in Gobi. There however, as well as in the oasis of Fezzan, also touched at by the caravans, this immoral habit is based on mercenary motives. A. Erman, Reise um die Erde.

[18] Ausland.

[19] According to Waitz, and also Darwin, Descent of Man, vol. i. p. 301 :—

BIRTHS IN JEWISH FAMILIES.

				Boys.			Girls.
In Prussia	...	...	...	113	...	...	100
Breslau	...	...		114	...	...	100
Berlin	...	...	...	208 (?)	...	...	100
Leghorn	...	...		120	...	...	100
Livonia	...	...	...	120	...	...	100

[20] Waitz, Anthropologie, vol. i.

not based on actual calculations, and are therefore of little scientific value.   Campbell, a thoroughly trustworthy observer, asserted on the other hand that boys and girls are born in equal numbers in the Siamese harem.[19] This refutes the theory so often put forward, that polygamy causes female births to predominate, polyandry the male ; so that Nature as it were adapts herself to the matrimonial laws prevalent in different localities.   The experiences of breeders of animals also contradict this hypothesis, for in the case of racehorses, greyhounds, and Cochin China fowls, the equal balance of the sexes in the births is undisturbed by the strict polygamy which prevails.[20]   German statistics, however, afford good evidence of the preponderance of boys at the first birth.[21]

But as social beings, we are subject to a moral order, and this is decidedly unfavourable to polygamy.   The history of oriental dynasties teaches us that the brief duration of the governing races is always to be traced to the intrigues of ambitious wives ; that the ennobling sentiment of brotherly love is totally wanting there, and that every son of a royal house is apt to hate his half-brother as his most inveterate enemy.   Even in ordinary families envy and jealousy estrange the children of different mothers.

Polyandry is less widely spread ; it must not be confounded with the community of wives of the military castes to whom celibacy was prescribed as a vow of the order, such as the Naiars of Malabar,[22] and formerly certain Cossacks.[23]   The true form of

---

[19] Darwin, Descent of Man, vol. i. p. 268.

[20] Ibid. vol. i. pp. 304-306 :—

BIRTHS.

Number of Cases.			Male.			Female.
25,560 Racehorses	...	...	99·7	...	...	100
6,878 Greyhounds		...	110·1		...	100

Of 1001 Cochin China chickens hatched, there were 487 cocks and 514 hens.

[21] Welcker, Bau und Wachsthum des Schädels.   According to the birth registers of Halle, in the case of first births there were 114 boys to every 100 girls, and in the genealogical pocket calendar of German princely families, there were 116 male births to 100 female, while in the total births of Germany the numerical proportion is 106 : 100.

[22] Grauf, Ostindien.

[23] C. von Kessel, Ausland, No. xxxvii.   1872.

polyandry occurs among the nations connecting Asiatics and Americans, namely, the Eskimo, the Aleutians, the Koniaks, and the Kolushs,[24] among whom the sexual relations are abnormal in other ways. In America the Iroquois and certain tribes on the Orinoco are also accused of polyandry by Sir John Lubbock. It is also said to have been found in the South Seas, among the Maori of New Zealand, and on several small islands. It occurs more frequently in Southern India, among individual tribes of the Nilgherri hills, among whom custom allows all the brothers as they grow up to become the husbands of the eldest brother's wife; and, conversely, the younger sisters of the wife become the wives of this conjugal community. The aborigines of Great Britain, in the time of Cæsar, had the same habit.[25] Community of wives is limited to brothers and other relations in Thibet, where this unnatural habit is attributed to motives of economy.[26] Poverty is also the cause of the occasional occurrence of polyandry among the Herero of South America.[27]

The origin of the custom of avoiding marriages among blood relations is one of the most obscure but instructive problems of ethnology. Recent experience enables us to infer that such admixture of blood is injurious, for if both husband and wife suffer from the same bodily defects, they will transmit it in an enhanced form to their progeny. Deafness, short sight, sterility, idiocy, and mental derangements make their appearance early, or break out with violence, in the children of parents who have transmitted the germs of these diseases.[28]

---

[24] Waitz, Anthropologie, vol. iii.

[25] De bello gallico, lib. v. cap. xiv.

[26] Von Schlagintweit, Indien.

[27] G. Fritsch, Die Eingebornen Südafrika's, p. 227.

[28] Even this hypothesis is not free from all doubt. In the community of Batz, 3300 inhabitants, situated on a peninsula to the north of the mouth of the Loire, and where the emptying of natural saltpans is the only occupation, intermarriages among relations have been customary from time immemorial. Thus in the year 1865 no less than fifteen ecclesiastical dispensations for marriages between cousins were procured. Voisin, who spent a whole month there, did not find, as the result of forty marriages between blood relations, respecting which he collected complete pedigrees, a single case of the diseases which usually threaten such alliances. Anthropological Review, vol. vi. London, 1868.

But this knowledge, which can only be gained by lengthened observation, is unattainable by unsettled and childishly heedless races, so that it is exactly among such that a horror of incest is developed most strongly. According to this theory, we should most especially avoid marriage with a sister, who, as regards blood, is the same as ourselves, and stands as near again to us as mother or daughter, with whose organism our own only half agrees as to descent; yet this particular marriage was prescribed to the Inca of the kingdom of Peru,[29] nor could the Pharoah of Egypt select a more fitting consort than his own sister.[30] In ancient Persia marriage with a sister or a mother was not merely allowed, but the intermarriage of relations was looked upon as a meritorious act,[31] and it is known that the Greeks, at least, allowed marriage with half-sisters even if they did not actually approve of them.[32] While these highly civilized nations did not recoil from such alliances, the less civilized felt a terror of them which was probably salutary : it is quite exceptional that the Veddahs of Ceylon allow the brother to espouse his younger sister.[33] It is less surprising that every form of incest is considered permissible [34] among the Aleutians and Koniaks, and probably among other nations on the shores of Behring's Straits, for they are all notorious for their licentiousness.

The Australians, on the contrary, adhered strictly to the rule that no man was allowed to marry a woman who even bore the same family name as himself.[35] Marriages among people of the same surname were also strictly avoided among the Samoyeds and Ostiaks.[36] The Hurons and Iroquois tolerated no marriages between relations.[37] The Kolushs, who are divided into the two branches of the Crows and the Wolves, forbid all marriages

---

[29] Garcilasso, Commentarios reales. Only in default of a sister were the other female relations taken in succession.

[30] Ebers, Durch Gosen zum Sinai.

[31] Duncker, Gesch. d. Alterthums.

[32] Martin Haug, Allgem. Zeitung. 1872.

[33] Tylor, Primitive Culture, vol. i. p. 51.

[34] Von Langsdorff, Reise um die Welt.

[35] Captain Gray as quoted by Eyre, Central Australia, vol. ii. p. 330.

[36] Castrèn, Vorlesungen.   [37] Charlevoix, Nouvelle France, vol. iii.

between members of the same tribe.[38] In the same spirit the Arowaks of South America permit no espousals within their own clans;[39] and in their carefully kept pedigrees it is the rule that the children belong to the tribe of the mother. We may cite instances from Africa also. The Hottentots punish incest with death; and among the Kaffirs loss of property is the penalty of marriage with the most distant relations, although they permit of a double marriage with two sisters.[40] The Fan negroes, in the west of Equatorial Africa, although they are notorious cannibals, regard marriages between those of the slightest consanguinity as a crime, invariably obtaining their wives from another tribe.[41] The Batta of Sumatra, who are also cannibalistic, punish marriages between members of the same horde with the death of both the guilty parties.[42] Among the Hindoos the prohibition extends to the sixth degree of relationship; and with them also identity of name is regarded as a sufficient impediment to marriage.[43] The same is the case with the Chinese,[44] who, as a nation, call themselves Pih-sing, or the *hundred families.* Nevertheless, in modern times, there are four hundred family names which are inherited not from the mother but, as in Europe, from the father. An American missionary of the name of Talmadge knew a village of 5000 inhabitants who nearly all bore the same surname, and are therefore unable to form alliances among themselves.[45] Traces of these wide-reaching ideas of incest have been preserved among the nations which practice wife-stealing, for as the different tribes were usually separated by enmity, forcible abduction was the only means of effecting a marriage. Hence ethnographists betray an imperfect knowledge of the subject when they speak of this custom as practised by the Australians as a barbarism, although the Australian women regard this ancient practice not as maltreatment,

---

[38] Waitz, Anthropologie, vol. iii.

[39] Martius, Ethnologie, vol. i.

[40] Ausland. 1859.

[41] Du Chaillu, Ashango Land, p. 427.

[42] Tylor, Early History of Mankind, p. 359.

[43] Colebrooke, Essays on the Religion and Philosophy of the Hindus.

[44] Huc, Das chinesische Reich.

[45] Morgan, Systems of Consanguinity.

11

but as a homage, and it is a favourite game of their boys and girls.[46]   The same custom prevailed among the extinct Tasmanians,[47] among the Papuans of New Guinea, the Fiji Islands,[48] the Aino on the Kurile Islands,[49] and among the Fuegians.[50]   Every Ostiak or Samoyed,[51] every Lapp, even in the present day, must by craft or force seize a girl of another tribe, as was formerly the habit of the Finns (Suomi).[52]   Ethnologists will agree with us in interpreting Livy's account of the rape of the Sabines as a faint tradition of an ancient Roman custom, by which they were prohibited from marrying within the tribal community.   In later and quieter times wife-stealing survived only as part of the wedding festivities.   One evening in Khondistan, Campbell saw a lad who was carrying on his shoulder a burden wrapped in a scarlet cloth, pursued by a crowd of women and girls, pelting him with stones, bits of bamboo, and other missiles.   It turned out afterwards that the victim was on his wedding journey, and was carrying his young wife in the scarlet wrapper, while the whole affair was only intended as a representation of the pursuit of a wife-stealer.[53]   In its last stage the capture becomes a mere game between the bridegroom and the bride, of which the result is always prearranged ; yet it is said that among the Maori, a girl who, on such an occasion, has an earnest desire to escape, is able to evade an unwelcome suitor.[54]   Kennan, who witnessed a similar wedding game among the Koriaks, affirms that the bride must always give a tacit consent to her own capture.   Even in Europe a feigned attack is often enacted as a marriage ceremony.   Among the Slovaks the bridegroom and his companions actually arm themselves to approach the bride's house, which is closed as if awaiting a siege.[55]   In old

---

[46] Dumont d'Urville, Voyage de l'Astrolabe, vol. i.

[47] Waitz (Gerland), Anthropologie, vol. vi.

[48] Williams, Ausland.   1859.

[49] Mittheilungen der Wiener geog. Gesellschaft.   1872.

[50] W. Parker Snow, Off Tierra del Fuego, vol. ii. p. 359.

[51] Castrèn, Vorlesungen.

[52] J. A. Frijs, Wanderungen in der drei Lappländern.   Globus, 1872.

[53] Campbell, Khondistan.

[54] Waitz, Anthropologie, vol. i.

[55] Klun, Die Slovenen.   Ausland, 1872.

Bavaria the custom of abduction still continues as a marriage sport, termed " Brautlauf" (bridal run), which in old northern was called "Quânfang" (wife capture).[56] Among the Patagonians, with whom Musters spent some time, purchase-money is secretly paid to the parents, while the bride herself is suddenly stolen.[57]

Where too great consanguinity is not avoided, and wife-stealing is not encouraged, the suitor was obliged to purchase the bride from the parents; the woman then becomes the property of the husband, and may be left by him to a legal successor. Among the Caribs of Venezuela,[58] and in equatorial West Africa, the eldest son inherits all the wives of his deceased father, with the sole exception of his own mother.[59] Schweinfurth asserts the same of Munza, the sovereign of the remarkable kingdom of the Monbuttoos on the Uellé.[60] On the Gold Coast the vacant throne was occupied by the prince who gained possession of the paternal harem before the other brothers.[61] This throws light on certain incidents in the Old Testament history. Absalom took possession of his father's wives in the sight of all Jerusalem, in order to proclaim to the whole people that he had expelled David from the throne.[62] In the same spirit Solomon orders the execution of Adonijah, because he begged to have Abishag, David's last favourite, as his wife, thus betraying designs upon the throne.

Where the purchase of the bride is still a reality, as among the Kaffirs, comparatively high prices are paid,[63] nor is the inclination of the chosen bride at all consulted. Among more advanced people, on the contrary, as, for instance, the Abipones and the Patagonians, the purchase becomes invalid or is cancelled if the girl refuses her assent.[64] Marriage was originally a purchase among the Germans, the suitor paying over the price to the individual

---

[56] Sepp, Die Schimmelkirchen. Alleg. Zeitung, 1873.

[57] Ausland. 1872.

[58] Gumilla, El Orinoco ilustrado. Madrid, 1741.

[59] Du Chaillu, Ashango Land, p. 427.

[60] In the Heart of Africa.

[61] Bosman, Guinese Goud-Tand-en Slavekust.

[62] 2 Sam. xvi. 22.

[63] Gustav Fritsch, Die Eingebornen Südafrikas.

[64] Dobrizhoffer, Gesch. der Abiponer. Musters, Unter den Patagoniern.

in whose power the maiden or the widow chanced to be, to the father, brother, or guardian.[65]   As the wife thus fell under the guardianship (vormundschaft) of the husband, this legal act was also termed a *mundkauf*.   Again, in Iceland and in Norway the wife was purchased ;[66] and the English, as late as 1549, in their marriage ritual, preserved traces of this ancient legal procedure.[67] It is a long-known fact that in ancient Rome the ceremonial form of marriage contract (confarreatio) was customary only among patricians, while the plebeians effected their marriages by a merely formal purchase (coemptio).   Where Islam prevails the wife must even now be bought.[68]   Manu's law, which abolished the customary bridal gift of a yoke of oxen, indicates a great refinement and softening of manners.[69]   The bridegroom is instead welcomed as a guest in the house of his father-in-law on the wedding day, and receives the bride with the forms usual in the case of ceremonial gifts.[70]   Divorce is open to the husband at his own will wherever polygamy prevails.

Sir John Lubbock has ventured to maintain that in the primitive state mankind did not live together connubially, but that the women of a tribe were the common property of all the men. For this barbarous idea he has also invented a barbarous word, for he speaks of this condition as " hetarism."   He recognizes traces of it even now in Australia, appealing to statements made by John Eyre.[71]   He could certainly have no better testimony, for Eyre is inspired with such sympathy for these perishing races, that he would certainly not have recorded unfavourable facts concerning them, either maliciously or recklessly.   He does say that the Australians with whom he became acquainted did not value conjugal fidelity in their women ; but his statements refer

---

[65] J. Grimm, Deutsche Rechtsalterthümer.   1854.

[66] Paul Laband in Zeitschrift für Völkerpsychologie.   1865.

[67] Friedberg, Das Recht der Eheschliessung   In the Netherlands, in Spain, according to West Gothic law, and in Longobard law, traces of the purchase of brides still exist.

[68] Warnkönig, Juristische Encyclopädie.

[69] Duncker, Geschichte des Alterthums.

[70] Colebrooke, Essays on the Religion and Philosophy of the Hindus.

[71] Central Australia.   1845.

only to the tribes in the vicinity of the Murray River, who were already in frequent intercourse with European settlers. Such intercourse has nearly everywhere corrupted the manners of the natives. The supposed habit of hetarism is moreover contradicted by Eyre's own statement,[72] that paternal authority is entirely unlimited, and, on the other hand, by the traits which he gives of the passionate tenderness of fathers for their children. Other observers attribute jealousy in a special degree to the Australian men, and it is asserted that they take bloody vengeance on the adulterer.[73] Neumayer, moreover, who spent many nights among the natives, never noticed any breach of propriety or morality.[74] When we remember that, from a horror of consanguinity, the Australians marry only women with a different family name, the hetaristic state appears very unlikely, and we may regard the facts communicated by Eyre as a local degeneration of manners, confined to the southern portion of the continent, where there really are tribes in which the husband's brothers call the wife by a like name.[75]

The hypothesis that at a remote age marriage was unknown to the human race is hardly credible. Even among animals we sometimes find a strict pairing, that is to say, among monkeys,[76] predatory animals, ungulates, ruminants, and among song birds, chickens, and birds of prey. Darwin has also disputed the probability of a community of wives among prehistoric man, on the grounds that the males of many mammals are extremely jealous, and are furnished with weapons with which to fight for the possession of the females. The Veddahs of Ceylon, whom we should expect to find most primitive, have, as we have already seen, a beautiful proverb that death alone can part man and wife.[77]

In the fact that the chase, which is the most primitive means

---

[72] Central Australia. 1845. [73] Waitz (Gerland), Anthropologie, vol. vi.

[74] Zeitschrift für Ethnologie. 1871.

[75] Waitz (Gerland), Anthropologie, vol. vi.

[76] In Borneo, between the Padass and the Papar, Lieut. C. de Crespigny came upon a family of Mias (Orang-outang), consisting of the male, female, and two young ones of different ages. Their connection must therefore have lasted some time. Proceedings of the Royal Geogr. Society, vol. xvi.

[77] Darwin, Descent of Man, vol. ii. p. 318.

of obtaining a subsistence, is rarely followed by women, we find a reason why the rearing of children could succeed only when both the father and mother supported them in their tender years. The statistics furnished by modern society show, in the case of illegitimate children who are provided for by a mother only, and by her insufficiently, that the mortality is far greater than among legitimate children brought up in the parental house.

An American scholar, Lewis Morgan, has recently published an excellent work on the terms used to express relationships in no less than 139 different languages, chiefly American, but also including Asiatic, Malay, and European tongues.[78]   By this new scientific expedient Morgan thinks it possible to raise in a slight degree the veil which shrouds the sexual life of dim past ages. Among the Mongoloid people of Asia, among the Dravidas of India, among the aborigines of America, and the nations of the Malay family, we find a system of names for blood relationships entirely differing from our own.   The descendants of a common ancestor or ancestors, if they are of the same generation, give each other the name of brother or sister; they call all male members of the previous generation fathers, and of the following one, sons.   A man will therefore designate as his brothers, not only all the sons of his father, but also all the sons of his father's brother, and all the grandsons of his great uncle.   He will address as his sons not only his own children, but all the sons of his brothers, all the grandsons of his father's brother, and all the great grandsons of his great uncle.   The children of his sister, on the contrary, he speaks of as his nephews or nieces; the brothers of his mother as uncles.   Conversely, a woman will address as mother, not only her parent, but also her mother's sisters, as well as the daughters of her grandmother's sisters.   All the children of her sister, all the grandchildren of her mother's sister, all the great grandchildren of her grandmother's sister, she calls her children; the children of her brother, on the contrary, are her nephews and nieces.[79]   But we must not forget that in all these

---

[78] Systems of Consanguinity and Affinity in the Human Family.   1871.

[79] Lafitau describes carefully this system among the Iroquois and Hurons. Mœurs des sauvages amériquains.   1724.

languages no proper terms exist for brother or sister, but specific words must be used for the elder and younger brother, for elder and younger sister. Even Hungarian has no proper name for brother and sister, but must have recourse to circumlocution.[80]

The great majority of nations made less distinction in speech between various degrees of consanguinity than between the different generations, and between the various ages in the generations indicated. This simplest form of things, as it prevails among the Iroquois and Seneca, as well as among the Tamuls, was susceptible of various refinements and modifications, so that this branch of knowledge has thrown a new light on to the mental relationships of the several races of kindred. It is a pity that this American scholar believes himself to have discovered, in this unusual method of viewing the degrees of kindred, traces of past times in which marriage was unknown. He, too, supposes that hetarism was once habitual, and that a state occurred later, in which the sons of one mother lived in common with all their sisters. The duty enjoined on the Hebrew brother-in-law, of raising offspring to his brother's widow, may perhaps be regarded as an inheritance from these early ages, for we have found this ordinance amongst a great number of other nations, to which we must add the negroes of the Gold Coast.[81] On the other hand, we should remember that the patriarch Jacob leads home two sisters one after the other, and that, as we stated above,[82] in Southern India marriages are concluded between a number of brothers and several sisters. Among the Kanaks of the Hawai Islands it was customary, under the name of Pinalua, for brothers to have their wives in common, and sisters their husbands.[83] We can scarcely venture, however, to designate these peculiar customs as invariable preliminary stages of actual marriage; we should rather, perhaps, regard them as local variations. That at any time and in any place the children of the same mother have propagated themselves sexually, for any long

[80] Steinthal, in the Zeitschrift für Völkerpsychologie.
[81] Bosman, Guinese Goudkust. Utrecht, 1704.
[82] See above, p. 22.
[83] Morgan, Systems of Consanguinity.

period, has been rendered especially incredible, since it has been established that even in the case of organisms devoid of blood, such as the plants, reciprocal fertilization of the descendants of the same parents is to a great extent impossible. The theory gains no weight from the fact that Malay, Asiatic, and American Mongoloid nations, the Dravida of India, and some few negroes, in their speech distinguish peculiar relationships, for there cannot possibly be any allusion to sexual procreation when a man calls the great grandson of his great uncle his son, or when a woman speaks of the great granddaughter of her great aunt as her daughter. It is also noteworthy that of the eighty American languages examined by Morgan, two only have no specific expressions by which the woman designates the brother of her husband, and the husband of her sister, as her brothers-in-law,[84] so that in the great majority of cases no community of wives among brothers, and no community of husbands among sisters existed. It is precisely nations in the most primitive stage which have the greatest abhorrence of incestuous marriages. Neither could community of wives nor polyandry exist in those races among whom the couvade, or paternal child-bed, was customary.[85] Moreover, when we consider that all the languages in which the titles, father, brother, son, are attributed to the various members of the family according to whether they are descended from a common ancestor in a nearer, equal, or more remote degree, have proper names to distinguish the elder or younger brother, or father's brother, and the elder or younger sister, or mother's sister, it is evident that it is not the degree of consanguinity that is denoted, but the succession of the generations and the rank in the family, because these grades involve important consequences in domestic intercourse, such as the superior dignity of the elders, and yet more probably, more or less imperative duties of "vendetta." It is also a well-known fact that the aborigines of the present United States carried on sanguinary wars, and concluded formal treaties, to decide which nation was to bestow upon the other the title of grandfather, uncle, or elder brother. In other places the descendants of a common ancestor or ancestors formed a corporation reciprocally bound to

---

[84] Morgan, Systems of Consanguinity.   [85] See above, p. 223.

one another. Among the negroes of the Gold Coast, when a culprit was condemned to pay a fine which he was unable to raise, the father and the uncle, or other relations, were liable, and if necessary were sold as slaves.[86] In the same way, on the Palawan Islands, each head of a family, who is also the eldest, was held accountable for his kinsmen.[87]

At present the progenitor almost everywhere has paternal power over his descendants ; while among the more barbarous people he generally exercises over the wife the rights of a proprietor. Yet there are many nations in which all family rights are derived from the mother. Bosman affirms of the natives of the Gold Coast, that all children take their position from the mother, whoever the father may be. They are considered free or slaves, according as the mother was free or a slave.[88] The same usage existed among the ancient Lycians, who took their names not from their father but from their mother.[89] In the same manner the Australians always inherit family name and caste from the maternal side.[90] The habit is common also to the Fijians,[91] the Maori of New Zealand, and the Micronesians of the Marshall Archipelago, among whom nobility or rank is inherited from the mother.[92] The same principle is observed where the young husband enters the house of his father-in-law and passes into his family. This occurs among the Dyaks of Borneo, and it is very significant that there the father-in-law is more highly revered than the actual father.[93] Likewise, among the Itelmes of Kamtshatka, the husband belongs to the Ostrog of his wife.[94] These family institutions were also widely spread in America. In Guayana the child followed the

[86] Bosman, Guinese Goud-Tand-en Slavenkust. 1704. Winwood Reade, Savage Africa. 1863.

[87] C. Semper, Palau-inseln.

[88] Guinese Goud-Tand-en Slavenkust.

[89] Herodotus, lib. i. cap. 173.

[90] Waitz (Gerland), Anthropologie, vol. vi. There are some other instances in A. Bastian, Rechtsverhältnisse. 1872.

[91] Ausland. 1859.

[92] D. G. Monrad, Das alte Neuseeland. 1871. Journal des Museum Godeffroy. 1873.

[93] Spenser St. John, Life in the Far East. 1862.

[94] G. Steller, Kamtschatka.

mother in all social respects, so that the offspring of a Macushi Indian woman and a Wapishiana would be considered to belong to the Macushi tribe.[95]   These views of rights were yet more decidedly marked among the Iroquois and Hurons of North America.   The relationship to the father was regarded as very slight, and the children were dependent on the mother.[96]   She alone possessed the right of adoption to supply the place left vacant when a son had been murdered.   Hence the women decided whether the prisoners of war should die at the martyr's stake or be received into the tribe.[97]   They were even honoured with the right of decision as to war or peace, as the former might give opportunity of gaining prisoners of war; this was not, however, done in earnest, for in reality they were kept from all knowledge of important political enterprises.[98]   Though the young husband during the first years of his marriage owed his parents-in-law certain services, the wife, on the other hand, was bound to work in the fields of her parents-in-law, and to provide their household with wood.[99]   The clear conception of such domestic institutions as these has been by no means aided by the fact that the Jesuit Lafitau applied to them the word "guneocracy," used by Strabo,[100] as if at any time, or in any place, however barbarous, women ruled in the house, and the men were under their control.   J. J. Bachofen has indeed written a comprehensive work to spread the scarcely credible opinion that, in the earliest stages of human society, the mothers were considered the heads of the family, as if the so-called children of nature had recognized, not the right of the strongest, but the right of the weakest.   Bachofen was only able to prove his assertion by adducing ancients myths, on which he put a forced interpretation. He holds the existence of female supremacy to be sufficiently established by the fact that, in ancient Egypt, the men occupied the weaver's stool; and, regardless of the exhaustive researches of

---

[95] Appun, in the Ausland.   1872.
[96] Charlevoix, Nouvelle France.
[97] Ibid.   [98] Ibid.
[99] Lafitau, Mœurs des sauvages.   1724.
[100] Strabo, Geogr., lib. iii.

Martius, he yet maintains that the Amazonian communities of South America existed outside the imagination of Spanish explorers.

The custom that the children belong to the mother in all social respects docs not necessarily indicate that the paternity was regarded as uncertain, but that the bodily relation to the mother was held to be incomparably stronger, just as, until quite recent times, physiologists have adhered to the opinion, that in the generation of offspring the function of the father must be considered quite subordinate. The strange ideas of procreation which are held by the so-called savages, are illustrated by the superstition of the Saliva Indians on the Orinoco, that every woman who gives birth to twins must necessarily have been guilty of adultery.[101] The view of the subject to which we have alluded explains the occurrences of the heirship of nephews, that is to say, the right of inheriting from the brother of the mother to the exclusion of his own off-spring. Thus among the Tuaregs the dignity of chief is always transferred to the sister's sons.[102] On the Gold Coast the son in-herited from his maternal uncle, the daughter from the mother's sister,[103] and even now the throne of Ashanti does not pass to the next heir of the body, but to the son of the brother or sister.[104] Heirship of nephews was also found by Livingstone among the Kebrabasa negroes on the Zambesi.[105] In the Antilles, the sister's children, as the nearest relations, at least excluded the brother's children from the succession.[106] The heirship of nephews is also customary in America among the Kolushs and other coast tribes in the north-west,[107] among the Montagnais in Labrador,[108] and also among the Hurons and Iroquois.[109] This social insti-tution was formerly far more widely diffused and perhaps pre-vailed in all those nations in which the children followed the tribe of the mother. When Europeans, in Africa and America,

[101] Jos. Gumilla, El Orinoco ilustrado. 1741.
[102] Bulletin de la Soc. de Geogr. Paris, 1863.
[103] Bosman, Guinese Goud-Kust. 1704.
[104] Winwood Reade, Savage Africa. p. 43. [105] Zambesi, p. 162.
[106] Oviedo, Historia general, lib. v. cap. 3.
[107] Waitz, Anthropologie, vol. iii.
[108] Youle Hind, Labrador. 1863.
[109] Charlevoix, Nouvelle France.

inquired into the cause of this family arrangement, they were invariably answered that no doubt could exist as to the relationship to the sister's children, whereas that on the father's side might be questioned. This certainly sounds as if conjugal fidelity was wanting, and as if very loose morals had prevailed; yet it is more probably due to an erroneous apprehension of the physiology of paternity, as the heirship of nephews occurs among so many nations of the strictest morality, such as the Kolushs above mentioned. Winwood Reade, who draws unfavourable pictures of the negroes of Western Africa, yet says that, notwithstanding the fact that the nephew is regarded as heir both in Dahomey and among the Adiya of Fernando Po, the first or, at any rate, the second commission of adultery is punished by death; nay, he even admits that in West Africa, if a girl disgraces her family by a false step, expulsion from the tribal community ensues.[110]   The heirship of nephews is also habitual among nations such as the Iroquois and Hurons, who are examples of severe self-restraint. Young couples were obliged to live together as brother and sister for an entire year to prove that higher motives than the gratification of sensual pleasure had brought them together.[111]   Joseph Gumilla says similarly of the Red Indians, "They are all highly sensitive to the infidelity of their wives, though the Caribs alone inflict exemplary punishment upon them; the whole community aiding to slaughter the guilty individuals in public." At another time he mentions an Indian woman who poisoned herself that she might not break her marriage vow. Uncertainty with regard to paternity cannot have led to the heirship of nephews in those races which observe the custom of the male child-bed.[112]   Hence, until strong evidence is adduced, preference of the sister's children before the actual bodily heir, and the reverence for the mother's brother, ought not to be regarded as a sign of conjugal immorality.

As no other suitable place may be found, we must be allowed here to add that kissing is not everywhere the custom. Darwin

---

[110] Savage Africa, pp. 48–61. 1863.

[111] Lafitau, Mœurs des sauvages. Charlevoix, Nouvelle France.

[112] El Orinoco ilustrado. 1741. There were, however, even gross breaches of conjugal fidelity.

has already informed us that in the South Seas this expression of affection is unknown to the Maori of New Zealand, the Tahitians, the Papuans, and the Australians, and also, in America, to the Eskimo and Fuegians.[113] Winwood Reade terrified a negro girl by kissing her, for in Western Africa such caresses are not usual ; Bayard Taylor likewise found among the Lapp women a decided aversion to this form of contact. It is of course impossible in the case of all those nations which slit open the lips and insert small pieces of wood, such as the tribes on the coast of Behring's Sea, the Kolushs, the Botocudos of Brazil, and the negroes of Central and Southern Africa.

VIII.—THE GERMS OF POLITICAL LIFE.

THE germs of civil life exist in the family. The Chinese, more than any other people, have strengthened this tie ; among them reverence for parents is developed into a kind of religious worship. One of the most sacred duties which unites the members of the family is the " vendetta," an institution not entirely deserving of our abhorrence, for we ought to respect it as the first attempt at legal protection. In past ages all the nations of the world observed this duty, which has been retained to our own days in Corsica and Albania. Confucius imposed upon a son the duty of carrying arms until he had taken and slain his father's murderer. The extinct Tasmanians also regarded such vengeance as a duty.[1] In like manner among their kinsmen, the Australians, all the members of a tribe were responsible for every sanguinary act committed by any of their number.[2] Martius describes this custom as common to all nations of Brazil, and notices it also among the Macushi and Arowaks of Guayana.[3] Among the Fijians the duty of vengeance was transmitted from father to son, and from the latter to the nearest relations.[4] This duty of defence

---

[113] This caress is despised by the Marquesas Islanders (see Langsdorff, Reise um die Welt), and probably by all Polynesians ; perhaps all nations among whom the Malay kiss is customary.

[1] Waitz, Anthropologie, vol. vi. [2] Ibid. vol. **vi.**

[3] Ethnographie, vol. i.

[4] H. Greffrath, in the Zeitschrift für Ethnologie. 1871.

serves a useful purpose, even if the chastising hand does not over-take the malefactor himself, but falls only on one who belongs to the same confederation.

It may seem strange that the sympathy of the ethnologist should be enlisted in favour of this doctrine of duty, but the following event, which happened in Arabia, will be sufficient explanation. In the year 1863, an Italian named Guarmani was sent to Nedshd by the Emperor Napoleon to buy thoroughbred horses. In the beginning of March, 1864, as he was wandering about with the Beni Ehtebe, a horde of Bedouins, they were attacked by their enemy, Emir Abdallah Ibn Feisal ibn Sa'wd. The conflict lasted several days, until at last an unexpected ally came to the aid of the Beni Ehtebe. Among the auxiliaries of the Emir were the Beni Kahtan who, during the successive days of hostilities, from the 9th to the 14th of March, had constantly skirmished with the Beni Ehtebe, but at the same time remained at a prudent distance. When the victors examined the field of battle they did not find among the slain a single individual of the Kahtans, whose entire party had seized the first available opportunity to fly. When we remember that the law of vengeance requires an accurate account not only of all deaths but of all bodily injuries, it is significant that, on the other hand, none of the Beni Ehtebe ascribed his wounds to any of the Beni Kahtan.[5] The Kahtan horde had always lived in peace with the Ehtebe, and had only followed the Emir to the battle on compulsion. In this instance, in which these two tribes by mutual consent had only pretended to fight, the law of vengeance showed its beneficial influence, for if any wounds had been inflicted, they would have given rise to a series of acts of violence descending to distant generations. We thus see that the "vendetta" was a protection to life. Hence, if an Arab kills his own relation no avenger pursues him, for he has injured him-self, nor does the murder of an outlaw or one expelled from his tribe involve consequences of any kind.[6] Where vengeance is

---

[5] Guarmani, Itineraire au Neged septentrional, in the Bulletin de la Société Geogr. Paris, 1865.

[6] Von Maltzan, Sittenschilderungen aus Südarabien, vol. xxi. p. 123. Globus, 1872.

regarded as a duty, he who does not execute it is regarded with contempt.[7] As retribution has thus been developed into an affair of honour, it is very difficult for these sanguinary feuds to end. They are most easily ended by the equalization of the number of deaths and wounds on both sides. The balance in any other case must be made up in money's worth. The Aneze Bedouins require for the life of a freeman, fifty female camels, a dromedary, a mare, a black slave, a coat of mail and a gun ;[8] some tribes demand money to the value of £50, and others only half as much.

As manners become gentler, compensation in money's worth becomes the practice, and hence is developed the custom of weregild, or blood-money. Wherever such penalties were imposed, the "vendetta" formerly prevailed. In Guinea, in Bosman's[9] days, that is, in the beginning of the eighteenth century, the death of every freeman was atoned for by heavy fines, which were paid to the relations. In Siam, contrary to our ideas of justice, a smaller sum is paid for the killing of an old man than for that of men in the prime of life.[10] The old Germans paid the were- gild partly to the family of the slaughtered person, partly to the community.[11] Among the Kaffirs justice has so far advanced that the fines are paid to the chief instead of to the injured parties, as if the wrong had been inflicted on the society or the person who represents it.[12] They justify the fact that the kinsmen are left without compensation, by the beautiful saying, that one cannot eat one's own blood.[13] The "vendetta" de- mands an equivalent retribution, according to the scriptural words,

---

[7] Among the Kuki, a tribe in Southern Asia, the kinsmen of a man killed by a tiger looked upon themselves as dishonoured until they had slain a tiger. Tylor, Primitive Culture, vol. i. p. 282.

[8] Burckhardt, Notes on the Bedouins. London, 1830.

[9] Guinese Goud-Tand-en Slavekust.

[10] Brossard de Corbigny, in the Revue maritime et coloniale, tom. xxxiii.

[11] Tacitus, Germ. cap. 12. Pars multae regi, vel civitati, pars ipsi, qui vindicatur, vel propinquis ejus absolvitur. Comp. J. Grimm, Deutsche Recht- alterthümer, and G. Geib, Lehrbuch des deutschen Strafrechtes. Leipzic, 1861.

[12] Fritsch, Eingeborne Südafrika, p. 97.

[13] Maclean, Kafir Laws and Customs. Mount Coke, 1858.

an eye for an eye, a tooth for a tooth, a life for a life. The Roman system of penal justice was also founded on this conception. At the time of the laws of the Twelve Tables, retribution was still exacted, at least for severe bodily injuries, unless the person wronged preferred a compromise.[14]

In every part of the world where man has taken possession of a thing either for use or pleasure, he has considered himself its proprietor. Even animals exhibit some apprehension of the rights of possession ; birds seem to feel this in regard to the nest which they have built. A monkey which was in the Zoological Gardens in London, and which had weak jaws, made use of a stone to open nuts, always hiding it in the straw after using it, nor would he allow it to be touched by any other monkey.[15] The Pomeranian dogs of our carters watch the goods of their masters, and evidently behave as guardians of the property. Appun, who spent many years among the natives of Guayana, assures us that the property of the individual is held sacred by the other inhabitants of his hut.[16] At a very early stage the conception of rights of property even in immovable objects arises. Hunting tribes always regard the hunting-ground as the property of the tribe collectively. The Brazilians avail themselves of rivers, waterfalls, mountains, rocks, and trees, as boundary marks.[17] A fight between two hordes of the Botocudos, at which the Prince of Wied was present, was the consequence of an invasion by one tribe of the hunting-ground of another tribe.[18] Among the Australians, whom ethnology was wont to look down upon as the most degraded people, property in soil and territory was strictly respected. Benilong, a native of New South Wales, had inherited Goat Island from his father, and intended to leave it to a friend.[19] Divisions of the inheritance during the lifetime of the owner occur among them, and the rights of the proprietor

---

[14] Si membrum rupit, ni cum eo pacit, talio esto ; Table VIII. H. E. Dirksen, Ueversicht der Zwölftafel-Fragmente.

[15] Darwin, Descent of Man, vol. i. p. 44.

[16] Ausland. 1872.

[17] Martius, Ethnographie, vol. i.

[18] Reise nach Brasilien. 1820.

[19] Dumont d'Urville, Voyage de l'Astrolabe.

were so rigidly respected that no one was allowed to fell trees or kindle fire on the territory of another without his leave. A state of society in which ownership is not recognized is therefore unknown.

Where stationary populations have fields under cultivation, the boundaries of the land are carefully and clearly marked out. Boundary stones are to be seen on the northern Nicobar Islands, which are densely peopled, while there are none in the southern islands, in which there is still sufficient space.[20] Among the old inhabitants of Cumaná on the Caribbean Sea, the Spaniards saw the field marked off by cotton strings, and to tamper with these was looked upon as a crime.[21] The inhabitants of the Venezuelan shores regarded theft as the most reprehensible offence, and punished it by a cruel death.[22] It is a most arbitrary act on the part of a despotic government when, in districts so densely peopled as British and Malayan India, the Crown exalts itself into the sole proprietor of soil and territory, farming out the land to the subjects. The same state institution existed in ancient China.[23] In Peru, during the time of the Incas, private property was impossible, for a strict community of goods prevailed, or rather, there was one sole proprietor, the Son of the Sun, who through his officials imposed the statute-service on his subjects, and divided amongst them all the produce of their labour. Nor was this system confined to Peru ; the Caziques of the Antilles [24] and the chiefs of the Otomaks in the modern Venezuela used it also. Where a divine origin is ascribed to the chiefs, and they are regarded as superior beings, property can only be held by them. Among the true Polynesians, and the hybrid Polynesian nations, all that the prince touches or treads upon becomes *taboo*, or not lawful for any one to touch. The troublesome precautions to which the chiefs were obliged to submit in order to avoid the unwished-for consequences of the law have often been told; how, for example, they are carried across tracts of land to prevent tabooing them.

[20] Waitz, Anthropologie, vol. i. p. 440.
[21] Petrus Martyr, De orbe novo, Dec. viii. cap. 6.
[22] Gomara, Historia de las Indias, cap. 28, 68.
[23] Plath, Gesetz und Recht im alten China.
[24] Peschel, Zeitalter der Entdeckungen.

The organization of the national life is most closely dependent on the mode of gaining a livelihood. Where man associates with his fellow-men, a governing authority springs up. The loosest of all social bonds are those of the nomadic hunting tribes of Brazil, which consist of a few families or often of only one. But even these have their hunting-grounds to protect, and require a leader, at least in times of war. Among all hunters and fishermen the power of the chiefs is very limited, and often not even hereditary. The Indians of North America, the Australians, the Bushmen, and the Eskimo, allow their chiefs very slight authority: for hunting and fishing are the employments in which the individual least requires the aid of his fellows. "In an ant's nest," exclaims Peter Gumilla,[25] with reference to the Indians of the Orinoco, "there is more order and authority than in the nations concerning which I have been writing." Another Jesuit, Charlevoix,[26] judges more favourably of the North American Indians. "Without any visible ruler," he says, "they enjoy all the advantages of a well-regulated government."

Pastoral tribes are usually found under patriarchal leaders, for the flocks generally belong to a single master who is served by the other members of his tribe in the capacity of domestics, or by former flock-owners once independent and subsequently impoverished. In the northern parts of the Old World, as well as in Southern Africa, great national migrations are nearly if not quite peculiar to pastoral life; the history of America, on the contrary, tells only of the invasions of barbarous hunting tribes into the civilized territories of prosperous populations. That entire nations should desert their former dwellings, press onwards, and wander over vast regions of the world, is inconceivable, unless they are accompanied by flocks yielding the requisite sustenance on the march. Cattle-breeding on steppes necessitates a change of abode. When nations become stationary, and husbandry commences, the desire for slave labour at once arises. Hunters who support themselves and their families only by constant exertion, can find no employment for bondsmen in their household. It is different even where fishing is practised, for in that case we some-

---

[25] El Orinoco ilustrado.   [26] Nouvelle France.

times find slavery, as on the north-west coast of America, among the Koniaks and Kolushs, and among the Ahts of Vancouver's Island [27] who, we may remark in passing, cut the hair of their bondsmen. Sooner or later slavery invariably leads to despotism, for he who possesses the greatest number of slaves is apt to use them to oppress the weaker. Slavery prevails throughout the whole of Central Africa, and therefore, whichever way we look in those regions, we see nothing but despotisms growing up on the ruins of other despotisms.

By the distinction of freemen from bondsmen, society becomes organized into ranks: an order of nobility is found even among negroes, although but rarely, as on the Gold Coast or in Congo.[28] The same occurs where a conquering race subjugates an alien nation. Physical characters are then usually regarded as tokens of superior descent; indeed, the Indian expression for caste, *varna*, is equivalent to *colour*,[29] alluding to the colour of the skin. When the kings of Spain raised a native American to the nobility, the formula was "that he might henceforth consider himself as a white man." It is difficult to explain how distinctions according to descent arise in hunting tribes. Yet among the Australians there are three castes which allow no intermarriages,[30] although it has nowhere been observed that any members of a tribe enjoyed a preference over the others. Our information concerning the supposed order of nobility among these races is still very imperfect.[31] If it is confined to the Coburg peninsula in the north,[32] it is probably due to an immigration from the islands to the north. For among the Malays, as well as among their kinsmen the Polynesians, there is an order of nobility which is generally subdivided into many grades.[33] Among the Tongans Mariner found, besides

---

[27] Waitz, Anthropologie, vol. iii. and Sproat in the Anthropological Review. 1868. Even among the Botocudos, slaves made prisoners in war are said to have been seen. Prinz zu Neuwied, Reise nach Brasilien.

[28] Antonio Zucchella, Missione di Congo, ix. 1712.

[29] Adalbert Kuhn in Weber's Indischen Studien.

[30] Earl, in the Journal of the Royal Geographical Society, vol. xvi.

[31] Reise in der Fregatte Novara, Anthropologie.

[2] Waitz (Gerland) Anthropologie, vol. vi.

[33] For instance, in the district of Holontal, in the Northern Celebes. Riedel, Zeitschrift für Ethnologie. 1871.

the princes, a higher and lower nobility, and two classes of plebeians.[34]   Aristocratic privileges and the institutions of caste are rampant also among the Papuan-Polynesian hybrid nations as well as among the inhabitants of the Fiji group or the Palau Islands.   As we possess very inadequate information respecting the true Papuans of New Guinea, and the power of the chiefs is described as very dubious, and as the New Caledonians (who are, however, probably not pure bred) seem to recognize no distinctions of rank, save the dignity of the chief, it is probably due to Polynesian influence alone that so many Papuan hybrid races have organized themselves into castes.

In America we find aristocracy of birth among the Kolushs on the coast of Alaska, and among their neighbours the Haidahs of Queen Charlotte's Island.   In both these places families bear the figures of animals as crests.[35]   Among the more southerly tribes on the north-west coast of America, those of noble birth were distinguishable by the artificial flattening of the head, for this mark, as we have seen, was conferred only on the free-born.[36]   The Iroquois made no differences of rank ; the Algonkins and their southern neighbours, on the contrary, separated themselves into nobles, commons, and slaves.[37]   In South America the Peruvian children of the sun founded a twofold nobility in their empire ; for, in addition to the numerous Incas or descendants of the blood royal,[38] they established the curacas, or local chiefs, in the vanquished provinces, and these were allowed to pierce their ears like the children of the Sun.[39]   Among the Guarani tribes and the Abipones there is also a marked distinction between people of high and low descent.   Old women, as Dobrizhoffer relates, whose wealth consisted solely in the wrinkles of their faces, boasted loudly that they were not descended from plebeian

[34] Tonga Islands.   Edinburgh, 1827.

[35] Waitz, Anthropologie, vol. iii.   Ausland, 1868.

[36] See above, p. 21.

[37] Lafitau, Mœurs des sauvages amériquains.   1724.

[38] Clements Markham is of opinion that the title of Inca was originally given not only to the ruling house, but to all the tribal heads of the Inca nation. Journal of Royal Geographical Society, vol. xli.

[39] Garcilasso, Commentarios, lib. i. cap. xxi.

parents. In conversing with nobles, the syllables *in* or *en* were appended to all verbs and nouns, according to whether the person addressed was a man or woman.[40]

IX.—THE RELIGIOUS EMOTIONS OF UNCIVILIZED NATIONS.

In all stages of civilization, and among all races of mankind, religious emotions are always roused by the same inward impulse, the necessity of discerning a cause or an author for every phenomenon and event. Those nations which have remained childlike combine with this an incapacity of conceiving the objects of sensory perception as inanimate. We shall shortly show that they attribute voluntary acts and human sensibility even to stones and rocks. The Dyaks of Borneo ascribe a psychical nature, called *semungat*, or *semungi*, not only to animals but even to plants. They regard unhealthiness in a plant as a temporary absence of its invisible *ego*, and when the rice perishes, its soul is said to have flown away.[1] When Philips the missionary complained of the heat on a sultry day to a young Fuegian, the boy anxiously exclaimed, "Do not call the sun hot or it will hide itself, and the wind will blow cold."[2] As the objects of the visible world are conceived as animated, volitional, and emotional, they may be deemed the originators of those misfortunes of which the true cause is unknown. The process of thought which results in these feelings among uncivilized races in intellectual obscurity is clearly illustrated by a frequently quoted anecdote given by the African traveller, Lichtenstein.[3] The chief of the Amaχosa, a Kaffir tribe, had given orders that a piece should be broken off a stranded anchor. Soon afterwards the man died by whom the order had been carried out, and as the Kaffirs, in common with many other nations in all parts of the world, ascribe the death of every man to supernatural causes, the injured anchor from that time received

---

[40] Geschichte der Abiponer. 1783.
[1] Spenser St. John, Life in the Far East, vol. i. p. 176. 1862.
[2] Ausland. 1861.
[3] Reisen im sudlichen Africa. Berlin, 1811.

marks of veneration from the Amaχosa. The Australians of New South Wales think it a crime to whistle in the vicinity of rocks, for, as they told Dumont d'Urville, some of their tribe who once whistled at the foot of a precipice were therefore killed by falling blocks of stone.[4] The proverb that avalanches are loosened by the sound of the bells on the mules' backs is certainly not founded on experience, but points to some old superstition of the same type as the Australian instance already given. We may here mention that the Wuka or Papuan hill people of New Guinea take their oaths near a high mountain, under the impression that it will fall upon them in case of perjury.[5] Near the Attar river in Pegu, about forty years before the visit of the Countess Nostiz,[6] a huge thingan tree, which was to be cut down and made into a war canoe, in its fall chanced to kill more than a hundred people ; the spot was at once regarded as bewitched, and a chapel for the Nat, or wood spirit, was erected on the stump of the tree. The King of Coomassie having died in 1698, and his bitter enemy, the Dutch superintendent of the Fort of Elmina, soon afterwards following him to the grave, the negroes who worship their dead as divine beings, looked upon the death of the latter as the work of their prince who had gone before him.[7] In all these cases we easily detect the weakness in the intellectual powers by which the temporal sequence of events is deemed necessarily to imply causal connection. Thus the Itelmes of Kamtshatka worshipped the water wagtails as the authors of spring, because a more propitious season set in at the time of their arrival :[8] a similar logical fallacy is indicated by the old proverb that " one swallow does not make summer." It was invariably the originators of alarming or desired events which attracted religious veneration. A native Mexican historian[9] tells us that the renowned king

---

[4] It is remarkable that on the Tonga Islands all whistling is avoided as being disrespectful to the gods. Mariner's Tonga Islands.

[5] O. Finsch, Neu-Guinea.

[6] Helfer, Reisen in Vorderasien und Indien. Leipzic, 1873.

[7] Bosman, Guinese Goud-Kust. 1704.

[8] G. Steller, Kamtschatka.

[9] Ixtlilxochitl, Histoire des Chichimèques. Prescott, Conquest of Mexico, vol. i. p. 194.

Tezcucos Netzahualcoyotzin worshipped an unknown god under the name of Cause of Causes. This craving after an invisible author or cause is the inducement to attribute a divine control over the destinies of mankind to lifeless objects, which are, however, regarded as animated. This is the obvious explanation of the origin of fetishism.

Every object that attracts the glance of the savage, who espies a ghost in every corner, may become in his eyes the abode of a deity. Fragments of plants, snake-skins, feathers, claws, shells, stone pipes, living beings, whole species of animals, in short, whatever first presents itself to the mind of the Red Indian, excited by long fasting, he thenceforth recognizes and worships as his guardian spirit.[10] The selection of the objects worshipped is however important, for by neglecting the commonplace for the sublime, it may transform fetishism into the belief in a supreme and morally perfect Being. Man remains ignoble only so long as his worship is given to portable objects, for these, together with their supposed divine power, are liable to become the property of a possessor. The services of these guardian spirits are then enjoyed by an owner. Laban, when he missed his household gods, pursued the patriarch Jacob ; and Rachel, who had stolen them, was able by her cunning to conceal them from his search. Long subsequent to the Mosaic legislation, down to David's times, the Hebrews kept their Seraphim or Penates in their houses.[11] Even where the intellect has attained the purest conception of God, the heart still clings tenaciously to the old objects of its childish veneration : no nation has yet completely purified itself from superstition, that is to say, from the remnants of earlier religious notions.

Sekedshket, who built cities in Turkistan in the hazy past ages, received several fetishes as part of the dowry of his Chinese wife ; and idol fairs were occasionally held in Bokhara.[12] When the fetish belongs to the movable properties or, as it were, to the household of the master, it is punished for its supposed obduracy

---

[10] Charlevoix, Nouvelle France.

[11] I Sam. xix. 13–19, and Ewald, Israelitische Geschichte.

[12] Vámbéry, History of Bokhara.

or malignity whenever it does not grant the wishes of the supplicant. When a misfortune befalls the Ostiak, he throws his idol on the ground, beats and ill-uses it, or breaks it to pieces.[13] About twenty years ago, Rastus, the last pagan Lapp in Europe, on some occasion deprived his divine bauta stone of its customary offering of brandy. When shortly afterwards two of his reindeer were killed by lightning, he angrily threw the pieces of the dismembered animals to his idol, exclaiming, " Take that which thou hast slain ; " he then immediately embraced Christianity.[14] Before every great enterprise the negro of Guinea, if no old and tried fetish is at hand, selects a new one ; whatever his eye falls upon as he leaves his house, be it a dog, a cat, or any other creature, he takes as his deity and offers sacrifices to it on the spot. If the enterprise succeeds the credit of the fetish is increased ; if it fails, the fetish returns to its former position.[15]

In all parts of the world stones have attracted the devotion of man. It is not surprising that worship was often offered to meteorolites which, falling red hot, penetrated into the ground. A stone which fell near Chicomoztotl, or the Seven Caves, an important spot in the mythological topography of the ancient Mexicans, was worshipped by them as the son of the divine couple, Ometeuctli and Omecihuatl.[16] The black stone, the chief object of worship of Mohammedans in Mecca, is said to have shone brightly at first, but very soon to have turned black on account of the sinfulness of mankind.[17] It is undoubtedly a remnant of the fetish worship of the pre-Islam Arabs, as is also the stone now built into the Mosque of Omar at Jerusalem, which carried the prophet heavenwards and then fell down, or rather still hovers in the air.[18] Owing to other conceptions easily interpreted, phallic-shaped stones, which are perhaps single pillars left standing out of a row of basalt columns, are worshipped in the Fiji

---

[13] Pallas, Voyages. 1793.

[14] Globus. January, 1873.

[15] Bosman, Guinese Goud-Tand-en Slavekust.

[16] J. G. Müller, Americanische Urreligionen.

[17] Sepp, in the Allgem. Zeitung. 1872.

[18] Baierlein, Nach und aus Indien.

Islands.[19]   Only recently Theodor Kirchhoff was shown a fragment of rock in Oregon to which the Umpkwa Indians are wont
to make pilgrimages.   The prophets of Israel and the devout
kings of Judah contended incessantly against the worship of the
"high places," which were probably tall, pointed stones symbolical of the Most Holy.[20]   Even Jacob anointed the stone
at Bethel on which he had rested.   In Celtic Europe we find
stone circles as places for worship, and also trilithic cromlechs
or stone tables, which served either as places of sacrifice or for
the faithful to crawl through.   Even in A.D. 567 a Council at
Tours was obliged to threaten excommunication against stone
worship; and in England similar interdicts were issued in the
seventh century by Theodoric, Archbishop of Canterbury, in the
tenth by King Edgar, and again in the eleventh by Canute.[21]   This
error is more pardonable in our eyes when the objects worshipped
are the mountains' crests.[22]   We do not allude to the consecration
of particular summits, such as Olympus, as the seat of the epic
deities, or of Sinai as the mountain of legislation, although with
reference to the latter we will observe that, on the heights of
Serbâls, there is a stone circle which the Bedouins only enter
without their shoes.   There is also one on which they lay gifts
on the adjacent Jebel Munâdshât, called by the Arabs "the
mountain of the dialogue" (that, namely, of Moses with Jehovah).[23]
The veneration of footprints, such as that of the god Tezcatlipoca
which the ancient Mexicans showed at Quauhtitlan,[24] or that of
Tiitii at Samoa, in the group of Navigator's Islands,[25] and, finally,
the footprint of Buddha on Adam's Peak at Ceylon, does not
belong to this category, but is a form of relic worship.   On the
other hand, we may mention the Shaman stone of the Mongolian
Burats, a rock on the peninsula of Olchon on Lake Baikal,
and the mountain of Tyrma, or Tirmak, on which the Guanches,

---

[19] Williams, Fiji and the Fijians.
[20] Ewald, History of the Children of Israel.
[21] Sir John Lubbock, Origin of Civilization, p. 209.
[22] Rüppell, Reise in Abyssinien.
[23] G. Ebers, Durch Gosen zum Sinai.
[24] J. G. Müller, Urreligionen.
[25] Tylor, Early History of Mankind, p. 143.
12

the aborigines of the Canary Islands, took their most solemn oaths, and from which enthusiasts voluntarily cast themselves as sacrifices.[26] Pausanias found stone worship established among the inhabitants of Phara, and on another occasion states that in old times all Greeks worshipped stones instead of images,[27] adding that they gave them the names of the different forces of nature; but it is doubtful whether this was a genuine stone worship, or only the remains of one that was genuine.

There is perhaps something alien to the German mind in stone worship, but the old pagan blood which is in us makes us more sympathetic on hearing that trees or groves were regarded as deities, or the abodes of deities : even now we understand the emotions of our forefathers when St. Boniface felled the Saxon oak. The murmur of the quiet wood, the roar of the forest during a storm, the crashing and creaking of the timber, the apparent struggle of a leafless tree with its gnarled branches rent by the storm, give us the impression of standing face to face with an animated being, and only too readily do we give way to the illusion of the actual presence of the supersensual powers. Tree worship formerly extended over all the world. On Loch Siant, in the Isle of Skye, there is even now an oak wood of such sanctity that no twig may be broken.[28] Wherever a solitary cedar springs up in a forest of fir trees, or there is a clump of seven larches, the Samoyed approaches the spot with awe. The Ostiak deems a tree sacred on which an eagle has built its nest for several successive years.[29] No twig of the groves of the Mundakhol, a Dravida tribe in India, may be injured.[30] On the other side of Jordan trees may still be seen from which are suspended sacrificial gifts, especially tresses of hair.[31] On his march to Sardis in Lydia, Xerxes adorned a sacred plane tree with ornaments of gold, and left a guardian to protect it.[32] In Africa, again, the huge monkey bread-trees, or

---

[26] Peschel, Zeitalter der Entdeckungen.   [27] Pausanias, vii.

[28] Sir John Lubbock, Origin of Civilization, p. 192.

[29] Castrèn, Vorlesungen. Pallas, Voyages.

[30] Zeitschrift für Ethnologie. 1871.

[31] Wolff in the Ausland. 1872.

[32] Herodotus, lib. vii. cap. 31.

Adansonia, receive the offerings of the devout. Adolf Bastian observed the same custom in Burmah.[33] Tylor speaks of a sacred cypress worshipped in this manner in Mexico ; Möllhausen of an oak on the western Colorado ; and at the outlet of Lake Superior stands the great ash tree to which the Red Indians bring offerings, as they do to the solitary Wallitschu tree on the pampas near Patagones (*Carmen*), visited by Darwin.[34] Other instances are the grove of Dodona, the Homeric plane-tree at Aulis, of which Pausanias[35] saw the remains ; the veneration accorded to the pepal (*Ficus religiosa*) and the Indian fig-tree (*F. indica*) by the Brahminical Hindoos and the Buddhists ; the sacred aspen of the Kirghiz,[36] the pear-tree lately felled in the Walser Feld, and the great ash Yggdrafil of our myths. A different form of tree worship is connected with the sojourn of holy personages, as was the case with the grove of Mamre because Abraham dwelt there, or the sycamore at Matarieh, under the shadow of which the Madonna is said to have rested in the flight to Egypt. The meaning of tree worship varies with the species of gift which is offered. The Arabs, who in pagan times offered sacrifices to trees, hanging their weapons on them,[37] regarded the trees as the seat of a god, or even as a god itself. Where, on the other hand, as Mungo Park saw[38] in the Mandingo country, the trees are laden with rags and shreds, Bosman[39] had already observed that in Guinea the sacred groves and trees were more assiduously visited in times of pestilence. Tylor mentions the existence in Europe of a superstition that a disease may be taken from the house of the sick person with a piece of his property, and conveyed to some other object—a tree or, better still, to another man. In Southern Europe young girls frequently offer to sell nosegays to the travellers which come from the house of a sick

---

[33] Zeitschrift für Völkerpsychologie u. Sprachwissenschaft. 1868. Bowers, Bhamo Expedition. Berlin, 1871.

[34] Journal of Researches, p. 68. 1845.

[35] Pausanias, lib. ix.

[36] Nöschel, Reise in die Kirgisen Steppe.

[37] L. Krehl, Die Religionen der vorislamitischen Araber.

[38] Reisen im Innern von Afrika. 1799.

[39] Guinese Goud-Tand-en Slavekust.

person.[40]   The author remembers being carefully warned in his boyhood never to pick up a flower lying on the road, "for one cannot tell what disease the person may have who threw it away." It must be understood that this prohibition extended only to flowers. The Suaheli in Eastern Africa offer food to the demons of disease : they do not eat it themselves, but place it in some footpath that a passer-by may consume it, and thus take the pestilence upon himself.[41]

Of all animals serpents have been most frequently worshipped. Snake worship, or the Naga religion, has spread most widely in India, as is testified by names of places such as Nagapoor, Widshanagara, and Baghanagara.   Even now the cobras or hooded-snakes are publicly worshipped by the Brahmins at the Feast of Nagapanshmi.   Moses in a weak moment allowed the brazen serpent to be made, which was afterwards transported to Jerusalem with other sacred objects, and was only removed from the Temple in 720 B.C. by the pious King Hezekiah.   Even within the limits of Christianity we find the sect of the Ophites, who continued or renewed snake worship, unless the greater part of what is imputed to them is untrue.[42]   The worship of serpents still continues in full vigour in the negro kingdom of Dahomey,[43] and has spread with slavery to the New World, where it is said to have recently taken firm root in Hayti.

Besides the world-wide veneration for wells, and for mineral springs in particular, running water has been regarded as divine, especially by the Hindoos.   On the magnificent mountain heights where the Ganges and the Jumna issue from glaciers, and in the plains over the pool which forms the source of the Nerbudda, sanctuaries and places of pilgrimage have been erected.[44]   Bathing in the holy rivers is supposed to have a sanctifying influence ; there are devout Hindoos who carry the water of the Ganges from Benares to Ramesseram, near the southern point of India, to wash their

---

[40] Tylor, Primitive Culture, vol. ii. p. 150.
[41] Journal of the Anthropological Institute, vol. i.
[42] Tylor, Primitive Culture, vol. ii. p. 243.
[43] Bosman, Guinese Goud-Kust.
[44] H. von Schlagintweit, Indien und Hochasien.

native idols,[45] although the distance is little less than that between Madrid and Berlin. The ancient Persians also regarded running water as sacred; but in contrast to the Hindoos they endeavoured to guard it from pollution, so that the erection of bridges, which put a stop to wading through the rivers, was considered a work of piety.[46] Although even the divinities of the ocean were not quite secure against the chastisements of barbarians, for a Persian king flogged the Hellespont with rods,[47] yet a better state of things dawned when men raised their eyes to seek the unknown Creator in the starry skies. The worship of sun, moon, and constellations, which is common among the Mongolian nations of Northern Asia, has spread from thence over both parts of America. Although religious emotions appear in human societies far earlier than the distinction between good and evil, and therefore have nothing to do with the subsequent laws of morality, yet as soon as intercourse between the members of the same confederation is regulated by strictly observed customs, human institutions are believed to be derived from the commands of the Deity, and from this time religion becomes the most effectual means of education and improvement.[48] In the endeavour to glorify the morality of the Deity, the religious impulse unconsciously advances the refinement of human society. When the conception of the fetish is extended to all visible objects, the sun, as the symbol of all that is pure and bright, seems capable of exerting the greatest influence in exalting the dignity of human intercourse. We refer especially to the government of the Peruvian Incas, who claimed descent from the day-star, and by means of conquest extended their strict laws and an admirable semi-civilization from Quito to Chili. But even the Apatsh points to the sun, and says to the white man, " Do you not believe that this deity sees

---

[45] K. Graul, Reise nach Ostindien.

[46] Duncker, Geschichte des Alterthums. 1853.

[47] Herodotus, lib. vii. cap. 35.

[48] Fritz Schultze similarly says (Fetischismus. 1871): " The fact that the savage is so absolutely under the dominion of his Mokisso (fetish) and of his oath, constitutes an important educational element of fetishism. The savage imposes duties on himself—he controls himself."

our actions, and chastises us if they are wicked?"[49]   A Huron
woman hearing the perfections of God extolled by a Christian
priest, exclaimed, "I had always pictured to myself our Areskui"
(by which she meant the sun and the Great Spirit) "as of the
nature which you ascribe to your God."[50]

As the sun is not merely a visible object, but is also a source of
the forces of nature, sun worship leads to the adoration of phenomena only indirectly perceptible by their effects.   This advanced
form of the demand for causality marks a great and happy chapter
in the history of the evolutions of every nation that has attained to
it.   Tree worship sooner or later necessitated the experience that
the decay caused by old age or, even earlier, by the devastations
of wood-eating parasites, or by a stroke of lightning, destroyed the
plant-god.   In the last case especially, it was evident that humbler
and perishable powers are controlled by still higher forces.   Nations
worshipping the forces of nature must necessarily have reached
a higher intellectual maturity, for divine interposition is traced
only in those phenomena of the material world, natural causes
of which are as yet inconceivable to the human understanding;
hence there must have been a previous attempt at explanation,
whereas thoughtless minds make no such researches.   It is only
in certain agricultural nations that we find the worship of the
forces of nature.   To such atmospheric changes are of supreme
importance, for on these depend superfluity or want.   The deifica-
tion of Force, that is, of something imperceptible to the senses,
can be maintained in its purity only in a priestly caste or as an
esoteric doctrine; but the uninitiated, who did not understand
the meaning of the enigmatical language of the worship of nature,
and received the allegories as literal realities, necessarily invested
the invisible with flesh and blood.   From an adjective applied
to Force arose a proper name for the Deity; from the name
again originated a conception of a Being, which was thought of as
male or female in accordance with the grammatical gender of the
customary appellation; the imagination, once thus called into play,
added fresh dreams to this romance of things divine.   It is at

---

[49] Frœbel as quoted by Tylor, Primitive Culture, vol. i. p. 286.

[50] Lafitau, Mœurs des sauvages amériquains, vol. i. p. 127.

once evident that the type of the language greatly influenced these creations. Hence languages which make a distinction of grammatical gender, such as those of the Aryan, Semitic, and Hamitic nations, are especially adapted for the fabrication of myths. Yet the functions of language must not be over-estimated, for we find myths of gods and goddesses among nations such as the Polynesians and the people of Central America, whose grammar is destitute of genders. Thus even Bleek [51] has made the mistake of looking for the worship of ancestors only in nations using the prefix-pronominal languages, although it exists among the Chinese whose language has no grammatical forms.

Delbrück has ingeniously employed the heroic fable of Hippolytus and Phædra to illustrate the manner in which language, as it were, automatically evolves myths. It had originally no other foundation than the phenomena visible in the evening sky from the first appearance of the crescent until the disc of the moon has become full. We may venture briefly to repeat his explanation. Any Greek scholar can perceive that the name Hippolytus indicates one who drives with loose or unharnessed horses. In the world of poetry this is done by the sun-god alone. The moon, on the other hand, is glorified as Phædra, the lustrous or brilliant, for the great majority of nations have thought of the sun as masculine and the moon as feminine, and only a few, among which are the Germans and the Hottentots, have reversed these genders. It is well known that on every succeeding day the crescent moon is retarded by a considerable span behind the sun as it hastens on its western course. After twelve days at most, the sun is just sinking as the full moon rises on the opposite side of the horizon. Thus the waxing moon apparently pursues the sun, but is unable to catch up the quicker traveller. But, according to the growing myth, Hippolytus is flying from Phædra. Now, when a generation grew up which applied other adjectives to the sun and moon, and who had forgotten the original signification of Hippolytus and Phædra, although a proverb was perhaps still preserved concerning Hippolytus flying before the pursuit of Phædra, the question might well arise, why should Hippolytus fly from Phædra

---

[51] Ueber den Ursprung der Sprache.

if, as her name suggests, she shines in all the beauty of her sex? In this stage of the conception, as Delbrück adds, the legend was completed by the notion that perhaps Phædra was the step-mother of Hippolytus. When the myth had once acquired this form, it was woven into the story of the house of Theseus, forming an admirable subject for a tragedy. Euripides, Racine, and his translator, Schiller, would probably have been surprised had it been shown them that their heroes were the sun and moon. Perhaps it may be said that it was unnecessary to suppose fear of incest as a motive for the flight of Hippolytus from Phædra : it would have been more natural to suppose that he already loved some other maiden; hence it is very remarkable that other nations give exactly the same interpretations to these natural phenomena. The Khasia in North-western India relate that at every fresh change the moon is inflamed with love for his stepmother the sun, who throws ashes in his face as a mark of abhorrence, and that for this reason the moon's disc is spotted.[52] The Eskimo say that the sun, which they regard as feminine, smears the face of her brother, the moon, with soot when he presses his love upon her. The inhabitants of the Isthmus of Darien also maintain that the so-called "man in the moon" was guilty of incest with his sister.[53]

The action of myth-making must in the course of time, especially while writing was not in use, have entirely obscured the original meaning of any form of nature worship, so that it was at last necessary to deify the same power under another name, only to reinvest it with an anthropomorphous shape. This is probably the reason that among Aryan nations so many deities play the same part, and that the functions of the atmosphere in particular are represented under so many forms. But every system of gods indicates a craving for a Supreme Being to whom all other powers must sooner or later be subordinate. For instance, it is impossible that a people undergoing intellectual development should persevere in worshipping the sun, for soon or later there must arise the doubt which was expressed by the Inca Huayna Capac

---

[52] Hooker, Himalayan Journals, vol. ii. p. 276.

[53] David Cranz, Historie von Grönland. Petrus Martyr, De orbe novo.

(+ 1525 A.D.),[54] namely, that the day-star cannot possibly be the creator of all things, for the progress of life proceeds without interruption during the night. This case again corroborates our proposition that all religious emotions proceed only from the desire for acquaintance with the Creator, and that the worship of a deity is extinguished the instant that it ceases to satisfy the requirement of causality. The divinity of the sun was not so long or so successfully tenable as that of the changeless, self-moving heavens, which were always regarded as masculine in contrast to the feminine fertile earth. The heavens and the earth were worshipped by the Hurons, and are still worshipped by the Chinese. Sky worship occurs also among the negroes of the west coast of Africa.[55] The Latins employed the same word for God and the heavens;[56] and that the heavens and the Supreme Deity were one, in ancient times, amongst the Germans also, may be inferred from the pagan idioms, " Heaven help you !" or " Heaven preserve this child." [57] Even in ancient Mexico we perceive that a multiplicity of gods makes a classification according to rank necessary, and that this involuntarily tends towards a monotheistic conception. In the celebrated admonitions of an Aztec mother to her daughter, reference is made to a single God, " who sees every secret fault." [58] Sahagun, who preserved this remarkable contribution to moral history, has indeed been accused of colouring ancient Mexican paganism with Christian views ; but Waitz has justly defended the trustworthiness of his account, saying that Spanish priests were more disposed to give adverse representations of the pre-Christian state of the Americans as the work of the devil than to say too much in their favour.

If the value of religion be estimated solely by its effects as a means of education, the worship of the forces of nature is capable of raising human society to high grades. Among nations of austere morals we also find austere deities and the conception of a just regulation of the world, whereas, in the other case, liber-

---

[54] A. von Humboldt, Ansichten der Natur.

[55] Tylor, Primitive Culture, vol. i. p. 321.

[56] *Sub divo* or *sub dio* was equivalent to " under the open skies."

[57] " Der Himmel behüte dich " and " der Himmel erhalte dir dieses Kind."

[58] Sahagun. See Prescott's Conquest of Mexico, vol. iii. p. 424.

tinism and vice are perceptible in the creations of religion, which are invariably related to the moral level of the social condition, as are the dark lines in a spectroscopic image to the source of light. The Polynesian Tongans, or Friendly Islanders, firmly believe that their gods approve of a life of virtue and resent vice, so that the guardian spirits watch over men only so long as they behave honourably, and at once abandon the reprobate.[59] But worship of the forces of nature is of little permanent service in the social education of nations. When the object contemplated as divine has once been invested in the imagination with human traits, the representative arts are nearly always employed at the very first fabrication of the myths ; and however the sculptor or painter may exalt the human form in his representation of the deity, in the eyes of the multitude, eager for objects of veneration, the material image immediately becomes an idol performing miracles, and, as a movable chattel, becomes the property of a community, and, by the folly of the majority, ultimately sinks into a fetish.

Religious veneration takes another direction when it involves belief in a future life. This belief has been found almost without exception among the aborigines of America as well as among the Polynesians, Papuans, and Australians, among the greater number of Asiatics, among the ancient inhabitants of Europe, and all the Hamites of Northern Africa from the Nile to the Canaries. When direct evidence is wanting, belief in immortality may be inferred from the mode of burying the dead. If we had no better information as to the notions of the Egyptians respecting a future life, we could still clearly recognize their expectations in the circumstance that they provided their mummies with wheat in order to supply them with seed-corn after the resurrection. In the same way the ancient Babylonians evinced a hope of another world by placing date stones in their tombs ;[60] the same remark applies to the people dwelling on the shores of the Caribbean Sea, who place maize seeds in the hands of their dead. The sacrifice of human beings at the graves of chiefs or kings, such as that prescribed by

---

[59] Mariner, Tonga Islands.
[60] Rawlinson, The Five Great Monarchies.

the Adah, or "great custom," testifies a belief in immortality in Dahomey, and the strangling of the wives at the death of a prince affords like evidence of a similar belief in the Fiji Islands. Again, if we knew no further details as to the opinions of the intellectually gifted Hottentots, formerly so greatly underrated,[61] it would be enough that, previous to burial, they place the body of the deceased in the same position which it once occupied as an embryo in the mother's womb. The meaning of this significant custom is that the dead will mature in the darkness of the earth in preparation for a new birth. As uncivilized nations, as we have seen, regard all objects as animated, they do not restrict the future life to human beings. The Itelmes of Kamtshatka believed in a renewal of all creatures, " down to the smallest fly." The Jesuits Acosta, Lafitau, and Charlevoix assert that the Inca-Peruvians,[62] the Iroquois, and other North Americans imagined, exactly after the fashion of the Platonic visions, the existence in the invisible world of a sort of prototype or essence for every living being.[63] The Fijians go still further, for they not only believe in a paradise for men and animals, but they hope that every cocoa-nut will there be made anew.

It is only among negroes that a denial of immortality has yet been found. "Can a dead man come out of his grave unless he is dug up?" said the chief Commoro in the Latuka country to the east of the White Nile, when Sir Samuel Baker in vain attempted by cross questions to force him to acknowledge his belief in a future. The first idea of immortality has probably been always evoked by the apparitions of dreams. As long as a negro dreams of a dead person, fear is inspired by his memory ; the spirit which has apparently come back demands food, and holds out threats of misfortunes to those still on earth, but the memory of a grandfather has long been extinguished and excites no further uneasiness. If, in Equatorial Africa, says Du Chaillu, inquiries are made after a person long since deceased,

---

[61] Kolbe, Vorgebirge der guten Hoffnung.

[62] Clements Markham, Journal of the Royal Geographical Society, vol. xli.

[63] Lafitau, Mœurs des sauvages, p. 360. Charlevoix, Nouvelle France. Also Tylor, Primitive Culture, vol. ii. p. 245.

the answer is that it is all over with him.[64] One of the current sayings then is, that at death all is past. It is possible that in the last case the witness quoted had not succeeded in gaining the confidence of the negro. Sproat, an excellent ethnologist, who had nearly fallen into errors such as we suspect in the case of Du Chaillu, very strikingly observes : " A traveller must have lived among savages for years as one of themselves before his opinion of their intellectual condition is of any value." [65] In Central and Southern Africa especially the idea of immortality is the source of great uneasiness. The negroes of the Gold Coast sacrifice slaves at a burial that they may serve the deceased in the other world.[66] In the Congo land Winwood Reade [67] assures us that a son killed his mother merely because he expected that as a glorified spirit she would render him more powerful assistance. Wherever the Bantu languages are spoken, that is to say, throughout Southern Africa, the souls of deceased parents are invoked for aid.[68] Rebmann has noted down a prayer of this sort from the lips of a negro in the Tshagga country on the East Coast ; and another of the Kaffirs in Natal to a deceased chief runs literally : " O Mossé, son of Motlanka, look upon us ! Thou, whose breath (fumée?) is seen by every one, turn thine eyes upon us this day and shield us. Thou our god ! " [69] The Bushmen also prayed in Livingstone's presence at the grave of an ancestor.[70] As divine descent is attributed to the chiefs in Polynesia, it is not surprising that sanctuaries are erected to them after their death, as Mariner frequently relates of the Tongans. It is due to Polynesian influences that at Tanna, an island of the New Hebrides, the deceased chiefs are thanked for the blessings of the harvest.[71]

Permanent worship of the dead has been very appropriately

---

[64] Explorations and Adventures in Equatorial Africa.

[65] Anthropological Review, vol. vi. 1868.

[66] Bosman, Guinese Goud-Tand-en Slavekust ; and Tylor, Primitive Culture, vol. ii. p. 116.

[67] Savage Africa.

[68] Krapf, Reisen in Ostafrika.

[69] Casalis, Les Basoutos.   [70] South Africa.

[71] Turner, quoted by Tylor, Primitive Culture, vol. ii. p. 114.

described as ancestor worship. Thus the Caribs of the West India Islands saw their immortal heroes in the constellations. Worship of the dead has been developed with peculiar strength among the Chinese, who built special temples for the deceased emperors. When their moral philosopher, Confucius, was canonized, he received the first sacrifice from the hand of an emperor in 194 B.C., and in A.D. 57 festivals were established, and sanctuaries erected in his honour. Hero worship is also apt to be extended to founders of religions, and thus Buddhism has been gradually alienated from its original purity and has degenerated into relic worship.[72] Even Napoleon III. who, like the old kings of France, was so eager to play the part of the eldest son of the Church, paid homage to ancestor worship, if the recently published will of April 14th, 1875, is genuine. " We must remember," writes the Emperor, " that those we love look down upon us from heaven and protect us. It is the soul of my great uncle which has always guided and supported me. Thus will it be with my son also if he proves worthy of his name." [73]

To the question, whether in any part of the world a nation has ever been found utterly destitute of religious emotions and ideas, we will venture to give a decided negative. In every stage of his mental development man feels a craving to discover an agency for every phenomenon, and an author for every event. As long as the powers of the understanding are small a fetish satisfies the demand for causality, but as the intellectual sagacity of nations increases, the powers of credence are diminished, and the conception of God acquires dignity, until it finally becomes the noblest and highest product of the human mind. Similarly, while the intellectual faculties are advancing, the first crude attempts to discover the unknown Creator constantly tend to the rejection of the first solutions, and ultimately to the hypothesis of a supreme incomprehensible Being. Yet history and ethnology tell of innumerable races of men who never raised themselves to such a height, and even of many who fell back from the nobler notions which they had acquired into gross errors of the understanding,

---

[72] Justi in the Ausland. 1871.
[73] Alleg. Zeitung. 1873.

which they have been unable to shake off for hundreds, nay, for thousands of years. These superstitions we shall speak of as Shamanism, and we will attempt to examine their origin.

X.—SHAMANISM.

WHEN in future we speak of Shamanism, this word must be understood in a comprehensive sense to include magic and ritualism of every description. The name itself originated from a corruption of Cramana, as the Buddhist anchorites and penitents are called in India. The term Shaman, however, has been hitherto applied only to the magicians of Northern Asiatic races. Their functions consist chiefly in working cures by magic, for among all barbarous nations, in present and past times, sickness and death are ascribed to witchcraft,[1] which the Shaman has to counteract by his secret remedies.

In Siberia and both continents of America the magician usually sucks the part of the body which is paining the invalid, and then produces from his mouth a thorn, a beetle, a stone, or some other unexpected object, which he shows to the anxious bystanders as the cause of the evil which he has detected and conquered by his intervention. The Shamans among the Dyaks of Borneo[2] and those in South America on the Orinoco,[3] operate in the same way. A priestess of the Fingo Kaffirs—for there are female operators also—who had pretended to extract a number of magic seeds from the body of the patient, was unmasked by the wife of a missionary. Previous to the operation she had swallowed some tobacco leaves as an emetic.[4]

Another branch of the business of a Shaman depends on their power of communicating with the invisible powers, occasionally

---

[1] This is the case among the Australians (Latham, Varieties), the Kutshin or Loucheux Indians of Hudson's Bay territory (Ausland, 1863), and the Hottentots (Kolbe, Cap der guten Hoffnung).

[2] Spenser St. John, Life in the Far East, vol. i.

[3] P. Jos. Gumilla, El Orinoco ilustrado.

[4] Tylor, Early History of Mankind, p. 355.

with departed spirits, and receiving from them revelations as to the future. On these occasions the performer is able to put himself into a state of nervous excitement, in which his mouth foams and his limbs are convulsed.[5] Hence Shamans in all parts of the world like to select, as their pupils, boys of epileptic tendencies.[6] Dwarfs or albinos are preferred by the negroes.[7]

The proceedings of the Siberian priests and of the so-called medicine-men of the North American Indians are so similar, that the similarity constitutes one of the evidences in favour of the hypothesis that the New World was peopled by races once belonging to Northern Asia. The sole difference between the Siberian Shaman and the North American medicine-man [8] is, that in his operations the former uses a magic drum, the latter a magic rattle; both wear fantastically decorated cloaks. The North American medicine-man reappears in South America under the names of Piaye, Piaï, or Paye, and he also carries a magic rattle (maracca) formed of a hollow gourd filled with hard seeds.[9] Lastly, separated from their fellow-craftsmen by the entire breadth of the Atlantic, there are the Mganga in South Africa, who carry neither drum nor rattle, but a magic horn, and who devote themselves to the work of calling down the much-desired rain on those dry countries.[10]

As illness is ascribed to the influence of a magician, death also, even when caused by the debility of old age, is believed to be due to the operations of evil powers. Hence, in every part of

---

[5] See an example among the Kares in Burmah, in A. Bastian's Völker des östlichen Asien, and with regard to the Kaffirs, comp. Fritsch, Eingeborne Südafrika's.

[6] It is so among the Tatars on the Southern Yennessei (Globus). Other examples in F. Schultze, Der Fetischismus.

[7] Winwood Reade, Savage Africa, p. 363.

[8] Catlin, North American Indians.

[9] P. Gumilla, El Orinoco ilustrado ; Dobrizhoffer, Geschichte der Abiponer ; Appun in the Ausland, No. 29. 1872.

[10] Among the Natchez of Louisiana, in America, the Shamans busy themselves with conjuring the weather. Charlevoix, Nouvelle France. It has been suggested that the word *maracá* is derived from the Spanish *matráca ;* but, independently of the difference of accentuation, the word *maracá* exists in the Tupi language. See Lexicon in Martius' Ethnographie, vol. i. p. 513.

the world in which Shamanism has carried on its malpractices, there is the strange delusion that man might indefinitely prolong the duration of his bodily existence, were it not curtailed by the malice of a wizard. This superstition is prevalent not only among races such as the Australian,[11] though this has been unjustly ranked too low; but even the Abipones assured the Jesuit Dobrizhoffer,[12] that deaths would cease if the magicians would renounce their deplorable arts. The Patagonian Casimiro confessed to Lieutenant Musters [13] that, after the death of his mother, he had caused a woman to be murdered to whose bad influence he did not hesitate to attribute this calamity. Let us now pass far away from the Patagonians to the island of Tanna, one of the New Hebrides in the South Seas, peopled by Papuans, a race of men having nothing in common either physically or in language with Northern Asiatics, Americans, or South Africans. Here, again, Shamans are to be found. They, too, make it their business to procure rain, and are believed to be the creators of flies and mosquitoes. Their special interest for us, however, is their power of inflicting diseases and death whenever they can procure a Nahak from any individual. This word properly signifies refuse, but is more specially applied to neglected remnants of food; these ought not to be thrown away but carefully and secretly burnt or buried. If a Papuan magician finds a banana rind which has been thrown aside, he rolls it up in bark with a leaf, and when night falls he sits down by a fire and slowly burns the Nahak. If the whole is transformed into ashes, the spell has taken effect, and the person to whom the refuse belonged will certainly die. But news of the nocturnal deed spreads immediately and rapidly. Hence, if there is any one in the neighbourhood whose conscience accuses him of neglecting the remains of his food, or who is already prostrate with illness, he gets his friends to blow a blast on the shell trumpet as a sign that the Shaman is to cease his work of destruction. The next morning money is offered for the restitution of the Nahak. The missionary Turner [14] relates that

---

[11] Eyre, Central Australia, vol. ii. 1845.
[12] Dobrizhoffer, Geschichte der Abiponer.
[13] Unter den Patagoniern.   [14] Nineteen Years in Polynesia.

he was deprived of many a night's rest by the unearthly sounds of the shell trumpet, for several of these plaintive signals were sometimes audible in different directions. It is unquestionable that the Papuan Shamans seriously believe in their own arts, for whenever one of the craft is overtaken by illness or the fear of death he also sends out a shell trumpet. It is only against the illnesses introduced into the island by Europeans that the natives confess that all counter charms have proved ineffectual. The Nahak ceremony reappears with little variation on the Marquesas island of Nukahiva,[15] which is inhabited by pure-bred Polynesians; it exists also in the Fiji Islands under the name of an " act with leaves," [16] and even in Australia the death of a sick person is considered certain if a malevolent Shaman has burnt the Pringurru, a sacred piece of bone which is also used for letting blood.[17]

Passing round almost a third part of the world, from Australia to South Africa, we find that the Kaffir princes, before they go out to war, raise the courage of their followers by displaying a fragment of clothing, the shaft of a spear, a snuff-box, or any other property of their opponents which they have been able to procure. The court Shaman has a magic liquid ready prepared, in which in the presence of the assembled community he steeps and dissolves some portion of the captured treasure. The chief has only to swallow this draught to possess irresistible power over his antagonist. This explains the fact that a Kaffir king, whenever he moves to a new hut, has the old one carefully swept out, and that, as Theophilus Hahn relates, an entire kraal (village) has been burnt down, only to prevent the enemy from obtaining any household implement by means of which to exercise a spell.[18]

Let us dwell a little longer on the unquestionably strange uniformity of such superstitions. We might perhaps account for it by supposing that Papuan and Kaffir races once inhabited a common home, and then separated by a series of migrations. But this would imply periods which must be reckoned by thousands of years, for the differences between these races are very great, and

---

[15] Langsdorff, Reise um die Welt.
[16] According to Williams in the Ausland. 1858.
[17] Eyre, Central Australia.   [18] Theophilus Hahn in the Globus. 1871.

such alterations take place as slowly as geological processes. Nor must we satisfy ourselves by fancying that these superstitions are only due to the yet inexperienced intellects of so-called savages. It is but lately that the superstition flourished among ourselves that the parings of nails, and hair which has been cut off, ought to be carefully destroyed. An Italian scholar, Caroline Coronedi, has lately stated that even now, at Bologna, combed-out hairs are carefully burnt, as they are particularly liable to be employed in the arts of witchcraft.[19] Tylor even gives full credit to the report that a witch was burnt in 1860 at Camargo, in Mexico.[20] The similarity of these superstitions almost forces us against our will to believe that the intellectual powers of man are a mechanism, which, under the influence of like excitations, necessarily performs the same acts.

Of all nations the South African Bantus suffer most from this mental malady of Shamanism. Whenever a death occurs, inquiries are made of the Mganga, or local Shaman, as to its author. He has the credit of possessing superior knowledge. To Shamanism must also be referred all interpretation of signs, the institution of oracles, and also the spirit-rapping of modern days. When the seer indicates a suspected person, a trial by ordeal takes place. Here we at once encounter a new form of necromancy, for faith in decision by ordeal is based on the illusion that there is an invisible regulating power which, when properly interrogated, cannot fail to declare infallible verdicts. Trial by ordeal is still habitual among the Dravida races in India,[21] and among Brahminical Hindoos, and in Southern Arabia it was maintained among our own ancestors long after the Christian era.[22] In the persecution of witches, the water ordeal was still in use until the sixteenth and seventeenth centuries. Jacob Grimm thought that the last traces of the superstition occur in the modern duel.[23] The Papuans of New Guinea also hold it possible to ascertain the guilt or innocence of an accused person by the process of immersion,[24] and a similar

[19] Ida von Düringsfeld in the Ausland. 1872.

[20] Tylor, Primitive Culture, vol. i. p. 138.

[21] Jellinghaus in the Zeitschrift für Ethnologie, vol. iii. 1871.

[22] Maltzan in the Globus, vol. xxi. 1872.

[23] Deutsche Rechtsalterthümer.   [24] Otto Finsch, Neu-Guinea.

method is employed by the negroes of the Gold Coast.[25] Otherwise in South Africa (where it extends from the Atlantic tribes to the Masai), trial by ordeal generally takes the form of swallowing a goblet full of Mbundu juice. If the poisonous beverage does not at once act as an emetic, the guilt of the accused is proved. When the small-pox broke out on the Rembo in Mayolo (2° south lat., 11° east long.) in 1865, Du Chaillu saw victims of this Shamanistic deception perish by the side of the victims of the pestilence.[26]

The judicial trials, accompanied by the torture of the accused, of the Amaχosa Kaffirs,[27] have been strikingly described by Maclean. Belief in the efficacy of the black art is all the more difficult to eradicate, owing to the fact that the accused sometimes confesses that he has worked charms. It is beyond question that such attempts at magic actually take place, for Martius[28] the traveller caught a revengeful slave in a Brazilian hut in the act of performing her nocturnal incantations. It is difficult to see how this vicious practice is to be done away, for although the miracles of the Shamans frequently fail, this, in the eyes of the prejudiced, affords no proof of the nullity of the means employed, but merely that the medicines or incantations were too weak to counteract the evil work of some distant Shaman. All observers of foreign races of mankind unanimously assure us that the wizards themselves are among the deceived, and firmly believe in their own arts.[29] The Siberian Shamans, the North American medicine-men, the Brazilian Piaï, the South African Mganga, the Australian and Papuan magicians, live apart from their tribes, educate their disciples by fasts and self-mortifications, and only thus reveal to them the treasures of their occult knowledge.

The ultimate idea of Shamanism, which, under all its numerous names and guises, is always fundamentally the same, is based on the superstition that man is able to communicate with the invisible

---

[25] Bosman, Guinese Goud-Kust.

[26] Du Chaillu, Ashango Land, p. 175.

[27] Kaffir Laws and Customs. Mount Coke, 1858.

[28] Ethnographie, vol. i.

[29] So says Dobrizhoffer of the Abipones (Geschichte der Abiponer), and Mariner (Tonga Islands), of the Polynesian inhabitants of the Friendly group.

powers, and to force them to obedience. In either case symbolical practices and incantations are employed, and these have preserved their efficiency because human reason is so weak that one affirmative instance, ineradicably impressed upon the memory, completely outweighs nine negative instances, which are speedily forgotten.

In its highest refinements this self-deception is able to insinuate itself into the purest minds. It attaches itself to symbolism and ritualism, and is in operation wherever a definite but not necessarily inevitable effect is expected from a symbolical act. When pious people in Protestant countries wish to obtain a revelation to guide them in the difficulties of life, they open a psalm book, expecting a divine answer in the first psalm or verse on which their eye may fall. They thus unconsciously make a covenant with the God within them that, when interrogated in this manner and with full faith, he is bound to bestow an answer.

Nothing is more capable of Shamanistic abuse than prayer, for it becomes a magic spell the instant that the words of the supplicant are supposed to have any sort of influence on the divine will. That such errors have taken root in some places is easily seen in the fact that repetitions of prayers are employed in an extreme degree ; and the Buddhists are so deeply sunk in this self-deception that they have invented prayer machines, which are revolving cylinders, on which is rolled a paper with the prayers inscribed upon it. The intention is to outwit the Deity by this apparatus at each revolution of the cylinder, for he is supposed to accept the prayers as though spoken. Ingenious Mongols have even set such prayer-rolls in motion by wind and water-wheels, and thus endeavoured to gain the rewards of piety.

Sacrifice tends to lead men into yet greater error. The purest motives, an overflow of gratitude, the avowal of a fault and the desire for its expiation may lead the believer to the altar. Imperceptibly, and almost inevitably, another aspect of sacrifice introduces itself behind this purer view. The Deity is then regarded as the recipient, and the donor expects a return for his benefits.[30]

---

[30] Tylor (Primitive Culture, vol. ii. p. 400) justly calls to mind that in English, and, we may add, in German, sacrifice signifies a self-inflicted loss.

Thus the Homeric heroes, invoking the aid of their invisible protectors, reminded them of the many libations which they had offered up to them.[31] But the superstition is most evil in its effects when symbolism is associated with the sacrifice. Nowhere has self-deception of this sort obtained such complete mastery over intelligent and even sagacious thinkers as in India; for the Brahmins are the chief of all Shamans—systematically educated, refined by depth of thought, and supported by the practice of a thousand years. Their most powerful charm is the juice of the Soma plant (*Sarcostemma viminale*) with which they reinforce their sacrifices. Like the Mganga, or South African rain-makers, they summon the desired wet weather; for only when invigorated by their sacred rites is the thunder-god Indra able to open the clouds and extract from them the fertilizing shower. A creative power is attributed to the sacrifice, for Brahma is supposed to be omnipresent in all offerings.[32] According to their doctrine, penances, if prolonged for an unlimited period, as were those of Vishvâmitra, at last confer such mighty power on the sufferer that the epic gods fear lest he may destroy both heaven and earth. But as, according to the Shamanistic hypothesis, by means of prayers and hymns, and above all by sacrifice, accompanied by effectual symbolical acts, the gods may be forced to perform the desired services, the logical conclusion is that penances, prayers, and sacrifices are stronger than the gods. Thus the Indians obtained the conception of Brahma, a spiritual power existing in the ritualistic mysteries and predominating over the gods. The Brahmins themselves, as the initiated to whom alone were known the occult meaning and the efficacy of the practices and sayings, were ultimately obliged to lay claim to superhuman qualities, and exalt themselves into incarnate deities. According to their doctrine, all success depended on the proper performance of sacrifice. To this act they owed their rank and prosperity. The sacrifices themselves, simple at first, became more and more complicated. Before long they required more than one day, then weeks, months, and years, and at the same time, by constant quadrupling, the number of officiating priests rose to sixty-four, according to Martin Haug, who

---

[31] Iliad, i. 37–42.   [32] Martin Haug, Alleg. Zeitung. 1873.

was the first European to penetrate the deepest secrets of the Brahmins.[33]

If the essence of Shamanism consists in the performance of some form of sorcery which rules the powers held to be divine, and extorts from them the fulfilment of a desire, or the disclosure of future events, it is obviously indifferent whether the method employed consists in shaking a rattle, in sacrifice, prayers, fastings, penances, or in the interrogation of the entrails of animals or the flight of birds. All nations have succumbed to this illusion; few have entirely shaken it off. It survives in full strength in America, in Siberia, in Buddhist Asia, in Brahminical India, under the various forms of the Amulet of the Mahommedans, the trial by ordeal, the rain-making of the Africans, and the Nahak tricks of the Papuans. We, ourselves, have only lately abolished trials for witchcraft. The great Kepler was obliged to return to his Suabian home in order to rescue his aged mother from death by fire, with which Protestant Shamanists were threatening her. From all this it is manifest that the moral education of mankind by means of religion has nowhere encountered greater dangers than from Shamanistic delusion. When any symbolical act is supposed to possess a supernatural effect, the rite is placed, like Brahma, higher than the deities.

XI.—THE DOCTRINE OF BUDDHA.

THE Aryans spread themselves over the Punjaub and the plain of the Ganges at the expense of a barbarian aboriginal population, which they excelled in mental endowments and physical beauty. The possession of these advantages characteristic of the race, led to the prohibition by Manu's legislation of mixed marriages, and to the most uncharitable regulations of caste. The priests, as the initiated, had, as we have seen, exalted the knowledge of the Shamanistic practices, of prayers and sacrifices, into a power superior to the old gods, who were reduced to the subordinate

---

[33] Martin Haug, Brahme und die Brahmanen.

office of guardians of the world. Brahma, in its oldest historical sense, means prayer,[1] and the Brahmins were originally called the people who pray. Brahma subsequently appeared, in an anthropomorphic aspect, as the god of prayer, and later still as the creator of the world. The priest had now the task of distorting the doctrines of the Vedas by skilful interpretation into conformity with the tenet of the transmigration of souls, taught by religious philosophy in the Brahminical books of ritual.[2]

Brahma, or the universal soul, was proclaimed to be the only real existence, while the world perceptible to the senses was an illusion, the work of Maja, or deception, and unsubstantial as the image of the moon reflected by calm waters. To see through this illusion, to proclaim that the world is nothing, to hail Brahma as the only existence, as Thou, to acknowledge Self as one with him, implied the liberation of the Ego from the illusions of the world of the senses, and reabsorption into Brahma. Like this doctrine of the Vedântâ, the Sankhja philosophy looked for the release of the human soul from its incarceration in the body, and regarded all objects of perception as illusions, but it expected liberation not by absorption into the Deity, but by a withdrawal of the soul into itself, and an alienation from the world of matter. The great maxim of the Vedântâ was, I am the The, I am Brahma; the Sankhja school, on the contrary, said, I am not the The (Nature).[3]

The people of India held, and still hold, to the conception of the indestructibility of the soul. A tendency to melancholy and weariness of life has existed in them from the earliest times. A never-ending series of transmigrations of the soul threatened them at every step. There are very few among ourselves sufficiently happy to care to begin their own lives anew with their disillusions and hours of dejection. In the words of the apostle, the creature groaneth for deliverance. The Hindoo was tortured and oppressed by the idea of a perpetual and unavoidable renewal of his present existence; the eternally revolving wheel could never

---

[1] J. Muir, Sanscrit Texts. London, 1872.
[2] Duncker, Geschichte des Alterthums.
[3] Köppen, Die Religion des Buddha. Berlin, 1857.

stop, and with his imagination disturbed by weird, numerical expressions, he looked out into an eternity, the horizon of which receded with each step which he himself took. Even the highest castes yearned for deliverance of the soul, but to the oppressed eternal existence seemed eternal torture.

According to the traditions handed down, Siddhârtha, the son of Cuddhôdana, king of Kapilavastu, of the tribe of Gautama and the house of Sâkja, appeared in the sixth century B.C., bringing a hope of salvation to the Indian people.[4] The sight of bodily evils, of sickness, age, and death, caused him to meditate how man could escape the misery of earthly existence. The doctrines of the Brahminical school did not satisfy him. He recognized the powerlessness of prayer, sacrifice, and penance. Even this destruction of Shamanistic errors would give him a high rank among the founders of religion. But it was not only to the initiated and as a mystery that he declared his doctrine, but, in complete contrast to the Brahminical system, he preached publicly and in the language of the people :[5] it was not to select castes, but to mankind in general that he addressed himself. Buddhism was at no time restricted to one nation, but has remained open to the whole world to the present day. Sâkjamuni, which was the nickname given to the founder of a new religion, proclaimed, on the contrary, that his doctrine was a law of grace for all.[6] The beautiful legend of his favourite scholar Ananda, closely resembling the story of the woman of Samaria, mentioned in the fourth Gospel, is well known. He asks for a draught from a girl of Chandâlâ, who is drawing water, and when she hesitates, fearing she might contaminate him by her touch, he says, " My sister, I do not ask what is thy caste or thy descent, I beg for water if thou canst give it me."[7] Another of the stories of Christ was foreshadowed in the legend of the poor man, who filled the alms-box of Buddha with a handful of flowers, though the rich could not accomplish it with ten thousand bushels ; and again, by the story of the lamps which kings and chancellors had lighted in

---

[4] Chr. Lassen, Indische Alterthumskunde.

[5] Bournouf, Introduction au Buddhisme indien. 1844.

[6] Ibid.   [7] Ibid.

honour of Buddha and which were extinguished, while the one brought by the poor woman burnt alone all through the night.[8]

Buddha's life, as we know it, was somewhat monotonous. By the renunciation of worldly power and the pleasures of the senses, bearing his alms-box in his hand, the Indian prince proved the sincerity of his doctrine of duty. He lived to an advanced age, and saw his ancestral city of Kapilavastu devastated by the enemy of his house. With Ananda he wandered in the starlight among the still smoking ruins, and stepping over the corpses of the slain, and the bodies of mutilated maidens in the streets, administered consolation to the dying. From thence he endeavoured to drag himself also to Kuçinagara, a distance of seventy miles, but, unable to reach the town, sank down under a çala tree not far from it, overcome by violent thirst. The death struggle soon set in, and he expired with the words, "Nothing is durable."[9]

The salvation contemplated by Buddha refers solely to the superstition of the transmigration of souls ; salvation can therefore be found in this doctrine only by those who share in this superstition. Transmigration always results from criminality in a previous existence, so that sin is the origin of all earthly misery. By its adhesion to existence and its craving for it at death, the soul is forced into a new sphere. For on the extinction of life nothing remains of the soul but the sum of its good and evil works, and of the latter a new birth is the normal consequence.[10]

The Buddhist view of the world, as it was taught by Sákjamuni himself, or perhaps only by his disciples, seems almost due to mental malady. Life itself appeared as the greatest of burdens, and to escape from its renewal, "to break through the eggshell," to escape the necessity of perpetual transmigrations, seemed salvation in the highest degree. The fundamental idea of Buddhism was comprised in the so-called four truths : that our misery is derived from existence ; that this misery arises only from

---

[8] Köppen, Die Religion des Buddha.

[9] O. Palladius, Das Leben Buddha's. Arbeiten der russ Gesandtschaft zu Peking. Berlin, 1858.

[10] Köppen, Die Religion des Buddha.

13

continued connection with the world of the senses; that by shaking off this connection release from existence is obtained; and, lastly, that there is a way to such a release. This way to the heights of Buddhism requires self-denial and unresisting absorption in one's self. The last and highest state which the righteous can attain is called Nirvâna, though it has always been disputed whether Nirvâna can be called a state. Buddha himself reached the Nirvâna by degrees. First, he experienced the sensation of liberation from sin, next, he destroyed the satisfaction of this feeling by a longing for the highest goal, then this longing was also reduced to complete indifference, with which however was mingled a satisfaction with the indifference itself. But this satisfaction was to disappear likewise, and happiness, pain, and memory were to be lost in infinite space or nothingness; but in nothingness he still preserved the consciousness of nothingness; finally, this also was extinguished in complete repose, undisturbed either by nothingness or by anything other than nothingness. The Nirvâna, or highest goal of Buddhism, as to the meaning of which the various sects are not agreed, was therefore originally and literally an extinction, a total annihilation which precluded any new birth. Hence the northern or neo-Buddhists went so far as to consider thought itself the root of ignorance, the admission of an idea as an obscuration of the intellect, and they looked for liberation from ignorance in the absence of thought.[11]

The moral doctrine of Buddha was thoroughly pure and chaste, in many ways harmonizing with the Christian system. First stands the prohibition against killing any living thing. This led to the abolition of capital punishment in India, at least, at the period at which Buddhism held the reins of government, but at the same time it prevented the extermination of predatory and parasitic animals. Respect for property, conjugal fidelity, truthfulness, avoidance of calumny, insult, or contempt, resistance of all covetous and envious emotions, of anger and vengeance, are enjoined on all believers. As in Christianity, the highest duty of the Buddhist is love to one's neighbours, but this term extends to all creatures, so that the erection and maintenance of refuges

---

[11] Fr. Spiegel on Wassiljiew's Researches.   Ausland, 1860.

and hospitals for animals are regarded as good works, equal to the institution of almshouses for needy men. Self-conquest, says an old proverb, is the best of all conquests.[12] Mankind is to be trained to gentleness, mercy, and consideration, and Buddhism itself set a good example of religious toleration, and by scarcely ever disgracing itself by the persecution of those who held different opinions.[13] The humility which was also to distinguish the priests was in contrast to the arrogance of the Brahmins. It is therefore hard to over-estimate the favourable effects of Buddhism in the softening of manners. The religion has been extolled for having educated mankind without having recourse to the conception of a deity, without prayer, without bribes or threats of another world, and yet in spite of this gained four hundred millions of votaries. The Buddhists had apparently shaken off the gods, or rather the gods were degraded into the willing auxiliaries of Buddha, at whose wish, even if unexpressed, they were supposed eagerly to assemble. But as their Shamanistic knowledge of wisdom, prayers, and the power of rites and penances, placed the Brahmins above the gods, so Buddha, by his virtuous life and by the strength of his devotion, acquired a nature far above that of the Vedic gods : he worked miracles and saw into the past and the future.[14] The distressed may therefore confidently cry to him ; he will listen to the mariner and rescue him from the storm.[15] Buddhism, in the form it necessarily assumed before it was accepted by four hundred millions, is not recognized by ethnology as an ethical atheism, but merely as ancestor or hero worship. Soon after the death of the founder, and not without the instigation of his disciples, began a relic worship, which may be described as a reversion to fetishism. The ashes of the deceased were distributed between eight cities, and over these relics arose sanctuaries to which pilgrimages were made.[16] As Buddha, before

---

[12] Köppen, Religion des Buddha.

[13] Comp. the rock inscriptions of King Açoka with regard to tolerance. Max Müller, Essays. Leipzic, 1869.

[14] Bournouf, Introduction.

[15] Ibid.

[16] Stanislas Julien, Histoire de la vie de Hiouen-thsang. Paris, 1853. Lassen in d. Alterthümer.

his glorification, had passed through previous careers, not only as man, but also in various animal forms, in many temples even hairs, feathers, or bones were worshipped as having been derived from the animal bodies which he had formerly abandoned.[17] Not only the founder himself, but a host of sanctified Bodhisattvás received homage, so that we see the highly revered Chinese pilgrim Hiouen-thsang visiting the images of these patron saints, and in devout rapture imploring oracular signs in answer to his questions asked with due rites.[18] Prayer, that is to say, Shamanistic invocation, was certainly alien to the mind of Sákjamuni or Gautama, but it was in the midst of his four hundred million votaries that rosaries and prayer cylinders were invented. It sounds strange that enthusiastic admirers extol Buddhism because it holds out neither bribes nor threats. In the eyes of Buddhism this world is itself a purgatory, a wheel that has revolved from eternity ; and birth into the blissful regions of the gods or into the horrors of hell, the unclean body of the animal, or, lastly, into lower or higher castes, enticed or terrified the righteous or the sinner. The Buddhist doctrine has not disdained using the fear of an infallible retribution as a means of discipline.

Nor has Buddhism done anything to cure the natives of India of the superstition of the transmigration of souls ; on the contrary, it maintained this dogma, and has even infected other nations with it as with a disease. It did not upset the distinctions of caste, but allowed them a social existence, although it showed a preference for the oppressed and despised in its promises of a speedy deliverance. Its boasted tolerance towards other religions is moreover of doubtful value, for it did nothing to raise alien notions of the Deity from their debased condition. Buddhism retained the Vedist heaven of the gods, and was contented to leave untouched the love of Shamanistic sorcery of the Mongolian tribes. Purer and riper conceptions can only gain the mastery by expelling the less pure and the less ripe. The estimate of the adherents of Gautama's doctrine as four hundred millions, includes the whole Chinese people, who, though worshipping heaven and earth as well

---

[17] Tylor, Primitive Culture, vol. i. p. 408.

[18] Stanislas Julien, Histoire de la vie de Houen-thsang. Paris, 1853.

as the dead, yet venerate Confucius as a moral legislator, and have in fact accepted from Buddhism only the figure of Buddha, adding one more false god to other false gods.[19]

The Buddhist doctrine was not preached to an elect people but to all mankind, and its history is like that of Christianity among the Jews; for it enjoyed many centuries of undisputed sovereignty, and was then extinguished among the natives of India, or has at least been expelled from the continent, and is now to be found only in Ceylon. In the west, in Kabool, Taberistan and Kurdistan, Buddhism has been driven out by the sword of Islam. At an early period it was divided into a northern and a southern school. Ceylon, Burmah, Siam, and the Malayo-Chinese countries in general, belong to the southern and older school, the writings of which, composed in Pali, were in all probability established at the third Buddhist council in the third century B.C. In Java, where Buddhism had successfully expelled Brahminism, it succumbed to Islam in the fifteenth century. The writings of the northern school which, although in Sanscrit, are more modern, only received their final form at the fourth council, about the time of the birth of Christ. New Buddhism is adopted in Nepaul and other Himalayan districts, in Thibet by the Mongolian tribes, and in China and Japan. The first missionary is said to have reached China as early as 217 B.C.; but it was not till A.D. 65 that the emperor Ming-ti established the doctrines of Gautama as an authorized religion.[20] The new believers worship a large number of Bodhisattvás, beings who, though only a grade lower than Buddha, and equally able to enter into the Nirvâna, yet through compassion, and to obtain the deliverance of their fellow-men, renounce this privilege in order to assist pious souls who call on them in prayer. Since the time of the Mongol emperors, the head of the church of Thibet, who resides at Lása, is held to be an incarnation of the Bodhisattva Padmapáni. His title, Dalai Lama, or Ocean-Lama,[21] first originated in the fifteenth century, when the northern church was divided on the question of the

---

[19] Max Müller, Essays.   [20] Ibid.

[21] Thibetan *bla-ma*, superior, from *bla*, above. Friedrich Müller, Reise der Fregatte Novara ; Anthropologie.

celibacy of the priesthood. The supreme head of those who permit the marriage of the priests lives at Taschilhúnpo, under the title of Bogda Lama. This Lama is also considered to be the incarnation of a Bodhisattva, namely, of Amitábha, or, in Thibetan, Odpagméd, and he bears the title of Pan-tshen-rin-po-tshe.[22] The two heads of the church are now reconciled, and with true Buddhist tolerance each sends his benediction to the other.

XII.—THE DUALISTIC RELIGIONS.

MAN views in its relation to himself every phenomenon which he encounters, and hence regards as animated whatever disturbs his comfort, whether it is heat or cold, drought, hunger, pain, disease, or death. An inexperienced mind can hardly conceive that good and evil proceed from the same hand. In history, as in creation, we see contradictions which are hard to reconcile with the hypothesis of a benevolent and just system of the world. The same God who created the sublime firmament with its glorious luminaries, the beautiful earth, the flower, the dewdrop with its resplendent colours, the innocent eye of the child, filled his own world with fever, with poison, with vermin, with war, with barbarous cruelty in the animal kingdom, in which it commonly happens that one animal is incapable of development without torturing and destroying another, devouring its very intestines. Long and difficult is the progress to the conception of a Leibnitz, that, with all its dark sides, the world perceptible to the senses is not only the best according to human standards, but the best of all possible worlds[1] Men of undisciplined intellect never attain to the perception that evil is but a limitation of the pleasures of existence, and, insatiable in enjoyment, they ask why the joys of life should be in any way hindered, limited, or ended. Still less do they see that even bodily pain is usually nothing else than an unasked but true warner against dangers, the approach of which threatens our lives or our health.

---

[22] Von Schlagintweit, Indien und Hochasien, vol. ii. p. 86.

[1] Tentam Theodic. Pars ii.

Unable to trace comfort and discomfort to a single source, all races of mankind in the earlier phases of intellectual development have employed the expedient of assigning these opposite effects to invisible beings, and have fancied themselves surrounded and watched by a host of mischief-makers as well as by benevolent protectors. As soon as this work of the imagination was accomplished, mankind was able to pass through various phases of improvement. In the first and lowest stage a reconciliation with the invisible tormentor is attempted. In a hymn of the Madagascans, Zamhor and Niang are addressed as creators of the world; and it is added that no prayers are offered to Zamhor, as the good God does not require them.[2] Among the Africans of Congo[3] and the Hottentots[4] we find worship of the evil combined with the neglect of the good Spirit. The negroes of the Slave Coast say God is so glorious and so great that he does not trouble himself about the base human world.[5] In America precisely the same ideas prevail among the Patagonians, for they also worship only the malicious Gualitschu.[6] Dobrizhoffer described the Abipones, who served only the gods of darkness, as worshippers of the devil.[7] Appun,[8] who gives the names of the good and bad spirits recognized by the Arowak, Warrau, Arecuna, Macuschi, Carib, and Atorai tribes of Guayana, adds that the Creator himself is deemed such an infinitely exalted being, that he does not concern himself with individuals. Among the Botocudos the sun and moon represent the two natures of the Godhead.[9] The ancient Egyptians assigned the parts of their dualism to Hesiri (Osiris) and Set; the Chaldeans to the planets, Jupiter and Venus being the propitious, Saturn and Mars the pernicious stars; the vacillating Mercury always adhered to the rulers for the time being of the astrological heavens. The worship of the horrible Siva may also be regarded as an attempt at conciliation,

---

[2] Roskoff, Geschichte des Teufels, vol. i. p. 47.

[3] Winwoode Reade, Savage Africa, p. 250.

[4] Kolbe, Cap der guten Hoffnung.

[5] Bosman, Guinese Goud-Kust. 1704.

[6] Musters, Among the Patagonians.

[7] Geschichte der Abiponer   [8] Ausland, 1872.

[9] Von Martius, Ethnographie, vol. i. p. 327.

and a so-called devil worship has continued to exist in Western Asia among the Yesidi, in the midst of purer religions which have obtained the mastery everywhere else. A great moral improvement must have taken place in man before he offered his homage to the well-disposed divinity, for he is then no longer influenced by fear, but by an impulse of gratitude. To our surprise, it is in this stage that we find the Australians of New South Wales, who offer their sacrifices not to the malignant Potoyan, but to a good power under the name of Koyan.[10] With regard to many Indian tribes in the neighbourhood of the Orinoco, who believed in a bad spirit under various appellations, Father Gumilla[11] states positively that that they paid him no honours.

Although races intellectually immature describe the disposition of the invisible powers as good or bad, they do not mean to distinguish between moral and immoral. Good and bad is nothing more than agreeable and disagreeable. The answer of the Bushman is sufficiently well known, who, in reply to the Christian missionary, gave as an instance of a bad action that some one should steal his wife, and, as an instance of a good one, that he should steal some one else's wife.[12] But as a gregarious being, man very soon perceives and understands in lapse of time, with increasing keenness, that social life imposes upon him duties to his neighbour. Even in the lowest stage the infraction of social enactments is looked upon as an offence. But the social laws are only recorded in the customs of the horde, the tribe, or the nation. The employment of the vendetta is certainly a moral action wherever it has not been replaced by better institutions. The Brazilian Tupinamba hope that the virtuous will be gathered to their fathers in the happy gardens of the other world ; but by virtue they mean brave defence of the property of the tribe, slaying many foes, and devouring the slain.[13] Moral commandments only attain their highest perfection when their relation is extended to the whole of mankind, when the rights of man are respected in foreign

---

[10] Dumont d'Urville, Voyage de l'Astrolabe. [11] El Orinoco ilustrado.
[12] Waitz, Anthropologie, vol. i.
[13] Lery, quoted by Tylor, vol. ii. p. 86.

nations, and the duties of man are fulfilled towards alien races. Whatever may be his distance from this goal, which though recognized by Christianity is still unreached in the Christian world, man is everywhere tempted to value his own pleasure and advantage more highly than the social commandment laid upon him. But in proportion as the moral conceptions amplify the conception of the Deity, so does religion operate as the most powerful lever of improvement: the invisible author of existence appears as the legislator, and as the judge of right and wrong. The Erânians in Persia were the first to connect religion with morality.

Search among their antiquities has invariably indicated that the Persian and Indian Aryans, at a date not yet determined, inhabited a common home, and shared the same religious conceptions. They imagined the invisible world to be filled with beings exercising an influence over the destiny of mankind, and these beings they named Deva and Ahura. Whether a religious division took place in consequence of the separation, or the separation in consequence of a religious division, the Erânians afterwards regarded the Ahura as benevolent, the Deva (in modern Persian, *div*, English, *devil*) as inimical powers. Conversely, among the Indian Aryans the Deva (Latin, *deus*) are considered the beneficent, and the Erânian Ahura evil powers.[14]

Among the Erânians there was a consecrated caste, called Soschianto in the oldest sacred writings, in ancient times exactly corresponding to the Indian Atharva, for both consisted of priests of fire.[15] In Media the Magi, whose name first occurs in the inscriptions of Darius, performed the functions of the Soschianto and Atharva.[16] They wore white raiment, refrained from animal food, and worshipped the forces of nature personified, or the highest forms of fetish, the sun (Mithra), the moon, the stars, the earth, running water, and especially fire. Among these priests rose

[14] In the oldest portions of the Rigveda Samhitâ, the expression Asura is still used in a good and elevated sense. Martin Haug, Religion of the Parsees.

[15] From the latter is derived the Atharva Veda. Atharva means provided with fire.

[16] Fr. Spiegel, Das Leben Zarathustra's. 1867.

the founder of a religion, Zoroaster, or more correctly Zarathustra.[17]
He is first mentioned in Greek literature about 470 B.C. by
Xanthus the Lydian, who dates his appearance at hundreds or
thousands of years before Xerxes. He is certainly of very high
antiquity.[18] Difficulties also occur in assigning the place of his
birth, and although it is generally said to have been Ragha or
the present Rai near Teheran, it must be added that he subsequently lived in Bactria, and that it was probably there that his
doctrine first took root.[19]

Zarathustra proclaimed that among the many benevolent Ahura
there was a Mazdâo, or creator of the world,[20] who rewarded
good and evil. This supreme being combined in itself a white or
holy (*çpento mainyus*) and a dark or evil spirit (*angro mainyus*),
so that the division into Ormazd and Ahriman did not form a
part of the pure doctrine of Zoroaster;[21] according to his tenets,
both good and evil proceeded from the same creative power. In
an old hymn in the Parsee liturgy, the soul of Nature is represented as appearing before God, and complaining that the world
is devastated by the oppression of the evil one. It also begs for
the creation of a being powerful enough to release it for ever from
its affliction. But it did not seem good to God to exempt mortals
from the conflict with the evil one, which tends to fortify the
power of good with which they were endowed. But, at the request
of the soul of Nature, he showed it the prototype of Zarathustra,
by whose appearance the champions of good should receive such
support that the victory of light would be secured for ever.[22]

But this more profound doctrine became obscured in the

---

[17] The name is translated variously by Windischmann (Zoroastrische
Studien), by Fr. Spiegel (Leben Zarathustra's), and by Martin Haug, who
explains it as the title of a high priest, and gives the founder the name of
Spitama.

[18] M. Haug (Lecture on the Original Speech of Zoroaster) does not think it
permissible to place it earlier than 2300 B.C. Rapp, on the contrary, has
adduced many reasons for fixing the period between the eleventh and thirteenth
centuries B.C.

[19] Rapp has skilfully set forth the evidence in favour of Bactra.

[20] Haug, Religion of the Parsees.   [21] Ibid.

[22] Ferdinand Justi in the Ausland.   1871.

course of time. The light side and the dark side of the Divine
will were separated. Since then the lords of light and of darkness struggle for the victory which is, however, decided from the
beginning. Ormazd alone knows of the existence of Ahriman,
and has three thousand years in which to form an army of immortal fellow-helpers before the latter moves. When Ahriman
at length rises to the conflict, he encounters a well-prepared
antagonist. The struggle lasts three thousand years without a decision. Only in the next and final period of three thousand years
is Ahriman reduced to impotence.[23] In this conflict mortal man
is to partake; he is to choose between light and darkness, to
conduce to the victory of the Good by the influence of his works,
and not increase Ahriman's prospect of success by bad actions.
It was certainly not easy to invent anything more influential in
fostering the better impulses of man than the promise of being
regarded by God himself as a contributor to the victory. Connected with this was the doctrine of the resurrection from the
dead, a genuinely Zoroastrian dogma, of which the earliest notice
reached the West at the end of the fourth century B.C., through
Theopompos.[24] The dead were supposed to rise to an eternal
life in bodies needing no change of substance, casting no shadow
and requiring no sustenance. For three days after the last dying
breath the soul still hovers near its bodily shell. But at the fourth
dawn an angel of death drags it to the bridge of the soul-catcher
(Tshinvat Peretu) and before the judge Straoscha, who tests
the good and bad works in the balance. The righteous man is
met with celestial greetings by an embodiment of his virtuous
life in the form of a maiden in the full beauty of youth, slim and
broad-bosomed, with white arms and noble countenance. To the
godless the embodiment of his conduct appears as an ill-favoured
girl, the sight of whom recalls to his remembrance all his lies and
acts of injustice. According to the verdict, the soul either passes
over the bridge to the sphere of hymns of praise (*garô demâna*) or
is cast down by evil spirits into the gulf of destruction.

Similar ideas respecting the trial of the soul after death are
diffused over the whole world. We need not dwell on the judg-

---

[23] Wendischmann, Zoroastr. Studien.   [24] Ibid.

ment of the dead as conceived by the Egyptians, as it is sufficiently well known. But according to the creed of the Badagas
in Tamul India, the souls are obliged to pass by a column of fire
which consumes the sinful, and it is only after perils that they
reach the land of the blessed by a bridge of rope.[25] Jesuit missionaries record that the Hurons believe that the souls of the
departed are obliged to pass over the river of death on the trunk
of a tree; during the passage many are seized and thrown over
by the guardian of the bridge, or by a dog.[26] Tylor, who has
sedulously collected other examples of the myth of the bridge of
the soul, found it also in an old English dirge, in which the words
" The brig of dread no brader than a thread " occur.[27]

The striking Erânian conception of a moral dispensation of
the world did not prevent the continuance of an old fetishistic
superstition, which was, however, skilfully reconciled with the
fundamental idea of the Mazdayasna, or the doctrine of Zoroaster.
Thus Mithra, or the sun, was adored as the eye of Ormazd,
although created by himself. The Shamanistic drinking of the
Haoma likewise preserved its magic influence. But, above all, fire
is even now worshipped as the son of Ormazd; hence no conflagration may be extinguished save with earth; no light blown out,
for every breath is a pollution, for which reason the priests in their
sacred functions and other Parsees while engaged in prayer cover
their mouths. Fire is contaminated by cooking and smith's work,
and the moral law of the Parsees everywhere insists on cleanliness.
Running water enjoys the same protection from pollution. For
this reason it was meritorious to build bridges in order to obviate
wading through the rivers. As the dead could neither be burnt
nor thrown into the water, nor can the equally sacred earth be
defiled by them, the bodies were exposed as a prey to birds in
circular places, surrounded by walls, which were called *Towers of
Silence.*[28]

---

[25] Baierlein, Nach und aus Indien.

[26] Tylor, Primitive Culture, vol. ii. p. 92.

[27] Early History of Mankind, p. 451.

[28] In Media also corpses were not laid in the ground before they had been
covered over with melted wax; or they were buried, as in the royal vaults at
Persepolis, when the flesh had been stripped from the bones. That Cyrus,

Among the followers of Zarathustra the notion of sin was very variable, for it might consist in an offence against Shamanistic precepts, in other words, in contamination, or else in an action morally reprehensible. Of the latter sort, lying was regarded as a heavy disgrace,[29] deceit as worse than robbery. Theft was a crime, if only because it is done in secret ; to lend money seemed culpable, because it was liable to result in the deception of the creditor.[30] The moral law of Parseeism insisted and still insists on probity and purity; even to our own times no other religious organization has enjoyed an equal degree of respect from those of other creeds. The first Gospel also makes kindly mention of the Magi who came from the East.

XIII.—THE MONOTHEISM OF ISRAEL.

NOTHING is more significant in the moral history of the human race than the development of a monotheistic conception of God. In the legends and narratives so ingenuously and undoubtingly related in the Old Testament, we may see, as in an entirely correct mirror, the slow ripening of this conception, which was so often in danger of annihilation. Because in early childhood we all imbibed the truth that the Holy and Eternal must be indivisible, we overlook the difficulties which necessarily encountered the diffusion of this idea when it was novel, hesitatingly and vaguely held by few, and rejected by the majority for the sake of other and older conceptions. Before reaching a belief in the Divine unity, a people must have passed through long periods of intellectual and moral development, for, as Tylor[1] truly remarks, monotheism has never been met with in a tribe of so-called savages. Implicit reliance

---

who was a fire-worshipper, should have condemned Crœsus to the stake is scarcely credible ; it would be less incredible that the Lydian king wanted to burn his god Sandon (F. Justi). Rapp, on the contrary, supposes that the funeral practices above mentioned were not customary in Western Erán, but were peculiar to the East alone.

[29] Herodotus, i. 138.
[30] Duncker, Gesch. des Alterthums.
[1] Primitive Culture, vol. ii. p. 333.

can, however, be bestowed on biblical history only from the date at which the people of Israel adopted the art of writing, that is, from the time of the exodus from Egypt, or not much before.[2]

In their earlier days the Hebrews made use of other names than Jahveh for the Supreme Being, and it is a suspicious fact that one of these (Elohim) is in the plural form, and that in swearing a solemn oath three Gods were successively addressed.[3] It has already been mentioned that household gods (seraphim) still received worship even in David's time.[4] Shortly before the Babylonian captivity, Josiah ordered the destruction of two altars of sacred stones before the gates of Jerusalem.[5] The Scriptures themselves expressly testify that in the earliest ages the Jews did not adhere to the pure religion of God. Hence, if the Egyptians worshipped a Supreme Being under the name of *I am that I am*,[6] the conjecture is not entirely to be rejected, that Moses, being initiated into the mysteries of the Egyptian worship, was the first to attain monotheistic views ; yet, owing to the obscurity which surrounds the early history of the people of Israel, an assertion such as this can neither be strictly proved nor strictly refuted. But it seems hardly credible that a single mind, however ardent and highly gifted, could have converted an entire nation completely unprepared for such a change to a totally novel interpretation of the world. The conception of an indivisible God must, in common with all processes of this world, have been of slow development. In the Old Testament story we frequently see this conception on the point of extinction, or obscured like the sun by a passing cloud on a gloomy day. Even Moses was not unshaken, or he would never have set up the brazen serpent in the desert as a protection against the snakes in the peninsula of Sinai. This fetish was only destroyed by the devout King Hezekiah, at a time when a far purer and clearer conception of God had become general. Traces of Shamanism are also retained in the trial by ordeal in accusations of adultery. The suspected woman is to

---

[2] The mention of signet rings in Joseph's time (Gen. xxxviii. 18, 25) would point to a somewhat earlier date.

[3] With Gen. xxxi. 53, comp. Ewald, Israelitische Geschichte, vol. i. p. 371.

[4] See above.   [5] Ewald, vol. iii. p. 757.

[6] G. Ebers, Durch Gosen zum Sinai.

drink water in which has been soaked a paper inscribed with curses,[7] just as the Mohammedan priests of the present day pretend to cure sick people with water in which written texts of the Koran have been washed.[8] That women also attempted to conjure up the dead is proved by Saul's secret visit to the witch of Endor : even in Josiah's time an oracle which existed at Jerusalem was held in much esteem. Immediately after Joshua's death a deplorable license had taken possession of the public mind, and Jahveh worship was polluted with human sacrifices, which were continued in use up to the time of the kings.[9] In old days Jahveh was considered only as the shield of the Hebrew race exclusively, as a tutelary spirit of greater powers than the deities of the hostile tribes.[10] Thus Jephthah sends word by his messenger to the king of the children of Ammon : " Wilt thou not possess that which Chemosh thy god giveth thee to possess ? So whomsoever the Lord our God shall drive out from before us, them will we possess."[11] Jahveh's power was even considered to be locally restricted, for God undertook to "go down into Egypt" with Jacob.[12] The sensuous view was sometimes carried so far that the forces of nature are regarded as vital manifestations of God, and the conception of God is almost reduced to a monotheistic worship of nature. The extreme beauty of the language employed must not obscure the significance of the fact that an audible voice was perceived in the thunder, and the cold or warm breath of Jahveh in frost and thaw.[13] Undoubtedly, the limitations to our intellectual faculties always compel us to reinvest the incomprehensible essence of God with the nature of man ; even the Gospels speak of the paternal emotions of God ; but it is a different thing when we are constantly aware that we are using anthropomorphic terms, in default of truer, just as even in the exact sciences we are not

[7] Numbers v. 19.

[8] The way in which Shamanistic notions had taken root may be seen from Job vi. 6-10.

[9] No sophistry can diminish the shock to humanity which we experience in reading the narrative of Jepthah's daughter (Judges xi). Respecting the human sacrifices under Saul and David, comp. 1 Sam. xiv. 23, 45, and 2 Sam. xxi. 6.

[10] Exod. xv. 11, and xviii. 11.   [11] Judges xi. 24.

[12] Gen. xlvi. 4.   [13] Job xxxvii. and xxxviii.

always able to avoid figurative expressions.   But when the Bible
represents Jahveh as being gratified by the savour of sacrifices,[14] it
uses language such as Homer would have used.   The conception
of the Jahveh to whom Moses on Mount Sinai is obliged to recall
the promises given, and who, infirm of purpose, withdraws his
threats,[15] is childish, and therefore destitute of sublimity.   Here,
again, we are reminded of scenes such as were enacted on
Olympus in the epic periods of the Greeks.   Even the dress of
the priests with its ornaments and embroidery is traced back to
Divine ordinances,[16] and we are sorry to read that Jahveh suggested and abetted the embezzlement of vessels of gold and silver
borrowed by the Israelites.[17]   The conception of the Supreme
Being remained long thus meagre, corrupt, and human in its
weakness.

The deep significance of the history of Israel consists in this :
that by its experiences and sufferings this nation was driven to
a conception of God, ever increasing in profundity and purity.
Of all the nations of antiquity the Jews alone possess a history
which strives to recognize the control of a moral dispensation of
the world in earthly events.   It was written in exile[18] in a sorrow-
ful mood, where the priesthood no longer existed, so that no
hierarchical craft came into play, as has sometimes been supposed.
The preceding period of the kings had given the experience that
religious license was nearly always followed by worldly ruin, but
the Scriptures did not conceal the fact that pious rulers sometimes
fell into adversity, or fortune smiled favourably on recreants to the
end.   By their misfortunes during the time of the kings, the Jews
acquired their firm trust in God.   "With the Assyrians," exclaims
Hezekiah, according to the Scriptures, "is an arm of flesh, but
with us is the Lord our God to help us, and to fight our battles." [19]
Thus Eliphaz admonishes the despairing Job how many that
" plow iniquity and sow wickedness " are consumed by the blast

---

[14] Lev. i. 9.   [15] Exod. xxxii. 9–14.
[16] Exod. xxviii. 33, 34.   [17] Exod. xi. 2.
[18] According to Ewald (History of Israel), the Book of Kings was written
in the middle of the Babylonian captivity.
[19] 2 Chron. xxxii. 7, 8.

of God.[20] The Jews had distinctly recognized that the strength of a nation can only be founded on a firm reliance on the moral dispensation of the world. From their own history they had derived the lesson that they had always been victorious as long as morality prevailed amongst them, and that departure from the law resulted in their being carried away into captivity.[21] The consolation and light which they derived in the hour of their affliction from this knowledge is echoed in the verses of the psalm, "Though I walk through the valley of the shadow of death, I will fear no evil, for Thou art with me."

There are individual traits which show that before, during, and after their exile, in their religious views they discarded their former childlike crudeness. Ezekiel no longer recognizes the God of the Old Testament who never forgave, but always revenged the sins of the forefathers on the third and fourth generations. "The father shall not bear the iniquity of the son, nor the son the iniquity of the father." Even the man overburdened with sin, if he turns away from his sins in true repentance may hope for forgiveness, "for," as the prophet represents the Lord saying, "Have I any pleasure at all that the wicked should die? and not that he should return from his ways and live?" In a psalm ascribed to David,[22] compassion as of a father is promised to all who fear God. The maxim of the son of Sirach that [23] we must forgive our neighbour before asking forgiveness for ourselves is among the foreshadowings of Christianity. The Israelites were indebted to the prophets for their liberation from Shamanistic errors. As we have already noticed the dangers with which all sacrificial worship threatens the moral tendencies of the religious emotions, we will recall the much-admired warning of Isaiah,[24] "Your country is desolate, your cities are burned with fire: your land, strangers devour it in your presence, and it is desolate, as overthrown by strangers. And the daughter of Zion is left as a cottage in a vineyard, as a lodge in a garden of cucumbers, as a besieged city. Except the Lord of Hosts had left unto us a very small remnant, we should have been as Sodom, and we should have been like upon

---

[20] Job iv. 7–9.　　[21] Ezech. xviii. 20.　　[22] Psalm ciii. 13.
[23] Ecclesiasticus xxviii. 2.　　[24] Isaiah i. 7.

Gomorrah.[25] Hear the word of the Lord, ye rulers of Sodom; give ear unto the law of our God, ye people of Gomorrah. To what purpose is the multitude of your sacrifices unto me? saith the Lord: I am full of the burnt offerings of rams, and the fat of fed beasts; and I delight not in the blood of bullocks, or of lambs, or of he goats. When ye come to appear before me, who hath required this at your hand, to tread my courts? Bring no more vain oblations; incense is an abomination unto me; the new moons and the sabbaths, the calling of assemblies, I cannot away with; it is iniquity, even the solemn meeting. Your new moons and your appointed feasts, my soul hateth: they are a trouble unto me; I am weary to bear them. And when ye spread forth your hands, I will hide mine eyes from you: yea, when ye make many prayers, I will not hear; your hands are full of blood. Wash you, make you clean; put away the evil of your doings from before mine eyes; cease to do evil; learn to do well; seek judgment, relieve the oppressed, judge the fatherless, plead for the widow. Come now, and let us reason together, saith the Lord: though your sins be as scarlet, they shall be as white as snow; though they be red like crimson, they shall be as wool."

Even Samuel is represented as saying that Jahveh is better pleased with obedience than sacrifice.[26] The prophets explicitly denied that sacrifice in any way binds the Deity as in a sort of reciprocal covenant, and guarded against the error that the slightest coercion was exercised upon the Divine will by any kind of ritual. As soon as inward moral purity and the avoidance of social crimes are insisted upon as a Divine law, the province of ethics coincides with that of religion. When strict and righteous conduct is regarded as the proof of reverence for the Supreme Being, the exaltation of the Divine will induces man to strive, consciously or unconsciously, to raise the value of his own existence by the fulfilment of higher duties.

The conceptions of God himself become more and more re-

---

[25] On this passage Steinthal observes, " The transition from the comparison of misfortune to the equality in wickedness of Judah and Sodom has always appeared to me of such overwhelming force, that I doubt whether in all rhetorical literature there is another such striking passage."

[26] I Sam. xv. 22, and Ewald Hist. of Israel. Psalm li. 18, 19.

moved from crude sensuousness. It was as a nomad that Jahveh went down to Egypt with Jacob, but on the other hand we read that no one can escape from the omnipresent God of the Psalmist, even "with the wings of the morning." [27] God, unlimited in space, is also recognized as eternal. He is conceived of as existing before the visible world of matter ; nor do human ideas of time affect one to whom "a thousand years are as one day, or as a watch in the night."

Thus, without observation, and not suddenly but by gradual transitions, a constantly new and newer God is revealed, purer and more moral, corresponding to the purer and more moral views to which the Jewish people were matured, when they had been educated to greatness and purified by sore trials.

The Scriptures lie open to every one, and in them we can pass through in history what the Hebrews experienced in their own persons.

As the monotheism taught by the prophets was a true gain, it necessarily proved its worth in the hour of unspeakable calamity, when the inhabitants of Judea were led into captivity at Babylon, as the ten tribes had previously been by the Assyrians. Of Zion and the temple there remained only the bare walls, and a garrison was quartered in the desolate spot to warn away any who might come to perform their secret devotions in the sacred places. The future was completely dark ; there gleamed no ray of the most distant hope that this once strong and envied people, who were now dispersed and scattered over the great kingdom of Babylon, should ever be reunited. When, to use the words of their singer, they wept by the waters of Babylon, and hung their harps upon the willow trees, because they could not sing the Lord's song in a strange land, their deeply troubled minds answered their self-inquiries as to the future with the cruel words, "All is over." It was over with Judah and Zion even as the kingdom of the ten tribes had already passed away.

When the period of their kings, during which they ruled from the sea to the desert, had passed away with its terrible conclusion like a vanished dream, and when fully restored to consciousness,

---

[27] Psalm cxxxix. 9.

they found themselves transported into the midst of the Asiatic marvels of Babylon and surrounded by sensual pleasures, where it was possible for any one of them to stifle his yearnings after his home in rocky Palestine, by abandoning himself to the enjoyable realities of the moment—to the varied luxuries and revelries of the voluptuous capital beneath the groves of the Euphrates, and to the superfluity of artificially irrigated gardens.   This was done by the greater number : they employed their exile in earning a better livelihood, and perhaps thought it a fortunate dispensation that they had been delivered from the poverty-stricken monotony of their former lives.   Had all accommodated themselves to their new position in a manner so spiritless and worldly-wise, nothing would now have remained of Judaism but the name of a people in cuneiform writing, which modern erudition would decipher as *hebr* or something similar : one name more among the other meaningless names.

But the uncorrupt nucleus of the Jewish nation did not forget, but transmitted to the following and succeeding generation the yearnings after the places where its higher emotions had been imparted to it.   The exiles closely observing their new masters, seeing a nation stronger and more wisely governed, favoured by nature and enriched by skill and technical dexterity, yet degrading itself daily by the absurdities of idolatry, acknowledged to themselves that they still remained the chosen people.   To us, who are able to survey the subsequent course of history, the exile seems most like the curve of a parabola round its focus.   Judaism had not ended, for the very thing to which it owed its highest value, the conception of the unity of God, was destined merely to alter the direction of its course to a higher enlightenment.   Misfortune did not harden the Jews, but when they ate their own bread with tears they were softened towards all the suffering that they beheld around them.   Each of us who has striven to obtain clear ideas, has attained some explanation of the world, which is not merely the sum of what he has discerned for himself or gained from the experience of others, but of all that has happened to him or before him.   The historical adventures of a nation greatly affect such results as the creation of a religion of its own, the adoption of a strange one or the maintenance of an adopted one.   Emmanuel

Deutsch [28] was thus enabled to show that even in the earlier writings of the Talmud, the same tendency to gentleness and humanity appear, which rendered Christianity preëminently the ideal religion of the heavy-laden, and whence for more than eighteen centuries it has derived its best strength. These Talmudical passages belong to the period of the Babylonian captivity, the time of woe and oppression, and it is to this purifying school of misfortune that the tone of justice and softness, of tenderness and charity to others is due.

XIV.—THE DOCTRINES OF CHRISTIANITY.

THE Hebrews who had known the cosmical views and the theistic conceptions of the Erânians more or less correctly before the captivities, but learned them with full accuracy during the captivity itself, could not remain entirely unaffected by this mental contact and impregnation. To this we must primarily ascribe the fact that in scattered portions of the Old Testament, an incarnate instigator of evil suddenly appears, although the already vigorous conception of the unity of God does not allow conception of the devil as an Ahriman equal in rank to the Deity, but only as the minister of the Lord and an instrument in his designs.[1] But far more important in its effects than the acquisition of Satan, of which little use is made, was the acquaintance with the Erânian opinions of the immortality of the soul as well as the doctrines of the resurrection of the dead, and of a judgment of their course of life. These ideas were originally so alien to the Israelites that in the time of Christ the Sadducees [2] still rejected a future life as contrary to the

---

[28] Quarterly Review, October, 1867.

[1] Ewald (Hist. of Israel) attributes the book of Job to the time of the last kings of Judah, but he also shows that the knowledge of the Zarathustrian dogmas made itself felt in the religious conceptions of the Hebrews in the 10th, and more plainly in the 8th century, especially in the more liberal apprehension of the opposition betwixt good and evil. As to the few passages in the Old Testament besides Job, in which Satan appears, comp. Roskoff, Geschichte des Teufels.

[2] Matt. xxii. 23.

Scriptures. Even to the disciples the doctrine was so new that they questioned what the rising from the dead should mean. Many passages in the Old Testament actually deny every hope of another world. The righteous is rewarded with promise of a long life and a numerous offspring, or else actual worldly abundance in garner and cellar is held out as a recompense for religious reverence and strict worship. "What profit is there in my blood when I go down to the pit?" cries the Psalmist to the Lord. "Shall the dust praise Thee? shall it declare Thy truth?" In Job we find the entirely desponding expression that there is hope of a tree if it be cut down that it may sprout again, but that when the sons of men lie down they shall not be raised out of their sleep.[3] The conclusion of this dramatic poem is unsatisfactory. The glimpse which we should have expected into a world of glory does not open on the trials of the sufferer, but Job is restored to health, supplied anew with flocks and progeny, and dies full of years. The Old Testament, indeed, speaks repeatedly of an abode of the dead, which in our translation is termed hell, but which must not be regarded as a place of moral atonement, but as Job portrays it, as a dark region full of everlasting terrors. Moreover, this Sheol, which corresponds to the Hades of the Greeks, is nowhere mentioned in the legislative ordinances of the Old Testament. The germs of other and more elevated views appear only in the later portions. The consolatory doctrine is taught that man was God's idea, and therefore had existed from the beginning. As this doctrine is otherwise to be found only in books of less consideration, it is an important fact that it occurs in Jeremiah also (i. 4). If another beautiful chapter in the Book of Wisdom, in which the expectation of a Nirvâna is rejected as a doctrine of the wicked, is not received on account of its apocryphal origin, on the other hand, we have the doctrine of the preëxistence of man, as God's idea, in Psalm cxxxix., which Ewald ascribes to Zerubbabel.[4] In the Proverbs [5] the same view is expressed in

---

[3] Job xiv. 7–12.

[4] The doctrine of the preëxistence of man before birth is, according to Schrader, of Assyrio-Babylonian origin.

[5] Prov. viii. 22–31.

poetic words, and by elevated similes, which sound like a fore-shadowing of our modern cosmogonic science. "The Lord," it is said, "possessed me from the beginning of his way, before his works of old. I was set up . . . . or ever the earth was. When there were no depths . . . . when there were no fountains abounding with water. Before the mountains were settled, before the hills was I brought forth. While as yet he had not made the earth, nor the fields, nor the highest part of the dust of the world. When he prepared the heavens I was there : when he set a compass upon the face of the depth : when he established the clouds above : when he strengthened the fountains of the deep : when he gave to the sea his decree, that the waters should not pass his commandment : when he appointed the foundations of the earth : then I was by him . . . . rejoicing always before him."

From these passages we learn that a well-calculated scheme of creation was assumed, in which individuals were already taken into consideration. But, as God's idea, man must also continue to exist to all eternity. Before briefly stating what is the main distinction by which ethnology separates the essential nature of the Christian doctrine from the religious impulses of other times, or of paganism, we must first emphasize the fact that the embodiment of the forces of nature in God which is found in the Old Testament,[6] is set aside by the maxim that God must be contemplated as a spiritual being.[7] The Gospels, indeed, attribute anthropomorphic language to the founder of their faith, inasmuch as God is spoken of as a father, but this is vindicated by the limits of the human intellect. We are incapable of imagining a spirit—for that which we choose to call by that name always resembles a thinking being like ourselves—inseparable from the functions of an organism. As long as we remain men, we shall always be forced to imagine the Divine in human form, but this is accompanied in the Gospels by a restriction of language. If God is to be addressed as Father we are told to apply to God alone the paternal name thus consecrated.[8]

---

[6] Job xxxvii., xxxviii. [7] John iv. 24, πνεῦμα ὁ Θεός.

[8] Matt. xxiii. 9, καὶ πατέρα μὴ καλέσητε ὑμῶν ἐπὶ τῆς γῆς· εἷς γάρ ἐστιν ὁ πατὴρ ὑμῶν, ὁ ἐν τοῖς οὐρανοῖς.

But there is one doctrine in particular which makes its appearance first and solely in Christianity, namely, the hypothesis of a benevolent Providence. To speak after the manner of Leibnitz, the plan of the best possible creation has been thought out to the smallest detail, to the number of hairs on the head of man, and the existence of the weakest creatures.[9]   In proportion as the recognition of such an idea is established, Shamanism of all sorts, the most dangerous error of mankind, is set aside. Although human reflection may perhaps overcome the grosser attempts to assume a feigned power over the course of nature by means of incantation and sorcery, there nevertheless remains much longer a reliance on symbolical actions, sacrifice, abstinence, penance, and prayer. The Indian Brahmins, as we have seen, by ingenious self-deceptions, deluded themselves into the belief that they, as possessors of such means, acquired a Divine nature. Although it was during the captivity that prayer first gained importance and power among the Hebrews,[10] even Zechariah was obliged to bid them beware of the enforced fasting and mourning by which they fancied they could alter the counsels of God. The true Christian, while assuming the existence of a benevolent Providence, must not require any Divine interference with the normal course of natural events. The Founder of our religion even distinctly forbade supplications for earthly objects, for before the request was offered provision was already made for all the real wants of man.[11] This necessary corollary of the doctrine of a benevolent Providence distinguished Christianity from all other religious creations. Christianity does not promise the realization of any wish, however small, intense, or pure. It is therefore impossible to stray further from the original and pure religion than when, on the supposition that earthly desires no longer reach the heavenly Father, a number of polytheistic intermediate beings are invented as intercessors, and by this circuitous course a reversion is made to Shamanistic prayer.

The form of prayer which Christ taught to his disciples is nothing

---

9 Matt. x. 29, 30.   10 Ewald, Hist. of Israel, vol. v. p. 23.
11 Matt. vi. 8, οἶδε γὰρ ὁ πατὴρ ὑμῶν ὧν χρείαν ἔχετε πρὸ τοῦ ὑμᾶς αἰτῆσαι αὐτόν.

more than an injunction to observe, as in a mirror, the moral and religious state of our *ego* at the moment, to fortify ourselves in holiness by the thought of God, by the desire that the kingdom of Christian opinions may penetrate into our minds, as well as by the remembrance that whatever may befall us is the will of a benevolent Providence. It brings home to us the warning to forgive those who may have done us wrong,[12] and, finally, the petition that the Christian faith may not be shaken, and that doubt may be more and more thrust out. The only earthly sound in this prayer is the petition for daily bread, if indeed this be not an exhortation that gratitude is due for every day that is vouchsafed to us. The Lord's Prayer requires extreme concentration of thought if its purport is not to pass through the human mind without result. But so ineradicable are Shamanistic tendencies, that, notwithstanding the Founder's warning against thoughtless repetitions[13] which immediately precedes the teaching of the Lord's Prayer, as the Paternoster in an unknown tongue, it has for many centuries been, not expressed in prayer, but in Buddhist fashion,[14] repeated by the counting of the beads of a rosary.

The essential point of this prayer, or self-communing, is the so-called third petition, which patiently and gratefully welcomes all that may be decreed for man in this world and the next, as the enactment of a benevolent Providence. Even severe strokes of destiny may turn to inward advantage, since, setting aside the cases in which they harden and embitter, they raise the mind into that disposition of gentleness and forgiveness which renders it most susceptible to Christian truth. The consolation of the new doctrine was not for the sound and strong, but for broken hearts.[15] But the self-training of the moral man has to begin with the dis-

---

[12] In a similar sense it is said by Jesus the son of Sirach, "Forgive thy neighbour the hurt that he hath done unto thee, so shall thy sins also be forgiven when thou prayest."

[13] Matt. vi. 7, μὴ βαττολογήσητε, ὥσπερ οἱ ἐθνικοί· δοκοῦσι γὰρ, ὅτι ἐν τῇ πολυλογίᾳ αὐτῶν εἰσακουσθήσονται.

[14] As the analogous Buddhist prayer-mills have already been mentioned, we will add that even among the ancient Erânians prayer was prescribed to be repeated 100 and 1000 times. Duncker, Gesch. der Alterthums.

[15] Luke v. 31.

14

cernment of his own faults. Forbearance towards fellow-creatures, conflict with one's own hardness of heart and uncharitableness, are the constantly reiterated precepts of the Gospels. The ordinances of the Old Testament were not upset but enhanced and refined. Not murder only, but all animosity; not adultery, but every culpable desire, were to be suppressed. No merit was to be assumed for recompensing love by love, for that was done by the heathen also, but, like God, who makes the sun to shine upon the just and the unjust, to return curses with blessings, hatred with benefit, insults with intercessions, was enjoined on Christians as a new code of duty.[16] The subjugation of human nature is everywhere required as a striving towards the kingdom of heaven, and an ennoblement of earthly society is enjoined. To the young man who wishes to bury his father, the Founder replies, " Let the dead bury their dead," [17] as if every one to whom his own salvation is not the chief concern were a living shadow. Parental and filial or fraternal affection, which is only enlarged self-love, is to be extended to all mankind.[18]

In human society, social rights necessitate their own observance. The progress of our race depends on a complete organization of work and functions which is inconceivable without strict observance of the rights of others. When the sense of truth and justice is blunted all society goes to ruin. This inexorable moral law ensures the social training of our race. But the Christian aspires to something higher than the refinement of the social instinct of mankind. Kennan, the traveller, praises the compassionateness of the Koriaks ; he never saw a child receive a blow, he never heard a hard word spoken to a woman; but those enfeebled by age or hopelessly ill are speared with great dexterity ; the father or mother is usually killed by the son, for the stern necessities of the nomadic life do not allow the migratory community to be burdened by the decrepit, and the social instinct places the general welfare above pity for the individual. If we acknowledge that maxims such as these are incompatible with the Christian code of duty, we admit that our morality rises above

---

[16] Matt. v. 44–46.   [17] Ibid. viii. **22.**
[18] Ibid. x. **37.**   Mark iii. 33.

and occasionally opposes the social instinct. Our care of those diseased in mind may be regarded as prudential egotism, for no one can foretell whether he may not derive benefit from this social protection. But we also provide for human malformations, such as cretins and idiots. Assuredly it would be more for the benefit of society to abandon such beings to their fate, and to apply the the expenditure required for their care to more profitable purposes. In not doing so we satisfy a sense of duty which cannot be traced to our social instinct.[19] Negro slavery and many systems of bondage were justified by the supposition that the bondsmen required discipline, that is, compulsion to labour ; that they throve much better under pressure, and that a great part of their services was lost to the world after their liberation. Nevertheless, every noble mind, abhorring coercion of every kind, would deem these sordid advantages too dearly purchased. But we owe this sensitiveness of conscience to the teachings of the Gospel implanted in us in youth.

When Christianity is charged with its persecutions of heretics, its inquisitions, its religious wars, the reproach applies only to those who transformed the doctrines of gentleness into the reverse. There has never been any dispute as to the morality of Christianity, but only as to the dogmas as established by the decisions of councils. Christ himself combated the party which assumed to represent orthodox Judaism : he who declared the Sabbath to be made for man, and who has left behind him the words so crushing to dogmatists, " In vain do ye worship me, teaching for doctrines the commandment of men."

The contemners of the doctrines of the Gospel in our times generally overlook the circumstance that all philanthropic efforts have found their strongest auxiliary in the Christian teaching. The abolition of negro slavery was already contemplated, but the accordance of equal rights for all in public life was more warmly advocated by the Christian sense of duty. We owe our present

---

[19] Among the ancient Mexicans, cretins were also taken care of (Oviedo, Historia general), but this was certainly from superstitious fear or as a fancy, just as in the Fiji Islands the chiefs were wont to maintain cripples for their own amusement.

care for the poor to the command to feed the hungry, and to clothe the naked.[20] Many other points which may perplex us in the doctrines of the Gospels may perhaps be founded on a misapprehension on the part of the disciples ; the sense of the words spoken in Syriac may have suffered more or less in the translation into Greek, or the obscurity of the metaphors may still be cleared up on better acquaintance with the East, as has been the case with the camel and the eye of the needle.[21] It is due to misrepresentations that Christianity is sometimes regarded as less enlightened than Buddhism, which is said to have gained four hundred millions of adherents without proclaiming either a recompense for good works or a punishment for bad actions. We have already described the true state of the case. The Buddhism of the four hundred millions is destitute neither of a glorious heaven nor of a hell with imaginative tortures. Even in its primitive purity the transmigration of souls acted as a terror to the transgressors of its commandments, for the son of Asoka was barbarously blinded only because, according to Buddhist interpretation, in a former existence he had put out the eyes of hundreds of gazelles.[22]

XV.—ISLAM.

BEFORE the appearance of their prophet the tribes of the Arabian peninsula were still in the shackles of fetishism. They worshipped stones, rocks, trees, and images, and also the sun, moon, and constellations.[1] Mohammed himself confesses that in his

---

[20] Mark vii. 7. Μάτην δὲ σέβονταί με, διδάσκοντες διδασκαλίας ἐντάλματα ἀνθρώπων.

[21] The lamented Lady Duff Gordon writes (Letters from Egypt) : "Yesterday I saw a camel go through the eye of a needle, *i.e.*, the low-arched door of an enclosure. He must kneel and bow his head to creep through, and thus the rich man must humble himself."

In the oases of Southern Algeria, the small doors near the great gates in the walls are also called the eye of the needle (F. Desor, Aus Sahara und Atlas).

[22] Bournouf, Introduction à l'histoire du Buddhisme.

[1] L. Krehl, Religion der vorislamischen Araber. Leipzic, 1863.

youth he adored the gods of his fathers. The meteoric stone in the Ka'aba at Mecca had long been the object of pilgrimages in connection with which fairs were held, and in order not to deprive his native city of this source of profit, Mohammed condescended to incorporate the worship of this stone into his religious system. The existence of invisible and supernatural beings, jins and angels, was also believed, and endeavours were made to obtain their good-will by worship. Even in very early times the Bedouins acknowledged a creator of the heavens and a ruler of the world under the denomination of Allah, a name derived from the verb *lâh*, which signifies trembling and shining.[2] On other grounds its relationship to the Hebrew El, or Eloah, and with Alâhah, the old Arabic name for the sun, is also conjectured.[3] A future life was denied, so that it was Mohammed's doctrine of resurrection which especially repelled the higher classes of his countrymen.[4]

The prophet, who was left an orphan at an early age, and was in his youth obliged to adopt the humble occupation of a sheep and goat-herd, improved his position in life by marrying at twenty-four a rich widow at least fourteen years older than himself. He suffered all his life from hysterical attacks, and for that reason alone would have been regarded by the races of Africa, Northern Asia, and America as a powerful Shaman. Like all such, he also firmly believed that his revelations were extraneous, and that a higher power spoke by him. When in advancing years his enthusiasm gradually subsided, and practice gave him the power of evoking at will convulsive ecstasies, which were so great as to produce foaming at the mouth, he delivered revelations for the most trivial purposes. Before bringing home his eighth wife, she required that her marriage should be decreed by the word of God, which was given at her demand.[5] Having sworn to another of his wives to reject a Coptic lady whom he loved, but afterwards repenting of his promise, he procured a revelation from God assuring him that such oaths to women were not obligatory.[6] Thus the

---

[2] A. Sprenger, Das Leben des Mohammed, vol. i. p. 250.

[3] Von Kremer, Herrschende Ideen des Islam, p. 3.

[4] A. Sprenger, Das Leben des Mohammed, vol. i. p. 358.

[5] Der Korân, Sura xvi.

[6] For instance, see Von Kremer, Ideen des Islam, pp. 80, 81.

youth, self-deceived by Shamanism, was at an older age transformed into a crafty impostor. To reconcile the miracle of revelation with reality, it was supposed that the will of God was made known to the Prophet only in its purport, and that time was required to clothe the meaning in that poetical prose which soon so deeply affected the minds of the believers, that pious Moslems, on unexpectedly hearing the menaces of a verse of the Koran, repeatedly fell down unconscious from mere terror, and are even said to have died in consequence.[7] Mohammed, as a proof of the Divine nature of his inspirations, advised the sceptics, if they believed the Koran was devised by him alone, to try to write even one or two Suras like his.[8]

The Koran itself contains one hundred and fourteen psalms or Suras, differing in length from a single verse to the dimensions of a sermon. Narratives of judicial punishments taken from biblical and ancient Arabic legends, are mixed up, as in a heap devoid of order, with social ordinances and the actual Divine revelations. By arranging them according to the date of their origin we can gain an insight into the growth and development of the new faith, which is merely a recoining of Jewish and Christian thoughts. The predecessors of the Prophet among the Arabs were the Hanyfes, who worshipped a creator and expected a resurrection of the dead, followed by a judgment of moral acts. Mohammed called himself a Hanyfe, and Abraham the founder of Hanyfism, which in his mouth meant a purified monotheism, which is well called Islâm, a significant word which implies direct opposition to atheism as well as polytheism.[9] The Prophet was profoundly influenced by the dogmas of the Ebronite Jewish Christians at Jerusalem and Pella, who recognized only the first Gospel as genuine, and rejected the doctrines of the incarnation and redemption.[10] Mohammed himself visited Jerusalem more than once; he honoured Christ and his sister, as he deemed the Holy Ghost, and even the immaculate conception of the Virgin Mary was included in his dogmas.[11] The Prophet at first attempted

---

[7] Von Kremer, Ideen des Islâm.   [8] Koran, Sura x.

[9] Sprenger, Das Leben des Mohammed, vol. i. p. 72.

[10] Ibid. vol. i. p. 22.   [11] Koran, Sura xxi.

to found a Jewish Christian community among the Arabs. But as he was probably never able to read, it often happened that he made erroneous appeals to the Old Testament and the Gospels. When he was reproached with such mistakes, he took refuge in the evasion which has from that time been maintained by all Moslems, that the revelations in the Old and New Testaments are of Divine origin, but from vile and interested motives had been so distorted and corrupted by Jews and Christians, that it was necessary that they should be revealed again to the Prophet, fresh and unfalsified. "To thee, Mohammed," it is said in the fifth Sura, "we have given the book of truth, which confirms the law of Moses and the Gospel. Had God so willed it, he would have made of you, ye peoples, one nation, but he has separated you by different laws in order to try the obedience of each to the law which is revealed to him."[12] Later, however, there was no more question of such tolerance and equality. On the 16th of January, 624, the Prophet decreed an alteration of the Kibla, or direction in which prayers were to be said; the face was previously turned towards Jerusalem, but henceforth it was to be directed towards Mecca, although, as if to quiet his own conscience, the Prophet adds in the same Sura which inculcates this ordinance "Direct your prayer where you will, God is there, for God is omnipresent and omniscient."[13] Against Christian dogmas, and especially against the doctrine of the Trinity, he directed the 112th Sura, which contains the entire creed of the Moslem, and is to be repeated at the most sacred moment of the pilgrimage, while kissing the black stone of the Ka'aba. It runs, "Speak! God is one! The eternal God! He does not beget, he is not begotten! No creature is like unto him!"

The moral decrees enacted by the Prophet on the strength of his Divine mission, were arranged in imitation of the Sinaitic laws, in the following two series, each of five precepts :—1. To acknowledge no other gods but God; 2. to show respect to parents; 3. not to kill children on account of dread of starvation; 4. to preserve chastity; 5. to protect the life of others except where justice demands the contrary. To this first series are attached as injunc-

---

[12] See Koran, Sura cxi.   [13] Sura xx.-xxiv.

tions ; 6. inviolability of the property of orphans ; 7. just weights and measures; 8. no overburdening of slaves ; 9. impartiality of judges ; 10. sacredness of oaths and of the covenant with God.[14] The Mosaic law certainly surpasses this decalogue in point of simplicity. The Prophet obviously racked his brains in order to reach the normal number, and after all inserted mere police regulations. The consecration of the Sabbath was not ordained : Mohammed maintained that it was imposed upon the Jews only on account of their perversity, because they persevered in the celebration of the Saturday, and not as Moses wished of the Friday.[15]

The authorization of four lawful wives and an unlimited number of female slaves betrays the weakness of the Prophet, who set no bounds to his own love of pleasure. But it would be unjust to regard polygamy as the essential contrast between Islam and our own religion. Long before Christianity, monogamy was the law among many nations, and still is so among pagan races ; moreover, in the earliest times it was possible while belonging to the Christian Church to have several wives. In common with all nations in a low state of civilization, the Arabs in the time of their heathenism had imposed upon themselves highly complicated dietary prohibitions. The Prophet limited these interdicts to the flesh of swine, of hunted animals, and of blood.[16]

To procure credence for his revelations, the Prophet endeavoured to alarm his followers by the threats of the resurrection and a day of judgment. In this the fiery force of his poetic language was of service, and he neglected no opportunity of recalling the judgments already accomplished in biblical and ancient Arabic legends. On the other hand, in wearisome reiteration, he promised the believers and the righteous an Elysium, according to the popular taste—a shady garden with bubbling fountains, delicious fruits, luxurious couches, and a race of houris who united every charm that could eternally satisfy eternal desire. It is true the Koran contains passages which reduce these entrancing descriptions to the level of metaphors adapted to human comprehension,[17] that others represent the contemplation of the

---

[14] See Koran, Sura **vi.**   [15] Sura xvi.
[16] Sura vi.   [17] Sura ii.

glory of God as the reward of the righteous,[18] but the extra-ordinary attraction of Islam was based on the literal interpretation of these sensuous promises; later traditions have taken care to satiate the greedy expectations of the faithful with fabulous de-lineations of this paradise.[19]

The most objectionable doctrine in the Koran is the denial of free-will in man. The destiny of each person is predetermined and recorded, so that the course of life is related to this record as the acting is to the text of a dramatic poem.[20] Damnation is decreed for those on whom it falls by an irrevocable counsel of God ; for, continues the Koran, had Allah so willed it, all men would have believed, but without His will no soul would attain to faith.[21] The doctrine of predestination was always maintained by the orthodox, and although the more liberal sects clearly recog-nized the incompatibility of preordination and punishment with Divine justice and mercy, and held milder views, the weak-minded mass of believers adhered to the letter. On account of this doctrine no priesthood could ever gain ascendancy in the society of Islam, for there was nothing to bind or to loose. Moreover, the Caliphs and their successors were always at the head of the faithful.[22]

In addition to the Koran, the Sunna, or book of customs and legal practice, wherever it does not stand in contradiction with revelation, has full authority, and contains ordinances on social and criminal matters, as well as precepts with regard to food and apparel. In addition to this, legal force is imputed to the Record, or Hadyth, which contains such traditional utterances of the Prophet as can be traced back through good witnesses to himself.[23]

In Persia these legal authorities were not recognized, and hence arose a division among the faithful into the Sunnites, adherents of the Sunna, and the apostates, or Shyites.

---

[18] See Koran, Sura lxxv.

[19] Comp. the description of Paradise in M. Wolff's Mohammedanische Eschatologie. 1872.

[20] Sprenger, Das Leben des Mohammed, vol. ii. p. 307.

[21] Koran, Sura x., also lxxvi. Kremer, Ideen des Islâm, p. 9.

[22] Ibid. p. 280.   [23] Sprenger, Das Leben des Mohammed, vol. iii. p. 77.

Shortly after its establishment Islam overran Egypt and Northern Africa ; at the beginning of the eighth century it passed over the Straits of Gibraltar, and maintained itself in Western Europe until the fall of Granada, in 1492. In the same century in which it was driven back from Spain to Africa, it succeeded in gaining a footing in Southern Europe in the eastern peninsula, and in 1453 it obtained the dominion over the straits which divide our quarter of the world from Asia Minor.

In the beginning of the eighth century the Arabs pushed their conquests into the territory of the Indus, but their principalities of Mooltan and Mansora soon fell off from the Chalifate. Arab communities existed in all the towns on the coast of Malabar, though Islam was then merely tolerated in those regions. It was was only in the year A.D. 1000 that it obtained a firm footing in India among the Ghazuwids,[24] and under Baber, the founder of the kingdom of the Great Moguls, the chief power in the peninsula fell into the hands of Mohammedan princes. In Sumatra the doctrine of the Prophet first became predominant in 1206 in the kingdom of Atschin, and in the kingdom of Malacca shortly after its foundation in the year 1253, while in Java it did not supplant Buddhism until after the fall of the state of Madschapahit, in 1478. It reached the island of Celebes in 1512, yet the Buginese were still vainly resisting its spread even in 1640. Islam still continues its progress eastwards. Its furthest limit in that direction is a small mosque at Dobo in the Aru Islands, a dependency of New Guinea.[25] But in New Guinea itself there are many new converts among the Papuans.[26]

In Africa the doctrine of the Prophet was first naturalized in the Mediterranean districts. It made its way across the desert into Bornou between 1086 and 1097, but early in the same century it had spread to the great kingdom of Sonrhay, on the middle Niger, and in the beginning of the thirteenth century it extended to the rulers of Melli on the Upper Niger.[27] It reached Wadai, Darfur,

---

[24] Reinaud, Geographie d'Aboulféda. Introduction.

[25] Wallace, Malay Archipelago, vol. ii. p. 276.

[26] Otto Finsch, Neu-Guinea.

[27] Heinrich Barth, Nord- und Centralafrika.

and Kordofan only in the beginning and the middle of the seventeenth century.[28] Whether the Tuareg were formerly Christians, as Barth conjectures, requires further confirmation, and, again, whether in the former kingdom of Ghana, lying westwards of Timbuctoo, Christianity succumbed to Islam only in 1075, and in Nubia, where according to reliable records it still prevailed in the first half of the fourteenth century.[29] Even at present Islam is slowly expelling Christianity from Abyssinia. Within our times the Fellatah have carried it to Adamaua, far into the interior of pagan Africa. The doctrine of the Prophet imposes no change of habits on the Africans. The negro who embraces Islam is assured that he rises higher, and by reason of his purer doctrine is nearer to God than the Christians. Lastly, in Africa the promulgators of the doctrine of the Prophet are poor and unpaid, whereas the missionaries, although they preach contempt for riches, surround themselves with profusion. In the opinion of a clear-sighted observer, these are the reasons why the Christian religion gives way to Islam among the negroes.[30] This doctrine has recently been victorious in China. It had early been diffused there ; partly by way of Kashgar and the fertile districts on the southern slopes of the Thianshan, partly by sea, following the great mercantile routes to the places on the coast, until towards the end of the ninth century, on the downfall of the Thang dynasty, a persecution of foreigners and the extermination of the Mohammedans took place.[31] A short time ago a governor established himself at Talifu, in the south-west of the Celestial Kingdom, among the Mohammedan Chinese, and seized a portion of the province of Yunnen. The English who had entered into commercial transactions with this infant state by way of Burmah, were full of praise of the honesty and morality of the Panthays, as these new adherents of Islam were named.[32] According to more recent accounts the Chinese again destroyed this new creation in 1872.

[28] Waitz, Anthropologie.

[29] Fr. Kunstmann, Afrika vor den Entdeckungen der Portugiesien. 1853.

[30] Gerhard Rohlfs in Ausland. 1870.

[31] Peschel, Geschichte der Erdkunde.

[32] A. Bowers, Bhamo Expedition. 1871.

XVI.—THE ZONE OF THE FOUNDERS OF RELIGIONS.

" KNOWLEDGE of the natural characters of different regions of the world," says Von Humboldt, in one of the most profound passages of his Physiognomy of Plants, "is an essential part of the history of the human race and of its culture.   For although the beginning of this culture is not determined by physical influences alone, yet its direction and the national character, the gloomy or cheerful temper of mankind, depend largely on climatic conditions. The sky of Greece had great influence on its inhabitants!   The colonists in the beautiful and favoured districts between the Euphrates, the Halys, and the Egean Sea began early to recognize moral loveliness and tender feelings.   When Europe had sunk back into barbarism, and religious enthusiasm had suddenly brought the sacred East into prominence, our forefathers again brought home from those genial valleys more gentle manners. The poetry of the Greeks and the ruder songs of the primitive people of the north mainly owe their peculiar character to the forms of the plants and animals, to the mountain valleys which surrounded the poet, and to the air which he breathed.   Turning only to familiar objects, we all feel different emotions in the dark shade of beech-trees, on hills crowned with scattered fir-trees, or on the grassy plain where the wind rustles through the trembling foliage of the birch.   These plants of our native land severally evoke in our minds melancholy, elevating, or gladsome images. The influence of the physical upon the moral world, the mysterious interaction of the sensible and of that which lies beyond the senses, endows the study of nature, when raised to higher points of view, with a peculiar charm which is as yet too little recognized."

It would be a pleasant task carefully to trace the inward connection betwixt the greatest events in human society and the scenes in which they occurred.   No one could better help us in our preparation for such researches than Buckle, according to whom, nothing is simpler and more intelligible than the reaction of the place of abode upon the mental phenomena.   Where nature terrifies man by portentous objects of alarm, the imagination is more fully developed than the intellect, and belief in miracles is most luxuriant. "Italy, Spain, and Portugal," says Buckle, "are, of all countries in Europe, most frequently visited by earthquakes; earthquakes intimidate the mind of man, consequently the belief in the interference of supersensual powers with the physical order of the world has been more stubbornly maintained among the inhabitants of Southern Europe than in other parts." The terrible catastrophe which befel Lisbon more than a hundred years ago, although it stands alone in magnitude, may in some degree justify us in considering Portugal among the countries in which earthquakes most frequently occur, but Spain, although not entirely exempt, is not a country either specially or even severely visited by earthquakes. Japan, which so often trembles under the trident of Poseidon, is peopled by a cheerful race of men, given to tricks and jests, and heedless on subjects of religion. Russia, again, is almost entirely free from earthquakes, yet Italy has long been cleansed from a system of exorcism such as still prevails in the Greek Church.

"In the tropics," Buckle continues, "nature appears still more violent and terrible in contrast with human pusillanimity, and hence among the inhabitants of India the imagination is preëminently peopled with illusions. There," he says, "obstacles of every sort were so numerous, so alarming, and apparently so inexplicable, that the difficulties of life could only be solved by constantly appealing to the direct agency of supernatural causes. There the terrified imagination beheld such visions of horror as Civa, or his consort Durga-Kali, the palms of whose hands were constantly reddened with fresh blood, and whose necks were adorned with a string of human skulls."[1]

As Indian culture was especially developed in Hindostan proper, that is to say, in the district of the Ganges, exclusive of Bengal, nature, according to Buckle's views, ought there above all to have filled the minds of the population with sensations of fear and awe. Earthquakes do not occur, indeed, but they are replaced by terrific hurricanes. The Bay of Bengal is certainly the source of those cyclones or circular storms which have visited

---

[1] History of Civilization.

Calcutta twice within the last few years.   The range of these
scourges is however confined to the coast, and their devastations
never extend beyond the limits of Bengal.   The Himalayas are
also supposed by Buckle to have exercised an intimidating effect,
but they are either invisible from the thickly populated districts,
or appear only as a beautiful boundary on the northern horizon.
When Buckle spoke of pestilences invading tropical Asia with
specially destructive footsteps, he was thinking only of the cholera
which just at the time he wrote was making a fresh progress
through Europe.   But our quarter of the world was visited in
former times by the black death and the plague—destroying angels
which might well be compared with the relatively modern epidemic of India, so that the temperate zone was no more exempt than
the tropics.   Strangely enough Buckle does not even mention the
most fatal evil genius of India, namely, famine, the most active
of gravediggers, which even now, when rains fail and rivers run
low, occasionally causes greater destruction than any pestilences or
cyclones, and transforms densely populated districts into deserts ;
this happened in 1770, at the beginning of the British rule, when
ten out of five-and-twenty millions of Bengalese perished in consequence of a failure of the crops.   If the dangers and anxieties
inherent in a place of abode exercise a control such as Buckle
attributes to them over the dispositions of the people, the Dutch
ought to be far more credulous than the Belgians.   Constantly,
but more especially at the time of the syzygies of the moon, they
are threatened by an adversary as pitiless as the earthquake,
namely, the sea, which they, inhabiting a territory below the level
of the sea, have robbed of its rightful property.   This power,
though expelled, has frequently avenged itself, as, for instance,
when the Zuyder Zee and the Dollart were filled by a sudden
inroad, and all the villages with their inhabitants were swallowed
up.   Lastly, in every nation sailors and miners ought to be more
superstitious than any other craftsmen, for they are peculiarly
exposed to freaks of the forces of nature quite beyond calculation,
yet no one has ever stated that this is the case in any perceptible
degree.

Hence we must admit that the greater perils of life in any place
of abode have not been the cause of an excessive development

of the imagination. Even Alexander von Humboldt's beautiful saying in regard to the reaction of the Grecian sky on the Hellenic temperament is unconvincing. If one spot on earth deserves the name of paradise rather than another, it is assuredly Mexico, with its lakes, its splendid vegetation, its distant scenery, rendered beautiful by snowy volcanoes, its perpetually bright weather, and its bracing mountain air. But it is under these delightful skies that the gloomy disposition of the natives of Anáhuac has evolved all the horrors of a dark and bloody worship.

Let us, then, rather attempt to ascertain whether the habitual food of the nation stands in causal connection with the phenomena of their temperament. Hindostan, the abode of Brahminism, and Central China, the home of Confucius, are almost equally exposed to sun, and are covered by a similar vegetation. Nature, as Buckle was obliged to admit, is in both places equally great and almost equally terrible ; this may at least be strictly asserted of Southern China, and yet in the Celestial Empire imagination has taken quite another direction than in India, or rather, it has scarcely taken any direction at all. The Chinese eat everything, even Holothurians, or sea-cucumbers (Trepang), the very sight of which makes those who are unaccustomed to them shudder. Orthodox Hindoos of high caste, on the contrary, abhor every kind of animal food. But it was not always so. In the time of the Vedas the consumption of animal food was not yet prohibited, and at the same time the Vedic religion was not darkened by the creation of bloodthirsty deities, nor filled with horrors and terrors as in later times. The depression of spirits, the inclination towards the prodigious and grotesque, the weariness of life, the dread of an endless series of transmigrations, first began to develop among the Hindoos simultaneously with the transition to a purely vegetable diet. Probably every one knows by personal experience that our mental functions are dependent upon nutriment ; for the genuine unconscious sleep, which is profound and refreshing, flies from us when the stomach is heavily overloaded. But hunger also, like all other cravings, even if partially satisfied, exercises control over the imagination. This biological fact was and still is the origin of the rigid fastings prescribed by religions so widely different, and made use of by Shamans in every quarter of the world, when they wish to enter into communication with the invisible powers.   As often as the usual order of nutriment is interrupted or even disturbed, as soon as it ceases to be regular, the imagination acquires unusual power, and in this shaken or enfeebled condition is more susceptible to that which it ascribes to supersensual operations.

Here, then, we fancy that we have at last found the key that gives us an insight into the control exercised by physical laws in the province of mental phenomena.   But turn again to Buckle, although it will this time be not as a counsellor but as a warning.   "As regards the daily food," he observes, "the date is in Africa what rice is in the fertile districts of Asia.   The date palm is indigenous in all countries from the Tigris to the Atlantic, and it provides millions of human beings with daily sustenance both in Arabia and nearly the whole of North Africa."   He adds, moreover, that in various places even camels are fed with dates, which is only exceptionally the case, and then proceeds to say that rice contains an unusual amount of starch, namely, between 83 and 85 per cent., and that dates possess precisely the same nutritious substances, with the single difference that the starch is already converted into sugar.   In his opinion this observation is a revelation, for in India, as in Egypt, he beholds the people, devoid of all will, yielding themselves completely to the priesthood.   Only those who have not observed the effects of wine and other alcoholic beverages, or of tea, coffee, tobacco, and narcotic substances in general, either on themselves or others, will deny that the nature of the food reacts upon the mental powers of man, that the temperament evoked by different sorts is different.   But we are still far from having ascertained anything in regard to the permanent effects of daily food, especially as the human stomach has to a great degree the power of accommodating itself to various food substances, so that with use even narcotics lose much of their effect.   Lastly, Buckle deceives himself and the credulous reader when he states that the old Egyptians were date-eaters.   We are far from disputing that they knew and cultivated date palms, for we should be at once met by an appeal to their ancient monuments, which bring their daily life before us as in a picture book. But we deny that the date was a constant or even an important article of food; on the contrary, we maintain that it was only an auxiliary or supplementary food of the Pharaonic people.[2] Buckle can hardly suppose that the Joseph of Bible history gathered up dates into the royal garners during the seven years of plenty. Nor can he imagine that during the seven years of scarcity Jacob sent his sons to Egypt to buy dates. When, in the days of Moses, Divine plagues were inflicted upon Egypt a hailstorm destroyed, not the date groves, but the barley and the flax, and spared the other crops, which had had not yet sprung up. The date is the daily food only in the date oases of Arabia, and to a much greater extent in those of North Africa, in Fezzan, and Southern Algeria, that is to say, on the edge and in the midst of the Sahara; there it trains up independent and warlike desert tribes which have not the most remote mental relationship to the rice-eating Hindoos, but are of a completely different character.

Indirectly we can ascertain that religious creations are in no way dependent on the kind of nourishment used by the population. These same Hindoos, whose unbridled fancy created during the epic times the most atrocious deities, were also the greatest story-makers that ever existed. It has long been known that the series of stories, which is of Indian origin, reached the West under the title of the Thousand and One Nights through the Arabs, and that besides this collection there are whole series of narratives which are sometimes put into the mouth of a skeleton, or of a clever parrot, or a wooden image which has suddenly come to life. Buckle recognizes in the numerical exaggerations of the Hindoos, with their countless ages of the world, and even in their language, which possesses an expression for a number of fifty-one places, a servile reverence for remote antiquity; we are more inclined to discern in this a predisposition for arithmetic, for the same people who played so eagerly with quantitative conceptions, benefited human culture by the contri-

---

[2] The merit of the Arab conquerors in first instituting and diffusing the cultivation of dates in Egypt is an acknowledged fact. H. Stephan, Das heutige Aegypten. 1872.

bution of an educational instrument second only to the invention of written characters, namely, the art of indicating the value of the numbers by their position, or, as we are wont carelessly to express ourselves, the invention of Arabic numeration. We are by no means the first to point out the obvious fact that the creation of religious and of profane fictions are merely to be regarded as different manifestations of the same intellectual capacity. Nations possessed of epic and dramatic creative powers, and those which are fond of building, painting, and sculpture, have also the faculty and the impulse requisite to people an Olympus with varied figures, which are either cheerful or gloomy according to the predominant disposition of their authors. But it may easily be shown that the creation of fictions is not confined to the rice-eating Hindoos. Fictions and legends of striking power have been collected from the scanty population of Iceland. There grain no longer ripens, and shrubs alone will grow ; one single mulberry-tree, standing in a sheltered situation at Akreyri, is proudly exhibited by the natives as *the tree* of the island. The people live only on animal food, the produce of cattle-breeding and fishing. Even were it admitted that many of the beautiful legends were only preserved by the Icelanders, and were derived from their old northern home, it is certain that a great number were invented in Iceland itself ; even had they originated in Norway, cattle-breeding and fishery decidedly predominated there also, and in former times far more than now. Hence we perceive that the activity of the imagination is quite independent of whether the daily aliment consists exclusively of vegetable or animal substances.

It would appear from this that there is no apparent connection between the greater precariousness of life at any given place of abode, or between the national food and the local religious creations. But we may, perhaps, find something serviceable where we should least expect it, among the old Arabian geographers. Although they were disciples of the Alexandrian Greeks, and familiar with the Ptolemaic division into degrees, in their popular expositions of their science they nevertheless distributed the earth into climates, or, as we are wont to express it, into climatic zones. These zones were not always of the same breadth, but were about seven degrees, more or less. Each zone was supposed to possess certain products, animal, vegetable, and mineral, in special per fection; even towards the close of the Middle Ages, our schoolmen believed that black men were to be found only on or close to the equator, and that gold and precious stones never occur beyond the limits of the second zone. In the language of this sys- tematic error, Shemseddin,[3] who was named after his native city of Demeschqi (Damascus), stated that people of light colour and high intellectual-endowments are limited to the third and fourth climates, or between 29° and 33° 49' north latitude, and that in these zones were born all great founders of religion, philosophers, and scholars, himself included. This zone begins a little to the south of the parallel of Mecca (21° 21') a great deal to the south of the parallel of Kapilavastu (27°), the birthplace of Buddha Gautama ; on the other hand, its northern margin does not in- clude Rai (Raghes) near Teheran, and still less Balch (Bactra). As we have already mentioned it was in one of these towns that Zoroaster was born. Yet there is some truth in the observation of the Arabian geographers, that the founders of the higher and still existing religions, Zoroaster, Moses, Buddha, Christ, and Moham- med belong to the subtropical zone. For the birthplace of the latest of the prophets alone falls within the tropics, though only by about seventy-four miles. We make no mention of Confucius, not on account of the high latitude of his birthplace in the dis- trict of Yentshau, in the province of Shantung, but because we should degrade the other founders of religion were we to reckon the Chinese moralist among their numbers.

The fact that the zone of religious founders does not lie within temperate latitudes, might be explained by the suppo- sition, that it was only in the presence of advanced intellectual development that mankind was able to add a yet higher dignity to human existence by allegiance to ideal objects, and that it was exactly in the subtropical climates that the most ancient social organizations had flourished. But even when civilization in its advance had passed outside the tropics, subtropical Asia still remained the fruitful parent of religions. Christianity did not

---

[3] Nouvelles annales des voyages, 6ème série, vol. vi. 1860.

make its appearance in the over-refined European empire of the Romans, but in Palestine. Islam came into existence six hundred years later, not in Byzantium, but in Arabia. In the cold of the temperate zone, man has always been obliged to struggle hard for his existence, working more than praying, so that the burden of the day's labour constantly withheld him from deep inward meditation. In warm countries, on the contrary, where Nature facilitates the acquisition of the necessaries of life, and the sultry hours of mid-day prohibit any bodily exertions, opportunities for mental absorption are far more abundant.

The place of abode is not however quite without influence on the direction taken by religious thought. The three monotheistic doctrines, Judaism, Christianity, Islam, originated with the Semitic nations, yet the tendency of the race was not exclusively to monotheism, for other Semites, such as the Phœnicians, Chaldeans, and Assyrians, took other courses, while even among the Jews reversions to polytheism were frequent, and in Egypt especially the people of God sank completely into idolatry. The perpetual reappearance of monotheism received powerful support from the surrounding scenes of nature.

All who have been in the desert extol its beneficent influence on the health and spirits. Aloys Sprenger declares that the air of the desert invigorated him more than that of the high Alps or of the Himalayas, and in a letter to the author he says : " The desert has impressed the Arabs with their remarkable historical character. In the boundless plains, the imagination which guides the youth of men is filled with images quite different from those suggested by forest country. The thoughts thus acquired are rather noble than numerous; out of his own consciousness of power man evolves for himself a yet bolder personality—a personal God by whom he is guided in his wanderings." Lastly, in nomadic life, it frequently happens that a herdsman roams about in solitude for weeks, tortured by hunger and thirst. Even the healthiest then suffers from illusions of the senses. In this state it often occurs that the forsaken wanderer hears voices speaking and calling to him ; hence in Arabic there is a special word *Hâtif* for voices of this sort. In Africa, again, *Ragl*, derived from *Radschol*, the man, signifies such anthropomorphous ocular illusions.

Every traveller who has crossed the deserts of Arabia and Asia Minor speaks enthusiastically of their beauties ; all praise their atmosphere and brightness, and tell of a feeling of invigoration and a perceptible increase of intellectual elasticity; hence between the arched heavens and the unbounded expanse of plain a mono-theistic frame of mind necessarily steals upon the children of the desert. The confusion of the Egyptian pantheon, the beautiful images of stone, the sacred animals, and human figures with emblematic heads and symbols, were not forgotten by Moses, the priest of Heliopolis, until he fled to Sinai, the oldest rock known to geology, and which, according to Oscar Fraas, is still uncovered by the smallest particle of any more recent formation, seeming as if it had never been submerged beneath the sea, had never risen up, never moved. Here in the wilderness it was necessary that the old Jewish race, with its Egyptian paganism, should be buried, before monotheism as a result of the thoughts and sights of the desert, could rise and strengthen itself in a new race. In other parts of the Scriptures the healthy influence of the desert is likewise testified. The zealous Elijah retired into the desert ; John the Baptist also preached in the desert of Jordan, clad as a Bedouin, in a raiment of camel's hair, and living on locusts and wild honey. Christ also prepared himself for his career by passing forty days and forty nights in the desert. Lastly, Mohammed, although born in a city, imbibed the milk of a Bedouin foster-mother, lived for a long time as a shepherd, and in his caravan journeys crossed the deserts between his own country and Pales-tine. The pilgrimages to Mecca, although far more ancient than Islam, are of no little service in strengthening the faith, inasmuch as they are preceded by a journey across the desert. But even inde-pendently of this, the followers of the Prophet live in the vicinity of deserts, for the doctrine of Mohammed has spread almost ex-clusively in the zone of Eastern Monsoons, and only in very late times extended into Africa as far as the Soudan. In India it was unable to extend beyond very narrow limits, and that only with political assistance.

This is probably all that can be accurately ascertained in regard to the influence of the nature of the country on the tendency of the religious feeling of the population. The desert contributes materially to awaking monotheism, because, from the dryness and clearness of its atmosphere, it does not expose the senses to all the attractive phantoms of forest scenery, the sunbeams as they play through the openings in the trees on the trembling and shining leaves, the marvellous forms of the gnarled branches, creeping roots, and storm-stricken trunks; the creaking and sighing, the whispering and roaring, the hissing and rustling, and all the voices and sounds in wood and forest, amid which the illusion of an invisible animation is so apt to overcome us. Neither do curling mists sweep and steal over the desert as on damp meadow lands. These cloud forms, as they rise over the forests of New Guinea, are venerated by the nations of Doreh as visible manifestation of their good spirit Narvojé. It may therefore be asserted that with the extermination of the forests, not only is the climate of the locality altered, but poetry and paganism have also been struck with the axe. But if a sunny land is favourable to monotheistic emotions, yet at the same time every religious creation is but an expression of the mental endowments of the race. The Semites never possessed any genuinely epic literature, and their dramatic literature was extremely scanty, for they were destitute of the Aryan capacity for framing such productions. It would be an error to trace all the intellectual productions of nations to previous physical conditions alone. They are assuredly subject to a normal course of development, and are nothing more than the necessary expression of a series of causes. But the historical destinies of the nations are certainly among these causes. "It is an old maxim," says Delbrück,[1] "that it is in the experiences of life that each individual finds or loses his God."

---

[1] Zeitschrift für Völkerpsychologie und Sprachwissenschaft, vol. iii.

THE RACES OF MANKIND.

THE RACES OF MANKIND.

In an earlier chapter we found that in any one race all the physical characters, such as the shape of the skull, the proportions of the limbs, and the colour of the skin, vary materially; that even the character of the hair must not be considered a persistently distinctive mark, and hence that, in the classification of the human species into groups or races, all the predominant characteristics must be taken into consideration. Though the limits of such groups are often easy, they are more often very difficult to define. We must not draw them where the common characteristics of one group merge by slight gradations into the common characteristics of another group, for on historical authority such gradations must be traced to intermarriage, and would be represented by hybrids.

On this principle we shall be obliged to separate mankind into seven groups, races, sub-species, or species, whichever expression may be preferred. The first includes the inhabitants of Australia and Tasmania; the second, the Papuans of New Guinea and the adjacent islands; the third, the Mongoloid nations, among which we reckon not only the Asiatics of the Continent, but also the Malayo-Polynesians and the aborigines of America; the fourth, the Dravida of Western India of non-Aryan origin; the fifth, the Hottentots and Bushmen; the sixth, the Negroes; the last consists of the Mediterranean nations, answering to the Caucasians of Blumenbach. The vindication both of the separations and associations of this system of seven groups must be reserved for the chapters which treat of each respectively. Moreover, we hold it to be the duty of ethnology to estimate the social, moral, and

15

intellectual development of the individual races.   The maturity of
the different social conditions of mankind does not, however,
accurately correspond to the various endowments of races, but
depends also on the advantageous or disadvantageous nature of
the place of abode ; so that the reaction of this on the history of
the civilization of each group of mankind must be considered.

I.—THE AUSTRALIANS.

THE physical characters of the inhabitants of the continent of
Australia, of the islands on the coast, and of Tasmania, separate
these into a distinct group.   With skulls of which the average
index of breadth is 71, and the index of height is 73, they belong to
the high dolichocephals ; they are both prognathous and phanero-
zygmatic.   The nose is narrow at the root, widening greatly below,
but does not curve as does that of the Papuans.   The mouth is
wide and unshapely.   The third upper molar tooth has usually
three roots, a formation which is of rare occurrence among
Europeans.[1]   The body is thickly covered with hair ; the hairs,
which are black, and in section are distinctly elliptical, stand out
round the head, forming a shaggy crown ; but being weaker than
those of the Papuans, they are frizzly, and have a tendency to
become matted.   In the peninsula of Coburg straight hair and
obliquely set eyes are also to be met with, but these characters
are due to intermixture with the Malay trepang-fishers who visit
that part.   Many of the natives of that district even speak the
Macassar language ;[2] rock inscriptions in Buginese or Macasssar
characters also prove the presence of Malays.[3]   The colour of the
skin is always dark, sometimes black ; sometimes, on the south
and south-east coast, light copper red.[4]   In all these points the
Tasmanians exactly resembled the Australians, except that the

---

[1] Latham, Varieties of Man.

[2] Earl, Journal of the Royal Geographical Society, vol. xvi. 1846.   This
explains the anomalous Australian institution of nobility mentioned in a former
chapter.

[3] Waitz (Gerland), Anthropologie, vol. vi.   [4] Ibid.

growth of their hair was more Papuan in character, that is to say, more tufted.[5] The few skulls that have been measured show a greater width as well as height, namely, 74 in both cases.[6] The way in which they reached the island has puzzled many, for the Tasmanians are erroneously supposed to have had no boats. They had however raft-like canoes;[7] nor was any great skill required for a migration of Australians across Bass's Straits, which are studded with islands. The proof that such voyages were made is to be found in the circumstance that the Tasmanians bore scars on their skin of the same form as those of the Australians.[8] Their island was colonized by Europeans in the year 1803. The last native died in 1869. The true history of their remorseless extermination has been told by an inhabitant of Tasmania.[9]

The nearest of kin to the Australians and Tasmanians are not the African negroes, and still less the aborigines of Western India, but the Papuans. Yet, in addition to physical differences, they are distinguished from them by the structure of their language, for the Australians employ no prefixes, defining the meaning of the root by suffixes. A few faint resemblances in the pronouns of the Australian and South Indian or Dravida languages, have induced Bleek, on very insufficient grounds, to infer a linguistic kinship between these peoples.[10] In the Australian languages the words, which are polysyllabic, begin with a consonant and end with a vowel or semi-vowel.[11] But, according to vocabulary, the Australian languages are separable into countless subdivisions. It is therefore more remarkable that the same family names are found in West and South Australia and in Carpentaria.[12] Although many Australian dialects are poor in numerical expressions, it is not the case that the natives were unable to distinguish larger numbers, for they use eighteen different terms for children, according to

---

[5] See some instructive copies from photographs in Mantegazza's Archivio per l'Antropologia. 1871.

[6] B. Davies, Thesaurus Craniorum, pp. 272, 358.

[7] Waitz, Anthropologie, vol. vi.   [8] Ibid.

[9] James Bonwick, The Last of the Tasmanians.

[10] Journal of the Anthropological Institute. 1872.

[11] Fr. Müller, Allegemeine Ethnographie.

[12] Grey, quoted by Eyre, Central Australia, vol. ii. p. 329.

whether the child designated is the first to the ninth-born boy, or the first to the ninth-born daughter.[13]

Before discussing their intellectual and social condition, it will be well to glance at their place of abode. Nowhere can the retarded development of mankind be more readily accounted for by the unfavourable configuration of the country than in Australia. Situated in a remote region of the globe, and too small to constitute a world of its own, Australia was so much undervalued that, until quite recently, no civilization had approached it. It was the last of all the continents to be discovered. Of all the discoveries it was the longest neglected, that is to say, for full two hundred years ; and when it was first colonized by Europeans, it was thought only fit for a place of banishment for the outcasts of society. Its coast line is, with the exception of that of Africa, more circular than that of any other part of the world ; in other words, its circumference bears the smallest proportion to its superficies. Its only two projections are the peninsula of Carpentaria, or Cape York, and the island of Tasmania, which, as we have stated elsewhere, is a partially submerged tongue of the continent, and very poorly represents the pointed projections of the other southern continents of South Africa and South America. Yet, however inadequate these projections may appear, one at least, Cape York, has exercised a great influence as the only path by which, till quite recently, Australia maintained any intercourse with higher civilizations. For Cape York is connected with New Guinea by a chain of lofty rocky islands ; and as we must look upon Australia as originally uninhabited, and upon its present dusky population as the results of an immigration at a period immeasurably remote, the passage by Torres Straits must have been the most convenient route for tribes with little inclination for sea voyages. It is even possible that the Australians made their way from New Guinea to their present home on dry land ; for along the chain of islands the depth of the sea in Torres Straits is nowhere more than ten fathoms (60 feet),[14] and the bottom may easily have sunk as much as this since the appearance of man, for in Sardinia, sixty metres above

---

[13] Journal of the Anthropological Institute. 1872.
[14] Jukes, Voyage of H.M.S. *Fly.*

the sea, potsherds have been found mixed with marine testacea and mud in a fossil state.

The vocabularies collected by the scientific expedition under Captain Blackwood prove, moreover, that the tribes at Cape York speak a language allied to that of the inhabitants of the islands in the Endeavour Straits, of the Murray Islands, and likewise of Masid and Errub, all of which lie to the east of the entrance to Torres Straits.[15] Thus, if we follow the track of the language we are led on almost to the coast of New Guinea. The Papuans, who inhabit these islands, are distinguished from the Australians by such distinct racial characters that, as Jardine has observed, a practised eye can easily discern among the Australians of Cape York the huge figures of individual emigrants from New Guinea ; nevertheless, from these migrations, which take place even now, and from the above-mentioned traces of affinity of language, we see that there has always been communication between New Guinea and Cape York ; these facts are the only indications of the road by which the first human beings may have reached the Australian continent. This at once justifies us in attributing historical importance to the peninsula of Cape York, the only medium by which the continent of Australia in some degree maintains its now very broken connection with the Old World. It was only by this same channel, by which it received its first human inhabitants, that, till recently, it received a few products of a rude civilization. For, notwithstanding their bloodthirstiness and cannibalism, the Papuans of New Guinea are in comparison to the Australians a refined people, whose spacious dwellings appear like stately palaces beside the leaf huts of the Australians. Some of them have already rendered the tribes of Cape York familiar with the use of the bow and arrow, which considerably increases the certainty of their aim. To the Papuans also is due the great improvement in shipbuilding that has taken place, for the old bark canoes are now supplanted by long pirogues with outriggers, after the Papuan model ; and, lastly, the first rudiments of husbandry have spread from New Guinea to the islands northward of Cape York, although these are limited to the planting of tubers

---

[15] Latham, Opuscula, p. 234.

and other edible roots.[16]   So that if Europeans had appeared in
the Indian Ocean some five hundred years later, and had the Australians longer enjoyed their insular repose, the influence of the
Papuan tribes might very easily have raised the inhabitants of this
continent to a state which would have placed them on a level
with the nobler hunting tribes of South America.

According to the conjecture of one of our greatest authorities
on Australia, the elevation of the surface of the sea by only a
few hundred feet would be sufficient to resolve this continent into
clusters of numerous islands, for the mountainous districts which
mainly lie on the margin round the central plains are in many
places separated by depressed tracts of low country.[17]   There
are, however, some plateaux in the heart of the country.[18]

So far as we are as yet acquainted with Australia, its most
striking feature is the absence of lofty mountain chains, and consequently of great rivers.   Thus its remote position on the globe,
and its deficiency of projections and indentations of outline, are
combined with a want of variety in its elevation.   Unfortunately,
also, its greatest elevations, the so-called Alps, which reach an
altitude of 7000 feet, are situated in the most remote corner of
the continent, while the only great river system, of which some
thousand miles have proved navigable for steamers, lies on the
side most distant from the civilized regions of the Old World.
The highest mountains of Australia, or, we might rather say, the
eastern slopes of the continent, resembling in form the Ghauts
of India, are moreover directly hurtful to the continent, for the
lofty coasts of the east intercept the damp monsoon, forcing it
to deposit its rain on their slopes, so that it reaches the plateaux
considerably exhausted and able to bring them only a very small
amount of moisture.[19]   If in place of this range a high chain of
mountains had risen on the western margin of the continent, as
in South America, while the eastern margin, on the contrary,

---

[16] Jardin, Journal of the Royal Geographical Society, vol. xxxvi.   1866.

[17] Meinecke, Australien, in Petermann's Mittheilungen.   Gotha, 1871.

[18] Comp. Forest's Observations in the Interior of West Australia; Petermann's Mittheilungen.   Gotha, 1871.

[19] The coast rivers therefore do great damage by these inundations, as in
1867, when the Hawkesbury suddenly rose 62′ above its average level.

was flat or moderately undulating, a river, if not so magnificent as the Amazon, yet of the size of the Orinoco, would have been developed, and the natives of its shores might perhaps have reached the grade of the Brazilian hunting tribes.

By the exploration of about two-thirds of the surface of Australia, the old delusion has been exploded that the interior is entirely occupied by a desert void of vegetation. If Australia really possesses a Sahara, it must be a very limited one, confined to the centre of the western arm of the continent. All the other districts enjoy a short but violent rainy season. In the centre of the continent Mackinlay [20] found himself stopped, if not seriously endangered, by floods ; for on nearly half the horizon nothing but an unbounded surface of water was to be seen, from which projected only the tallest trees and a few island-like elevations of ground. J. M. Gilmore experienced the same in the extreme west of Queensland. [21] This sudden discharge of moisture from the atmosphere is followed by an equally sudden evaporation, so that a few weeks after the inundations the soil is again parched with drought. In consequence of this irregular distribution of moisture, the known part of Australia [22] consists mainly of grass land, with park-like woods or trees bordering the rivers, although great tracts of brushwood are frequent. This would not in itself have been prejudicial to the development of human society had it not been combined with the unpropitious geological structure of Australia.

The appearance of the tertiary strata has as yet been noticed in two places only. The rocks are either crystalline or their strata belong to the earliest ages, seldom more recent than the carboniferous period, and are scarcely ever as old as the variegated sandstone. This implies in other words that this portion of the globe has never been submerged since the secondary and tertiary periods, but has been exposed without regeneration or reparation to all the depredations of the atmosphere, and has thus lost more

[20] Journal of the Royal Geographical Society, vol. xxxiii.

[21] Petermann's Mittheilungen. 1872.

[22] A shepherd, John Ross by name, states that he has discovered at 24° 30′ S. lat. and 137° E. long., not only rich pastures, but also standing and running water extending about 240 miles, and adapted for steam navigation, &c. Sir R. Murchison in the Proceedings of the Royal Geographical Society. 1871.

and more of the charms of its original form.[23] The highest part of its mountainous formations of the primary and secondary period must have been worn down by long-continued disintegration and aqueous action, and thus have been levelled towards the general surface.   Even this would not have been so injurious had not the communication by land which existed between Australia and the great mainland of the Old World also been interrupted.   But the isolation of Australia took place at an immature period, namely, when the development of the fauna had advanced only to the stage of marsupials and rodents, and not as far as the ungulates. While in the Old World the continued struggle for existence secured improved animal forms by a progressive advancement, to which those of the archaic marsupial character were obliged almost completely to give way, the struggle in Australia was confined within much narrower limits, and hence, with slight alterations, its animal creation remained stationary at the point which it had reached when the isolation first took place.   The most ancient continent of the world shelters the oldest mammalian forms.   First we notice the absence of carnivora, for the dingo, or Australian dog, probably immigrated only with man, although it is now found wild in hunting-packs.   Even if, as might be conjectured from the discoveries of their remains in ancient bone-caves, they entered Australia before mankind, this occurred, nevertheless, within a recent geological period.   As powerful antagonists, beasts of prey exercise a favourable effect on the education of mankind, so that their absence forms one of the disadvantages of the place of abode.   The absence of ungulates is yet more to be regretted, for it at once barred man from the possibility of raising himself to the highest grade of civilization.   With the exception of the dog, probably no Australian animal has allowed itself to be tamed ; a certain degree of intelligence seems to be requisite when an animal is to be received into the society of man as his supporter or assistant, and the deficiency of intellect in marsupials renders them unfit for this purpose.   As we all know, Australia is especially adapted for the breeding of sheep, cattle, horses, and camels, but these creatures, which are so

---

[23] Hochstetter in Petermann's Mittheilungen. 1859.

important to civilization, were unable to reach this continent which was unconnected with the Old World. It may, therefore, be truly said of Australia that it is an island without the advantages of an island climate, a country of productive steppes without the ungulates of the steppes, a land of insular tranquillity, or, in other words, of a languid struggle for existence, and an asylum for animal and vegetable forms of past ages. But if we correctly understand the processes of animated nature, quiet involves stagnation, for the mammalian forms of Australia seem like living fossils when compared with those of the Old World. When the first ship landed animals from the Old World, the seclusion of Australia was over and it ceased to be an island, for a bridge, although only a flying one, again united it with the Old World ; then the prematurely interrupted struggle for existence was renewed, but it was now between creatures armed and adapted for fighting and others unused to strife : it was inevitable that the last surviving and superseded forms of past ages should succumb, that the Australian fauna should find a place in palæontological books, and the kangaroo hunter disappear with the kangaroo. This has ever been the course of Nature ; always eager in pursuit of novelty, it acknowledges only the right of the strongest, and the strongest must always be something new ; were the newer the weaker, it would be suppressed almost before it came into being.

European travellers landing in Australia have always met with natives or their traces. Where one explorer perchance fancied that he was passing through a desert, on the same spot the next comer found himself surrounded with blacks. In the remarkable lake district which Sturt assumed to be an uninhabited region, Mac Kinlay in his journey across the continent in 1861, 62, was surprised by the density of the population ; the latter in turn found no natives between 26° and 22° south latitude, though almost at the same time MacDouall Stuart, in his second journey through Australia, found himself, six degrees more to the east, in the midst of natives, just as he was crossing the tropics in the exact centre of Australia, on the 3rd of March. On the 5th of January, 1861, shortly before reaching the tropics, Burke and Wills also perceived fresh traces of natives whom they actually met further to the north.

Leaving the inhabitants of the peninsula of Carpentaria out of

consideration, we find the tribes of the mainland in very different
stages of civilization, and differing also very materially in physical
respects.   Hitherto the piteous objects at King George's Sound,
in the south-west corner of the continent, of which Dumont
d'Urville procured drawings, have been generally regarded as
samples of Australian humanity.   We were wont to imagine them
emaciated skeletons, with narrow pelvises even in the women,
meagre feeble limbs, and swollen bellies ; but according to all
explorers the type improves towards the interior.   In the lake
district, at the north-east limit of South Australia, MacKinlay found
the handsomest tribes that he had seen on the continent.   Landsborough in April, 1862, in 23° south latitude, on the Thompson
River, far from the coast, and Stuart in the north, met with natives
whom they agree in describing as fine and powerful men.   The
settlers on the shores of Queensland also say that the natives of
that district are well-built and strong-limbed.   The social development visibly deteriorates both from north to south and from
east to west ; that is to say, in proportion to the distance from
Cape York, the chief point which has served to connect Australia
with the Old World, the customary mode of life of the natives
becomes more and more degraded.   For example, before the
introduction of the Papuan pirogue the tribes of the peninsula
of Carpentaria had long possessed boats, although the best specimens were not better than the bark canoes of the Red Indians
of North America.   On the east coast of Queensland, observers
on board H.M.S. *Fly* were unable to discover any such canoes
south of Rockingham Bay, (18° south lat.)[24]   In Botany Bay,
Cook found that the natives had pieces of bark which served as
boats, and the tribes on the Murray were no better provided.[25]
In the neighbourhood of Port Essington, on the north coast, the
people used rude floats, and Ferd. Müller who, with Gregory,
discovered the Victoria River and Sturt's Creek, also observed
among the tribes of the interior only floats of two or three trunks,
which, for fear of alligators, were used in crossing.   Lastly,
Gregory's ship *Dolphin*, when lying behind Dampier Island, on

[24] Jukes, Voyage of H. M. S. *Fly.*
[25] George French Angas, Australia and New Zealand.

the north coast (1861), was visited by natives who used trunks of trees in their natural form instead of boats. The Australians of the south coast have not been met with on the sea. James Browne [26] assures us that the West Australians of Swan River are not only destitute of any boats, but are even unable to swim.

At King George's Sound the natives have only leaves for roofs; they spread a covering of leaves over curved stakes, the ends of which are inserted in the ground. In New South Wales, Queensland, and on the shores of the Bay of Carpentaria, the curved bark of a tree placed on the ground serves as a protection from the weather for a single person, or several pieces of bark spread upon a framework of stakes gives shelter to several. Thus the Australian builds no permanent dwelling, but lives as a roving hunter in a tent made of leaves or bark. Yet in West Australia there are wooden huts and spacious buildings in the peninsula of Coburg, and others with two storeys in the Cape York district.[27] In the two latter cases, however, the favourable influence of Malays and Papuans may be inferred.

The Australians when first discovered were living in the age of unpierced stone implements. Their arms and hunting weapons were projectiles, the most important being the spear, of which the point was either hardened in the fire for hunting purposes, or provided with barbed hooks for harpooning fish, or armed with sharp flints or shells for fighting purposes. The boomerang is found among all the tribes of the north, west, south, and east coasts, with the exception of the inhabitants of Cape York and a few tribes on the Lower Murray. Shields for defensive purposes are used by all the tribes both on the coast and in the interior, except in West Australia. The people of the east coast manufacture lines and hooks for fishing, the latter being made of birds' claws or mussel shells, while on the west coast nets are used for fishing purposes.[28] The wish to cover the body as a matter of sentiment is as yet unfelt in Australia, but on the west, south, and east coasts, cape-like cloaks, made of the skins of animals, are

---

[26] Petermann's Mittheilungen. 1856.'
[27] Waitz (Gerland), Anthropologie, vol. vi.
[28] Lubbock, Prehistoric Times, p. 430.

thrown round the shoulders as a protection against bad weather. Many tribes also fasten straps round their loins, which are drawn tighter in times of scarcity in order to diminish the feeling of emptiness. An attempt at clothing is first met with at Cape York, where the influence of the Papuans is evident.[29] The monuments and works of art of the Australians consist almost solely of decorations of burying-places, and of hollow boat-like coffins, which latter do not occur only on the east coast, for one containing the body of a child was noticed by MacDouall Stuart on May 12th, 1861, in the Ashburton mountains, in the northern half of Australia, and is described by him as the most artistic native production he had seen. There are also figures of men and animals drawn in chalk and ochre on the rocks of the Victoria River, which were observed by Gregory and Müller[30] in 1856, as well as still more remarkable etchings, an inch in depth, on the rocks of the east coast; in those, for instance, at Camp Cove, near Sydney, rude outlines of men and animals may be discerned. The women of the tribes on the Murray, and in New South Wales, showed great dexterity in plaiting baskets of rushes.

In the previous enumeration of weapons, we purposely omitted to mention the wummera, or throwing-stick, an invention common to all Australian tribes without exception, and indicates much greater intelligence than the boomerang, which, although more surprising on account of the eccentricity of its flight, is always an uncertain missile, the discovery of which was probably the result of accident. The throwing-stick fastened to the palm of the hand, or held by the three last fingers, and provided at the fore end with a diagonal groove in which the spear is laid, doubles the throwing power of the human arm. If it be imagined, says Jukes, that the forefinger is the same length as the throwing-stick, and that while the spear is held with the thumb and middle finger, the last joint of the forefinger is bent round the end of the spear, this explains the increase given by the throwing-stick to the initial velocity of the spear.[31] Unfortunately, it cannot be positively ascertained that the Australians did not borrow this invention, for the New

---

[29] Journal of the Royal Geographical Society, vol. xxxii. 1862.
[30] Ausland. 1859.　　　[31] Voyage of H.M.S. *Fly.*

Caledonians also use a throwing-sling, although not the throwing-stick. A similar plan is followed in other places : by the Aleutians and their neighbours the Eskimo, and was used by the ancient Mexicans.[32]

The fact that the intelligence of the Australians is by no means contemptible has only been recognized since we have gained an insight into their languages. If the profusion of forms briefly expressing minute relations were to decide the rank of a language, we and all the nations of Western Europe might envy the miserable tribes of King George's Sound, for their language possesses four more case-terminations than Latin, and a dual as well as singular and plural. The verb is as rich in tenses as Latin, and has also terminations for the dual, and three genders for the third person; in addition to active and passive, it has reflective, reciprocal, determinative, and continuative forms. In point of structure of language, the highly cultured Polynesians, and even the ancient Chinese, must yield to the inventive Australians. We also find among them attempts at poetry and the names of renowned poets. Although their songs are rude they nevertheless contain expressions which no longer occur in daily intercourse.[33] They have, moreover, many pretty and picturesque names for the constellations. They regard the Milky Way as a reflection of the River Darling, in the waters of which their dead are fishing, and the Clouds of Magellan as two old witches, transfixed to the sky for their crimes.[34] The most surprising fact is that they have names for eight different winds. They are peculiarly inventive in expressions of courtesy, which they both require and bestow freely in conversation.

We have already stated that a great dread of incest prevails amongst them, and that wife-stealing is therefore customary ; that they hold the duties of " vendetta " sacred, recognize property in immovable objects, and inherit the family name from the mother. Even in such a condition as that of the Australians, society is

---

[32] O. Langsdorff, Reise um die Welt. David Cranz, Historie von Grön land. Tylor, Primitive Culture, vol. i. p. 69.

[33] Reise der Fregatte Novara, Fr. Müller.

[34] Waitz (Gerland), Anthropologie, vol. vi.

regulated by various institutions. The Australian languages are indeed said to be without an expression for chieftain,[35] and we look in vain among the western tribes for anything that might even in a broad sense be termed a priesthood. In New South Wales and in Queensland, which are the most highly civilized districts of Australia, we find on the other hand the Koradshi, who have so far discarded the vulgar terror of the dark that they will spend a night on the graves of dead men. By their Shamanistic arts they are likewise able to give comfort and reassure sick people, and they also know how to apply slight palliatives, blood-letting among others. It is a curious fact that among the wretched people of the west coast, the inviolability of ambassadors is respected till the gaping wound by which such a messenger is marked is completely healed.[36] Experience in Queensland and New South Wales shows that the modern Australians were quite capable of rising to a higher condition, for in those parts many learnt to speak English with fluency and correctness, became skilful and bold riders, and as shepherds were preferred to Europeans, on account of their adroitness in the bush, and also because it was found possible to train them into efficient guards for the more remote runs.

That their condition has hardly improved is partly due to the isolation of their native land, which impeded any contact with other nations. Hence the inhabitants of Cape York were first influenced by Papuan immigrants, and they in their turn influenced for good their southern neighbours; for instance, on the east coast, according to Angas, all the new popular songs, and the dances which accompany them, have been propagated from the north in a southerly direction.[37] But the degraded condition of the Australians is principally due to their ignorance of agriculture, while they are not strictly maritime people like the Fuegians and the Eskimo. They were thus obliged to content themselves with the produce of the chase, with the fish and shell-fish which they were able to obtain on the seacoast and the banks

---

[35] H. Wilkes, United States Exploring Expedition, vol. ii. p. 186.

[36] Browne in Petermann's Mittheilungen. 1856.

[37] Australia and New Zealand, vol. ii.

of the rivers, and with the nutriment afforded by wild roots. While thus dependent on chance from day to day, man does not as yet recoil from cold-blooded animals, such as caterpillars, lizards, ants, and worms. As hunters destitute of bows and arrows, even the throwing-stick would not have ensured them against frequent times of scarcity had they not made great use of prairie fires. But the chase itself necessitated frequent change of abode. When the pools left by the last rainy season began to dry up, the natives were obliged to leave their hunting grounds and repair to the well-known spots where water still remained in deep pools. Thus it may perhaps be the steppe-like nature of the country which has kept the natives from agriculture in any form.

Recent explorers who, though hardy and meritorious, were usually uneducated men, have frequently stated that Australian grass consists of oat and barley grass. It would be natural to suppose that in such an extensive and sunny region of steppes some wild species of cereals should exist,[38] and this is actually the case, and in relatively, if not absolutely, greater variety than in America. Thus in the marshes near Sturt's Creek and on the Victoria, Ferdinand Müller, the botanist, found wild rice, which the natives ground between two stones, and the edible seeds of a wild cereal of the genus Pannicum, or millet, and occasionally in North-western Australia a species of wild oat. On April 28th, 1861, MacDouall Stuart, in his second attempt to cross the continent, discovered at Tomkinson Creek a species of corn resembling wheat, except that the grains were smaller and the straw much tougher. In the autumn of 1861, when staying near the remarkable lake district between 28° and 26° south latitude somewhat to the east of the longitude of Adelaide, MacKinlay noticed a leguminous vetch-like plant growing on the lands covered by the floods of the rainy season. The natives swept up the fallen seeds, cleaned them by winnowing, ground them to flour, and baked them into flat cakes. It is probable from the same seed that the tribes on Cooper Creek made the Nardu bread, with which they for a time prolonged the lives of those unfortunate men, Burke and Wills,

---

[38] Landsborough, Journal of the Royal Geographical Society, vol. xxxiii.

who were the first persons to cross the continent of Australia, on their return from Cape York. Howitt, who there rescued King, their last surviving companion, describes (Cooper's Creek, Sept. 1st, 1861), the plant which probably produces the Nardu seeds as resembling clover in foliage, but covered with a silvery down, which envelops the seeds also while fresh. When the weed dies, the seeds, which are flat and almost oval, literally cover the ground, and when they have been separated from the sand, they are crushed by the natives and made into bread.[39]

These facts are of great importance, as proving that the manufacture of flour and the baking of bread are older than agriculture. Various reasons may be adduced to show how it happened that the natives never thought of multiplying these useful products by artificial cultivation, thus supplying themselves with provisions, diminishing their dependence on the produce of the chase, freeing themselves from the necessity for wandering, and consequently rendering it possible to rear a more numerous posterity. Australia, especially in the tropical parts, possesses a great variety of fruit trees, so that scarcely any explorers return without bringing home some new or nominally new discovery of this description. Even bananas are said to grow wild in the Carpentaria country, and in the north, Ferdinand Müller came upon a grape-bearing creeper which he considers identical with our vine. In the south, the so-called Hottentot fig, which is the fruit of a species of mesembryanthemum, is a natural article of food. The adoption of agriculture by the Australian people was, however, delayed less by the fruits, which remain in an edible condition only for a short time, than by edible roots, which, unlike the cereals, required no careful preservation. The peninsula of Carpentaria produces the true yam (*Dioscorea Carpentariæ*), while the south yields the roots of the sorrel, an oxalis, and the grass-tree, which is a species of Xanthorhea. The root of the latter is dug up by the women with pointed sticks, and is always kept as the last resource in case of failure of the chase. On the Swan River, on the west coast, kangaroos are so plentiful in places, that when the natives were promised ninepence a head for them, they brought in such

[39] Petermann's Mittheilungen. 1862.

a number that the settlers fed their pigs with them. The late James Morill, who lived for seventeen years among the coast tribes of Queensland, near Cape Bowling Green, also states that food was plentiful. It may be said that Australian society was not yet ripe for the transition to agriculture, that is to say, was not sufficiently dense, for the population is estimated at not more than 200,000, by many at only 60,000, for which the hunting grounds were more than adequate.

Yet the digging up of roots is so troublesome, and the food so little nutritious, that it appears strange that as, by the abundant growth of the cereals enumerated, Nature had so clearly shown them the method and the advantages of agriculture, the Australians should never have thought of putting seeds into the ground. It is only because habit has blunted our apprehension of the extraordinary, that we fail to perceive that an unusual degree of intelligence is implied by the first scattering of seed in the expectation of a result. The ancient Greeks, who were nearer to the first movements of human civilization than we are, and from whom the great first steps were not hidden, regarded a purposive invention of agriculture as beyond the intellectual powers of man, and therefore ascribed it to a deity, just as the Egyptians, amongst other honours, gave to their Osiris the credit of having taught mankind the art of sowing seed. The first cultivation of plants, even if practised only by migratory hordes in their summer quarters, contains the germ of all future progress, for man then ceases to depend on the chance of finding a supply of natural roots. When his strength is not perpetually exhausted by the exertion of hunting, man has time left for the invention of improvements. The high degree of intelligence often met with in hunting tribes is quite absorbed by the chase itself, as it is constantly and keenly directed to the observation of the nature of both the game and the hunting ground. The chase is also fatiguing to the body, so that in default of some other mode of gaining a maintenance, intellectual development, which always requires physical repose, is out of the question.

II.—THE PAPUANS OF AUSTRALIA AND ASIA.

THE Papuans of Australia include the inhabitants of New Guinea, the Pelew Islands, Tombara (New Ireland), Birara, the Solomon group, the New Hebrides, New Caledonia, with the adjacent Loyalty Islands, and lastly of the Fiji archipelago. The distinctive characters of their race are preserved in the greatest purity in New Guinea, although even there, especially in the western half, intermixtures with the Asiatic Malays have recently taken place. In the other islands mentioned, the Polynesians have intruded themselves among the older populations, and have materially influenced the language and manners, but their influence upon the physical characters has been much less, so that the inhabitants of the Pelew and Fiji groups, as well as of New Caledonia, may be unhesitatingly reckoned among the Papuan race. In the Carolines and Mariannes, or Ladrones, Polynesian and Papuan blood is intermingled, but the former preponderates, so that, as hybrids, these so-called Micronesians are more correctly placed in the next group of nations.

The most distinctive mark of the Australian Papuans is their peculiarly flattened, abundant, and long hair, which grows in tufts and surrounds the head like a periwig, or a crown, eight inches high, which is however probably much aided by constant care and the aid of a three-pronged comb.[1]   This tufted matting of the hairs is also common to the Hottentots, whose hair does not however grown so long or so thick; perhaps close miscroscopic comparison would show different causes for the tendency.   The Papuans are also distinguished from the aborigines of the Cape by the abundant growth of their beard, and by their general hairiness.[2]   The skin of all Papuans is dark, almost black in New Caledonia, brown or chocolate colour in New Guinea, blue-black at Fiji, this peculiar colour being due to the growth of a light-

---

[1] See illustration in Wallace's Malay Archipelago, vol. ii. p. 306.

[2] Nieuw Guinea ethnographisch en natuurkundig onderzocht en beschreven. Amsterdam, 1862.

coloured down upon the skin.[3]   Welcker's measurements show
that the New Caledonians have an index of breadth of 70, an
index of height of 77 ; in other Papuans the numbers are 73 for
the one and 75 for the other, which show that the form of the
skull is narrow and high.   This agrees with the results obtained
by Barnard Davis in the cases of the inhabitants of the Solomon
Islands, the New Hebrides, and New Caledonia ; he found 72 as
the index of breadth and 76–79 of height.   The Papuans must
therefore also be ranked as dolichocephals.   The jaws are prognathous, although not to so great a degree as occurs in extreme
cases among negroes.   The lips are fleshy and somewhat intumescent.   The broad nose is hooked, giving the countenance
the Jewish cast noticed by all observers.   It is noticeable in
the inhabitants of New Caledonia and of Annatom in the New
Hebrides,[4] in the Fijians, and in the inhabitants of Errub and
Darnley Islands,[5] of the north coast of New Guinea near Dorey,[6]
of the south coast on the River Utanata,[7] and, lastly, of the
Pelew Islands.[8]   We gather from descriptions that the Papuans,
independent of local variations, are of medium stature, or at least
certainly not tall.

Wallace considers the inhabitants of the islands on the coast
of New Guinea, such as Waigiou and Mysol, and likewise of the
Aru and Ké groups, as well as those of Larat and Timor-Laut, to
be pure Papuans, while we find on the more westerly islands, on
the Molucca group, including Halmahera, the Banda Islands, the
eastern half of Floris, as well as on Chandana and all the islands
to the east of it, the remains of an aboriginal population, once
belonging to the Papuan race, but now much mixed with Malay
blood.   It is far more difficult to determine the race of the
aboriginal population of the Philippines and those islands which
on geological grounds must be assigned to Asia and not to

---

[3] Waitz (Gerland), Anthropologie, vol. vi.
[4] Waitz (Gerland), vol. vi.   [5] Jukes, Voyage of H.M.S. *Fly*
[6] Wallace, Malay Archipelago, vol. ii. p. 305.
[7] Natuurlijke geschiedenes der nederlandsche overzeesche bezittingen. Land
en volkenkunde door Salomon Müller.
[8] Karl Semper, Die Palau-Inseln.   Leipzic, 1873.

Australia.[9]   We shall not adopt the ordinary names of Melanesians, Alfurs, Harafurs, Negritos or Australian negroes, for all these appellations have been so loosely used that their application has become ambiguous.[10]   For instance, certain Alfurs on the island of Celebes are described as having physical characters which clearly show that they are Malays ; and it has become customary in the Dutch settlements to describe as Alfurs any so-called savages, even when they are undoubtedly of Malay origin, as in the case of the Batta of Sumatra, and of the Dyaks of Borneo.[11] We therefore prefer to call the remnants of the aboriginal population of these islands Asiatic Papuans. To these belong the Aëta of the Philippines, who have preserved their racial characters in full purity ; but this applies only to the few bands on the northeastern shore of Luzon.   In Petermann's Mittheilungen for 1876, Dr. Meyer proves that the so-called Negritos of the Philippines are pure Papuans.   Karl Semper found their average stature to be 4 feet 7 inches in the case of men, and 4 feet 4 inches in that of women.   In common with the Australian Papuans, they have woolly crimped crowns of lustreless hair and flat noses widening below.   Their skin is not black, as the Malay name of Aëta would lead us to expect, but of a dark copper-colour.   The lips are a little intumescent, and the jaws slightly prognathous.   These hunting tribes, unlike Malays, use bows and arrows.[12]

If we may judge from a photograph copied by Jagor,[13] the Negritos of Mariveles, and the Negritos of the north of Luzon might be classed as Aëta.   At present we should be justified in classing this aboriginal people, which has now been supplanted and nearly extirpated by the Malays, with the Australian Papuans. We assign to them the value of a subdivision, but it is as a precaution, for we require more accurate researches than have yet been made to enable us finally to decide as to the position of their race.   Several skulls which reached Berlin through Schetelig

---

[9] On the natural limits of Asia and Australia, see Peschel's "Neue Probleme der vergleich. Erdkunde," p. 26. Leipsic, 1869.

[10] Waitz, Anthropologie, vol. v.

[11] Riedel in Zeitschrift für Ethnologie. 1871.

[12] Karl Semper, Die Philippinen. 1866.   [13] Reisen in der Philippinen.

as those of Negritos of the island of Luzon, had, according to Virchow's measurements, a relative breadth of 80·8 to 90·6, with a relative height of 77·6 to 82·3. They were therefore brachycephalic, of small height, prognathism, chiefly due to the position of the alveoli, was strongly marked in them, and the zygomatic arches were very prominent. The skulls were too greatly brachycephalic not to render us doubtful as to their relationship with the Papuans of Australia. It is quite possible that the form of these heads was of artificial origin, as Virchow strongly suspects. Moreover, Karl Semper states that the skulls in question all came from the mountains of Mariveles in the neighbourhood of Manila, the population of which has long ago lost its purity by intermixture.[14] Scattered remnants of a former aboriginal population of Papuan race were also seen by Wallace at Sohoe (Sohu) and Galela on Halmahera. They have the Papuan crown of hair, are bearded, and are hairy on the body, but are at the same time as fair as the Malays.[15]

Lastly, far to the westward are the Mincopies [16] of the Andaman Islands, a small race of men resembling the Papuans in the growth of their hair. As they shave their heads quite smooth with shells or the fragments of broken glass which are occasionally washed upon the shore, this statement may appear somewhat strange,[17] yet the tufted matting of the hair was observed on Mincopie prisoners at Moulmein, by A. Fytche, who describes their skin as "sooty, not black," and notes the total absence of beard.[18] Those who depend exclusively on the character of the hair may regard the Mincopie as the western advanced post of the Papuan race, and must suppose that the latter, at some remote period, spread from the mainland of Southern Asia eastwards to the Australian Ocean.[19] This would be as good as proved, if, on account of their abundant beards and frizzly hair, accompanied, according to Logan's description, by a brown or black complexion, we may class the Semangs of the peninsula of

[14] Die Palau-Inseln.   [15] Malay Archipelago.
[16] See above for a description of their manners, p. 147.
[17] Helfer, in a description of a Mincopie in his journal, says: "His hair, shorn on both sides, formed a curly comb of wool."
[18] Petermann's Mittheilungen. 1862.   [19] Waitz, Anthropologie, vol. v.

Malacca, who are a diminutive race of men, physically and intellectually feeble, and now in process of extinction, with the Asiatic Papuans.   Latham, who has investigated their language, classes them with the Negritos, which according to him implies relationship with the Aëtas, and he scarcely admits that they bear any resemblance to the Andamanese, but places them unhesitatingly in the Malay group.[20]

The languages of the Australian Papuans make use of roots of one or more syllables, and effect the definition of meaning by prefixes and suffixes, of which the primary signification has generally disappeared.   Herr von d. Gabelentz, who examined and compared the languages of ten Papuan islands, discovered, amid all other differences in the vocabularies, an agreement in the mode of word structure.   Besides this, a relationship with the Polynesian languages was everywhere shown; at any rate, the personal pronouns were analogous, and also several adverbs of place and a large number of prefixes.   Among the latter is *faka*, which appears in all Papuan and Polynesian languages only as a prefix, but in Fiji may still be used as an independent word or as a suffix.[21]   The investigation led to the general conclusion that the Papuan languages have more in common with the Polynesian than could arise from merely borrowing from one another.   These unquestionable facts involve a great problem, for from the agreement of the languages a common origin was inferred in the case of two races which are very distinctly separated by their physical characters.   But the results obtained by Herr von d. Gabelentz admit of another interpretation.   The vocabularies which he examined were collected in the Fiji group, on the New Hebridean islands of Annatom, Tanna, Erromango, and Mallikolo, on Marré and Lifu in the Loyalty group, on the adjacent island of New Caledonia, and lastly in Bauro (San Christoval) and Guadacanar of the Salomon group.   Intermixture with Polynesians in all these islands has been proved, in consequence of which the Papuans have adopted Polynesian customs and manners.   A fuller examin-

---

[20] Opuscula. London, 1860.

[21] Von d. Gabelentz über die melanesischen Sprachen in the transactions of the philolol. histor. Classe der Kgl. Sächsgesellsch. der Wissenschaften. 1861.

ation of the Papuan languages of New Guinea than any which, as we believe, has yet been made, can alone explain the linguistic relationship.

The Papuan of New Guinea is clearly distinguished from the reserved and cautious Malay by his noisy, talkative, petulant, and inquisitive nature, and by his constant restlessness. The Papuans of New Guinea, the Fiji group, and New Caledonia, cook in earthen vessels, which are never found among Polynesians. The inventive powers of the Fijians are shown by their habit of dyeing and stamping their clothing material made of bark (Tapa), with gaudy patterns, like those of chintz, by means of carved wooden stamps or stencil-plates of banana leaves. The people of Humboldt's Bay in New Guinea, when the Dutch sailors gave them paper and pencil, which they could certainly never have seen before, drew fishes and birds with a firm hand.[22] Wallace gives great weight to the fact that the Papuan decorates his house, his boat, and his utensils with carvings, and thus exhibits an artistic impulse of which the Malay race is almost entirely deficient.[23] But this latter is certainly only true of the Asiatic Malays, and in this case it may be ascribed to the circumstance that the trades and arts of semi-civilization were neglected and extinguished after a lengthened commercial intercourse with nations of superior refinement. The Polynesian Malays, on the contrary, greatly excel all Papuans in artistic carvings and tatooings. These latter, as their wide distribution over the sea shows, ventured upon the ocean early and perhaps earlier than the Malays, but have since then been far outstripped by the latter in nautical skill. The Papuans use unpierced stone implements,[24] though in the west of New Guinea the knowledge of iron ore and the art of smelting has become general. From the fact that bellows with tubes and pumps of Malay type [25] are used in the latter process, we may infer that this advance came from the West.

After the age of maturity the women always wear the liku, or

---

[22] Nieuw Guinea ethnographisch onderzoocht. 1862.

[23] Malay Archipelago, vol. ii. p. 447.

[24] J. G. Wood, Natural History of Man.

[25] O. Finch, Neu-Guinea.

fringed girdle; among the men a cloth above the loins is customary, but on secluded shores and islands, a piece of bamboo, a rolled up leaf, a gourd, or a shell is considered sufficient for purposes of decency.[26]   Complete nudity in men is rare, but is said to occur in New Ireland.[27]   Bows and arrows as hunting weapons are found only in New Guinea and its immediate vicinity. Captain Cook observed from a distance on the south coast of this island a tube in the hands of the natives, who placed it as if for taking aim, after which a cloud seemed to issue from its mouth. If a report had been heard at the same time we should have had to suppose that the Papuans used fire-arms.   But, according to Salomon Müller, a fine dust is blown from the tube, and signals are made by the direction of the cloud.[28]

The Papuans live on the produce of such agriculture as the cultivation of trees. They possess only seedless varieties of the bread-fruit tree, so that they must have borrowed it from other nations.[29]   Their fields and gardens are fenced.   The New Caledonians build water conduits of great length to irrigate these.[30]   They have no pigs, which with dogs are otherwise universal among the Papuans, and are their only domestic animals.

This race has deeply degraded itself by cannibalism, which prevails in New Guinea, New Caledonia, the Fiji Islands, and probably in other parts inhabited by this race.

Otherwise the Papuans of New Guinea and the smaller islands are praised for their. chastity and morality, their respect for parents, and their brotherly affection.[31]   In the New Hebrides old people are buried alive, but it is probably, as in the Fiji Islands, at their own desire.   The belief in a future life is strong; and as the state in which man abandons this world is believed to be his condition in the next, premature death is preferred to total debilitation.   The horrible scenes which Williams describes at

---

[26] Peschel, Zeitalter der Entdeckungen, pp. 321, 454.   Prince of Wied, Reise nach Brasilien, vol. i. p. 377.

[27] Père Lesson, Voyage autour du Monde.   Paris, 1839.

[28] Natuurlijke Geschiedenis der nederlandsche overzeesche bezittingen Land en Volkenkunde.   1839.

[29] Waitz (Gerland), Anthropologie, vol. vi.

[30] Knoblauch.   Ausland.   1866.   [31] O. Finch, Neu-Guinea.

the burying of a living Fiji chief, whose wives were strangled at the same time, are not unfavourably explained by this superstition ; indeed the custom which is found in the Loyalty Islands of killing the mother or aunt of a loved dead child that it may not be quite forsaken in the other world, is almost pathetic.[32] With this is closely connected the worship of the dead, whose skulls are set up as household gods, invoked for signs, and appealed to for assistance in difficult undertakings. This custom cannot have been borrowed from the Polynesians, as it has been observed among the Papuans of New Guinea. In the latter place are found large, high, empty buildings, erected on piles, which are used as temples or places of devotion.[33] The Papuans hold dualistic opinions, for they hurl all manner of imprecations at an evil being called Manuvel, while they offer worship and sacrifice only to the good guardian spirit, under the name of Narvojé.[34] There are no professional Shamans among the nations of pure race, but each individual studies to interpret the future. The innocence of persons accused is tested by ordeal, either by boiling water or by prolonged immersion. In New Guinea, and wherever Polynesian visitors have not introduced their customs and social tenets, freedom and equality prevail, and the power of the chiefs is therefore nominal.

The Papuan race has attained its highest intellectual and social development in the Fiji Islands, where, owing to frequent intercourse with the Tongans, it has very readily adopted Polynesian inventions and institutions. Among these are the drinking of Yakona, or Kava, the division into guilds or castes, and, lastly, the institution of taboo, which the chiefs have carefully fostered as a means of increasing their power. It is only necessary to trail their garments over the fields in order to consecrate to their own use all the produce which they had touched. The chiefs of Mbengga, an island off the south coast of Great Fiji, bore the title of *Gali-cuva-ki-lagi*, or "subject to Heaven alone." The small island despots were in constant strife, and their history is in many points comparable with that of the Peloponnesian war. A kind

---

[32] Fiji and the Fijians.

[33] Waitz (Gerland), Anthropologie, vol. vi.

[34] O. Finsch, Neu-Guinea.

16

of diplomatic corps existed at the various courts, and was familiar with political arts.[35]   When embassies were sent, sticks and nets were used to aid the memory.   This seems a first attempt at symbolical embodiment of thought, and a proof of a need for writing.   In the Pelew Islands strings with knots and loops serve for the exchange of news, or to authorize any commission entrusted to a third person.   In the local dialect they are called *rusl*, and it is a significant fact that this word is now applied also to the letters of Europeans.[36]   The Fijians are polite and polished in their conversation : according to Williams, their languages contain expressions which exactly correspond to the French *Monsieur* and *Madame*.[37]   Even in presence of Europeans they retain a strong feeling of national pride, which to us seems like ignorant conceit.[38]

They are extraordinarily rich in mythological fictions, which are recited in rhythm as well as rhyme, and in magniloquent language. A European, who told them the stories of the Arabian Nights, gained a considerable sum of money from his auditors.   As in all Papuans, belief in a future life is so powerful that it leads to suicide and human sacrifice on the graves of the deceased.   As a matter of course, this is accompanied by a worship of the dead, in addition to which Ndengei, the creator of the world and of mankind, is adored under the symbol of a serpent.[39]

Among their industrial inventions is a net, as a protection against mosquitoes : the neighbouring Polynesians have neither these nets nor earthen vessels, such as are made by the Fijians of red or blue clay, and are remarkable for their true and graceful outlines.   Although in shipbuilding they are the pupils of the Polynesians, yet they manufacture canoes one hundred and eighteen feet long, and twenty-four feet wide, fit them with masts of sixty-eight feet in height, and decorate them profusely with carvings.   For these purposes their tools are only unpierced

---

[35] Horatio Hale, Ethnography, p. 51.

[36] Karl Semper, Die Palau-Inseln.

[37] Williams, Fiji and the Fijians.

[38] Waitz (Gerland), Anthropologie, vol vi.

[39] Williams, Fiji and the Fijians.

stone axes, and rat's teeth for the finer sculpture ; brain corals, and the skin of the sting ray are used as files, and, lastly, pumice-stone for polishing.

They have advanced so far in the science of war as to fortify their villages with moats or canals, and to lay in stores of food, nominally sufficient for four years. Unluckily, they are more inclined to cunning than to heroic courage, and they are also generally accused of craft, falsehood, and inordinate distrust. It is among this undoubtedly highly gifted and active people that cannibalism did and does especially prevail.

III.—THE MONGOLOID NATIONS.

To this race belong the Polynesian and Asiatic Malays, the people of South-eastern and Eastern Asia, the inhabitants of Thibet, some of the hill tribes of the Himalayas, as well as all Northern Asiatics with their kinsmen in northern Europe, and, lastly, the aboriginal population of America. Their common characters are long straight hair, which is cylindrical in section; almost complete absence of beard and hair on the body; a dark-coloured skin, varying from a leather-like yellow to deep brown, or sometimes tending to red; and prominent cheek-bones, generally accompanied by an oblique setting of the eyes. Their other characters occur in so many gradations that the local types pass into one another, as will be shown in each group. The linguistic characters alone afford grounds for subdivision.

I.—THE MALAY RACE.

The Malay languages are distinguishable by a community of roots but not of words. This indicates that the members of this family of nations separated before the structure of the language had assumed fixed principles. The primitive language itself developed independently and stood alone in the world. Its defining roots are sometimes placed before and sometimes after the main word. The Polynesian dialects are poorer in sounds and have remained more archaic; the Western or Asiatic dialects are richer, and in them the morphological and material elements of the groups of roots are at the same time more closely united by transformations of sound.[1] The home in which this primitive language was developed was situated in South-eastern Asia, either on the great islands of the Sunda or on the projection of the continent. From this centre a portion of the family, now become maritime, swarmed out towards the east, peopling the islands of the South Seas as far as the Hawai group on the north, and Easter Island on the extreme east. This branch of the Malays came into frequent contact with the Papuans, thus giving rise to the hybrids which are called Micronesians.

The time at which the Polynesian Malays separated from their Asiatic kinsfolk cannot as yet be even approximately determined. An able botanist, Berthold Seemann, who was taken from us prematurely, has indeed remarked that the palm wine, which is obtained from the sheath of the cocoa-nut tree blossom, is called toddy, or taddy, by the Malays of the Sunda Islands. As this word is derived from Sanscrit,[2] it would appear to have been the Brahminical Hindoos who first introduced the important art of preparing palm wine into the islands of Southern Asia. Now, as the cocoa-nut palm probably spread from east to west, and occurs in all tropical islands of the South Seas, as its nuts are the daily food of the inhabitants of the atolls, or coral groups, and its milk is often the only means of appeasing thirst, it is hardly credible that if the Polynesians before their migration knew the secret of preparing palm wine, they should ever have disused it. But as this beverage was entirely unknown to them at the time of the first visits of Europeans, their emigration must have taken place before the arrival in Java of Sanscrit-speaking Indians, hence certainly before the beginning of the era of the Saka or Salivana, which was introduced about the year 78 B.C.[3] But this argument points to a period too recent. The evolution of the varieties of the language required a far greater lapse of time. We may also add that the

---

[1] Fr. Müller, Reise der Fregatte Novara; Anthropologie.

[2] Berthold Seemann, Dottings on the Roadside, p. 153.

[3] Crawford, Dictionary of the Indian Islands, p. 137.

art of manufacturing earthen vessels was not yet known to the Polynesians in their original home at the time of their migration, for they all cook their food by means of heated stones. On the other hand, the custom of consecrating persons or things so that they must not be touched was already established in this original abode, for traces of the institution of taboo are still preserved in the form of interdicts in the island of Timor and among the Dyaks of Borneo.[4]

The prevalent eastern monsoons and westward currents offered no insurmountable obstacles to the eastward diffusion of the Polynesians from the west, for there are plenty of contrary winds and counter currents. That these obstacles were formerly much over-estimated is proved by the map of Tupaia,[5] a Polynesian who was familiar with all the island groups between the Marquesas to the east, and the Fiji archipelago in the west, so that in Captain Cook's time intercourse from Tahiti must have extended throughout forty degrees of longitude. Comparison of Polynesian dialects and the traditions of the natives afford further means of ascertaining the order in which the various colonizations succeeded each other.

The inhabitants of Rapa-nui, or Easter Island, maintain that they come from Oparo or Rapaiti (27° 35' s. lat., 144° 20' w. long.), and therefore, on their voyage to their own country, must have touched at Pitcairn's Island and abandoned it again, for remains of old stone structures are still standing there.[6] According to the native traditions they landed, four hundred in number, under a leader or king Tu-ku-i-u, or Tocuyo, who is also called Hotu, or Hotu Motua.[7] From the time of their arrival to the present day twenty-two chiefs have succeeded to the government, so that if the average duration of each reign is reckoned at twenty years, the colonization of the island does not date further back than the

---

[4] Waitz (Gerland), Anthropologie. Spenser St. John, Life in the Far East, vol. i. p. 175.

[5] United States Exploring Expedition, 1846, where this map is for the first time correctly explained by Horatio Hales.

[6] Waitz, Anthropologie, vol. v.

[7] Palmer, Visit to Easter Island, in the Journal of the Royal Geographical Society, vol. xl. 1870.

year A.D. 1400. The tradition will gain in weight if the three wooden tables of hieroglyphics, which were recently found among the Easter Islanders and carried off by Europeans, contain the list of the kings' names, in early attempts at writing.[8]

The inhabitants have made hundreds of high but very rude stone images with human faces, of a very friable trachyte lava, and have set them up throughout the island, perhaps in memory of the dead.[9] They also built great stone terraces which recall the Morai of the other Polynesians. Lastly, ruins have been found of spacious buildings of stone slabs, which though now in a dilapidated condition, must have been inhabited within 150 years, for on their walls are pictures in white, red, and black, representing sheep, horses, and ships with their rigging,[10] and Roggeween was the first seafarer to open intercourse with the inhabitants in 1721. On good grounds it has been conjectured that a civilized people, now extinct, were in possession of Easter Island before the arrival of the present Polynesian inhabitants, but as yet these suppositions have received no confirmation. On the other hand, the present inhabitants confirm the experience that when a handful of people stray into an ocean solitude, and live there without the incitement of intercourse with others, they gradually lose the accomplishments and capacities which they possessed before their separation. Though the other Polynesians now erect only wooden buildings, yet the remains of ancient stone edifices have been found on various islands of the South Seas.[11]

Names of islands and of places in the Samoan group (Sevaii, Upulu, Lefuka), reoccur in the Sandwich Islands in the forms Hawaii, Upolu, and Lehua. Yet the first settler of the Sandwich Islands did not come directly from the Samoan group, even if their original home was there. Islands of the Marquesas archipelago, such as Noukahiva and Taowatte, are mentioned in their old songs,

---

[8] Meinicke, in the Zeitschrift für Erdkunde. 1871.

[9] According to the prints in the Revue maritime et coloniale, and photographs which we have received, these sculptures strongly resemble the well-known wooden Tiki images of New Zealand.

[10] Palmer, Visit to Easter Island in the Journal of the Royal Geographical Society, vol. xl. 1870.

[11] Waitz (Anthropologie, vol. v.) gives a list of these remains.

as is also Tahiti.[12]   As the dialect of the Kanaks or Hawaians is closely allied to that of the Marquesas Islanders, Horatio Hale considers it to have come from the latter, while its legends and proverbs even point back to Tahiti.[13]   The lists of kings contain sixty-seven names, but of these at least twenty-two must be rejected as fabulous, so that, allowing an average of twenty years for each reign, we must place the colonization of the group in the middle of the tenth century.[14]   It was only after the emigration of the Kanaks that the important discovery was made in Tahiti and in the Marquesas Islands that bread-fruit may be preserved for a long time if allowed to ferment, for the practice was unknown in the Sandwich Islands.[15]   Here again we perceive how unfavourably local separation, which hinders the spread of useful discoveries, affected remote islands.

The first visitors from over the sea landed considerably earlier in the Marquesas group, in the dialects of which Tongan and Tahitian peculiarities reappear, from which circumstance it may be inferred that it was colonized from the Society and the Friendly Islands.   It was from Vavau, or one of the Friendly Islands, that the Noukahivian chief Gattanewa, or more correctly Keatanui, led the first inhabitants to the group which became their home, and the names of no less than eighty-eight other rulers might be enumerated.[16]   This would take us back to the first centuries of our era, unless we must make allowance here also for fabulous personages at the beginning of the list.

There are no traditions respecting the first colonization of the Low Archipelago ; the local vocabulary contains an extraordinary number of peculiarities, whereas the syntax agrees with that of the Tahitian dialect, so that an immigration from the Society Islands probably took place.[17]   The traditions of the Maori of

---

[12] J. J. Jarves, History of the Hawaian or Sandwich Islands. Boston, 1844.

[13] Waitz, Anthropologie, vol. v.

[14] H. Hale assumes thirty years as the duration of a reign.   If this is preferred the above calculation can be altered.

[15] Von Langsdorff, Reise um die Welt.

[16] Tylor, Early History of Mankind.

[17] Waitz (Gerland), Anthropologie, vol. v.

New Zealand are, on the contrary, vivid, for they profess to know
the number and names of their ships, and the points on the
shore at which their forefathers landed. The northern island was
first reached from the east, yet the Maori call their early home
Hawaiki, thus pointing to the Samoan group, although Hawaiki
subsequently came to mean a far off land of bliss, the home
to which departed souls were destined to retûrn.[18] The Maori
did not bring with them the domestic animals of their native
land, yet their language has retained the Polynesian word for
pig, *puaka*.[19] Their forefathers must have known the cocoa-nut
palm, for the Polynesian word for the nut occurs in the Maori
language, although only applied to an implement used in sooth-
saying.[20] The list of the New Zealand chiefs extends backwards
for eighteen or twenty generations, so that scarcely 400 years can
have elapsed since the first colonization. Stragglers are moreover
said to have arrived from Hawaiki about a century ago, and to
have brought the Kumara, or sweet potato, to New Zealand.[21]

Earlier or later colonizations of the smaller groups of islands
have been proved; and even if no great weight can be attributed
to the calculations given above, it is certain that the islands of the
Pacific were gradually peopled from Samoa or Navigators' Islands,
and since this may have happened at a period not very remote,
traditions of an immigration have nowhere entirely died out.

The Polynesians fished but did not hunt.[22] They lived also on
the produce of the cocoa-nut groves, the bread-fruit, and a few
tuberous plants, such as the Taro and the sweet potato. The dog
and the pig were their domestic animals, the absence of which
in New Zealand is probably due to the circumstance that during
the long passage the live stock on board the vessels was eaten;
for in other respects the colonization of new islands was always
well planned. The distribution of land and water in South-
eastern Asia was of itself an inducement to seek for trans-oceanic

---

[18] Schirren (Wandersagen der Neu Seeländer) and Hochstetter place
Hawaiki in the lower world, and allow it only a legendary signification.
Gerland, however, has skilfully vindicated the older opinion of H. Hale.

[19] Waitz (Gerland), Anthropologie, vol. v.

[20] Tylor, Primitive Culture, vol. i. p. 80.

[21] Hale, Ethnographie.   [22] See above, p. 184.

abodes, for nowhere else in the world have former continents been resolved into islands of such various degrees of size. The low coral reefs are inadequately protected against storms and surf; atolls are occasionally destroyed, and their inhabitants obliged to seek a new home. The Polynesians, in common with all Malays, are clever seamen; they are indebted to their own ingenuity for the single or double outrigger which secures their narrow sailing craft from being upset by the rolling waves.

Their manufactures are those of the age of polished but unpierced stone implements. The spear and club are the usual weapons of war. They are without earthen vessels, but cook their food by means of heated stones. Their dwellings consist of posts with roofs of leaves, and their clothing of bark of the paper mulberry tree, although the cotton plant grows wild in the the islands.

The religious emotions of the Polynesians manifested themselves in worship of the forces of nature personified, whose deeds and conduct, interwoven with geological legends, are as cleverly and fancifully adorned with myths as is the Greek Olympus. The Maori of New Zealand, detestable as they are, on account of their cannibalism, yet possess beautiful legends of the Creation, according to which, thought, as the subtlest element, first germinated in the primordial night, and was followed by desire; or, according to a different version, thought arose first, then the spirit, and lastly, matter.[23] Beside the forces of nature, the chiefs after death also received divine honours,[24] and oracles were instituted at their shrines. The priestly order was well versed in all the juggleries of Shamanism, but was held in far less respect than were the princes, who boasted of divine descent, and were certain of worship after death. Closely connected with this was their privilege of tabooing, a right which enabled them by touching a field to render it unlawful for others to set foot upon it, or to eat the produce of the harvest. Taboo, however, in some forms, could be inflicted by those of lower rank. It served also as a protection to property, and enforced the observance of useful police

---

[23] Waitz (Gerland), Anthropologie, vol. vi.
[24] Mariner, Tonga Islands, vol. ii.

regulations.[25] Any breach of this interdict was unheard of, for temporal and eternal punishments menaced the reprobate. Unconscious infraction of this institution led to sanguinary acts of vengeance on the part of the nations against the Europeans, and Captain Cook, although received by the Sandwich Islanders as a god both before and after his death, perished in expiation of breach of taboo. The misapprehension of this custom long blackened the character of the Polynesians. A Maori perhaps came to the house of a European settler and begged for a drink ; after refreshing himself he would either break the glass or quietly carry it off, since it had been consecrated by contact with him, and was unfitted, therefore, for use by any other individual ; but the person robbed ever after entertained a deep grudge against New Zealanders in general on account of this supposed act of base ingratitude. The difficulties caused in daily life by this strange institution were partly counterbalanced by the fact that slaves made prisoners in war were free from the regulations of taboo.

The Polynesian communities were divided into princes, nobles, and plebeians. The forms of intercourse were adjusted according to these gradations, and the gratification of aristocratic vanity was amply provided for by rigid etiquette. In the Society Islands we moreover find the association of the Arreoi, a confraternity half social, half artistic, for the performance of dramatic dances. To this society, divided into seven grades distinguished by tattoo marks, belonged princes, nobles, and commons, men as well as women ; the children of these last were killed as soon as born. The Arreoi wandered from island to island to perform their festal games, and were everywhere entertained with merrymakings. They have been justly praised in that, as cultivators of art, they have diffused higher culture and social polish.[26]

The Asiatic Malays, who remained nearer their original home, are still to be met with in the peninsula of Malacca, or it may be that they have returned to it again. They inhabit the large islands now under Dutch rule, the Philippines and even Formosa. It has

---

[25] Langsdorff, Reise um die Welt, vol. i.

[26] Waitz (Gerland), Anthropologie, vol. vi.

long been known that the civilized agricultural inhabitants of the shores of this last island spoke a Malay language ; [27] but in the mountains of the interior there is a savage warlike tribe, called by the Chinese Chinwan, or "barbarous savages." They were supposed to be akin to the Philippine population. Schetelig, who first investigated their language, came to the conclusion that these Chinwans have only borrowed a sixth part of their vocabulary from their Malay neighbours, from whom they differ otherwise in language, and are physically closely allied to the continental people of China.[28]

It might have been supposed that the vast tract of the Indian Ocean, destitute of islands, would have set a limit on the west to the migratory impulse of the Malays. The similarity of Malagassic and Malayan words was observed both by Sir Joseph Banks, who as botanist accompanied Captain Cook on his first voyage, and by Hervàs, the philologist ; but it is only since Wilhelm von Humboldt's researches in the Kawi language that the fact has been established that, while the islands of Rodriguez, Mauritius, and Bourbon were found uninhabited at the time of their discovery by European seafarers, Madagascar was peopled by Malays.[29] Traces of the custom of taboo occur there, for by a *Kiady* which is a tuft of grass on the point of an erect pole, the guardians of the fetishes are able to prevent any intrusion on the part of unconsecrated persons into the holy places.[30] No tradition has been preserved among the Malagassees themselves, although their immigration may have been much more recent than the separation of the Polynesians from their Asiatic kindred. According to Ellis,[31] the Hovas of Madagascar in smelting iron ore use a sort of bellows with two bamboo tubes, through which alternately the air is expelled by the motion of a pump. This ingenious invention occurs nowhere

[27] Latham, Opuscula.

[28] Schetelig, in the Zeitschrift für Völkerphysiologie and Sprachwissen-schaft, vol. v.

[29] Banks in Hawksworth, Discoveries in the South Sea, 1773. Hervàs Catálogo de las Lengues ; Madrid, 1800. W. von Humboldt, Ueber die Kawisprache. 1836.

[30] Lieutenant Oliver, Journal of the Anthropological Society. 1868.

[31] Three Visits to Madagascar.

else except in the Malay islands; and Tylor[32] therefore seems justified in the impression that the colonization of Madagascar took place only after the working of iron was practised in the Sunda Islands. In connection with this circumstance, it is noticeable that the Hovas breed the zebu, or Indian buffalo, though the indigenous cattle of Madagascar are like the African species.[33] If with this we connect the fact that the inhabitants of the southern coast of Ceylon and of the Maledives speak the Malay language, this throws some light on the way by which the ancestors of the Hovas reached Madagascar.

It is very difficult to estimate rightly the natural capabilities for social organization of the Asiatic Malays, for they lost their independence at an early period. First Brahminical and, later, Buddhist settlers brought to Java[34] Indian learning, Indian religious arts, and Indian characters, as well as a chronology; nor were Sumatra and the peninsula of Malacca unaffected by their influence. On the extinction of Buddhism the old temples on the Sunda Islands fell into ruins. Since that time the Malays have adopted Islam, the precepts of which now constitute the framework of social justice. The oldest events of their written history point to a kingdom in Sumatra of which Menang-Kabao was the centre, and whence seafaring adventurers started, nominally in the year 1160 A.D., to establish themselves at Singapore. From that time it was mainly the Arabs who imparted their culture to the nations of the Sunda Islands. The Dyaks of Borneo and the warlike Batta of Sumatra have alone remained almost untouched by foreign influences. The former in their self-evolution have scarcely raised themselves higher than the Polynesians. Until stopped by Rajah Sir James Brooke, the primitive custom of taking heads was in force amongst them, a custom probably characteristic of all Asiatic Malays, for it has recently been observed by Bechtinger in Formosa[35] and in the fifteenth century it still prevailed among the

---

[32] Early History of Mankind, p. 215.

[33] Lieutenant Oliver, Journal of the Anthropological Society. Schweinfurth has however shown that the buffalo occurs in every part of the Soudan. In the Heart of Africa, vol. i. p. 63.

[34] Friedrich Müller, Reise der Fregatte Novara, Anthropologie.

[35] Ausland. 1872.

Batta in Sumatra.[36] The meaning of this strange custom of procuring from anywhere, by force or craft, a head or skull, which was
taken as a precious possession to the grave, is explained by the
popular superstition, that in the abode of the departed the former
owner of the skull would be the slave of its later proprietor.[37] We
have already assigned due credit to the Batta, who are cannibals,
for having invented an alphabet of their own, though it is merely
an imitation of the Indian characters.[38]

The Asiatic Malay is reserved, taciturn, obsequious to superiors,
harsh to inferiors, cruel, revengeful, and susceptible to insult, yet,
on the other hand, he is gentle to children, dignified, and polished
in manners. Wallace, who lived for a long time among both
Malays and Papuans, considers the latter to be the more highly
gifted race.

We find the third group of Malays east of the Philippines,
and north of or close upon the equator, in the Marianas, the
Pelew group, the Carolines, as well as on the Ralik, Rádik, and
Gilbert Atolls. Recently they have all been given the name of
Micronesians. The inhabitants of these islands are hybrids of
Polynesians and Papuans, but in language, customs, and social
institutions, they are Polynesian. Among the inhabitants of the
Pelew Islands, however, Papuan blood predominates, so that they
should not be classed in the Malay race. But further east, the
type becomes more Polynesian, though even at the extreme limit
of the region which they inhabit, the Micronesians are distinguished
from the pure Polynesians by the frizzliness of their hair, while
on approaching Japan oblique setting of the eyes grows more
frequent.[39]

Among Asiatic as well as Polynesian Malays, dolichocephals are
very rare ; when they occur, as in the Carolines, they only confirm
the statement that the Micronesians must be regarded as a hybrid
people. The cranial index of breadth in Polynesian, is, however,
perceptibly lower than in the case of Asiatic Malays, hence the

---

[36] Kunstmann, Indien im 15 Jahrhundert.
[37] Tylor, Primitive Culture, vol. i. p. 452.
[38] Junghuhn, Die Battaländer, vol. ii.
[39] Semper, Die Palau-Inseln. 1873.

former rank among the mesocephals, the latter among the brachy-cephals.[40] In both divisions of the Malay family, the height of the skull is as great or perhaps a little greater than the breadth.[41] Prognathism is moderate in degree, but the zygomatic arches are more or less prominent. All the nations of this family have a dark but never a completely black skin; while among the Asiatic Malays it is of a dirty yellow hue. The characters which they have in common with other members of the Mongolian race are black straight hair on the head, and a scanty growth of beard and of hair on the body, the latter being, moreover, artificially removed. The nearer their abode to the continent of Asia, the more frequent is the oblique setting of the eyes. In this they very closely resemble the populations of the eastern portions of the Old World. Not only have they more resemblance to them than to any other races of mankind, but no distinct line of difference can be drawn between them, as the types merge into one another. Hence a Chinese origin has been wrongly ascribed to the inhabitants on the Nias and Battu islands, on the west coast of Sumatra.[42] Semper, to account for resemblances in various tribes in the Phillipines and among the Iraya to the Japanese and Chinese, supposes an admixture of blood, although he admits that " only in a few cases some slight historical evidence can be found."[43] Wallace decides the matter when he writes,[44] " I was much struck when, in the island of Bali, I saw Chinese traders who had adopted the costumes of that country, and who could then hardly be distinguished from Malays, and, on the other hand, I have seen natives of Java who, as far as physiognomy was concerned, would pass very well for Chinese." Latham speaks of the physical characters of the Malays as " truly Indo-Chinese,"[45] and in another passage he says that the Mongolian type is more marked in the Micronesians than in the Chinese,[46] which can, however, be admitted only in regard to the inhabitants of the Marianas. We believe, with

---

[40] Comp. the tables of Barnard Davis, Thesaurus Craniorum, and above.

[41] This character is more conspicuous in Welcker's measurement than in B. Davis's, but only because the latter measured the " greatest breadth."

[42] Waitz, Anthropologie, vol. v.   [43] Die Philippinen.

[44] The Malay Archipelago, vol. ii. p. 453.

[45] Man and his Migrations.   [46] Varieties of Man.

Moritz Wagner, that the shape of skull, the form and colour of the face, as well as the whole physical constitution of the Malay race, is so nearly allied to the Mongolian that, in similar apparel, the two races are hardly distinguishable. We shall therefore not be contradicted if we class the Malay race among the Mongoloid nations. Yet their linguistic characters entitle them to a separate place. We subdivide them into Micronesian hybrid nations and Polynesians, or, if it be preferred, into Pacific and Asiatic Malays. The latter are better subdivided again, as by Frederick Müller, into—1. The inhabitants of the Philippines, termed Tagals and Bisaya; 2. the Malays in the restricted sense, as inhabitants of the peninsula of Malacca, and in Sumatra, the Atchinese, Passumahs, Rejangs, and Lampongs; 3. the Sundanese in the west; 4. the Javans in the eastern part of Java; 5. the Batta in Sumatra; 6. the Dyaks of Borneo; 7. the Macassars and Buginese in the island of Celebes. Lastly, this race includes scattered members settled in the islands of Formosa, Ceylon, and Madagascar.

II.—SOUTHERN ASIATICS WITH MONOSYLLABIC LANGUAGES.

To this group belong primarily the inhabitants of the eastern peninsula of India, whom we will speak of as Malayo-Chinese, rather than by their inappropriate epithet of Indo-Chinese. With these are allied the people of Thibet and the southern slopes of the Himalayas on the west, and the Chinese on the north and north-east. They all have straight, black hair, very little beard or hair on the body, a coloured skin, usually of a leather yellow, and obliquely set eyes. Narrow skulls are extremely rare amongst them. According to their index of breadth these nations rank in part among the mesocephals, and in part among the brachy-cephals. The height of the head is either equal to its breadth, or not infrequently surpasses it. Prognathism is not universal, and is always moderate in degree. But very few skulls have been measured. Even Barnard Davis had at his disposal only twenty-one Chinese heads of both sexes, a very insufficient number, by means of which to find the average proportions of 350 millions of human beings scattered over one of the greatest empires of the world.

Owing to the uniformity of the most important physical characters of the various races, they can be distinguished only by their languages. The language of the Bod-dschi, the inhabitants of Thibet, although strictly monosyllabic, nevertheless possesses prefixes which are written but not pronounced,[1] thus proposing an obscure and as yet unsolved problem to comparative philology.[2] Numerous small tribes, whose names we need not enumerate, inhabit the Himalayas, especially their southern slopes. They much resemble the Thibetians in physical characters and in language, but are only partially pure-bred, having usually Indian blood in them. Among those of pure breed are the Leptscha of Sikim.[3] It must be noted that the nomadic Sifans of the Chinese provinces of Schensi and Sse-tschuen also belong in language to the group of Thibet nations.

Another group centres round the Burmese, whose linguistic type we have already noticed. With them are allied the inhabitants of Aracan, the Khyeng, in the mountains dividing Aracan from the Irawaddy, and the small tribes between this last river and the Brahmaputra. The Thai, or Siamese, form another division ; the Laos nations in the interior of Siam are separated from these only by varieties of dialect. The still barbarous Miaotse, or Miautsi, in the highlands of the southern half of the Chinese empire, who are there regarded as aborigines, are said also to belong to the Thai group.[4] On the other hand, the Anamese in Tonkin and Cochin China stand alone.

Unconnected with any of the previous groups are the Kares in Pegu and in southern Burmah, the Mon in the delta of the Irawaddy, the Khos or aborigines of Camboja, the Tsampa on the coast to the east of the mouths of the Mekong, who in the

---

[1] The names of the towns Thashilhúnpo and Tassisudon are, for example, written b Kras shis lhun po, and b Kras shis chhos krong. Von Schlagintweit, Indien und Hochasien.

[2] Whitney, Language and Study of Language.

[3] Von Schlagintweit.

[4] Friedrich Müller, Allgemeine Ethnographie.

time of Marco Polo had set up a kingdom, the Kwanto, who are
the aborigines of Tonkin, who must not be confounded with the
Anamese, and the Moi, or Myong, in the mountains which separate the Nukong from Tonkin.[5] The Kho language in Camboja
and the Mon language in Pegu are said to be much more nearly
allied to each other than to the Thai language, which is spoken in
the intervening country.[6] These smaller tribes are of but little
interest to ethnologists. They are no longer in a primitive condition, and such civilization as they have adopted is of foreign
origin, a graft on a wild stock. This is true even of the greater
states, Burmah, Siam, and Tonkin. For, although in all these three
countries considerable remains have been discovered of handsome
but now mostly ruined edifices, their buildings all bear the stamp
of Indian origin and of the Indian taste which was introduced
with Buddhism. However, they all belong to the post-Christian
period and are of no high antiquity. Tonkin, on the other hand,
received its culture mainly from China, while Siam has in recent
times added Chinese methods of improvement to the Indian ones
which it previously possessed. We may therefore pass quickly
from the Malayo-Chinese in order to dwell longer on the Chinese
as the most civilized nation of the Mongolian race. We have
already pointed out the most important facts in regard to their
language.

Too many of our countrymen know noth'ng of the Celestial
Empire but the pigtail—though this was only adopted by the
Chinese in 1644, and will be laid aside on the fall of the Mandschu
dynasty—and the great walls, which are now neither guarded nor
repaired, and of which it is proverbially, though falsely, said that
they were erected to ward off the teachings of the West. For
centuries, according to the more cautious, for tens of centuries
according to the more confident, China has remained China without moving forwards or backwards. To disprove this error we
shall assign dates in the enumeration which follows of the innova-
tions which the Chinese, like other nations, have adopted ; from
which dates it will be self-evident that the inhabitants of the

---

[5] Friedrich Müller, Reise der Fregatte Novara ; Anthropologie.

[6] Latham, Man and his Migrations, p. 195.

Celestial Empire have progressively improved their condition partly by their own ingenuity, partly by the adoption of foreign ideas.

It is true that until the conquest of Pekin the Chinese spoke of Europeans as " barbarians " and " devils." We leave the question as to whether, had we been Chinese, we should not have done the same, and with justice, to any one who has heard the account given by a trustworthy and humane American of the barbarities of Europeans in China. A steamboat, which had undergone repair,[7] was to make its trial trip from Shanghai, and the chief people of the town were invited to attend. Among the guests was our American witness. The steamer went up the Woosang river, and sped with full power through the water ; a Chinese vessel was noticed further up so heavily laden with bricks as scarcely to obey the oars of the four native rowers. The stream being narrow, the Chinese tried to get out of the way, and worked with all their might. Still the heavy vessel did not move quite aside. The pilot therefore asked whether the steamer should stop? "No," cried the captain ; "go on." Pumpelly breathlessly awaited the result. The bow of the ship struck the brick barge so heavily that it swung round against the paddle-box. The steamer was shaken by the collision, but went on merrily. Pumpelly, looking over the stern, saw nothing of the boat or its crew, but one Chinese motionless in the water. The pleasure of the party was not however in the least damped by this interlude, especially when the officers had satisfactorily ascertained that the paddle-box was not seriously injured.

Another story may serve as a companion picture.[8] As Pumpelly was returning from the coal-mining districts in the north, the people of Tahwei-tschang mobbed him and his companion, Murray, a distinguished Chinese scholar attached to the English embassy. A mob is the same all the world over ! The Chinese crowd amused itself with witticisms on the strange figures, just as an English or American mob would have diverted itself with a pig-tailed Chinaman. But after joking for some time, a more angry feeling arose, and the Celestials flung all manner of repulsive

---

[7] Pumpelly, Across America and Asia.   [8] Ibid.

missiles at the foreign devils, regardless of the fact that they were travelling under the protection of three Mandarins. Murray turned his horse, raised his hand to enjoin silence, and began in excellent Chinese: "Oh people of Tahwei-tschang, is this the way you practise hospitality? Is this the way you obey the precepts of your philosophers to treat strangers within your walls tenderly? Have you forgotten the saying of your great master Confucius, 'That which I wish another not to do to me, I must not do to him?'" In an instant the scene was changed; the old Chinese benignly shook their heads, and the boys tried to efface the remembrance of their former misconduct by civilities. Let us ask ourselves what an English or American mob would have done, had a Chinese, in order to escape rude molestation, recited a text from the Sermon on the Mount.

It may be said of the Chinese more certainly than of any other nation of the Old World, that their knowledge is almost completely self-evolved. With the exception of vague reports by the historians and geographers of antiquity respecting a people in the far East who wove silken materials, the records of Arabian travellers of the latter period of the Abbasides are the first notices we possess of the social condition of China, which evoked both the surprise and admiration of their contemporaries. About five hundred years later the Poli returned from China to Venice, and their statements regarding the density of population and gigantic towns of the Celestial Empire sounded so incredible that the youngest of the travellers, Marco, received the scornful appellation of Messer Milione (million prater). It has long been acknowledged that the Venetian gave a faithful and accurate account of what he saw and heard. When Marco Polo, at the beginning of the fourteenth century, described the wonderful society in Eastern Asia, there was in truth much which Europe might envy the Chinese empire, and little which China could envy Europe as regards social order and industrial accomplishments.

The silken materials mentioned even by the prophet Ezekiel,[9] earned for the Chinese their earliest national name; and, as Klaproth proved long ago, the word for silk in the languages of the

---

[9] Chapter xvi. 13, and Fr. Spiegel, Ausland. 1867.

West is derived from the Chinese. According to their artificial and hence unreliable chronology, the Chinese had earthen vessels as early as 2698 B.C. ; but, according to Stanislas Julien, the porcelain manufacture was not developed until 185–87 B.C. Although in the Schuking mention is made of "sweet wine" under Thai-Kang, between 2188-59,[10] it must be remembered that a Chinese captain, Tschangkhien, only introduced the vine and vine culture into the middle empire in the year 130 B.C.,[11] and that even at the present day the Celestials eat the grape but do not press it. The sweet wine of the Schuking is therefore the produce of fermented rice, with the addition of a leaven of wheat, whereas the distillation of brandy became known only under the Mongolian rulers.[12]   In ancient China, that is to say, under the first three dynasties, tea was neither cultivated nor drunk, for the empire did not as yet extend to the natural habitat of the Yscha bush in the south. Tea-drinking is, moreover, said to have been introduced by Buddhist monks, and is perhaps not older than our era.   Paper was also an innovation in China, for its first spread was in A.D. 153, prior to which time tablets of bamboo were used in its place.   Indian ink is still chiefly made in China, although its quality has deteriorated since glue made of buffalo's instead of stag's horn has been employed as the vehicle for the lampblack.   Its first invention was between A.D. 220–419.   Printing by means of carved wooden tablets was invented in China in A.D. 593 or 583, and was described in Radschideddin's "Dschemma et tewarikh."   Stanislas Julien and Paul Champion even assert that the art of printing with movable types was invented in the period King-li (A.D. 1041-49.)[13]   Of course it was not in alphabetical letters, but in the abridged syllabic characters of Chinese writing, on movable pieces of porcelain, which were put together.   This art necessarily fell into disuse again, as type-printing can only be successfully applied with the use of alphabetical characters.   In a monosyllabic language, such as

---

[10] Tableaux historiques de l'Asie. 1826.

[11] Plath, On the Wild Vine (*Vitis amurensis*) in Northern China. Ausland, 1869. Comp. Petermann's Mittheilungen. 1869.

[12] Huc, Chinesisches Reich.

[13] Stanislas Julien and Paul Champion, Industries anciennes et modernes de l'empire chinois. 1870.

Chinese, it was easy to invent a hieroglyphic for each root, but as the language did not require it, the roots were not divided into their separate sounds, nor were the sounds symbolized. Of all the nations of the world the Chinese are the only people who read, write, and print, without having invented orthography.

The polarity of a freely swinging magnetic needle was known to the Chinese as early as A.D. 121 ;[14] and they certainly made spectacle-glasses earlier than the people of the West. Gunpowder they also knew long before Europeans, though they used it only for fireworks. Even now the Chinese do not use money, that is to say, stamped pieces of precious metals, but employ scales and weights in all commercial intercourse ; paper-money, on the contrary, has been in circulation since 119 B.C. The last two dynasties, the Ming and the Mongolian, fell victims to the assignat system ; and if the *Pekin Gazette* should ever bring us tidings of an over-issue of Mandschu treasury bills, we may be sure that the last grains in the hour-glass of this dynasty are running out.[15] The Chinese are skilful in the use of numbers. They are not only the inventors of the abacus, but, according to Sir John Bowring, they use the finger-joints of the left hand as figures to aid mental calculations to the amount of 99,999, each successive finger, beginning from the little one, possessing a higher decimal value.[16] The so-called macadamization of streets is an extremely ancient invention of the Chinese, which we began to imitate in 1820. The Greek expression used in the account of the Last Supper in the Gospel of St. Mark, certainly implies that Christ and his disciples used their fingers in eating ;[17] but the Chinese under the second dynasty, that is to say, more than a thousand years before our era, made use of chopsticks of bamboo, and soon after of ivory.

Before giving an account of the antiquity of Chinese culture, we must commend the Chinese as trustworthy and diligent historians. Their authentic history reaches back to Yao, or, according to the

---

[14] Klaproth, Lettre sur l'invention de la boussole. 1834.

[15] Klaproth, Sur l'origine du papier-monnaie in the Journal asiatique. Paris, 1822.

[16] Ausland. 1868.

[17] Schmoller, Geschichte der deutschen Kleingewerbe. 1870.

usual reckoning, which however allows too long, to the year 2357. According to Legge, the Chinese chronology is accurate as far back as 826 B.C. ; Plath, who is not to be suspected of hasty conclusions, goes back as far as the year 841. At the commencement of the third dynasty the dates already vary by eleven years, that is to say, we must place this event either in 1122 or 1111 B.C. The time of the first dynasty and the reigns of Yao or Schün cannot be more accurately fixed than as belonging to the nineteenth or twentieth century before Christ. Hence criticism rejects dates which go back to two and three thousand years.[18]

The Chinese empire has, however, endured for nearly four thousand years, within which period its development was affected by a disease exactly similar to that suffered by the German empire in the middle ages, and in which a decline of imperial power was followed by the rise of small predatory states, until under the Thsin the royal power was erected again in greater strength than ever. When compared with that of the Chinese empire, the duration of the states created by the Mediterranean races, of the Chaldean empire, of the sovereignty of the Assyrians, of the new Babylon and the monarchy of the Achæminidæ, and even of the Roman empire, appear insignificant ; Egypt alone, with its families of kings, traceable up to the thirty-ninth century before Christ, is yet more venerable. But just as nations must have lived in social order in the valley of the Nile long before the time of Menes, so was a state of order already in existence before the first chronicles of the Chinese empire. As early as the reign of Yü, the founder of the first dynasty, canals were cut. The minister of public works occupied a high position in the royal council ; and arable land was taxed at its estimated value.[19] In ancient China there already existed an active police, a passport system, toll-keepers, game laws which were in force during the breeding season, laws to prevent the taking of eggs from the nests of song

---

[18] Legge, Chinese Classics. J. Chalmers has demonstrated that in the period between 2154 and 1718 B.C. no less than sixteen eclipses in the sign of Scorpio were visible in China, so that it is quite optional which of those eclipses is to be considered as the one which took place in the reign of Tshung-kang.

[19] J. H. Plath, Verfassung und Verwaltung China's unter den drei ersten Dynastien.

birds, and edicts against carrying arms or furious riding in the
streets of towns. If we are to credit a statement made A.D. 282,
China had a population numbering 13,553,923 heads in Yü's
time; but James Legge thinks that all ancient censuses are
valueless calculations by later Chinese scholars.[20] The rule of the
first dynasty was bounded by the great angle formed by the
Hoangho in the province of Schansi, and it was very long before
it extended to the Yiangtse-kiang. It was only in 537 B.C. that
Tschekiang was incorporated ; and since 214 B.C. Southern China
(that is to say, Fokien, Kuang-tung, Kuangsi, Kueitscheu to the
south of the Nanling mountains), was acquired by colonists as
peacably or, in fact, more peacably than, under our own eyes, the
United States have stretched beyond the Mississippi into the
far West. China grew in extent as late as A.D. 1255, when the
Mongols added Yunan ; indeed, the island of Formosa only came
into possession of the empire in 1683.[21] Within the last twenty
years not only the trans-Amourian district, but large portions of
Mandschuria have been ceded to Russia ; Kashgaria was lost
by a rebellion, and a Mohammedan state has risen in the south
of Yunnan ; but we must remember that these losses occurred
during a time of internal disorder. The Mandschu dynasty is evidently enfeebled, and China is preparing for a change of dynasty,
a social malady such as it has already several times suffered and
overcome, always to gain fresh strength under a new race of
sovereigns.

Before we proceed to examine how far the nature of the country
promoted the development of Chinese society, we must first
ascertain the physical and intellectual capacities and the natural
disposition of the people. The great variety of circumstances to
which the Chinese can accustom themselves is especially noteworthy. Notwithstanding the difference of temperature, this people
thrives equally well at Kiachta or, more correctly, at Maimatschin,
on the boundaries of Siberia, where quicksilver freezes every year
in the thermometer, as in the hot-house warmth of Singapore,

---

[20] Legge, Chinese Classics.

[21] J. H. Plath, Verfassung und Verwaltung China's unter den drei ersten
Dynastien.

where the nutmeg was cultivated as an article of commerce previous to the last outbreak of the pestilence. The Chinaman has all those qualities which, when unchecked, speedily result in over-population; he is a kind father, looking for his greatest happiness in his children, frugal to excess, of exemplary economy, an indefatigable worker, scorning any Sabbath rest, and in trade more crafty than a Greek. The very children transact business; bargaining and taking pledges are their favourite pastimes.[22]

The Chinaman still adheres closely to that first stage in which the organization of human society begins. Each command emanates from the paternal lips; obedience is the first sacred duty of the child, who if he injures his parents is liable to capital punishment. The absolute power of the monarch is based on the legal maxim that he is the father of his people. The extensive power of the civic authorities rests mainly on moral respect, for the standing army of China, consisting only of eight bodies of Mandschu soldiers, each of 10,000 men, is quite inadequate in this huge empire. The officers of public security are also extremely few, so that the Mandarin of a province or a town is totally destitute of any means of coercion. Our admiration, not to say our envy, is raised when we see 350 millions undisturbed in their occupations although a most insignificant sum is expended on state officials. Such a thing is conceivable only in a society which has practised school-like discipline for thousands of years, which bestows no office without a successful examination, where every privilege must be earned, where there is no hereditary but only a personal aristocracy. We must, however, bear in mind the dark side of this parsimony in the expenses of government. Pumpelly was several times in great danger owing to the total impotence of the Mandarins in insurrections of civic mobs. Life and property enjoy only imperfect security in China: pirates swarm round the coast, and there has scarcely ever been a time in which rebellion was not raging in some part of the great empire. The liking for secret societies, which the Chinese carry with them wherever they go, is the great cause of the civil strifes which rage everywhere.

---

[22] Huc, Das Chinesische Reich.

Chinese family names are of great antiquity. While in Europe even royal dynasties can hardly trace their founder at a distance of a thousand years, in China there are descendants of Confucius who are able not only to trace their descent from this great philosopher, but who also boast that their ancestor could prove the existence of his family name as early as 1121 B.C. This explains the meaning of the contemptuous inquiry which the Chinese are in the habit of addressing to Europeans : " Have you got family names too ? " by which they mean, Are they as ancient as ours ? [23]

It has already been said that Confucius did not found a religion. He adhered to the worship of Heaven and Earth as he found it in the so-called classical books of the ancient empire. At the time of his birth (551 B.C.) China had been split up into thirteen larger principalities and a number of predatory states. The philosopher rose to a position answering to that of mayor of one of the former, and later to that of Minister of Justice, but abandoned the service of the state in disgust at the prevailing system of concubinage, and subsequently, as a state pensioner of the Duchy of Wei, occupied himself with literary works on the national antiquities. He lived comfortably but without extravagance, and always travelled in his own carriage. He died calmly, but with no prayer, at an advanced age, in 478 B.C., without the comfort of wife or child, recognizing the slightness of the influence of his teaching, and without hope of better times. When one of his disciples questioned him as to a future life, he answered indirectly, " Were I to say that the departed were possessed of consciousness, pious sons might dissipate their fortunes in festivals of the dead, and were I to deny their consciousness, heartless sons might leave their fathers unburied." [24] His moral teaching, which had for its highest object social utility, was therefore far inferior to the Buddhist doctrine. To the question of a disciple whether the duty of man could not be comprised in a single word, he answered, " Does not retribution do this ? Thou shalt not do unto others that which thou wilt not that they should do unto thee." When another disciple desired to know whether injury

---

[23] James Legge, Life of Confucius, p. 55.   [24] Ibid. p. 101.
17

was to be requited with benevolence, the master replied, "Wherewith wilt thou then requite benevolence? Requite injury with justice, and benevolence with benevolence." [25] It was in the same spirit that, as we have already seen, he inculcated the duty of avenging murder by murder. To escape unwelcome visitors he often falsely gave himself out to be ill, and on one occasion he deliberately broke a solemn promise. On being taken to task for it he quietly said, "The oath was compulsory, and the spirits do not hear such."

Laotse was the contemporary of Confucius, but his influence was less. In language which was, as Rémusat has said, Platonic in its elevation and obscurity, [26] he taught the existence of a supreme Being resembling the Logos, as creator of the material world. The Taoteking, [27] book of faith of Laotse and his followers, the Taosse, is in fact so full of obscurities that even the name of Tao and of the supreme Being admit of a variety of interpretations. The moral doctrine of this philosopher was thoroughly pure ; like Buddhism, it taught gentleness and toleration. But his disciples and followers, who styled themselves doctors of Reason, soon brought contempt upon themselves and the Tao doctrine by despicable Shamanistic tricks, and have since then become the object of public scorn. [28]

A glance at the scene of this peculiar civilization is sufficient to show that the compact form of the country was neither advantageous nor injurious. The shores and the surrounding seas offer no inducement to navigation. When we notice that the Chinese are even at the present day equally bad as sailors and as shipbuilders, it must not be forgotten that they were originally an inland people, and that it was only at a late period that their empire extended to the sea and along the coast. It was not with Chinese, but Indian and Javan vessels, that Fahian the Buddhist returned to China from Ceylon and Java, in the beginning of the fifth century. It was only in A.D. 630 that nutmegs, camphor, aloe wood, carda-

---

[25] James Legge, Life of Confucius, p. 101.

[26] Abel Rémusat, Mélanges asiatiques, vol. i. p. 91.

[27] Laotse, Taoteking, Ed. Plaenckner, p. 7.

[28] Gützlaff, Geschichte des chinesischen Reiches, p. 75. 1847.

mons, and cloves first reached China by sea.[29] The Chinese did not know of Sumatra till A.D. 950. The leaden coins which are found at Singapore belong to this and the next century.[30] The best refutation of the statement that the Chinese never extended their voyages beyond Malacca, is to be found in accounts of Arabian travellers. We know moreover from Marco Polo, that under Kublha Khan enterprises against Madagascar were already contemplated, and from Makrisi's statements that in A.D. 1429 a Chinese vessel, which was unable to dispose of its wares at Aden, went up the Red Sea as far as the port of Jidda.[31] But as Chinese civilization was at its height long before these voyages, we may safely assert that the form of its coast had but little influence, and that only at a late period, on the civilization of the Celestial Empire.

The fact that the Chinese territory belongs to the Old World, is of far greater importance, for thus the best cultivated plants and the most important domestic animals were either indigenous or could reach it by transmission from one nation to another. China was in this respect far better adapted for civilization than America, not to speak of Australia. Of its valuable products, its copper and, above all, its tin ore are of most importance. The veins of this latter metal are widely and scarcely distributed over the world ; but without tin no bronze can be produced. The knowledge of bronze has everywhere preceded that of iron, and has always initiated a new phase of culture. As the requisite ores existed in their country itself, we need not hesitate to believe the Chinese when they date back the working of the metals to the mythical ages.

The original nucleus of the Chinese community was situated in a fertile lowland, bordered on the north by the declivities of the Gobi. The great wall runs along the edge of this declivity. "It marks," says A. von Humboldt, in a remark on Bunge's travels, "a natural boundary, in the proper sense of the word, while no better locality for a political boundary could be chosen." In the steppes all was dead, but the traveller had but to take one more

---

[29] Plath, in the Ausland, p. 1213. 1869.
[30] Waitz, Anthropologie, vol. v. p. 119.
[31] Et. Quatremère, Mémoires sur l'Egypte, vol. ii. p. 291.

step to stand at the edge of the abrupt cliffs of Northern Asia, and to see the most luxuriant life welcoming him.[32]   As far as Pumpelly was able to follow the great wall in a westerly direction, the declivity is broken into promontories and indentations exactly as if the sea had at one time worn against a steep coast.   So that the eastern provinces of China are recently emerged lowlands, and their soil is, generally speaking, reckoned extremely fertile.

These advantages of soil were also aided by peculiarly favour able meteorological conditions, for the regular fall of abundant monsoon rains during the early summer, following a warm and dry spring, quickens vegetation in its period of growth, and thus affords one of the advantages otherwise peculiar to the tropical zone.[33] Owing to these circumstances, the bamboo, the canes of which are used for so many domestic purposes, is able to grow in unusually high latitudes in China.   The canals which run through the plains show that the difficulty of irrigating the country is not great. Farinaceous plants must always have been abundant in China, or they could at least easily have been spread by cultivation.   Plath says that the chief crops of the ancient kingdom consisted of two grasses resembling millet (*Milium globosum, Panicum verticilatum*), of *Holcus sorghum*, and above all of wheat.[34]   Rice, which is the principal field produce of the southern half of China, reached the country only at a late period.   It is only in the south, beginning about the 30th degree of latitude, that tea and silk are cultivated. That the Chinese do not obstinately reject importations from other countries is proved by the fact that they have acquired rye, oats, and buckwheat from Mongolian or, more probably, from Turkish tribes, and have adopted the cultivation of maize since the discovery of America.   Peas and beans, cucumbers and melons, onions and leeks, were cultivated even in the ancient empire.   The most important domestic animals of the Old World, such as oxen, sheep, horses, pigs, fowls, and dogs, were there, but camels, asses, and goats were unknown.   Perhaps owing to Buddhists scruples, the ox is seldom eaten; and it is remarkable

---

[32] Correspondence with Berghaus, vol. ii. p. 30.

[33] Grisebach, Die Vegetation der Erde, vol. i. p. 489 et seq.

[34] Nahrungsweise der alten Chinesen, p. 1212.   Ausland, 1869.

that there are no dairies in China. Pigs furnish the principal part of the animal food consumed ; these, unlike the European breed of domestic pigs, are descended from the *Sus indicus* of Pallas,[35] so that they must have been domesticated by the Chinese themselves. Animals and plants, suitable for domestication, were therefore either indigenous or easily made their way into China at an early period. Yet this, with the conditions favourable to agriculture which we mentioned above, and the presence of valuable ores, are the only conditions advantageous to the development of Chinese culture contributed by the district itself. The geographical position of the empire was advantageous only in that the Chinese had thousands of years for peaceful self-evolution before the danger of disturbance from nations of superior strength arose. They were surrounded by neighbours of like descent, whom, at an early period, they surpassed in civilization. Invasions of migratory hordes only briefly interrupted the persistent growth, for the conqueror, having attained the throne, soon adapted himself to the intellectual supremacy of those whom he governed. Mongols and Mandschus founded dynasties, but the only thing changed in China was the name of the governing dynasty.

Industry and philoprogenitiveness have caused the Chinese people to increase to more than 350 millions. Social training was absolutely necessary for a population of such density. All increase of population on any given surface necessitates further refinement of the social compact. Without protection of life and property, without observance of conjugal fidelity, without purity in courts of justice, a large community is incapable of thriving, but must necessarily perish by internal decay. The census itself gives evidence of social refinement, which is always accompanied by industrial progress. When we have to deal with thousands of years and millions of human beings, chance, as the father of invention, certainly plays a great part. It becomes the instructor of handicraft, and it constantly increases the store of experience. It was thus inevitable that the Chinese, who two thousand years before Christ were numbered by millions, should have acquired a technical skill which is even now more or less startling to us.

---

[25] Von Nathusius, der Schweineschädel, p. 175.

But at this point it stopped. It is everywhere noticeable that the Chinese do not advance beyond a certain grade of intellectual development. They have independently invented a character of their own, but only with syllabic and not phonetic symbols ; they had long been acquainted with the art of engraving, but no longer used the movable types formerly employed. They had discovered the polarity of the magnetic needle, but had never used it as a compass ; they were acquainted with the nature of gun-powder, but had no knowledge of the gun ;[36] they had invented the abacus, but not the positional value of the figures ; they had observed astronomical events for thousands of years, but allowed the division of the zodiac to be introduced from abroad.

Carl Ritter dwells on the idea that the history of culture would have taken a different direction had it been possible for the Chinese and the Roman empires to come into closer contact. Reinaud, the Orientalist, who was for a long time the President of the Asiatic Society of Paris, tried to prove in his last work that under the first Roman emperors the impending contact with China was discussed much as at the present time : a great deal is superfluously written respecting the collision of the English and Russian powers in Central Asia. Perhaps the result of a contact between Roman and Chinese culture has been exaggerated in imagination. The only result affecting Europe would probably have been the introduction of the culture of the silkworm a few centuries earlier.

Such a contact might have reacted more beneficially on China. Its isolation in the east of Asia, which was formerly favourable to its aggrandizement, now threatens its future. The expression used by Adolf Bacmeister with reference to the people of South Africa, is in this case almost literally applicable : " The evolution of the original nature of any historical people is very differently affected if, on the one hand, the nations which it encounters, with which it has intercourse, and with which it learns to measure itself, are entirely or nearly such as itself ; or, on the other hand, if its history has caused it to struggle in the arena with

---

[36] The Chinese expression for cannon is a foreign word from the West. Huc, Das chinesische Reich, vol. ii. p. 78.

foreign powers, and, constantly strengthening itself by conflicts with fresh forces, to found, widen, and expend its existence, or perchance to lose it gloriously."

Our own respect for the achievements of Chinese culture can hardly be surpassed. Of all highly civilized nations they owe least to foreign promptings, whereas until the thirteenth century, we, that is to say, the Europeans, and especially the Northern Europeans, owed almost everything but our language to the teaching of other nations. We are the pupils of nations which now live only in history, but the Chinese were their own teachers. But comparing the course of our own development with that of theirs, we see what is wanting to them, and on what our own greatness depends. Since our intellectual awakening, since we have come forward as the propagators of the treasures of culture, we have indefatigably toiled with the sweat on our brows in search of something, the very existence of which was unsuspected by the Chinese, and which they would think dear at a platter of rice. This invisible object we term causality. We have admired the Chinese for an incalculable number of inventions, and have appropriated them, but we are not indebted to them for a single theory or a single glance into the connection or the first causes of phenomena.

III.—COREANS AND JAPANESE.

In addition to the people discussed in the last chapter, the inhabitants of the peninsula of Corea and of the Japanese archipelago have the characters of the Mongolian race. The Japanese, whose index of breadth is 76, are mesocephals, while the height of their skulls almost equals the breadth. It is only the polysyllabic character of their languages which prevents their being placed in one group with the Chinese and Malayo-Chinese. Their language is nearer the Altaic type, for they have the same loose combination of the morphological elements and have other rules of verbal structure in common. In these fundamental features the Japanese language corresponds so accurately with the Corean that the two may have had a common origin, but our present knowledge does not enable us to say that this must necessarily be the case.[1]

The Japanese migrated from the continent to their present abode, and afterwards peopled the Loochoo Islands further to the south. From Nippon and the southern islands they drove out the aborigines, in all probability Ainos, who now hold their own only at Yezo and the Kuriles. Ethnology cannot dwell long on the Japanese, though they are an intellectually gifted people and easily assimilate the improvements of foreign civilization.

As long ago as 1860, a steamboat manned and commanded by Japanese made its way across the Pacific to San Francisco and back. But their history, even when only partially authentic, extends only to Zinmu, or into the seventh century B.C., and they have hitherto always borrowed their civilization from China, though they have developed for themselves what they have thus adopted. Thus they invented a phonetic alphabet of forty-seven letters, retaining, however, the Chinese syllabic symbols also. They have improved and stamped with their own character many branches of industry originally Chinese, such as the manufacture of porcelain and the production of steel. Their humour and waggishness are expressed in their caricatures, which are of great vivacity, and evince an accurate observation of nature, but are spoilt by false drawing. They are the only Asiatics who have a chivalrous and keenly susceptible sense of honour, analogous to the Spanish Pundónor. In other respects also they approach more nearly in character to the people of the West than any other Mongoloid nation : their instinct of cleanliness distinguishes them most favourably from the Chinese.

The Coreans are also indebted to the Chinese for their present social condition, while we know nothing of their earlier civilization.

---

[1] Whitney, Language and the Study of Language, p. 329.

III.—THE MONGOLOID NATIONS IN THE NORTH OF THE OLD WORLD.

The country from the bay of Okotsk to European Lapland is inhabited by people who, with the exception of the Russians who have advanced eastward, live by hunting, fishing, and cattle-breeding, and who have continually changed their abodes and intermingled with one another from their earliest historical times. Conquerors have again and again appeared among them, who have united these independent hordes and enabled them to act in concert. With our present knowledge it is impossible to assert or deny that this vast territory was ever inhabited by various races. At any rate constant intermixture of blood has obliterated earlier differences, and hence we find physical characters of every gradation, from those of the pure Mongolian to those of the civilized inhabitants of the West. This group of nations, which Castrèn has named Altaians, is closely allied to the Eastern and Southern Asiatics. The colour of the skin is yellow or yellowish brown, the hair of the head cylindrical, stiff, and black; the beard and hairy covering of the body is slight or totally wanting; the eyes are usually obliquely set, the cheek-bones very prominent, the nose flattened, the skull extremely broad and low. The purity of the Mongolian characters of the Northern Asiatics gradually decreases towards the west. The Samoyeds resemble the Tungus in the shape of their face; the Ostiaks are like the Finns and Russians.[1]

Under these circumstances we must divide this group of mankind into five large branches, as was done by Alexander Castrèn; namely, Tungus, true Mongols, Turks, Finns, and Samoyeds. Fortunately, the structure of the languages of all these nations agrees completely in its main features. The meaning of the roots is defined by a second appended root, in other words, always by suffixes. Prefixes are never employed. These languages have also many roots in common, though not enough to prove a common primitive language; it is equally probable that they have been borrowed. These languages are moreover characterized by more

---

[1] Pallas, Voyages, vol. iv. p. 90; H. u. K. Aubel, Ein Polarsommer, p. 258.

or less strict laws of euphony. In Moschka, however, the harmony of vowels is not so fully developed as in Turkish or Finnish, or more probably it has been obliterated by foreign influences. Yet distinct traces of these phonetic laws have been preserved.[2] Two consonants never occur at the beginning or end of a word, and the principal vowel determines the terminal vowel.[3] These remarkable points of resemblance may perhaps have been developed at a later period, but the burden of proof lies with those who maintain this opinion. A common origin is not so certain in the case of these languages as in that of the Aryan group, and the wide separation between the Mongolian and Mandschu languages seems very suspicious to some people.[4] On the other hand, we must not forget that none of these nations possess any ancient literature. Were we able to compare the languages in their earlier form, we should readily ascertain whether we were or were not justified in uniting them into a whole.

To the Tungus branch of this group belong in the first place the Mandschu, who conquered the Chinese empire in 1644, and founded a sovereign dynasty. The other Tungus tribes have received the name of Orotshongs, or reindeer herdsmen. Some Tungus call themselves Boji, or men, others again Donki, or people. The Tungus of the shores of Okotsk are called Lamuts from *lamu*, the sea. The Tshapodghirs have penetrated further to the west than any other Tungus, namely, to between the Yenesei and Tunguska, while there are other Tungus tribes as far north as the bay of Chatanga on the Frozen Ocean. It is impossible to point out any contributions of these nations towards the civilization of our species, though it is probable that the Chinese may have learnt from the Tungus some things which we now attribute to their own invention.

The Mongols are the second branch of Northern Asiatics. They are sometimes called Tatars, and sometimes, on account of

---

[2] A. Ahlquist, Mokscha-mordwinische Grammatik, § 14, p. 3. Petersburg, 1861.

[3] A. Castrèn, Ethnologische Vorlesungen über die altaischen Völker, p. 18. Petersburg, 1857.

[4] Whitney, Language, p. 315; compare with this W. Schott in the Abhandlungen der Berliner Akademie, pp. 267 and 285. 1869.

a pun made by St. Louis, Tartars. This term must no longer be used in ethnological writings, for it has been so often misapplied, and has become so ambiguous, that we are obliged to infer from the context, if not actually to guess, whether by Tatars we are to understand Turks or Mongols. The term Mongolian was long of very vague application in the language of ethnology. We have a double list of these hordes which were originally called Mongols and those which were subsequently falsely so termed.[5] History applied this name to the hordes which invaded the West under Gengis Khan and his successors, of whom the greater number spoke Turkish.

Ethnologists now reckon but four branches of true Mongols: the Eastern Mongols, the Kalmucks, the Buriats, and the Hazara or Aimauq. To the Eastern Mongols the Chinese originally gave the nickname of Tata, and it was only later, that is, since the eighth century, that they were called Mungku (Mongols).[6] They inhabit the eastern half of the Gobi, and are divided into two hordes, the Schara towards the south, and their northern neighbours the Kalka. These people being destitute of history we cannot point out any services which they have rendered to civilization. The next branch, the Kalmucks,[7] call themselves the Ölöts, the peculiar people, or Durban oirad, the four allies. The names of these hordes are the Dzungar, Turgut, Choshod, and Turbet. A Kalmuck kingdom was founded in 1671, but it lasted less than a century, and then fell under the Chinese rule. The Kalmucks have continued their migrations to within the most recent times. They first reached European Russia in 1616, and a portion of them wandered back to China in 1771, amid untold perils and hardships. Some hordes have also swarmed out across the southern border of the Gobi.[8]

The Buriats are distinguished from the latter only in language.

---

[5] F. von Erdmann, Temudschin der Unerschütterliche, p. 168.

[6] Castrèn, Vorlesungen, p. 37.

[7] This name is sometimes derived from the Turkish word *Khalimak*, those left behind; sometimes from the Mongolian *Gholaimak*, fire-horde, or again from *Kalmuck*, fiery people. Fiadoff in Journal of Anthr. Institute, vol. iv. p. 401.

[8] After the fall of the Yuen dynasty a swarm of Kalmucks, made up of Dzungars, Turguts, and Choshods, migrated to Koko-noor. Howorth in the Journal of the Anthropological Institute, vol. i. p. 232.

These lived at Lake Baikal and in its vicinity at the time of Gengis Khan, and with no great opposition subjugated the Cossacks in 1644. These three Mongolian branches have all accepted Buddhism, though retaining their Shamanistic juggleries. They are very phlegmatic, good-humoured people. The appearance in their midst of Gengis Khan, who was destined to raise himself from a humble origin to be a mighty conqueror, was therefore the more extraordinary.

Far removed from the rest of the Mongolian brotherhood are the Hazara, who lead a nomadic life between Herat and Cabul, and spoke Mongolian as late as the time of the Sultan Baber.[9] Their physiognomy is also so distinctly Mongolian in type, that travellers have never differed as to their ethnographical position. The Hazara are divided into western and eastern tribes, of which the former are Sunnites and the latter Shiites. The western Hazara are sometimes called Aimauq, but this word is equivalent to horde,[10] and, as it has been applied to other Mongolian tribes also, we recommend its future disuse in ethnology.

The Tungus and Mongols are few in number, and many of their tribes are dying out. The case is quite different with the Turks, the third branch of the Northern Asiatic group. According to the old oriental traditions, one of Japhet's eight sons was named Turk. He dwelt on the Ili and Issikol, and from one of his descendants sprang the twins Tatar and Mongol. We must regard legends such as these as attempts at ethnological classification, and they show how nearly related the Central Asiatics held themselves to be. The Turks of the West have so much Aryan and Semitic blood in them that the last vestiges of their original physical characters have been lost, and their language alone indicates their previous descent. Turcomans, Uzbeks, Nogaians, and Kirghiz, on the other hand, approximate to the Mongols; from whom the Buruts and Kiptshaks differ only in the colour of the face. So says Vambéry; but he adds that the grammar of the Mongolian language is by no means identical with that of the Turkish, although it has adopted three-fourths of the vocabulary.[11]

---

[9] Fr. Spiegel, Eránische Alterthümer, vol. i. p. 344.
[10] Castrèn, Vorlesungen, p. 42.   [11] Geschichte Bochara's, vol. i. p. 130.

It is now usual to distinguish the following nationalities of the Turks: Uighurs, Uzbeks, Osmanlis, Yakuts, Turcomans, Nogaians, Basians, Kumuks, Karakalpaks, and Kirghiz. In the story of the journey of the Grecian ambassador Zemarchus, A.D. 569, mention is made of a Turkish Khân, called by the Byzantines Dissabulos, and by the Chinese Ti-theu-pu-li, who had set up his court at Talas, an important commercial town of the middle ages, in the present Burut territory.[12] This old Turkish kingdom was destroyed by the Uighurs, or, as they are called by the Chinese, Kaotsche, a moderately civilized people who have retained traces of Zoroastrian doctrines, but who were later converted to Buddhism [13] and finally to Islam. In the fifth century they already wrote and had a literature of their own; they inhabited the two slopes of the Thianshan, part of which they still occupy. Their present western neighbours are the Uzbeks, a Turkish tribe, named after Uzbek, a chief of the Golden Horde (1312–1342); these have some Mongolian blood. This tribe at its first appearance in history inhabited the northern end of the Caspian Sea, from whence it spread under the descendants of Timur to the Sir Daria; [14] after the sixteenth century it conquered Turkestan, and it is still the predominant tribe in the Khanates of Khiva, Bokhara, and Kokand, as well as in Kashgaria. The Seldschuks, who in A.D. 1030 yet inhabited the present Turcoman desert, came from the same regions, breaking in on the west, and afterwards, as Osmanlis, appearing as conquerors in three quarters of the world.

With some exaggeration it has been said that an Osmanli from Constantinople can make himself intelligible to a Yakut on the Lena. But it is certain that the branches of the Turkish language separated by this enormous distance are strangely alike. The hardiness of the Yakuts has already been mentioned. The American traveller Kennan, not only describes them as industrious people, but adds that of all the aborigines of Siberia they are the only ones whose numbers do not diminish but increase. Their

---

[12] Menandri, Excerpta de legat. Corpus script. Hist. Byzant., ed. Niebuhr, pars i. pp. 295–302 and pp. 380–384.

[13] Stanislas Julien, Journal asiatique, p. 58.

[14] Vambéry, Geschichte Bochara's, vol. ii. pp. 35, 36.

language,[15] when Erman was in Siberia, had also become the universal means of communication for travellers and merchants, for Russians, Tungus, and Buriats, from Irkutsk to Ockotsk, and from the Frozen Ocean to the Chinese frontier.

The fifth branch above enumerated consists of the Turcomans in the steppes and deserts to the east of the Caspian, and south of Lake Aral; they were dreaded as kidnappers, who, on their excellent horses, were in the habit of surprising the villages of Khorassan in earlier times, and infested the shores of Mazenderan in their pirate boats, until the Russians suppressed this scandalous trade. They supplied the slave markets in Khiva, Bokhara, and Kokand, thus causing a constant intercrossing of Turkish and Erânian blood. This has probably taken place since the oldest times, for when the Turkish tribes conquered Kashgaria, Fergana, and Khorassan, they found ancient Persian town populations, the Tadshiks of modern ethnology, who by earlier travellers were also called Sarts; though Robert Shaw had deprecated such a confusion of terms. The Sarts of Kashgaria have indeed all the physical characteristics of Erânian descent, but they speak Turkish. Prior to Shaw, and quite independently, the German traveller, H. von Schlagintweit had recognized marks of Aryan descent in the town populations of Kashgaria.[16] Cases such as these, in which the language and the physical characters of a tribe assign it to different positions, stand to ethnology in much the same relation that pseudomorphic phenomena occupied towards mineralogy. If a crystal is dissolved by percolating water and carried away out of the matrix, another mineral penetrating into the cavity may fill it up and appear as a fictitious crystal. Analogously it happens that nations have adopted the language of an alien race, or, conversely, the language holds its ground in a country while the race is gradually altered by an admixture of blood.

The invading hosts which Central Asia from time to time sent into the West, here and there left behind them fragmentary populations, which the elevated valleys and tablelands of the Caucasus sheltered from extermination. Among these remnants of the

---

[15] Reise um die Erde, vol. iii. p. 51.

[16] H. von Schlagintweit, Indien und Hochasien, vol. ii. p. 40, and R. Shaw.

Turkish group are the Nogaians on the left bank of the Kuban and the island of Krim; the Basians on the east and west of Mount Elburz, in whose misfortunes Freshfield (the first person who ascended Mount Elburz) has endeavoured to enlist our sympathies; and, lastly, the Kumuks in the lower portion and on the right bank of the Terek, and on the shore of the Caspian Sea. Another Turkish tribe, the Karakalpaks, or Black-caps, has descended from their former home on the Volga to the lower portion of the Sir Daria. Lastly, the Kirghiz, that is to say, the three hordes between the Ural and Lake Balkash, including the Buruts, are of all Turks most nearly allied to the Mongols in their physical characters, and by their family names, such as Kyptshak, Argyn, Naiman, give evidence of Mongolian descent, or at least of intermixture with Mongols.[17] According to an interpretation given by Radloff, their name arose from the circumstance that one of their hordes was called *Kyrk*, the forty, and another *Jüs* (Dschiis) the hundred.[18] They call themselves Kasaks, or riders.

It is difficult to assign to the Turko-Mongolian nations their true rank in the history of civilization. It is certain that many of these tribes have remained nomadic even to the present day, and will probably disappear without having ever become stationary. The fairly advanced civilization of the Uzbeks in Kashgaria and Turkestan, and of the European Osmanlis, might be due to their admixture with Aryan and semi-Semitic races. But the early civilization of the old Uighurs and the social capabilities of the Yakuts, prove that the pure-bred Turkish tribes were also fully capable of the higher forms of social life. The invention of leather tents and the manufacture of felt, the breeding of horses as milch animals, the taming of the sheep with fat tails, and perhaps of the Bactrian camel, are achievements which are probably derived from Central Asia and a remote antiquity. Still it is hard to say to which branch of the Northern Asiatics these improvements in domestic life are to be ascribed.

The fourth division with which we have next to deal, consists of the nations of the multiform Finnish group, which is again divided

---

[17] W. Radloff, Türkische Volksliteratur in Südsibirien, vol. iii. p. 14.
[18] Zeitschrift für Erdkunde, vol. vi. p. 505. 1871.

into four branches, namely, the Ugrian, Bulgarian, Permian, and the true Finnish. Their original homes were in part more to the east and south than at present, in the Ural and Altai mountains, from which circumstance the race is often collectively termed the Ural-Altaic.[19] Under the head of Ugrians, Castrèn included the Ostiaks on the right bank of the Ob, the Voguls on the eastern slopes of the northern Urals, and the Magyars. A hundred years ago Saijnovics, a travelling companion of Hell, proved that the latter belonged to the Finnish family,[20] and a comparative grammar has thrown further light on the position of their language.[21] The Bulgarians on the Danube can no longer be placed in the Bulgarian branch, for according to language and physical characters, they belong to the Sclavonic family, and have also completely absorbed into themselves the remnants of the former Bulgarians of the middle ages. For while the Bulgarians of the Volga maintained their government until the thirteenth century, and their nationality until their permanent subjugation by the Czars of Moscow, the Bulgarians of the Danube forfeited their language in the tenth and their independence at the beginning of the eleventh century.[22] The inhabitants of the insulated Tsherimis, Mordvin, and Tshuvash districts on the Volga, who are quite surrounded by Russians, are Bulgarians. The name of the Tsherimis signifies in the Mordva language the Easterns. The Mordvins again call themselves Mokshans in the east, and Ersans in the west. Ruybroek called them Moxel, Merdas, and Merduas; and Herberstein called them Mordva. A more or less veiled paganism is found among them,[23] and their archaic peculiarities attract the attention of ethnologists. The Permian branch received its name from the Permians, who lived on the waters of the Kama, in Bjarmaland, as it was called in old Scandinavian.

---

[19] Comp. the travelling maps of Ujfalvy, Migrations des peuples touraniens, pp. 120 and 130.

[20] Saijnovics wrote a book in 1770, entitled Idioma Ungarorum et Lapponum idem esse.

[21] Michael Weske, Untersuchungen zur vergleichenden Grammatik des finnischen Sprachstammes. Leipzic, 1872.

[22] Robert Roesler, Romänische Studien, p. 239.

[23] Von Haxthausen, Studien über Russland, vol. ii. p. 16.

Their kinsmen are the Zirianians further north towards the Frozen Ocean, and the Votiaks on the north bank of the Viatka, who however call themselves Udy, or Ut-murt.

The fourth, which is the true Finnish branch, has spread over the northern and eastern shores of the Baltic Sea, and received from German neighbours its European appellation which is connected with Veen, turf or bogs.[24] They moreover call their country Suomi, swamp and sea-land, and themselves Suomalaisia.[25]

There is no longer any doubt that Tacitus and Ptolemy knew of these people under the name of Fenni and Phinni in or near their present place of abode.[26] Their dialects distinguish them into the Suomi on the Gulfs of Finland and Bothnia, the neighbouring Karelians, the Vesps, or North Tshud, on the south-western shores of Lake Ladoga, the Vods, or South Tshud, to the north-east of the town of Narva, both in course of extinction, the Krevins who have died out in Courland since 1846, the Livonians, now reduced to two thousand individuals, also in Courland on the Gulf of Riga, and the Ehsts a numerous and compact body. Allied to these tribes by consanguinity are the Lapps, or Kvans, of Scandinavia and Russia, whose language, in Castrèn's opinion, was only two thousand years ago the same as that of the Suomi. These only migrated to their present place of abode at a late period.[27]

The consanguinity of the Finnish group with the nations of the Mongolian race is most distinctly recognizable in the Voguls, who resemble the Kalmuks far more than is the case with the Ostiaks.[28] Carl Vogt recognized the characteristics of the Mongolian race even in the Lapps of Norway, in the narrow slit eyes, horizontally set, broad cheek-bones, wide mouth, short nose, and yellow complexion.[29] The Finns of the Baltic have borrowed from their Teutonic and Slavonic neighbours a number of words for civilized

---

[24] H. Guthe, Die Lande Braunschweig und Hannover, p. 62.

[25] Prof. Hjelt in the Verhandlungen der Berliner Gesellschaft für Anthropologie, p. 117. 1872. This derivation has recently been contested by Sjögren, and the proper name of the Finns is provisionally pronounced to be without explanation.

[26] Forbinger, Alte Geographie, vol. iii. p. 1124.

[27] Ujfaloy, Migrations des peuples touraniens, pp. 118–120.

[28] Castrèn, Vorlesungen, p. 128.   [29] C. Vogt, Nord-Fahrt, p. 166.

implements, and with the words the objects also. This gives an idea of their condition before the acquisition of these. The only domestic animals which they bred were dogs, horses, and oxen, and the only cereal which they cultivated was barley. In summer they lived in leather tents, in winter, like all Polar nations of the Old World, in semi-subterranean yourts. It is therefore possible that the Ostiaks and Voguls of the present day represent the state of their western kindred in olden times.[30] Unfortunately, the history of the language of the Baltic Finns does not extend beyond the year 1542. But their epic poems, collected in the Kalevala, certainly belong, at least in their present form, to a very recent period. While the Mongolian and Tungus dialects have remained more pure but also poorer, and the Mandschu has hardly freed itself from monosyllabism, in the Ugrian group, Magyar and the Finnish of the Baltic have almost reached the stage of the inflected languages.[31]

Besides these people the Bashkers, Meshtsheriaks, and Teptiars, on the European slopes of the Central and Southern Urals, speak Turkish languages, but are reckoned in the Finnish group on account of their physical characters, and must therefore be regarded as Turco-Finnish hybrid nations.

The fifth branch of the so-called Altaic group of nations, by the Russians termed Samoyeds, originally came from the Saian mountains, near the sources of the Yenesei and the Ob. We still find there the Samoyed Soiots, on the northern slopes of the Saian chain the Karagasses and Kamassintzi, and to the east of the Yenesei the Koibals.[32] From these, their southern kinsmen, the Samoyeds, have spread as breeders of reindeer to the north of the continent from the White Sea to the Bay of Chatanga. In ancient Yugria, on both sides of the Sea of Ob, lives the tribe of Yuraks, and further east the Tawgi. As the same family names occur among these northern Samoyeds as among the Kamassintzi of the south, the emigration must have taken place downwards

---

[30] Prof. Ahlquist über die Culturwörter in den westfinnischen Sprachen. Ausland, 1871. No. 31, p. 741 et seq.

[31] Whitney, Language and the Study of Language, p. 320.

[32] Pallas, Voyages, vol. iv. p. 433.

along the Yenesei. In point of language the Samoyeds are nearest allied to the Finnish division, and in this to the Bulgarian branch. Through fear of incest the Samoyeds do not intermarry with the Ostiaks of the same family names pointing to a near relationship.[33] It is very possible that in some future classification of nations the Samoyeds will not be ranked as a separate division of the Altaian family, but only as a branch of the Finnish. The term Altaian was originated, as we have observed, by Castrèn, and the supposition that even the Finns formerly inhabited the Altai mountains is based on the fact that names of waters in the Yenesei district, such as Oja, Yoga, Kolba, mean in Finnish and Lapp, brook, water, and fishing-water, and that in its upper course the Yenesei itself is called Kem, which signifies stream in the Finn language only, where it appears in the form of Kemi and Kymi.

V.—NORTHERN ASIATICS OF DOUBTFUL POSITION.

This chapter is not a description of a new group of the Mongolian family, but a candid confession that the system which we set forth is given in an incomplete condition, as there are three distinct tribes which cannot be included in any of the greater divisions. The first of these are the Ostiaks of the Yenesei, who have nothing in common with the Ostiaks of the Ob, except their ill-chosen name. They live on the upper course of the Yenesei as far as the confluence of the lower Tunguska, first on the left bank only and afterwards on the right also. Their language, which has nothing in common with the Ural-Altaic typical tongue, has six dialects, of which we will name only the Assan, Arinzi, and Kottish, the latter of which was spoken by only five persons in Castrèn's time. These Siberian tribes are now reduced to one thousand individuals and must inevitably die out, principally owing to the fact that hunting and fishing are their only means of livelihood.[1] In their physical constitution the Ostiaks of the Yenesei are, moreover,

---

[33] Castrèn, Vorlesungen, pp. 82, 84, and 107.
[1] Latham, Varieties, p. 268. Castrèn, Vorlesungen, pp. 87, 88.

in no way distinguished from their Siberian neighbours, so that they certainly belong to the Mongolian race, but occupy an independent position within it.

Both these remarks apply to the Yukagiri, who now live on the polar sea of Siberia, eastward of the Lena. In 1809, Hedenström found in the islands of New Siberia vestiges of former Yukagiri settlers who were even then extinct.[2] Their language is altogether different from that of the Ural-Altaic group.[3] They call themselves Andon domni.

It is far more difficult to define the position of the third race, which has given itself the name of Aino, or Ainu, the people. As we have already stated, they were the oldest inhabitants of the Japanese islands, but are now met with only in Yesso. With them must be classed the inhabitants of southern Saghalien, of the Kurile Islands, and the Giliaks on the Lower Amoor[4] and in northern Saghalien.[5] Their language has been pronounced akin to the Japanese, but without sufficient reason.[6]

At the sitting of the Anthropological Society of Berlin, December 16th, 1871, Herr von Brandt, the German Consul in Japan, exhibited photographs of Ainos, the expression of whose faces was very like that of the Japanese. The inhabitants of the island of Paramushir at the southern point of Kamtshatka, who speak a Kurilian dialect, have "obliquely slit eyes" which is one of the most easily recognizable characters of the Mongolian race.[7] The skulls of these people have almost the same index of breadth as those of the Japanese, namely, 76–78·8; but their index of height, 69–76, proves to be considerably lower, though this is not a very important difference.[8] We are far more puzzled by

---

[2] F. von Wrangell, Reisen längs der Nordküste von Siberien.

[3] Whitney, Study of Language, p. 330.

[4] Petermann's Mittheilungen, 1857, p. 305 ; 1860, p. 99.

[5] Wenjukow maintains on the contrary that the language of the Giliaks is different from that of the Tongus as well as of the Kurilians, who speak Aino.

[6] Whitney, Study of Language, p. 329.

[7] According to Russian authorities in the Zeitschrift der Wiener geogr. Gesellschaft, vol. xv. § 12, p. 558. 1872.

[8] Verhandlungen der Berliner Gesellsch. für Anthropologie, pp. 27–29. 1872.

their luxuriant growth of beard, the bushy, curly hair of the head, and general hirsuteness,[9] which latter, although not more abundant than in Europeans, is highly significant in the midst of smooth-skinned races. This peculiarity alone would suffice to separate the Ainos from other Asiatics as a distinct race, did not all our information respecting them depend on such scanty and cursory statements that only later and better-instructed ethnologists will be able to decide as to their position. It is not quite impossible that they may be related to the Aëta, for the Asiatic Papuans may have spread across the Loochoo Islands to the Kuriles. We do not make this conjecture with any confidence, but only in order that the dialects of the Aëta may be compared with the Aino languages. It is only when this investigation has led to some result, whether affirmative or negative, that their true position can be more satisfactorily assigned to the Aino.

VI.—THE BEHRING'S NATIONS.

Under this head we include a number of North Asiatic and American tribes which, for the most part, either inhabit the shores of Behring's Straits or have migrated, like the Eskimo, from its shores to Greenland. The name of Hyperborean Mongols, which Latham employed, is inapplicable to this group, as we mean it to include nations as far as the Straits of Juan de Fuca. Only some of these tribes are united by a common type of language. The physical characters are more satisfactory, for they form a transition from the Mongol-like Siberians to the aborigines of America. This transition justifies our intention of not separating the Americans as a distinct race, but of connecting them with the Mongolian Asiatics. All the people named have reddish or brownish dark-coloured skin, stiff cylindrical hair, and, with one exception, no beard, and scarcely any hair on the rest of the body.

(*a*) *Itelmes, or Kamtskadals.*—These characters together with their narrow slit eyes caused George Steller to describe the

---

[9] Blakiston, Journey in Yezo, in the Journal of the Royal Geographical Society, vol. xlii. p. 80.

Itelmes, or Kamtskadals, as of decidedly Mongoloid appearance.[1] The words of their language are found by the separable combination of roots ; and if Kennan is correct in his assertion that they use prefixes, they are distinguished by this from the Ural-Altaians as well as from the Eskimo.[2] They live chiefly by fishing; the dog, which they harness to sledges, is their domestic animal. In comparison with other Behring's nations, they are very unskilful sailors. Their only social institution was the duty of "vendetta" in the inhabitants of an Ostrog. The husband belonged to the family of his parents-in-law. Shamanism was in full force, though there was no actual caste of sorcerers, but each individual conjured the spirits at his own peril. Belief in a future life led frequently to suicide : fathers allowed themselves to be strangled by their children or were thrown to the dogs. It was supposed that the poor would be recompensed for their sufferings in the present world by superfluity in the next.[3] The musical talents of the Itelmes are of a very high order, for they have even composed part songs.[4] Steller saw dances and dramatic representations, which usually consisted of comic imitations of their foreign visitors. Adolph Erman praises their honesty, gentleness, and "innate refinement of manners."[5] Much that he tells us of their self-sacrificing hospitality is touching, and Kennan has recently experienced the same. In Steller's time water was their only beverage, so that the decoction made from the fly agaric can only have become customary at a later period.

(*b*) *Koriaks and Tshuktshi.*—Steller says of the Koriaks who live on the Sea of Okotsk and as far north as Kamtshatka, that in stature, face, hair, and the deep tones in which they speak, they are as like the Itelmes as "one egg is to another."[6] This can

---

[1] Steller, Kamtschatka, p. 298.

[2] Latham (Varieties, p. 274) asserts, without giving evidence, that the Kamtskadal language has some community in the vocabulary with Corean and Japanese. This is probably only in words of civilization which have been borrowed in intercourse.

[3] Steller, Kamtschatka, pp. 277, 294, 270, 271.

[4] Ibid. p. 332.

[5] Reise um die Erde, vol. iii. p. 422.

[6] Kamtschatka, p. 251.

only be true of the fishing population on the coast, for the Koriaks of the interior, who live a patriarchal life in tents on the produce of their herds of reindeer, are described as people of more than average height; they are therefore taller than the Itelmes, whom they do not resemble either in hospitality or in obliging and kindly treatment of strangers. In their physical characters, Kennan describes these tribes as of North American type.[7] Unlike most of the Behring's nations, they are untainted by erotic vices, and are at the same time jealous husbands. Unfortunately, they are only too fond of intoxicating themselves with the decoction of fly agarics, which, in spite of the strict prohibition of the Russian government, is brought to them by unconscientious merchants.

The old people of this tribe and of the Tshuktshi[8] allow their own children to kill them with lances, presumably believing that man will enter on a new life at the exact age at which he left the world, and that it is therefore better not to empty the cup to the dregs.

The Tuski, or Tshuktshi, are as closely related to the Itelmes in language as are Spaniards to Portuguese. They live in almost entire liberty on the coasts of the Behring's Straits breeding reindeer, and on the shores of the Frozen Ocean as fishermen. They are sometimes termed Reindeer Tshuktshi to distinguish them from the Namollo, with whom they were formerly combined. They are powerful men, able to walk lightly under burdens of 200 lbs. A Tshuktshi boy, whom Colonel Buckley took from Plover Bay to San Francisco, was always supposed to be a Chinese; the same mistake has been frequently made about two native Aleutian sailors in a town in which Chinese and Japanese are to be met with in every street.[9] In conclusion, the Tuski sail on the Behring's Straits in leathern boats with a framework of whalebone, and make use of a sail, probably in imitation of European ships. They tie inflated sealskins to the outside of the boats to guard against capsizing, after the manner of Polynesian outriggers.

(*c*) *The Namollo and the Eskimo.*—Quite at the north-eastern corner of Asia, on Behring's Straits, and along the Frozen

---

[7] Tent Life in Siberia, pp. 117 and 218.
[8] Whymper, Alaska, p. 98.   [9] Ibid. p. 273.

Ocean, the Tshuktshi border on the Namollo, with whom they were formerly confused. They differ little from their neighbours in manners and habits. Lütke [10] noticed their well-marked Mongolian features, prominent cheek-bones, small noses, and frequently obliquely set eyes. We also know that the Namollo language is allied to the Eskimo. [11] Chamisso, who had an opportunity of comparing the Namollo of the Gulf of St. Lawrence with the Eskimo in Kotzebue Sound, observes that the population of the north-east point of Asia as well as all Americans from Behring's Straits to the Eskimo of Baffin's Bay, belong to " the same race of men, with a conspicuously Mongolian form of face." [12] The Eskimo, whose name is derived from Esquimantsic in the Abenaki language, or from Ashkimeg in the Ojibwa dialect, which, in both cases, means " eaters of raw meat," [13] call themselves In-nu-it, a plural form of *in-nu*, the man. Their words are always formed by means of suffixes, [14] and so far the method is the same as in the Ural-Altaic group, though the most important character, the harmony of the vowels, is wanting in the Innuit language. Although the Eskimo language is in no exact sense incorporative, it will soon be shown that it is a transition between the Ural-Altaic and the American types. At the time of the visits of the Northmen to America, that is, about A.D. 1000, the Innuit lived somewhat to the south on the Atlantic coast ; and at the beginning of last century they might occasionally be seen in Newfoundland. [15] It was only in the middle of the fourteenth century that they appeared in Greenland. [16] Barnard Davis gives as the cranial indices of the Greenland Eskimo a breadth of 71 and a height of 75, and of the Eskimo of eastern North America, 70 and 75 for the same dimensions. But these characters are worthless, for the skull is artificially shaped. [17] In the case of the western Innuit, among whom this habit is supposed to be unknown, and who, therefore,

---

[10] Voyage autour du monde, vol. ii. p. 264. 1835.

[11] Waitz, Anthropologie, vol. iii. p. 301.

[12] Otto von Kotzebue's Entdeckunge Reise, vol. iii. p. 176. 1821.

[13] Charlevoix, Nouvelle France, vol. iii. p. 178.

[14] Steinthal, Typen des Sprachbaues, p. 220.   [15] Charlevoix.

[16] David Cranz, Historie von Grönland, vol. i. p. 333.

[17] See above, p. 58.

have skulls of natural form, 75 is the index of breadth, and 77 the index of height ; hence they are mesocephals in whom the height is greater than the breadth.[18] In other points the Innuit exactly resemble the northern Asiatic populations in all physical characters, especially in skin and hair. The oblique setting of the eyes, and the broad flat faces, are recognizable even in the Eskimo of Greenland,[19] although intermixtures with German blood have frequently taken place there. The Namollo and Eskimo are not tall people ; but we have already contradicted the old and erroneous statements as to their dwarfish size.[20] Their women are not prolific,[21] or rather productiveness is considered undesirable, so that this race also will not escape extinction.

Under the name of Angekoks we find among them genuine North Asiatic Shamans, who prepare themselves for their magic cures and incantations by such prolonged solitude and fasting that, as Cranz ingenuously remarks, "their imagination becomes disordered."[22] They worship a benevolent creator named Torngarsuk or Anguta.[23] When they hear the praises of an Almighty God from the mouths of missionaries, many of them imagine that their Torngarsuk is intended.[24] Opposed to him stands a baneful female deity said to be without a name. Not only do they believe in a future life, but also in a future punishment for malefactors and the unrighteous.[25] In their legends the Innuit tell of an Arctic paradise called Akillnek, and have narratives of travelling adventures, in which the oriental bird, the roc, is replaced by gigantic seagulls. Among them has also been found the story of the girls who, when bathing, turn, not into swans—which are unknown—but into ducks. Hall, who lived among them so long, says they are the best-hearted people on the face of the earth. Their intelligence is proved by the fact that they quickly learnt dominoes,

---

[18] Barnard Davis, Thesaurus Craniorum, pp. 219–224.
[19] Die zweite deustche Nordpolfahrt, vol. i. p. 135.
[20] See above, p. 81.
[21] D. Cranz, Historie von Grönland, vol. i. p. 212.
[22] Ibid. book iii. vol. i. p. 268.
[23] So called by Hall, Life with the Esquimaux, p. 524.
[24] David Cranz, vol. i. pp. 264, 265.
[25] Hall, Life with the Esquimaux, p. 524.

18

draughts, and even chess.[26] Leopold von Buch, when travelling in Arctic Norway, persuaded himself that human society could hope for no intellectual gains from the inhabitants of those regions where the full strength of man is consumed in the struggle against the asperity of nature to procure the bare necessaries of life. This would apply with far greater force to Polar America. The Eskimo, it is true, have not inferred the flattening of the earth from certain disturbances in the moon's course ; they have not analyzed water into its two component gases, nor have they founded a universal religion, but, relying on their own strength and skill, they have entered zones in which day and night are as long as seasons : they have proved that man can still hold his own where a nine months' winter turns the land to stone, where no tree can grow, and where there is not even enough drift wood to serve for the shaft of a spear. Of the bones of Arctic mammals killed in the chase, they have laboriously constructed sledges, and put together spears, which, lashed round with the sinews of animals, are sufficiently substantial to enable bold hunters to kill the white bear in close combat. They have found out how to build huts of snow as quickly as tropical natives build them of branches and leaves ; nay, they have constructed arched vaults of stone, which had not occurred to any of the civilized people of Mexico. They know how to warm their huts with train-oil lamps, and how to melt snow and ice over them that they may allay their thirst. They possessed in sledges, which were unknown in other parts of America, a means of accomplishing land journeys ; to move these they had harnessed to it draught animals, namely, dogs ; while in America, the most advanced stage of such art was to be found only among the Incas of Peru, who use llamas as beasts of burden, though not as draught animals. It is an achievement in the history of civilization to have peopled the highest latitudes of the earth, and the Eskimo performed this unenviable task when they were themselves still in the stone age. Now, indeed, they procure iron from the Danes for lance and harpoon points ; but Northern Greenland had long been inhabited by them before

---

[26] H. Rink, Eskimoisk Digtekonst, in For Ide og Virkelighed, p. 222 et seq. Copenhagen, 1870.

Europeans ventured to approach it. The first ship which penetrated into Baffin's Bay in 1616, under Captain Bylot, opened
a communication with the natives. It was only in 1818 that the
elder Ross, who was the second to enter those latitudes, appeared,
and in his track followed the whale-fishers, who brought with them
the first iron. But the Eskimo tribe which lives on the other side
of Smith's Bay has certainly been settled there for several generations, perhaps for centuries.

The Eskimo have contributed in no small degree to the increase
of European science by giving their assistance to both the older
and more recent explorers of the North-west Passage. Sir Edward
Parry was indebted to a remarkable Eskimo woman, Iligiuk, for a
map, which led to the discovery of the Fury and Hecla Straits.[27]
The Eskimo Hans, who accompanied the celebrated Kane, and
his successor Hayes, guided the sailor Morton to beyond the
eighty-first latitude, the most northerly point ever reached on the
coast of Greenland. When we follow the records of the older and
newer explorers in the regions of the North-west Passage, and see
their ships shut in by the winter ice, and the Arctic night, which is
to last three or four months, begins, we cannot help fearing that
the European, notwithstanding his control over matter and force,
may be unable to cope with the severity of Nature, and that his
life and liberty must depend on the caprice of the coming season ;
then when the cry resounds on board ship, " The Eskimo have
come ! " it seems as if the portals of the Arctic prison-house were
opened by a friendly hand. Like assistants in the darkness appear
beings of our species, whose cheerfulness is unaffected by cold and
obscurity, and who contentedly wander and range over regions in
which Nature seems armed with all the horrors of one of the
circles in Dante's hell.[28]

We need not say much of their skill on the sea. It is well
known that they have two sorts of vessels ; some large and
capacious, the so-called women's boats (Umiak), in which families

---

[27] Captain Lyon's Private Journal, pp. 160 and 226. Hall has made copies
of two Eskimo maps, which could scarcely have been drawn more true to
nature by Europeans.

[28] Inferno, xxxii. v. 22–30.

travel from place to place, and the men's boats (Kayak), in which a single hunter goes in search of sea animals. The English and the Americans of the United States are the ablest judges of the build and management of boats. Both, however, speak with admiration, and almost with envy, of the Eskimo who, with his double paddle and sense of balance worthy of a tight-rope dancer, makes his Kayak dance over the waves.

The identity of their language with that of the Namollo, their skill on the sea, their domestication of the dog, their use of the sledge, the Mongolian type of their faces, their capability for higher civilization, are sufficient reasons for answering the question, whether a migration took place from Asia to America or conversely from America to Asia, in favour of the former alternative ; yet such a migration from Asia by way of Behring's Straits must have occurred at a much later period than the first colonization of the New World from the Old one.

Akin to the Namollo and the Eskimo both in language and in blood are the inhabitants of the northern and western portion of what was formerly Russian America, who have also been called Alaskan Eskimo. They live on the shores of Behring's Straits, on the peninsula of Alaska, and the adjoining coast towards the east, nearly as far as Mount St. Elias. They are divided into thirteen tribes : the Koniaks, or Konaks, of the island of Kodiak, the Tshugatshi on Prince William's Sound and the peninsula of Kenai, and eleven others, the names of which all end in *mjuts* or *mutes*.[29] To the latter belong Whymper's Malemutes who, like all the rest, are distinguished from the Eskimo and Namollo only by their dialect. Men of six feet high may be seen among them, so that the dimensions vary considerably in this race. Trade has always been carried on between the Behring's nations of Asia and America. The Tshuktshi pass over to Diomedes Island, and the Malemutes cross from the extreme north-westerly point of America, to exchange reindeer's hides for furs. The trade is so brisk that the clothing of the natives several hundred miles up the Yukon river consists of Asiatic skins obtained from the Tshuktshi.[30]

---

[29] For their names see Waitz, Anthropologie, vol. iii. p. 301.

[30] Whymper, Alaska, p. 149.

O. von Kotzebue, who sailed along both shores of Behring's Straits remarks that the inhabitants of St. Lawrence's Island speak the same language as the tribes on the American coast, and call them brothers. "Altogether," he says in another passage, "I find so little difference between these two peoples that I am much inclined to consider them as derived from the same stock."[31] Similarly George Steller states that the inhabitants of Choumagin Islands, on the south coast of Alaska, are as like the Itelmes of Kamtshatka as one egg is to another.[32] All this goes to prove that migrations took place from the Old World to the New. On the other hand, it is not likely that the Eskimo spread from America to Asia, because of all Americans they have preserved the greatest resemblance in racial characters to the Mongolian nations of the Old World, and in historical times their migrations have always taken place in an easterly direction.

(*d*) *Aleutians.*—Between the peninsulas of Alaska and Kamt-shatka lies, in regular curve, a chain of volcanic islands, destitute of trees and generally enveloped in mist. They are called the Aleutians, as are their inhabitants. The latter are connected with the Eskimo only by a number of words common to both, which may however have been merely interchanged ; in other respects their language is isolated.[33] They are a Mongolian race[34] whose precocious marriages we have already mentioned.[35] All the Behring's nations are more or less good sailors, but the Aleutians seem to excel even the Eskimo in dexterity. Their hide canoes for one person are, as Erman informs us, about 60lbs. in weight, and when occupied by an Aleutian weighing 140lbs. draw so little water that the section submerged offers only 0·056 metre's resisting surface. With a

---

[31] Entdeckungsreise in die Südsee, vol. ii. p. 105, and vol. i. p. 159.

[32] Steller, Kamtschatka, p. 297.

[33] According to the short sketch given by Lütke (Voyage autour du monde, vol. i. p. 243), in the structure of their words they also use prefixes, which are totally wanting in the Innuit language.

[34] A German traveller (Allgemeine Zeitung, p. 4300. 1873) is induced by the form of their face to consider them as descended from castaway Japanese.

[35] The same erotic views are prevalent among them (Langsdorff, Reise um die Welt, vol. ii. p. 43; W. H. Dale, Alaska, p. 402) as among the Namollo (Lütke, vol. ii. p. 197), the Itelmes (Steller), and the Reindeer Tshuktshi (Wrangel).

canoe of this sort a native accomplished 214·8 kilometres, or rather more than 132 miles in 27½ hours, while a pedestrian could at most carry a weight of 60lbs. twelve miles in a day, and would therefore require eleven days to go the same distance.[36] The canoe enables the Aleutians to rival the speed of the largest marine animals, and the pursuit of these forms a part of his daily means of sustenance.[37]

(*e*) *Thlinkites and Vancouver Tribes.*—On the coast south of Mount St. Elias, and on the islands on the coast as far as Dixon's Sound, dwell people whom the Russians term Kaliushes, or Kolushes, but who call themselves Thlinkites, or "men." To the south of them live the Haidahs of Queen Charlotte's Island. On the opposite mainland, the Hailtsa, or Hailtsuk, extend from latitude 53½ to 50°. Some tribes, such as the Cowitshin and Clalam, inhabit not only Vancouver's Island, but also the mainland on the Frazer River and Puget Sound. It is difficult to procure skulls from this coast district, nor could they afford us much instruction, for in Vancouver, as in Oregon, it is the fashion to disfigure them artificially; and the process is not confined to mere flattening, but dolichocephalism is artificially produced.[38] The complexion is almost as fair as in Southern Europeans, but the hair is black and stiff.

Among the Thlinkites and Haidahs [39] a little more beard occasionally appears than is otherwise the case among Asiatic and American Mongols. Very prominent cheek-bones, a depressed base of the nose, and wide, fleshy snub-noses still prevail.[40] The Tshinuks who live in Oregon to the south of Puget Sound, and who flatten the head artificially, still have the obliquely slit Mongoloid eyes,[41] which on the other hand are wanting in the Haidahs. The

---

[36] A. Erman in der Zeitschrift für Ethnologie, vol. iii. § 3, p. 167. 1871.

[37] An accurate drawing of the structure of this excellent vessel is given by Langsdorff, Reise um die Welt, vol. ii. p. 39.

[38] Barnard Davis, Thesaurus Craniorum, p. 231.

[39] R. Brown in the Reports of the British Association held at Norwich in 1868, p. 133.

[40] Also among the Kolushes according to Von Langsdoff, Reise um die Welt, vol. ii. p. 96.

[41] Waitz, Anthropologie, vol. iii. p. 324.

inhabitants of the coast are not one in language with the people on the other side of the Rocky Mountains, nor have they even a common language among themselves. But as the physical characters do not admit of any separation into different races, and an observer such as Lütke expressly says, that the inhabitants of Queen Charlotte's Islands are not to be distinguished in this respect from the people living on the shores of the Behring's Sea, it seems best to class them with the inhabitants of the extreme north-east of Asia, especially as they resemble these in manners and customs far more than the hunting tribes beyond the Rocky Mountains. They also are good sailors, and know how to build vessels of graceful and well-considered lines. However, it is without doubt the nature of the coast which has evoked and developed their skill on the sea, and hence we must not ascribe it to a tendency of the race and therefore infer a common descent. In the same way the custom of piercing the cheeks or lips and inserting small plugs, which is common to the coast populations of America from Kotzebue Sound to Vancouver Island, would at the most indicate that a close reciprocal intercourse has caused the spread of this vitiated taste. The American Behring's nations were acquainted with iron prior to the arrival of the Russians and Captain Cook's visits to the coast. Provisionally, and until thorough researches enable us to suggest any thing better, we may suppose that Japanese, who visited the Kuriles and Kamtshatka before the Russians, brought to the North iron or iron utensils, which thence spread to America by the trade between the shores. With the exception of the Kolushes, whose conjugal morality is praised by Von Langsdorff,[42] we find among all the Behring's nations, even among the Eskimo, erotic vices of the worst description, disregard of conjugal fidelity, the resignation of wives and sisters in token of hospitality to a guest, and at the same time precocious marriages.[43] If George Steller was right in ascribing the tendency to such aberrations to the predominance of fish as the staple food, this character common to the Behring's nations is attributable to their place of abode. We find among them all more or less taste for art, which shows itself in carving. Among the Kolushes every

---

[42] Reise um die Welt, p. 113.   [43] See above, p. 397, note [35].

large vessel bears the name of some object, generally an animal, a figure of which adorns the bows. Any peculiarly successful decorations of this sort are much esteemed and are rewarded with a slave.[44] Among the Haidah of the Charlotte Islands, again, the nobles bear copper shields, on which are engraved crests.[45] They are also very fond of dramatic dances and theatrical representations, which are performed with masks, as is the case with the Thlinkites, and even some tribes in Oregon,[46] as well as with all the inhabitants of Vancouver's Island.[47] Social conditions were far more highly developed among the Thlinkites and Vancouver tribes than on the other side of the Rocky Mountains. The houses were stationary, which was necessitated by the fishery, and were sometimes like barracks. The chiefs possessed great power; a distinction into nobles and plebeians had arisen, and slavery existed among the Kolushes, the Haidahs, and the Vancouver tribes.

VII.—THE ABORIGINES OF AMERICA.

If the human species has peopled the world from a single centre of creation, and if its cradle is not in America, the New World must have received its first inhabitants from the Old. When they entered the Western Continent they were certainly still in a very barbarous stage, although their language possessed the rudiments of its future character, and although they may have known how to produce fire, and used bows and arrows. We cannot suppose that these immigrants made long voyages, but at most that they crossed Behring's Straits. It is not impossible that the first migrations took place at a time when what is now the channel of Behring's Straits was occupied by an isthmus. The climate of those northern shores must then have been much milder than at the present day, for no currents from the Frozen Ocean could have penetrated into the Pacific. That the severance of Asia

---

[44] Lütke, Voyage autour du monde, vol. i. p. 212.   W. Dale, Alaska, pp. 413 and 417.
[45] R. Brown, as above.   [46] Waitz, Anthropologie, vol. iii. p. 335.
[47] Whymper, Alaska, p. 58.

from America was, geologically speaking, very recent, is shown by the fact that not only the straits [1] but the sea which bears the name of Behring is extraordinarily shallow, so much so indeed that whalers lie at anchor in the middle of it.[2] But it is always dangerous to rely on geological events which themselves require more accurate proof. We therefore prefer to assume that at the time at which the Asiatics passed over into America, Behring's Straits already possessed their present character. We must, however, remember the first question which Gauss the great mathematician addressed in 1828, at Berlin, to Adalbert von Chamisso the circumnavigator, namely, whether the coast of America was visible from any point in Asia, that in such a way the two worlds might be connected by a triangle. Chamisso was able to answer this query in the affirmative,[3] so that no accidental discovery need be supposed, for the Asiatics of Behring's Straits, when they crossed over to America, saw their goal before their eyes. Luxurious Europeans, indeed, think it strange that people whom we must suppose still without any means of protection, could have continued to exist in a climate so severe. But they forget that the children of the north are more comfortable in severe weather than in a milder temperature. " When, in winter mornings," wrote George Steller, " I was freezing under my featherbed and fur coverlets, I saw the Itelmes, and even their little children, lying in their *kuklanka* naked and bare half-way down the chest, without coverlets or featherbeds, and yet were warmer to the touch than I was." In another place he adds that the Kamtskadals always place a large vessel filled with water, which they cool with pieces of ice, by their side at night, and drain this to the last drop before the break of day. But the case of the Fuegians is yet more convincing, for the first immigrants to America were probably as undeveloped as these people, many of whom endure all weathers in total nudity. Darwin, who saw a woman in this state, adds, " It was raining heavily, and the fresh water, together with the spray, trickled down her body. In another harbour not far distant, a woman

---

[1] Lütke, Voyage autour du monde, vol. ii. p. 209.

[2] Whymper, Alaska, p. 94.

[3] Chamisso, Gesammelte Werke, vol. i. p. 146.

who was suckling a recently born child came one day alongside the vessel, and remained there out of mere curiosity, whilst the sleet fell and thawed on her bosom, and on the skin of her child."

A few pages further on he says again, " We were well clothed, and though sitting close to the fire were far from too warm ; yet these naked savages, though further off, were observed, to our great surprise, to be streaming with perspiration at undergoing such a roasting."[4] This is sufficient to convince any one that even for beings on the level of the Fuegians, a climate such as that of Behring's Straits would not impede a migration from Asia to America.

But the proof that the aborigines of America took this road consists in their Mongoloid characters. In the last chapter it was shown that the Asiatic and American tribes of Behring's Straits are so much alike as to be mistaken for one another. In the United States even adherents of the doctrine of the plurality of the human species have admitted that all the aborigines of America resemble each other as much as "full-blooded Jews," and that the Mongolian is the only race with which they can properly be closely connected.[5] A. von Humboldt, moreover, attributes to the natives of Mexico all the Mongolian characters, with the sole exception of the nose, even the obliquely set eyes,[6] which latter peculiarity he also ascribes to the Chayma in the north-east of Venezuela.[7] The obliquely set eyes and prominent cheek-bones of the inhabitants of Veragua were noticed by Moritz Wagner, and according to his description, out of four Bayano Indians from Darien, three had thoroughly Mongolian features, including the flattened nose.[8] James Orton the traveller was also struck by the likeness of the Zaparo of the Napo River, east of the Cordilleras of Quito, to the Chinese.[9] In 1866 an officer of the *Sharpshooter*, the first English man-of-war which entered the Paraná River in Brazil, remarks in almost the same words of the Indians of that district,

---

[4] A Naturalist's Journey round the World, pp. 213, 220.

[5] Morton, Types of Mankind, p. 275.

[6] Essai politique sur la Nouvelle Espagne, vol. i. p. 381.

[7] Reisen in die Æquinoctialgegenden, vol. ii. p. 13.

[8] Naturwissenschaftliche Reisen, vol. i. pp. 128 and 313.

[9] The Andes and the Amazon, p. 170.

that their features vividly reminded him of the Chinese.[10]   Burton describes the Brazilian natives at the falls of Cachauhy as having thick, round Kalmuck heads, flat Mongol faces, wide, very prominent cheek-bones, oblique and sometimes narrow-slit Chinese eyes, and slight moustachios.[11]   Another traveller, J. J. von Tschudi, declares in so many words that he has seen Chinese whom at the first glance he mistook for Botocudos, and that since then he has been convinced that the American race ought not to be separated from the Mongolian.[12]   His predecessor, St. Hilaire,[13] noticed narrow, obliquely set eyes and broad noses among the Malali of Brazil.   Reinhold Hensel,[14] says of the Coroados that their features are of Mongoloid type, due especially to the prominence of the cheek-bones, but that the oblique position of the eyes is not perceptible.   Yet the oblique opening of the eye, which forms a good though not an essential characteristic of the Mongoloid nations, is said to be characteristic of all the Guarani tribes in Brazil.[15]   Even in the extreme south, among the Hiullitches of Patagonia, King saw a great many with obliquely set eyes.[16]

Those writers who separate the Americans as a peculiar race fail to give distinctive characters, common to them all, which distinguish them from the Asiatic Mongols.   All the tribes have stiff, long hair, cylindrical in section.   The beard and hair of the body is always scanty or totally absent.[17]   The colour of the skin varies considerably, as might be expected in a district of 110° of latitude ; it ranges from a slight South European darkness of complexion among the Botocudos to the deepest dye among the Aymara,[18]

[10] Nautical Magazine, vol. xxxvi. p. 564.   London, 1867.

[11] R. Burton, Highlands of Brazil, vol. ii. p. 403.

[12] Reisen durch Südamerika, vol. ii. p. 299.

[13] Voyage au Brésil, vol. i. p. 424.

[14] Zeitschrift für Ethnologie, vol. iii. p. 128.   1869.

[15] Orbigny, L'homme américain, p. 62.

[16] Latham, Varieties, p. 415.

[17] This was remarked even by the Jesuit Charlevoix (Nouvelle France, vol. iii. p. 311) and Catlin (North American Indians, p. 328) and more recently by Musters (Among the Patagonians, p. 172).   That bearded men appear occasionally among the Comantschs, will surprise no one who knows how many Spanish women these predatory hordes have carried off into slavery.

[18] See above, p. 89.

or to copper red in the Sonor tribes.[19] But no one has tried to draw limits between races on account of these shades of colour, especially as they are of every conceivable gradation. American skulls often have projecting jaws, but, as in the Asiatic Mongols, prognathism is never very great. Pruner Bey[20] states that the shape of the American skull is very variable. "The heads of the Botocudos," he continues, "do not differ essentially from the Chinese; those of the Toltec nations are like those of the Javanese, and those of the New Zealanders may be compared with those of the Redskins." According to Welcker's skull measurements, the average breadth varies from 74 in Brazilians to 80 in Caribs and Patagonians. Thus they vary as much as in the Asiatic Mongolian group. Yet, except in the case of the Araucanians,[21] Barnard Davis has not ventured to state the proportions of breadth and height in the case of the aboriginal population of America, although a considerable number of skulls were at his disposal. But on both continents the children's heads are shaped by artificial means. This was customary in North America not only among the Flatheads of Vancouver's Island and Oregon,[22] but occurred also among the Algonkin tribes in the east of the United States.[23] In the southern continent this practice obtained among all the civilized nations of the Andes, and hence we find in skulls of the Muysca, the old inhabitants of Quito and Peru, indices of breadth as high, and even higher, than 100. At present, therefore, it is impossible to say within what limits the breadth and height of uninjured American skulls vary ; but the few individual tribes in which it has been accomplished proved to be mesocephalic or brachycephalic, as was to be expected, if they belong to the Mongolian race.

The narrow-slit and often obliquely set eyes, which have been remarked in individual tribes in both continents as far as the

[19] Waitz, Anthropologie, vol. iv. p. 200.

[20] Resultats de craniométrie. Mem. de la Société d'Anthropologie, vol. ii. p. 13.

[21] Breadth 80, height 80. Thesaurus Craniorum, ɪ. 357.

[22] See above, p. 398.

[23] Hence the French called the tribes with artificially and entirely round skulls "têtes de boule." Charlevoix, Nouvelle France, vol. iii. p. 324.

extreme south, may be regarded as a mark of Mongolian ancestry (atavism). Although they are not essential marks of all the nations of Northern Asia, they occur only in the Mongolian race, for Fritsch has now satisfactorily proved that they do not occur in Hottentots, and that their limited local appearance in Australia may be attributed to a mixture of Malay blood.[24] In only one physical character some American tribes differ from the Asiatic Mongols. A small snub nose with a low bridge is typical in the latter; whereas in the hunting tribes of the United States, and especially among the chiefs, we meet with high noses. It is known, moreover, that the Mexicans and other civilized nations of Central America, represented the faces of their gods with very prominent noses, so that some few individuals among these also must have had this marked feature. This deviation from the Mongol type occurs in South America even in high latitudes: among the extinct Abipones, as well as among the Patagonians of the present day, the so-called eagle nose was and is no rarity. But a peculiarity which appears only locally, and is not common to all the aborigines of the New World, can not be regarded as characteristic of race.

A complete separation of the American from the Asiatic Mongols could only be founded on the internal diversity of the languages. Yet the greatest divisions in the present system have been based on physical characters. We will now inquire whether the type of their languages does not clearly indicate that the Americans, before their immigration into the New World, were in the same stage of development as the Ural-Altaic nations. As we have already seen, the American languages are peculiar in that the structure of the sentence is merged in the form of the word, on which account they have been called polysynthetic. If this is true, it has been a great mistake to attribute an entirely isolated position to the Innuit language. Like the Ural-Altaic languages, it employs suffixes only for the definition of meaning, but it is also capable of forming a complex sentence in a single word; in other words, it is polysynthetic. The Greenlander uses a single word to express the idea,

---

[24] See above, p. 322.

"he says that you, also, are going in haste to buy a beautiful knife."[25] But it is most important to recollect that this loose combination of roots is not genuine incorporation, for in the American languages the connected syllables are always curtailed of some sounds. Steinthal, as we have seen,[26] says that the fullest development of incorporation is in the Mexican Nahuatl language, which places the object between the subject and the verb, and resolves all the three into one whole. But this method is not quite peculiar to American languages, for it occurs also in the Ural-Altaic family, in the Ugrian and Bulgarian groups, in the Magyar, Ostiak, Vogul, and Mordvin languages. In the last of these, and also in the Moksha dialect, the inflected words and objective personal pronouns are closely interwoven in the Mexican manner.[27] This fact shows us that, in the midst of strictly suffix languages, some adopted incorporation : we here see the internal relationship of the American and the Ural-Altaic languages.

There are many inventions, customs, and myths common to Northern Asiatics and the natives of America. We need not attach much weight to the fact that the leathern tent occurs on both continents, for no great thought was required in its invention. The resemblance in all points of the Siberian Shaman to the North American medicine-man is of less importance, from the fact that the Shamans of other quarters of the world correspond as closely. It is more significant that the war dances and Shamanistic customs of the Ostiaks are repeated in a minutely identical form by the Kolushes.[28] Many of the legends of the Old World have reached the New. The story of an adventurer who climbs up to heaven by a high tree, and then lets himself down again, either by a leathern strap, by a wisp of straw, or by tresses of hair, and sometimes by the column of smoke from a hut, is told by the Ugrian tribes,[29] and by the Athabaskan Dogrib Indians of the extreme north of

---

[25] Knife beautiful to buy go   haste will likewise thou also he says.
    sauig- ik-   sini- aṛiaṛtok- asuar- omar-   y- oṭil- tog- og.

[26] See above, p. 124.

[27] In Moksha *palasamak* means, thou kissest me, and *palaftärämak*, if thou wouldst not have kissed me. Ahlquist, Mokscha-mordwinische Grammatik, p. 60. Petersburg, 1868.

[28] Adolf Erman, Reise um die Erde, vol. i. p. 675.   [29] Ahlquist, p. 109.

America.[30] Legends, however, float like winged seeds over wide regions, and are therefore of little weight as evidence of common descent; still they indicate an ancient intercourse. It is far less likely that superstitious ideas should have been thus interchanged. But the Itelmes of Kamtshatka consider it very sinful to take up a burning stick otherwise than with the fingers, as, for instance, with the point of a knife;[31] and in the same manner it is forbidden to the Sioux or, more properly, the Dahcotas, to take glowing brands or embers from the fire with an awl or a knife.[32] Charlevoix relates that the tribes on Hudson's Bay show great respect to the bear.[33] When they have killed one of these animals his head is painted over with great ceremony, and songs of praise are sung in honour of the victim. Throughout Siberia bears are held in respect. The Giliaks on the Amoor,[34] the Aino,[35] the Yenesei Ostiaks,[36] and lastly, the true Ostiaks, have the same feeling; these last hang the skin of the animal on a tree, pay it homage in every way, and beg the animal's pardon for having killed it. They also swear by the bear.[37] It may be suggested that this similarity of habit is also due to intercourse at some past period, but if so, it is very suspicious that useful inventions, such as the manufacture of earthenware, were not also diffused by this intercourse; but, when first visited by Europeans, the Itelmes of Kamtshatka, the Aleutians, the Kolushes, and in part the Assiniboins, cooked only by means of stones.[38]

It has never been disputed that, according to their physical characters, the peoples of America belong to a single race, but there are also many mental features common to the inhabitants of both parts of the continent. The similarity of the North American

[30] Tylor, Early History of Mankind, p. 443.

[31] Steller, Kamtschatka, p. 274.

[32] Tylor, Early History of Mankind, p. 354.

[33] Nouvelle France, vol. iii. p. 300.

[34] Petermann's Geogr. Mittheilungen, p. 305. 1857.

[35] Watson in *Nature*, April 2, 1872, p. 424.

[36] Castrèn, Ethnologische Vorlesungen, p. 88.

[37] Pallas, Voyages; Erman (Reise um die Erde) records precisely the same, vol. i. p. 670.

[38] See above, p. 167.

medicine-man and the Shaman of Brazil has already been mentioned.[39] The remarkable masquerades witnessed by Spix and Martius, and more recently by Bates, among the Tecuna tribes on the Amazon,[40] we have already found among the Kolushes;[41] they recur again among the Aht of Vancouver's Island,[42] and the Moqui Indians of the "seven villages."[43] Sexual excesses of the most detestable description, namely, those associated with the appearance of man in female attire, were observed by Herr von Martius among the Guaycuru in the states of La Plata,[44] by the first Spanish discoverers among the people of the Isthmus of Darien,[45] and by Cabeça di Vaca[46] among the tribes in Louisiana and Texas, and vices of the same nature are prevalent among all the Behring's nations, even among the Tshuktshi on the frozen ocean of Siberia.[47] Men in women's clothes occur among the hunting tribes of the United States, and, strangely enough, among the old Illinois, who, according to their own traditions, migrated to their present dwelling-place from the west.[48] Among the peculiarities of the Red Indians are the customary modes in which nations address one another, as, for instance, the title of grandfather which the Delawares have secured to themselves by compact; and the Iroquois in the same way imposed upon the subjugated Hurons the condition that they should in future always be addressed as younger brothers.[49] The same custom occurs in Brazil, where the tribes address one another as grandfathers or uncles. In the legends of the Mexicans and the inhabitants of the Antilles, living beings are supposed to have first proceeded

[39] See above, p. 263.

[40] Martius, Ethnographie, vol. i. p. 445. Bates, Naturalist on the Amazon, p. 409.

[41] See above, p. 400.

[42] Whymper, Alaska, p. 58.

[43] Waitz, Anthropologie, vol. iv. p. 208.

[44] Ethnographie, vol. i. p. 75.

[45] Gomara, Hist. de las Indias, cap. 68. Petrus Martyr, De orbo novo, Dec. iii. cap. 1.

[46] Ramusio, Navigationi e Viaggi, vol. iii. p. 270.

[47] See above, p. 397, note [35], and p. 399.

[48] Charlevoix, Nouvelle France, vol. iii. p. 303.

[49] Waitz, Anthropologie, vol. iii. p. 22.

from caves, and caves play a similar part in the legends of creation current among the Tehueltecs.[50]   These examples would suffice to prove a mental relationship between the inhabitants of the two continents, but in addition to this the resemblance in the structure of the languages indicates a common derivation.

Let us now cast a glance over the regions inhabited by Americans.   The fact that the people of the Old World had attained a much greater control over nature than had the denizens of the New, has always been ascribed to the obviously superior form, and to the division of labour of the West.   Yet this advantage was confined to two districts only of the New World, namely, Europe with the Asiatic and African shores of the Mediterranean, and the south-east portion, where Asia and Australia are brought nearer to each other by peninsulas and chains of islands ; though this portion has never been especially favourably distinguished by its civilization.   It may here be questioned whether on the whole the New World does not appear more propitiously organized than the Old.   In graceful outline and slender form the land of the so-called western hemisphere is far more pleasing to the eye than the somewhat cumbrous masses of the Old World. But even if the upright form and apt arrangement of Europe be considered sufficient to account for the superiority of occidental civilization over any civilization to be found in America in the year 1492, this explanation does not meet the fact that China is capable of a civilization almost equally superior, though there the advantages of an advantageous arrangement of the land either did not exist or came into play only when the culture of that country had long been superior to any civilization in Anahuac, or in the empire of the Incas of Peru.

The various districts of the Old World must have other advantages in common, by which the education of mankind is far more powerfully promoted than has been the case in the two Americas. It is strange that as yet no one has looked for and discovered the cause of the superiority just where it lies most obviously before us, namely, in the greater extent.   Asia alone is rather larger than the New World, and as Europe and Africa together are

---

[50] Musters, p. 99.

nearly as large as Asia, it follows that the New World is only half as large as the Old. A more accurate estimate of the difference is as follows :—[51]

OLD WORLD.		NEW WORLD.	
	Square miles.		*Square miles.*
Europe ...	3,700,000	North America ...	8,600,000
Africa ...	12,000,000	South America ...	7,000,000
Total	15,700,000		
Asia ...	17,500,000		
Total	33,200,000	Total ...	15,600,000

Neglecting for the moment to take into account the way in which the disposition of this double extent of the Old World differs from that of the New, we will first ascertain the immediate consequences resulting from the greater extent. In the first place, we may suppose that in a district of twice as great extent, twice as many vegetable and animal species may exist. The younger De Candolle, the best authority on the subject, declared that in the present incomplete state of botanical statistics, it was impossible to compare the number of vegetable species in the Old and New World respectively, but that botanists had good reason to expect that it would ultimately appear that, on account of the general direction of its mountains from north to south, America, relatively to its size, is somewhat richer in vegetable species than the Old World. This prepares us to acknowledge that America, though half the size, has more than half the number of vegetable species of the Old World. But the latter is absolutely the richer of the two.

If it be richer in wild species, it should be richer in cultivated plants also. We occasionally have heard it maintained that the only domesticated plants or animals obtained by the Old World from the New World are maize, potatoes, the turkey, the guinea-pig, and the Muscovy duck. We shall, however, soon perceive that the New World is not so poor as it is apt to be represented. Confining ourselves to the most important cultivated plants, we find in the—

---

[51] These figures, though only approximately correct, give a correct view of the proportionate areas.

OLD WORLD.	NEW WORLD.

CEREALS, LEGUMINOUS PLANTS, ETC.

Wheat	Maize
Rye	Mandioca
Barley	Potatoes
Oats	*Chenopodium Quinoa*
Millet	Sweet Potatoes
Buckwheat	....
Negro Millet	....
Kaffir Corn	....
Rice	....
Lentils	....
Peas	Mesquite Tree
Vetches	....
Beans	....
Yams	Yams ?
Bananas	Bananas ?

FRUITS OF THE TEMPERATE ZONES.

Vines	Catawba Grapes
Apples	....
Pears	....
Plums	....
Cherries	....
Apricots	....
Peaches	....
Oranges	....
Figs	....
Dates	....

FIBROUS PLANTS.

Cotton	Cotton
Flax	*Agave Americana*
Hemp	....
Mulberry, with the Silkworm	....

SPICES.

Pepper	Vanilla
Ginger	Spanish Pepper (*Capsicum annuum*)
Cinnamon	....
Nutmeg	....
Cloves	....
Sugar Cane	....

NARCOTICS.

Tea	Paraguay Tea
Coffee	Cocoa
Poppy (Opium)	Tobacco.
Hemp (Hashish)	Coca

Both lists are defective, but were we to enumerate the less important articles, the only result would be to show yet more clearly that the cultivated plants of the Old World have been of more service to mankind than those of the New. We have, moreover, given the New World credit for the yam, although it is more probable that the eastern part of India is its native country ; and we have also credited it with the very valuable banana, as some botanists still maintain that at least a variety which they distinguish as *Musa paradisaica* is a native of the New World. In order to avoid wearying the reader, we have made no comparison between the fruits of the Old and the New World, and leave it to others to decide whether the Old or the New World has gained the most by exchange. Our orchards have not been enriched by a single contribution from America. This, however, by no means proves that the New World was naturally not so well provided as were the eastern continents, for all our fruit-trees in their present form are the produce of industry, and have been improved by careful selection and artificial propagation. It is therefore rash to deny that trees and shrubs may exist in America, whose insipid wild fruits could be rendered palatable by careful cultivation.

Artificial cultivation has had but little effect on annual plants propagated by seed ; among these are numerous kinds of cereals, while America has produced maize alone. As in their common characters they belong to the grasses, it is important that, according to De Candolle's statistical review, the Old World, and Asia especially, is comparatively richer in grasses than the New, for whereas in the latter the grasses rarely amount to as much as 10 per cent. of all the flowering plants in the various districts, usually only 9, occasionally only 7 per cent., they usually amount to 10, and often to 12 per cent. in the eastern continents. Among the grasses, the cereals particularly affect sunny stations, while, as compared with the Old World, much larger regions of America are overshadowed by forests.

In the animal kingdom the number of species is yet more unequal in the two Worlds. To one contemplating for the first time the domestic animals of both hemispheres; that is to say, animals which have been, or which we may suppose might have been tamed; the poverty of the New World must be very striking. There are, in the—

OLD WORLD.	NEW WORLD.
Reindeer	Reindeer
Cattle of various sorts	Bison
Camels ⎫ Dromedaries ⎰	⎧ Llamas ⎩ Vecunas
Pigs	⎧ Peccaries ⎩ Waterhogs
Elephants	Tapirs
Dogs	Prairie Dogs
Cats	....
Sheep	.... , ᵱ
Goats	....
Horses	....
Asses	....
Domestic Fowls	⎧ Guinea Fowls ⎩ Turkeys
Geese	....
Ducks	Muscovy Ducks

It should be noticed that of the domestic animals of the New World, the reindeer, the bison, the turkey, and the Muscovy duck belong exclusively to North America; and that the varied services performed by the domestic animals of the Old World entitle them to a superior rank. All these are bred, more or less, for the sake of their flesh; but, in addition to this, the reindeer, the camel, the horse, the goat, and the cow, are kept for the sake of the milk which they produce. We might add the sheep and the ass, although, in their cases, the milk is only a secondary advantage. In its llama species America is well provided with wool-bearing animals; but we have the sheep, the goat, the camel, and the dromedary. As beasts of burden and draught the New World possessed only the llama, though the reindeer and the bison occur and might also have been domesticated; we, on the other hand, besides the reindeer and the ox, had the camel, the ass, the horse, and the elephant, not to mention the dog, which the Eskimo, at least, have used as a draught animal. The lack of draught animals implies the absence of the plough, the sledge, and the carriage. But as all the animals above enumerated live not in the forest, but in grassy plains bordering on the deserts, or even in the deserts themselves, and as we may describe the New World as mainly a forest country, and the Old as mainly a region of steppes, this accounts for the fact that the eastern hemisphere is richer in the number of its species of graminivorous mammals; man, seeking his own advantage, easily selected from among these those which were capable of feeding and clothing him, carrying his burdens or doing his work.

All who, since Zimmermann, have turned their attention to the geographical distribution of animals, have noticed the fact that the Old World abounds far more than America in large and powerful mammals. The largest animal in South America is the tapir; the most powerful in the northern continent is the grisly bear. The New World has none of our larger animals : the elephant, the rhinoceros, the hippopotamus, the giraffe, and the camel. The distribution of the other animals in the two hemispheres is equally significant. These are, in the—

OLD WORLD.	NEW WORLD.
Lions	Pumas
Tigers	Ounces
Crocodiles	Alligators
Catarrhine Apes, some anthropo-morphous and tailless	Platyrrhine Apes with pliant and prehensile tails

Compared with the lion, the cowardly puma is ignoble. Continents as small as North or South America could hardly produce such a splendid forest ranger. The poet in calling the lion the king of the desert, supplies us with an apt epithet. But the monarch is entitled to a royal hunting-ground, which even now, although greatly narrowed, extends through the whole of Africa and Western Asia, and formerly included European territory too. The tiger also, the royal tiger, as the magnificent but terrible beast is justly termed, has a vast range of territory, for he roves from the Caspian Sea to the Amoor, where the Russians in their advance some twenty years ago, became aware that his habitat extended as far as, and even beyond, the fur-bearing animals, while in the south he has penetrated to the extreme point of Asia in the peninsula of Malacca ; he can even swim across an arm of the sea to destroy hundreds of human beings annually in the island of Singapore. This animal is represented in the New World only by the blood-thirsty but smaller and far less courageous ounce, which attacks man only when driven by necessity.

These contrasts have long been recognized and plainly expressed in the saying, that the New World is more favourable to vegetable life, and the Old to animal life. The tall forests of the temperate zones, as well as the so-called primeval forests of the tropics, pre-clude the development of a rich fauna, or admit only of one which is able to climb and live in tree tops. In the dense forests on the western slopes of the Rocky Mountains, a profound stillness prevails, according to Lord Milton's description, unbroken by the sound of any animal. On the other hand, in grass countries, and especially where, as in the prairies of North America, the forest still appears in isolated fragments, or scattered as in a park, we find great herds of bisons, and, in Africa, troops of antelopes and gazelles. The greater abundance of steppes in the Old World explains the fact that the animal kingdom of the eastern hemisphere exceeds the American fauna in number of species and of individuals, but not that the largest, the strongest, and the cleverest animals all occur in our portion of the globe. But this, again, is really caused by the greater extent, inasmuch as its consequence is a more animated struggle for existence. We ought to regard this struggle not so much as a necessary evil as a necessary blessing, for it is this which increases the strength of every creature, and forces enfeebled indi-viduals or species to make room for the stronger, and which accurately represents in nature that which in political society is called open competition, which gives all the prizes to those fore-most in the press, and mercilessly crushes those who lag behind. For our purpose we need only notice that in small secluded regions, for example, in islands, the struggle for existence is soon at an end, and the balance is undisturbed until some new competitor appears upon the scene of conflict. This may also be expressed by saying that the intensity of the struggle for existence increases propor-tionately with the size of the regions, so that it was far more energetic in the Old World than in the New, and that as a consequence of this continued pressure forwards, and of a more rapid adaptation of organisms to present circumstances, the largest, strongest, and cleverest creatures were necessarily to be found in the Old World.   It is easy to conceive that in a larger space a pause in the struggle can rarely occur, and then only for a short time. Long before Darwin, Leopold von Buch [51] had observed : " The individuals of continental species spread and, with increasing distance and change of station, develop varieties, which, on account of the great dissimilarity which they have acquired, are no longer capable of being crossed with the other varieties, or of being brought back to the principal type ; these ultimately become persistent, independent species, which, perhaps by other channels, come across other varieties equally changed, the two differing greatly and no longer capable of mixing. . . . . This is not the case in islands."

Hence, if on a larger extent of land the struggle for existence is more intense, because each variety follows rapidly on the heels of the other, this is the simplest explanation of the fact that the creatures of the Old World are in advance of those of the New, for not only is the square mileage of our continents twice as great, but weight must be given to the fact that America is divided into two quite distinct battle-grounds—into two continents with different natural kingdoms, each of which has its greatest length from north to south, instead of stretching like the countries of the Old World from west to east.   The form of the New World seems as if designed to cover as many latitudes as possible, that of the Old World as if meant to extend over as many degrees of longitude as possible within the same latitudes.   As most species and genera of both kingdoms are bounded by certain polar and equatorial limits (or more correctly by maximum and minimum isothermal boundaries), a far greater range is obviously open to each individual species in the Old World than in the New.   How considerably the dimensions of the battle-ground is increased in the Old World by the fact that its main direction is from east to west, may be seen from the following comparison of proportions under the same latitudes.

---

[51] Physikal Beschreibung der canarischen Inseln, vol. i. p. 133.   1825.

IN NORTH AMERICA. g. g. miles.

In 50° North Lat.	Parallel of Vancouver's Island and Newfoundland			725
40° ,,	,, Parallel of Philadelphia			575
30° ,,	,, Parallel of New Orleans			450

IN THE OLD WORLD.

50° ,,	,, Parallel of the South-west point of England ...			1450
40° ,,	,, Parallel of Naples and Pekin			1620
30° ,,	,, Parallel of Cairo			1690

If it is proved that in the larger regions the struggle for existence is carried on with greater intensity, it follows that the survivors on the wider scene of conflict must necessarily be superior to the survivors in the narrow region. For example, if plants of the Old World were to come unobserved into the New, or were they when already there to escape from the supervision of man, that is to say, from gardens into the open, they would supplant the American species with much more vigour than the American species under converse circumstances would supplant our vegetation on the eastern continents; in other words, European plants, either wild or escaped from cultivation, would spread in America far more rapidly than would American plants in Europe or in any part of the Old World. Experience actually confirms this theory, so that trans-atlantic botanists have themselves termed America the garden of European weeds. Appearing first at Buenos Ayres, wild European plants, such as lucerne, the ladies' thistle, and the teasel, have clothed the steppes for miles; the native grasses have been obliged to give way to our rye-grass species (*Lolium perenne* and *L. multiflora*) and to the *Hordeum maximum* and *H. pratense.* In North America, the small-flowered mullein and the common prunella have taken complete possession of some parts of the coast. 158 European species and eight from other parts of the world have made their way into America since 1492, while only thirty-eight plants have made their way into Europe from all quarters of the globe.

Every unprejudiced reader will, before this, have recognized for himself that the irresistible spread of the races of our hemisphere over the New World is exactly analogous to the victorious progress of our so-called weeds. The struggle for existence was very active at the time of the great migrations. It is true in-

19

vasions by barbarian hordes into the territory of civilized nations are usually regarded as great calamities to mankind ; but, perhaps, a little reflection will convince us that most, if not all of them, have proved beneficial. For the present, let us consider only the last but one of these great phenomena, namely, the incursion of the Mongols who, in an incredibly short time, poured down from their home on the Onun and Kerulen, in the Siberian Dauria, to the Danube, and whose appearance had a favourable influence upon Europe, although not equal in degree, yet of the same kind, as the sudden appearance of the Arabs. Where such struggles for existence arise, whatever may be their end, our race is eventually brought to a higher development ; for either the older cultured nations succeed in forming a barrier against the advancing flood, and they become strengthened in the conflict, or if they succumb from weakness it must be because the supplanter was more vigorous than the supplanted. Even though a noble civilization was thus overthrown and its glories became buried in the soil, and the plough finally passed over its buried pavements, yet the victorious barbarian had one advantage over the conquered Roman, namely, his youth and the prospect of a more glorious future.

(*a*) *The Hunting Tribes of the Northern Continent.*—All the nations of America constitute a single branch of the Mongolian race, but for the sake of convenience, the inhabitants of the northern and southern continents are separated, and these are again distinguished into the so-called hunting tribes and the civilized nations. Language is the only means of forming a further and final subdivision. But we must be prepared to find a great number of languages, for hunting necessitates a system of small and widely scattered hordes, which, as has been already shown, is apt to break up the language into dialects which finally become completely dissimilar. Careful research is, however, able to trace the common derivation of the many languages. The languages of North America have been thus treated by Buschmann, on whose researches Waitz based his classification, which was afterwards embodied in the form of a map by Otto Delitsch. We need not therefore burden ourselves with an enumeration of uninteresting names, but it will be enough to specify the larger groups.

The immediate neighbours of the Eskimo and the other Behring's nations of the north-west coast, are the Kenai and Athabaskan groups, which, notwithstanding their great dissimilarity, still retain traces of a former affinity of language. The Kenai, of whom the Yellow Knife or Atna tribe [52] is best known, live chiefly on the Youcon river. The Athabaskans live further east, occupying the country between Hudson's Bay and the Rocky Mountains, about as far as the British boundary extends. Better known tribes are the Chippeways (different from the Objibeways), the Coppermine, Dogrib, and Beaver Indians. To this group belong also the Tlatskanai, Umkwa, and Hoopah, who have migrated far from their original homes in the north to the neighbourhood of the sea-coast of Oregon. The Athabaskan Navaho tribe have wandered even further to the south, eastward of the Colorado, to the highlands of New Mexico; and even the dreaded Apatshes, who range from the western Colorado to the Mexican provinces of Chihuahua and Coahuila, also belong to this group. Lastly, another Athabaskan tribe, the Lipani, live north of the mouth of the Rio Grande del Norte, so that this group is distributed over a district extending from the Arctic circle to the Gulf of Mexico.

Extending from the Rocky Mountains, near the sources of the Missouri, but especially in the northern States eastward of the Mississippi, dwell, or rather dwelt, at the time of the discovery, the Algonkins. The extreme west of the region over which they are distributed is occupied by the Blackfeet Indians; the shores of Lake Superior by the Objibeways, and the districts south and west of Hudson's Bay by the Knistinaux, or Crees. To the east of the Mississippi, and belonging to the Algonkins, were the Leni Lenappes, who constituted the "five nations" of the Delawares, which also included the Mohicans. To their language geography is indebted, among other names, for Massachusetts, Connecticut, Alleghany, Savannah, Mississippi. Other well-known Algonkin tribes are the Susquehannoc, Pampticos, Shawanos or Shawnees,

---

[52] Properly Ah-tená. *Tená*, or *tinneh*, signifies " people," and all the tribal names have this suffix. Hence the Kenai would be better named the Tená tribes. W. Dale, Alaska and its Resources, p. 428. Boston, 1870.

Illinois, Sauk, Musquakkee or Foxes, Menomennee or Wild-rice people.

A third group, the Iroquois of Canada, were surrounded by the Algonkins. In the year 1700, the tribes of the Senecas, Cayugas, Onondagos, Oneidas, and Mohawks formed the league of the "five nations," of which the Tuscaroras became a sixth member in 1712. The Hurons, or Wyandots, were allied to them in language, but were, however, in a constant state of warfare with the Iroquois confederation. They formerly received from the allied tribes the title of "father," but having been conquered, they were forced to consent to address the other Iroquois as "elder brothers." By a treaty made in 1591, the Iroquois were allowed to address the Delawares only by the title of "uncle," though the latter were addressed by all other tribes as "grandfather."

The fourth group consists of the Dahcotas, better known by their nickname of Sioux. They inhabit grassy plains in the territory of the United States, between the Rocky Mountains and the Mississippi, as far south as Arkansas. The group includes the Assiniboins, the Winnebagos or Winnepegs, the Iowa Omaha, Osages, Kansas, Arkansas, Menitarees, the Crows or Upsarokas, and the Mandanas.

The Pawnees and Riccaras stand alone in and about the Rocky Mountains, between the upper course of the north fork of the Platte river and Arkansas. In the south-east of the United States were the Choctaws and Chikasas, allied in language with the Muskogees or the union of Creek tribes, of which the noble Seminoles, whose name signifies "fugitives," were formerly the oldest member. South and North Carolina were inhabited by the Cherokee tribes, which are quite distinct in language from the surrounding tribes. In the same way the former inhabitants of Texas can neither be united into a common group nor attached to any other groups. Among them were the Keioways, the Paducas, the Caddos, or Cadodaquius, to which belong the Tejas, or Texas, and the remarkable Natchez on the Lower Mississippi.

(*b*) *The Hunting Tribes of South America.*—On the Southern Continent a high degree of civilization occurs only on and near the Andes. Brazil, the Guayana territories, and Venezuela are entirely occupied by so-called hunting tribes, some of which are still in the lowest stages of social and intellectual development. Their languages are even more varied than those of North America, and no scholar has seriously attempted to reduce this confusion to order. Old charts professing to show the distribution of language have given rise to the error that a single language prevails through-out Brazil, to which the name of *lingoa geral* (common Indian language), or Guarani, is given. Von Martius was the first to show that this Tupi language, although understood by individuals in every tribe, really prevails only in two districts, remote from one another, namely, between the Tapajos and the Xingu, both affluents of the Amazon, and in the province of Chiquitos. Be-side these, a more dense Tupi population occurs in Paraguay, in a district on the right bank of the central Paraná. Other Tupi tribes have strayed as far as the Atlantic coast, and only few provinces of Brazil are without some traces of them. North of the Amazon, on the contrary, they are totally wanting.

Martius makes a distinct group of the Lenguas or Tongue Indians, so called because they pierce the lower lip. By the Tupi they are called Guaycuru, or runners; they inhabit the western bank of the Paraná and Paraguay, and are remarkable for their rude manners. To other tribes between the sources of the Paraná and the Madeira, Martius gives the collective name of Parexis, or Poragi, signifying "highlanders." The enormous territory drained by the Tocantin is occupied by the Gês, also called Crans, which means "chiefs," or "sons." Unlike the Tupi, who sleep in hammocks, they use a low trestle. The Crens, or Gueras, who are scattered between Parahiba and Rio das Contas, are allied to them. Cren, like Cran, signifies "the chiefs." To the Crens belong the Botocudos, the Coroados, the Puris, and the Malalis. Martius gives the collective name of Guck or Coco hordes to several Indian tribes in the interior of the provinces of Bahia, Pernambuco, and Piauhy; as these words, as titles for a maternal uncle, are common to them all. To these belong the Indians on the Amazon, who call themselves Ore Manoas, which means *we the Manoas*, and the Macusi and Maypures in Guayana and Venezuela. There are a few national names in North America, but in Brazil there are only tribal names, of which Herr von Martius collected no less than 106 on the Rio Negro alone. Consciousness of nationality implies higher social development and common historical achievements, which are wanting here. The tribes on the Amazon are but little better. There we find the warlike Mandrucu, hybrids related to the Tupis, who are conspicuous for their strict discipline, the use of trumpet signals in battle, and a regular service of outposts in times of war. On the Rio Negro live the Miranhas, formerly cannibals, and otherwise known for the production of excellent hammocks, each of which costs the labour of six weeks. Where the Amazon approaches the confines of Peru, we come upon the Tecunas, whose masquerades have already been mentioned; and on the boundaries of Venezuela we find the Uapes, whose spacious buildings we have noted. Guayana is mainly occupied by two tribes, who do not, however, occupy separate districts, namely, the Arowaks, or Flour people, so called because in them we have to respect the inventors of the art of preparing tapioca, and the Caribs (since the seventeenth century erroneously called Caraibs), to whom the Spaniards attributed everything most odious, and who remained notorious for their barbarity, until the experiences of A. von Humboldt and the Brothers Schomburgk showed them to be an uncorrupted race, full of good impulses.[53]

The northern and southern continents of America resemble one another in many great features, and especially in their shape, for both consist of great triangles, the apices of which are towards the south. But their vertical structure is also similar, inasmuch as on the western shore the Cordilleras rise from the Pacific Ocean, and plateaux are intercalated between their ridges. As a necessary consequence of this analogous structure, we find no forests eastward of the slopes of the Rocky Mountains and the Cordilleras, or in their "rain shadow," but open steppes, which are called prairies in North America, savannahs in Central America, llanos in Venezuela, and pampas on the Argentine rivers. It is only to the east of the steppes that the great forest districts are found stretching over

---

[53] As Richard Schomburgk observes, they do not poison their arrows although the curare plant (*Strychnos toxifera*) grows in their territory. Reisen in Britisch Guiana, vol. ii. p. 429. Leipzic, 1848.

the Atlantic shores of the northern and southern continents. In the grassy plains of South as well as of North America we look in vain for the social phenomena which have been everywhere evoked by corresponding regions in the Old World. We there note the absence of nations representing the Berber tribes of Northern Africa, the Bedouins of Arabia, the Turks of Turkestan, the Mongols of the desert of Gobi, or the Lapps and Samoyeds of the far north of America. Neglect of cattle-breeding is often attributed to the American aborigines, but the assertion is inaccurate, for, strictly speaking, it is only the production of milk which is totally uncared for. Von Martius states [54] that there is a special expression in the Tupi language, or *lingoa geral*, of Brazil, for the taming wild animals, implying that the animals are to be induced to lay aside their ferocity. Most natives of Brazil take pleasure in intercourse with animals. They are in the habit of attaching monkeys and parrots to themselves, and by feeding the latter on fish they produce red and yellow feathers when the plumage is green. Their huts are often like menageries. But in the history of civilization, the breeding of animals first acquires much significance when man purposes by this means to provide for his own future maintenance, and discontinues the habit of living from hand to mouth on the wild products of nature. On the Amazon a sufficient number of turtles might be taken to supply food during the whole year to the inhabitants of the shores, but no efforts are made to obtain them, except in the dry season when the animals come to land. For this reason almost every family possesses a closed tank near its dwelling, in which a number of live animals are stored for the rainy season. [55] Orellana, [56] the discoverer of the Amazon found these domestic precautions in use among the natives. Many Brazilian tribes were also formerly, as they still are, in the habit of breeding guinea-fowls (*Grax*) for the sake of their palatable flesh. On the coast of Venezuela, the Spanish sailors saw domestic animals, which they described as rabbits, geese, and pigeons. [57] In the Antilles the prairie dog

---

[54] Ethnographie, vol. i. p. 672.   [55] Bates, Amazon, p. 321.

[56] Oviedo, Historia general, vol. iv. p. 553.

[57] Gomara, Historia de las Indias, cap. 75. .

was bred, and in Hayti the guinea-pig. Peccaries and tapirs easily become accustomed to the proximity of man, and were and are still often tamed by the Brazilians, but they do not breed in confinement.[58]

There is, however, no reliable record that any of the tribes of the northern continent, east of the Rocky Mountains, always excepting the Eskimo, were in the habit of breeding animals for domestic purposes prior to the discovery. Yet North America, unlike the southern continent, had the advantage of a gregarious animal which was in every way adapted to encourage a nomadic life. We mean the buffalo, or bison, which, with the exception of one small district, does not appear on the western slopes of the Rocky Mountains, and on the east does not extend very far beyond the Mississippi. When captured young, the bison allows itself to be tamed and trained; and it has also formed a useful hybrid race with European cattle. As it was neither bred nor even preserved by the natives, it is obvious that the Redskins are wanting in the inclination or the patience for taming animals. The native wild duck was not domesticated until European settlers did so; and the turkey, which was a domestic animal in Mexico, was found only in a wild condition on the territory of the United States. The northern continent is inhabited by the reindeer (cariboo), which has been everywhere tamed in the Old World, but never by the Canadians of the New World. The dog is indeed found among the tribes of the Hudson's Bay territory as a domestic animal, and trained for hunting, but it is probable that it was domesticated only after the immigration of the Eskimo, who had seen the dog used as a draught animal in their Asiatic home. But as the inclination to domesticate animals was naturally very weak in the North American Indians, there was no conceivable reason why they should tame the bison, for hunting supplied them with as much meat and as many skins as they could require. No nation in America ever thought of using milk as food. The use of milk belongs entirely to a very late and high stage of development in nomadic life. Even at the present day, the great herds of cattle on the pampas and llanos yield nothing but meat

---

[58] Darwin, Plants and Animals under Domestication, vol. ii. p. 150.

and skins; indeed, the abundant secretion of milk in cattle takes place only after prolonged domestication. While in England a cow yields forty pints of milk daily,[59] the Damara in South Africa, a nomadic people, obtain from their animals at most three pints, and their cows refuse their milk as soon as the calf is taken from them.[60] Hence we may infer that the people who first collected animals into herds did so only for the sake of the flesh, and that use of the milk began much later, and in consequence of skilful selection. The steppes and the forest districts of the New World are, therefore, inhabited only by hunting and agricultural tribes.

In South America there are no traces of building east of the Andes; but in North America there are dome-shaped tumuli, round, flat-topped mounds, and circular earthworks; some of them contain graves and covered passages. They are very scarce in the New England States, and are rarely found west of the Mississippi, but extend from the upper course of the Missouri and the great lakes to the south on both slopes of the Alleghanies as far as Florida. These remains are most numerous on the Ohio. Most archæologists have ascribed them to an extinct people of "mound-builders," whom they suppose to have migrated either from Mexico to the north-east or from the north-east to Mexico. Had these monumental edifices been nothing more than an offshoot from the civilization of Nahuatl the intrenchments would necessarily become more plentiful in proportion as they approach the high-lands of Anáhuac; but their traces are lost in Texas, where, as in Chihuahua, according to Cabeza de Vaca's reports,[61] dwelt extremely barbarous and half-starved tribes, who lived on fish, roots, and the fruit of the prickly pear (*Opuntia tuna*). The descriptions given by the Spaniards of the intrenched villages of the Indians in the former slave states, and Jaques Cartier's sketch of the Iroquois city Hochelaga,[62] the present Montreal, in Canada, answer sufficiently to the form of these earthworks as we can

---

[59] Darwin, Plants and Animals under Domestication, vol. ii. p. 300.

[60] Anderson, Südwestafrika. Barrow (South Africa) reckons two quarts of milk to a South African cow.

[61] Ramusio, Navigationi et Viaggi.

[62] Relation originale de Jaques Cartier, ed. d'Avizac, p. 23. Paris, 1863.

imagine them from the numerous ground-plans and sections in Schoolcraft's comprehensive works on the antiquities of the United States. We, therefore, fully share the opinion of Samuel F. Haven,[63] who supposes the ancestors of the present Indians to have been the authors of these erections, and who has shown that as late as 1800 a mound was erected over the body of an Omaha chief, and that Lewis and Clarke found many newly made earthworks on the Upper Missouri. It is true that Europeans have never actually seen the Red Indian hunters carrying out such structures as the "walled lake," an artificial reservoir for purposes of irrigation in Wight County (Iowa),[64] but, on the other hand, Charlevoix states that the Iroquois formerly built much more spacious dwellings, though, like many other half-developed races, they neglected their old arts after coming into contact with Europeans.[65] The builders of these mounds and intrenchments were, therefore, the forefathers of those Redskins who were supplanted by the European settlers. Like their descendants, they lived by the chase, and perhaps remained in the same condition for some centuries previous to the arrival of the discoverers.[66]

But hunting prevents an advance to any high degree of civilization, for the moral development of nations is closely dependent on their mode of sustenance. The earliest and long isolated central points of human society existed only where population could easily become dense, as on the Nile and in China; for it is only after a certain degree of concentration of the population that a division of labour is effected, which in many primitive civilizations is expressed by a distinction into castes. But in a territory which contains only a certain amount of game, the chase, on the contrary, can support only a fixed and scanty population. If a tribe multiplies beyond the supply of meat afforded by its territory, the men are urged partly by want, and partly by the consciousness of their superior numbers, to invade the hunting-grounds of their neigh-

---

[63] Archæology of the United States.

[64] Kapp, Vergleichende Erdkunde, 2nd ed. p. 615.

[65] Nouvelle France, vol. iii. p. 335.

[66] The above was published in the Ausland, 1868. It is important that Tylor, a thoroughly trustworthy observer, has reached the same conclusion. Primitive Culture, vol. i. p. 57.

bours. The inevitable consequences are feuds, in which the stronger tribe either extirpates or drives out the weaker, in which latter case the weaker must in its turn drive out some other tribe or perish. Strong hunting tribes may, therefore, spread but cannot become dense.

. The progress of civilization in America, if it had not been interrupted by the arrival of the Europeans, could only have taken place if maintenance by agricultural products had more and more replaced the maintenance by the produce of the chase. As far as the polar limits of maize, namely, as far as the St. Lawrence and great lakes, and even further to the north, at least, in the territory of the Hurons, we find hopeful beginnings of agriculture among the hunting nations. Everywhere there are traces of husbandry, except in the Hudson's Bay territories eastward of the Rocky Mountains, among most of the Athabask tribes, who are, however, far more barbarous than their more southerly neighbours. Even in the forest country nature provided some gratuitous articles of food, namely, in addition to berries and roots, water rice (*Zizania aquatica*) on the Canadian lakes and the Upper Mississippi, the juice of the sugar maple in the spring, and lastly, the fruit of wild plums and wild vines. Maize, beans, gourds, and tobacco are expressly mentioned by Cartier[67] as the agricultural produce of the Canadian Iroquois, near Montreal; and it may be said in general that, advancing from higher to lower latitudes, agriculture more and more supplied the wants of the natives. For a period as long as may have elapsed from the formation of the first in-trenchments to the arrival of the Europeans, the Redskins have remained stationary in the phase in which agriculture, hunting, and fishing supplement one another. Yet the fact that they have never advanced to pure agriculture must not betray us into denying that they had any disposition towards a higher civilization. It is too frequently overlooked that hunting does develop the intellectual powers of a people, although at the same time it consumes them. Skill in hunting requires an accurate knowledge of wild animals and their habits. The Redman pos-sessed the most thorough acquaintance with his hunting-ground

---

[67] Voyage de Jaques Cartier au Canada en 1534. First journey.

and its stock of game; he easily succeeded in outwitting even the most crafty animals, and his keen observations, and his clever interpretations of the smallest signs of life in the open air, have always greatly surprised civilized men, whose own senses are so much less acute. He has never been wanting in sagacity to unravel the connection and the details of any incident of the forest from the most insignificant indications, but all the sagacity he possesses is expended in the pursuit of an animal or an enemy. There can be no doubt that men of unusual talents have appeared among these nations as frequently as among ourselves, yet none of them became founders of religions, philosophers, or regulators of society, but only famous hunters, fortunate leaders, or admired orators at tribal meetings. It must also be remembered that hunting affords supreme enjoyment, and that agriculture has nothing to offer in compensation for the excitement and delight of the chase.

In inquiring into the causal connection between the configuration of countries and the degrees of civilization, a reason must be found for the fact that social instincts are more mature in the inhabitants of the steppes and forests of North America than in those of the southern continent. It is a fact that in the latter, all the tribes of the steppes and forests, with the exception of the Muras on the Amazon, and a few other tribes, practised agriculture in addition to hunting and fishing. The produce of their cultivation was even more varied than in the north, for in addition to maize it includes the manioca root, from which a poisonous juice must be carefully expressed before it becomes edible. The cultivation of the indigenous palm is also noteworthy. But as palms are much slower in bearing fruit than annual or biennial plants, their cultivation shows forethought, and implies abandonment of a roving life. Moreover, it has already been shown that in some districts the papunha trees (*Guildma speciosa*) bear only seedless fruits; this palm must therefore have been cultivated by man for a long period, and the seedless variety can have been propagated only by offsets. But if the South American hunting tribes rivalled the North Americans in agriculture, and even excelled them in the culture of trees and domestic animals, they were entirely outstripped in other achievements.

The rudest tribes in the Hudson's Bay territory occupy a far higher position than the Botocudos of Brazil, for example, who have remained stationary in the lowest phase of civilization to be found in the New World. In all South America (of course, always excepting the nations of the Cordilleras), great or complete nudity, sometimes of one, sometimes of the other, and sometimes of both sexes, was the rule ; whereas in North America it was only exceptional. The natives of South America cannot claim superiority on account of the yarn and cotton tissues which they used, for not only did the native women of Georgia in De Soto's time wear white clothes made of the alburnum of the mulberry tree,[68] as the Spaniards thought, but great skill has always been shown there in the preparation of leather also, and in its manufacture into clothes, which were richly decorated with feathers, and which are even now much admired. Another peculiarity which distinguished the North American tribes, not only from their equals but also from many civilized nations, was their use of clothing[69] for their feet, for which purpose they employed mocassins, or half-boots. Snow shoes were, perhaps, not used before the arrival of the Eskimo, who, probably, first brought this invention from Asia to the New World.[70]

No trace of mining has been met with among the hunting tribes of South America. Among the natives of the United States, on the contrary, the discoverers found many copper ornaments and utensils. Copper was worked in Alabama and various places east of the Mississippi, but the most important mines were situated on Lake Erie. Some archæologists have somewhat hastily concluded that this was the seat of a people of very ancient civilization, entirely distinct from the hunting tribes of modern times. But the achievements of the old North Americans have always been undervalued. Even the rude Athabaskan tribes dug for copper, for in the 18th century they used to bring this ore to Fort Churchill, the most western station of the Hudson's Bay Company, and it was mainly

---

[68] Oviedo, Historia general, vol. i. p. 556.

[69] The Patagonians also use mocassins. Musters, Among the Patagonians, p. 174 ; Catlin, Rambles, p. 259.

[70] Herrera, Historia de las Indias occidentales, Dec. vii. lib. 2, cap. 1.

to discover the source of this metal that Samuel Hearne [71] undertook his expeditions, which resulted in the discovery of the Coppermine River and its outflow into the Arctic Sea.   The owner of the
mining district on Lake Erie was a chief of the Fond du Lac tribe,
and according to the number of his ancestors that he could name,
his pedigree reached back to the beginning of the 12th century.

A German miner who had been director of one of these mines,
states that the old Redskins loosened the rocks by firing piles of
wood, and by saturating them with water, and from the blocks of
metal obtained they separated pieces with stone hammers, and
shaped them by cutting with flint knives and striking with hammers, " for the ancients were not acquainted with the process of
smelting."   This fact has, however, not been proved, at least as to
Lake Superior; and, on the other hand, it is maintained that cast
copper utensils have occasionally been found.[72] There is, therefore,
not the slightest necessity for refusing the credit of these mining
achievements to the ancient Iroquois, in whose territory the famous
copper mines were situated, or for referring them on very doubtful grounds to the Aztecs of Mexico.   It is true that obsidian
blades have been found in tombs eastward of the Mississippi,
and even on Lake Ontario, and that this mineral can only have
been procured from Mexico.   But these pieces of obsidian are no
better evidence of a migration of the Aztecs than the discovery of
coins with Kufic inscriptions prove a visit of the Arabs to Iceland.
Articles made of nephrite, which must have come from a great
distance, and which dated from the reindeer period, were met with
at Schussenried, and show that even then commerce must have
been widely spread.   If a close relation with Aztec culture is to
be inferred from the discovery of obsidian blades in the United
States, we might insist with equal justice on the influence of the
ancient population of Poland on the French of the reindeer period,
because horns of the Saiga antelope were excavated from the caves *
of Périgord. [73]

---

[71] Reise zum Eismeer, pp. 4 and 14.   Berlin, 1797.

[72] Rau (Archiv für Anthropologie, 1871) has however again stated positively
that the ancient inhabitants of the United States were not acquainted with the
art of smelting.

[73] See above, pp. 37 and 209.

The superiority of the civilization of the hunting tribes of the northern as compared with those of the southern continent is most clearly seen in their social organization. In the north, by comparisons of language, ethnographers have succeeded in uniting the tribes into nations, and in defining the territories occupied by these nations. In Brazil, Guayana, and Venezuela such a classification is unattainable, for in these countries, instead of nations there are merely bands, and artificial names have to be invented for the groups of hordes allied in language. In North America, on the contrary, the Algonkin nations lived in compact territories, into which the Iroquois had intruded on the western slope of the Alleghanies. These nations make their appearance in history when already united into confederations declaring war and peace, and making treaties; occasionally, although only for a short time all the hunting tribes were even leagued together in one great alliance against European oppressors. Certain international ordinances were likewise observed by all the tribes; as, for example, that peace should always prevail throughout the sacred territory of the Red Pipestone.

Lastly, and in our eyes of most importance, we notice among the North Americans the rudiments of a communication of ideas by means of symbolic writing. It is true these inscriptions were legible only to those who knew the meaning of the symbols, and their reference to a particular event, yet these records served to refresh the memory. South America, eastward of the Cordilleras, is destitute of such hopeful indications, and it is therefore indisputable that the inhabitants of the northern continent (independently of its civilized nations, to whom, however, the same observation may apply) had attained a far higher civilization than the inhabitants of South America. It is therefore necessary to ascertain the extent to which the physical features of the two countries have caused this unequal distribution of civilization.

All must recognize the great advantage enjoyed by North America in its closer vicinity of the Old World, so that plants, animals, and human beings which migrated across Behring's Straits, spread over the northern continent before reaching the southern. Just as at a later period the Eskimo immigrated from Asia, and as skill in traversing the sea spread from Kamtshatka across the Aleutian Islands and the west coast of North America, a number of ideas and inventions made their way from Asia to the tribes of the northern continent. According to our theory that America was peopled from Asia by way of Behring's Straits, the northern continent must have been the earlier home of the Americans, from which South America was discovered as a New World ; this must have been accomplished by the expulsion of weaker hordes who were driven from the northern half by stronger ones. The northern continent, as the earlier inhabited, was also more densely populated than the southern.

To the east of the Andes of the southern, and of the Cordilleras of the northern continent, the forest and steppes have not developed any very perceptible difference between their inhabitants. At the most it may be said that the Dahcotas, or Sioux, of the North American prairies, whose places of abode almost exactly coincide with the range of the bison, appear more barbarous than their neighbours eastward of the Mississippi, and from Cabeza de Vaca's experiences, it is quite evident that the aborigines of Texas, as well of Chihuahua as far as the Pacific watershed, were incomparably more degraded than even the Dahcotas.

But if we compare the social development of the various hunting tribes in the northern and southern continents, there is in both countries a sensible improvement as we approach the shores of the Gulf of Mexico and the Caribbean Sea ; in other words, in South America, the nations who dwell more to the north, and in North America, the nations who dwell more to the south, are, on an average, the most civilized. The most barbarous tribes of South America, such as the Botocudos, Coroados, Puris, and Lenguas, all belong to the south of Brazil ; but, on the Amazon, Spix and Martius met with great advances in the social condition. If we could fully trust the accounts of the first discoverers under Orellana, the upper course of this great river flowed by many populous villages, in which there were temples, and idols moving on wheels. Later visitors have, however, perceived no signs of such things, and even if they existed, it is not impossible that they belonged to tribes which had been expelled from the civilized empire of the Incas. To the north of the Amazon live the gentle Arawaks, among whom the woman already occupies an honourable position,[74] and whose priests preserve the history of the tribes for the instruction of the young. Near them and among them, as far as the gulf which bears their name, are spread the Caribs, who irrigated their fields by artificial water-courses, marked off their plantations with cotton strings, and held fairs, in which salt took the place of money. Here, therefore, the outward state of human society constantly improves from south to north.

Conversely, in the northern continent, the southern neighbours of the rude Athabaskan tribes in the Hudson's Bay territory are the agricultural Algonkin nations, who live to the north of the Iroquois ; these latter, again, are favourably distinguished by their mining works on Lake Erie, and by the careful arrangements of their fields in Michigan and Indiana, designated by archæologists as garden-beds; to their territory also belong remains of intrenched villages which are especially frequent and numerous on the Ohio. On the south, the nearest neighbours of the Iroquois were the so-called Appalachic nations, of whose condition the first account was given by Hernando de Soto's freebooting expedition. Among them the Spaniards came upon temples which seem to have been something superior to the so-called "medicine huts" of the northern Redskins. Their chiefs possessed far greater authority than among the other hunting tribes, and in South Carolina or Georgia the government was actually in the hands of a woman, with whom the Spaniards negotiated as with a monarch, a circumstance which clearly proves that the chieftancy had become hereditary in families, and that the women were no longer employed as domestic beasts of burden. Among the Seminoles of Florida, the Spaniards found fixed rafts used as bridges across the lagunes ; and real bridges [75] are mentioned in the land of Appalache, that is to say, in Georgia or South Carolina. It is therefore not surprising that remains of old roads have been discovered in Florida, for the existence of bridges implies a frequent traffic across the country.

Further westward on the Ohio, the remains of ancient circular

---

[74] Richard Schomburgk, Reisen in Britisch-Guiana, vol. i. p. 227 and vol. ii. p. 314.

[5] Herrera, Indias occidentales.

fortifications of Indian villages lie very closely together. It has been somewhat hastily inferred that the Ohio valley was thickly peopled by an agricultural population, who were extirpated by barbarous hunting tribes before the arrival of Europeans. But other archæologists have suggested that simple natives frequently abandon their abodes, sometimes from superstition, and sometimes on account of an outbreak of disease.[76] Hence, although all the old intrenched villages already discovered were certainly not inhabited at the same time, it is, nevertheless, manifest that the present southern states of the American Union were formerly far more densely peopled than at the time when the European emigrants took possession of their territories ; that is to say, as densely peopled as when visited by the Spaniards under Hernando de Soto in 1540. At that time there were not only villages but true towns. Of these the largest seems to have been Mavila, the present Mobile. It was surrounded by a wooden wall plastered with clay, and protected by towers, probably mere scaffoldings with breastworks. Within the wall stood eighty large houses or, rather, barrack-like edifices, each supposed to have afforded shelter to one thousand persons, and from the flat roofs or balconies of which missiles were showered down upon the Spaniards. Hernando de Soto with his advanced guard was obliged to endure a conflict of nine hours, and the battle was not decided until the arrival of the main body, then still six hundred strong. The Spanish accounts speak of 11,000 enemies destroyed by fire and sword, while the conquerors lost forty-five horses and eighty-three soldiers, either on the spot or in consequence of their wounds. Where places so populous as Mavila had already sprung up, there can have been no hunting life, for tribes living by the chase never built cities.

If we could thus assure ourselves that the population of both continents became more dense towards the shores of the American Mediterranean, that is to say, the double bay of the Gulf of Mexico and the Caribbean Sea, and that these had half renounced the hunter's life, we must be persuaded that the favourable influence of a mild climate upon agricultural pursuits, combined

---

[76] P. Gumilla, El Orinoco ilustrado.

with the vicinity of the sea, facilitated this important transition to a higher state. Had the arrival of Europeans in the New World been delayed one or two thousand years, the civilized people of Mexico and Yucatan might have entered into communication with the Appalachic and Caribbean nations, and perhaps civilizations might have grown up in the New World also, comparable to those which existed on our Mediterranean about the time of Herodotus.

(c) *The Civilized Nations of North America and their Kinsmen.* —In the review of the hunting nations of North America, the tribes of Oregon, California, New Mexico, and Mexico have been passed over. Nor do we now propose to give a dry list of names, which can be better understood on an ethnographical chart. But we must notice one important result of Buschmann's researches. He united a large number of New Mexican and North Mexican languages into a single family, which he named Sonora. He paid special attention to the phonetic system, the numerals, and the grammar of the Tarahumara, Tepeguana, Cora, and Cahita languages.[77] All these possess common family features; all have more or less adopted a vocabulary from the Nahuatl. This is also the case with the language of the Moqui, who inhabit six of the famous "seven cities," or villages, north-west of Zuñi. Others allied in language to the Sonora family are the Utahs, Pah Utahs, the Diggers of California, and the Shoshons, or Snake Indians, which latter, before their expulsion by the Blackfeet, lived on this side of the Rocky Mountains, and now reside on the other side, on the Snake River, to which they have given their name. The Comantshes, the dreaded robber-tribes of Northern Mexico, also belong to this group. According to Maillard, they observe a division of the year into eighteen months of twenty days; in other words, they use the Mexican calendar. Buschmann still leaves it doubtful if we are to regard the Sonora languages—which, moreover, differ widely from one another—as the further-developed branches of a single stock, a Nahuatl primordial language; but it is certain that they all show traces of close intercourse with the ancient Mexicans. Nahuatl, the language of the latter, was spoken in full

---

[77] Abhandlungen der Berliner Akademie der Wissenschaften. 1863.

purity only in and about the lake district of the Mexican highlands. But, as is proved by the Aztec names of places, Nahuatl languages were locally scattered at extraordinary distances. Thus, in the neighbourhood of the South Pacific, they pervaded Guatemala; they appear with ancient ruined temples in the Mexican style in Honduras, and extend southwards to the Lake of Nicaragua. They cease entirely at Costa Rica. In the north they are spread over the whole of the present Mexican empire, with the exception of Cohahuila. But they reappear in Texas, and end in New California at the 37th degree north latitude [78] with the exception of scattered names which have reached the 50th degree of latitude. It is far inland in latitude 35, among the present Zuñi of New Mexico, that we must look for Cibola, or the " Country of the Seven Communities," discovered by Fra Marco, a monk from Nice, and shortly afterwards (in 1540) visited and described by the Spaniard Francisco Vasquez de Coronado. He found there small villages with stone houses, two or three storeys high, built like fortresses without an entrance, so that the roofs had to be mounted by ladders. The inhabitants cultivated maize and beans, reared turkeys, clothed themselves in woven stuffs, of which the threads were spun of some vegetable fibre that was not cotton, and wore head coverings exactly like those of the Aztecs of Mexico.[79] The same style of architecture is yet retained among the so-called Pueblo Indians, and was last described and depicted by Möllhausen.[80] The language of the Pueblo Indians is in no degree connected with the Nahuatl. Somewhat like these buildings were probably the so-called Casas Grandes, southwards near the Gila and at Chihuahua, respecting whose inhabitants so much has been written just because as yet we know nothing about them. Civilized nations lived therefore to the north of Mexico as far as the 35th degree of latitude.

The partial community of vocabulary of the Nahuatlecs and the present Snake Indians, induces us to suppose that the former may in ancient times have resembled the Shoshons, for either the Shoshons turned to the north after their contact with the Nahuat-

---

[78] Buschmann, Astekische Ortsnamen. Berlin, 1853.
[79] Coronado in Ramusio's Navigationi e viaggi.
[80] Möllhausen, Reise nach der Südsee.

lecs in the south, or else the Nahuatlecs originally lived with the Shoshons in the north before they emigrated to Mexico. After the power of their kinsmen, the Toltecs, had fallen, hordes of barbarians constantly invaded Mexico from the eleventh to the fourteenth century A.D. Among these were the Nahuatl Tlascaltecs, and the Nahuatl Aztecs. Both came from the north, that is to say, in the last instance, only from the north of the present Mexico; still it is enough that their migration was in a southerly direction. On their first appearance in Mexico, they are said to have been still very barbarous in comparison with the refined Toltecs, but this merely proves that they did not bring their highest civilization with them from their northerly home, but first developed it in the south, although at the time of the irruption they had reached a degree of culture about equal to that of the Casas Grandes on the Gila, or the City Indians of Cibola in the year 1540.

It is impossible to say, on the other hand, whether it was in the present Mexico, in Guatemala, in Honduras, or in Nicaragua, that the Toltecs first took up their abode. No one, however, has undertaken to prove that it was in Nicaragua, for the Aztec names of places in that district are probably derived from a later colonization, which is also the case with Honduras. In Guatemala, the seat of one of the oldest centres of civilization, in addition to names of Aztec extraction, there are names of places and local languages derived from another civilized nation, the Quiché, who are, again, linguistically allied to the Maya, their neighbours on the peninsula of Yucatan. At the time of the discovery, the social development of the Quiché and the Yucatecs was equal to that of Mexico. When the Toltecs enriched them with their civilization, they may already have raised themselves independently to a high grade of civilization. Contact with people as civilized as the Quiché and Maya certainly were, must have had a beneficial effect upon the Nahuatls when they came from the north. It is worth noting that Aztec names of places are totally wanting in Yucatan, which probably indicates that the Maya nations must have equalled the Nahuatls in the progress of culture, for colonies are always founded by preference among inferior nations.

In the empire of Mexico itself, besides Nahuatl, entirely different languages were spoken by the Otomi, the Mixtecs, and Zapotecs, the Matlaziacs and Tarascs.[81]

In South America all the civilized nations live either on the plateaux between the ridges of the Cordilleras or on the shores of the Pacific. Thus the empire of the Muysca, or more correctly of the Chibcha, grew up on the highlands of Bogotá on the right bank of the Magdalena River. Further south, as far as Chili, but keeping to the ridges of the plateaux, dwelt nations speaking kindred languages; namely, the so-called Quichua tribes in Quito and Peru, and on Lake Titicaca, the Colla, now better known under the name of Aymara, which has been erroneously attributed to them. These latter were formerly regarded as the most ancient civilized nation; their language was supposed to be the so-called court language of the Emperors of Peru,[82] and the temples of the sun on Lake Titicaca were believed to be the earliest buildings of the civilized races of South America. Now, however, we must look for their earliest abode in Cuzco itself. The Cara, or inhabitants of Quito, who also spoke a Quichua dialect, were said to have ascended the River Esmeralda, and to have taken possession of the plateaux.[83] They manufactured artistic works in cast gold,[84] and also instruments of bronze, and, like the Peruvians, observed the beginning of the solstices on pillars of stone visible at a great distance.[85] Entirely different from the Quichua nations are the Yunca tribes, who lived near the coast streams on the western slopes of the Andes, but were split up into locally separate states. They have left behind them innumerable remains of spacious buildings of comparatively high art, and they were in the habit of skillfully irrigating their land.[86] The Incas of Peru, without doubt,

---

[81] Orozco y Berra, in his Geografia de las lenguas de Mexico (1864), has given a linguistic map of Mexico, the only good feature in the whole book, as the author openly confesses that he has not philologically examined the languages, and being also unacquainted with Buschmann's researches, spreads anew errors long exploded.

[82] Thoroughly refuted by Markham, Journal of Royal Geographical Society, vol. xli. 1871.

[83] Velasco, Histoire du royaume de Quito. Paris, 1840.

[84] Benzoni, Mondo nuovo. Venice, 1565.

[85] Joseph de Acosta, Historic natural y moral de las Indias.

[86] Markham, as above.

must have learnt as much from them as they in their turn had to communicate.[87]

At the time of the emperors, the Rio Maule formed the boundary between Peru and Chili. To the south lived the Araucanians and their kinsmen the Patagonians. In the present Chili these people called themselves Pehuenches, or the "Westerns;" from Valdivia to Terra del Fuego, Huilliches, or the "Southerns;" in Patagonia, Tehuellsches; and, lastly, on the pampas between the Rio Negro and La Plata, Pehuelches, or the "Easterns." The old Abipones and the present inhabitants of the Gran Chaco, the desert to the west of the Paraguay, were closely allied to them in intellect and manners. Both Araucanians and Patagonians in some degree partook of the benefits of the Inca-Peruvian civilization;[88] at any rate, they resemble the inhabitants of the plateaux much more than the hunting tribes of Brazil, even if they cannot be classed among the civilized nations.

To account for the advanced social conditions in ancient Mexico and in the empire of the Peruvian Incas, many who underrated the talents of the so-called Redmen, assumed that the best germs of civilization were carried by chance from the Old World to the New. Now it was Egyptians from the Platonic island of Atlantis, or at the time of the circumnavigation of Africa under Neku; now it was Carthaginians from the colonies on the coast of the present Morocco, who were said to have made their way to Brazil; now it was Northmen, who in their voyages of discovery reached the good "wine country" (Virginia) in Central America, and in the guise of Votan, the name of a hero or an idol of the Chiapanecs, the old northern Woden was detected; now it was said that Malay Polynesians, drifting from the South Sea, landed on the western shores of America; now it was imagined that descriptions of some parts of the New World might be recognized in Chinese records of an eastern land named Fusang. All these passing guesses were so ill-founded that they were easily refuted, and never obtained real credit.

---

[87] Miguel Cavello Balboa (Histoire du Pérou) gives ancient lists of the sovereigns of Yucatan, with a sketch of their history.

[88] The Quichua terms for the higher numbers had spread as far as the Pehuelches. D'Orbigny, L'homme américain.

Yet the possibility must not be disputed that mariners from the Old World might be cast away in America, for we actually know of at least one case of this description. In December, 1731, a bark, manned by five or six men, arrived at Trinidad, which had been caught in a storm on its passage from Teneriffe with a cargo of wine to one of the western Canary Islands, and had ultimately been carried by the trade wind to the West Indies.[89] But it is idle to suppose that one or more individuals are able to convey the civilization of their own country like freight in the hold of a ship to distant worlds. Europeans comparing themselves with Australians are apt to fancy themselves demi-gods in the midst of beings only semi-human. Each imagines that were he thrown among a tribe of such savages, he would bestow on them a share of the blessings of our civilization; that these favoured beings would honour him as their benefactor and their saviour; and even that the appearance of the " bearded man " would be remembered as a religious legend, and his second coming be awaited as the dawn of an age of prosperity, just as the Aztecs promised themselves a fresh growth and exaltation of their condition on the reappearance of Quetzalcoatl. But the real result of such a case is clearly shown by the fate of James Morill, an unfortunate sailor who spent seventeen years among Australian tribes. At the end of these seventeen years the natives led exactly the same life as before, while Morill ate shell-fish with them, slept like them under a slight shelter of leaves, had discarded his clothing, almost entirely forgotten his mother tongue, and he, the demi-god, had sunk into an Australian. Nor can we take comfort in the supposition that although a single individual must succumb to this fate, yet several, a ship's crew for instance, cast away in the New World, would have effected greater results. History proves the contrary. In his first voyage Columbus left behind him at Hayti forty Spaniards well equipped in a small stronghold, amid a good-humoured and almost defenceless population, and on his return a few months later he found nothing but corpses and the remains of a conflagration. The fate of Hernando de Soto and his companions, in his expeditions across the south of the United States,

---

[89] P. Gumilla, El Orinoco illustrado.

is even more instructive. When they landed in 1540 they were well equipped, but they never received any supplies from their own country. Their horses perished, their firearms became useless for want of powder, their daggers rusted and broke, their clothes and shoes wore out, till finally they marched and fought, dressed and armed like Indians. It is evident that a high degree of civilization cannot be transmitted by a small number of individuals, for progress in culture takes place only in dense populations and by means of a division of labour, which fits each individual into a highly complex but most effective organization. If any one member is separated from this whole, he appears far more helpless than the child of nature, and for all practical purposes he is of no more value than is the stray wheel of a broken watch for telling the time.

The phenomena of American civilization thus originated independently and spontaneously, and, what is still more remarkable, the respective civilizations of the northern and southern continents developed themselves entirely without reciprocal contact or aid, for the Mexicans were as little aware of the existence of the empire of the Incas as were the Peruvians of the splendours of Tenochtitlan or of Palenque. The geographical knowledge of the Aztecs extended only to the Lake of Nicaragua, as far as which their language was spoken, or single bands of colonists had penetrated who spoke Nahuatl. On the other hand, according to a record, which is however of doubtful authority, the Inca Huayna Capac is said to have received tidings of the appearance of bearded strangers (under Balboa in 1513) on the western shore of the Isthmus of Darien. But when we consider that shortly before the discovery of America the Peruvian Incas had conquered the empire of Quito (1487), and that no particular difficulties impeded their further advance, it is possible that a communication between the civilized nations of South and Central America, and an interchange of their resources, might have taken place in the course of the 16th and 17th centuries without the intervention of the Europeans. The distance between Mexico and Cuzco is about 2900 miles, whereas Babylon, Nineveh, Athens, Sidon, and Tyre were only from 320 to 780 miles from Memphis on the Nile; from this far greater separation of the two centres of American

20

civilization, we become aware that the division of the New World
into two continents was much more unfavourable to the quick
progress of civilization, even had the inhabitants possessed intellectual powers equal to those of the people of the Old World.
The inland seas, and especially the highland lakes, have exercised
a peculiar power of attraction on the civilized nations of the New
World. Lake Titicaca was formerly, though erroneously, considered the earliest seat of Quichua civilization, but under the
later Incas it was the seat of the famous manufacture of Cumbi,
the finest llama cloth.[90]   The temple pyramids of the Toltecs
were reflected in the lakes of Anahuac ; the sanctuaries of the
Chibcha tribes were situated on the Lake of Guatavita, with the
shores of which is connected the legend of the golden personage
(*el dorado*), who when he bathed washed off the pulverized metal
into its waters. The islands on the Peten Lake in Guatemala were
selected as a residence by the Iztaes in their migration southwards
after the destruction of the empire of Mayapan, in the year 1420;[91]
and previous to the discovery of the Lake of Nicaragua, a refined
population had become extraordinarily dense on its shores. Hence,
at first sight, there is a great tendency to attribute to inland seas a
peculiarly great influence on the advancement of social conditions.
But on further investigation their influence is seen to be more
limited. South of the 40th degree north latitude the New World
is singularly destitute of inland seas, and this is especially the case
with South America as compared with Africa, to which it bears
such a close resemblance. It is therefore conceivable that many
civilized tribes halted in their migrations, fascinated by the sight
of a bright expanse of water in the interior of the country. In
the celebrated pass of the Andes, between Valparaiso and the
ruins of Mendoza, of which the splendid scenery was never better
described than by Pöppig, is situated a small mountain pool
named by the nations "the eye of the Inca," an expression which
seems to indicate that the so-called Redman was not entirely
insensible to the charms of scenery.[92]   Lakes on elevated plains

---

[90] J. Acosta, Hist. natural y moral.   Madrid, 1792.

[91] Morelet, Reisen in Central America.   Jena, 1872.

[92] Pöppig, Reise in Chile, Peru, etc.

usually lie in shallow depressions, and round their margins rise gentle slopes peculiarly fitted for purposes of agriculture. The lakes themselves supplied food in the shape of fish, and in Mexico they harbour on their sedgy banks millions of edible and palatable insects' eggs (*Corixa mercenaria*), which are baked into cakes. Populations would therefore be more apt to grow dense on the shores of these inland seas than in other places, but it would be a mistake to attribute to them any decisive influence on the development of the social conditions of the New World.

The later and rapid growth of the empire of the Incas from small beginnings, in the course of five centuries at most, or perhaps of only three, has been very satisfactorily accounted for by Squier. The germ of the Peruvian empire was developed on the Punos or bare table-lands, which rise to a height of from ten to sixteen thousand feet between the double or triple chain of the Andes. Between the western slopes of these mountains and the Pacific Ocean stretches a narrow fringe of coast, on which rain never or rarely falls, and which is moistened by mists during six months at most. It is only where coast rivers flow from the Andes into the sea that agriculture and the cultivation of trees is in any way possible. But the coast rivers are few and far between, while the intervening spaces are complete deserts. Thus single tribes might well maintain themselves for a long time, separately and independently of one another, but when the first great state arose on the table-land, the coast populations, which were separate and weak, were successfully overthrown, and by these acquisitions the power of the monarchy on the table-land was increased. Where the rainless fringe of coast terminated to the south, namely, in the present Chili, the sway of the Incas reached its limits. Towards the interior it was in like manner unable to descend the eastern slope of the Andes through the forest district to the plains of the Amazon, where rude hunting tribes still range in undisturbed barbarism.

All South American civilization, including that which was not Peruvian, that of the Chibcha on the plateaux of Bogotá and Tunja, on the right bank of the Magdalena river, was therefore closely connected with considerable mountain heights, and the same phenomena are repeated, although not so invariably, in North America. It is very easy, and especially so to us who live in the temperate zone and avoid torrid regions, to recognize the favourable influence on the course of civilization of the high plateaux within the tropics. Their inhabitants, we say, escape the enervating atmosphere of the sultry lowlands ; they were obliged to provide clothing and shelter as a protection against the weather; to avoid starvation, they were early obliged to till the ground and to store provisions, and they were even soon forced to congregate and organize societies, in order to meet the requirements of their abode with greater ease. True as all this may sound, it does not account for the strange fact that nations should voluntarily have sought out regions in which the difficulties of maintenance were greater. In the Old World, moreover, civilization was always favoured by the lowlands. It occurs there at the sea level, by the side of great rivers, such as the Nile, the Tigris, and the Euphrates. The Chinese too maintain that their civilization was not developed until they had descended to the Hoang-ho. When the Brahminical Aryans entered India they first spread themselves over the plains of the Ganges ; they did not ascend the slopes of the Himalayas, but they drove the original inhabitants into the Vindhya mountains and the jungles of the table-land of Deccan, where they still propagate their race in accessible deserts, without having changed their mode of life for perhaps three thousand years. Thus in the Old World it is everywhere the case that the civilized nations, as the stronger, seek out the more convenient lowlands and expel the weaker aborigines into the mountains. This is the case also in all the islands and peninsulas of Southern Asia, where the Malays have always taken possession of the coast, while the uncivilized Papuans were obliged to seek refuge in the hill country of the interior. Mountains are almost always impediments to civilization. Unlike plains, they admit of no close assembly of the inhabitants ; they hinder or stop active intercourse between the scattered communities, and as we ascend their narrow valleys to the central ridge, it seems as if we approached, not indeed the end of the world, but the outer edge of all higher civilization. Table-lands are more favourable to advance than mountain chains, but yet we must remember that they have been mounted only by nations which have been expelled from the more convenient lowlands by stronger opponents. It might therefore be imagined that in the higher strata of air even weakly tribes would be invigorated, yet nowhere in the history of the Old World can it be shown that civilization has descended from the heights to the plains. Hence in South America there must have been peculiar conditions which attracted civilization to the table-lands. The education of the civilized natives of South America is due to three natural products of the Peruvian plateaux, namely, the llama in its various species, the potato, and the Chinoa bean (*Chenopodium Quinoa*). The Inca Garcilasso,[93] who has given a detailed description of the state of civilization in ancient Peru, repeatedly remarks on the extraordinary lack of animal food in those regions. It was only on the occasions of the great drives of game organized by the Incas that the lower ranks obtained the flesh of the llama, and then in all probability merely because it would otherwise have been spoilt. On other feast days they ate as a delicacy a small mammal (according to Garcilasso a rabbit), which they carefully reared, but when this was soon after imported into Spain, it was there thought so unpalatable as not to be worth the trouble of breeding. In the rainless coast districts fish was the only animal food. It was therefore not necessarily the weakly inhabitants who, driven out by stronger tribes, sought refuge on the Punos of Peru or Quito, but, on the contrary, bold and spirited men were probably the first to ascend the chain of the Cordilleras, in order to hunt and tame the shy llamas on the plateaux. Yet as maize ripens there only in a few sheltered spots, they would never have been able to establish dwellings on these lofty heights, or to build noble temples of the sun on the islands of Lake Titicaca, had not the potato and the Chinoa bean thriven at altitudes equal to those of our mountain tops. That Brazilian hunting tribes did not migrate from the side of the Atlantic to the highlands of Peru, but that on the contrary the Puno was ascended from the shores of the Pacific, may be assumed, because we find in the hands of the inhabitants of the Andes, even as far as Terra del Fuego, a weapon which no forest hunting tribe ever invented, but which on the other hand is

---

[93] Commentarios reales. Lisboa, 1609.

especially common among shepherds, namely, the sling and its varieties, the lasso and the bolas, or casting-line.

Before ascertaining to which of the four independent civilized nations, the Toltec-Mexican, the Yucatec, that of the Incas of Peru, or of the Chibcha of Cundinamarca, the highest rank is due, it must be mentioned that the cultivation of maize was common to all. In Mexico maguey and cocoa were also cultivated, and, in Peru and Bogotá, the potato, the Chinoa bean, and the coca bush. Artificial irrigation is found everywhere, but the use of guano as manure was confined to Peru. The Mexicans bred the turkey, the Peruvians trained the llama as a beast of burden. Bridges and causeways were constructed by all the nations above enumerated, but the high roads of the Peruvians, paved with stones and shaded by rows of trees,[94] were unquestionably superior.[95] A postal service was organized both in Mexico and in the empire of the Incas.[96] None of the four civilizations were without stone buildings, but the Peruvians alone constructed arches.[97] The Chibcha still lived in the age of unpierced stone implements. The same may be said even with regard to the Yucatecs and Mexicans, for although they were acquainted with copper and bronze, the use of metal implements was very unusual, for the sharp flakes and knife blades of obsidian were efficient substitutes. The weapons were the same among all the four civilized nations, except that the Peruvians had not the wooden swords of the other three, while they alone carried battle-axes and lances with bronze blades. The northern nations used gold dust enclosed in quills, bars of tin and copper, and also cocoa beans, as money. The Incas of Peru were acquainted with weights and scales in their commercial transactions, and the Chibcha even used discs of gold as the medium of exchange. Were we to continue the list, the result would tend to show that the Peruvians excelled the Chibcha in many,

---

[94] Francisco de Xerez, Conquista del Peru, in Barcia, Historiadores.

[95] See the description of the Imperial road from Cuzco to Quito in Carate, Historia del Peru.

[96] The Chaski, or runners, brought sea fish to the Imperial kitchen at Cuzco in forty-eight hours, a distance of about 315 miles. Acosta, Hist. natural y moral.

[97] Rivero y Tschudi, Antiguëdades peruanas. Vienna, 1851.

and the northern nations in a few points of civilization. But the latter possessed a calendar of 365¼ days, whereas the Peruvians were satisfied with observing the sun's rising point (azimuth) at the time of the solstices by means of stone pillars. The Mexicans possessed maps from which the Spanish conquerors derived important information, while the Peruvians only made embossed plans of towns. The Peruvians were far poorer, inasmuch as, except hieroglyphics,[98] they used only the Quippu, or knot writing, similar to that of the Chinese in former times,[99] or to that which we have already met with among the Papuans,[100] and such as existed even among the hunting tribes on the Orinoco, where, on the commencement of a journey, the husband used to leave his wife a cord on which were as many knots as the days of his intended absence, one of which she untied every evening. These knotted cords also served as an acknowledgement of debt; on the payment of each instalment, the creditor unfastened one of the knots.[101] But Quippu writing is little fitted to preserve the memory of events and names, for which reason the credibility of the Inca-Peruvian history is open to considerable doubt. The Mexicans, on the other hand, possessed a series of characters expressive of rebus-like syllables, and also a collection of symbols each representing an idea. The Maya of Yucatan had reached a still higher grade. Even if they borrowed their calendar from Mexico, they were the inventors of a phonetic character consisting of twenty-seven partially homophonous letters and several syllabic signs.[102]

The local distribution of the primitive civilizations in the New World points to several important conclusions. We saw that in South as well as in North America the Atlantic side invariably belonged to these rude hunting tribes, and the western portion towards the Pacific to the civilized nations. Von Frantzius has

---

[98] Acosta, Historia natural y moral. J. J. von Tschudi has given a sample of these records in his Reisen durch Südamerika.

[99] Whitney, Language.

[100] See above, p. 346.

[101] Gumilla, El Orinoco ilustrado.

[102] Diego de Landa, Relation des choses de Yucatan, Paris, 1864; and Von Hellwald in the Ausland. 1871.

shown that this is the case in Central America also. Many of our readers may remember how in the adventurous wanderings the Spaniard, Cabeza de Vaca, travelling westwards from Texas, as he passed into the Atlantic watershed, left behind him the miserable squalor of the Redskins and found himself surrounded by kindly, well-fed, agricultural nations, to whom he owed his ultimate deliverance.   It might, at most, be objected that, contrary to this rule, a civilized region on the eastern shore of the continent, and belonging geographically to the Atlantic margin, was to be found in Yucatan, but the true eastern margin of the New World in Central America is probably formed by the Antilles, and it is quite permissible to look upon the Caribbean Sea and the Gulf of Mexico as two inland seas, the union of which is prevented by the interposition of Yucatan—a physical formation which is in itself sufficient to raise this peninsula into a region favoured by rapid increase of civilization.   But the physical reason why the western half of America exclusively belonged to the civilized nations is to be looked for in its comparative dryness. A superabundance of rain discharges itself upon the western coasts of both continents only in high latitudes, and the existence of dense forests always depends upon a large quantity of rain. Great unbroken forests, however, occupied the regions to the east, in Brazil as well as in the United States.

On the Pacific slopes of America it may further be observed that the condition of the inhabitants perceptibly improves on approaching and passing the tropics : a fact which is true even of the hunting tribes, and corroborated by similar experiences in the Old World. Warm countries when sufficiently watered will always most richly repay tillage, and it is only where there is a considerable profusion of food easily procured that a dense population becomes possible. In low latitudes it is not until a certain control has been obtained over nature by human intelligence and social organization, that civilization is able to penetrate into the more inclement regions. It is also an important point that Mexico is situated where the northern continent abruptly narrows into a peninsula. Even in a mature state of civilization, and still more in an earlier stage, nations easily resolve on a change of abode ; as the only passage from the northern to the southern continent was this contraction of the mainland, they necessarily pressed more frequently upon one another there than elsewhere. In Mexico, therefore, new blood was always entering, and it was thus that the antiquated Toltec government was reinforced by the migrations of youthful Nahuatl nations from the north.

But the elevation of North America was unusually favourable to migrations in the direction of the equator. The diffusion of human civilization has so many points of analogy with the migration of animal and vegetable species, that we find a resemblance also in the New World. The highlands and Cordilleras of North America enabled the plants and animals of colder regions to spread themselves far to the south. They acted as bridges by which the tropics were entered in higher and cooler strata of air. South America possesses no true firs or pines, but conifera have been able to spread from North America to the Isthmus of Darien on the mountain ridges, and Andreas Wagner fixes the termination of the North American fauna at the point which Shouw had defined as the southern boundary of the pine family.[103] There is, however, no exact limit, for the faunas of North and South America overlap. Just in the same way the people who lived in the North were able to seek out new homes, and to pass quickly by the tropics, without being obliged to descend into the hot and feverish tract lying along the coast, which only long habit during many generations could render habitable to their race.

A favourable region will not only accelerate the intellectual development of its inhabitants sooner or later, but it will invariably become the spoil of the most capable nations, for the strength which makes itself felt in history is in great measure based upon capacity. The fact that the Nahuatl nations, in their migrations, preferred the highlands of Mexico to all other districts as a dwelling, is accounted for by their system of husbandry. Like all Americans, they cultivated the only cereal of the New World, the maize, which, although it produces remarkably rich harvests in Mexico, could be cultivated with equal success in many other places. But on these plateaux, in addition to maize, grows the

---

[103] Abhandlungen der bayerischen Akademie der Wissenschaften.

Maguey (*Agava mexicana*) from the flower buds of which a juice is drawn in astonishing quantities, which the ancient Mexicans converted into their favourite beverage, metl or pulque.[104] At their feet also lay the torrid line of coast which furnished them with all the fruits of the tropics, amongst others, the cocoa, which they already knew how to mix with pods of vanilla.

The fact is therefore explained that of the many tribes which successively passed through Central America, the most highly gifted chose the table-lands of Mexico, where they had the advantage of coming into contact with the Maya and Quiché of Yucatan and Guatemala. The local position of the youthful civilizations was therefore not accidental, but was due to the physical features and the situation of the countries as well as to the consequent distribution of animals and plants, and it was to a certain degree unalterably predestined even at the time when the first Asiatics reached the north-west of the New World.

---

[104] De Candolle regards Mexico as the botanical home of this Agave. The prohibition against drinking of pulque, and the severe punishments inflicted on drunkenness in the later empire of the Aztecs, is the best proof of the seductiveness of this beverage (Prescott, Mexico, vol. i. pp. 137, 157). Perhaps it may have been an excessive consumption of pulque which sapped the strength of the ancient Toltecs.

IV.—THE DRAVIDA, OR ABORIGINES OF WESTERN INDIA.

BEFORE the irruption of the Brahminical Aryans, Western India and Beloochistan were inhabited by a race which is now commonly termed Dravida. Their skin is generally very dark, frequently quite black. In this point they resemble negroes, although they are without the repulsive odour of the latter. Their most noticeable feature is their long black hair, which is neither tufted nor straight, but crimped or curly. This clearly distinguishes them from the Mongoloid nations, as does the fact that the hair of their beard and bodies grows profusely. Coarse and refined, noble and ignoble forms of face are intermingled. The intumescent lips occasionally recall the negroes, but the jaws are never prominent.[1] All who have studied the ancient history of India are agreed that, although the organization of castes existed at the time of the composition of the Vedas,[2] it was only at a later period that intermarriages were strictly prohibited. Frequent intermixtures with the aborigines must previously have taken place, and they are still common in Southern India between male Brahmins and Sudra women. Hence, even the highest castes, among which we must still look for the purest Aryan blood, are not distinguished from the aboriginal population by any marked characters. "The skull of the Brahmin," observes Barnard Davis,[3] on the strength of numerous measurements, "does not differ from other Hindoo skulls." Welcker came to the same conclusion,[4] and gives 73 as the index of breadth for high as well as for low castes, while Davis found it to be 75, a rare instance of agreement, for the difference of two per cent. is merely due to different systems of measurements. The height of the skull does not always exceed the breadth, or at most by a small percentage. The Indians are therefore also dolichocephals

---

[1] H. von Schlagintweit, Indien und Hochasien, vol. i. p. 546.

[2] Martin Haug, Brahma und die Brahmanen. 1871.

[3] Thesaurus Craniorum.
Kraniologische Mittheilungen, p. 157. Comp. Appendix A.

of medium height. Isidor Kopernicki[5] has also recently compared 83 Hindoo heads with 15 of gipsy origin, and has given us figures which agree with those above stated. The inhabitants of India thus form at the present time but a single race, and the separation of the populations resident between the Himalayas and the Vindhya mountains from the Dravida of the Deccan, is based solely on the fact that the former speak languages which are descended more or less directly from Sanscrit.

The non-Aryan inhabitants of the peninsula and Beloochistan are divided according to language into Dravida proper, and the more central populations from the south of the Ganges to about the 18th degree of latitude, which latter, to avoid inventing a new name, we shall follow Friedrich Müller in calling the Munda family, and under this name include the Kolh, the Santal, the Bhilla, and other smaller tribes. This division is justifiable because their languages, which are allied to one another,[6] belong to a totally different group from that of the Dravida.[7] These so-called jungle tribes maintain themselves on the produce of the chase and of agriculture, and still make great use of stone implements. In Sinbonga they worship a benevolent creator, but they also offer sacrifices to the evil powers. They believe in magic, and in consequence trials of witches and trials by ordeal are customary among them. In addition to this the worship of Civa has made its way among them.[8]

Among the Dravida proper are the Brahui of Beloochistan, while the Beloochs themselves are Eranians.[9] The language of the former, which was long ago placed among the Dravida by Christopher Lassen,[10] extends from Shal in the north to Jalaván in the south, and from Kohak in the west to Harrand in the east. The Brahui are a rude, hardy, and uncorrupted tribe, given to hospitality, and of unalterable fidelity. Locally separated from

---

[5] Archiv für Anthropologie, vol. v. p. 285. 1872.

[6] Jellinghaus (Zeitschrift für Ethnologie, vol. iii. 1871) observes that the language of the Santals and that of the Munda Khol are more closely allied than high and low German.

[7] Whitney, Language and the Study of Language, p. 327.

[8] Jellinghaus, as above.   [9] Fr. Spiegel, Eranische Alterthumskunde.

[10] Zeitschrift für Kunde des Morgenlandes, vol. v.

these, quite in the south of the Indian peninsula, five Dravidical civilized languages were developed; namely, on the margin of the west coast, the Tulu, or Tulava, which is now spoken only in the neighbourhood of Mangalore by about 150,000 inhabitants; secondly, on a small strip of coast adjoining, as far as the southern point, Malayalam, or Malabar; thirdly, from Cape Comorin to beyond the latitude of Madras, and from the ridge of the Western Ghauts to the Bay of Bengal, Tamil, the language of the Tamuls, to whom the northern half of Ceylon also belongs.[11] It is spoken by ten millions, and possesses an ancient litera-ture. Not long after the commencement of our era a Tamul academy was founded at Madura, under a king of the Pandja empire.[12] The appearance of Tiruvalluvers, the poet-king of the Tamuls, occurred on the other hand between A.D. 200–800. His principal work, the Kural, or "short lines," with four and three-footed strophes with initial rhymes and alliterations in the middle, is a didactic poem, with maxims on the moral aims of man, full of tender and true ideas, but vitiated by the superstition of the transmigration of souls, from which release is to be sought in the Buddhist method.[13]

The fourth civilized language of the Dravida family is Telugu, by the English called Gentoo, or the pagan language; it is spoken by fourteen millions, and maintains its existence along the east coast from the 14th to the 19th latitude, whence it extends into the interior to the meridian of Cape Comorin. From hence westwards the fifth Dravida language, Kannadi, or Canarese, the language of the Carnatic, is diffused among more than five millions of people. The language of the Tuda, a small tribe in the Nilgherry Hills, in the 11th degree of latitude, is a dialect of Canarese. The Gonds in Gondivana, and the Khonds of Khondistan, also belong to the Dravida nations. The latter were notorious for the human sacrifices which they annually offered to the deified earth. Captain Campbell, an English officer, however, succeeded between 1837–52 in persuading one

---

[11] Comp. the linguistic map in Berghaus's Physikal Atlas.
[12] K. Graul, in Ausland, p. 1160. 1855.
[13] K. Graul, Bibliotheca Tamulica.

tribe after the other to renounce this horrible worship by solemn treaty.[14]

The Paharia, in the line of mountains near Râjmahel, in Bengal, south of the Ganges, is connected with the languages above enumerated.

All these languages and dialects are closely akin, whereas Cingalese, or Elu, which prevails in the interior of the southern half of Ceylon, is alien in character. It has neither pronouns nor inflectional elements in common with the Dravida languages, and it thus maintains a solitary position, although the language is of the same type, and the connection of the various parts of the sentence is effected in the same manner.[15] Hence, especially as the physical characters are the same, there is no necessity for separating the Cingalese of Ceylon into a distinct race.

The Dravida languages define the sense of the roots by appended groups of sounds, and in so doing observe laws of euphony, which react from the vowel of the suffix on the vowel of the root stem, therefore in the converse direction from that observed in the Altaic languages. The Dravida nations have, nevertheless, been placed in a so-called "Turanian" family, on account of the similarity of system in the formation of words, but this hazardous step has already been condemned by philologists;[16] an ethnological system, however, which attributes the chief importance to physical characters, can only enjoin caution against this mistake. In the Dravida languages we already detect rudimentary distinctions of grammatical gender, inasmuch as the substantives are divided into a "high and low caste." All words designating superior beings, men, duties, or spirits belong to the high caste; and all others, which express animals, other visible objects and ideas, are of the low caste.[17]

The masculine formula is constructed with the suffixes *ân, on, ôn,*

---

[14] He relates all the incidents in his comprehensive work, Thirteen Years Service amongst the Wild Tribes of Khondistan, by John Campbell. 1864. The information which he gives respecting wife-stealing among the Khonds has been already noticed.

[15] Fr. Müller, Reise der Fregatte Novara, vol. ii. p. 218.

[16] Whitney, Language and the Study of Language, p. 327.

[17] K. Graul, Tamil Grammar.

the contraction of *avan* (masculine), the feminine with the suffixes *âl, al*, the contraction of *aval* (feminine). *Magan* is therefore the son, *magal* the daughter ; *illân* the master of the house, *illâl* the mistress of the house.[18]

V.—HOTTENTOTS AND BUSHMEN.

In the southern parts of Africa, near the Atlantic coast, and on the side more remote from the Indian Ocean, live a race of men, partly split up into tribes, but mainly distinguishable into Hottentots and Bushmen. The first of these names signifies stammerer, and was given to them by the Dutch in ridicule of their clicking sounds. It is now replaced by Koi-Koin, or the men, the title which the Hottentots themselves use. The Bushmen are called *Sān*, the plural of *Sāb*, by the Hottentots. Tufted matting of the hair is common to both divisions, but it also appears among other South Africans, although in a less degree. The Bushmen are distinguishable from the latter chiefly by the leathery yellow or brown colour of their skin, which becomes much wrinkled at an early age. Their finger-nails also are never lightly coloured as is the case with the Bantu negroes.[1]

The women of both these divisions are remarkable for steatopygy,[2] that is to say, the fatty cushions of the buttocks project above like inverted steps, and then gradually merge into the thighs ; in other words, the arrangement is the reverse of that which occurs in other races.[3] A less trustworthy character is the elongation in the women of the *labia minora* and of the *praeputium clitoridis* (Hottentot's apron), for similar deviations occur not only in Africa, but also in America.[4] The beard is scanty, and the rest of the body is almost entirely hairless. According to Welcker, the relative breadth of the head is only 69, but, as the skull widens towards

---

[18] Fr. Müller, Reise der Fregatte Novara.

[1] Fritsch, Eingeborne Südafrika's, pp. 264, 279.

[2] Theophilus Hahn asserts that this formation occurs also in men during youth.

[3] According to the result of the dissection of the Afandy who was brought us to Tübingen as a corpse in 1866. Archiv. für Anthropologie, vol. iii.

[4] Dr. Ploss in the Zeitschrift für Ethnologie, vol. iii. 1871.

the back, the index would rise a few per cent. if the calipers were inserted at the widest place. But the skulls are yet more remarkable when we consider the occiput, for the height is even less than the breadth, so that these people belong to the low dolichocephals. The jaws are usually prominent; but the prognathism is moderate in degree. The cheek-bones also project laterally. The lips, although very full, are not so intumescent as in the South African negroes. Near the root of the nose the nasal bones often project but little beyond the adjacent parts, so that the snub nose makes its appearance only a little way above the mouth. The opening of the eyes is narrow, but not oblique, as Barrow has stated, having probably been deceived by the habit common among the Koi-Koins of contracting their brows as a protection against the dazzling sun. The Bushmen, who have all these characters in common with the Koi-Koins, are, in their turn, distinguished from the latter by secondary peculiarities. Their stature is considerably smaller than that of the Koi-Koins, although the tribes to the west of Lake Ngami are described as taller. It remains for future travellers to decide whether a former original population, once much more widely spread and akin to the Bushmen, are not represented by the Obongo, a dirty yellow race of low stature, ranging from 4 ft. 4 in. to 5 ft., with tufted matted hair, and skins covered with down, whom Du Chaillu met with in equatorial West Africa, and described as timid people inhabiting the forests[5]; by the dwarf-like Acka, or Ticki-Ticki, whose dwelling-place is situated to the south of the Uellé, and therefore not in the Nile district of Dr. Schweinfurth;[6] lastly, by the small Doko in the south of Kaffa, respecting whom Krapf[7] received information from a somewhat untrustworthy source.[8]

The latter are distinguished from the Hottentots by the absence of secondary sexual characters, with the single exception of steatopygy. The men do not exceed the women in height; and the pelvises of the two sexes are so much alike as to be mistaken for

---

[5] Ashango Land, pp. 316–320.

[6] Im Herzen von Afrika, vol. ii. p. 136. Leipzic, 1874.

[7] J. L. Krapf, Reisen in Ostafrika, vol. i. pp. 76–79.

[8] Behm on the Bushman territory in Petermann's Mittheilungen, 1858, and in the same work on the pigmy nations of South Africa. 1871.

one another, and even the feeble development of the mammary glands is strikingly similar in male and female Bushmen.[9]

The Bushmen and Koi-Koin form a single race; they are, as Theophilus Hahn observes, the children of the same mother. It is true that in language they have in common only the clicking sounds, which are produced by applying the tongue to the teeth, or to various parts of the gums, and suddenly jerking it back. One of these sounds is used by Europeans to express annoyance, and another by drivers as an encouragement to their horses. Except the clicking sounds, and a few words which have been interchanged,[10] there is no resemblance between the San and the Koi-Koin languages.[11] The dialects of the Bushmen differ widely from one another, as is usual in all hunting tribes, although a certain kinship is always recognizable;[12] but we are as yet totally without information respecting the system pursued in their formation of words.[13]

The Koi-Koin language, on the contrary, is of great ethnological interest.[14] Dr. Moffat was the first to discover in it a resemblance to the language of ancient Egypt. This was also the opinion of Lepsius, and was also acknowledged by Pruner Bey.[15] Even Max Müller has sustained the assertion,[16] and Whitney has repeated it.[17] Lastly, Bleek admits that, in the phonetic signs for the genders, the Hottentot language agrees more closely with ancient Egyptian or Coptic than with other languages, but that it also contains traces of Semitic forms.[18]

---

[9] Fritsch, Eingeborne Südafrika's, pp. 407, **415.**

[10] Theophilus Hahn in the Globus. 1870.

[11] Fritsch, Drei Jahre in Südafrika, pp. 253, 254.

[12] Theophilus Hahn, VI. and VII. Jahresbericht des Dresdener Vereins für Erdkunde.

[13] A description of the manners of the Bushmen has already been given. See p. 146.

[14] S. G. Morton, Types of Mankind, p. 253. 1854.

[15] L'origine de l'ancienne race egyptienne. Mémoire lue à la Société d'Anthropologie, Aug. 1, 1871, p. 430.

[16] Science of Language, vol. ii. p. 2.

[17] Language and the Science of Language, p. 347.

[18] Reineke Fuchs in Afrika. Weimar, 1870. Bleek still clings to the common origin of the Hottentot and Hamito-Semitic languages.

Von Gabelentz, Pott, Friedr. Müller, and Theophilus Hahn have pronounced against the relationship, and we should not have recurred to this old dispute, did it not plainly show that the dialects of the Koi-Koin must be very highly developed, and, in fact, so highly that Martin Haug supposes that their higher and more refined constituents have been acquired by contact with a civilized people. It is impossible to say whether this people is the same as the ancient Egyptians.[19] Not a single fact, however, speaks in favour of any such contact. Hence, until strict proofs are adduced for these conjectures, we must persist in maintaining that languages may be raised and polished by nations which have been unjustly called savages. The social condition of our forefathers at the time of Tacitus was little better than that of the Koi-Koin, but their language was even then Aryan in dignity.

The Nama and other dialects of the Koi-Koin attach highly abraded phonetic forms to the end of the roots. From *koi* human being, comes *koi-b* man, *koi-s* woman, *koi-gu* men, *koi-ti* women, *koi-i* person, *koi-n* people. We select this example that we may add that from *koi*, human being, is derived *koi-si* kindly, *koi-si-b* philanthropist, *koi-si-s* humanity.[20] As many anthropologists reproach primitive nations with the assertion that their languages contain no expressions for abstract ideas, or no word for God or morality, we take this opportunity of pointing out that the Hottentots, who were once placed in the lowest grade, possess this said word for kindliness.

As they have already been in communication with Europeans for several centuries, we shall obtain the best information respecting their manners and customs from the older descriptions, of which the most valuable is undoubtedly that given by Kolbe in the first decade of last century.

At the time when the Portuguese first saw them, the Hottentots were said to be cattle-breeders,[21] but not given to agriculture,

---

[19] Anthropologisches Correspondanzblatt, p. 21. 1872.

[20] Nama Grammatik von Th. Hahn in the VI. and VII. Jahresbricht of the Dresden Vereins für Erdkunde, p. 32.

[21] The Angra dos Vaqueiros, or the landing point, of Bartolomeo Dias (Barros, Da Asia) was the present Bay of Algoa. Peschel, Zeitalter der Entdeckungen, p. 94.

contenting themselves with wild fruits and roots, which latter, however, it was unlawful to dig up until the ripe seeds were shed.[22] For shelter they used a low dome-shaped framework made of sticks, which were sunk into the ground, bent and lashed together, and then covered with rush-mats. Their clothing consisted of leathern aprons and cloaks; they wore sandals, and both sexes— the women from feelings of modesty—covered their heads with fur caps. Spears, darts (kiri), and shields for parrying blows were their weapons; and for hunting purposes they carried bows and poisoned arrows. Like all Africans, they knew the arts of smelting iron ore and of working the metal.[23] They were in the habit of training oxen for riding purposes in very early times. Cooking was done in earthen vessels. From honey they made an intoxicating drink; and, owing to their strong tendency to such beverages, brandy drinking has become a national vice among them. In addition to this they, in common with the Bantu negroes, had long indulged in the pernicious practice of smoking Dacha, or hemp. The contempt with which they are regarded by Europeans is perhaps principally due to their uncleanliness. The custom, incredible as it sounds, that, on the conclusion of a marriage, the Shaman defiles the bridal pair with his urine, is said actually to continue among the Nama tribes. Yet, let us not forget that, notwithstanding their uncleanliness, the Neapolitans and Irish, as well as the gipsies, are members of the Aryan family; and also that the drinking of the urine of oxen was enjoined on the Brahminical Hindoos as a purification from all manner of iniquities. Revenge, slight respect for parents, and the custom of exposing, the aged and decrepit in deserts, are also flaws in the character of the Hottentots. Their love of freedom—or rather of indolence— has greatly diminished their number, and their total extinction is almost inevitable. They lived in tribes under chiefs, who shared their dignity with the elders of the community. Occasionally the single tribes concluded treaties of defence against common enemies. The Kei-χous, or "red people," still call themselves a royal

---

[22] Kolbe, Vorgebirge der guten Hoffnung, p. 460.
[23] Kolbe, p. 453. Theophilus Hahn, VII. Jahresbericht der Dresdner Geogr. Gesellschaft. p. 9.

tribe, from which it may, perhaps, be inferred that the Koi-Koin were formerly, if only for a short time, united into a nation by some skilful ruler. Polygamy is allowed, but is seldom practised. Kolbe states that a woman is never ill-used, but more recent observers do not confirm his assertion. It may be that the better customs of old times have been corrupted by the bad example of the Boors. Like the neighbouring Bantu negroes, the Koi-Koin exhibit skill in all forensic arts on the occasions of public judicial proceedings. The duties of the vendetta are not quite extinct, but the infliction of fines is generally held to be sufficient.

Great obscurity still prevails as to the religious ideas of this remarkable people. It is only certain that the Koi-Koin worship the moon, which is regarded as of the masculine gender. Their belief in a life after death is proved by the custom of giving to the corpse at its burial the same attitude as in the maternal womb, and they also break up their kraals after every case of death to avoid the proximity of the grave. Ancestor worship has been proved to exist among the Korana tribe, who worship a great chief of former times under the name of Tsui-χoab.[24] It is much more difficult to decide whether the Hottentot Heitsi-Eibib was an historical hero. Stones are piled on tumuli in his memory, and dances are executed in his honour, so that the Namaqua, in speaking of the members of their tribe, say " they still dance," or " they dance no more," to express their persistence in paganism or their conversion to Christianity. Little light is afforded by the fables told of the death and deeds of this enigmatical being. He is said to have died and been born again more than once, so that many consider him identical with the moon-god.[25] There were also Shamans among the Hottentots, who exercised power over rain and sunshine, and cast out the spirits of disease. Of course, belief in charms existed also, but the persecution of witches did not produce such evil consequences as among the Bantu negroes.

Any one who is capable of valuing the development of their

---

[24] Bleek, Reincke Fuchs, pp. 59-64.

[25] Theophilus Hahn, Die Nama-Hottentotten ; Globus, vol. xii. p. 276. 1867.

language, is also able to appreciate the fact that Hottentots readily learn foreign languages and speak them correctly. Any one who in the examples given in Bleek's Reineke Fuchs admires their power of remodelling fables of animals of foreign derivation, so as to suit African understanding, will no longer allow that the Koi-Koin are among the lowest of human races, but will rather attribute to them a very high position among the semi-cultured nations. They undoubtedly possessed every disposition for social improvement, but the dearth of water in South Africa, which always compels its inhabitants to renew their wanderings, has prevented them from becoming stationary, and has at the same time precluded any density of population.

Before concluding this brief sketch, we must call attention to a remarkable coincidence of specific resemblances between the Koi-Koin and the Papuans of Fiji. Not only are the tufted matting of the hair and the narrow shape of the skull common to both, but in women of the Papuan race there is also a tendency to steatopygy.[26] We must attribute less importance to the point that in both races men and women eat apart, from the fact that this practice is not uncommon elsewhere. It is more remarkable that the Fijian women when mourning for the dead cut off joints of their fingers, and that the same mutilation is practised by the Koi-Koin as a rule, especially among women, more rarely among men. But the direct coincidence of the legends concerning the mortality of man is very strange. Two gods, the Fijians relate, disputed whether eternal life should be conferred upon mankind. Ra-Vula, the moon, wished to give us a death like his own ; that is to say, we were to disappear and then return in a renewed state. Ra-Kalavo, the rat, however refused the proposal. Men were to die as the rats die, and Ra-Kalavo carried the day. According to Anderson, the Koi-Koin have transformed the legend in the following way. The moon sent the hare on an embassy to man to say, " As I die and am born again, so shall ye die and come to life again." But the hare gave the message wrong, for he used

---

[26] At least among the people dwelling on the shores of the Utenata River, in New Guinea. Natuurliche Geschiedenis der nederlandsche Bezittungen. Saloman Müller.

the words "As I die and am not born again." When he confessed his mistake to his employer, the moon hurled a stick at the
hare and slit his lips. The faithless messenger took flight, and
still ranges timidly over the face of the earth.[27]

The temptation is great to explain the coincidence of decisive
physical characters, strange customs, and even a peculiar legend
by supposing either that the Koi-Koin and the Papuan Fijians
were derived from a common ancestry in primordial times, or at
least that they lived so near together as to exchange customs and
legends. But neither hypothesis is tenable. On closer examination, the Koi-Koin are sufficiently distinguished by the colour of
the skin, the absence of hair on the body, and by the lowness
of the skull. Among these people the amputation of the finger-
joints is affected during youth, and seems to be superstitiously
regarded as a sort of charm.[28] It occurs, moreover, among the
Polynesians and in the Nicobars.[29] Thus there remains only
the similar connection of the moon with the hope of immortality.
But this merely corroborates the old maxim that among different
varieties, in different regions, and at different times, the same
objects have given rise to the same idea. Hence the psychical
identity of human nature ought no longer to be disputed.

VI.—THE NEGROES.[1]

THE Negroes inhabit Africa from the southern margin of the
Sahara as far as the territory of the Hottentots and Bushmen, and

---

[27] Another version of the myth of immortality exists among the Bantu
negroes. Casalis, Les Bassoutos, p. 255. Paris, 1859.

[28] The same custom is noticed among the Kaffirs by Maclean (Kafir Laws
and Customs). The Bushmen are also said to sacrifice the end joints of their
fingers on occasions of illness, beginning with the little finger of the left hand,
believing that the illness will be removed with the flowing blood. Barrow,
Travels, vol. i. p. 289.

[29] Tylor, Primitive Culture, vol. ii. p. 402.

[1] With this and the preceding chapter compare Richard Andrée's Chart of
the Tribes and Languages of Africa, in Meyer's Conversations-lexicon.

from the Atlantic to the Indian Ocean, although the extreme east
of their domain has been wrested from them by intrusive Hamites
and Semites. Most negroes have high and narrow skulls. According to Welcker[2] the average percentage of width begins at 68 and
rises to 78. The variations are so great that, among eighteen
heads from Equatorial Africa, Barnard Davis found no less than
four brachycephals. In the majority dolichocephalism is combined with a prominence of the upper jaw and an oblique position
of the teeth, yet there are whole nations which are purely mesognathous. It is to be regretted that in the opinion of certain
mistaken ethnologists, the negro was the ideal of everything
barbarous and beast-like. They endeavoured to deny him any
capability of improvement, and even disputed his position as a
man. The negro was said to have an oval skull, a flat forehead,
snout-like jaws, swollen lips, a broad flat nose, short crimped hair,
falsely called wool, long arms, meagre thighs, calfless legs, highly
elongated heels, and flat feet. No single tribe, however, possesses
all these deformities.[3] The colour of the skin passes through every
gradation, from ebony black, as in the Joloffers, to the light tint
of the mulattoes, as in the Wakilema, and Barth even describes
copper-coloured negroes in Marghi.[4] As to the skull in many
tribes, as in the above mentioned Joloffers, the jaws are not
prominent, and the lips are not swollen.[5] In some tribes the
nose is pointed,[6] straight, or hooked;[7] even "Grecian profiles" are
spoken of, and travellers say with surprise that they cannot perceive anything of the so-called negro type among the negroes.[8]

According to Paul Broca,[9] the upper limbs of the negro are com-

[2] Thesaurus Craniorum, p. 210.

[3] The typical negro is a rare variety even among negroes, says Winwood
Reade (Savage Africa, p. 516).

[4] Nord- und Central Afrika, vol. ii. p. 465.

[5] Mungo Park, Reisen, p. 14. Berlin, 1799.

[6] Among the Batonga between the Cameron Mountains and the Gaboon.
Winwood Reade, Savage Africa, p. 515.

[7] Among the Quissama Negroes in Angola. Hamilton, Journal of Anthrop. Institute, vol. i. p. 187.

[8] See Hugo Hahn's account of the Ovakuengama and Ovambo. Petermann, Mittheilungen, p. 291. 1867.

[9] Anthropological Review, vol. vii. London, 1869.

paratively much shorter than the lower, and therefore less ape-like than in Europeans, and, although in the length of the femur the negro may approximate to the proportions of the ape, he differs from them by the shortness of the humerus more than is the case with Europeans. Undoubtedly narrow and more or less high skulls are prevalent among the negroes. But the only persistent character which can be adduced as common to all is greater or less darkness of skin, that is to say, yellow, copper-red, olive, or dark brown, passing into ebony black. The colour is always browner than that of Southern Europe. The hair is generally short, elliptic in section, often split longitudinally, and much crimped. That of the negroes of South Africa, especially of the Kaffirs and Betshuans, is matted into tufts, although not in the same degree as that of the Hottentots. The hair is black, and in old age white, but there are also negroes with red hair, red eyebrows, and eye-lashes,[10] and among the Monbuttoo, on the Uellé, Schweinfurth even discovered negroes with ashy fair hair.[11] Hair on the body and beards exist, though not abundantly ; whiskers are rare although not quite unknown.[12]

The negroes form but a single race, for the predominant as well as the constant characters recur in Southern as well as in Central Africa, and it was therefore a mistake to separate the Bantu negroes into a peculiar race. But, according to language, the South Africans can well be separated, as a great family, from the Soudan negroes.

I.—THE BANTU NEGROES.

To them belong the known parts of South Africa up to the equator ; and their district extends even to the 5th latitude of the northern hemisphere. Their languages are recognizable by their peculiar defining prefixes,[1] and they also have a large number

---

[10] For instance on the Gaboon. Comp. Walker in the Journal of the Anthropological Society, vol. vi. London, 1868.

[11] Im Herzen von Afrika, vol. ii. p. 107. Leipzic, 1874.

[12] Gerh. Rohlfs, Reise von Kuka nach Lagos. Petermann's Mittheilungen.

[1] See above, p. 121, et seq.

of roots in common. For the sake of convenience they may be divided into east, west, and inland tribes.[2] The eastern tribes are again divisible into the people of Zanzibar, including the Suaheli, the Mozambique nations from the coast to Lake Nyassa, the Betshuans further inland, and, lastly, the so-called Kaffirs. The tribes of the interior are the hordes, as yet little known, of the Ba-yeiye, the Ba-lojazi, the Ba-toka, the Ba-rotse, etc. Still more numerous are the western tribes in the Atlantic districts. They are separable, first, into the Bunda nations, including the Herero[3] (erroneously called Damara), the Ovambo and their kinsmen, the Nano, or Ba-nguela, in Benguela, and the A-ngola in Angola. The second division of the western group is represented by the Congo negroes, consisting of the true Congos and the Mpongwe. Lastly, to a third division belong a number of north-western languages, such as the Ba-kele in the Di-kele, the Benga on the Gaboon, the Dualla in the Cameron Mountains, and the Isubu, and the language of the totally naked Adiya of Fernando Po, who have but recently made their appearance there.[4] Finally, the remarkable Bafan or Fan negroes must be mentioned, who not long ago migrated from the interior to the coast, and who make remarkable toothed iron missiles, like those of the Sandeh, or Niam-Niam, and some of the Hamite tribes of Nubia.[5]

II.—THE SOUDAN NEGROES.

We shall begin their enumeration at the Niger and, advancing westwards and describing the shape of a horse-shoe, return to the

---

[2] Bacmeister in the Ausland, p. 580. 1871.

[3] Their language is used for intercourse by many other tribes. Hahn, Peter-mann's Mittheilungen, p. 290. 1867.

[4] Like all other islands of the Atlantic, it was found uninhabited by the Portuguese. The Adiya, on the contrary, came from the Gaboon district, from which they were expelled by the Mpongwe. Windwood Reade, Savage Africa, p. 63. The name of Adiya is said to signify merely dwellers in villages. Bastian, San Salvador, p. 317. Bremen, 1859.

[5] Du Chaillu, Explorations and Adventures, 1861. It is possible that the name of Ba-fan was only given to them by their neighbours, but in that case they ought perhaps to be placed in a totally different group.

21

White Nile. In the lower course of the Niger, the Ibo language is spoken, and from the Benue upwards the Nuffi language, neither of which has hitherto been examined. Westwards follows the Ewhe language, which includes the dialects of Joruba; Dahomey, and that of the Mahi, which appears further inland. Allied to these are the languages of the negroes on the Gold Coast who speak Odshi, as do the Ashantees, the Akim, the Akwapim, the Akwamboo, and the Akra. There are many tribes also on the Ivory and Pepper Coast, among which the Kru are best known, on account of their heroic stature and their skill on the sea. In language they are more nearly allied to the Ashantees and Fantees than to the Mandingo, from whom, however, they have borrowed a large number of words. Mande, which is the language of the Mandingo, includes many dialects. Among them is the language of the Vei,[1] who possess the art of writing, and also the Soso and Bambara. These latter form the word by additions to the roots, and some of their suffixes are used independently, thus affording a clue to the meaning when employed for purposes of definition.[2] The Mande negroes have spread between the 10th and 15th degrees of latitude, from the coast to the upper part of the Niger. Between the Gambia and the Senegal (which river now, as in ancient times, divides the negroes from the Berbers), live the Joloffers, the finest of the negro races, whose language still stands alone. The small space between the River Gambia and Scherboro is thickly occupied by the various languages of the Sererer, or Sárar, and Fulup family, in which, as among the Bantu negroes, prefixes are used.[3]

Turning further inland, to the countries belonging ᴛo the district of the Niger, the first people encountered are an enigmatical people, which has conquered and penetrated far into the interior. These are the Fulbe (singular Pulo), called Fulah by the Mandingo, Fellani by the Hausaua, Fellata by the Kanuri. The term Fulbe means "the Yellows" or "the Browns," and was meant to express the contrast with black negroes.[4] Mungo

---

[1] S. W. Koelle, Outlines of a Grammar of the Vei Language, p. 2. London, 1854.

[2] Steinthal, Die Mandenegersprachen, p. 67. Berlin, 1867.

[3] Koelle, Polyglotta africana. London, 1854.   [4] Ibid.

Park,[5] who saw them in the west, speaks of their fair colour and glossy hair. A well-formed nose and small lips are universally attributed to them, but such peculiarities occur also among other negroes, and vary too much to be a mark of race. Barth[6] also observes, that as early as twenty years of age " an ape-like expression effaces their Caucasian features." By their dignity, polish, great respect for property, and also by their artistic taste, the Fulbe are very favourably distinguished from other Africans. Their type has, however, long ago lost its purity by intermixture with negro women. Yet in the central parts of the kingdom of Sokoto, that is to say, far in the interior, Rohlfs still found several among the Fulbe of yellowish white colouring, and " an European form of face." Only the hair was " brilliantly black and crimped."[7] Were we therefore to depend solely on the character of the hair, we should be obliged to classify the Fulbe among the negroes. Rohlfs considers, however, that philological research can alone show the true position of this race in a system of ethnology. According to Barth, their language has much in common with the Hausa, but these resemblances have been borrowed in recent times. The names of numbers again recall the prefix languages of Southern Africa, and the language as a whole is really akin to that of the Joloffers, who are true negroes, and to Kadshaga, the language of the former kingdom of Ghana, which otherwise stands quite alone. The Fulbe did not originally belong to Senegal, for in the 7th century A.D. they were still cattle-breeders and hunters in the oases of Tauat and in the south of Morocco; their progress, as, for instance, the adoption of the cultivation of rice and cotton, was due to the influences of the Kadshaga. They are therefore either an extreme variety of the negro race or an early hybrid people of half-Berber, half-Soudan blood. To constitute them a separate race, or to suppose them to have migrated from Asia in prehistoric times, must be left to other and more imaginative ethnologists.

Midway between the source and the mouth of the Niger live

[5] Travels in the Interior of Africa.

[6] Petermann's Mittheilungen, No. 34, p. 45. Appendix, 1872.

[7] Caillié says the same of the Fulbe in Futa Djalon. Voyage à Tembouctoo, vol. i. p. 328. Paris, 1830.

the Sonrhay, whose language occupies an entirely isolated position. But it must be observed that, according to Barth, the languages of the nations living nearest to the southern edge of the Sahara first received their grammatical form by contact with Berbers and Arabs. Up to this time they had "neither declension or conjugation, but simply joined the infinitive or substantive root of the verb to an object or a person." The influence of the Berber language was far more powerful in this direction than that of Arabic.[8]

The euphonious and rich Hausa language is spoken between the Niger and Bornou. In its words of number it has some relationship to ancient Egyptian, and is even placed by Lepsius among the Libyan languages, but these analogies are probably due to borrowing. It is worthy of note that Herodotus was acquainted with the Hausa, under the name of Ataranta, in their present places of abode.[9] In Logona a language is spoken which belongs to the Masa group. Barth held the Wandala or Mendara language to be related to the Hausa; Rohlfs, on the contrary, considered it to be allied to the Kanuri.[10] The latter, the language spoken in the kingdom of Bornou, has points of resemblance to the Téda, which extend to the essential nature of verbal structure ("das innerste Wesen der Wortbildung"). The Téda, Tebu, or Tibbu occupy the district west of the Libyan desert, and are in possession of the salt mines of Bilma and of the oasis of Fesan, where their representatives are of the negro type.[11] Barth identifies them with the Garamantes of the ancient geographers, in which case the evidence of the language would tend to show that a branch of the negro race had spread across the desert to the neighbourhood of the Mediterranean. But Barth has probably misinterpreted the facts, for the negro type of the Fesans may be traced to intermarriages with Soudan women. Nachtigal, who was better acquainted with the Téda, perceived

---

[8] Henr. Barth, Centralafrikanische Vocabularien. Gotha, 1862.

[9] Barth (Vocabularien) derives ἀτάραντες in Herodotus from *a-tara,* the assembled (confederates), and *tara* in Hausa means to assemble.

[10] Appendix to Petermann's Mittheilungen, No. 34, p. 21.

[11] Von Maltzan, Tunis und Tripolis, vol. iii. p. 325. 1870.

nothing of the negro in their features,[12] while the Kanuri realize the ideal ugliness of the race.[13] But Nachtigal accounts for the resemblance of the Téda and Kanuri languages by supposing that the latter was developed by the adoption of Téda forms. On this theory the Téda do not belong to the negro race.[14]

Bagrimma in Baghirmi, and a family of languages in Wadar, which is named Maba, are separate languages further eastwards. In the towns of Darfur and Kordofan both Arabic and Barabric are spoken, and nothing is known as to the position of the language of the natives of the country. The lowest of all negro tribes inhabit the district of the White Nile. From latitude 11° southwards, we find the Shillook, the Nuehr, the Dinka, and west of the latter the Luoh (Djurs), the Bongo (Dohr), and the Sandeh (Niam-Niam).[15] The relationship of these languages has not yet been examined, and nothing is known except that the Luoh (Djurs) and the Bellanda tribes are offshoots from the Shillook.[16] Lastly, the Bongo (Dohr) language is said to have some affinity to the Maba of Wadai and the Bagrimma on the one hand, and to the Nuba on the other.[17] The languages of the Elliab, the Bohr, and the Bari tribes are still unclassified, as is that of the remarkable Monbuttoo, who are estimated at a million individuals, and inhabit a district of 81,000 square miles on the Uellé.

In their physical character the Dinka and Shillook negroes closely resemble the Fundi negroes on the Blue Nile, the founders of the kingdom of Sennaar in the sixteenth century, which they maintained for three centuries. The Fundi are mesocephalic, but very prognathous; their hair is several inches long, and becomes crimped; their skin, which has a strong odour, varies from brown to blue-black, with the exception of the hand and the sole of the foot, which are of a flesh-coloured red; the finger

---

[12] Petermann's Mittheilungen, p. 280. 1870.

[13] Zeitschrift für Erdkunde, vol. vi. p. 344. 1871.

[14] Dr. Nachtigal in Petermann's Mittheilungen, p. 328. 1871.

[15] We follow the linguistic chart of G. Schweinfurth and his observations in the Globus. The bracketed names are taken from the Dinka language.

[16] Schweinfurth, Zeitschrift für Ethnologie, vol. iv. Supplement, p. 61. 1872.

[17] Hartmann, Nilländer, p. 210.

nails also are of an agate brown. The lips are fleshy, but not intumescent ; the nose straight or slightly aquiline, as among many negroes of Southern and Western Africa.

An attempt has been made to separate the Fundi into a race apart from the negroes and to constitute them a Nubian race. A more unlucky name could hardly have been found, for the Nuba, or Nôbah, are the inhabitants of the mountain districts and the plains in Kordofan who resemble the Fundi in all the characters enumerated, except that, as dolichocephals with extremely crimped hair, they are of a still more negro type.[18] But it is quite incomprehensible how they can be connected with the Fulbe of West Africa. The Berthâ negroes are directly allied to the Fundi in physical characters, language, and manners.[19]

It may seem premature to examine whether the elevation and shape of Africa have exercised a good or evil influence on its inhabitants, for there are still vast regions in it of which we possess no information. The unknown portions of Africa have gradually been reduced into a nearly circular district, of which the equator forms the diameter, and containing an area which is variously reckoned at 1,485,000 and 1,260,000 square miles. Australia, with its adjacent islands, extends over a surface of 2,805,000 square miles, so that the *terra incognita* of Africa is not as much as half the size of Australia. Africa itself is estimated at 20,000,000 square miles, of which 25,000 must be deducted for its islands, and thus the unknown centre forms about one-ninth or one-tenth of the continent. This unknown region may contain many unexpected features ; high table-lands, perhaps, or snow mountains, lakes as large as the Caspian Sea, or streams which constitute an entire river system. In addition to the African races already known, a new one may there be discovered, either having nothing in common with the others, or, as a detached fragment of the race, may show traces of a common origin, either with the North Africans or with the Hottentot family of the south. Nor is it impossible that in this unknown interior an African civilization may have been developed of a social value equal to

---

[18] Hartmann, Nilländer, p. 291. E. Rüppell, Reisen in Nubien, p. 153. Frankfort, 1829.

[19] Hartmann, as above, p. 283.

that of the Toltecs in Central America, or of the Incas of Peru on the plateaux of the Andes. None of these supposed discoveries are however likely, with the exception of that of new lakes and larger river districts in the neighbourhood of the equator, for if there were no enclosed basins retaining a portion of the tropical rains, which cannot be wanting there, more abundant rivers would reach the coasts which are already known.

Difficulty of approach is the fundamental feature of the African continent. The outline of its surface is, unfortunately, not only entirely destitute of peninsulas but also of receding or projecting angles. The projection of the east coast at Jardafun, the promontory of spices as it was termed in ancient geography, is the only peninsula; the open bay of Guinea, the only representative of an oceanic gulf, and the gulfs of Sidra and Khrabs the only considerable indentation of the coast of Africa.

In addition to the unfavourable outline of the sea-coast, there is also a lack of rivers, such as the Amazon, to open up the country. All the rivers of Africa, the Nile itself included, are but indifferent means of communication. The Niger runs through thickly populated districts, yet it is without any navigation worth mentioning. The Africans are inferior to all other people in nautical skill. The Kru negroes, on the Grain Coast, are the only blacks who are fit and willing to engage themselves as sailors on board European ships. In South Africa a river of the second magnitude is sufficient security against hostile oppressors. The tribes under the great conqueror, Mosilikatse, extend their incursions only as far as the right or southern bank of the Zambesi, for they do not dare to think of crossing such a river. As crocodiles frequent all the rivers of Africa, excepting in the north and the extreme south, it would be natural to suppose that ferry boats would have been found in all the more populous villages. This is, however, often not the case; but Africans frequently build bridges. There were probably no bridges, except those built by the Romans, in Germany during the times of Cæsar and Tacitus. In Africa they are common. It is not surprising that Livingstone repeatedly mentions them in his marches, as the territory through which he passed was that of somewhat gifted tribes, but even among the negro races on the western affluents of the White Nile, and therefore in the lowest grade of African civilization, we find wooden bridges of "fabulous length." [20]

The difficulty of approaching Africa by sea is more unfortunate on account of the impenetrable character of many of its vast inland regions. The line of deserts which extends obliquely from the Atlantic through the north of the country, and even across the Nile to the Arabian Gulf, divides the continent, as regards the history of civilization, into two quite separate parts ; for while the northern border was influenced for good by the course of Mediterranean culture, the southern portion was more thrown back upon its own resources. During the period of Roman colonization, only one geographical expedition passed beyond the Sahara, and it is still doubtful whether it penetrated to the Soudan itself or only as far as one of the great oases. [21] The difficulties of crossing the Sahara were far greater in old times, for it was only after the beginning of our era that camels were introduced into the Berber countries as a beast of burden—a remarkable innovation, and one which was as important to Africa as the beginning of the railway system to us. Even plants are far more effectually restricted in their migrations by deserts than by narrow arms of the sea, for while the floras of Northern Africa and of the Mediterranean shores of Europe agree most closely, on the other side of the Sahara a new vegetation makes its appearance, differing entirely from the flora of North Africa. These impediments and barriers also obstructed the march of civilization, under which head we include all advantages wrested from Nature by human ingenuity, the ennoblement of its gifts, the easy acquisition and the improvement of food in its various forms, inventions for the curtailment of labour, the organization of social life, and lastly, the highest blessings of mankind—self-knowledge, the striving after better things, after ideal prototypes, or, in a word, Religion. But, on the other hand, justice requires that, in estimating this obstructive power of deserts, many, although not

---

[20] Petherick, Central Africa, vol. i. p. 236.
[21] Vivian de Saint Martin, Le Nord d'Afrique. Ptolemy, however, mentions the rhinoceros, and the country must therefore have been in the Soudan (Geogr. lib. i. cap. 8).

invariably advantageous, social and moral phenomena mentioned by recent travellers in the Soudan as special inventions of the Africans of those parts must be taken into consideration, and we are thus enabled to form a more just appreciation of the capacity of development possessed by negro races, as has already been done by Gerhard Rohlfs.

The advantages of a continent as the scene of human civilization do not depend solely on its own physical features, but also on the proximity or remoteness of its situation in regard to other especially favoured regions. From this point of view Africa is a peninsula of the eastern hemisphere. Supposing that the Isthmus of Suez were a strait, and that the whole of Africa lay some ten degrees further south and west, so as to form an insular continent deprived of its connection with the Old World, its condition would be far less propitious than at present, and much more like that of Australia at the time of its discovery. Its land connection with Asia Minor, and its vicinity to Arabia and to Southern Europe, enable Africa to enjoy advantages which were impossible to the American race. Its northern and eastern shores, at least, allowed of the favourable influence of Asiatic civilization.

One of the effects of the advantageous geographical position of Africa was doubtless the fact that the art of smelting iron ore, and of its manufacture into implements and weapons, was spread throughout the entire continent. Wherever travellers have penetrated into the interior they have found the Africans in the midst of the so-called iron age. All the tribes in whose territory iron ore is found know how to raise the glow of coals by a current of air to a heat equal to the flame of the blow-pipe. The African bellows consists of a pair of hollow wooden cylinders closed at the top with leather pouches, and terminating below in an earthenware tube, from which the air is expelled by alternately raising and depressing the pouches. The metal smelted in the charcoal fire is of particularly good quality, so that many negroes justly prefer their own excellent iron utensils to the English importation of impure metal.

Where nature aided the early maturity of human society, the most ancient forms of culture sprang up. The Old World had a centre of this description in the happily situated district between the sister rivers of Mesopotamia and the Nile. If Africa had been more distant from this centre its condition would have been proportionately lower. The facts actually observed greatly confirm this hypothesis; for the highest refinements existed in the oldest times on the Nile, and extended as far as the first natural obstacle, while the southern point of the continent was occupied by the lowest grades of human society.

Before increased powers of navigation had overcome the obstacle offered by the oceans, which may be said to have been fully accomplished only in the last few centuries, the old inhabitants of the Atlantic shores of Africa lived at the end of the world without neighbours beyond them, or, at least, on the boundaries of the impassable. It is generally the case that the conditions of the interior of Africa are far more propitious than those of the Atlantic coast. It is only within the last two centuries that the stronger and more intelligent inland tribes have made their way to the sea. Throughout Guinea the Portuguese found only very barbarous tribes, while towards the interior, great states had already fallen into decay on the Niger, and others had in turn flourished on their ruins. Even now it may be roughly said with reference to the western side of Africa, that the African of the interior is superior to the African of the coast. As regards the Soudan, we need only recall Rohlf's vivid descriptions; but in the south the same phenomenon is repeated. The negro monarchies of the Makololo, Lunda, Mosilikatse, and Cazembe, all lie far inland, and, according to Speke and Grant, the negro states of Karagwe and Uganda also appear much more orderly and prosperous than any that were seen either on the way thither or on the return journey. Travellers when they ascend the Nile, and leave Khartoum behind them, pass in their boat only through naked and barbarous tribes on either shore. It might be supposed that on penetrating further south-west, that is to say, more inland, the same conditions would be met with; but there is some reason to suppose that the contrary is the case. The Niam-Niam, for instance, the most westerly people with whom we are acquainted, are far superior to such tribes on the White Nile, as the Shillook, Dinka, Nuehr, Kitsh, in clothing, skilful ironworks, buildings, and social organization.

If they are only advanced posts of other more highly cultivated negro tribes, it is just possible that some great monarchies may even yet be met with in the south of Darfur.[22]

In comparing the regions of Africa lying beyond the Sahara with the two continents of America, previous to the arrival of Europeans, many great differences between their respective civilizations are noticeable. In the two Americas there are many hordes which live exclusively by hunting and fishing, also tribes which practice agriculture as well as the chase, and even purely agricultural people in Mexico, Yucatan, the states of the Isthmus, in Peru, and on the plateaux of Bogota. In Africa there are no people so degraded as some of the Athabaskan tribes in the Hudson's Bay territory, or as the Botocudos, Coroados, Puris, or Fuegians of South America. But, on the other hand, no negro, Kaffir, and still less any Hottentot tribe, ever attained such a degree of culture as the Nahuatl nations of Mexico, the Yucatecs and the Peruvians. They never attempted independently to fix the meanings of the spoken words by symbols or phonetic signs. In the Soudan we look in vain for monuments in any degree comparable with the step pyramids of Cholula, the elaborately decorated buildings of Yucatan, the stone streets of the Incas, or the ruins of the Temple of the Sun on Lake Titicaca. The Mongoloid race of the New World was far superior to the Africans beyond the Sahara in intellectual talents, especially as the progress of culture in America was in no way due to foreign influence.

The degree of civilization was, however, much more uniform in Africa; husbandry and cattle-breeding, and even genuine dairy-farming, were universal there. As a peninsula of the Old World, Africa was more favourably situated than America for such progress in the mode of sustenance. The only cereal of America is maize; in Africa there are two, the negro millet, or Dochn (*Panicum*, or *Pennisetum distichum* and *P. dyphoideum*), and Kaffir corn (*Holcus sorghum*, or *Sorghum vulgare*). Unfortunately, our knowledge of the distribution of plants is not yet sufficient to decide whether these, which are now thoroughly African cereals, were

---

[22] The above was printed in the Ausland in 1870. Since then Schweinfurth has given an account of the kingdom of the Monbuttoo.

developed by cultivation in Africa itself, or were merely introduced into the country. Tropical America possesses some edible roots ; the mandioca and, in the temperate parts, the potato, and also in the highest districts another cereal, the Quinoa bean. Africa, on the other hand, possesses the " bread-roots," which, Barth informs us, serve as the daily food in some villages of Adamaua, and also earth nuts. With regard to the latter (*Arachis hypogaea*) we are uncertain whether they were first cultivated in Africa. As to fruit-trees, the two countries are evenly balanced, or America has slightly the advantage. The Doom and oil palms belong to Africa, and also the butter-tree (*Bassia Parkii*). Even if the negroes were not the first to improve any of their indigenous cereals, they yet readily availed themselves of all the gifts of civilization offered to them by strangers. Although they may have received the first seed from Egypt or Abyssinia, it was rapidly diffused throughout the entire continent, just as maize, the manioc root,[23] wheat, barley, the sugar cane, etc., have now in many districts spread far into the interior. Even on the Zambesi, where Europeans had never been seen before, Chapman [24] noticed that the natives had grafted good sorts on wild fruit-trees.

Cattle-breeding in the New World was only rudimentary, while goats, sheep, and cattle are common throughout the whole of Africa. They were certainly not domesticated there, but were received by the negroes in a domesticated state, so that here again the advantage of the peninsular connection of Africa with the Old World is evident. The Africans have been unjustly reproached for not having trained the elephant as did the Hindoos ; but the African elephant is a different species from the Asiatic, and is probably not so easy to tame.[25]

The mode of sustenance in the Soudan and South Africa may be fairly correctly inferred from the nature of the country. The

---

[23] Even among the Bongo negroes to the west of the White Nile, Schweinfurth (Heart of Africa) saw fields of maize ; and among the Monbuttoo on the Uellé, he observed the cultivation of the *Jatropha Manihot*.

[24] Travels into the Interior of South Africa, vol. ii. p. 202.

[25] Livingstone infers from Roman coins that the African elephant was tamed in former times ; but it is doubtful whether the characteristics of the African variety are clearly recognizable.

Soudan, heated by the perpendicular rays of the sun, and watered by tropical rains, is a land of wood and corn; agriculture therefore chiefly prevails, and cattle-breeding is unimportant. It is possible for the population to become comparatively dense; and the government is a strict absolutism. Great kingdoms and large towns rise and fall again in rapid succession, for each despotism endures only as long as the vigour of the despot, which is not always inherited by the next sovereign, and very rarely by the third. Polygamy further endangers the certainty of succession, and consequently causes wars among the claimants of the throne. All true negroes adhere either to a rude animal and fetish worship or to Islam.

The explored parts of South Africa may be described as a table-land, the edges of which rise opposite the two oceans. It lies in the zone of the trade winds; as its rainy seasons are uncertain, park-like steppes abound more than dense forests; cattle-breeding therefore predominates, and there is little agriculture, consequently the populations are less strongly organized, but, like all nomads, are loosely combined. The kraal frequently replaces the village with stockades, or the towns peculiar to the Soudan. There are many despots with power over a large extent of territory, but they reign only for a short time. South Africa has no continuous history such as that of which the negro kingdoms to the south of the Sahara are so proud. We have already noticed the fetishism of Central Africa, the ancestor worship of the Bantu negroes, their Shamans, and their trials by ordeal. We have also had occasion to praise the Kaffirs for their custom of paying over their "weregild" to the chieftains. It must be added that, of all semi-civilized nations, the negroes have most thoroughly elaborated their social jurisprudence. African judicial proceedings attract the curious as a theatrical performance does us; and in the contesting parties there is no want of dramatic excitement or lavish expenditure of eloquence and cunning.[26] The Bantu negroes are masters in the art of perplexing an opponent by cross-questioning.[27] Bishop Colenso declares that his scepticism as to the Mosaic history of creation was first aroused by the objections of his Kaffir pupils in Natal. In social disputes the first

---

[26] Casalis, Les Bassoutos, pp. 242, 243. 1859. [27] Ausland, p. 1044. 1863.

appeal may be made from the decision of the village justice to the chief of the district, and from him again to the head chief.[28] Sentence is given by a council of old men learned in the law, according to precedent and the principles observed in previous verdicts. If the case is unlike any former one, help is asked of the legal authorities of other tribes. It has even happened that, in a difficult legal question, the strangers who had been appealed to were also unacquainted with any case of precedent, and finally it was decided to give no verdict, for fear of establishing a new and perhaps an erroneous principle. Among the Bantu negroes a more refined idea of justice is shown, by their considering the practise of causing abortion as punishable,[29] and inflicting a penalty also on the doctor by whose assistance the deed was accomplished. In cases of defamation of character compensation must be made to the injured person, for "good reputation is wealth."[30]

The affection of negro children for their parents, or at least for their mother, is touching. The Herero (Damara) swear "by the tears of their mother."[31] Mungo Park[32] heard a Mandingo lad exclaim, "Strike me, but do not speak contemptuously of my mother." Mandingo mothers deserve this affection, continues the same traveller, for they take great care of their children's morals. The greatest praise in the mouth of these mothers is "my son has never told a lie." Their poets and bards need never starve, for the Mandingo reward them liberally for songs in honour of the deeds of their nation.[33] Very many proverbs giving golden rules for life are used by the Soudan and Bantu negroes. In the Joruba a half-witted person is indicated by the saying that he does not know how much nine times nine is.[34] The chief wish of the Mandingo is to die in the place where he was born. No water seems so sweet as at home, no shade so refreshing as the shadow of the Tabba tree of his own village. When a

[28] Maclean, Kaffir Laws and Customs, p. 143. Mount Coke, 1858.

[29] Ibid. p. 111. [30] Ausland, p. 1069. 1863.

[31] Anderson, Reise in Südwestafrika, vol. i. p. 247.

[32] Reisen im Innern von Afrika, p. 237. 1799.

[33] Mungo Park, as above, p. 249.

[34] Tylor, Primitive Culture, vol. i. p. 240.

negro of the Gold Coast dies away from home, his friends try to
bury him in his native place.[35] Although some few tribes disgust
us by their indolence, Otto Kersten [36] cites instances of East
African negroes which show that they voluntarily endeavour to
improve their circumstances by industry. The inhabitants of
the Gold Coast exhibit their patience and skill in the manufacture of chains of the finest gold wire, which, as Bosman justly
remarks, can scarcely be imitated in Europe.[37] Schweinfurth pro-
nounces the steel chains of the Monbuttoo negroes to be equal to
any similar productions in Europe.[38] In the Soso country, a
southern district of the kingdom of Sokoto, the negroes pave the
inside of their courts with a sort of mosaic.[39] Ladislaus Magyar
speaks of flint locks made by the natives of Bihé ; Hamilton
also saw guns among the Kissama negroes, which had been
made after Portuguese patterns, and in Bambara, Bambook, and
Bornou, the negroes make gunpowder, and contrive to procure the
necessary saltpetre in their own country.[40] It must be added
that the Hausa and Fulbe, in Sokoto, and also the Joloffers, manufacture a useful sort of soap from a decoction of earth nuts mixed
with a lye of wood ashes.[41] But the most ingenious achievement
on the part of a negro is the creation by a Vei of an original
character, consisting partly of a syllabic, partly of simple phonetic
signs. In his youth, it is true, the inventor was educated by
Europeans, and was able to read, but he had to make an
alphabetical analysis of his own language before he could invent
the characters.[42]

The negroes possess in a high degree both the power and the
inclination to adopt the benefits of foreign civilization, but, on the
other hand, they are extremely deficient in inventions of their

[35] Mungo Park, as above, p. 261. Bosman, Guinese Goudkust, vol. ii. p. 15.

[36] Von d. Decken's Reisen in Ostafrika, vol. ii. p. 302.

[37] Guinese Goud Tand-en Slavekust, vol. i. p. 123.

[38] In the Heart of Africa.

[39] Gerhard Rohlfs in Petermann's Mittheilungen ; Appendix. 1872.

[40] Waitz, Anthropologie, vol. ii. p 97. Barth, Nord- und Centralafrika,
vol. iii. p. 245.

[41] Gerhard Rohlfs, as above, p. 56. Mungo Park, as above, p. 305.

[42] We owe our knowledge of this remarkable fact to Lieutenant F. E.
Forbes. S. W. Koelle, Grammar of the Vei Language.

own. While in other countries travellers have much to say about strange implements, in Africa they are silent. All the household utensils of the negroes occur elsewhere also. The only instance of the inventive powers of negroes which we can cite, is the Marimba, a musical instrument made of hollow gourds, which are fastened, according to size, on a hoop which the performer carries on a frame. He makes the shells vibrate by the blows of a hammer, and, as may be supposed, extracts low notes from the large, and high notes from the small cups.[43] Even the training of oxen for riding is not certainly an invention of the negroes, but is far more likely to have been due to the Galla or other people of Hamite origin on the Nile.

After all that has been said, it would be quite unjustifiable to pronounce the negro incapable of rising to a higher state ; and yet to attribute the low grade of present civilization solely to the nature of the continent, would be to ignore entirely the difference of intellect in the various races of mankind. The advantage of Africa consisted, as we saw, in the fact that it was within possible though not easy reach of the Old World. From the latter the negroes have derived almost everything that has improved their condition. If this race had made its appearance in Australia, they would scarcely by their own strength have risen above the state of the Australian natives. Hence, in our estimate of natural talents, we must rank them far below the aborigines of America, who quite independently reached a far greater maturity. On the other hand, if Africa had been better formed, and had it been as accessible as Europe, the negroes would have raised themselves much sooner, and might now perhaps have enjoyed about the same social advantages as the Malayo-Chinese.

VII.—THE MEDITERRANEAN RACE.

To the nations with which the history of ancient and modern civilization in the West has especially to deal, Blumenbach gave the name of Caucasian, but the name has been abandoned as it

---

[43] Livingstone, Travels in Southern Africa, vol. i. p. 332.

led to mistakes. The term "Mediterranean Nations" has now been generally substituted for Blumenbach's Caucasians, and we shall therefore use it. The Mediterranean nations include all Europeans who are not Mongoloid, all North Africans, and all Western Asiatics, and, lastly, although as hybrids, the Hindoos of Northern India must be classed with them on account of their language.

The prevalent forms of skull are mesocephalic and brachy-cephalic, yet it is only in a single case that the average index of breadth exceeds 82°. The height of the skull generally decreases proportionately with the increase of breadth. Prognathism and prominence of the cheek-bones are equally rare. In the northern nations the colour of the skin is quite fair; it is darker in Southern Europe, and becomes yellow, red, and brown in North Africa and Arabia, and in the gipsies. The hair of the head is never so long or so cylindrical as that of Mongoloid nations, never so elliptic in section or so short as in negroes, but is gene-rally curly. The most bearded and hairy nations occur among those races, and the North Africans alone have less beard and hair on the body. The nose has always a high bridge, and is never broad or flat as in negroes or Mongols. The lips are usually thin and never intumescent. In no other race are refined and noble features so frequent; nowhere else is that ideal of beauty so often attained, which is in reality the same among all races, for, as Rohlfs significantly remarks, a woman with so-called Caucasian features is considered beautiful by the negroes of the Soudan. With few exceptions, the languages of all the Mediter-ranean nations are marked by grammatical genders and a highly developed morphological structure. The race itself is divided into the Hamite, Semite, and Indo-European families. The Basques stand alone, and several tribes in and about the Caucasus remain unplaced.

I.—HAMITES.

This family occupies the whole of North Africa as far as the Soudan and the coast districts of Eastern Africa northward of the equator. It is divided into three branches: the Berbers, the ancient Egyptians, and the East African. In addition to the Guanches, or aboriginal inhabitants of the Canary Islands, the Berbers include the Libyans, the Moors, the Numidians and Gaetulians of the old geographers, who were already acquainted with the true name of all these nations ; namely, Amazig, or Mazig. Amazigh, or Amazirgh, in the Berberic languages signifies "the free or independent.[1] It is true that North Africa has been occupied by many other nations, mostly Semitic, and also by North European conquerors, yet the Berber strain was everywhere able to maintain itself in full purity in the level country. In Morocco the Berbers who yet remain free from Arab blood still call themselves Masig, but their language is termed Shellah, or Tamashigt.[2] To them belong, first, the Sanhadsha of the Western Sahara, the Azanagues of the Portuguese discoverers. The central region of the great African desert is occupied by the Tuareg, who call themselves Imoshag, and their language Ta-Masheg (Mazig language), or Ta-Mashigt. Among the pure Berbers of Algeria are the Kabyls of the French, a corruption of *qabâil,* which signifies the "tribes." In Tunis the Berbers bear the name of Suawua, and in the south-east of this dominion they are called Jebaliya.[3] The inhabitants of Siwah, the oasis of Jupiter Ammon, the Garamantes of ancient geography, are also of Berber origin. Lastly, the Tédas, or Tibbu, of the Eastern Sahara, must be classed with them.[4] In the hieroglyphic inscriptions, all these people bear the name of Temhu, and are recognizable on the Egyptian monuments by tattoo marks in the shape of a cross, which are said to be still customary among Kabyl women.[5]

The ancient Egyptians, called Retu in the hieroglyphics, are still more or less purely represented by the Fellâheen, the peasantry of the Lower Nile, but in the greatest purity by the Coptic Christians of the towns.

Of the Hamites of East Africa, the inhabitants of the Nubian

---

[1] Movers, Das phönizische Alterthum, part 2, pp. 390–395.

[2] Rohlfs, Erster Aufenthalt in Marokko, pp. 56, 62.

[3] Maltzan, Tunis and Tripolis, vol. i. p. 100.

[4] See above, p. 468.

[5] Recherches sur l'origine des Kabyles. Le Globe. Genève, 1871.

Nile districts, who call themselves Berâbra, or Berbers, most resemble the ancient Egyptians.[6] They were formerly Christians, until the fall of the Berber Nilitic empire of Dongola in 1320. Between the Nubian Nile and the Red Sea live tribes called Blemmyer by the old geographers,[7] Bedsha in the Axumitic inscriptions, and also by Arab geographers. Their purest representatives are the Bishareen, the Hadendoa, and some of the Beni Amer, who, in addition to a corrupt Arabic, speak Tobedauie, a more ancient Hamite language with three genders.[8] Between the Blue Nile and the Atbara rove the nomadic tribes of the Awlâd Abu Simbil and the Shukurieh, which latter are not descended from Arabs, although they speak a corrupt Arabic.[9] The Kababish live as shepherds between the Nile and Kordofan; and on both banks of the White River, above the mouth of the Blue Nile, live the Hassanieh. Both are pronounced to be Arabs, although in type they are East African Hamites. The Niam-Niam, or Sandeh, have very long hair, and are copper-coloured.[10] Perhaps future ethnologists will place these also among the Hamites. To the eastern group belong also the Dankali (sing. Danakil), who inhabit the most southerly African shores of the Red Sea as far as the Straits of Bab-el-Mandeb. The next are the Galla, who are partly distributed in Abyssinia, and live partly in a compact body in the east of the interior of Africa, from 8° north to 3° south latitude. The name of Galla, which is equivalent to "immigrants," is quite unknown to them; they call themselves Orma, or Oroma, which means "strong brave men."[11] With the exception of the southern tribes, they and their wives always appear mounted either on horses or oxen. They have nothing in common with the negroes but the colour of the skin, and this is free from any repulsive smell.[12] Their hair is long and curly, and their beard

---

[6] Hartmann, Nilländer, pp. 215, 235.

[7] Lepsius, Standard Alphabet, ed. 2, p. 203.

[8] Werner Münzinger, Ostafrikanische Studien, pp. 341, 344.   Schaffhausen, 1864.

[9] Hartmann, ibid, p. 263.   [10] Schweinfurth, The Heart of Africa.

[11] Krapf, Reisen in Ostafrika, vol. i. p. 94.

[12] Otto Kersten, Von d. Deckens Reisen in Ostafrika, vol. ii. p. 374.

tolerably luxuriant ; their features are regular and agreeable, not infrequently sharply cut, and rather European than Semitic.[13] The Galla are a warlike, manly people, conscious of their own strength, and of a moral and noble character.

The position of the Somali is less certain ; they occupy the eastern promontory of Africa from near Bab-el-Mandeb to the Juba on the Indian Ocean, and border on the Galla district on the west. Otto Kersten [14] describes the Somali of Bardara as of lofty stature (men 5 ft. 7 in., women 5 ft. 3 in.), with long thin faces, beardless chins, piercing eyes, and a woolly head of stiff thick hair from six to eight inches long, and which is said to be always crimped. Guillain adds that a curly head among the Somali invariably indicates a cross with Arab blood. Some tribes of the Somali believe themselves to be descendants of the Koreishites of Mecca, and others of the Ansari of Medina. It is therefore quite possible that on closer examination the Somali may entirely lose their position as Hamites, and be regarded in future as mongrels between negroes and Semites. It is noteworthy that Kersten eulogizes their noble and manly character, although it was among them that the undertaking of Baron von der Decken was destined to end fatally. The position of the Eloikob, or Wakuafi, is also very obscure, as well as that of the Masai, both of which nations have become the terror of all negro tribes in equatorial East Africa, on account of their warlike and kidnapping expeditions.

There is a deplorable scarcity of skull measurements of the Hamite family. According to Welcker, the skulls of Egyptian mummies and of Kabyl heads measure $75°$ in height and $74°$ to $75°$ in breadth. They are therefore on the border between dolicho- and mesocephaly. Even among the Egyptians the jaws project a little, and prognathism increases the further we ascend the Nile. The straw colour of the skin gradually darkens, as we advance, into red brown, deep bronze, or dark brown. In approaching the equator the hair becomes shorter and the beard more scanty. Hartmann is right in his assertion that an approximation to the negro type thus takes place proportionately with the distance from

---

[13] Richard Brenner, in Petermann's Mittheilungen, p. 462. 1868.

[14] Von d. Decken, Reisen in Ostafrika, vol. ii. pp. 318, 325.

the shores of the Mediterranean. "On closer observation" says Münzinger, "the candid traveller no longer knows where the true negro begins, and his belief in the absolute distinction of race diminishes more and more." These gradual transitions must at present be ascribed to intercourse with negro slaves until further light is supplied by a thorough comparison of languages. Let us rather try to solve the question why the Hamite family was the first of the members of the Mediterranean race to acquire a high civilization and become the instructor of all neighbouring nations.

If we turn over the pages of Rosellini and Lepsius, or better, if we set these works aside, on account of their cumbrous form, and turn to Wilkinson, we shall be able to watch the ancient Egyptians at their daily work. The bricks were made in moulds as at the present day; in the walls are built doors, turning on vertical hinges, and fastened with bolts. The furniture of the dwelling-houses seems quite familiar to us; there are even patriarchial arm-chairs, and camp-stools opening in the shape of St. Andrew's cross. The women turned the spindle and produced yarn, which was elsewhere woven into striped or checked materials. In the carpenter's shop, the master and his apprentices wielded the hatchet, mallet, hand-saw, chisel, plane, and gimlet.[15] The articles produced there were varnished by other workmen, who used a broad paint-brush, such as our brushmakers still keep for sale. The goldsmith used not only files and pincers of all sorts, but, strange to say, the blow-pipe, which was however worked by bellows, moved by the feet, and of very indifferent form.[16] In the cellar might be seen coopers, acquainted with the action of the siphon, making liquids flow through bent tubes from one vessel to another.[17] There is no doubt that it was wine which was thus treated, for the vine was introduced in the old empire and was assiduously cultivated in the new one, and even after the intrusion of Islam it still held its place in Fayum, whence it only recently disappeared in consequence of the vine disease.[18] In the women's apartment, Egyptian ladies arranged their hair with a

[15] Brugsch, Gräberwelt, p. 24.

[16] Wilkinson, Manners and Customs of the Ancient Egyptians. London, 1873.

[17] The date of this monument is about 1450 B.C.

[18] R. Roesler in Ausland, p. 776. 1867.

wooden comb before a metal mirror, and even used wigs and false hair. On the Nile, fishermen threw their drag-nets just as we see it done at home. At certain festivals the fishermen tried to push each other out of the boats with poles. This fisherman's tournament is more congenial to us than the bull-fights which were already instituted : it may be remarked that cattle were even then branded with their owners' mark on their hide. Of amusements there was no lack. Here flutes might be heard, accompanied by lutes, guitars, zithers, and harps.[19] Elsewhere mora was played, dice were thrown, or draughts were played upon a board. The tastes of children were even attended to ; leather balls were made of eight segments of spheres sewn together, wooden dolls were given to little girls, and there were even jumping figures which, on pulling a string, tossed their arms and legs in the air to amuse babies crying in their nurses' laps. Tricks rivalling those of this toy were performed by professional acrobats in shows, from whom the performers of our fairs seem to have taken a lesson. In short, in examining the records of old Egyptian life, we come across our oldest and most familiar experiences at home, and we are inclined to confess that, until the time when machinery and steam power was set in motion amongst ourselves, the Egyptians were not inferior to us in mechanical apparatus, or even that we have inherited from them the most important articles of our household furniture.

Yet this conclusion would be too hasty, for directly or indirectly the Egyptians also owed no little to their neighbours in Western Asia. The monuments, indeed, show us that pigeons and ducks were already bred, and that geese were artificially fattened,[20] yet we miss a later product of Eastern culture, namely, the domestic fowl, which was unknown to Homer and Hesiod, and in the times of the Old Testament, although Aristotle and Diodorus describe the artificial hatching establishments of the Egyptians.[21] Even the camel and the sheep do not appear on the monu-

---

[19] Lauth, On Ancient Egyptian Music. Sitzungsberichte der Münchener Akademie. 1873.

[20] Brugsch, Gräberwelt, p. 14.

[21] Von Hehn, Culturpflanzen und Hausthiere, p. 226. Berlin, 1870.

ments of the ancient kingdom, and the horse itself is unrepresented in these "stone picture-books" prior to the irruption of the shepherd kings.[22]   The domestication of the horse was the work of a family of nations far removed from Egypt.   The invention of the carriage was also not Egyptian ; this was a great improvement upon the movement by cylinders, and in its age an advantage as decisive as the opening of railways in our century.   The fact that the Egyptian word for carriage is borrowed from Semitic languages, indicates the source from which this instrument of culture reached the Nile.[23]   Horse-riding was not customary in Egypt, although Grecian scholars hold it to be the birthplace of this art.[24]   Admiration and surprise are still roused by the buildings erected by the people of the Nile ; their temples, their avenues of sphinxes, gigantic stone statues, and their pyramids. The latter are trustworthy records of the early maturity of the social condition, for their erection implied a surplus of labouring power, large accumulations of provisions on the building site, easy means of communication, laws of villenage, and regular taxation.   All this is also indirectly confirmed by the circumstance that in the new kingdom legal authority was established by the independence of the judicial order, which was bound by oath to protect the law against the caprice of despots.[25]   The erection of the first pyramids is ascribed to the third successor of Menes, the founder of Memphis.   They were still standing in the Grecian period, and Lepsius [26] believes that their ruins are still extant. The most moderate chronologist places Menes at 3892 B.C., and in his time the Egyptians had long been architects, sculptors, painters, mythologists, and theologians.[27]

The strongest evidence of the extraordinarily high antiquity of Egyptian civilization is its calculation of time.   It was based on a

---

[22] H. Brugsch, Histoire d'Egypte, vol. i. p. 25.

[23] G. Ebers, Aegypten und Mose, vol. i. p. 222.

[24] According to the Scholiasts of Apollonius, King Sesonchosis is supposed to have invented riding.

[25] G. Ebers, Durch Gosen zum Sinai, p. 543 et seq.

[26] Zeitschrift für ägypt. Sprache und Alterthumskunde, p. 91.   1870.

[27] According to the canon given by H. Brugsch (Histoire d'Egypte), his reign would fall in the years 4455-4395.

civil year of twelve months, each divided into three weeks of ten days, to which were added five intercalary days. The Egyptians were perfectly aware that these 365 days did not exactly correspond to the true solar year, for they knew that it was only at an interval of 1461 years that Sirius was visible at Memphis before sunrise in the first thoth, or month. This led them to adopt the Sothis or Sirius periods of 1461 civil years. One of these periods ended in the year 1322 B.C., consequently it must have begun in the year 2782, and the duration of such a period must have been determined on, at least, one previous occasion. Thus the first observation of the early rise of Sirius on New Year's day must have taken place in the year 4242 B.C.[28]

The conjecture that in those ancient times the Egyptians used only stone implements, is mainly founded on the circumstance that circumcision was performed with stone knives as among the Hebrews, who borrowed this practice from the Egyptians. But in reality this fact merely justifies another inference, namely, that circumcision was introduced in the stone age. The instruments used on solemn occasions are very unwillingly changed, lest the ceremony itself should lose the sanction of antiquity. Flint knives are still used by the Arabs in the peninsula of Sinai for scraping their sheep after shearing.[29] Even in ancient tombs bronze implements are found with an alloy of twelve to fourteen per cent. of tin. The Egyptians derived pure copper or bronze compounds from the Semitic nations, and it is doubtful whether they were early acquainted with tin in its pure form.[30] It is still unknown from what place tin reached Eastern Asia, and who brought it there. Iron, and perhaps steel, both originally far more valuable than bronze, do not occur in the old empire, but only in the new.[31] When it is asserted that the granite sculptures, which were executed under the fourth Manetho dynasty, could not have been produced without iron implements, it is entirely overlooked that the Incas of Peru performed achievements quite as great in

---

[28] Lepsius, Chronologie der Aegytper, part i. p. 165 et seq.

[29] G. Ebers, Durch Gosen zum Sinai, p. 531.

[30] Lepsius, Die Metalle in den ägyptischen Inschriften, pp. 105, 114. 1872.

[31] Ibid.

hewing and polishing stones, although they were totally unacquainted with iron.[32]

It has long ago been stated that the annual inundations of the Nile frequently effaced the landmarks, and that the Egyptians were very early obliged to study the science of mensuration. Yet we must not rate their achievements too high. The researches of Lepsius [33] respecting the Egyptian ell have proved that the unit of measurement was not accurately determined, and that the buildings therefore frequently exhibit great inaccuracies in the quantities. From a work of Aloys Sprenger,[34] however, it seems highly probable that the Egyptians measured a degree from Syene along the Nile about 700 B.C. Just as at the beginning of our century German scholars thought it incumbent upon them to obtain the highest honours at Paris, so the Greeks, possessed with a thirst for knowledge, made a pilgrimage to the country of the Nile. We know this with regard to Pythagoras, Thales, Solon, Anaxagoras, Eudoxus, and Herodotus. Democritus of Abdera first recognized the fact that the Greeks had nothing more to learn from the Egyptian geometricians.

All the services we have enumerated as rendered by the Egyptians to art and manufacture, to social organization and the sciences, are surpassed by an invention destined to hasten the maturity of civilization in the East by thousands of years. About three thousand years B.C. we already find hieroglyphic inscriptions of King Snefru, that is to say, during the transition from the third to the fourth dynasty.[35] The hieroglyphic symbols were already the representatives, some of phonetic groups or syllables, some even then of simple sounds. The written word was frequently elucidated by an adjoined symbol or emblem, the so-called determinative sign. Although the oldest records contain phonetic writing also, it may yet be inferred from the appearance of this determinative sign that, at a period prior to the oldest records, the Egyptians were satisfied with a purely symbolic and emblematic character.

[32] Rivero y Tschudi, Antigüedades peruanas, pp. 212, 231, et seq.

[33] Die altägyptische Elle, p. 5 et seq. 1865.

[34] Ausland, p. 1020. 1867.

[35] Ebers, Durch Gosen zum Sinai, pp. 138, 139.

A papyrus roll exists, named after Prisse, and dating from the twelfth dynasty, that is, from before the irruption of the Hyksos, written in an abbreviated running hieroglyphic character, which reached its highest perfection in the fourteenth century B.C., that is to say, before the exodus of the Jews. From this originated, in the eighth century B.C., the demotic or popular writing—a character with alphabetical sounds; but the Semites had previously adopted several of these; at least thirteen if not fifteen of the Phœnician letters were derived from the hieratical characters.[36]

In examining how far the nature of the country was accessory to this early ripening of civilization, our thoughts turn at once to the Nile and the regular rise and fall of its surface. According to the observations made in 1848–61, at the dam at the point of the delta,[37] the stream is at its feeblest in the month of May. It is true that in February the sun has already produced rains, which have filled the river beds of the White Nile, yet the greatest amount of rain falls between April and August. In the low lands the Nile begins to swell gradually from the latter half of June to the latter half of July, and from that time it increases with extreme rapidity. Meanwhile the tropical rains have descended upon Habesh, and have found their way into the Blue Nile, and somewhat later into the Atbara. In the middle of August the Nile reaches its high-water level, and remains at the same height till the third week of October, after a maximum of high water itself has occurred in the beginning of the month and has again disappeared. From the end of October the surface falls very steadily, at first somewhat faster than later on. In October the Nile contains about twenty times the volume of water which it had in May, or rather it does not contain it between its banks, but sends it right and left towards the desert.

The fertilizing effect of the Nile is due to the floating matter in its waters. Its mud has repeatedly been analysed,[38] recently

---

[36] Ebers, Ageypten und die Bücher Mose's, vol. i. p. 147.

[37] Heinrich Barth in die Zeitschrift für Erdkunde. New series, vol. xiv.

[38] Leonard Horner gives eight different analyses. Philosophical Transactions, vol. cxlv. London, 1855.

by W. Knop,[39] who detected very little organic matter, but found in the fine clays, known by all as existing in the Egyptian mud, the highest power of absorption (135) combined with the greatest number of siliceous bases (13.42), which produce the most useful effects on agriculture. Now we know that the White Nile, since it passes through lakes which act as a filter, is poor in floating minerals, and its greenish hue is produced only by vegetable particles. Its waters therefore serve only to fill the bed and for purposes of irrigation in dry seasons, but not for fertilization. The fertilizing elements are contributed by the Blue Nile and the Atbara.[40] Other streams also overflow the districts near their mouths; yet none distribute such rich blessings as the Nile. The hydraulic mechanism of this great river is unique. Under the microscope the Nile mud appears in the form of homogeneous grains of from $\frac{1}{80}$ to $\frac{1}{100}$ millionth part of an inch in diameter, which, when traversed by a ray of light, reflect the most beautiful prismatic colours.[41] It is known that the Nile receives the Atbara as its last tributary, and then flows through fourteen degrees of latitude in a double curve, while the desert winds absorb its surface. The tract is so arranged that no other tributary again contaminates the pulverized clays with coarse detritus. From Assouan, or the last cataract to Cairo, the fall amounts to eleven, and below Cairo, to only four feet in 100,000; even from Wadi Halfa, the second cataract to Assouan, the fall diminishes to nine inches in the English mile, so that even in this part but little coarse sand can be carried down. But it is owing to its slow speed that only the fine floating particles, or pulverized clays, can be carried forward. Let us remember that were the speed of the river to diminish to 0·5 feet in the second, even the finest particles must also sink to the ground. If the Nile ever slackened to this degree it would no longer reach Lower Egypt of a chocolate brown colour, but as a clear stream.[42] But science can foresee such a condition.

---

[39] Landwerthschaftliche Versuchsstationen, vol. xv. 1872.

[40] S. Baker, Nile Streams of Abyssinia.

[41] Leonard Horner, Philosophical Transactions, vol. cxlv.

[42] The mean speed of the Nile, which is, however, less important than the highest, is 2½ miles in the hour. Sir John Herschel, Physical Geography.

With the diminution of the fall in the last reach the speed must diminish also. If the bed of the Nile at the cataracts consisted of soft sandstone instead of hard syenite, the Nile would long ago have deepened its bed and decreased its fall to the extreme minimum ; but the hardness of the rocks in the district of the cataracts has hindered the occurrence of this calamity. Above Philæ an old Nile mark is actually seen 28–38 feet above the present level ; and under Amenemha III.[43] of the twelfth dynasty, the river actually flowed on a bed twenty-five feet higher.[44] The time of the wonderful powers of the Nile is therefore unquestionably limited.

At the present day the Fellah, without previous labour, still throws the seed from his boat into the wet mud when the water is partially withdrawing from the plains ; [45] yet, as early as the age of the pyramids, the fields were ploughed or loosened with the pickaxe,[46] while the seed itself was trodden in. In the cultivation of plants for commerce the soil is much manured ; but this was certainly not the case in ancient times. The present yield of wheat is from eight to twenty fold, of barley from four to eighteen, of maize from fourteen to twenty, of Durrah (*Sorghum vulgare*) from thirty-six to forty-eight fold.[47] Kaffir corn is not mentioned among the agricultural produce, and was perhaps not cultivated in ancient times,[48] in which case civilization is indebted for it to the negroes.

Whatever may be said to the contrary, Herodotus is right in maintaining that the earth nowhere yields agricultural produce in return for so little labour as in Lower Egypt, and gives back the seed so plentifully. The population in the delta of the Nile was thus enabled to become extremely dense. But on the other hand these natural advantages fell into worthy hands. Had the irrigating and fertilizing apparatus of the Nile been situated on the western

[43] According to Brugsch (Histoire d'Egypte), he reigned from 2653–2611 B.C.

[44] Lauth, Aegyptische Reisebriefe ; Allgem. Ztg. p. 1334. 1873.

[45] Leonard Horner, Philosophical Transactions for 1858. A. von Kremer, Aegypten. Leipzic, 1863.

[46] Ebers, Durch Gosen zum Sinai, p. 468.

[47] Heinrich Stephan, Das heutige Aegypter, p. 82. Leipzic, 1872.

[48] E. Ringer, Botanische Streifzüge, in Transactions of the Vienna Academy, vol. xxxviii. p. 100.

coast of South Africa, it would indeed have worked wonders, but not such great prodigies of civilization as in Egypt. The mouth of the Nile is close to the isthmus which connects Asia with Africa, therefore its advantages could not long remain concealed. Whether national migrations were directed from Africa to Asia, or whether tribes were driven into Africa from the already over-crowded parts of Western Asia, they invariably reached the Nile, and the permanent possession of the low country would finally accrue to the race which could best turn to account the advantages it offered for the rapid increase of the population.

II.—SEMITES.

This branch of the Mediterranean family peoples Western Asia and parts of Eastern Africa. It possesses all the characters of the other members of the race, is more bearded than the Hamites, and is more frequently gifted with expressive features, thin lips, high and generally aquiline noses, and well-marked eyebrows. The colour of the skin varies from a rather dark shade to a deep brown. Measurements of the skulls of this family are scanty. According to Welcker's tables the Jews are almost mesocephalic, but yet rank among the low brachycephals. The Arabs, on the contrary, approach the limits of dolichocephalism, but must still be classed among the high mesocephals. Lastly, the Abyssinians, with an index of breadth of 69° and an index of height of 76° are high, negro-like dolichocephals. But we have little guarantee for the fact that the skulls from Habesh belong to the descendants of true unmixed Semitic immigrants.[1]

Those who have studied the ancient Egyptian and the Semitic languages, long ago conjectured that, at a period which is at present beyond the reach of research, the Hamites and Semites developed their languages in a common primeval home, at least

---

[1] We expressly deny that the above words refer to a book which appeared at Gotha in 1872, under the title of "The Semites in their Relations to the Hamites and Japhites" (Die Semiten in ihrem Verhältniss zu Chamiten und Japhiten).

as far as the roots of the pronouns. In the Old Testament also a system of ethnography of the Mediterranean nations is sketched,[2] in which, in the naïve language of the patriarchal state, it attributes the names of countries, nations, or towns to fictitious heads of families. Thus the Jews represent their ancestor Eber to be the grandson of Arphaxad, but Arphaxad is the district of Arrapachitis near Ptolemæus, not far from Ararat, and still called Albak.[3]

At the time when the national genealogy of Genesis originated, likenesses which were afterwards lost may have been recognizable in the various races. As the Cushites were derived from Ham, while the Canaanites were regarded as the descendants of Cush, and the Phœnician town of Sidon is described as the eldest son of Canaan, the Old Testament favours the opinion that the Semite and Hamite families were very nearly allied in old times. The text of the Bible nevertheless contradicts itself more than once; Havilah, for example, is in one place counted among the Cushites, and in another among the Arab sons of Joktan.[4] Now, if the ethnographer, or rather the Elohistic and Jahvistic ethnographers of Genesis, based their system solely on the colour of the skin, as is frequently maintained by those versed in biblical archæology, modern science can attribute no value to their statements, for it must even then have been the case that the slight gradations of colour which occur varied from district to district, and in each horde the extreme varieties must have been connected by transitions.

Modern ethnology must judge only by language and its remains, of which the type has already been described.[5] They admit of a somewhat marked division into Northern and Southern Semites. The northern people may be again subdivided into Aramaians, Hebrews, Canaanites, Assyrians, and Babylonians. Aramaic was spoken in the north of Syria and in Assyria, but is now extinct except in two isolated spots, the dialects of which are different. Between Mosul and Diarbekr, and as far as lakes Van and Urmia on the north-east, live Nestorian Christians, who without reason call themselves Chaldeans, and speak a corrupt

---

[2] Gen. x. 1–32.   [3] F. Spiegel in the Ausland, p. 1035. 1872.
[4] Gen. x. 7 and 29.   [5] See above, p. 122.

Aramaic.[6] The second fragment of the language occurs near Damascus,[7] which is described in the Bible as the ancient Aramaic centre.[8]

In language the Hebrews were so nearly allied to the Canaanites, and to the Phœnicians in particular, that Phœnician inscriptions may be readily deciphered by the aid of Hebrew.[9] In the year 400 B.C., Hebrew became extinct as a national language, and was supplanted by Syriac, or Aramaic, while Samaritan, a hybrid language between Aramaic and Hebrew, still for a time found a link between the two. The third North Semitic branch is the Assyrio-Babylonian, the language of cuneiform characters of the "third genus," for the deciphering of which a reliable key has been secured by the discovery of the explanatory tablet at Nineveh Koyyunchik. This character is not invariably a phonetic character, nor when it is, is it always a syllabic character. Like the hieroglyphic and hieratic writing, it possesses determinative signs, but they are conventional and not symbolic ; and it has also a number of difficult idiograms,[10] many of which, however, are now explained, and which were probably old verbal emblems or symbols, abridged in the cuneiform characters. There is now no doubt that the Assyrians and Babylonians spoke a common language, and that this language was Semitic.[11] It was less like Aramaic than the Hebrew-Canaanite, and formed a link between the northern and southern Semitic groups.[12]

The genealogical table in Genesis, which describes Nimrod, the founder of Babel, Erech, Accad, and Calneh, as the son of Cush, has long been recognized as a later intercalation.[13] The

[6] Ritter, Erdkunde, vol. ix. p. 679 ; vol. xi. p. 211.

[7] Friedr. Müller, Reise der Fregatte Novara.

[8] 2 Sam. viii. 5, and Knöbel, Völkertafel.

[9] Whitney, Language and the Study of Language, pp. 295–297.

[10] Eberhard Schrader, Die assyrisch-babylonischen Keilinschriften. 1872.

[11] Ibid.

[12] Eberhard Schrader in the Zeitschrift der D. Morgenland. Gesellschaft. 1873. A. H. Sayce (An Assyrian Grammar, 1872) arrived at the same conclusion without knowing the work of Schrader.

[13] A. Knöbel, Die Völkertafel der Genesis, p. 339. Giessen, 1850.

statements in Genesis are the only evidence that Semite immigrants mingled in Babylon with an older Hamite population, and the circumstance is therefore not free from doubt. The Assyrian inscriptions testify that at least 900 years before Christ the inhabitants of Babylon were called Kaldi (Chaldeans).[14]

But before Semitic Chaldeans founded their supremacy in Babylon in the 18th century B.C., an empire existed near the mouth of the Euphrates, of which Ur was the capital, and whose kings did not bear Semitic names.[15] There the oldest form of the cuneiform character was invented, which is called by some Accadian and by others Sumeric, but from which, without doubt or dispute, the Assyrio-Babylonian character was first derived. The language of this ancient people was first called Turanian by J. Oppert, or, to use plainer words, Ural-Altaic, and as far as words of number and pronouns are concerned, is more nearly allied to the Finnish branch than to the Turkish.[16] But, strangely enough, although the words are otherwise always formed by a loose attachment of suffixes, as is the case in the Altaic group, the verb forms its definitions chiefly by prefixes,[17] and is thus completely alien to the type of North Asiatic languages. Unfortunately, the investigation of the Accadian or Sumeric language is entirely dependent on the progress made in the study of the Assyrio-Babylonian character. We shall therefore long remain without full certainty, but in due time we shall undoubtedly solve this most attractive problem of ethnology.

The Southern Semites separated themselves from the common stock as a second branch. In ancient historical times they spoke Pre-Arabic, which separated again into the Arabic of the Ishmaelites, whence are descended the old language of the Scriptures and the modern Arabic dialects, and, secondly, into the language of the Qahtanîtes, which was again subdivided into Himyaritic, whence originated the present Ehkyly of Southern Arabia and ancient Ethiopian, whence are derived the extinct Gabez, or state language,

---

[14] Schrader, Zeitschrift der D. Mgld. Ges. p. 398.
[15] Lenormant, Etudes accadiennes. Paris, 1873.
[16] Ibid.
[17] J. Oppert, Journal asiatique. Paris, 1837.

and the still extant Amharic in Habesh.[18]   Thus, previous to the conquest of Egypt by the Arabs, Southern Semites had already crossed the Red Sea from Yemen and Hadhramaut, and peopled Abyssinia.   These events certainly took place in pre-Christian centuries, the date of which cannot as yet be accurately determined.   As we noticed in the last chapter, the language of Arabia has now spread into Nubia among Hamite tribes, who are therefore inclined to attribute to themselves a Semitic origin.[19] The only ones who appear justified in so doing are the Shua, or Shiwa, and the Jalin and Shukurieh.[20]

All Europeans must honour the Semites as well as the Hamite Egyptians as more ancient civilized nations to whom we owe innumerable intellectual spurs and aids to civilization, even in comparatively recent times.   The invasion of the Arabs first dispelled the monkish darkness which threatened to overwhelm Europe, and fresh light illuminated our quarter of the world from the inventions and valuable knowledge which the crusaders brought home from Palestine.   According to the foregoing explanations, the Chaldeans of the land of Sinjar (Shinar), one of the oldest civilized nations of Western Asia, belonged to the Semites.   Like the Egyptians they inhabited a desert; as the former made use of the Nile so did they use the overflow of the Mesopotamian rivers, especially of the Euphrates, for artificial irrigation.[21]   In the upper and middle part of its course this river is so rapid that now, as in old days, the leathern boats are only used down stream, and having reached their destination, are carried back on beasts of burden to their starting-point.   Further south the Euphrates becomes more tranquil, and approaches the Persian Gulf as a still but deep river.   In April it overflows its right bank and leaves lakes and marshes behind it in the hollows, in which grow tall rushes eight or nine feet high.   From May to November a brazen sky overarches Sinjar, the temperature rises to 39° Reaumur, and even behind thick walls to 30°, without producing any relaxing

---

[18] Von Maltzan in the Introduction to A. von Wrede's Journey in Hadhramaut.

[19] Hartmann, Nilländer, p. 269.

[20] W. Münzinger, Ostafrikanische Studien, p. 563.

[21] Herodotus, lib. i. cap. 194.   Comp. also Ritter, Erdkunde, part xi. p. 64.

effects on the intellectual power of the population, as is also the case in Egypt, India, and Yucatan. From November to December light showers fall again. Trees only grow on the margins of the shores, and then only tamarisks, acacias, poplars, pomegranates with their brilliant flowers, and palms laden with branches of amber-coloured dates. Throughout large districts, the Euphrates, once so flourishing, is now terribly still. The wind raises up clouds of sand, and smothers the prolific soil of the marshes without hindrance from any one.[22] High above the plain tower strangely shaped hills, which on nearer approach are recognized as huge ruins made of baked bricks. There was nowhere any want of clay for making unbaked bricks, and an excellent mortar was supplied by the still existing bitumen wells near Hit. These ruins are the remains of the first and oldest towns known to the writers of Genesis, namely, the Chaldaic Ur, now Mugheir ; Erech, now Warka ; Nipur, or Calneh, in the language of the Bible, now called Niffer ; and, lastly, Babel, now Hilah and Borsippa, the " tower of languages." [23]

These towns were founded under the second ruling dynasty of Berosus, to which the date of 2286 B.C. is assigned,[24] though the imperfect chronology has been supplemented by artificial additions. The great structures of Ur rose in terraces. The surfaces of its walls were decorated with blue enamel, polished agates, alabaster, pieces of marble, mosaics, copper nails, and gold plates. Rafters of palm-wood supported the roof, though there were also early attempts at arched vaults. In the tombs we come upon sarcophagi, which consist of two earthenware vessels fitted together ; and at the side of the dead we find polished flint utensils, bronze implements, gold ear-rings, and brass armlets.[25] One of the oldest records is the cylindrical signet of the ancient king Uruch, the value of which depends not so much on the fact that it preserves to us the fashion of the court of those times, as because the use of a seal indicates the existence of a written character. Even if the inventors of this oldest form of writing did not belong

---

[22] Pauline von Nostiz. Helfer's Reisen, vol. i. p. 256.

[23] J. Oppert, Inscription de Nabuchodonosor, pp. 13–15. 1866.

[24] G. Rawlinson, The Five Great Monarchies, vol. i. p. 153.

[25] See above, p. 179.

to the Semitic family, the meteorological achievements of the
Chaldeans are beyond dispute. Even now the face of every dial
is a witness to their wisdom.[26] The first metrical weight was
determined by the Euphrates, for the Babylonian talent corre-
sponded exactly with a Babylonian cubic foot of water at the
mean temperature of that country.[27] We owe to the Chaldeans
the division of the year into months and week, and the names
of our seven days. They divided the circle into 360 degrees,
and these again into sixty fractions. Their figures reached to a
hundred, yet they also had special signs for sixty or a Sossos, as
well as for the Saros, or square of the Sossos. Earthenware tablets
found near Senkareh actually contain directions for distinguishing
the unit and the Sossos by their position from right to left; in
other words, the invention of the positional value of figures is due
to these people. The Chaldeans even had a mode of writing
which was essentially like our expressions for decimal fractions.
Let us add that, with their sexagesimal division, the Babylonians
originated the talents, minæ, and shekels, which became the
monetary standard of Western Asia. Bars of silver had however
to be weighed and tested when used in commercial transactions.
To give to money an easily recognizable value, to stamp gold and
silver into coins, was reserved for the Greeks of Asia Minor,
while the Semites and the nations descended from them continued
the use of bars long after this invention.

To other Semitic nations the West is indebted for its religious
training. These creations have already been under consideration,
so it only remains for us to examine the share which the type
of the language had in the institution of monotheism. The old
Aryans designated natural phenomena, or the forces of nature,
according to the impressions made by these on their senses; and
as in these languages the radical and significant phonetic elements
were very soon effaced, the name, as we have already shown,
became incomprehensible and gave rise to endless myths. The
Semites, on the contrary, gave to their gods names referring to

---

[26] J. Brandis, Münz- Mass- und Gewichtsystem, p. 20. Berlin, 1866.

[27] J. Brandis. According to J. Oppert the Babylonian foot was 315 millimetres in length. Journal Asiatique. 1872.

abstract qualities, such as El the Strong, Bel, or Baal, the Lord, Belsamin the Lord of Heaven, Moloch the King, Eliun the Highest, Ram, or Rimmon, the Exalted. It was inherent in the type of languages with three consonants that the distinctive sounds remained unimpaired by phonetic decay, and they thus incessantly reminded the Semites of the derivation of the word. The names of the Semite gods, although mere adjectives at first, subsequently became personal appellations, so that the different designations of a single being were transformed into the designations of different beings. Had the Jews not forgotten the signification of El, the Almighty, they would not also have worshipped Baal, the Lord, as a different deity. Thus even the Semitic languages were no protection against polytheism, although temptation was more rarely offered. But the Semites from the first attributed abstract names to their deities, less on account of their language than of their inherent tendency to spiritualize all things.

Ethnology has as yet nothing to do with the important inquiry of our times, as to whether the Semites shared a comparatively small home with the Indo-Europeans, and possessed in common a vocabulary of monosyllabic words. Even the most recent examination of this kind,[28] distinguished from its predecessors by a scientific method, has resulted in no decision, but has only revived the hope that, sooner or later, full evidence may be afforded of a primitive community of language between the three great families of the Mediterranean race, which are so closely situated in respect to each other.

III.—EUROPEANS OF DOUBTFUL POSITION.

Among the inhabitants of Europe, several nations which unquestionably belong to the Mediterranean race in their physical characters, must be separated from them on account of their languages. These are the Basques and certain tribes in the Caucasian countries.

[28] Friedr. Delitsch, Studien über indogermanisch-semitische Wurzelverwandtschaft. Leipzic, 1873.

(*a*) *The Basques.*—This is the name now given to the people of the north-east provinces of Spain, and of a small district in the south-west of France. About half a million in number, they speak Euscara, and call themselves Euscaldunac. The old geographers called them Iberians ; they then peopled the whole of Spain and the south-west of France, but were early driven towards the west and south by the Celts, and intermixing with them in the district of the present Catalanian dialect, constituted the Celtiberians. There is great difference of opinion as to the proportions of their skulls. According to Paul Broca [1] the Spanish Basques rank among the mixed semi-dolichocephals, while brachycephals preponderated among the French Basques. Their language, the Euscara, stands quite alone, or has mere analogies with the American type in the structure of words, in that it incorporates a number of prenominal relations into the verb, and also puts together fragments to represent words. The whole sentence does not however merge into a single word, and the substantives are subject to an inflection which has nothing in common with the American method. [2] Of all Europeans we must provisionally hold the Basques to be the oldest inhabitants of our quarter of the world.

(*b*) *Caucasian. Peoples.*—In addition to scattered tribes in or near the Caucasus, which have already been classed among the Turkish branch, or which have yet to be added to the Indo-European family, we come upon nations of the Mediterranean race whose languages as yet stand quite independently. Thus Daghestân, or the northern slope of the Eastern Caucasus, is peopled by the Avares, the Kasikumuks (not to be confounded with the Turkish Kumuks), the Akusha, the Kürines, and the Udes, who are all called Lekhi by the Georgians, Leksik by the Armenians, and by us Lesgians. Their westerly neighbours, whom the Daghestâns call Mizchegs, term themselves Nachtschuoi. Among their tribes is that of the Tshetshente, who fought obstinately for their independence under their Emir Shamyl, and which name was given to the whole group by the Russians, while

[1] Anthropological Review, vol. vii. pp. 382, 383. London, 1869.
[2] Whitney, Study of Language, p. 354.

the Georgians call them Kists. The western hill tribes are divided into the Abkhazi, who own both slopes of the Caucasus and the greater part of the shore, from the Ingur to the Kuban, and the Adigé, or Tsherkess, further to the west and north.

Between the Caucasus and the Anticaucasus, as Palgrave has happily called the northern slope of the Armenian highlands, live natives with kindred languages. These are, in the south-west and on Turkish territory, the Lazes ; in the coast districts to the north-west, the Mingrelians ; and in the valley of the Ingur to the south of the passes which lead to the Elburz, the barbarous, still almost independent Suanes, so well described by Freshfield, and, lastly, the Georgians, an inland people in the district of the upper and middle Kur ; they call themselves Karthuhli, but are termed Gruses by the Russians.[3]

IV.—THE INDO-EUROPEAN FAMILY.

The relationship in language of these highly developed nations, although long ago suspected, was first proved by Franz Bopp, and has since then been more and more fully recognized. They must all have inhabited one primeval home, and have spoken a primitive language common to them all. August Schleicher[1] has shown the gradual divergence of the branches from the stem, and of the the twigs from the branches in a genealogical table, which even now requires but little corrrection.

The Indo-European family divided at an early period into the Asiatic and European Aryans. The Brahminical Indians and the Eranians were the main branches of the Asiatic division. From the Sanscrit of the Brahminical Hindoos sprang the Neo-Indian languages, Bengalee and Orija, in Bengal and Orissa, Nepaulee and Cashmeree, in Nepaul and Cashmere, pure Hindoo and the Urdu, or camp language of the Great Moguls, which is mixed with many foreign ingredients, Punjaubee and Scindhee, and also

---

[3] The linguistic chart in Berghaus's Physikal. Atlas. Ethnographie, is fully sufficient for the present ethnology of the Caucasian territory.

[1] Die Darwin'sche Theorie und die Sprachwissenschaft, Plate i. Weimar, 1863.

Mahratha, or the Mahratta language. This branch also includes the language of the Siah Pôsh, or Blackclothes, in Kafiristân[2] and that of the enigmatical gipsies, who did not leave India before the year 1000 A.D., and entered our quarter of the world by way of Greece, and are proved to have been in Crete in 1322, in Corfu in 1346, and in Wallachia in 1370.[3]

The second branch of the Asiatic Aryans comprises the people who spoke Zend, the language of the Avesta, or ancient sacred writings of the Persians, as well as that of the cuneiform inscriptions of the first race of Persian sovereigns, and other nations akin to them. From Zend, mixed with Semitic elements, proceeded Pahlavi, and from the latter modern Persian.[4] To the Zend group also belong the Karduchs of ancient, the Kurds of modern geographers, a hill people of Western Asia, and also the Armenians, whose language resembles Pahlavi, and is supposed to be related to those of the Phrygians and Cappadocians ; thirdly, the Iron, or Ossets, of the Caucasus, who very significantly occupy the gorge of Dariel and both its outlets, the only natural road through the great mountain range, deeply dividing both the central chain and the northern line of hills ; also the Beloochs of Beloochistan, and, lastly, the Afghans of Afghanistan, who call themselves Bushtaneh, or Pushtaneh, and their language Pashto, or Pachto ; but it must be observed that, according to the most recent researches, this Pashto was an independent side-shoot from the bifurcation of the Eranian and Sanscrit branches. We must mention in conclusion the Tadshik of Turkestan, the agricultural slave population of the Khanates of Ozbeg, Khiva, Bokhara, Kokand, and Kashgaria.

European Aryans first separated into North and South Europeans. By North Europeans must here be understood the Letto-Sclavonic and the Germanic branch. The Letto-Sclaves were separated into Letts and Sclavonians, and the Letts again into true Letts and Lithuanians, to whom belonged the Prussians, whose language is now extinct. The East and South Sclavonians

---

[2] Trumpp, Sprach der Kafirn in Zeitschrift der D. Mgld. Gesellschaft. vol. xx. p. 391.

[3] F. Miklosich, Zigeuner Europa's. Vienna, 1873.

[4] Schläfli gives the names of the various hordes in Petermann's Mittheilungen, p. 62. 1863.

must be distinguished from the West Sclavonians. To the East Sclavonians belong the Russians, divided according to dialect into Great Russians, White Russians, and Little Russians, or Ruthenians, as they are called in Galicia.

The South Sclavonians, on the other hand, include the Slovak inhabitants of the South-east Alps in Austria, and the inhabitants of Croatia, Servia, Bosnia, and Herzegovina. While only slight differences of language distinguish the people above named, the Bulgarian of the Bulgarians of the Danube has become more alien. The inhabitants of Moldavia and Sclavonia are, on the contrary, Romanized South Sclavonians. In language the South and East Sclavonians are more nearly allied to each other than either is to the West Sclavonians. In addition to the Sclavonians of the Elbe, now Germans, the latter include the Vends of Lusatia, whose language forms a fragment which is rapidly diminishing,[5] the Poles in Posen, in the former kingdom of Poland, and in Western Galicia; thirdly, the Czechs in Bohemia and Meringia, and, lastly, the Slovaks in the northern principalities of Hungary.

The Germanic or second branch of North Europeans diverged into Goths, Scandinavians, and Teutons. The Gothic language has long died out, and is preserved only in the translation of the Bible by Ulfilas. The old northern language of the Scandinavians, on the contrary, still exists in Iceland and the Faroe Islands, and in its continental home has given birth to Dano-Norwegian and Swedish. The language of the Teutons is divided into the Northern or Low German dialects, such as Frisian, Saxon, Anglo-Saxon, Low German (Platt Deutsch), Dutch, and Flemish; and the Central and Southern German, which, as the language of literature, has become the most important in Germany since the time of the Reformation.

The Southern Europeans were more intricately subdivided. The first to dissever themselves were the ancient Greeks, whose language still exists in good preservation in the form of modern Greek. Their northern neighbours in Thracia and Illyria were

---

[5] The gradual collapse of this language since 1550 and 1750 has been shown by Richard Andrée in an instructive map. Das Sprachgebiet der Lausitzer Wende.

nations whose language has now disappeared, with one small exception in Albania. This is the Skipetar, the language of the hill people, called Arnauts by the Turks and by us Albanians. Their language certainly belongs to the Indo-European family, but it stands quite alone and without relationship in the same degree to any of the other members. The third branch consists of the Italians, who formerly spoke the Umbrian, Latin, and Oscan dialects. Corssen is said to have succeeded in discovering that Etruscan was another old Italian language ; but we are still anxiously looking for the publication of the evidence. The Romans raised Latin into the language of their empire, whence arose Portuguese, Catalonian, Provençal, Northern French, and the Ladine and Romantsh dialects in the Swiss and Tyrolese Alps, as well as the Furlanian dialect greatly mixed with Celtic in Friuli and Venetia, and, lastly, Roumanian in Siebenburgen and sundry Hungarian principalities, as well as in Wallachia and Moldavia. The last branch of the South Europeans is represented by the Celts, who formerly inhabited the Alpine countries and South Germany, and in France drove back the Basques, and peopled the British Islands. They have almost everywhere been expelled or partly Romanized and partly Germanized. The Cymric dialect has been preserved only in Brittany and Wales, the extreme north and west of its ancient territory, and the people still speak Gaelic dialects in the western counties of Ireland, in the Isle of Man, and in Scotland.[6]

The Indo-Europeans have the physical characters of the Mediterranean race in the fullest purity, the Hindoos only excepted : these latter have lost their purity of breed by intercourse with the Dravida. In Europe the shape of the skull varies from the medium form to those of great breadth. The height is always less, and often remarkably less, than the transverse section. Fair hair and blue eyes were very frequent among the North Europeans, even among the Gallic Celts, as they were described in ancient history, while their descendants, the French, afford evidence of the transient nature of these characters.

---

[6] Pure Gaelic is now spoken only in the north-east corner of Scotland, while it is spoken mixed with English to the west of a line curved to the east, extending from the Moray Firth to the mouth of the Clyde. Murray, Transactions of the Philological Society. 1870-72.

To describe the intellectual advantages and the social development of the Indo-European nations is a task at which historians have long been labouring. Our task is only to inquire what favourable or unfavourable influences the nature of the place of abode, and of Europe in particular, has exercised on the early maturity of our civilization. Unfortunately, we can as yet only guess where to look for the primitive homes of the Indo-Europeans. But every geographer must reject the old opinion that our forefathers descended from the highlands of Pamir. This district is still one of the least known regions of the world; and, at any rate, inhospitable plateaux, fit only for cattle-breeding, were ill-chosen as the primordial home of a high civilization and a cultured language.

The selection of Turkestan, and of Bactria in particular, is far more likely to meet the favour of students of Indian and Erânian languages. When the ancient vocabulary of the primordial Aryan age is restored by collecting the roots common to all the members, we at the same time obtain an outline of the social condition of these nations in the most ancient period. We thus learn that they already tilled the ground, ploughed it with oxen, used carriages with wheels, kept cattle for the production of milk, and ventured on a neighbouring sea in rowing-boats, but did not use sails.[7] It is more than doubtful whether they smelted metals, especially as the name for bellows[8] is not derived from the primordial place of abode. As they were not there acquainted with the ass and the cat, both ancient domestic animals in Africa, they had not as yet interchanged any of the treasures of civilization with the Egyptians. The fact that they subsequently borrowed the name for camel from Semitic languages is decisive against Bactria. As they had the same terms for snow and winter, and the other seasons afterwards received different names, we may be certain that in ancient Arya there was an alternation of hot and cold months. In these primitive abodes dwelt bears, wolves, and otters, but there were neither lions nor tigers. By these indications we can accurately define the home of the Indo-Europeans. It lay eastward of Nestus, now Karasu, in Macedonia, which in

---

[7] J. Muir, Original Sanskrit Texts, part ii.
[8] Adolph Pectet, Les origines indo-européennes. Paris, 1859.

the time of Xerxes was the limit of the range of the European lion [9] It was also further north than Chuzistan, Irak Arabi, and even than Assyria,[10] where lions are still to be met with. It cannot have included the highlands of West Iran and the southern shores of the Caspian Sea, for tigers still wander in search of prey as far as those districts.[11] Hence from all the facts here cited, every geographer will probably agree that the Indo-Europeans occupied both slopes of the Caucasus as well as the remarkable gorge of Dariel, and were in the habit of visiting either the Euxine or the Caspian Sea, or perhaps both. It is usually objected to this argument that, in the course of their migrations, the European families abandoned the territory of the lion and the tiger, and with the animals forgot their names also. But this requires stronger evidence, for the Maori have preserved the name for the domestic pig and the cocoa-nut, although neither existed in New Zealand. Had the ancient Aryans seen and fought against such magnificent animals in their own country, their names would certainly have been retained even though with an altered signification. The burden of proof lies with those who have selected Bactria as the most fitting home for the Indo-Europeans.

We have only now to inquire whether Europe, as a residence, did or did not conduce to accelerate the progress of civilization. The land and water are so intermingled in this quarter of the world, that even Strabo, who was so imperfectly acquainted with the neighbouring continents, praised Europe as being highly integrated ($\pi o \lambda u \sigma \chi \dot{\eta} \mu \omega v$). In our continent, which is itself a peninsular prolongation of Asia, the outlines are again peninsular in shape, for in the South three projections of this sort encroach on the Mediterranean, and in the North, Scandinavia and the Cimbric peninsula almost come in contact, and it is still evident that even Great Britain, before the shallow Channel had been

---

[9] Herodotus, lib. vii. cap. 125, 126.

[10] On the range of the lion in Western Asia, comp. Layard, Nineveh and its Remains,

[11] Carl Ritter, On the range of the lion in the Zeitschrift für Erdkunde, vol. i. of new series. 1856.

excavated by the sea, was also a projection from the main body. As a consequence of these numerous projections, gulfs of the sea everywhere penetrate the continent.

Straits caused by the approximation of mainland to mainland are as rare as they are important. Australia, the continent which possesses none, was therefore neglected longer than any other. The first inhabitants of America, in all probability, came across Behring's Straits. Europe has not only the Cattegat and the Sound, but forms with Africa and Asia the straits of Gibraltar, of Sicily, and of the Hellespont and Bosphorus, of which the two latter divide the Mediterranean into three separate basins. With each of these points are connected events which have changed the course of history. It was necessarily where Sicily is nearest to the coast of Africa that the greatest naval power of antiquity arose, for the two basins of the Mediterranean could be most efficiently controlled from that point, especially as, in old times, navigators never ventured to lose sight of land. At this spot Carthage rose, grew, and fell. The other strait takes its present name from Djebel-Tarik, the rock of Tarik, for Tarik there crossed over with the Arabs from Africa to Spain, an enterprise which would probably never have been attempted, owing to the low state of navigation in those times, had the two continents been separated by a broad channel instead of by narrow straits. The Arabs brought with them the riper knowledge of the East, and, in a measure, also the then forgotten learning of Grecian antiquity. With the Bosphorus and the Hellespont is connected the fall of Constantinople in 1453, which by a marvellous dispensation was destined to prove a blessing to future times; for, put to flight by the Osmanli, the Byzantines brought to mediæval Europe the long lost literary treasures of the best Grecian period, and through them the Greek language became the common property of scholars, and the source of the new light of the sixteenth century. Even now these straits still threaten the inhabitants of Europe with new trials. In modern times a somewhat highly gifted people has gathered strength, and in the form of the Russian empire is ready to press forwards to the open ocean. Its shores are confined to those of two inland seas, which may be compared to two rooms of which other nations possess the keys. In winter the Baltic freezes, and Sweden becomes united to the Danish islands, so that navigation is suspended. The Black Sea flows out through a double valley, so narrow that either point may be brought under a cross-fire of artillery. Any people of like strength would endeavour to make their way to a more open sea, and hence, whenever the captive impatiently shakes the bars of his geographical prison-house, the nations of the West tremble for their peace.

In consequence of its highly complex form, our part of the world possesses the greatest length of coast line in proportion to its superficial extent. Behm's new and beautiful chart of the distribution of population in Europe, has shown that with the exception of the Landes, the Maremma, and the " iron-bound " coast of Jutland, the number of inhabitants is relatively greater on the sea-shore than in the inland districts. This map also teaches us that every elevation of ground diminishes the density of population, or, as it were, loosens it. It is therefore very significant that, of all the quarters of the world, Europe has the lowest mean altitude. It is essential to all progress of culture that men should not be separated by great distances.

The advantageous coast line is further aided by meteorological advantages which could scarcely have been better arranged by professional experts. Owing to the deep indentation of the sea, all harsh contrasts are neutralized, and the warmth is so evenly distributed throughout the year that temperate summers succeed to moderate winters, and even in the south of Ireland, myrtles, laurels, camellias, and oranges live all the year in the open air. A hasty glance at atlases with isothermal lines will be quite sufficient to assure us that, of all parts of the world, Europe enjoys cooler summers and milder winters than any of the corresponding regions under the same latitudes.[12] The narrow peninsular form, and the direction of the great axis of our continent, is also very favourable to the equal distribution of moisture. When, as on the eastern shore of Australia, or the western shore of America, coasts extend from south to north, and the rain-bearing sea winds immediately deposit their moisture on the slopes of high moun-

---

[12] A. von Humboldt, *Kleine Schriften*, vol. i. p. 438.

tains, the ridges are immediately succeeded by almost rainless zones, as in the cases named. Nothing of the kind can occur in Europe, where, much to our annoyance, the rain clouds of the Atlantic often shroud the whole of Northern Europe as far as Russia, for there are no elevations of ground running from north to south to disturb their even distribution at the expense of the inland districts. Our principal line of mountains, the Alps and their eastern prolongations, rather serve to emphasize the separation of the continent into two climatic regions, into Northern and Southern Europe, a zone in which the foliage falls in autumn, and a Mediterranean shore clothed with evergreen bushes and plants; the one inhabited by nations which brew beer and make butter, the other by nations which tread the grape and press the fruit of the olive tree. Only in the far east of the continent, on the shores of the Black Sea and the Caspian, the steppes form a third zone with different conditions of life; they occupy a district which is at first narrow but rapidly increases in extent. These sudden contrasts of climate necessarily gave rise to international commerce at an early period, for the people of the north, as well as those of the south, were able to offer products which, if only as novelties, would be acceptable.

The advantages of high integration are simply shown by the ease with which variously gifted nations are enabled to interchange their respective products. But man's best products are his happy and sanctifying thoughts, which, when once framed, extend their fertilizing or consolatory influence for thousands of years, and from generation to generation. Among these sanctifying thoughts must be classed the creations of religions; among the fortunate thoughts, those inventions, among others, which control our domestic life and daily habits. Civilization, culture, and morality are but the sum of lucid thoughts, mostly inherited by us, and of Asiatic origin. No civilized people stands high enough to be incapable of adopting anything new from the so-called savage nations, or not to have already adopted something from them. The use of forks in eating was, for instance, only spread through the north of Europe in the 17th century,[13] and was at first

---

[13] Lubbock, Prehistoric Times. p. 443.

regarded as an undesirable innovation. If the nations of antiquity had not left us this utensil, or if, like the Chinese even at the present day, we made use of chopsticks, our travellers might perhaps bring the fork to Europe as a novelty from the cannibals of the Fiji Islands. The Romans learned many things in their intercourse with the Celts of Gaul, from whom they first obtained soap,[14] and learnt how to tin and plate metal vessels.[15] From the Celtic nobles they learnt to hunt wild beasts, and they were interested in falconry by our German forefathers.[16] The ancient Britons, again, were the first to apply a mineral manure to agricultural purpose, namely, marl; and, according to a somewhat obscure account given by Pliny, they already cut their corn by machinery and horse-power.[17] On the other hand, the Northmen, the boldest seamen in the world, became acquainted with the use of sails only after the time of Tacitus.[18]

It was from foreign nations that we first acquired a knowledge of our most important narcotics during the last three or four centuries. Tea came from the Chinese, and coffee from the Arabs. Chocolate was first drunk by the Spanish conquerors from the imperial kitchen of the Mexican Emperor Mocteuzoma, or Monteuzoma,[19] and when Spanish spies returned from the interior of Cuba in 1492, they told the discoverer of the New World that the harmless Indians of that island rolled up the leaves of a weed called tobacco, and put them in their mouths in order to imbibe the smoke from the ignited end. Cigars were in use in the Antilles, and Europeans first saw tobacco smoked in stone pipes by the Red Indians of North America, and taken as snuff in ancient Peru[20] and other parts of South America. Suspended nets for sleeping were an invention of the New World, and the German expression *Hängematte* is not only a translation but also a phonetic imitation of the original word *hamaca*, which

---

[14] Ausland, p. 139. 1866.
[15] Mommsen, Romische Geschichte, vol. iii. p. 217.
[16] Hehn, Culturplanzen, p. 270.
[17] Pliny, Hist. nat. lib. xvii.
[18] Germania, The Suiones of Tacitus are the inhabitants of Sweden.
[19] Prescott, Conquest of Mexico, vol. i. p. 135.
[20] Ibid. Conquest of Peru, vol. i. p. 140.

has been well rendered by the French *hamac* and the English hammock, and which comes from the language of St. Domingo. The use of artificial flies for angling, and the selection of the particular kind according to the species of fish, the season; and the weather, was first learnt by the English from the Indians on the rivers of Guayana ; the Portuguese were taught to manufacture tapioca by the natives in Brazil.[21]   The simplest and, at the same time, the unusually picturesque male garment, the poncho, which is now worn in every part of Spanish America, was the national costume of the brave Araucanians.[22]   Even in boat-building we might learn something from unjustly despised people such as the Eskimo, whose kayaks were the model of our pleasure-boats decked at bow and stern.

Therefore, if even in our mature condition intercourse with undeveloped races is still beneficial, it was infinitely more important to our race in its earlier times that the accessibility and openness of our part of the world allowed free admission to the intelligent nations of Asia and Africa.   But it would be a misapprehension of the history of civilization to conclude that because they inhabited a highly integrated region, the Europeans would necessarily have been in all ages conspicuous for their achievements.   The French cave men of the Dordogne, who hunted the wild horse with stone implements for the sake of its flesh, in an age when the prehistoric elephant still ranged over Northern Europe, were quite unaffected by the fact that the quarter of the world in which they lived was semi-peninsular in shape, and broken up by many sounds and gulfs.   In the lowest stages of our development, when care for daily wants is almost the sole aim of life, when the only want that is not animal in kind but, strange to say, æsthetic, is provisionally satisfied when, for instance, pretty shells strung upon a band adorn the throat or ankles, neither coast line or elevation, or any other geographical characters, were of any value in softening the rudeness of human nature.

As the superiority of the organization of Europe consisted in its accessibility to foreign culture, its inhabitants, as far as our

---

[21] See above, p. 422.

[22] Waitz, Anthropologie, vol. iii. p. 510.

historical knowledge reaches back, have always, until four or five centuries ago, received rather than spread the benefits of civilization. For this reason it was important that as an Asiatic peninsula, Europe formed part of the Old World, for vast tracts of country are especially rich in those species of animals and vegetables which are best adopted for entering into social relations with the inhabitants; and it is a fact, that more than half the forms which adorn the landscape of the Mediterranean shores are derived from the East. Only the vine, the fig-tree, the laurel of Apollo (*Laurus nobilis*), and the oleander, have yet been found as fossils in Provence.[23] In all probability the evergreen oak, the myrtle, and the pine, were also indigenous plants. The olive, on the contrary, which was found in the Greek island of Santorin, under a very ancient stratum of lava, first came to Italy by ship with with Greek settlers in 600 B.C. The vine which yields the fiery wines of the South came from the southern slopes of the Caucasus by way of Thrace; it was followed by the pheasant from the banks of the Phasis, and by the apricot from Armenia. From Persia came the plane-tree, the peach, the rose, and the lily, while it was at a late period that melons, gourds, and cucumbers, which are all products of the steppes, reached the West, and were brought from Turkestan by the Sclavonians. It was in Phœnicia that the Greeks first saw date palms; as the inseparable companions of the Arabs, these trees appeared in Spain after the conquest, and landed with the Saracen pirates on the shores between Nice and Genoa. From Semitic Asia comes also the cypress, the paradise apple, the caraway, and mustard, while Northern Europe is indebted to Rome for the lime, and to Greece for the pea. From Italian gardeners our ancestors learnt to ennoble the sloe into the damson by grafting Damascene scions; and the agriot from Cerasus on the Black Sea was placed on the wild cherry-tree. The domestic fowl migrated, in the first instance, to Greece from India, and across Persia; while the peacock was brought from Ophir (Abhira at the mouth of the Indus) by the ships despatched to India by Solomon and Hiram.

It was thus mainly the eastern countries which poured their

---

[23] Charles Martius in the Revue des deux Mondes, vol. lxxxv.

23

riches into the south of Europe, and the New World had comparatively little additional to bestow : a single cereal, maize, a single tuber, the potato, and, as common ornaments of southern landscapes, the aloe and the prickly pear.

But it was not only the gifts of Ceres, not only the ornaments of our gardens and groves, and the tempting fruits of our orchards, that migrated from the East to the Mediterranean ; for the noblest intellectual riches came by the same road. The art of separating the spoken word into its separate sounds, and of rendering these sounds visible by means of symbols, was first received by the Grecians from Asia Minor. Egyptian and Assyrian models first incited them to give life to stone in works of sculpture and architecture. Lastly, from oriental lands, from the desert more especially, where sun and stars unceasingly shine in a calm and cloudless sky, where pious enthusiasm is more frequently aroused, and the gift of prophecy is more readily kindled, were spread the more enlightened religions, and by their means a notable softening of manners. Little more than a thousand years ago, the Arabs brought to us from India an invention only surpassed in ingenuity by that of phonetic writing, namely, our numerical figures, and the art of determining their rank in the decimal arrangement by their positional value.

Although we must respect the East as the mother of the highest inventions, of all the pleasant improvements of household existence, of all intellectual enlightenment, yet its people have remained stationary, even to the present day, in the lower stages of human society, that is to say, in the phase of despotic government, more or less modified by an administration of theocracy, but never free from the curse of polygamy, which renders brotherly affection impossible ; the result is a constant series of intrigues in the harem and revolutions in the palace, and constant changes of dynasty. With this defect it might have been foreseen that if some other family of nations, the Aryans for instance, were capable of organizing a better and more worthy social state, its abode would inevitably sooner or later have attained the highest development.

Of all Aryan nations the Romans were unquestionably the most conspicuous for statesmanlike talents. No one knew better

than they did how to regulate a community by laws, how to train
an army, how in peaceful intercourse to settle questions respecting property and service according to sound views of justice and
equity. In the East despotisms arose on the ruins of despotisms;
among the Aryans of the West were developed the first germs
of political society. But, happily for mankind, the Romans had
made their home on a central peninsula, for, as Strabo already
noticed, the Latin sovereignty of the world was due to the central
position of Italy. Thus it happened that shortly before the commencement of our era, the centre of civilization moved for the
first time from the southern to the northern shores of the Mediterranean, and from its extreme east to the middle, from the
Levant to the west.

If, as geographers and ethnologists, we estimate the course of
history, the greatest achievements of the Roman Empire were the
long conflict with Spain, the rapid conquest of Gaul and the
British Isles, and the partial invasion of Germany. Inconspicuous
and commonplace works are, from this point of view, the highest.
The Romans established roads, milestones, and posts; as our
language testifies, they first taught the art of building stone houses,
and of surrounding them with circular ditches and breastworks.
The effect of the foundation of the towns was to distinguish the
people into a civic and rural population, and, at the same time,
the first instruction was given in the art of governing such communities. Among the Celts of Gaul and Britain this revolution
grew, but the prolonged advantage of Roman government cost
the sacrifice of the native language, so that the Basque dialect
could hold its own only in the inaccessible mountains and remote
districts of Aquitaine, and Celtic only in Wales, Scotland, and
Ireland. The Germanic tribes owed the preservation of their
language to the greater severity of their climate, the impractica-
bility of their plains, the shorter duration of the Roman
dominion, and their brave resistance, and also to the protection of their huge mountains, for while Latin easily entered and
diffused itself in the open and prosperous country of Gaul, which
those very qualities rendered more susceptible of earlier civilization, it was not able to penetrate into Germany by the shortest
road, that is to say, from the south, but was compelled to take an

indirect course by the south-east and west, so that to the inaccessibility of the Alps the maintenance of the German language is due.

With the growth of political civilization in Northern Europe, the value of geographical features gradually changed. The streams suggested the sites of towns, trade and commerce flourished, and the northern shores of the Mediterranean obtained what they had previously possessed only in a small degree, a country of political importance in their rear. At this period the prosperity of Marseilles revived, Barcelona became a place of the first rank, Seville rose somewhat later, and the maritime power of Genoa came into existence, which, after the subjugation of Pisa, strove to obtain the supremacy of the Mediterranean. Predestined to cast all these completely in the shade, to survive all rivals, ultimately to become the predominant maritime power, Venice was founded in an incomparable situation, at the head of the Adriatic of which we may regard the Red Sea, the oldest marine road to India, as the continuation.

While the southern coast of Europe still appeared the most fortunately shaped region of the world, the maritime powers of Italy themselves brought about a change which entirely altered the import of the coast line of Europe, and we can even accurately point out the time at which the lustre of the Mediterranean shores began to fade. In the year 1318 Venetian galleys first conveyed Indian or, in other words, oriental wares, by sea through the Straits of Gibraltar to the Antwerp market. Single ships, indeed, had previously taken this course, but the perils of the sea and the fear of pirates had hitherto rendered land carriage preferable to sea freight for mercantile purposes. This advance in navigation led the seamen into the Atlantic Ocean. It was almost immediately followed by the rediscovery of the Canaries, the finding of the Azores, which latter lie two-fifths of the way to America. The Mediterranean sailors did not pass unnoticed along the coast of Portugal, which is most advantageously situated for trade by sea. Lisbon became a sea town of the first importance; the Portuguese and Spaniards, timid at first, gained practice on the African coast before making voyages on the open seas; a New World was discovered in the West, and a marine road to India, while the Mediterranean sank at first slowly, and then with increasing rapidity, into the character of an inland sea. The greatest geographical advantages were thenceforth enjoyed by the nations which occupied the oceanic shores of Europe, whose maritime tendencies only needed a stimulus. In proportion as the countries across the sea gained in importance every century, in the character of a rejuvenated and duplicate Europe, the value of the oceanic coasts became higher and higher.

This aspect of history is always surprising. We previously admitted that at the reindeer period the outlines of our continent were as yet negative advantages to its inhabitants; we subsequently ascertained that the most ancient rise to a higher civilization occurred in the district of the Nile, near the point of contact between Africa and Asia, and that by its geographical proportions and indentations, the southern shore of Europe was, as it were, providentially prepared for the reception of oriental culture ; but that these processes came to a stop when the value of the conditions of nature were altered by the progress of human achievements. Hence we must regard action as superior to any outlines of land or sea, and indeed as superior to all else.

These historical conclusions teach the temporary character of all advantages of geographical position. In the chain of the history of civilization the Mediterranean was a mere link which was only for a short time surrounded by the highest lustre. So also Europe can only for a time remain the scene of the highest achievements of the human race. The ancient Greeks, as inhabitants of islands, sharply cut peninsulas, isthmuses, valleys, and villages separated by mountains, enjoyed all the incentives and advantages of political seclusion favourable to the evolution of intellectual heterogeneity, but adverse to great national achievements. Thus, when their course was run, they sank into historical oblivion. Similarly Europe is now the most suitable region for the development of nations with strongly marked idosyncrasies. It was almost inevitable that compact and separate states or societies should be formed in Spain, the British Isles, Scandinavia, Italy, the Illyrian peninsula, in France with natural boundaries on them, and Germany with similar boundaries on two sides, and even European Russia seems to be a somewhat distinct region. It is a question whether the development of a number of strongly characterized nations may not soon appear as small and contemptible as the separate life of Athens, Lacedemonia, Corinth, and Bœotia appeared when the time had come for larger historical existences.

In a world to the west of us, facing a world that is old, and growing older, and in a region situated between two oceans, a young and mixed nation occupies nearly the whole of a continent which could easily support three times the population of China, nearly 1000 millions. Here a new society is growing up which triples its numbers every ten years, so that it may perhaps enter upon the twentieth century with a population of 100 millions. If at some future time the higher problems of history are solved upon this stage the nations of Europe must resign their importance in history. As soon as the sun reaches midday with us its first rays brighten the shores of the New World. Thus it is with human culture also. Europe is now in the meridian of its course, and morning is already breaking over them. But the sun moves on; it does not remain as at Joshua's command; and as the configuration of our quarter of the world is, in a geological point of view, only a transient phenomenon, so also will its importance in the history of civilization be unable to escape the fate of all perishable things.

APPENDIX A.

TABLE OF SKULL MEASUREMENTS,

From Welcker's Craniological Contributions to the Archiv für Anthropologie.

LENGTH OF THE SKULL = 100.

Source of Skulls.	Index of breadth.	Index of height.	Difference.	Source of Skulls.	Index of breadth.	Index of height.	Difference.
I.				**IV.**			
Caroline Islands ...	68	74	+ 6	Abyssinian	69	76	+ 7
New Caledonia ...	70	77	+ 7	Fellaheen ...	69	76	+ 7
Australian	70	75	+ 5	Modern Egyptian ...	71	76	+ 5
Papuan	73	75	+ 2	Arab	74	76	+ 2
New Zealand	73	76	+ 3	Egyptian Mummy ...	74	75	+ 0.3
Alfur	74	79	+ 5	Cabul	75	75	+ 0.6
Bligh Island	74	79	+ 5	Guanche	75	72	− 3
Marquesas Group	74	76	+ 2	Jew	78	71	− 7
Nicobar Islands ...	74	78	+ 4				
Tahiti	75	80	+ 5				
Chatham Island ...	76	79	+ 3	**V.**			
Sandwich Islands	77	81	+ 4				
				Rajpoot	66	72	+ 6
				Leptsha	69	73	+ 4
II.				Ganges Mussulman	69	72	+ 3
Dyak	75	77	+ 2	"Hindoo" ...	70	75	+ 5
Balinese	76	77	+ 1	Thakur	70	74	+ 4
Amboynese	77	77	+ 0.4	Sikhs	71	75	+ 4
Island of Sumatra	77	78	+ 1	Bhots of Thibet ...	72	75	+ 3
Macassar	78	78	− 0.5	Cashmir	72	73	+ 1
Javanese	79	80	+ 0.4	Average of four ⎱	72	73	+ 1
Buginese	79	80	+ 0.4	Hindoo castes ⎰			
Menadorese ...	80	81	+ 1	Bhils, Gods, and Kols	73	75	+ 2
Madurese	82	82	− 0.1	Nagas and Khassias	73	74	+ 1
				Bais	73	73	+ 0.3
				Cingalese ...	73	77	+ 4
				Gorkhas	74	74	+ 0.5
III.				Brahmin	74	74	− 0.3
				Soudras	75	73	− 2
Moravi Negro ...	68	74	+ 6	Himalayan Bhots	75	75	− 0.4
Senaar and Darf	68	72	+ 4	Gipsies	76	74	− 2
Ashanti	69	75	+ 6				
Kafir	69	74	+ 5				
Donko Negro ...	69	76	+ 7	**VI.**			
Hottentot	69	70	+ 1				
"Negro"	70	73	+ 3	Sion	75	72	− 3
Mozambique Negro	70	75	+ 5	Swedes	75	71	− 4
Soudan Negro ...	71	76	+ 5	Dutch	75	71	− 4
South Guinea Negro	71	75	+ 4	English	76	73	− 3

APPENDIX A (*continued*).

Source of Skulls.	Index of breadth.	Index of height.	Difference.	Source of Skulls.	Index of breadth.	Index of height.	Difference.
Icelandic	76	71	− 5	Ancient Greek	75	74	− 1
Danish	76	71	− 5	Scotch	76	73	− 3
Swiss	81	75	− 6	Portuguese	76	75	− 1
Hanoverian	77	72	− 5	Italian	79	75	− 4
From near Jena	77	72	− 5	French	79	75	− 4
Holstein	77	71	− 6				
Bonn and Cologne	77	72	− 5				
Austria	79	75	− 4	**IX.**			
Hesse	79	72	− 7				
Suabia	79	73	− 6	Ehst	75	74	− 1
From near Halle	80	74	− 6	Japanese	76	75	− 1
Bavaria	80	74	− 6	Chinese	76	78	+ 2
Franconia	80	73	− 7	Tatar	77	76	− 1
				Finnish	79	75	− 4
				Magyar	80	76	− 4
VII.				Bashkir	80	76	− 4
				Kalmut	81	74	− 7
Lett	75	72	− 3	Tungus	81	71	− 10
Modern Greek	77	74	− 3	Turk	82	78	− 4
Serb	79	76	− 3	Lapp	82	73	− 9
Little Russian	79	75	− 4	Buriat	83	76	− 7
Polish	79	75	− 4				
Roumanian	80	76	− 4				
Russian	80	77	− 3	**X.**			
Rutherian	80	77	− 3				
Slovak	81	76	− 5	Eskimo	70	74	+ 4
Croatian	82	78	− 4	Brazilian	74	75	+ 1
Czech	82	76	− 6	Mexican	76	78	+ 2
				North American Indian	77	75	− 2
VIII.				Patagonian	80	77	− 3
				North-west American	80	76	− 4
Irish	73	70	− 3	Carib	80	74	− 6
Ancient Roman	74	71	− 3	Old Peruvian	95	87	− 8
Spanish	74	73	− 1	Flatheads	100	87	− 13

APPENDIX B.

TABLE OF SKULL MEASUREMENTS.

From B. Davis's "Thesaurus Craniorum," pp. 352–359.

LENGTH OF THE SKULL = 100.

Source of Skulls.	Number of Skulls.	Breadth.	Height.	Source of Skulls.	Number of Skulls.	Breadth.	Height.
EUROPEAN.				Thai	6	84	87
				Chinese	21	76	79
Ancient British	17	79	71				
,, ,, ...	81	79	75	**AFRICAN.**			
,, ,, ...	147	77	75				
Ancient Scotch ...	7	79	72	Berber	4	73	74
Ancient Roman-British	14	76	71	Guanche	22	75	74
Ancient Roman and Roman-British }	8	75	70	Negro	17	73	74
				Dahomey Negro ...	12	72	73
Ancient Roman and Roman-British }	43	76	73	Ibo Negro	3	73	77
Anglo-Saxon	36	76	72	Joruba Negro ...	4	69	74
,, ,, ...	11	75	74	Equatorial Tribes ...	17	76	76
English	39	77	73	Hottentot	3	76	73
Irish	31	75	71	Zulu Kaffir	4	72	76
Merovingian Frank ...	5	74	75	Bushman	4	73	72
French	26	78	73				
Spanish	5	78	74				
Italian, Ancient Roman	8	76	77	**AMERICAN.**			
Ligurian	4	85	79				
Italian	7	75	73	Eskimo, Eastern ...	6	72	75
Lapp	9	80	73	Eskimo, Western ...	4	75	77
Swedish	12	75	72	Eskimo, Greenland ...	10	71	75
Fries	5	78	73	Araucanian	7	80	80
Amsterdam	5	79	74				
Netherland	23	80	73.				
Prussian	8	80	74	**AUSTRALIAN.**			
German	2	79	71				
Finnish	8	82	78	Australian	15	71	73
Russian	10	78	73	Tasmanian ...	10	74	74
Turkish	3	84	78				
				OCEANIC.			
ASIATIC.				Sumatran	7	76	78
				Javan	25	81	80
Hindoo of High Caste	6	75	78	Madurese	7	81	81
,, ,, ,,	3	75	75	Celebes	6	79	79
Hindoo of Low Caste ...	20	76	78	Dyak	14	77	80
,, ,, ,,	27	75	74	Bisaya	8	80	79
,, ,, ,, ...	54	75	76	Negrito	3	77	77
Mohammedan Indian	22	74	75	Papuan	3	77	77
Khond tribes ...	2	73	74	Salomon Island ...	3	72	76
Nepaulese	6	76	77	New Caledonia ...	4	70	79
Leptsha	13	76	77	New Hebrides	9	72	77
Bodos	12	76	78	Maori	7	75	80
Bodshi	14	76	75	Marquesas Islands ...	27	78	77
Mishmi	3	78	79	Kanak	116	80	81

INDEX OF NAMES AND SUBJECTS.

INTERNATIONAL SCIENTIFIC SERIES.

NOW READY.

No. 1. FORMS OF WATER, in Clouds, Rain, Rivers, Ice, and Glaciers. By Prof. JOHN TYNDALL, LL. D., F. R. S. 1 vol. Cloth. Price, $1.50.

No. 2. PHYSICS AND POLITICS; or, Thoughts on the Application of the Principles of "Natural Selection" and "Inheritance" to Political Society. By WALTER BAGEHOT, Esq., author of "The English Constitution." 1 vol. Cloth. Price, $1.50.

No. 3. FOODS. By EDWARD SMITH, M. D., LL. B., F. R. S. 1 vol. Cloth. Price, $1.75.

No. 4. MIND AND BODY. The Theories of their Relation. By ALEX. BAIN, LL. D., Professor of Logic in the University of Aberdeen. 1 vol., 12mo. Cloth. Price, $1.50.

No. 5. THE STUDY OF SOCIOLOGY. By HERBERT SPENCER. Price, $1.50.

No. 6. THE NEW CHEMISTRY. By Prof. JOSIAH P. COOKE, Jr., of Harvard University. 1 vol., 12mo. Cloth. Price, $2.00.

No. 7. THE CONSERVATION OF ENERGY. By Prof. BALFOUR STEWART, LL. D., F. R. S. 1 vol., 12mo. Cloth. Price, $1.50.

No. 8. ANIMAL LOCOMOTION; or, Walking, Swimming, and Flying, with a Dissertation on Aëronautics. By J. BELL PETTIGREW, M. D., F. R. S., F. R. S. E., F. R. C. P. E. 1 vol., 12mo. Fully illustrated. Price, $1.75.

No. 9. RESPONSIBILITY IN MENTAL DISEASE. By HENRY MAUDSLEY, M. D. 1 vol., 12mo. Cloth. Price, $1.50.

No. 10. THE SCIENCE OF LAW. By Prof. SHELDON AMOS. 1 vol., 12mo. Cloth. Price, $1.75.

No. 11. ANIMAL MECHANISM. A Treatise on Terrestrial and Aërial Locomotion. By E. J. MAREY. With 117 Illustrations. Price, $1.75.

No. 12. THE HISTORY OF THE CONFLICT BETWEEN RE-LIGION AND SCIENCE. By JOHN WM. DRAPER, M. D., LL. D., author of "The Intellectual Development of Europe." Price, $1.75.

No. 13. THE DOCTRINE OF DESCENT AND DARWINISM. By Prof. OSCAR SCHMIDT, Strasburg University. Price, $1.50.

No. 14. THE CHEMISTRY OF LIGHT AND PHOTOGRAPHY. In its Application to Art, Science, and Industry. By Dr. HERMANN VOGEL. 100 Illustrations. Price, $2.00.

No. 15. FUNGI; their Nature, Influence, and Uses. By M. C. COOKE, M. A., LL. D. Edited by Rev. M. J. BERKELEY, M. A., F. L. S. With 109 Illustrations. Price, $1.50.

No. 16. THE LIFE AND GROWTH OF LANGUAGE. By Prof. W. D. WHITNEY, of Yale College. Price, $1.50.

No. 17. MONEY AND THE MECHANISM OF EXCHANGE. By W. STANLEY JEVONS, M. A., F. R. S., Professor of Logic and Political Economy in the Owens College, Manchester. Price, $1.75.

No. 18. THE NATURE OF LIGHT, with a General Account of Physical Optics. By Dr. EUGENE LOMMEL, Professor of Physics in the University of Erlangen. With 188 Illustrations and a Plate of Spectra in Chromolithography. Price, $2.00.

No. 19. ANIMAL PARASITES AND MESSMATES. By Monsieur VAN BENEDEN, Professor of the University of Louvain, Correspondent of the Institute of France. With 83 Illustrations. Price, $1.50.

No. 20. ON FERMENTATIONS. By P. SCHÜTZENBERGER, Director at the Chemical Laboratory at the Sorbonne. With 28 Illustrations. Price, $1.50.

No. 21. THE FIVE SENSES OF MAN. Price, $1.75.

D. APPLETON & CO., PUBLISHERS, 549 & 551 Broadway, N. Y.

THE INTERNATIONAL SCIENTIFIC SERIES.

D. APPLETON & Co. have the pleasure of announcing that they have made arrangements for publishing, and have recently commenced the issue of, a SERIES OF POPULAR MONOGRAPHS, or small works, under the above title, which will embody the results of recent inquiry in the most interesting departments of advancing science.

The character and scope of this series will be best indicated by a reference to the names and subjects included in the subjoined list, from which it will be seen that the coöperation of the most distinguished professors in England, Germany, France, and the United States, has been secured, and negotiations are pending for contributions from other eminent scientific writers.

The works will be issued in New York, London, Paris, Leipsic, Milan, and St. Petersburg.

The INTERNATIONAL SCIENTIFIC SERIES is entirely an American project, and was originated and organized by Dr. E. L. Youmans, who has spent much time in Europe, arranging with authors and publishers.

FORTHCOMING VOLUMES.

Prof. W. KINGDON CLIFFORD, M. A. *The First Principles of the Exact Sciences explained to the Non-mathematical.*

Prof. T. H. HUXLEY, LL. D., F. R. S. *Bodily Motion and Consciousness.*

Dr. W. B. CARPENTER, LL. D., F. R. S. *The Physical Geography of the Sea.*

Prof. WILLIAM ODLING, F. R. S. *The Old Chemistry viewed from the New Stand-point.*

W. LAUDER LINDSAY, M. D., F. R. S. E. *Mind in the Lower Animals.*

Sir JOHN LUBBOCK, Bart., F. R. S. *On Ants and Bees.*

Prof. W. T. THISELTON DYER, B. A., B. Sc. *Form and Habit in Flowering Plants.*

Mr. J. N. LOCKYER, F. R. S. *Spectrum Analysis.*

Prof. MICHAEL FOSTER, M. D. *Protoplasm and the Cell Theory.*

H. CHARLTON BASTIAN, M. D., F. R. S. *The Brain as an Organ of Mind.*

Prof. A. C. RAMSAY, LL. D., F. R. S. *Earth Sculpture: Hills, Valleys, Mountains, Plains, Rivers, Lakes; How they were Produced, and how they have been Destroyed.*

Prof. RUDOLPH VIRCHOW (Berlin University). *Morbid Physiological Action.*

Prof. CLAUDE BERNARD. *History of the Theories of Life.*

D. APPLETON & CO., PUBLISHERS, 549 & 551 Broadway, N. Y.

THE INTERNATIONAL SCIENTIFIC SERIES.

FORTHCOMING VOLUMES.

Prof. H. SAINTE-CLAIRE DEVILLE. *An Introduction to General Chemistry.*

Prof. WURTZ. *Atoms and the Atomic Theory.*

Prof. De QUATREFAGES. *The Human Race.*

Prof. LACAZE-DUTHIERS. *Zoölogy since Cuvier.*

Prof. BERTHELOT. *Chemical Synthesis.*

Prof. C. A. YOUNG, Ph. D. (of Dartmouth College). *The Sun.*

Prof. OGDEN N. ROOD (Columbia College, N. Y.). *Modern Chromatics and its Relations to Art and Industry.*

Prof. J. ROSENTHAL. *General Physiology of Muscles and Nerves.*

Prof. JAMES D. DANA, M. A., LL. D. *On Cephalization ; or, Head-characters in the Gradation and Progress of Life.*

Prof. S. W. JOHNSON, M. A. *On the Nutrition of Plants.*

Prof. AUSTIN FLINT, Jr., M. D. *The Nervous System, and its Relation to the Bodily Functions.*

Prof. FERDINAND COHN (Breslau University). *Thallophytes (Algæ, Lichens, Fungi).*

Prof. HERMANN (University of Zurich). *Respiration.*

Prof. LEUCKART (University of Leipsic). *Outlines of Animal Organization.*

Prof. LIEBREICH (University of Berlin). *Outlines of Toxicology.*

Prof. KUNDT (University of Strasburg). *On Sound.*

Prof. REES (University of Erlangen). *On Parasitic Plants.*

Prof. STEINTHAL (University of Berlin). *Outlines of the Science of Language.*

P. BERT (Professor of Physiology, Paris). *Forms of Life and other Cosmical Conditions.*

E. ALGLAVE (Professor of Constitutional and Administrative Law at Douai, and of Political Economy at Lille). *The Primitive Elements of Political Constitutions.*

P. LORAIN (Professor of Medicine, Paris). *Modern Epidemics.*

Mons. FREIDEL. *The Functions of Organic Chemistry.*

Mons. DEBRAY. *Precious Metals.*

Prof. CORFIELD, M. A., M. D. (Oxon.). *Air in its Relation to Health.*

Prof. A. GIARD. *General Embryology.*

D. APPLETON & CO., PUBLISHERS, 549 & 551 Broadway, N. Y

RECENT PUBLICATIONS.

Diseases of Modern Life. By Dr. B. W. RICHARDSON, F. R. S. 1 vol., 12mo. Cloth. $2.00.

"'Diseases of Modern Life' is a work which throws so much light on what it is of the utmost importance for the public to know, that it deserves to be thoroughly and generally read."—*Graphic.*

'The literature on preventive medicine has received no more valuable contribution than this admirably-written treatise by one of the most accomplished physicians of Great Britain, who has concentrated upon his task a great amount of scientific research and clinical experience. No book that we have ever read more fully merits the attention of the intelligent public, to whom it is addressed."—*The World.*

Comin' Thro' the Rye. 1 vol., 8vo. Paper covers. 75 cents.

"A very amusing and well-written story. The history of the youth of the Adairs is extremely amusing, and told in a bright and witty manner. . . . One of the pleasantest novels of the season."—*Morning Post.*

"It is a clever novel, never dull, and the story never hangs fire."—*Standard.*

Memoir and Correspondence of Caroline Herschel. By Mrs. JOHN HERSCHEL. With Portraits. 12mo. Cloth. $1.75.

"The unlimited admiration excited by the noble, heroic virtues, and the uncommon talents of the subject of the memoir, is overborne by the intense sympathy felt for her long life of unselfish and unregretted devotion to others."—*Chicago Tribune.*

General History of Greece, from the Earliest Period to the Death of Alexander the Great. By the Rev. GEORGE W. COX. 1 vol., 12mo. Cloth. $2.50.

"We envy those schoolboys and undergraduates who will make their first acquaintance with Greek history through Mr. Cox's admirable volume. It ought to supersede all the popular Histories of Greece which have gone before it."—*The Hour.*

"The book is worthy, in every way, of the author's reputation. . . . It is altogether a most interesting and valuable book."—*Educational Times.*

A Short History of Natural Science and of the Progress of Discovery from the Time of the Greeks to the Present Day. By ARABELLA B. BUCKLEY. With Illustrations. 1 vol., 12mo. $2.00.

"Miss Buckley, the friend of Sir Charles Lyell, and for many years the secretary of the great geologist, in this volume has given a continuous, methodical, and complete sketch of the main discoveries of science from the time of Thales, one of the seven wise men, B. C. 700, down to the present day. The work is unique in its way, being the first attempt ever made to produce a brief and simple history of science. The author has entirely succeeded in her labors, evincing judgment, learning, and literary skill."—*Episcopal Register.*

A Hand-Book of Architectural Styles. Translated from the German by W. COTLETT-SANDERS. 1 vol., 8vo. With 639 Illustrations. $6.00.

"There is a great amount of information in the book, in a small compass. For one who simply wishes to gain a full knowledge of the various styles of architecture, written in a clear and interesting manner, the volume has not its equal nor rival in the English language. This knowledge will be facilitated by the profuse illustrations, of which there are not less than six hundred and thirty-nine, nearly all handsome specimens of engraving, among which figure a large number of famous buildings, ancient and modern."—*Evening Mail.*

D. APPLETON & CO., 549 & 551 *Broadway, N. Y.*

Works of Charles Darwin.

JOURNAL OF RESEARCHES into the Natural History and Geology of the Countries visited during the Voyage of H. M. S. *Beagle* round the World, under the command of Captain Fitzroy, R. N. 1 vol., 12mo. 579 pages. Cloth. Price, $2.00.

"Darwin was nearly five years on board the *Beagle*. A keen observer, and a genuine philosopher, he has brought back to us a precious freight of facts and truths. The work has been for some time before the public, and has won a high place among readers of every class. It is not so scientific as to be above the comprehension of intelligent readers who are not scientific. Some facts and species, new even to the scientific, are brought to light. Darwin's transparent, eloquent style richly illuminates his observations. The weightier matters to which he alludes are interspersed among more familiar observations, such as would naturally be made by a traveler passing through new and wonderful scenes. It is an instructive and interesting book."— *Northwestern Christian Advocate.*

THE ORIGIN OF SPECIES by Means of Natural Selection, or the Preservation of Favored Races in the Struggle for Life. New and revised edition, with Additions. With copious Index. 1 vol., 12mo. Cloth. Price, $2.00.

"Personally and practically exercised in zoölogy, in minute anatomy, in geology, a student of geographical distribution, not in maps and in museums, but by long voyages and laborious collection; having largely advanced each of these branches of science, and having spent many years in gathering and sifting materials for his present work, the store of accurately-registered facts upon which the author of the 'Origin of Species' is able to draw at will, is prodigious."—*Prof. T. H. Huxley.*

THE DESCENT OF MAN, and Selection in Relation to Sex. With Illustrations. New edition, revised and augmented. Complete in one volume. 688 pages. Price, $3.00.

"This theory is now indorsed by many eminent scientists, who at first combated it, including Sir Charles Lyell, probably the most learned of geologists, and even by a class of Christian divines like Dr. McCosh, who think that certain theories of cosmogony, like the nebular hypothesis and the law of evolution, may be accepted without doing violence to faith."—*Evening Bulletin.*

THE EXPRESSION OF THE EMOTIONS IN MAN AND the Lower Animals. With Photographic and other Illustrations. 1 vol., thick 12mo. Cloth. Price, $3.50.

"Whatever one thinks of Mr. Darwin's theory, it must be admitted that his great powers of observation are as conspicuous as ever in this inquiry. During a space of more than thirty years, he has, with exemplary patience, been accumulating information from all available sources. The result of all this is undoubtedly the collection of a mass of minute and trustworthy information which must possess the highest value, whatever may be the conclusions ultimately deduced from it."—*London Times.*

INSECTIVOROUS PLANTS. With Illustrations. 1 vol., 12mo. Cloth. Price, $2.00.

"In conclusion, we lay this book down with increased admiration for Mr. Darwin as a discoverer and expositor of facts, and with great satisfaction at the increase to our knowledge of plant physiology given us, as well as the ample promise of further additions as the direct consequence of the present publication."—*London Athenæum.*

"In this work Mr. Darwin's patient and painstaking methods of investigation appear to the best possible advantage. It is impossible to read it without enthusiastic admiration for the ingenuity which he displays in devising tests to determine the characteristics of the plants, the peculiarities of which he is studying, and, as is always the case with him, he presents the conclusions arrived at in language so lucid that he who reads simply for information is sure to be attracted and charmed quite as much as the professional student."—*N. Y. Times.*

D. APPLETON & CO., PUBLISHERS, 549 & 551 Broadway, N. Y.

INSECTIVOROUS PLANTS.

By CHARLES DARWIN, F.R.S., etc.

WITH ILLUSTRATIONS.

1 vol., 12mo. Cloth. . . . . Price, $2.00.

"Mr. Darwin's book may be held up as a model of what a treatise should be that is addressed to intelligent readers, a majority of whom, it is to be presumed, have no special acquaintance with the matter under consideration. In style it is strongly marked with Darwinian characteristics. The opening passage, indeed, allowing for difference of subject, is drawn up almost precisely in the same way as that which ushers in Chapter I. of the 'Origin of Species.' We have laid before us the circumstances that led the author to pursue his researches in the first instance, so far back as 1860; then, step by step, we are treated to the history of those researches; fact is added to fact, inference to inference, till at length the body of evidence, direct and indirect, becomes so overwhelming, that there is as little chance of controverting Mr. Darwin's conclusions as there is for a fly to escape when once it has been caught in the cruel embrace of a sun-dew. The modesty, the perfect candor, the scrupulous care to acknowledge the labors of others, even in the most trifling particulars, are as apparent in this as in the rest of Mr. Darwin's books. These Darwinian characteristics, as we venture to call them, are only equaled by the apparently inexhaustible patience with which he has pursued his observations and experiments throughout many years."— *London Athenæum.*

"In this work Mr. Darwin's patient and painstaking methods of investigation appear to the best possible advantage. It is impossible to read it without enthusiastic admiration for the ingenuity which he displays in devising tests to determine the characteristics of the plants, the peculiarities of which he is studying, and, as is always the case with him, he presents the conclusions arrived at in language so lucid that he who reads simply for information is sure to be attracted and charmed quite as much as the professional student."—*N. Y. Times.*

"As a model of scientific inquiry, his work will scarcely find a parallel in any language. It is utterly free from the diffuse verbiage which corrupts the style of so many of the prominent German naturalists, and from the subtile refinements which so often throw an air of romance around the physical speculations of French writers. In English scientific literature it has no superior in acuteness of thought, candor of judgment, and felicity of expression.

"Mr. Darwin's manner is equally remote from the vehemence of the polemic and the indifference of the cold-blooded observer. His pages are warm with deep human interest, but an interest inspired by the love of truth and knowledge, not by personal passion. His anxious endeavor for accurate observation is evinced in every line of his writings, and, if he clings to theories with the earnestness of a discoverer, he clings still more devotedly to the facts of Nature which he undertakes to interpret. The scope of his experiments illustrates the rare fertility of his mind, as well as his wonderful patience. The thoroughness of their execution is fully equal to the ingenuity of their conception. No detail appears to escape his notice, no inadvertence mars the harmony of his statement, no unwise haste disturbs the clearness and serenity of his judgment, and even if one could be indifferent to his volume as a scientific production, it must still be admired as a masterpiece of intellectual workmanship."—*N. Y. Tribune.*

D. APPLETON & CO., Publishers, 549 & 551 Broadway, N. Y.

RECENT PUBLICATIONS.

THE NATIVE RACES OF THE PACIFIC STATES.

By HERBERT H. BANCROFT. To be completed in 5 vols. Vol. I. now ready. Containing Wild Tribes: their Manners and Customs. 1 vol., 8vo. Cloth, $6; sheep, $7.

"We can only say that if the remaining volumes are executed in the same spirit of candid and careful investigation, the same untiring industry, and intelligent good sense, which mark the volume before us, Mr. Bancroft's 'Native Races of the Pacific States' will form, as regards aboriginal America, an encyclopædia of knowledge not only un equaled but unapproached. A literary enterprise more deserving of a generous sym pathy and support has never been undertaken on this side of the Atlantic."—FRANCIS PARKMAN, in the *North American Review*.

"The industry, sound judgment, and the excellent literary style displayed in this work, cannot be too highly praised."—*Boston Post.*

A BRIEF HISTORY OF CULTURE.

By JOHN S. HITTELL. 1 vol., 12mo. Price, $1.50.

"He writes in a popular style for popular use. He takes ground which has never been fully occupied before, although the general subject has been treated more or less distinctly by several writers. . . . Mr. Hittell's method is compact, embracing a wide field in a few words, often presenting a mere hint, when a fuller treatment is craved by the reader; but, although his book cannot be commended as a model of literary art, it may be consulted to great advantage by every lover of free thought and novel sugges-tions."—*N. Y. Tribune.*

THE HISTORY OF THE CONFLICT BETWEEN RE-LIGION AND SCIENCE.

By JOHN W. DRAPER, M. D., author of "The Intellectual Develop-ment of Europe." 1 vol., 12mo. Cloth. Price, $1.75.

"The conflict of which he treats has been a mighty tragedy of humanity that has dragged nations into its vortex and involved the fate of empires. The work, though small, is full of instruction regarding the rise of the great ideas of science and philos-ophy; and he describes in an impressive manner and with dramatic effect the way re-ligious authority has employed the secular power to obstruct the progress of knowledge and crush out the spirit of investigation. While there is not in his book a word of dis-respect for things sacred, he writes with a directness of speech, and a vividness of char-acterization and an unflinching fidelity to the facts, which show him to be in thorough earnest with his work. The 'History of the Conflict between Religion and Science' is a fitting sequel to the 'History of the Intellectual Development of Europe,' and will add to its author's already high reputation as a philosophic historian."—*N. Y. Tribune.*

THEOLOGY IN THE ENGLISH POETS.

COWPER, COLERIDGE, WORDSWORTH, and BURNS. By Rev. STOPFORD BROOKE. 1 vol., 12mo. Price, $2.

"Apart from its literary merits, the book may be said to possess an independent value, as tending to familiarize a certain section of the English public with more en-lightened views of theology."—*London Athenæum.*

BLOOMER'S COMMERCIAL CRYPTOGRAPH.

A Telegraph Code and Double Index—Holocryptic Cipher. By J. G. BLOOMER. 1 vol., 8vo. Price, $5.

By the use of this work, business communications of whatever nature may be tele-graphed with secrecy and economy.

D. APPLETON & CO., Publishers, New York

THE POPULAR SCIENCE MONTHLY.

CONDUCTED BY

E. L. YOUMANS.

*This periodical was started (in 1872) to promote the diffusion of valuable sci-
entific knowledge, in a readable and attractive form, among all classes
of the community, and has thus far met a want supplied by
no other magazine in the United States.*

Eight volumes have now appeared, which are filled with instructive and interesting articles and abstracts of articles, original, selected, translated, and illustrated, from the pens of the leading scientific men of different countries. Accounts of important scientific discoveries, the application of science to the practical arts, and the latest views put forth concerning natural phenomena, have been given by *savants* of the highest authority. Prominent attention has been also devoted to those various sciences which help to a better understanding of the nature of man, to the bearings of science upon the questions of society and government, to scientific education, and to the conflicts which spring from the progressive nature of scientific knowledge.

THE POPULAR SCIENCE MONTHLY has long since ceased to be an experiment. It has passed into a circulation far beyond the most sanguine hopes at first entertained, and the cordial and intelligent approval which it has everywhere met, shows that its close and instructive discussions have been well appreciated by the reading portion of the American people. It has not been its policy to make boastful promises of great things to be done in the future, but rather to appeal to what it has already accomplished as giving it a claim upon popular patronage. But no pains will be spared to improve it and make it still more worthy of liberal support, and still more a necessity to the cultivated classes of the country.

THE POPULAR SCIENCE MONTHLY is published in a large octavo, handsomely printed on clear type, and, when the subjects admit, fully illustrated. Each number contains 128 pages.

Terms: $5 per Annum, or Fifty Cents per Number.

Postage free to all Subscribers in the United States, from January 1, 1875.

A new volume of THE POPULAR SCIENCE MONTHLY begins with the numbers for May and November each year. Subscriptions may commence from any date. Back numbers supplied.

Now Ready, Vols. I., II., III., IV., V., VI., VII., and VIII., of the Popular Science Monthly, embracing the numbers from 1 to 48 (May, 1872, to April, 1876). 8 vols., 8vo. Cloth, $3.50 per vol. Half Morocco, $6.50 per vol.

For Sale, Binding Cases for Vols. I., II., III., IV., V., VI., VII., and VIII., of The Popular Science Monthly. These covers are prepared expressly for binding the volumes of THE POPULAR SCIENCE MONTHLY as they appear, and will be sent to Subscribers on receipt of price. Any binder can attach the covers at a trifling expense. Price, 50 cents each.

ADDRESS

D. APPLETON & CO., Publishers,

549 & 551 Broadway, New York.

PHASED
DETERIORATION

Made in the USA